Against Capitalism and Bureaucracy

Historical Materialism Book Series

The Historical Materialism Book Series is a major publishing initiative of the radical left. The capitalist crisis of the twenty-first century has been met by a resurgence of interest in critical Marxist theory. At the same time, the publishing institutions committed to Marxism have contracted markedly since the high point of the 1970s. The Historical Materialism Book Series is dedicated to addressing this situation by making available important works of Marxist theory. The aim of the series is to publish important theoretical contributions as the basis for vigorous intellectual debate and exchange on the left.

The peer-reviewed series publishes original monographs, translated texts, and reprints of classics across the bounds of academic disciplinary agendas and across the divisions of the left. The series is particularly concerned to encourage the internationalization of Marxist debate and aims to translate significant studies from beyond the English-speaking world.

For a full list of titles in the Historical Materialism Book Series available in paperback from Haymarket Books, visit: www.haymarketbooks.org/series_collections/1-historical-materialism.

Against Capitalism and Bureaucracy

Ernest Mandel's Theoretical Contributions

Manuel Kellner

Translated by
Maciej Zurowski

Haymarket Books
Chicago, IL

First published in 2023 by Brill Academic Publishers, The Netherlands
© 2023 Koninklijke Brill NV, Leiden, The Netherlands

Published in paperback in 2024 by
Haymarket Books
P.O. Box 180165
Chicago, IL 60618
773-583-7884
www.haymarketbooks.org

ISBN: 979-8-88890-210-3

Distributed to the trade in the US through Consortium Book Sales and
Distribution (www.cbsd.com) and internationally through Ingram
Publisher Services International (www.ingramcontent.com).

This book was published with the generous support of Lannan
Foundation, Wallace Action Fund, and the Marguerite Casey Foundation.

Special discounts are available for bulk purchases by organizations and
institutions. Please call 773-583-7884 or email info@haymarketbooks.org
for more information.

Cover art and design by David Mabb. Cover art is a detail from *Construct
79, after Kathleen Kersey (for Morris & Co), Arbutus / Liubov Popova, textile
design 1922–23*, acrylic on wallpaper (2023).

Library of Congress Cataloging-in-Publication data is available.

Contents

Foreword to the English Edition

Ernest Mandel was not only the main leader of the Fourth International in the second half of the twentieth century and a world-famous economist, but he also rejuvenated Marxist theory with a revolutionary humanist perspective. Unlike so many other leaders who claim to have inherited the legacy of Leon Trotsky, Mandel never transformed this heritage into a dogmatic body of work or a set of universal recipes. His excessive optimism led him to be mistaken in some of his predictions, but he nevertheless elaborated analyses that remain necessary reference points for revolutionary Marxists today. There is a collection of essays paying tribute to Mandel, *The Legacy of Ernest Mandel*, edited by Gilbert Achcar (London: Verso, 2000), and an excellent biography by Jan Willem Stutje, *Ernest Mandel, A Rebel's Dream Deferred* (London: Verso, 2009). But Manuel Kellner's book is the first substantial exercise that systematically presents Mandel's economic and political thinking. The work had originally been submitted as a thesis to the University of Marburg, Germany. Kellner is one of the main leaders of the section of the Fourth International in Germany, as well as being an activist in the Die Linke party and the IG Metall trade union.

This remarkable book is a rigorous and accurate study of the ideas of one of the most influential Marxist intellectuals of his time. Kellner defines himself as a disciple of Mandel who gradually gained the necessary distance from his mentor to write about him. This is reflected in the structure of the book. In the first instance, Kellner presents, synthesises and explains Mandel's positions, and then discusses them critically in the final chapter. This is a pity, because it would have been much better if critical distance had been present throughout the book.

Kellner briefly reviews the main moments of Mandel's life: his participation in the resistance in Belgium, his internment in Nazi camps, his role as a leader of the socialist left in Belgium, and his contribution to the development of the Fourth International. The author does so by looking at the relationship between 'theory and practice'. But what really interests him is Mandel's contribution to a critique of contemporary capitalism: the historical/organic method of analysis, the theory of crises, late capitalism, the long waves of the economy. Kellner highlights what is essential: Mandel's analyses were not academic exercises, but directly linked to his struggle as an anti-capitalist thinker and activist!

Kellner also analyses what he calls 'Mandel's utopian dimension', that is, his conception of socialism as the final goal of the proletarian struggle. Mandel did give the concept of 'utopia' a rather pejorative meaning, but Kellner is right to give it a more positive dimension. Mandel's definition of socialism remained, on the whole, within the model of October 1917, that is, a republic of workers' councils. When the Fourth International adopted the resolution on 'Socialist Democracy and Dictatorship of the Proletariat' at its 1984 Congress, he took some distance from the Bolshevik experience, and drew inspiration from the revolutionary democratic ideas of Rosa Luxemburg. This was also the case in his fight against the Stalinist bureaucracy, and in his criticism of the 'dark years' of Lenin and Trotsky who were weighed down by a 'substitutionist' temptation – a temptation which also concerns social democracy and the Austro-Marxism of Otto Bauer.

The discussion on socialist strategy is the most important aspect of Kellner's book. He reviews Mandel's conceptions of the mass strike, transitional demands, the dual nature of the unions, class consciousness and the revolutionary party, the united front, and, of course, permanent revolution and internationalism. The main thread of his strategy, which is woven throughout these themes, is that of the self-organisation 'from below' of the subaltern classes.

In other sections of the book, Kellner discusses Mandel's work on Trotsky's theory of fascism and his writings on the Holocaust. While the former is arguably among Mandel's richest and most interesting contributions, the latter are far more problematic. Kellner acknowledges that Mandel had great difficulty in appreciating the 'specific' character of the Judeocide, and did not always escape the tendency to 'relativise' the crime as one of the many atrocities committed by imperialism and colonialism.

The last chapter, 'Evaluation and Perspectives', is one of the most interesting in the book because Kellner distances himself from the work of his master and outlines a number of criticisms. They concern in particular the problematic concept of the bureaucratised workers' state, which Mandel thought he could even apply to Pol Pot's Cambodia! But Mandel was an incorrigible optimist with his forecasts, whether about the revolutionary potential of Western Europe (since 1946!), or the improbability of a capitalist restoration in Eastern Europe after the fall of the Wall in 1989. Kellner mentions here, without totally agreeing with it, the distinction I had made in my own contribution in *The Legacy of Ernest Mandel* between Mandel's legitimate anthropological optimism, and that which is not grounded in historical forecasts.

Nevertheless, Kellner shows very well that the common thread which runs through Mandel's writings and his conception of revolutionary strategy was the self-determination and self-activity of the working class as the touchstones of the process of universal human emancipation.

Mandel's last text is a polemic with the North American 'Spartacist' sect. He was already suffering from a heart condition, but had decided to travel to New York for this debate, against the advice of his friends (including the author of this preface). In this text, Mandel recognises two important gaps in the theoretical baggage of revolutionary Marxism: the ecological crisis and the oppression of women. Manuel Kellner soberly notes that these tasks are still largely ahead of us.

In his last years, Mandel began to integrate the ecological crisis in a significant way in his thinking. But it was only in the 2000s that the Fourth International adopted an ecosocialist perspective – that is, an ecological refoundation of socialism – in its programme and strategy.

Michael Löwy

Against Capitalism and Bureaucracy:
Socialist Strategy in the Work of Ernest Mandel

∴

Foreword

The present study seeks to assess Ernest Mandel's political conception, starting from his analysis and critique of contemporary conditions, through his visions of the future and ideas for the revolutionary transformation of society. For this purpose, I essentially draw on Mandel's main body of work while only exceptionally considering newspaper and magazine articles and contributions to debates. An even remotely comprehensive examination of all that Mandel ever contributed would far exceed the scope of this work. Beyond my reconstruction of Mandel's positions, I will evaluate them critically – especially in the final chapter – and put their characteristic blind spots, weaknesses and problematic aspects up for discussion.

I would like to thank: my doctoral supervisor Prof. Dr. Georg Fülberth for his dedicated assistance; the Jakob Moneta Foundation for material support; Mandel's close political companion of many years Charles-Andre Udry (Lausanne), who devoted a full two days of his time to answering far too many questions when I began writing my manuscript; all those who agreed to be interviewed and give eyewitness testimony (see the list following the bibliography); Mandel's widow Anne Sprimont-Mandel, who gave me access to the Mandel archives at the International Institute of Social History (IISG) in Amsterdam; Mandel biographer Jan-Willem Stutje, who readily answered my questions about Mandel's life; the staff at the International Institute for Research and Education (IIRE) in Amsterdam for granting access to the IIRE archives, which contain numerous contributions by Mandel; my friends Kemal Bozay, Wilfried Dubois, Christoph Jünke, Angela Klein, Hans-Günter Mull and Carmen Wenzke, who always had an open ear for me, for their encouragement and willingness to discuss everything.

Since Ernest Mandel had considerable influence on the development of my own political positions, my approach to his theoretical work is not an outsider's perspective. I had to work hard to achieve the necessary critical distance from the object of my study. In that sense, my work has also helped me to gain more clarity about the foundations and problematic aspects of my own views. At the same time, I am certain that Mandel's theoretical contribution will remain important for future socialist and emancipatory debate and position-forming. I also believe that it will remain extremely inspiring – of course, only insofar as it is revisited.

Manuel Kellner

Introduction

Not much research is yet available on the work of Ernest Mandel.[1] If we leave aside polemics of a mainly factional character and texts on individual topics, this is even more true. The impression is reinforced if we confine ourselves to independent publications and to those in German. There has yet to be any critical account of Mandel's overall conception.

For instance, if we search the electronic catalogue of the German Library (http://www.dbd.de), which lists all German-language publications after 1945, for titles containing 'Ernest' and 'Mandel' as 'title keywords', we find 12 results. However, five of these refer to publications in which Ernest Mandel is co-author or interlocutor. Only seven titles (two of which are virtually identical) have him as their subject as a person, author or political figure.

In chronological order, they comprise the following publications: In 1971, one of the organisations that emerged during the 'organisational phase' of the extraparliamentary opposition (APO) and after the rapid disintegration of the Socialist German Student League (SDS), and which has long since disappeared almost without a trace, the Proletarian Front – Group of West-German Communists, published the second issue of its journal. The journal contains a composite review of 11 books, pamphlets and articles by Ernest Mandel published in German. Its author, Karl-Heinz Roth, is still well-known and continues to play a role in the debates of the German radical left.[2] This was followed by an undated collection reproducing a large number of newspaper articles and typescripts, leaflets, press statements and facsimile briefs and representing a wide range of viewpoints.[3] There is also an eight-page publication from 1972, edited by the 'Emergency Association for a Free University': it reprints without comment the justification given by West Berlin's then Senator for Art and Science, the Social-Democratic Party member Werner Stein, for rejecting Ernest Mandel's appeal

---

1   A list contained in the second volume of the third print edition of Wolfgang and Petra Lubitz's *Trotsky Bibliography* may give the opposite impression – see W. Lubitz and P. Lubitz 1999, from p. 549. However, the first impression is deceptive: it mainly comprises numerous obituaries, a number of book reviews, polemics by authors of rival Trotskyist groups, contributions to debates, articles in reference works and only very few independent publications. No distinction is made between independent and non-independent publications and unpublished works, making it difficult to gain an overview.

2   Roth 1971.

3   GIM 1972a. The reprinted texts date from the period from 21 January to April 1972. This A4 brochure comes without a title page or imprint. 1973 is the year of publication according to the catalogues of the German Library and the City University Library of Frankfurt/Main.

at the beginning of the summer semester (in January, Mandel had been the only person proposed by the Economics Department of the Free University of Berlin for a vacant lecturer position).[4]

Three further dossiers, also published in response to the rejected appeal and entry ban issued by the then interior minister, Hans-Dietrich Genscher, and the ensuing public debate apparently never found their way into the German Library. Firstly, a 'Documentation on the Ernest Mandel case', published by the Press and Information Office of the Free University of Berlin in April 1972.[5] Secondly, more 'Documentation and Analysis' published by Mandel's political supporters in the same month.[6] Finally, a pamphlet produced by the Socialist Office.[7] 1973 saw the publication of a booklet that reprinted two essays, originally published in German in 1969 in the *Kursbuch* journal. The first gives a useful overview of the Cuban 'planning debate' of 1963–65, in which the French economist Charles Bettelheim and Ernest Mandel participated with theoretical essays alongside Ernesto 'Che' Guevara and other Cuban leaders.[8]

This was followed in 1980 by the first book dedicated to the work of Ernest Mandel. It was authored by two GDR economists, Günter Krause and Klaus O.W. Müller, and is available in two editions: the original one issued by GDR publishers Theorie und Praxis and a West German licensed edition by the German Communist Party's publishing house.[9] This polemic targets Ernest Mandel as an exponent of the political economy of 'left-wing radicalism',[10] which, according to the authors, is a 'pseudo-left tendency'. The author of the present work responded to this in the journal *Die Internationale* with a review entitled 'The "True" Marxism of Ernest Mandel – or the Advantages of Polemics with a Stranger'.[11] Finally, in 1992 a small publishing house (known for printing just

---

4   Notgemeinschaft für eine freie Universität 1973.

5   This also contains Peter von Oertzen's article on 'liberal democratic order and council [soviet] system' – see Oertzen 1972, pp. 15–22; originally published in 1969 in *Politische Bildung. Beiträge und Materialien zur wissenschaftlichen Grundlegung und zur Unterrichtspraxis*, 1, 1969: 14 et seq.

6   GIM 1972a and GIM 1972b.

7   Sozialistisches Büro 1972.

8   Alonso and Santis 1973. See also Müller 1969a. The anthology contains writings by Ernesto 'Che' Guevara, Charles Bettelheim, Ernest Mandel and Fidel Castro among others. Bertram Silberman's account of this debate is much more extensive – see Silberman 1971. Ernest Mandel's contribution was published under the title 'Le grand débat économique' in French in *Partisans*, 37, 1967 and translated by this author into German – see Mandel 1981b. See also 'Das ökonomische Denken des Che' in Löwy 1987, pp. 37 et seq.

9   Krause and Müller 1980.

10 Cf. Krause 1977.

11 Kellner 1981.

about anything imaginable as long as a hefty financial contribution is provided) published an 'unconsciously scientific study', as the title warned. The treatise contained within is confused and shambolic to the point of incomprehensibility.[12]

So far, there is not a single work that is even remotely comprehensive, substantial and serious *at the same time*.

The user catalogue of the Archive of Social Democracy at the Friedrich Ebert Foundation in Bonn (http://library.fes.de) lists five publications under the entry 'mandel, ernest [about]'. One title is not in fact a text about Mandel, but contains a contribution from him. The other entries include: a paper by the Europa Union of 1974, in which a brief subchapter discusses Ernest Mandel's view on European integration; a lengthy review essay of Mandel's *Late Capitalism* by Paul Mattick, also 1974; an academic paper on the theory of long waves from 1985; and the aforementioned satirical book by Peter Freitag.[13]

Similarly, in terms of English- or French-language texts, I am only aware of very few publications dealing with Mandel's theoretical and scientific work.[14]

Ernest Mandel's political views and activities are the main subject of a stapled booklet published in Australia in July 1997, two years after his death.[15] It contains three lectures by the leading thinker of a 'Trotskyist' group from the US that has always been very hostile towards Ernest Mandel and the organised tendency that he represented, the Fourth International.[16]

Gilbert Achcar's anthology *The Legacy of Ernest Mandel* offers the most serious reappraisal of Mandel's theoretical oeuvre. It is based on a seminar held in Amsterdam in July 1996, one year after Ernest Mandel's death, and was first published in French and English in 1999, the following year in Japanese (according to the editor), and in 2003 in German.[17] However, as the editor points out in his introduction, only a part of Ernest Mandel's contribution to Marxism and a rather small part of his extensive writings, namely his theoretical work, were examined during the seminar and therefore in the volume. Achcar writes that he does not wish to abstract from Mandel's self-conception and continuous political practice or belittle this activity; he sees and appreciates that Ernest Mandel belonged 'to a species that has become increasingly endangered in this

---

12   Freitag 1992.

13   Häckel and Elsner 1974, Mattick 1974, Senftleben 1985 and Freitag 1992.

14   For instance, Vincent 1995 and a reply by Artous 1996.

15   See North 1997.

16   For the history of this tendency, see Alexander 1991, p. 471 et seq., p. 501 et seq., p. 539 et seq., p. 923 et seq. See also Wohlforth 1991 and Tourish and Wohlforth 2000, p. 156 et seq. Ernest Mandel deals with this group in Mandel 1967c.

17   See Achcar 1999a.

second half of the twentieth century: theoreticians of militant Marxism'.[18] The appendixes of these editions contain useful bibliographies of Mandel's writing in English, French and German respectively. However, the aim was not to provide an exhaustive list, but to limit it from the outset to the independent writings authored and edited by Ernest Mandel, i.e. books, pamphlets and contributions to books.[19] A complete bibliography of Mandel's writings, including his countless newspaper and magazine articles as well as written contributions to debates in the Fourth International, would surely be a substantial scientific project in its own right.

In almost every academic library, reference works of various kinds contain concise and lengthy biographical or bio-bibliographical entries on Ernest Mandel. Since the beginning of the 1980s in particular, he is featured in a number of such texts in Belgium, the US, Britain and Germany. Among these, the articles by Paul Mattick Jr in the *Biographical Dictionary of Marxism* (1986), by Michel Beaud and Gilles Dostaler in their work *Economic Thought Since Keynes* (1995) and by Shoichi Itoh in *Routledge Encyclopaedia of International Political Economy* Volume 2 (2001) are particularly noteworthy. Finally, there is an entry that Ernest Mandel wrote himself, which appeared in *A Biographical Dictionary of Dissenting Economists* (1992).

On 10 and 11 November 2003 a second, smaller conference also took place in Amsterdam. Entitled 'Theory as History: Ernest Mandel's historical analysis of world capitalism', it focused even more exclusively than the previous conference on Mandel's theoretical work. There do not seem to be any plans to publish the conference contributions outside the internet in the foreseeable future.[20]

In a few years from the time of writing, the state of research on Ernest Mandel as a personality, on his political activity and on his theoretical contributions will have changed fundamentally. The Dutch social scientist Jan Willem Stutje has begun work on a biography covering these three aspects (political activity, theoretical and scientific work, personal life) and comprising several hundred pages in January 2002.[21] A paper introducing his project has been published online.[22] Stutje has the opportunity to assess Ernest Mandel's extensive liter-

---

18   Achcar 1999a, p. 3.
19   More comprehensive but by no means complete bibliographies are available: Bendien 1987; Bendien 2000; Lubitz and Lubitz 1996. See also François Vercammen's neat and succinct breakdown in Mandel 1997a.
20   See https://search.iisg.amsterdam/Record/ARCH01971 (Ernest Esra Mandel Papers).
21   [This biography has now been published and translated into English: see Stutje 2009 – Translator.]
22   http://www.iisg.nl/research/stutje.doc.

ary legacy, the bulk of which is kept in a closed department of the International
Institute of Social History (IISG), and spend some five years in the halls of the
renowned institute. A partial result of this eminently knowledgeable, serious
and thorough research is now available, namely in an essay about Mandel's parents and the years of his illegal activity during the Nazi occupation of Belgium.
It has only been published in Flemish in a journal of contemporary history thus
far.[23]

I will not go into the numerous obituaries, reviews (or review essays) of
individual books by Ernest Mandel that can be found in periodicals.[24] As to
German-language writing on Mandel's theoretical and political contribution
that has not appeared in book form, aside from a review by Wolfgang Müller
published in a journal edited by the national board of the Socialist German
Student League (SDS), I find one major article to be noteworthy.[25] However,
it is difficult to access and has been little discussed, as it appeared in a rather
obscure source: namely the aforementioned composite review written by Karl-
Heinz Roth in 1971 for the journal of his political organisation at the time.
His essay is a sharp systematic critique which, although polemical ('a discussion of Mandel's neo-Kautskyist position on the critique of political economy',
'the dogmatism of the Fourth International'), is presented as criticism between
'comrades'.

The present work is the result of 32 years of Mandel reception and seven
years of effort to assess and present in detail Ernest Mandel's overall theoretical and political-strategical conception.[26] Owing to changing personal circumstances and the degree of 'distraction' caused by this author's political commitment, my work on this book was either more or less intensive at different times,
but never interrupted. The starting point was the reception of Mandel's work by
one of his disciples – i.e. someone who had to gradually acquire the necessary
critical distance to his subject. This process is apparent in the resulting text,
which initially reproduces, summarises and explains Mandel's positions, then
increasingly formulates critical questions and objections (note that I wrote the
final versions of the following chapter on 'Theory and Practice' and of the concluding chapter on 'Evaluation and Prospects' last).

By and large, Mandel's position is a coherently developed whole. His analysis
of contemporary capitalist class society, its prehistory and its contradictions,

---

23   Stutje 2003.
24   A number of essays have appeared on the tenth anniversary of Mandel's death after com-
      pletion of this work.
25   For Wolfgang Müller's essay, see Müller 1969b.
26   I have been studying Mandel's work intensively since I first met him in Brussels in 1972.

his critique of the bureaucracy in the workers' movement and in what he, following Trotsky, calls the 'bureaucratised workers' states' (beginning with the Soviet Union) and his positions on socialist strategy will be assessed in detail in this work. I will rely essentially on Mandel's major works and on his contributions published in book form. Only in exceptional cases will I consult his countless newspaper and magazine articles, his entries in anthologies also featuring other authors and his innumerable written contributions to discussions in the Fourth International. I have interviewed a number of Mandel's contemporaries (see appendix) and incorporated their testimony into my text in one way or another.

This text cannot be the final and conclusive assessment or critical appraisal of Ernest Mandel's theoretical and political legacy. Such a feat could only be achieved if the abundant material that has hitherto not been dealt with were examined collectively by representatives of the critical social sciences of different theoretical and political orientations. This work has fulfilled its purpose if it can demonstrate that it is worthwhile continuing the critical reappraisal of Mandel's theoretical legacy; that from a socialist and emancipatory perspective this legacy represents a part of the balance of the twentieth century; and that Mandel's approach is a relevant contribution in the context of addressing contemporary social problems and in the struggle to renew the labour movement and the cause of socialism.[27]

---

27 By all means, all the subjects addressed in this book that Ernest Mandel has approached theoretically and on which he has commented extensively are worthy of their own, more in-depth studies. My objective is to explain Mandel's overall political conception in its coherence, but also to reveal its inherent problems.

CHAPTER 1

Theory and Practice

1   Occupational Ban and Refusal of Entry 1972

On 23 February 1972, the German daily papers reported that a certain Ernest Mandel would not be offered a chair at the Free University (FU) Berlin after all, even though he had been the only candidate proposed by the department of economics, owing to his 'outstanding qualifications'. The political senate of West Berlin had rejected the appeal proposal on the grounds that Mandel was a 'staunch, avowed and practising opponent of the liberal democratic order', whose 'revolutionary destruction' he was planning: 'His aim is the creation of a council republic of a Trotskyist character, led by a national congress of workers' councils as the highest decision-making body on economic and socio-political issues. In this way the liberal democratic order set out in our constitution is to be destroyed completely' [our translation].[1]

Mandel disagreed, as did a number of socialist groups and personalities including social democrats like Peter von Oertzen and sections of the Young Socialist league (Jusos).[2] They argued that a socialist revolution as understood by Mandel did not involve the destruction of the 'liberal democratic order': in fact, Mandel wanted to abolish capitalism and introduce a socialist council democracy that would realise far more democratic rights and freedoms than even the most democratic bourgeois republic ever could. Alas, such arguments did not convince the political decision-makers. Mandel was invited by FU students to address a protest meeting against the decision.

Yet Willy Brandt's social-liberal coalition (whose declared ambition was to 'risk more democracy') and its liberal minister of the interior, Hans-Dietrich Genscher, issued an entry ban against Mandel because allegedly 'unrest' had to be expected: 'As requested by the State of Berlin, Mr Mandel has been put on the border surveillance list and turned back when attempting to enter the country at Frankfurt airport in order to travel to Berlin this morning', the minister of the interior declared on 28 February. According to him, the aim of the Trotskyist Fourth International was to organise a revolutionary uprising, and Mandel had been planning to move the headquarters of this organisation from

---

1   Berlin-West Senator für Wissenschaft und Kunst 1972.
2   See Oertzen 1972.

Brussels to West Berlin. That same afternoon in Berlin, a few thousand who joined the protest had to make do with a tape-recorded speech by Mandel. In an interview for *Der Spiegel*, Mandel explained with characteristic humour that he opposed capitalism but not the German constitution, which incidentally he had not read.[3]

Through several publications and books in German, Mandel had also become a well-known figure on the left in Germany. Suhrkamp Books printed relatively large runs of the German editions of *Marxist Economic Theory* and *Late Capitalism*.[4] Mandel's *Introduction to Marxist Economic Theory* served as educational material for quite a few left-wing organisations, including Socialist Youth of Germany/Falcons (sjd – Die Falken) and Young Socialists (Jusos) groups.[5] By now, *Introduction to Marxist Economic Theory* has reached its seventh edition. After Georges Simenon, Mandel is the most widely read Belgian author internationally.[6]

Mandel remained barred from West Germany until the late 1970s. As a 'Trotskyist', he was naturally *persona non grata* in the Soviet Union, the Warsaw Pact countries, and the People's Republic of China too. In the west, Switzerland, France, Australia, Spain and the US had banned him from entering.[7]

2   **Captured by the Nazis**

Ernest (Ezra) Mandel's parents were emigrated Poles of Jewish descent. His father Henri (Henoch) Mandel did not want to be a soldier in the World War and fled to the Netherlands in 1914. When the German revolution broke out in November 1918 and the Emperor was overthrown (who, as is well known, embarked on a trip to the Netherlands too), Henri Mandel moved to Germany and joined the Communist Party (KPD) immediately upon its foundation. In Berlin, he worked in the press agency that had just been set up by the young Soviet government and met Karl Radek, who acted as a kind of 'ambassador' of the Bolshevik leadership in the German revolution. The murders of Rosa Luxemburg and Karl Liebknecht in January 1919 shocked him profoundly. This, along with the overall setbacks of the German revolution, motivated him

---

3   See Mandel 1972b.
4   For the English-language versions, see Mandel 1968b and 1975d.
5   For the English-language version, see Mandel 1973b.
6   See Stutje 2003, p. 7.
7   See Berlin-West Senator für Wissenschaft und Kunst 1972.

and his wife Rosa to move to Antwerp in Belgium and put their political commitment on hold.[8]

Their first son Ernest Mandel was born in Frankfurt (Main) on 4 April 1923. Following medical advice, they had returned to Germany only for the purpose of his birth and then continued to live in Belgium. In 1930s Belgium, the young Ernest Mandel experienced the tough period of the looming Nazi invasion and saw the misery of the working-class families with whom his parents were associated, but also enjoyed the atmosphere of a revolutionary communist and anti-Stalinist family home. He learned to identify with the workers' movement and with the political struggle against exploitation and oppression in the cradle, so to speak. The family bookshelves were stacked especially with the classics of German-speaking socialist theoreticians like Karl Marx, Friedrich Engels, Rosa Luxemburg and Karl Kautsky, as well as issues of *Die Neue Zeit*, then the theoretical journal of German Social Democracy. Ernest Mandel's father taught his son the foundations of the Marxist worldview and faith in the revolutionary traditions and revolutionary potential, particularly of the German working class. The Moscow Trials of the mid- to late 1930s shocked Mandel's father, not least because Karl Radek, whom he had known personally and held in high esteem, was sentenced on absurd and slanderous charges in the second trial. He became active again and got acquainted with the supporters of the Left Opposition in Belgium.

In this period, the young Ernest Mandel met strike leaders and other movers and shakers from the various tendencies of the workers' movement. Disputes between the Social-Democratic, Stalinist-Communist and Trotskyist tendencies were ripe in this milieu. In the Revolutionary Socialist Party (SRP/PSR), a small organisation that represented the Belgian section of the Fourth International, he became acquainted with the archetype of the autodidactic and cultured workers' leader, but also with exiled members of the German section of the Fourth International whom his parents harboured. At the age of 13 he already considered himself an SRP/PSR 'sympathiser'. And even though these people were, in his words, 'not crazy enough to accept a child as a member', he was still allowed to attend numerous meetings and gatherings as a listener. The political organisation of which he had become a member in 1939 – i.e., at the age of 16 – used to engage in passionate debate and had a strong international orientation. It wrote articles especially for illegal dissemination in Nazi Germany, maintained contact with comrades in the German underground and corresponded with Trotsky in writing.

---

8 My account of Ernest Mandel's biography up to the end of World War II is essentially based on the detailed narration in Stutje 2003.

The news of Trotsky's assassination in 1940 came as a shock to the family. It was also the reason for a restructuring of the Fourth International (the organisation that had emerged from the Left Opposition led by Trotsky), which had been almost destroyed by repression, but also by resignation and disorientation.

These experiences left their mark on the young Mandel, not least with respect to his positive attitude towards the German workers' movement. For him, Karl Marx, Friedrich Engels and Rosa Luxemburg were like deceased close relatives. In 1944 he was convinced, like most other members of the Fourth International, that Germany was facing an imminent revolution not unlike that of 1918–19. When he was deported to Germany, he characteristically believed that he was being taken 'to the heart of the world revolution'.

At the time of Ernest Mandel's first conscious involvement, the SRP/PSR was a small but not marginal organisation. In 1933–36, some of its members were involved in leading workers' strikes, some of which had cross-enterprise, cross-industry and regional significance. The SRP had roots among miners, metal workers and dockers. However, 1938 was a year of serious defeats: members in Antwerp, for instance, were driven out from the wage labour market when an enterprise was shut down as a deliberate measure of political repression – and in 1940–41, harsh crackdowns against the left constituted an additional problem. The Belgian Trotskyists were actively involved in resistance against the Nazi occupiers. Ernest Mandel, who at that time was already a leading member of the Fourth International and considered a kind of intellectual prodigy thanks to his knowledge and his contributions to assessing the international situation, went underground. His father was editing a much-noted journal against the occupiers. The Trotskyists did not indulge in the widespread illusion that things would 'not get that bad' (they were aware that the Jewish population was genuinely facing extermination and were warning against it). At the same time, they were consistently internationalist and free from anti-German hatred. Their propaganda was aimed at the occupying soldiers too. In the first phase of the occupation, they acted 'without competition', as it were, because the Social Democrats were perceived rather as collaborators with the German occupiers and the Communist Party could initially publish its paper legally (after all, it was the period of the Hitler-Stalin pact).

When Ernest Mandel was arrested for the first time, he was taken to a prison in St Gilles near Brussels, which was operated by the Wehrmacht rather than the SS or Gestapo. His real name and identity – including his 'Judaism' – were determined within less than 24 hours. Despite this, he was treated as a 'political' prisoner. Presumably, the Germans wanted to find his father through him, whose illegal publication was a constant thorn in the side of the occupying forces. Friends and family managed to help Mandel escape by bribing the guards.

In March 1944, Ernest Mandel was arrested a second time. This time he was sentenced to forced labour and sent to a concentration camp – but not an extermination camp – in Germany. He made a very convincing impression on his fellow prisoners when arguing that Nazi Germany would lose the war and that this would open up revolutionary possibilities. He also eloquently explained what the Social-Democratic Party of Germany (SPD), the Communist Party (KPD) and the German confederation of trade unions (ADGB) should have done to stop Hitler's rise to power. Fellow prisoners helped him to escape – it is furthermore likely that former SPD and KPD members who were guards in the camp deliberately looked the other way because he had made an impression on them. He was arrested a third time just before he could reach the Belgian border – once again by the Wehrmacht, which once again sent him to a 'normal' concentration camp rather than an extermination camp. He remained there until he was liberated by US troops in April 1945.

Having been quite literally 'beheaded' by repressive measures at the beginning of the war, the Belgian section of the Fourth International was now very isolated. It was Abraham (Abram) Leon who rebuilt the organisation under conditions of illegality, launched the newspaper *La Voie de Lénine* (Lenin's Path) and wrote the first illegal leaflets. Under his influence, the Belgian section of the Fourth International adopted an orientation under the Nazi occupation that pushed it into two fields of activity: firstly, the broadest possible anti-fascist resistance with a focus on its proletarian core, and secondly, internationalist propaganda directed at German soldiers. This work was carried out in close cooperation with German comrades.

Ernest Mandel soon became a member of the central committee of the Belgian section, now known as the Revolutionary Communist Party of Belgium. In November 1943, he attended an international meeting of the Fourth International for the first time, namely a session of the newly set up provisional European secretariat. In February 1944, a few weeks before his second arrest, he attended the First European Conference of the Fourth International. Subsequently he remained active in the leading bodies of the Fourth International and its Belgian section. From the late 1960s onwards, the focus of his activities shifted permanently from political work in Belgium to the international level.[9]

---

9 See François Vercammen's 'Biographie d'Ernest Mandel (1923–1995)' in Mandel 1997, pp. 546 et seq.

3   Role Model Abraham Leon

The key leading personality among Belgian Trotskyists that substantially influenced Ernest Mandel in the last two years of World War II was Abraham
(Abram) Leon, born 1918.[10]

Even as a young man, Ernest Mandel authored draft resolutions in the Fourth
International, which he usually prepared together with Abraham Leon after
they had been debated in the Belgian group. These included 'The Tasks of
the Fourth International in Europe' (February 1942), 'The National Question'
(which, according to the assessment presented in that document, would arise
anew in countries under prolonged Nazi occupation) and a draft resolution
on the 'revolutionary liquidation of the imperialist war'.[11] The European section of a new international leadership was created with the participation of
Ernest Mandel in these years. However, the process was considerably disrup-
ted when Abraham Leon, the French Trotskyist Marcel Hic and Ernest Mandel
were arrested by the Nazis. Of these three, only Mandel survived the camps.

Abraham Leon had three years to make a lasting impression on Ernest Mandel. Apart from his great talent, a range of other qualities distinguished Leon:
his level of activism and readiness to put aside personal interests; his broad
horizons; his unsectarian approach to the workers' movement as a whole; and
his unbreakable revolutionary optimism, which constantly encouraged and
inspired his comrades under the stressful conditions of underground political
activism. His motto was, 'find a reason for hope behind every reason for despair!'

Ernest Mandel wrote a biographical sketch also containing an appraisal of
Abraham Leon's work which served as an introduction to Leon's posthumously published text, *The Jewish Question*. It offers significant insight into what
inspired Ernest Mandel throughout his life and how he viewed one of his most
important role models:

> Those who read his book will admire the clarity and vigour of his reason-
> ing and will be astounded by the maturity of a mind at the age of twenty-
> four years. Among those who learn the story of his life there may be some
> who will perhaps ask why a man of such remarkable qualities tied his
> destiny to a small revolutionary organization; they will praise his sincer-
> ity, his complete ideological honesty that caused him to live in complete

---

10   See Mandel 1997; Stutje 2003, pp. 23 et seq.
11   See Stutje 2003, pp. 27 et seq.

harmony with his ideas. They will ask themselves: Why did the Marcel
Hies, the Martin Widelins, the A. Leons, who were among the most gifted
European intellectuals, choose a movement which could promise them
neither success nor glory nor honours nor even a minimum of material
comfort, but which on the contrary demanded of them every sacrifice,
including their lives, and which required long ungrateful work, frequently
in isolation from the proletariat to whom they wanted to give everything?
And if they are able to recognize in these young revolutionists, along with
their intellectual gifts, exceptional moral qualities, they will then say to
themselves that a movement capable of attracting such men solely by the
power of its ideas and the purity of its ideal and capable of leading these
rationalist dialecticians to such heights of self-denial and devotion is a
movement that cannot die because in it lives everything that is noble in
man.[12]

Analogously to the outcome of World War I, the Trotskyists were hoping for
enormous mass movements that would carry the possibility of socialist revolution – although Trotsky himself had sometimes spoken, a little more cautiously,
of a period of some 10 years after the looming World War. Much to Mandel's
disappointment, the Trotskyists' expectations did not come true between 1943
and 1946.[13] Movements did emerge in Greece, France and Italy, and a broad
sentiment of questioning capitalism prevailed among the masses. In Great Britain and in the western sectors of Germany (in East Germany, capitalism was
abolished through the military might of the Soviet Union), there was instabil-
ity and a certain mood in favour of non-capitalist solutions too. However, the
hegemony of the traditional political leadership of the working class was far
from broken or even being questioned.

    In 1943–44, Mandel and Leon worked out a new understanding of the situ-
ation, i.e., a way to explain the unexpected overall absence of revolutionary
mass movements that was new in relation to the traditions of their movement.
Their analysis was more nuanced when compared to Trotsky's late writings
and his formulation in the *Transitional Programme* (which the Fourth International had adopted as its foundational document) that the crisis of humanity
could be reduced to the 'crisis of proletarian leadership'.[14] For Mandel and
Leon, 'betrayal' by the Social-Democratic and Stalinist leaderships was not a

---

12   Leon 2017, pp. 30–1.
13   See Mandel 1989a, p. 9.
14   See Alles 1989, p. 61.

good enough explanation. Why were these leaderships not only able to maintain their political and organisational hegemony in the working class, but even reinforce and increase it at a time when the working class – e.g. in Italy and France – was moving again, returning to collective action, and in some cases even going on the offensive? The starting point for Leon and Mandel's at least partially new way of grasping this problem was the notion of a general crisis of the workers' movement, caused by the dialectical interaction between the role of the 'reformist' or 'bourgeois' leadership – i.e. a leadership that respects the framework and limits of capitalism – and the specific deficiencies in class consciousness in the working class itself.[15]

This understanding would remain important to Mandel throughout his life – it was key for the development of his analyses and his uncompromisingly argumentative yet unsectarian attitude to the majority trends of the workers' movement. In 1946, Ernest Mandel became a member of the International Secretariat of the Fourth International, its innermost leadership core, at a time when the organisation was far from achieving the hoped-for breakthrough towards greater strength and effectiveness. Mandel helped the nuclei of the Fourth International in several countries to develop perspectives. For instance, he drafted the first comprehensive action programme for Groups of Revolutionary Communists (GCR), the Italian section of the Fourth International.[16] It was written in the spirit of the *Transitional Programme*, which had been adopted by the Fourth International upon its formal inception in 1938.

4   Political Work in the Belgian Workers' Movement

Mandel's role in the Belgian workers' movement up to the mid-60s was linked to the politics of 'entrism', which in this case meant the political work of the Belgian section of the Fourth International in its native social-democratic movement. It was a fruitful experience for him and important for the development of his strategic thinking as well as personal political style. It was also in the context of 'entrism' that Mandel joined the social-democratic party in Belgium, the Socialist Party (BSP/PSB). From 1954 to 1956 he worked as a journalist for its party newspaper, *Le Peuple*. His most important mentor in this context was André Renard, the general secretary of the social-democratic General Feder-

---

15   See Stutje 2003, p. 38.
16   Italian Section of the Fourth International: *Übergangsprogramm und sozialistische Revolution* (Transitional programme and socialist revolution). This text is available to me in German and in the form of an unpublished manuscript. It is dated 'Rome, 1962'.

ation of Belgian Labour (ABVV/FGTB). Renard was a charismatic personality. Formerly active in the resistance against the Nazi occupation and a left syndicalist politically, he was the most prominent spokesman for the strong left-wing tendency within this trade union association. Through Renard, Ernest Mandel became the official advisor of the ABVV/FGTB as part of his commission for economic research and a journalist for *La Wallonie*, the daily paper of the metal worker union.[17]

Mandel's research at the time was mainly dedicated to studying the composition and structure of the main fractions of capital in Belgium. He contributed significantly to an important analytical document of the Belgian workers' movement entitled 'Corporations and Economic Democracy' and in this context was involved in drafting a programme towards 'structural reforms'.[18] Read in conjunction with the classical revolutionary Marxist texts, this programme seems rather ambiguous (in the sense of making concessions to reformist policies). But if one wanted to, one could also interpret it in the sense of transitional demands (an idea developed at the time of the third and fourth world congresses of the Communist International, i.e. predating the Stalin era) and in the spirit of the *Transitional Programme* of the Fourth International of 1938 that drew on this idea. The Belgian section of the Fourth International had come to believe that its links with the left-wing 'Renardist' tendency potentially enabled the workers' movement to create the preconditions for the emergence of a new broad left; this also offered the possibility of a revolutionary Marxist party rooted in the working class and far exceeding the already existing small cadre in size.

The Renardist leadership not only saw to it that a programme of 'anticapitalist structural reforms' was drafted, but also sought to win over the membership of the trade union federation in a systematic campaign of persuasion. Mandel also took part in this and got acquainted with numerous delegates and active trade unionists, especially in Wallonia. It gave him the opportunity to get to know the workers' movement, the mindset, and the strengths and weaknesses of this working-class vanguard intimately (he defined as the 'vanguard' those who were not only active during mass struggles, but who also defended workers' interests and prepared the next struggles during periods of downturn and mass passivity).[19]

During this period, Mandel was crucially involved in launching two new weekly papers: *La Gauche*, which was edited by him and had a circulation of up

17   See Mandel 1997, p. 544 et seq.
18   Ibid.
19   See Mandel 1997, p. 545.

to 20,000 copies, and the Flemish-language *Links*. From 1956–57, these publications reached an ideologically broad readership within the social-democratic
and socialist left, both in proletarian and intellectual circles. By 'tendency'
standards, the readership was certainly heterogenous; however, it was capable
of taking initiative at the level of social struggles and political argument. For
Mandel, it was an important experience to see that a minuscule revolutionary
tendency can have a real impact on a broader level. In later periods, when this
influence was no longer present – or not to the same extent – he tried again and
again to convey to younger members the importance of this strategic approach,
of always seeking to re-establish this kind of living connection with broad layers of the workers' movement.[20]

The mass strike of 1960–61 was the peak of the movement. Mandel played an
active role in the strike, even if he temporarily sneaked out to attend an international conference of the Fourth International, which he did not want to miss
for anything in the world. For Mandel, the strike was a sign indicating that the
great socially transformative potential of the working class in western Europe
and in the industrialised capitalist countries in general could re-emerge. Particularly important for him was the transition from a collective but passive refusal
of work in the context of a 'normal' strike to the emergence of self-organised
collective activity, linked to active strike management and involving as many
workers as possible. In this way, people who are normally mere objects of other
people's decisions or victims of so-called 'material constraints' become actors –
actors who no longer compete with each other but act together in solidarity.
This emerges as a driving factor for the development of political consciousness
and for learning processes that would require much more time and extraordinary individual effort under 'normal' circumstances. Moreover, the logic of the
struggle between the striking workers and the supportive parts of the population on one side, and the bosses and the bourgeois state defending the interests
of capital on the other, pushes towards an expansion of self-organisation into a
variety of other areas – not only in material production, where workers might
take over management, but also in public life. Mandel liked to cite the example
of Liège, where you could only withdraw money from a bank or savings bank at
the time if you could produce a valid trade union membership card. He argued
that in such situations, the proletarian mass movement has the tendency to
take over the public administrative functions previously monopolised by the
bourgeois state (including security) and organise them democratically from
below, as bank employees, lower civil servants, family members and sympath-

---

20   See Mandel 1972d, p. 9 et seq.

isers from among the general population join in. In Mandel's interpretation, this is how the seeds of an alternative state emerge – a proletarian state in Marx's sense that is beginning to 'wither away' from the outset. It is therefore the point of origin for a self-governing new society of 'associated producers', a society without classes and without a state apparatus that is divorced from society or has the monopoly on violence. Moreover, the emancipatory effect of such processes is evident from the beginning. Within weeks or months, those previously excluded by circumstance from participating in higher forms of cultural life acquire a keen interest in many different subjects. They become critical, confident and creative.[21]

As is well known, the mass strike of 1960–61 – aimed against the anti-social austerity programme of a conservative-liberal government and pointing in the direction of socialising the large Belgian corporations – did not culminate in a socialist revolution. To explain the outcome, it was far from Mandel to resort to the general statement, so emphasised by Trotsky in the last years of his life, that the only thing lacking was a sufficiently strong and influential revolutionary party which might lead the movement towards victory. For him, the causes of failure were concrete – and if one wanted to draw lessons, one had to work out the causes from the concrete problems and choices facing the movement.

The Renardist leadership and its most popular figure, the charismatic André Renard, had great authority. In the decisive moment, Renard disoriented the movement. The division of the Belgian working class through the so-called 'language dispute' between Flemish and Walloons, which is rooted in the concrete history of the country and its regions, was the lever that pushed the movement back. It was substantially stronger in Wallonia than it was in Flanders. Radicalisation had reached new heights in Wallonia and increasingly turned the movement against the central government in Brussels. In Mandel's view, the Renardist leadership was responsible for diverting this radicalisation at the crucial moment from the idea of developing an alternative counter-society from below and fighting for the solidarity of the Flemish working class by any means necessary. In the final stages, Mandel and his comrades tried to direct the movement towards a nationwide 'march on Brussels' to overcome regionalism (although they had no objections to the proposal for a democratic federalism, which was particularly popular in the Walloon workers' movement). Renard, on the other hand, used mass meetings to proclaim a desire to 'close the borders' and cut Wallonia off from the Flemish part of Belgium. This fundamentally nationalist rather than socialist idea, which encouraged divisions

---

21   See Mandel 1961, p. 129 et seq.

in the working class, appeared to most of the movement as a 'radical' solution at the time. This change of mood, however, was the beginning of the end and sealed the fate of the movement, which was unable to implement its most important demands.

Despite this, the left-wing current in Belgian social democracy initially emerged strengthened on the back of the strike movement. It succeeded in pushing through the party's adoption of the FGTB's 'anti-capitalist structural reforms' programme against the will of the leadership – an accomplishment in which Mandel, *La Gauche* and *Links* played an important role. But even so, the reformist leadership remained in office and increasingly orientated itself towards a government coalition with the Christian conservatives. Confrontations with the left subsequently focused on this question. Opponents found to be violating 'party discipline' – i.e. by voting against the coalition policy – were soon subject to legal proceedings. When the coalition with 'the bourgeois' became reality, the social democrats not only agreed to social welfare cuts, but also to Belgium's neo-colonial intervention policy in the Congo and new legislation on 'domestic security', which the left interpreted as anti-strike laws in response to the great industrial action of winter 1960–61.[22]

At the 'congress of contradictions' of 1964, resolutions against support for *La Gauche* and *Links* and against the left-wing federalist forces of Wallonia finally set the course: the anti-capitalist left was to be pushed out. The left-led youth league of the party, Jeune Garde Socialiste (JGS), was likewise marginalised when a 'right-wing' rival organisation was set up. Mandel, whose affiliation to the Fourth International and its 'entrist' tactic had just been revealed and denounced by members of the party leadership in the daily papers, defended the position of the left and especially the 'right to form tendencies' at the 'congress of contradictions'. According to him, a right to different tendencies did *de facto* not exist if the left was not permitted to express its views openly in its own publications – especially since it had much smaller print runs than the official party press that reflected the views of the leadership. This was tantamount to a 'claim of infallibility' by the leadership, resembling the Pope or Stalin.

After this period, Mandel made efforts to build a new party to the left of social democracy. Several attempts failed, and once again regionalism played a role. But there were also left-wingers who had worked closely with Mandel in the previous years and who were shocked to learn that Mandel was 'in reality' a member of the Fourth International. Some, like Jacques Yerna and

---

22   My account of Mandel's role in the Belgian workers' movement and in the social-democratic Belgian Socialist Party (PSB) up to his exclusion is based on the historical work of Nicolas Latteur (2000).

Ernest Glimme, felt manipulated – like puppets whose strings had been pulled by obscure forces from behind the scenes. This highlights a problem of the 'entrist' tactic: the Trotskyists are in fact for transparency and open debate in the workers' movement. But when they entered traditional parties of the labour movement to be in touch with the most class-conscious workers, they usually had to hide their organisational affiliations. By doing so, they often created an air of secretiveness and distrust around themselves, which had a deterrent and demoralising effect even on those politically close to them.

After their failure to build a significant party to the left of the social democrats, the influence of Mandel and his comrades remained confined to relatively small circles again. *La Gauche* later became a limited circulation newspaper of the small Belgian section of the Fourth International and the JGS its small youth league. Although the Belgian section, too, grew and gained new momentum with the upturn of workers' struggles, the movement against the Vietnam War and the youth radicalisation of the late 1960s, it would remain a small organisation on the left fringes of the workers' movement to this day.

5   Role in the Fourth International and Contribution to Theory

Ernest Mandel continued his work on economic issues with great dedication: 1962 saw the original French-language publication of *Marxist Economic Theory*, and he deepened his analysis of *Late Capitalism*, initially referred to as 'neo-capitalism', and his interpretation of the *Long Waves of Capitalist Development*.[23] At the same time, he focused on the strategic question of whether socialist revolutions were possible in the developed capitalist countries and how to aid them politically. His reflections revolved around two main problems: firstly, the question what objective contradictions of capitalism could lead to revolutionary situations and, in this context, the danger of another world war bringing unprecedented devastation on account of new means of mass destruction (nuclear weapons). Secondly, the subjective preconditions for the development of revolutionary consciousness by the working class under conditions of relative prosperity in the context of a prolonged post-World War II economic upturn.[24]

There is no mechanical link between Mandel's economic works and his political and strategic reflections. Mandel often stressed the need to examine

---

23   Mandel 1968, 1975d and 1995.
24   See Ali 1995.

objective reality in a strictly scientific fashion, without being guided by political wishful thinking. At the same time, he tried to bring his political thinking into line with the developmental tendencies of contemporary capitalism that he was researching. He tried to develop his ideas in dialogue with other tendencies of the left, especially the left currents in the social-democratic and 'official' Communist parties.[25]

The essay 'A Socialist Strategy for Western Europe' (first printed in French in July 1965 in the *Revue internationale du socialism* edited by Lelio Basso) reflects Mandel's views at the time – they would be put to a practical test with the emergence of new anti-capitalist mass movements in the late 1960s.[26] As early as 1963, Mandel had a major part in a perspectives document of the Fourth International (adopted at its Seventh World Congress, i.e. the 'reunification congress' after the Trotskyist movement had been divided for 10 years) that spoke of a dialectics between three sectors of the world revolution: the developed capitalist countries, the poor and dependent countries, and the bureaucratised transitional countries.[27]

As mentioned earlier, from the mid-1960s onward the focus of Mandel's work permanently shifted to the international level. He felt the urge to merge his political tendency with the emerging youth radicalisation and use the new arising opportunities to build revolutionary organisations in the individual countries and internationally. It was in this context that he met Gisela Scholtz, who was active in the Berlin section of the Socialist Student League (SDS) and who became his companion and first wife. She died young in 1982, which came as a shock to Mandel – he found his loss difficult to overcome, and it became a decisive turning point for him. Although he did not lose his general qualities – his devotion to the cause he espoused, his enthusiasm and ability to enthuse others – to those who had known him well, he no longer seemed quite so 'youthful', carefree and indestructible. Private happiness returned to Mandel's life when he met his second life companion Anne Sprimont-Mandel (see eyewitness testimony by François Vercammen).

In Mandel's view, the groundwork for the events of the late 1960s had been laid by a constellation of different processes, ultimately finding expression in a new global awakening. The fact that he had predicted the turn of a prolonged economic trend and forthcoming shocks strengthened his predictive confidence, which would later prove a double-edged sword. For him, the prehistory

---

25   See Mandel 1997, p. 545.
26   Mandel 1965.
27   See Fourth International 1963, p. 5.

of May 1968 involved the long-term upsurge of strike movements in the rich developed capitalist countries, the revolts in Eastern Bloc states (East Berlin in 1953, Poland and Hungary in 1956), the onset of the Sino-Soviet conflict and the Cuban revolution – both of which contributed to the break-up of Stalinist monolithism in the 'official' Communist movement – and the successes of the anti-colonial revolution, especially the defeat of French imperialism in Algeria. These events matched the outline of a 'dialectical relationship between the three main sectors of the world revolution' drawn up at the seventh world congress of the Fourth International with Mandel's substantial input: i.e. of a contradictory interaction, which, however, held the possibility of a substantial turn of the international situation.

Mandel actively participated in the May 1968 movement, just as he tried to be close to mass movements with an anti-capitalist and emancipatory potential at every opportunity that offered itself.[28]

Ernest Mandel made efforts – not only in Belgium – to build individual sections of the Fourth International, the Fourth International as a whole, and revolutionary organisations in general. He did not limit himself to the role of the 'ideologist', speaker, theoretician, journalist and writer, but also took care of the more 'profane' problems of organisation building: arranging translations, calling for donations, setting up meeting and training facilities, creating offices and launching sympathiser organisations.

In Germany, too, his role in building and guiding the national section was significant (see eyewitness testimony by Helene Jungclas, Hans Peiffer and Helmut Wendler). He travelled the Asian continent and personally contacted comrades politically close to the Fourth International in India, Indonesia and Sri Lanka. One must remember that the local section of the Fourth International, the Lanka Sama Samaya Party (LSSP), became Sri Lanka's strongest mass workers' party (later, however, it took part in bourgeois governments and lost its revolutionary character as a consequence; today the Fourth International is represented in Sri Lanka by the 3,000-member strong NSSP).[29] Mandel attached great importance to relations with the US Socialist Workers Party (SWP), which had been the most important organisation of the Fourth International during World War II. However, Mandel's efforts always extended beyond relations with Trotskyist groups and organisations. He practised solidarity with Algeria, and by no means just verbally. At the time, the FI provided illegal

---

28   For Ernest Mandel's role in the Fourth International, in broader social and political movements and in public life since the early 1960s, I rely heavily on the biography written by François Vercammen – see Mandel 1997, pp. 546 et seq.

29   See Mandel 1997, p. 548.

logistical support for the Algerian FNL in Belgium and the Netherlands as well as in Germany and France.[30] In 1962, Ernesto 'Che' Guevara invited Mandel to join the economic debate in Cuba, which discussed paths to the construction of socialism. Mandel was close to the position of 'Che' Guevara, who was sceptical, even hostile towards policies based on propagandistic invocations of work ethic as well as purely individual incentives, which usually have a demoralising effect. Mandel emphasised the primacy of collective incentives that engender solidarity. He argued against a 'socialist market economy', for the greatest possible expansion of self-management and socialist democracy, for democratic majority decision-making especially with respect to big economic decisions that have overall 'strategic' relevance for the country's development (the bitter experience of Yugoslavia, in his view, was based on a combination of self-management at company level, which was very commendable in and of itself, with undemocratic decisions 'from above' on all issues that concerned the whole country and the overall orientation).[31] Subsequently, the Fourth International supported the 'Guevarist' continental movement in Latin America (from the OLAS conference onward) and the armed struggle of various guerrilla groups. In this context, it set up armed groups itself (especially in Argentina). There was a sharp and controversial debate on this orientation in the Fourth International. Mandel and the Fourth International majority were self-critical about it from 1974 onward, but their self-critique was not very pronounced.[32] Mandel was probably wary that stronger self-criticism might cut him off from radicalised young people in Western Europe and in Latin America.[33]

After 1968 Mandel became quite internationally renowned. He took part in countless events and meetings in many countries, spoke in panel debates as well as in small academic circles or Marxist educational seminars.[34] Mandel spoke convincingly and stirringly. He knew his subjects well and always supported his views with a variety of facts and examples. He appeared credible and knew how to captivate an audience for many hours. Mandel's popularity and outreach to larger audiences surpassed that of his small international organisation. Contrary to what an outside observer might assume, his personal effect on the members of the Fourth International was not solely owed to his theoretical competence and productivity.

---

30   Ibid.
31   See Mandel 1967b.
32   See Bensaïd 2002, pp. 103 et seq.
33   According to a message from Charles-André Udry (see Introduction).
34   See Lubitz 2004.

His proverbial 'revolutionary optimism' was one of his most typical characteristics.[35] Not unlike his role model Abraham Leon, he countered every reason to resign with two or three reasons for hope. Whether politicised young people, strike leaders, representatives of left-wing trade union movements, socialist-minded intellectuals or dissidents from the 'bureaucratised workers' countries' – Mandel addressed them all as equals or at least gave that impression. In the last years of his life, the constant exertion of travel, lectures and conversations became a burden and a danger to his health. It was only then that he tried to slow down, although he never quite succeeded.[36]

Much of Mandel's attention was dedicated to the contradictions of contemporary capitalism and the direction in which it would evolve, the chances for an emergence of revolutionary mass movements, questions of socialist strategy, and proletarian and revolutionary forms of organisation (trade unions, councils/soviets, revolutionary organisations, parties and internationals). Beyond this, Mandel's theoretical work also focused on his investigation of bureaucracy, Stalinism, and developments in the USSR and countries with a similar socio-economic structure and political system.[37]

Although the 'Trotskyist tradition' meant the world to him, Mandel was no dogmatic. He wanted to understand any new developments and apply the best analytical methods from the past to achieve this – yet without simply regurgitating the positions of the 'old masters'. Mandel's strengths and weaknesses were closely linked. With his extensive knowledge and use of many examples, he could 'knock out' partners in a debate or numb their critical impulses. His optimism and penchant for generalisation often gave rise to illusions which would later inevitably turn into disappointment. For a long time, Mandel had a fairly traditionalist view of progress, which he viewed as evolvement towards ever 'higher stages' in history. In this respect, he was an 'old school Marxist' par excellence, which is also why he espoused concepts that would make little sense if not for some predetermined 'higher development' – for example 'degeneration' (of leadership, parties or states) and historical 'diversions' (a term which implies that history has a predetermined path).[38]

Mandel advocated an 'open Marxism', which he understood as openness towards all schools of thought that aspired to universal emancipation.[39] At the same time, the coherence of Marxist theory, its programme and its compre-

---

35   Mandel 1997, p. 542.
36   See eyewitness testimonies by Livio Maitan and François Vercammen.
37   See Mandel 1997, p. 549.
38   Mandel 1979, p. 114 et seq.
39   See Mandel and Agnoli 1980.

hensive claim to validity were so important to him, it is fair to say that Mandel's openness was more of a general attitude, a willingness to engage in dialogue, but not to pursue joint theoretical work with representatives of other intellectual trends. Mandel's overly optimistic assessment of the events from 1989 to 1991 also showed weaknesses in his theoretical approach.[40] I will return to both aspects in the final chapter.

Mandel's contribution to the Fourth International manifesto *Socialism or Barbarism: To the Threshold of the 21st Century* reflects the problems he was facing in his final years, before he died of a second heart attack on 20 July 1995.[41] His role was initially to incorporate the revolutionary Marxist tradition, as understood by him, as clearly and fully as possible into the text. By doing so, he was following a tradition that Trotsky also used to invoke: according to him, passing on the unadulterated tradition to future generations becomes the foremost task especially in the face of frustrated hopes (this had also been one of the motivations for Trotsky's activity in his final years). However, as the debate within his organisation continued, Mandel began to grasp the full extent of uncertainty and doubt that had taken hold of the socialist left. He got involved in developing perspectives aimed at new generations for whom the splits and schisms of the communist world would largely be affairs of the past. Parts of contemporary global reality that are still tied to the October Revolution of 1917 by an umbilical cord or barely visible threads are no longer perceived as such. Barely anyone is interested which Marxist trend has been vindicated against others, especially in the assessment of events that are now history. There have been profound changes in our societies, in the wage-earning class, in the cultural atmosphere and in political debates. We must grasp these changes to develop revolutionary programmes and practices in a realistic fashion, but also without hiding or backtracking on the fundamental views that we still consider correct.[42] This is more or less what Ernest Mandel thought in the last years of his life.

Ernest Mandel suffered his first heart attack in December 1993. Even then, he did not slow down his political work in the Fourth International. He placed great hopes in the successes of the left in the Brazilian workers' movement (the Democracia Socialista tendency in the Workers' Party), in which the Brazilian section of the Fourth International plays a significant role. He formulated a catalogue of unresolved or insufficiently solved questions that he thought his

---

40   See Mandel 1997, pp. 549 et seq.
41   Ibid.
42   Mandel 1997, p. 550.

comrades should address in the future.[43] In his last will and testament, he referred to the Fourth International as 'the meaning of [my] life'.[44]

At the heart of Mandel's socialist strategy was the idea of the democratic self-organisation of the working class – in his view, this would provide a pole around which a general process of universal emancipation would become possible.[45] Apart from his books dedicated to the analysis of modern capitalism and a much-read *Introduction to Marxism*, Mandel produced theoretical papers on numerous topics.[46] One of his later publications was titled *Power and Money: A Marxist Theory of Bureaucracy*. It addresses the problem of bureaucracy in the workers' movement, in non-capitalist countries and in the bourgeois state. Of particular interest is the chapter on the temptation of 'substitutionism' since this issue affects not only mass organisations, but revolutionary tendencies and smaller groups too.[47] For Mandel, the temptation correlates with the degree of passivity in the working class or mass movement. In a later introduction to the German edition, Mandel wrote that 'revolutionary Marxism' – by which he mainly meant the Fourth International, including himself – had underestimated the negative impact of decades of (post-)Stalinist dictatorship on the consciousness of workers in the Soviet Union and in similar countries.[48]

The outcry of Seattle 1999 – 'The world is not a commodity! Another world is possible!' – the upsurge of a new international protest movement against neoliberal globalisation, defensive struggles of wage labourers against cuts, the social forum movement, and more recent efforts to build political forces against capitalism and to the left of neoliberal social democracy would have reinforced Mandel in his basic convictions – and perhaps tempted him to overly optimistic projections yet again.

Ernest Mandel's legacy merits not just another glance – some of its aspects are worth examining in greater depth. The present work can only be a beginning – or rather, a continuation of the work that began in July 1996 in Amsterdam at the conference on 'Ernest Mandel's contribution to Marxism'.[49]

---

43   Mandel 1995b, pp. 32–3.
44   Mandel 1997, p. 550.
45   Mandel 1979a, pp. 128–30.
46   In his essay 'Ernest Mandel (1923–1995): An Intellectual Portrait', Gilbert Achcar outlines the history of Mandel's most important theoretical publications. See Achcar 1999a, p. 3 et seq.
47   See Mandel 1992a, p. 103 et seq.
48   See Mandel 1992a, p. 5.
49   The transcribed conference talks were first published in French – see Achcar 1999b.

Critique of Contemporary Capitalism

1   Mandel's Historical-Genetic Critique of Capitalism

1.1   *Economic Theory and History*

Ernest Mandel considered himself the exponent of an orthodox Marxist critique of capitalism. For him, the capitalist mode of production had characteristic traits following a set pattern and pointing to the need for its demise and replacement with a different system. In 1992, three years before his death, he formulated a summary of ten such laws (1. The law of value; 2. The law of capital accumulation; 3. The law of surplus-value; 4. The law of equalisation of the rate of profit; 5. The law of concentration and centralisation of capital; 6. The law of the tendency of the organic composition of capital to rise; 7. The law of class struggle determination of wages; 8. The law of the tendency of the rate of profit to fall; 9. The law of the cyclical nature of capitalist production; 10. The law of the unavoidable collapse of the system):

1) Capitalism is generalised commodity production. Commodities and money (money being a commodity that can in principle be exchanged against any other commodity) must circulate. Therefore, commodities always have a price expressed in money. They can only be acquired with money. Commodity prices fluctuate in the short term because of the interaction of supply and demand. But these fluctuations gravitate around an axis that is ultimately determined by value. Value, in turn, is an expression of the production costs measurable in abstract human labour (in working hours). In the long term, production determines circulation and consumption.

2) Capitalism is production organised by the private owners of the means of production. These owners, the capitalists, buy the necessary elements for production in order to sell the produced goods and services as commodities. Their initiative is crucial for the capitalist economy. Because they are private proprietors who are in competition with each other, they make their decisions autonomously. Competition compels them to maximise profits, because without sufficient profits the individual capitalist can neither compete nor accumulate capital.

3) The only fundamental source of profit (and therefore of accumulation) is surplus-value. Surplus-value is the new value produced by human labour power minus the costs necessary to maintain and reproduce labour

power. From this arises the need of the capitalists to extract the greatest possible surplus-value from their workforce. The main means of achieving this are wage reductions, increasing the number of working hours, intensifying work and increasing labour productivity without compensation through corresponding increases in real wages.

4) Under capitalism, commodities are not merely products of labour, but products of labour appropriated and controlled by capital. Therefore, these products are not exchanged in proportion to work done; they do not generate profits proportionally to the direct contribution of labour to their production. Rather, the profits are proportional to the total capital invested. Capital is composed differently in the various sectors (particularly the proportion of expenditure on the material ingredients of production and on the remuneration of labour power varies from one sector to another). Profits can therefore differ greatly from the surplus-value that was generated directly in the production of the respective commodities. However, with respect to the economy as a whole and in the long term, the total price of production (that is: the production costs plus the average profit) is equal to the total value of commodities produced.

5) The centralisation and concentration of capital (which are, in turn, consequences of competition) result in limited competition. This creates the phenomenon of market control by monopolies and oligopolies. However, their control is not absolute: in the long term, the law of value prevails. In real terms, monopolies produce 'only' two rates of average profit, with the monopolistic sector appropriating a surplus profit (a rent). In the very long term, there is a tendency for the two different profit rates to align.

6) Capitalism has an intrinsic tendency towards permanent technological innovation because capitalists have an interest in reducing their production costs. Therefore, they want to 'reduce workloads', devalue labour as a factor and replace living labour with dead labour (the production of past labour). This creates a trend towards the automation of production. High accumulation rates can temporarily neutralise or revert the tendency of the declining growth rate of living labour. In the long term, however, the tendency towards stagnation or reducing the share of living labour in production prevails.

7) The relationship between surplus-value and wages is not only determined by the market, but also by 'moral' and 'historical' factors. Needs that are regarded as indispensable by society are essential for this – it goes without saying that this factor is subject to historical change. This basket of commodities, in turn, is determined by the results of class struggle

and the balance of forces between labour and capital. The fluctuations of the 'reserve army of labour' (the percentage of unemployed among the wage-dependant and unpropertied class) determine this balance of forces. Hence, the tendency of capital to 'reduce workloads' has at the same time the function of guaranteeing that wages do not rise above a certain threshold so that they do not reduce profit too much.

8) The rise in the organic composition of capital (the ratio between the expenditures for 'living' and 'dead' labour) leads to the tendency of the rate of profit to fall (the rate of profit being the ratio of surplus-value to 'dead' and 'living' labour). This tendency of the rate of profit to fall can be compensated by counter-tendencies, the most important of which is the growth of the surplus-value rate (i.e. the rate of exploitation, the ratio of surplus-value to wage costs). In the long run, however, the rate of surplus-value cannot grow proportionally to the rise in the organic composition of capital, and other counter-tendencies also subside in the long term.

9) Since competition is a prerequisite under capitalism, fluctuations in production and periodic crises are inevitable. The results of decisions taken by the autonomously producing individual capitals can be very different from their intentions. Thus all individual measures to increase profits can lead to a general fall in the profit rate. One reason for crises is, for instance, that production increases faster than effective (solvent) demand, or that the average rate of profit falls. Periodically occurring capitalist crises are simultaneously crises of overproduction (overaccumulation) and underconsumption (i.e. overproduction of commodities). Within 160 years, capitalism was characterised by seven-year cycles culminating in such crises. These cycles should be read as time periods within which value asserts itself as an axis. Prices gravitate around this axis, and profit rates level out towards a general average rate of profit. This is established through 'cleansing crises' in which 'superfluous' capital (from the point of view of capitalist production) is destroyed.

10) There is no linear tendency for crisis to worsen within the individual cycles, but there is a combination of different secular trends: a) The tendency of the rate of profit to fall; b) the declining share of living labour in the total cost of production; c) the territorial expansion of capitalism meeting its limits d) the intensification and radicalisation of class struggle. There is no purely economic law according to which capitalism will collapse. Nonetheless, increasingly violent upheavals (wars, revolutions, counterrevolutions) are probable consequences of the contradictions of this system. Thus humanity drifts towards two alternatives: social-

ism or the general disintegration of civilisation. Mandel's version of the 'breakdown theory' is based on a combination of economic, social and political factors.[1]

As is well-known, Karl Marx opens his critique of political economy in *Capital* Volume I with the commodity as the nucleus of the contemporary capitalist economic order: 'The wealth of societies in which the capitalist mode of production prevails appears as an "immense collection of commodities"; the individual commodity appears as its elementary form. Our investigation therefore begins with the analysis of the commodity'.[2] In the course of his presentation, the unfolding contradictions within the capitalist mode of production appears at least partially as unfolding contradictions within its elementary form, the commodity itself. When expounding on the theory of surplus-value, Marx only mentions in passing in which way it corresponds to earlier historical forms of exploitation: 'What distinguishes the various economic formations of society – the distinction between for example a society based on slave labour and a society based on wage-labour – is the form in which this surplus labour is in each case extorted from the immediate producer, the worker'.[3]

Mandel, on the other hand, opens his account of the Marxist critique of political economy with the historical origins of exploitation in general and the problem of pre-capitalist unconcealed exploitation based on direct relations of dependency. In this way he exposes the capitalist form of exploitation (explained through Marx's theory of surplus-value) as a form of exploitation that is concealed by the commodity form.

Similarly, Mandel does not initially present commodities as the elementary form of the capitalist mode of production, but as the form that the products of labour assume under specific conditions in pre-capitalist relations. While (dialectical) logic appears to dominate in Marx's *Capital* (although in part this is mere appearance, and interpretations of *Capital* suggesting otherwise are based on a selective reading of the text),[4] Mandel proved to be more of an adherent of (dialectical) historiography.[5] In the climate of a leftist reception of Marx at the time, this difference provoked criticism of Mandel, which did not leave him unaffected. He therefore dedicated the opening chapter of *Late*

---

1   See Mandel 1997, p. 470 et seq.

2   Marx 1990, p. 125.

3   Marx 1990, p. 325.

4   The eighth part of Marx's main work *Capital* Volume I, 'So-Called Primitive Accumulation' (Marx 1990, p. 872 et seq.), certainly supports the notion of a generic-evolutionary investigation in Mandel's sense – see Mandel 1968b, p. 19.

5   See Mandel 1968b, p. 17 et seq.

Capitalism to the underlying methodological problem: in 'The laws of motion and the history of capital', he expressed his desire to present a conscious and critical balance of history (genesis of the capitalist mode of production and its later development) and a deduction of categories based on dialectical logic.[6]

Either way, it seems to me that the historical-genetic presentation is a specific feature of Mandel's that offers didactic advantages to begin with. It makes Marx's critique of political economy – which 'ascends' from simpler, more easily comprehensible economic conditions to more complex capitalist relations that are more difficult to grasp – more accessible. The exposure of these relations as relations of exploitations thus gains plausibility. Marx self-critically drew attention to his 'coquettish' use of Hegel's language in parts of *Capital* Volume i.[7]

As early as 1963, during his lecture at an educational event organised by the Paris Federation of the United Socialist Party (psu), which is reproduced in *Introduction to Marxist Economic Theory*, Mandel succinctly formulated the theoretical justification of his view of the links between economic theory and economic history. In my view, he essentially maintains this view in the first chapter of *Late Capitalism*.

> The exchange value of a commodity, then, is determined by the quantity of labor socially necessary for its production, with skilled labor being taken as a multiple of simple labor and the coefficient of multiplication being a reasonably measurable quantity.
>
> This is the kernel of the Marxist theory of value and the basis for all Marxist economic theory in general. Similarly, the theory of social surplus product and surplus labor, which we discussed at the beginning of this work, constitutes the basis for all Marxist sociology and is the bridge connecting Marx's sociological and historical analysis, his theory of classes and the development of society generally, to Marxist economic theory, and more precisely, to the Marxist analysis of all commodity-producing societies of a precapitalist, capitalist and postcapitalist character.[8]

After this preliminary leap ahead, motivated by the methodological formulation of the question, let us first follow Mandel's usual mode of presenta-

---

6 See Mandel 1975d, p. 11.

7 See Marx's postface to the second German edition (1873), where he also quoted from a review – see Marx 1990, pp. 100–2. There, the aspect of historical development (analogously to the biological evolution of living organisms) plays an important role.

8 Mandel 1973b, pp. 31–2.

tion: the point of departure are those social conditions that allow labour productivity to grow above a certain threshold, so that a social surplus product is created. The necessary product that keeps the producers alive does not by itself allow for a social division of labour and social differentiation. The surplus product over and above this minimum allows the maintenance of a part of society that carries out activities other than the immediate production of food. This also creates the possibility of struggle over this surplus product and the development of a class society comprising an exploited class and a ruling class that lives off the work of the former. The labour of the exploited class is divided into necessary labour (to produce the necessary product) and surplus labour (to produce the surplus product appropriated by the ruling class). Exploitation through direct domination and dependence prevails, for example, in slave-owning societies or under feudal conditions, which involve the exploitation of serfs who spend much of their time working for the feudal lord.[9]

At the outset, surplus-value is merely 'the monetary form of the social surplus product'.[10] Capitalist surplus-value is also the appropriation of labour without offering anything in return, although this is disguised through the commodity and money form. Commodities are goods that are produced not for immediate use but for exchange; they have a use value but also an exchange value. From a certain stage of the social division of labour onward, a significant share of the products of labour can assume the character of commodities. The progressive generalisation of commodity production thus appears as the prehistory of capitalism (i.e. the mode of production in which advanced commodity production dominates the economy). The specifically capitalist form of alienation develops alongside this: the separation of producers from their products and from the means of production, work (including increases in working hours and number of days worked per year) as external obligation due to direct or indirect coercion, the separation of the mechanical-exhausting from the creative aspects of work, the replacement of personal relations (and be they relations of dependence) by the apparently impersonal bond of commodity and money relations.[11] The emergence of the law of value can be understood as the development of work towards regulated and measurable work and of parts of the economy towards a labour-time economy.[12] From the seventeenth

---

9   See Mandel 1973b, pp. 16–17; Mandel 1975a, p. 6; Mandel 1968b, p. 23; Mandel 1979a, p. 11.
10   Mandel 1973b, p. 17.
11   Ibid.
12   See Mandel 1968b, p. 49 et seq.; Mandel 1973b, p. 24.

century, peasants who worked for the urban markets and thus became commodity producers worked with increasing regularity. The same is even more true for work in manufacture and in the factory, which has no seasons, 'dead time' (actually 'living time' from the producer's point of view), days or hours of leisure according to the natural or human rhythm. An accounting system based on labour emerges. Mandel offers many examples of this from pre-capitalist societies. The transition from feudal compulsory labour to payment in kind, and from payment in kind to monetary contribution, also presupposes a transition to calculation in work-hours. In the eighteenth century, when peasants in western Europe regularly purchased handmade textile products (instead of producing them for their own use as they had done for hundreds of years), controlled equivalents based on the calculation of labour-time were established. Within the medieval towns, the working hours considered necessary for the artisan production of various products were very strictly defined. This calculation in work-hours is characteristic for 'small-scale commodity production', described by Mandel as an intermediate epoch between the time of pure use-value production (natural economy) and capitalism.[13]

Such are the concrete historical origins of determining the exchange value of commodities through socially necessary labour-time (the average time required with specific labour productivity) and the commodity relations (of the market) as an objective bond between independently producing producers. Because one hour of unskilled work cannot be equated with one hour of skilled work (to acquire the skills requires a certain number of work-hours), skilled labour is complex labour, i.e. simple labour multiplied by a coefficient 'based on the cost of acquiring a given skill'.[14] This analytical penetration of a specific social reality must not be mistaken for moral justification: from a socialist point of view, skilled labour does not entitle anyone to privileges.[15]

The concept of 'socially necessary labour' does not derive from moral judgement either.[16] Commodities can only function as commodities if they satisfy needs. Economic equilibrium is only possible if the overall purchasing power in society is used to buy the sum of all goods produced. Hence, 'too many' horse carriages and 'too few' automobiles were produced in Paris in the late nineteenth and early twentieth century. In the former case, more labour was spent than was 'socially necessary' because unsaleable commodities were produced

---

13   See Mandel 1973e, p. 28; Mandel 1979a, p. 34; Mandel 1968b, p. 23 et seq.
14   Mandel 1973b, p. 31.
15   See Mandel 1973b, pp. 30–1; Mandel 1968b, pp. 84–6.
16   Mandel 1973b, p. 32.

in that sector. The 'excess' production was tantamount to wasted labour. Conversely, the automobiles that were 'too few' could be sold at higher prices than would have been the case if their production had covered demand. Brokered through the market, these commodities allowed for a 'bonus' to be collected.[17]

Under capitalism, labour productivity is subject to permanent changes, and in many areas of production, the work done is above or below the given average labour productivity. Production with below-average labour productivity means that more work-hours are spent on the production of the same value, i.e. labour is wasted. Conversely, production with above-average labour productivity means an over-profit above the average profit. The pursuit of surplus profit (over-profit) is the driving force of capitalism. However, as a result of competition, above-average labour productivity sooner or later becomes the average labour productivity, which eliminates the surplus profit. This leads to a levelling of profit rates.[18] Surplus-value is the money form of surplus product, i.e. that part of the wage labourers' output that goes to the owners of the means of production without any compensation in return.[19] This occurs in a seemingly paradoxical way through the exchange of equivalents. The capitalist buys labour power at its value and in return receives the whole product of its value production, including the new value it creates. Thus surplus-value is the difference between the value produced and the value of the commodity labour-power (whose value is determined by the costs of its reproduction). The minimum wage is not physically but socially determined and variable, in particular through the growth of the productive forces. Any 'theory of absolute immiseration' (which suggests that it is a 'law' of capitalism that real wages constantly fall in the long term) is false and cannot possibly be deduced from Marx.[20]

The value produced can be measured by labour-time. Ten hours of work produce a value that corresponds to ten hours of work. If the costs of reproduction of the commodity labour power were equal to this value (assuming a ten-hour working day), no surplus-value would be produced (in a society without commodity production this corresponds to a situation where the total of production only serves the direct maintenance of the producers, where there can therefore be no surplus-value). In real terms, under capitalism the equivalent value of the wage is created in a mere fraction of the working day. Everything

---

17   Mandel 1973b, p. 34.
18   See Mandel 1968b, pp. 158–60.
19   Mandel 1979a, p. 39 et seq.
20   Mandel 1968b, pp. 150–1. Marx 1990, p. 14 et seq.

produced beyond and above this is surplus-value. If that were not the case, no capitalist would invest money in labour.[21]

Mandel cites three pieces of 'proof of the labour theory of value'. The first ('analytical') proof proceeds by breaking down the price of a commodity price into its constituent elements, almost to the point where the only remaining elements are material immediately found in nature and human labour. The second ('logical') proof draws on Marx's statements in the beginning of *Capital* Volume I: To be interchangeable, different commodities must have something in common, and this common quality cannot be physical. Their common feature is that they are all products of human labour, that is to say, of *abstract* human labour ('work sans phrase', as Marx called it), because the producers produce independently of each other for exchange. The measure of their exchange-value is the socially necessary labour in the production of these commodities. The third and final proof ('by reduction to the absurd') is based on the hypothetical idea of a society in which all production is automated. In this scenario, no surplus-value could be transferred from fully automated to semi or non-automated sectors of production (which is possible with partial automation). Such production could not possibly create monetary revenue. The products could not be sold. Their exchange-value would be eliminated – precisely because human labour has disappeared from production.[22] At this point Mandel resumes the historical-genetic mode of representation in order to address 'Capital in precapitalist society'. Between the age of natural economy (i.e. production purely for use-value) and capitalism there stretches a long period of 'small-scale commodity production' in which exchange has not yet been generalised and does not dominate society. Social division of labour means that producers produce different commodities and exchange them among themselves. Peasants purchase the products of craftsmen and vice versa. Money serves as a means of exchange (C–M–C). People are selling in order to buy. This changes with the emergence of the merchant as a distinct profession. The merchant buys in order to sell, i.e. to have more money after the exchange than before (C–M–C'). Without achieving the difference (M'–M) – i.e. a surplus – the trading activity would be pointless from the merchant's point of view. If a purchased value is increased by surplus-value, this is equivalent to the conversion of money into capital. In pre-capitalist society, surplus-value (in the hands of the merchant or usurer) is created in the sphere of circulation through the transfer of value from one person's hand to the hands

---

21   See Mandel 1973b, pp. 36–8.
22   See Mandel 1973b, pp. 38–42.

of another. In capitalism, surplus-value is created in the sphere of production through the increase of value in the whole of society, and thus without violating the exchange of equivalents. Capital has existed for some three thousand years, capitalism only for two hundred years. Capitalism is characterised by the penetration of capital into the sphere of production and the domination of the sphere of production by capital.[23] Similar to Marx's sarcastic description of the 'so-called primitive accumulation' of capital, Mandel does not deduce the 'origins of the capitalist mode of production' from general historical laws.[24] He argues that we are dealing with a concrete history, even if capitalism has assimilated its origins as permanent characteristics. Its points of origin are the separation of producers from the means of production, the monopolisation of these means of production by the capitalist class, and the emergence of a class of people who can only live by selling their labour to the bourgeois class.[25]

In the early middle ages, the majority of peasant-producers were serfs. They were unfree. They were bound to the soil, and the soil was bound to them – i.e. to their work. They did not have to sell their labour power because they could live off their work.[26]

In Africa in the nineteenth and early twentieth century, the inhabitants were stock breeders and cultivators of the soil who only possessed very primitive means of production. The yield from their lands was mediocre and the standard of living was low, but there was a relative abundance of usable land. For this reason, colonialism exerted massive extra-economic pressures to separate the mass of the population from its means of subsistence, the land. Land was transformed overnight into national domains owned by the colonising state or by capitalist corporations. The native population was deliberately resettled into reservations, i.e. land areas that could not sustain it. A head tax was introduced. Such measures forced the victims of these violent and oppressive measures to work for wages, even if it was 'only' during two or three months a year. Just as had been the case under early capitalism in Europe, ideological complaints about the 'laziness' of the people became commonplace. Nobody likes to work eight or 12 hours a day in a factory. Therefore, direct coercion is one of the 'idyllic' (Marx) processes in the implementation of the capitalist mode of production.[27]

---

23   See Mandel 1973b, p. 43 et seq.
24   Marx 1990, p. 871 et seq.
25   See Mandel 1973b, p. 45 et seq.; Mandel 1968b, p. 119 et seq.
26   Mandel 1968b, pp. 34–6.
27   See Mandel 1973b, pp. 46–8.

It became possible to monopolise the means of production when they became increasingly complex and expensive. The costs of building and operating a factory grew higher and higher. The industrial revolution saw the emergence of a class that could no longer acquire any means of production and was condemned to a life without property – it could therefore only sell its labour power. According to Mandel, this class is more numerous today than ever before – it is the 'modern proletariat' in the Marxist sense.[28]

1.2   *Independent Variables*

For Mandel, there has never been a 'pure' capitalism. In his view, capitalism has entered a stage of decay in 1914, or in 1917 at the latest.[29] However, capitalist relations have interacted with semi-capitalist and non-capitalist (pre-capitalist) relations from the outset. The 21 overproduction crises since 1825 cannot be explained by this. According to Mandel, they result from the contradictions immanent in the capitalist mode of production.[30] However, he considers such interactions important for rent theory, for example. Oil prices, for example, also follow the law of value in the long term, although they are superficially subject to political decisions. The October Revolution in Russia created a very effective 'exogenous factor' with strong repercussions for the development of capitalism.[31]

Society must be understood as an organically structured totality driven by its inner contradictions, leading to a process of self-reproduction of its totality. Capitalism's ability to adapt must not be underestimated. However, it is impossible to abolish the laws tied to the prevalence of money as capital and to the profit principle without abolishing capitalism itself. Therefore, the interaction of endogenous factors (i.e. factors determined by the laws of the capitalist economic system) and exogenous factors (political and other factors affecting the capitalist economy 'from the outside', as it were) is confined by the limits of the capitalist system itself. The exogenous factors are never absolutely independent. The capitalist system and its environment can in turn be interpreted as a 'system'. The exogenous factors are only partially autonomous factors.[32] Since Marxism wants to carry out a scientific investigation of social phenomena, it cannot simply resort to a formula along the lines of 'on the one hand, on the other hand' which assumes that the differ-

---

28   See Mandel 1968b, p. 116 et seq.; Achcar 1999a, p. 241 et seq.
29   See Mandel 1975d, pp. 19–20.
30   See Mandel 1968b, p. 349 et seq.
31   See Mandel 1997, p. 47.
32   See Mandel 1997, p. 474.

ent factors are roughly equally significant. Reality is always concrete. In the long run capitalism always produces crises, mass unemployment and misery and undermines the foundations of class peace and of social partnership. In Mandel's view, unscientific eclecticism can only be avoided if one recognises that the extra-economic factors are partially determined by the logic of the system.[33]

1.3   *Distinct Historical Characteristics*

The most evident extra-economic factor is the different respective significance of pre- and semi-capitalist conditions for each specific formation. The most important of the many resulting variables are for Mandel: 1) The relative importance of small-scale commodity production in society and the extent to which self-sufficiency limits the domestic market. This was very different, for instance, for China and for Japan between 1870 and 1920. 2) The degree to which the indigenous capitalist class can use the state as an instrument of 'primitive accumulation', which in turn depends on its relationship to the pre-capitalist classes, foreign powers, etc. This was very different, for example, for Italy and for France between 1780 and 1830 and between India and Japan between 1850 and 1900. 3) The specific historical roots and distinct traits of each national bourgeoisie, their relationship to the other classes and their 'specialisation' in the emerging world market. Thus the relations of the English bourgeoisie with the large landowners in the eighteenth and early nineteenth centuries were a significant factor in the level of food prices and therefore also in the level of real wages. The Dutch bourgeoisie, for instance, specialised in trade, transport and banking and was therefore unable to industrialise the Netherlands despite a surplus of capital; if anything, it contributed to the industrialisation of Britain. 4) The distinct political traditions of the three main classes under capitalism, which can have very deep roots. For instance, the relative weakness of central power in feudal western Europe aided the relative autonomy of towns. Hence, the bourgeoisie in Belgium, in the Netherlands, in England and in France had a long tradition of class politics and class movement, unlike the bourgeoisie in Prussia, Austria and Spain, let alone Turkey, Russia and China. For a long time, such differences crucially defined how much room for manoeuvre the bourgeoisie had against the proletariat. They were the reason for significant differences in wage levels regardless of economic power.[34]

---

33   See Mandel 1997, p. 475.
34   See Mandel 1997, p. 476.

2   Mandel's Contribution to Marxist Crisis Theory

Mandel's prime motivation for researching the capitalist economic cycle with
its recurring stages of recovery, upturn, boom, crisis and depression at specific intervals is not the desire to carry out a technical investigation or find
a means of counteracting crisis and depression within the framework of the
capitalist market economy. Rather, the objective is a critique of the capitalist
economic order. According to Mandel, crises are characteristic only of capitalist production. Earlier economic crises were essentially shortage crises due
to a lack of articles of consumption, whereas under capitalism crisis is characterised by the overproduction of commodities and overaccumulation of capital.[35]

Mandel considers the empirical observation of regularly occurring crises in
the history of capitalism a striking confirmation of a central tenet of Marx's critique of capitalism. He addressed this subject in a lecture on the *Long Waves of
Capitalist Development* at the RWTH Aachen University. Writing on the black-
board the 20 cycles that the capitalist economy had gone through up to that
point, he commented that he did not wish to fashionably 'pluck away at Marx's
beard', but 'comb it and groom it beautifully' instead. According to him, there
had been 20 'overproduction crises' in the history of capitalism since 1816, the
date when the first cycle had begun. What is more, he wrote 'q.e.d.' below the
dates: *quod erat demonstrandum* (as we were able to prove).[36]

In *Marxist Economic Theory*, Mandel cites 17 cycles of the capitalist world
economy from 1816–1958 and gives a concise account of the respective economic historical catalysts and circumstances.[37] The cyclical nature of the capitalist economy does not mean, however, that everything simply repeats itself
in an eternal cycle. Every time a crisis is mastered, every new upturn involves
changes from the previous cycle: 'The cyclical development of capitalist economy becomes particularly feverish through the extension of the basis of this
economy at the beginning of each recovery, and this happens through the sudden appearance of new markets for important sectors of the industry, which
thus stimulates the activity of the capital goods industry'.[38] This can occur
through geographic penetration into non-capitalist areas, through the deploy-
ment of new techniques that increase labour productivity, or through abrupt
changes in competition, for example because a powerful rival disappears due

---

35   See Mandel 1968b, p. 342 et seq.
36   This anecdote is based on the author's own recollection.
37   See Mandel 1968b, p. 358 et seq.
38   Mandel 1968b, p. 358.

to war or other events. 'Substitute sales markets', in particular government con-
tracts for military armaments, also played an important role in this regard in the
twentieth century.[39]

Unfortunately, Karl Marx did not leave a complete theory of capitalist overproduction crises to us. His original plan for *Capital* was to present this kind of
theory only in the sixth volume, which would have dealt with the world market
and crises.[40] Marxist theorists who investigate the question of overproduction
crises therefore rely on the explanations offered in the existing volumes of *Capital*, especially in the second, and in *Theories of Surplus-value*.[41] Ernest Mandel
criticises the use of reproduction models for crisis theory. He argues that they
are not meant to help explain overproduction crises – on the contrary, they
explain why under capitalism periodic stages of equilibrium are possible despite the 'anarchy of production' (i.e. despite the investment decisions of individual, autonomously operating producers and capitalists who are blind to the
overall social outcomes of their decisions).[42]

Mandel's own contribution to explaining capitalist overproduction crises
is best summed up as an attempt to fend off in 'monocausal' explanations.
In *Marxist Economic Theory* as well as in later comments on this subject,
Mandel opposed both pure 'underconsumption theory' and pure 'disproportionality theory', while regarding demographic explanations as a special form
of disproportionality theory.[43] For 'underconsumption theorists', the lack of
solvent demand is the crucial reason for crises, whereas 'disproportionality
theorists' stress the unavoidable occurrence of macroeconomic imbalances,
especially between 'department I' (the production of means of production)
and 'department II' (the production of articles of consumption). In this context, we can exemplify how for Mandel, the search for conclusive explanations
backed by empirical findings goes hand in hand with political motives. He consistently tries to demonstrate not only why certain views are one-sided and consequently wrong, but also why they have politically undesirable consequences,
or why they can be abused in the class struggle of capital owners against the
workers. Moreover, Mandel is motivated by his will to defend the explanatory
power of Karl Marx's observations and fend off claims that they are inconclus-
ive or contradictory.[44]

---

39   Ibid.
40   See Mandel 1968b, p. 96.
41   See Marx 1992, p. 307 et seq.; Marx 1863, chapter 17.
42   See Mandel 1968b, p. 361.
43   Mandel 1968b, p. 361 et seq.
44   See Mandel 1991c, p. 41 et seq.

Mandel was aware that the different emphases of various theorists who were all appealing to Marx pointed to certain tensions between Marx's different takes on the subject of overproduction crises. In the second volume of *Capital*, Marx explains the role of commercial capital in temporarily covering the increasing discrepancy between expanding production and limited demand.[45] Marx explicitly refers to the great significance of the relative 'poverty' of a large part of the population under capitalism:

> The periods in which capitalist production exerts all its forces regularly show themselves to be periods of over-production; because the limit to the application of the productive powers is not simply the production of value, but also its realization. However, the sale of commodities, the realization of commodity capital, and thus of surplus-value, is restricted not by the consumer needs of society in general, but by the consumer needs of a particular society in which the great majority are always poor and must always remain poor.[46]

A passage from *Capital* Volume III, which is also frequently quoted, appears to support the 'under-consumption theorists' even more clearly: 'The ultimate reason for all real crises always remains the poverty and restricted consumption of the masses, in the face of the drive of capitalist production to develop the productive forces as if only the absolute consumption capacity of society set a limit to them'.[47] Mandel, however, cites a detailed passage in the second volume of Marx's *Capital*, to which 'disproportionality theorists' might appeal no less legitimately:

> It is a pure tautology to say that crises are provoked by a lack of effective demand or effective consumption. The capitalist system does not recognize any forms of consumer other than those who can pay, if we exclude the consumption of paupers and swindlers. The fact that commodities are unsaleable means no more than that no effective buyers have been found for them, i.e. no consumers (no matter whether the commodities are ultimately sold to meet the needs of productive or individual consumption). If the attempt is made to give this tautology the semblance of greater profundity, by the statement that the working class receives too

---

45   See Marx 1992, pp. 272–3.
46   Marx 1992, p. 391.
47   Marx 1991, p. 52.

small a portion of its own product, and that the evil would be remedied if it received a bigger share, i.e. if its wages rose, we need only note that crises are always prepared by a period in which wages generally rise, and the working class actually does receive a greater share in the part of the annual product destined for consumption. From the standpoint of these advocates of sound and 'simple' (!) common sense, such periods should rather avert the crisis. It thus appears that capitalist production involves certain conditions independent of people's good or bad intentions, which permit the relative prosperity of the working class only temporarily, and moreover always as a harbinger of crisis.[48]

For Mandel there is no real contradiction between these two quotations. In his view, Marx refutes the 'reformist or liberal thesis' on the one hand, according to which an increase in mass purchasing power before the beginning of overproduction can contain crisis – but on the other hand, he also rejects the one-sided emphasis on disproportionality between the production departments, because production under capitalist commodity relations 'can never fully emancipate itself from sales to the final consumer'.[49] However, an increase in the sale of articles of consumption does not automatically lead to an increase in investment, i.e. in the sale of production equipment and raw materials. Instead, massive wage increases lower the profit rate, thereby limiting the accumulation of capital and thus accelerating rather than containing crisis. 'The basic causes of periodic crises of over-production are, at one and the same time, the inevitable periodic decline of the rate of profit, the capitalist anarchy of production, and the impossibility under capitalism of developing mass consumption in correlation with the growth of the productive forces'.[50]

Mandel also believes that it is wrong to explain periodic overproduction crises merely through the tendency for the average rate of profit to fall. In his view, although there is a close correlation between fluctuations in the profit rate and fluctuations in production, this does not provide a causal explanation for crisis, particularly with respect to mechanical interpretations, according to which the ultimate cause of crises is poor surplus-value production: 'In this vulgar sense, explanation of overproduction crises by the decline in the rate of profit alone is both wrong and dangerous'.[51] Moreover, this view abstracts from the problem of the realisation of surplus-value; after all, the production

---

48   Marx 1992, pp. 486–7.
49   Mandel 1992d, p. 72.
50   Ibid.
51   Mandel 1991c, p. 39.

of commodities comprising surplus-value does not yet solve the problem of selling those commodities at their value.[52]

Mandel considers the one-sided view 'wrong and dangerous' because it may prompt the conclusion that crisis can be avoided if real wages are reduced and in this way surplus-value and profit, investment, employment, etc. increased. It is an obvious 'argument' in favour of the owners of capital and class struggle from above: 'The working class in general, and the trade unions in particular, are thereby confronted with an agonizing choice between defending real wages and fighting unemployment: i.e. they are made responsible for the loss of jobs'.[53]

But it is not only the side of capital which embraces this logic:

> Needless to say, reformist proponents of class collaboration are only too ready to come forward with arguments of this kind, calling upon the workers to make the necessary sacrifices in order to 'save jobs' or 'restore full employment'. Experience, however, has shown time and again that this is not borne out empirically by the real course of the industrial cycle. It represents an ideological weapon designed to impose the burden of the crisis on the working class and assist an increase in the rate of surplus-value, which is one of capital's main goals during and after a crisis.[54]

In a footnote, Mandel refers to the German and Spanish experience in the second half of the 70s, when wage sacrifice undoubtedly led to an increase in profits and investment. However, since these were streamlining investments, the unemployment rate did not decrease at all.[55]

Mandel's critique of the 'three main variants of the monocausal interpretation of Marx's theory of crisis' denounces their inadequate explanatory power as well as their unfavourable implications for wage earners in their confrontation with capital (due to the lines of argumentation that can be derived from them respectively).[56] In the following paragraphs, we are again not concerned with Mandel's contribution to the specialist economic debate, but rather with the aspects of political argumentation related to this debate.

Proponents of 'pure' disproportionality theory like Mikhail Tugan-Baranovsky and Rudolf Hilferding saw the cause of industrial cycles and periodically

---

52   Ibid; see also Marx 1991, pp. 356–7.
53   Mandel 1991c, p. 41.
54   Ibid.
55   Ibid.
56   Mandel 1991c, p. 42.

occurring crises in the inability of capitalism to establish the necessary balance between the different areas of production through investment decisions taken by individual companies. This applies by way of example to the proportion between the production of means of production (department I) and the production of articles of consumption (department II). This problem and the progressive monopolisation in important areas of the capitalist economy gave rise to the idea of a 'general cartel' (Hilferding) – i.e. an organised capitalism that would overcome capitalist 'anarchy' and thus capitalism's susceptibility to crisis. Mandel rejected this idea as factually incorrect and a justification of reformist illusions.[57]

Mandel cites Karl Kautsky, Rosa Luxemburg, Nathalia Moszkowska, Fritz Sternberg and Paul Sweezy as Marxist exponents of underconsumption theory who assume a fixed proportion of the developments of department I and department II. According to them, as the organic composition of capital and the rate of surplus-value grow, the purchasing power for the acquisition of means of production increases at a faster rate than the mass purchasing power for means of production; because of this, a part of the means of consumption produced remains unsaleable, which is the cause of crisis. Mandel's counter-argument is that capitalist growth tends to produce a larger share of means of production in the total product, and that this does not necessarily lead to stagnation or a decline in production in department II. Stagnation or a decline in production in department II only occurs if the ratio of production in department I to that in department II grows more slowly than the ratio between the demand for means of production and the demand for articles of consumption. The obvious conclusion from the underconsumption theory criticised by Mandel is certainly not found in Rosa Luxemburg's work. However, it can be heard at every tariff dispute led by social-democratic trade union leaders in Germany, and it was typical of Keynesian models of crisis management: the claim that an increase in mass purchasing power can prevent or at least alleviate crises. Real wage increases and increased social expenditure redistribute the total income of society in favour of wage earners, so the argument goes, and their increased purchasing power in turn boosts capitalist investment and the economy as a whole. But according to Mandel, capitalist production is production for profit. Any redistribution that is not favourable to profit will therefore not stimulate capitalist investment, but rather slow it down.[58] While disproportionality and underconsumption theories favour reformist concepts

---

57   Ibid; Mandel 1968b, p. 366 et seq.
58   See Mandel 1991c, p. 45; Mandel 1968b, p. 363.

of either overcoming crises through 'organised capitalism' or by 'boosting mass purchasing power', 'pure' over-accumulation theory, which sees the cause of the crises in insufficient surplus-value production, serves the interests of capital. Mandel regards demographic attempts to explain crisis as examples of such theories. The first author with claims to Marxism who attempted such an explanation was Otto Bauer. His starting point seems unrealistic in today's world of permanent mass unemployment and was hypothetically assumed by Marx in Chapter 15 of *Capital* Volume III: the borderline case of 'absolute over-accumulation' of capital due to unemployment tending towards zero after a long period of prosperity, and real wages rising so sharply that the surplus-value rate and – consequently – the profit rate fall drastically. According to Mandel, such a situation, while conceivable on a purely theoretical level, corresponds neither to the actual conditions of real capitalism nor to its ability to create large industrial reserve armies when needed. The proposal of the Hungarian Marxist Ferenc Janossy to limit this effect to the stratum of particularly skilled workers also underestimates, according to Mandel, both the ability of capitalism to quickly produce appropriate skills and to make skilled work superfluous through technological innovation.[59]

Put forward by the bourgeois side, the line of argument is essentially that high profits mean high accumulation of capital, i.e. greater investment, more employment and more spending on luxury items as well as mass articles of consumption – and that high profits therefore rule out 'underconsumption' as a cause of crisis. To undermine this chain of thought, Mandel points out that simultaneous growth of production in departments I and II does not automatically mean growth in equal proportions. A simultaneous increase in the organic composition of capital and the rate of surplus-value in both departments in fact make it likely that mass consumption periodically lags behind the production output of department II.[60]

The investment decisions of companies are determined by past experience and future expectations. The present is unknown; current trends can only be estimated. The individual company managers may believe that due to competitive advantages, they can extract greater profits even against the general trend. This, Mandel argues, can result in an overproduction of commodities even before the general slowdown in the accumulation of capital occurs.[61] According to Mandel, all 'monocausal' and therefore one-sided explanations contain correct aspects which 'in the light of Volume 3's basic insistence upon

---

59   See Mandel 1991c, p. 47.
60   See Marx 1991, p. 192.
61   Ibid.

the tendency of the average rate of profit to fall' must be assimilated in a theory of the cyclical crises of capitalism. To this end, the various forms of capital accumulation during the cycle have to be examined.[62] During a strong upturn, a particularly large amount is invested in machinery and raw materials (department I) so that more articles of consumption can be produced (department II), which indeed creates a disproportion between the two departments. The additional means of production are sometimes only available for production after a certain delay, and when they enter production, they increase the production capacity of both departments by leaps and bounds. Even if output in department II grows more slowly than in department I, the high investment and profit rates mean that the solvent demand for articles of consumption cannot keep pace (even with rising real wages). Growing overproduction or overcapacity in department II is the result. Because the introduction of new means of production goes hand in hand with new technology, the organic composition of capital also increases; this pushes the rate of profit down, especially since under boom conditions the surplus-value rate cannot be sufficiently increased to compensate for this. Since part of capital can no longer achieve the average profit in productive investment, overaccumulation is the result. An extension of credit, in turn, only delays the matter. The result is an accelerated decline in investment in both departments, which finds expression in a sharp drop in commodity prices, production and employment. The ruin of weaker competitors, the devaluation of a significant part of capital and all other devastating effects of the crisis are at the same time the starting point for a new upturn.[63]

We must distinguish the debate about the causal relationships of the cycle from the function of cyclical crises for the capitalist system. According to Mandel – and as Marx had previously argued – these crises are 'healthy' as they ultimately represent a convulsive adjustment of prices to values that have actually fallen:

---

62   See Mandel 1991c, pp. 48–9.

63   Mandel 1991c, p. 50. Mandel 1968b, p. 368. There, Mandel attempts an 'outline of a synthesis'. Concluding the issue, he states on p. 371: 'The collapse of the boom is thus the collapse of the attempt to maintain the former level of values, prices and rates of profit with an increased quantity of capital. It is the conflict between the conditions for the accumulation of capital and for its realisation, which is merely the unfolding of all the contradictions inherent in capitalism, all of which enter into this explanation of crises: contradictions between the great development of the consumption-capacity of the broad masses; contradictions arising from the anarchy of production resulting from competition, the increase in the organics composition of capital and the fall in the rate of profit; contradictions between the increasing socialisation of production and the private form of appropriation'.

The effects of the crash, for the system as a whole, are healthy, however nasty they may be for individual capitalists. General devalorization of capital is not accompanied by a proportional reduction in the mass of surplus-value produced. Or (which amounts to the same) an identical mass of surplus-value can now valorize a smaller total amount of capital. Hence the decline in the rate of profit can be stopped and even reversed. Largescale reconstitution of the reserve army of labour, occurring during the crisis and the depression, makes possible a vigorous increase in the rate of surplus-value, not only through speed-ups but even through a cut in real wages, which in turn leads to a further rise in the rate of profit. Raw material prices generally fall more than the prices of finished goods, so part of constant capital becomes cheaper. The rise in the organic composition of capital is thereby slowed down, again pushing up the average rate of profit on industrial capital. A new cycle of stepped-up accumulation of capital, stepped-up productive investment, can now start, once stocks have become sufficiently depleted and current production sufficiently cut for demand again to outstrip supply, especially in department II.[64]

According to Mandel, the law of the tendency of the rate of profit to fall does not provide an immediate explanation for overproduction crises; it only shows the disharmony and discontinuity in the system of specifically capitalist growth, which necessarily takes place during phases in which upward and downward movement of the average rate of profit occurs. For him, the necessarily crisis-laden process already contains a *memento mori* of the capitalist mode of production. Mandel claims that his 'multi-causal' approach explains cyclical crises better than the various 'monocausal' approaches. In his view, this approach also more closely corresponds to Marx's own conviction.[65]

Mandel's attempt to explain cyclical crises of the capitalist mode of production allows for political conclusions at three levels. Firstly, from this perspective, only overcoming the capitalist mode of production altogether can offer a way out from the spell of specifically capitalist overproduction and overaccumulation crises. Secondly, workers can also use favourable economic cycles within the system to improve their living conditions by means of class struggle. Thirdly, however, the results of this system-immanent struggle of workers for their immediate interests are repeatedly called into question as soon as the economic situation worsens the conditions for pursuing their interests. This

---

64   Mandel 1991c, p. 51.
65   Ibid.

in turn puts revolutionary conclusions at least in the realm of possibility.[66] In addition to his contribution to the cyclical crises and the 'long waves of the capitalist development', Mandel contributed a theory of the necessary 'collapse' of the capitalist mode of production to the secular perspectives of the capitalist mode of production, although he did not link this to an automatic victory of socialism, nor did he advocate 'purely economic' theories of collapse.[67] Rather, he emphasised Rosa Luxemburg's slogan 'socialism or barbarism' or its modernised version 'socialism or death'. Put simply: if the exploited and oppressed allow everything – literally everything – to happen to them without defending themselves, then there is in principle no reason why capitalism could not continue to exist for a long time.[68] However, the general social structural crisis of the capitalist system, which Mandel saw unfolding, leaves no room for a future worth living under capitalist conditions.[69] Mandel's notion of the final crisis and collapse of capitalism ties in its economic core to an aspect of Henryk Grossmann's position, who – and on this Mandel does not agree with him – extrapolated the law of the tendency of the rate of profit to fall in such a way that the final crisis appears inevitable. Mandel considers this approach to have 'failed'.[70] What Mandel nonetheless regards as ground-breaking in Grossmann's approach is the idea that at a certain point in capitalist development, the tendency of the rate of profit to fall is augmented by the end of the growth of the mass of surplus-value, which finally also begins to fall. Mandel's argumentation in *Late Capitalism* on the consequences of the advance of semi-automated and fully automated production processes highlights the incompatibility of the capitalist mode of production with an ever-increasing displacement of living labour from the production process.[71] Mandel writes:

> So the extension of automation beyond a given ceiling leads, inevitably, first to a reduction in the total volume of value produced, then to a reduction in the total volume of surplus-value produced. This in turn unleashes a fourfold combined 'collapse crisis': a huge crisis of decline in the rate of profit; a huge crisis of realization (the increase in the productivity of labour implied by robotism expands the mass of use-values produced in an even higher ratio than it reduces real wages, and a growing proportion

---

66   Mandel 1979a, p. 88.
67   See Chapter 2, section 4, 'Long waves of capitalist development' in the present work.
68   Mandel 1990b, pp. 85–6.
69   Mandel 1995a, p. 7.
70   Mandel 1984a, p. 43.
71   See Mandel 1991c, p. 87.

of these use values becomes unsaleable); a huge social crisis; and a huge crisis of 'reconversion' (in other words, of capitalism's capacity to adapt) through devalorization – the *specific forms* of capital destruction threatening not only the survival of human civilization but even the physical survival of mankind or of life on our planet.[72]

For Mandel, theses of a 'post-industrial age' in which production is allegedly becoming increasingly replaced by services do not change these prospects. Rather, he identifies a significant trend of replacing services with goods and pushing out living labour through technological innovation in the service sector too.[73] For Mandel, the crisis of legitimacy arising from the fact that an increasingly highly qualified, technically and scientifically trained workforce is needed to operate and maintain increasingly expensive plants adds another dimension to the secular crisis of the capitalist mode of production. According to him, it is difficult for such workers to reconcile their self-confidence with their subordinate position in the company hierarchy. Permanent mass unemployment, on the other hand, results in the extreme exploitation of a growing stratum of unskilled workers and in escalating mass misery. Naturally, these developments can result in a general decline just as much as they might inspire solutions based on cooperation, solidarity and social equality. Overall, though, Mandel saw in the working class (in the broad sense of the term espoused by him) the potential for asserting a global socialist perspective.[74] The necessity of this perspective in order to prevent more unforeseeable global catastrophes – such as those that marked the twentieth century – is the essence of his conclusions from the study of capitalism's tendencies towards crisis.[75] Mandel analysed the economic situation in countless articles written for newspapers and journals; he tried to show the inevitability of further escalation of capitalist crisis based on available data; and he tried to deduce arguments for a socialist policy that would overcome the present system. On some crucial occasions, these contributions took on a more comprehensive character and were published in book form. After the worldwide stock market crash of 19 October 1987, he co-authored a book with Winfried Wolf analysing the causes of the crash.[76] Alongside sections summarising Marx's basic statements on the capitalist system and linking them to the latest developments, it also contains some essen-

72   Marx 1991, p. 230.
73   Ibid.
74   See Mandel 1979a, p. 41.
75   Mandel 1991c, p. 89.
76   Mandel and Wolf 1988.

tial theses of Mandel's analysis of 'late capitalism' – in particular, the thesis that credit inflation will expand to delay the dreaded big crash, with the result that the latent contradictions of the system are exacerbated.[77] The book is of particular interest because it was published shortly before the collapse of the Soviet Union and the Eastern Bloc, events that probably gave capitalism some 'breathing space' and re-legitimised in the eyes of many – albeit, from today's point of view, only for a fairly short time. In a 'postscript' written on 18 October 1989, Mandel and Wolf defend the text against assertions made by *Der Spiegel* in a book review of 9 October 1989, according to which they had once again been 'predicting the great economic collapse'. But they also note the growing anxiety of stock market players and bourgeois commentators. In support, they quote the *Frankfurter Allgemeine Zeitung*, which ran the headline, 'Fear is breathing down our necks' on the same day as their book was published.[78] Mandel made no crisis forecasts in the vein of Jehovah's Witnesses, who occasionally have to reschedule the date of the end of the world because it has once again passed – that would be a travesty. Mandel's most important motivator for his constant preoccupation with the capitalist economic situation, however, was certainly his desire to convince people of socialism. This is particularly evident in a section of the 'periodic overproduction crises' chapter in *Introduction to Marxism*. The passage also underlines the universally social rather than purely economic character of capitalist crisis as understood by Mandel:

> The economic crisis accentuates social contradictions and can lead to an explosive social and political crisis. It indicates that the capitalist system is ready to be replaced by a more efficient and humane system, which no longer wastes human and material resources. But it does not automatically bring about disintegration of this system. It must be overthrown by the conscious action of the revolutionary class it has engendered – the working class[79]

3   Late Capitalism

Mandel's point of departure for his concept of 'late capitalism' was similar to that which had prompted socialist theorists to discuss the 'monopolistic' or 'imperialist' phase of capitalism in the late nineteenth and early twentieth

---

77   See Mandel and Wolf 1988, p. 60.
78   See Mandel and Wolf 1988, p. 218.
79   Mandel 1979a, p. 54.

centuries. A quotation from Marx's *Capital* Volume I elucidates the horizon of expectations that lie behind such inquiries from a Marxist perspective:

> Along with the constant decrease in the number of capitalist magnates ... the mass of misery, oppression, slavery, degradation and exploitation grows; but with this there also grows the revolt of the working class, a class constantly increasing in numbers, and trained, united and organized by the very mechanism of the capitalist process of production. The monopoly of capital becomes a fetter upon the mode of production which has flourished alongside and under it. The centralization of the means of production and the socialization of labour reach a point at which they become incompatible with their capitalist integument. This integument is burst asunder. The knell of capitalist private property sounds. The expropriators are expropriated.[80]

Alas, it was not to be the death knell for capitalist private property. Instead, the capitalist mode of production entered a new expansionist phase. The task was to explain on what basis this had occurred and how. Rosa Luxemburg highlighted the advance of industrial capitalism into pre-capitalist and proto-capitalist societies, which breathed new life into the capitalist mode of production.[81] Rudolf Hilferding analysed the merging of industrial and banking capital into finance capital, arguing that a new 'organised capitalism' had to some degree overcome the capitalist 'anarchy of production', opening up the prospect of a more or less organic transition to socialism.[82] Lenin called 'imperialism' the highest stage of capitalism, defined by the following features:

> 1. The concentration of production and capital has developed to such a high stage that it has created monopolies which play a decisive role in economic life; 2. The merging of bank capital with industrial capital, and the creation, on the basis of this 'finance capital', of a financial oligarchy; 3. the export of capital as distinguished from the export of commodities acquires exceptional importance; 4. the formation of international monopolist capitalist associations which share the world among themselves, and 5. the territorial division of the whole world among the biggest capitalist powers is completed.[83]

---

80   Marx 1990, p. 929.
81   Luxemburg 1913, chapter 31.
82   See Hilferding 1981.
83   Lenin 2008, p. 89.

Seen from this perspective, the new lease of life that the capitalist mode of production gains from generating colonial extra profits has its price. The contradictions of capitalism, far from having been muted for good, emerge at a new level and deepen. The complete territorial division of the world, combined with the inherent compulsion of the capitalist mode of production to expand, pushes towards large-scale military conflicts like those that erupted during World War I. The imperialist phase of capitalism ushers in an era of wars, civil wars and revolutions. In light of this, the October Revolution of 1917 in Russia is the first breakaway from the world capitalist system and the beginning of a process of world socialist revolution.[84] Mandel's reasons for developing his theory of 'late capitalism', initially under the term 'neo-capitalism' (neither of these terms was to his liking since 'neo-capitalism' suggested too strong a break within capitalism, whereas 'late capitalism' appeared to imply a purely chronological sequence), are similar to the reasons that led socialist theorists to analyse the 'imperialist stage' of capitalism.[85] The challenge was to explain why, after World War II, the capitalist economic and social order saw another period of sustained upturn instead of perishing from the contradictions so forcefully pointed out by Marx, Lenin and others. This new economically expansive phase of capitalism allowed for a steady rise in the standard of living for a large part of the wage-dependent population – by no means without struggles, but nonetheless within a framework of disputes that posed no threat to capitalism and where negotiations and social consensus-building played a much greater role than they had during the interwar period (although one might well compare them to the New Deal era in the United States). At the same time, in his economic writings Mandel consistently rejects any interpretations of the new reality which suggest that capitalism and its classical contradictions had been overcome ('levelled middle class society', 'social market economy', 'welfare state', 'age of managers', 'service society', etc.).[86]

---

84   This view is articulated in 1919 in the 'Manifesto of the Communist International to the Workers of the World' (available at http://www.marxists.org/archive/trotsky/1924/ffyci-1/cho1.htm).

85   See Mandel 1975d, pp. 10–11.

86   Mandel writes in *Introduction to Marxism*: 'It is extremely important to do away with the myth that the present Western economy is no longer a real capitalist economy. The 1974–75 generalised recession of the international capitalist economy dealt a death blow to the theory which says that we are living in a so-called "mixed economy", in which the regulation of economic life by the state guarantees uninterrupted economic growth, full employment, and a high standard of living for all. Reality has once again shown that the requirements of private profit continue to dominate the economy, periodically provoking massive unemployment and overproduction ...' (Mandel 1979a, p. 62).

According to Mandel, one of the tendencies of capitalism's imperialist phase that have intensified in late capitalism is the concentration and centralisation of capital. This tendency has been empirically proven many times, and the same is true for the extensive cartelisation of the economy. In contrast to 'classical' imperialism up to World War II, though, the 'multinational corporation' has become the 'basic unit' in late capitalism (in present-day discourse, we tend to speak of multinationally operating or transnational corporations to avoid the false impression that 'multinationals' can detach themselves from their entrenchment in any given nation state).[87]

In the preface to the 1972 German edition of *Late Capitalism*, which is widely considered Mandel's key economic text, the author reaffirms the veracity of the claims he made in the 'Late capitalism' chapter of *Marxist Economic Theory*. Nonetheless, in his view the weakness of this chapter consisted in its 'its overly descriptive character, i.e. in the lack of a systematic approach to analysis, and especially in its lack of effort to deduce the present-day history of capitalism from the immanent laws of motion of capital' [our translation].[88]

It makes sense to begin by outlining the most important phenomena that in Mandel's view are characteristic of late capitalism. We will then examine what new elements he added in later efforts to 'systematise' his insights. At the end, I will outline what conclusions for his political ideas Mandel drew from his analysis of late capitalism.

In addition to the growing internationalisation and concentration of capital, late capitalism is characterised by accelerating technological innovation and shorter turnaround times for fixed capital. This brings with it increasing pressure on large corporations to plan their expenses and investment decisions for the long term and use the state to this end. Of course, the result is not a 'planned economy' since we are still dealing with production for the market. But within this framework, a tendency towards 'economic programming' emerges, affecting mainly those areas that can be influenced by decisions at all. There is an increasingly strong tendency towards 'wage guidelines' to allow for the exact calculation of wage expenses; furthermore, there is more pressure towards long-term collective bargaining on the part of employers' associations and trade unions, with the state acting as mediator and agent (namely in its role as 'employer'). If certain areas of production are not profitable in a given period, the state takes them over as required, namely to restructure and later return them to the direct control of big capital. Moreover, the state plays an

---

87   See Wolf 2000; Mandel 1979a, pp. 58–9.
88   Mandel 1972a, p. 7.

ever more important role as a guarantor of profits for the big monopolies. In
addition to the traditional means of control and guarantees, the state acts as a
commissioner, allowing for such profits to be financed from taxpayers' money.
This is particularly evident in the spectacular expansion of the arms industry
as a consequence of the east-west conflict.[89]

The downside of these developments is a tendency towards permanent
inflation, especially credit money inflation. The production of armaments
boosts the supply of money in circulation and increases purchasing power,
but without putting equivalent commodities into circulation. Under such circumstances, inflation could only be avoided under very specific, precarious
equilibrium conditions (which are impossible to achieve in practice). Public
debt is only a substitute for monetary inflation in this scenario, although in
practice often both occur at the same time.[90] According to Mandel, other features of contemporary capitalism reinforce this trend, which has in fact put
the world monetary system in a state of permanent crisis: a growing tendency
of the big capitalist corporations to finance themselves; accelerated depreciation and overcapitalisation of the large monopolies (against the background
of accelerated 'moral attrition' of machinery and equipment, which is downside of the pressure for permanent technological innovation). The latter feature
augments the classic overproduction crises (which before the publication of
Late Capitalism had been occurring in a subdued form) by keeping financial
and arithmetical depreciation below the actual renewal of fixed capital, thus
introducing money (e.g. the purchase of government securities) into the money
and credit cycle to which there is no corresponding countervalue in commodities.[91]

One of the aspects highlighted by regulation theorists who, like Joachim
Hirsch, speak of a 'Fordist mode of regulation' is the addition of new consumer
durables to the shopping basket of the average wage-dependent household
(cars, electrical household appliances, etc.).[92] The foundation for this is not
only higher labour productivity and the ability of trade unions to win higher
real wages with fairly little struggle or risk as long as there is near full employment (at least by today's standards), but also mass private debt in addition to
public debt. Consumer credit, on which part of this new 'consumption model'
is based, is also the reason for mass private bankruptcy of a growing proportion

89   See Mandel 1979a, p. 60 et seq.; Mandel 1968b, p. 485.
90   See Mandel 1968b, p. 526.
91   See Mandel 1968b, pp. 528–9.
92   See Hirsch 1971.

of wage earners, who can very quickly find themselves unable to meet their numerous instalment payment obligations.[93]

Like many other phenomena that Mandel analysed in the 1960s and 1970s, this one is only assuming dramatic proportions in the present era of mass unemployment and increasing social cuts.[94] In late capitalism, the ruling capitalist classes of the 'rich' metropolitan centres remain the masters of the world. They are facing dependent countries of the so-called 'third world', which have been drastically restricted in their development by the global conditions and are 'poor' to varying degrees. The special exploitation and plunder of these countries continues in late capitalism, but their position changes drastically.[95] During the rise of classical 'imperialism' (in Lenin's sense) from 1875 to 1914, the volume of world trade grew by about 900 % while world per capita income grew by less than 100 %. These figures, which say nothing about the distribution of wealth and income, demonstrate the degree of vitality or decomposition of a particular mode of accumulation.[96] After 1945, the world saw a 'new beginning' of world capitalism, built on the ruins that had been left behind by World War II and based on a drastically increased rate of exploitation (rate of surplus-value), but under considerably different global political conditions. The Soviet sphere of influence had expanded as a result of World War II. There were also revolutions like those in China and Cuba. A third of the world was no longer under the direct control of imperialist capital. The development of anti-imperialist movements and national liberation struggles in the so-called 'third world' resulted in the political independence of the vast majority of former colonies.[97] As an accumulation regime, late capitalism differs from classical imperialism primarily in that the appetite of the large capitalist corporations for profits over and above the average profit – which, according to Mandel, is the key driving force of the capitalist economy in the age of monopoly, the form in which competition primarily operates under these conditions – is far from satisfied by the attainment of colonial extra profits. Rather, the lion's share of the surplus-value on which capitalist profits are based is generated by the exploitation of wage

---

93   Mandel already wrote in *Marxist Economic Theory*, where he also provided figures to prove the spectacular increase in consumer credit from 1946–58, with reference to private household debt: 'In the United States, private indebtedness, which has become more and more disturbing, is a generator of inflation' (Mandel 1968b, p. 527).

94   The extent of excessive private debt and private insolvencies has virtually exploded compared with the first three post-war decades.

95   See Mandel 1979a, pp. 60–2.

96   See Mandel 1968b, p. 489.

97   See Mandel 1968b, p. 488; 1975d, pp. 158–60.

labour in the rich industrialised capitalist countries themselves.[98] This trend has continued to intensify to the present day and is empirically proven by way of numerous indicators in Attac's 'globalisation atlas'.[99]

The new distribution of power between the leading capitalist world powers – the supersession of British hegemony by the US and the ascendancy of European powers that had not been among the leading colonial powers – is mainly owed to the fact that the export of capital to poor countries that characterised classical imperialism went hand in hand with reduced investment in machinery and equipment in the 'mother countries', resulting in the relative obsolescence of the industrial base there. The mechanisms of plundering the poor and dependent countries that still operate in late capitalism and their significance for world capitalism will be discussed later.[100] At this juncture, I want to highlight the change in importance attributed to these mechanisms for capital accumulation in Mandel's analysis. This change is directly linked to the late capitalist trend towards permanent technological innovation and the constant revolution of the production process. Initially, this trend was linked to the technologies and product lines developed for World War II with the aid of government commissions, with electronics emerging as the technological revolution that was the most defining feature of late capitalism. The technological rent became the main source of monopolistic surplus profit. Starting from Marx's theory of the levelling of profit rates, Mandel assumes that two profit rates emerge, a normal and a monopolistic one. A process of levelling between these two profit rates does occur, but in an impaired and delayed manner. Once important reason for this is the inability of small capitals to deploy new technologies on the same scale as large corporations. In the short term, any significant technical innovation will proliferate under the pressure of competition in the market, at least in the realm of the large monopolies; thus the monopolistic rate of profit is quickly levelled out and the basis for technological rent lost. If the labour process is not further technologically revolutionised, the motivation to invest in production – i.e. the very motor of the capitalist economy – will wane.[101]

Fully in line with Marx, Mandel highlights a crucial contradiction especially of present-day capitalism: in the long term, the displacement of living

---

98   See Mandel 1968b, p. 480; Mandel 1975d, pp. 76–7; Mandel 2001, p. 325.

99   Whether in terms of the share of direct investment or trade flows, everything takes place predominantly within the 'triad' of the developed capitalist world: USA/NAFTA, EU, Japan/ASEAN. See Atlas du Monde Diplomatique, Paris 2003, pp. 22, 24 and 26.

100   See also Mandel 1968b, p. 480.

101   See Mandel 1968b, p. 423 et seq.; Mandel 1975d, pp. 91–3.

labour from the production process, which goes hand in hand with the constant revolutionising of the labour process, causes the tendency of the rate of profit to fall.[102] In Marx's critique of capitalism, living labour is not the source not of all wealth, but it is nonetheless the source of all value.[103] Despite a range of counteracting factors cited and studied by Mandel (e.g. falling prices for the elements of constant capital, increases in the rate of surplus-value, outsourcing of production to areas of lower labour productivity, etc.), he concludes that the capitalist system cannot evade the secular trend of falling profit rates as 'living' labour is increasingly replaced by 'dead labour'.[104]

In his effort to present both the characteristics of contemporary capitalism and the history of the capitalist economy as a simultaneous unfolding of the laws and internal contradictions of the capitalist mode of production, Mandel formulates a concept of six 'basic variables' of the capitalist mode of production. These variables are to some degree functionally related to each other, but nevertheless have a relative autonomy in the sense that they can all 'partially and periodically perform the role of autonomous variables'.[105] These are 1) the organic composition of capital in general and in departments I and II in particular; 2) the distribution of constant capital between fixed and circulating capital (again in general and in each of the main departments); 3) the development of the rate of surplus-value; 4) the development of the rate of accumulation; 5) the development of the turnover-time of capital, 6) the relations of exchange between departments I and II.[106] According to Mandel, the development of capitalism is essentially a function of the development and a correlation of these six variables. Fluctuations in the rate of profit are the 'seismograph' of its history. However, they are not the cause, but only results of the specific interplay of the cited variables. Some of these variables depend on the class struggle. The elementary struggle for wages, working hours and working conditions is itself to a large extent a function of the fluctuations of the reserve army and the rate of accumulation, but not in a mechanical or exclusive way.[107] Here again, Mandel's method cannot be called 'economistic' since it requires an analysis of the overall social situation and its developments.[108]

---

102 See Marx 1991, pp. 232–3.
103 See Mandel 1973b, pp. 36–7; Mandel 1991c, pp. 29–31.
104 Mandel 1968b, pp. 167–8.
105 Mandel 1975d, p. 39.
106 Ibid.
107 Mandel 1975d, p. 40.
108 See also Mandel 1975d, where Mandel writes on p. 40: 'Whether or not the rate of surplus-value does in actual fact rise depends among other things on the degree of resistance

In all the phenomena that Mandel analyses from these viewpoints, the movement of capital and the respective economic and social changes appear to correspond with 'attempts' on the part of capital to escape its fundamental contradictions and are ineffective in the long run. Thus, the bloated 'hypertrophic service sector' in late capitalism is an expression of poor prospects for profit in the productive sector. However, the consequence is not a 'service society' replacing the existing industrial capitalist society, but ultimately the mass replacement of services by surrogate commodities.[109]

In his summary chapter on 'Late capitalism in its entirety', Mandel's basic premise is that in spite of many contemporary illusions and ideological positions, contemporary capitalism has not been overcome by its characteristic new phenomena in the slightest. Yet at the same time, greater internationalisation when compared to the 'classical' imperialist age and the even more blatantly emerging social character of production point to the obsolescence of the nation state, private appropriation, and capitalist class society in general. Neither the monopolies nor the state have abolished the law of value. The task is to determine in what ways the law of value asserts itself in late capitalism (when compared to pre- and early capitalist stages and the early imperialist stage).[110] While in small-scale commodity production the law of value operates directly through the exchange value of commodities, in developed capitalism it operates through the levelling of profit rates as a result of the competition between capitals. The surplus-value generated is distributed in proportion to the total mass of capital employed by each individual enterprise: capitals operating at lower labour productivity transfer capital to those operating at higher labour productivity. This, in turn, tends to lead to an outflow of capital to the sectors that for this reason achieve higher profit rates. The outflow becomes permanent when it is matched by a change in the final consumers' structure of consumption. The function of the monopolies is to prevent or make it more difficult for them to achieve the 'normal' levelling of the profit rate that is normal in capitalism when free competition prevails. According to Mandel, they cannot achieve this in the long term, though.[111]

For Mandel, the starting point for investigating this problem is Marx's thesis that the entire mass of new value produced in society is determined by the sum total of the labour expended and cannot be changed, but only redistrib-

---

       displayed by the working class to capital's efforts to increase it'. See also Mandel 1970d; Mandel 1972c.

109   See Mandel 1975d, pp. 377–8.
110   See Mandel 1975d, p. 527.
111   See Mandel 1975d, pp. 528–9.

uted through the circulation processes. This is why the total social sum of production prices is equal to the total value produced by society.[112] Sustained monopolistic surplus-profits can therefore only be generated if the profit rate in the non-monopolistic areas is reduced below the average or if the overall social surplus-value rate is increased. Drawing on model calculations based on the simplified assumption that the entire department I is monopolistic and the entire department II non-monopolistic, Mandel shows that after a certain number of production cycles, the same means that produce an above-average monopolistic profit rate later undermine it or cause a declining monopolistic profit rate.[113]

Mandel sums up as follows:

> The more the monopolized sector expands, so the less becomes the margin between the monopoly profit and the average profit. This explains why it is not in the interests of the monopolized sectors to absorb all those sectors where 'free competition' remains. Indeed, they even stand to gain from the creation of new non-monopolized sectors in the economy. The classic examples in this connection are the so-called sub-contracts granted to medium and small enterprises ....[114]

A permanent transfer of surplus-value in favour of the monopolistic sector also requires a permanent change in the structure of consumption to the detriment of commodities produced in the non-monopolistic sector. This would have to be in a specific proportion to the redistribution of surplus-value, which is barely feasible under market economy conditions. On the other hand, the absorption of non-monopolistic sectors by monopolistic sectors in turn tends to undermine the basis for monopolistic surplus-profits. However, if the consumption structure does not change, the transfer of surplus-value is undermined by another mechanism. Slower accumulation in the non-monopolistic sector initially leads to a relative shortage of commodities produced there; this causes rising prices, including in relation to the commodities produced in the monopolistic sector, which periodically reverses the transfer of surplus-value. In the non-monopolistic sector, we can thus observe an accelerated accumulation of capital and an adjustment of the organic composition of capital to that of the monopolistic sector, which in turn amount to an overall social equalisation of the rate of profit. According to Mandel, the enormous expansion of

---

112   See Mandel 1975d, p. 528.
113   See Mandel 1975d, p. 529.
114   Mandel 1975d, p. 535.

advertising, market research and such arises from the need of monopolies to secure demand for their products in exact proportion to current accumulation and solvent demand, though this cannot be achieved in the long term.[115]

Mandel explains important specifics of late capitalism with refence to the reactions of monopoly capital to these problems:

> The threat of a fall in monopoly surplus-profits – i.e., the approximation of the monopoly rate of profit to the average rate, which is subject to a falling tendency, can only be averted by the constant expansion both of markets and of product differentiation ... This is the reason for the tendency towards the massive growth of Research and Development, the acceleration of technological innovation, the incessant search for technological 'rents' and the efforts to avert the dangers of conjunctural, and particularly structural, relative decline in the demand for specific commodities by international centralization of capital-the multinational corporations-and formation of conglomerates. The more this process advances, and the nearer the package of goods produced by the monopolies comes to comprise the whole range of social production, the smaller monopoly surplus-profits will tend to become and the closer the monopoly rate of profit will have to adjust to the average rate of profit. The monopolies will thus increasingly be dragged into the maelstrom of the tendency for this average rate of profit to fall.[116]

According to Mandel, the ability of monopolies to sustain a monopolistically higher rate of profit for a prolonged period of time depends on the 'undertone' of the period. He links this question to the theory of 'long waves of economic development'. During a long wave with a prosperous and expansive undertone, competition (classical price competition has largely been eliminated for the monopolies, but not competition as such, or else there would be no need for the large corporations to expand) has the effect of establishing a higher monopolistic profit rate. A long wave with a stagnant or depressive undertone such as the one that began in the second half of the 1960s, on the other hand, increasingly undermines the foundations for this.[117] Mandel attests a similarly limited effectiveness to the efforts of the late capitalist state to regulate the economy without overriding the capitalist mode of production and its laws. The forms of

---

115   See Mandel 1975d, p. 531 et seq.
116   Mandel 1975d, p. 539.
117   Mandel 1975d, p. 544.

state intervention typical of contemporary capitalism are measures to stimulate the economy, Keynesian deficit spending and state subsidies. In the longer
term, crisis-suppressing measures have the downside that they also suppress
the 'advantages' of crises for capitalism. Even if we assume that inflation can
ideally be avoided, the 'healthy' function of the crisis is also curtailed. After
all, crises are an eruptive process through which a capitalist market economy
asserts that capitals do not forever lag behind the demands of competition
and that labour is expended 'for free'. According to Mandel, increasing solvent
demand alone cannot stimulate the capitalist economy. What is additionally
needed most of all is an increase in the rate of surplus-value, which 'automatically intensifies the difficulties of realization to the extent that the conditions
of exploitation are improved'.[118] However, the problem of inflation can hardly
be avoided. This is because state orders and state production (which must not
deprive private capital of markets but supplement it, improve its general conditions of production and tap new sources of profit) only have a stimulating
effect if the corresponding state expenditures are not fully covered by taxes.
Instead, purchasing power has to be expanded by new forms of payment that
are brought into circulation, which in turn are not matched by a corresponding
circulating mass of commodities (infrastructure and armaments are traditional
state sectors).[119]

Infrastructure operations carried out by the state, in so far as they are financed by taxes which are also levied on workers and small owners, already
constitute a subsidy to capital. For Mandel, subsidy activity necessarily plays
a greater role as the structural crisis of the capitalist mode of production deep-
ens. In its early stages, capital tended to limit state activity as much as possible.
Direct and indirect subsidies boil down to a redistribution of surplus-value or
to an increase in the rate of surplus-value within certain limits that cannot
be exceeded, depending on the overall situation (unlike Paul Mattick, Mandel argues that government expenditure does not always mean deductions
from the surplus-value mass, but under certain conditions increases the overall surplus-value).[120] While in 'classical' imperialism banks and finance capital acted as clearinghouses for orientation in the distribution of the overall
surplus-value, the late capitalist state fulfils this function in close cooperation
with the monopolies. For Mandel, the fact that a growing number of sectors
falls under state responsibility is a symptom of the fact that capitalism is out-

---

118   Mandel 1975d, p. 550.
119   Mandel 1975d, p. 551.
120   Mandel 1975d, p. 554.

moded.[121] Nonetheless, without denying the temporary successes of the Keynesian measures that were part of the climate at the time, Mandel returns to the same questions he raised in the face of the great monopolies' attempts at programming:

> In the long run, the State cannot simultaneously improve the conditions of valorization of capital and reduce the difficulties of realisation. If the rate of profit declines, there will also be a fall in the accumulation of capital even if the market is expanding. If the rate of profit is high or rising, the accumulation of capital will still slow down if there is simultaneously a relative contraction of the market or the utilisation of capacity decreases. No combination of private and State regulation of the economy has managed to achieve in the long-run the miracle of a rising rate of profit and an expanding market (a high utilization of capacity in both Departments).[122]

In the synoptic chapter 'Late capitalism as a whole', Mandel turns to the proponents of 'state monopoly capitalism' theory, who all belonged to, or were close to, the official Communist Parties at the time. Mandel initially leaves aside secondary problems with the 'state monopoly capitalism' formula – according to him, it was originally coined by Lenin primarily to describe the war economy of the German Empire in 1917–18. He begins by outlining his view of the political motives behind this theory.[123] According to him, it is inextricably linked to the substitution of the antagonism between capital and labour by the struggle between the 'capitalist and socialist camps' and, as such, corresponds to the political needs of the Soviet party and state bureaucracy. Since the worldwide struggle will ultimately be won in a 'competition of systems' (labour productivity in the socialist camp will outstrip productivity in the capitalist camp one day), no revolutionary struggle for transitional demands is to be waged in the capitalist countries until then. The theory of state monopoly capitalism is augmented by the idea of winning over 'non-state monopoly' sections of the bourgeoisie as allies (this socio-political goal was theorised as an anti-monopolistic stage of 'advanced democracy' supposedly preceding a socialist revolution). Mandel rejects this idea and therefore the entire concept.[124] In the detail, however, the theory takes various forms. By way of example, Mandel

---

121   Mandel 1975d, pp. 552–3. As is well known, the neoliberal offensive and its policy of privatisation turned this wheel back again.
122   Mandel 1975d, p. 553.
123   Mandel 1975d, p. 515.
124   Mandel 1975d, pp. 514–15.

examines *Le capitalisme monopoliste d'etat* by Victor Cheprakov, an anthology of the same name edited by Paul Boccara that contains essays by French Communist Party economists, and *Zur Theorie des staatsmonopolistischen Kapitalismus* by Rudi Gündel, Horst Heininger, Peter Hess and Kurt Zieschang.[125] In a nutshell, the theorists of state monopoly capitalism view it, on the one hand, as a reaction to the intensified crisis and weakness of contemporary capitalism. On the other, they consider it a potential starting point for a pushback against the power of the monopolies: they believe that the anti-monopolistic forces can make use of the very same state apparatus which, after all, acts as a guarantor of the monopolies' interests, and into which these monopolies are merged to a substantial degree. In Mandel's view, the critique of capitalism as generalised commodity production is neglected or, as in the French authors' case, abandoned altogether.[126]

Mandel's summary and pointed depictions of contemporary capitalism as 'late capitalism', as a particular way in which the contradictions of the capitalist mode of production unfold, stresses the inevitable turn of the ascendant phase of this system into a phase of decline, even if it is still characterised by the features of the ascendant phase.[127]

The starting point is the growing rate of surplus-value and the falling prices for the elements of constant capital during and after World War II, which led to a recovery in the average rate of profit and accelerated capital accumulation. Moreover, it led to the massive introduction of technological innovations into the production process, which was partly fuelled by the arms industry. This upward movement of capitalism gains longevity through the capacity to keep the rate of surplus-value relatively high and moderate the effects of the increasing organic composition of capital through lower prices for its elements. This results in a high rate of growth, even if it is unevenly distributed across the different parts of world capital and a section of the capitalist class is expropriated (namely in the non-capitalist countries). During this period, monopolies in the advancing growth sectors secured technological surplus-profits for themselves, supplemented by the fruits of unequal trade with poor countries. Other sectors of the economy such as coal, agriculture and textiles suffered a decline in profits due to changes in the structure of demand. However, it was initially possible to transfer employees in these sectors to the growth industries and trigger corresponding new waves of industrialisation (in France, Italy, Japan, the Netherlands, the Scandinavian countries, the southern states of the US and some

---

125 Mandel 1975d, p. 516.
126 Mandel 1975d, p. 520.
127 Mandel 1975d, p. 560.

semi-colonies, but also through industrialisation within sectors such as agriculture, accounting, banking and services).[128] However, the solvent demand of the 'final consumers' cannot keep up with the high pace of capital accumulation for long, which results in overcapacities in the 'growth sectors'. At the same time, the industrial reserve army is absorbed to a great degree, resulting in a declining rate of surplus-value. The technological revolution brought about by electronics, the shorter turnover times of fixed capital, the growing importance of highly qualified labour and the increasing complexity and fragility of the entire system create the need for economic planning in the enterprises and for economic programming, private and public control of the economy by society as a whole. The technological revolution brought about by electronics, the shorter turnover times of fixed capital, the growing importance of highly qualified labour and the increasing complexity and fragility of the entire system create the need for economic planning in the enterprises and for economic programming, private and public control of the economy for society as a whole; at the same time, the dependency of the monopolistic extra profits, the profit rate, the sale of goods and the growth rate of the enterprises on the law of value cannot be abolished.[129] One of the tendencies threatening to 'tip over' the expansive tendency is the crisis of the monetary system, i.e. the erosion of the role of the dollar as world money and world credit money. This steady erosion of the function of the dollar makes it increasingly necessary to return to an internationally accepted universal equivalent that is free from the interference of individual nation states. The role of national monetary and credit policy in moderating the ups and downs of the business cycle is weakened. The multinational corporations and monopolies become subject to the law of value internationally the more they try to withdraw from it nationally.[130]

Mandel diagnoses a widening productivity and wealth gap between the rich north and the poor south. He predicts a growth of revolutionary liberation movements in the colonies and semi-colonies. And most importantly:

> The third technological revolution has brought about profound changes in the needs of the working masses in the metropolitan countries-including the need for qualitative changes in the form and content of work; but late capitalism is unable to fulfil these needs. Still less can it do so today as the outbreak of a universal struggle over the rate of surplus-value has even forced it in practice to deny 'rights' (especially full employ-

---

128   Ibid.
129   Mandel 1975d, pp. 559–60.
130   Mandel 1975d, p. 560.

ment and autonomy in wage negotiations) previously conceded to the proletariat. Social contradictions and tensions are thus intensifying in the metropolitan countries. Their roots lie in the growing universalization of a social crisis ....[131]

In his depiction of the structural crisis of capitalist relations of production as a whole and in the chapters on the state and the ideology of the late capitalist age, Mandel predicts intensified struggles over distribution and potential regression. Yet on the other hand, he looks upon the phenomena of contemporary capitalism with optimism.[132] Perhaps characteristically for the transitional period between the events of May '68 and the 1970s (when the potential 'tipping over' of the undertone of capitalist development was still widely underestimated), Mandel regarded these phenomena as possible points of departure for a comprehensive challenge to the system. He rejects any strategy aiming at their regulation within the framework of capitalism – instead, he regards them springboards for politicisation and for the development of a higher level of workers' problem awareness and class-consciousness. Likewise, he sees the more widespread training of technical intelligentsia and the greater role of highly qualified workers as a potential future challenge to the internal hierarchy and the capitalist power of command.[133] In keeping with the social climate of the 1970s, Mandel stresses the likelihood of revolts not based on processes of immiseration. He implies that future revolts will be motivated by unfulfilled expectations arising from decades of sustained upturn, social changes brought about by the third technological revolution, improvements in the living standards of many, and reforms made to stabilise the system. In his nuanced analysis of the role of the state in late capitalism (starting from an assessment of the emergence of the state in the context of class divisions and the social division of labour, the role of the state in capitalist class society in general, and the ways in which the bourgeoisie maintains its rule in bourgeois-parliamentary democracies), Mandel addresses the tendency of the repressive role of the state to increase. As the contradictions of capitalism intensify – between labour and capital, between the metropolises and the periphery, between the imperialist powers – the state apparatus and executive increasingly assume a separate, independent existence, displaying a tendency towards the 'strong state'. The technical role of the state is also becoming more important in late capitalism.

---

131   Mandel 1975d, p. 561.
132   See Mandel 1975d, p. 562, p. 474 and p. 500.
133   See Mandel 1975b, p. 258.

For Mandel, the late capitalist state is not just an instrument of social integration, it also plays an important role in economic life itself. This is due to the fact that in contemporary capitalism, the 'automatism' of the market economy no longer ensures normal and advanced capitalist reproduction. Overall, Mandel identifies a downright 'hypertrophy' of the state in late capitalism.[134]

Similarly, Mandel speaks of the state's growing 'ideological' role, and in this context, he cites aspects that present-day capitalism (the capitalism of 'neoliberal globalisation') has apparently overcome, in addition to factors that remain in place:

> The late bourgeois state attempts to counter the increased vulnerability of the system ... by making the dismantling of proletarian class consciousness – especially in its socialist form – a priority task. This implies control over a huge apparatus of manipulation to 'integrate' the worker into bourgeois society as a consumer, a 'social partner', a 'citizen' affirming the existing social order, etc. It implies the attempt to absorb any rebellion into reforms that can be easily integrated, systematic efforts to undermine class solidarity in the workplace (new forms of wage payment; antagonisms between 'indigenous' and 'immigrant' workers) and in society as a whole (all kinds of co-management and shareholding practices; concerted action; income policy, etc.).[135]

Likewise, with respect to ideology in late capitalism, Mandel cites aspects that still apply today, but also some that now appear outdated – for example the 'anything goes' mania of limitless technological feasibility.[136] With today's ecological awareness being significantly higher than that of the 1970s, the feasibility craze is somewhat less widespread nowadays. The belief that social contradictions can be overcome by sophisticated social engineering also hardly features in mainstream consciousness anymore. The dominant neoliberal politics of today are based on confrontation rather than integration. Even in the early 1970s, Mandel emphasised the regressive aspects of 'late bourgeois' ideo-

---

134   See Mandel 1972e, p. 436.
135   Mandel 1972e, p. 437, our translation.
136   See Mandel 1975d, p. 503. Mandel was himself in a sense a victim of the feasibility craze, for example when he wrote: 'But who can speak of limitations that man will never be able to break through, man who is stretching out his arms towards the stars, who is on the brink of producing life in test-tubes, and who tomorrow will embrace the entire family of mankind in a spirit of universal brotherhood?' (Mandel 1968b, p. 686). Mandel's vision of a future society appears here to be based on a naive belief in the titanic power of technological progress.

logy, which have since become more acute. Against the backdrop of increasing inequality and the absence of rights for many, the claim to universality typical of the ideology of the early bourgeoisie is steadily disintegrating. Instead of proceeding from the assumption of equal rights for all, certain groups of people are granted special 'privileges' – a recourse to concepts that appear archaic and pre-bourgeois. The generalisation of capitalist violations of the law (beginning with tax evasion) and the far-reaching impunity of the superrich for more or less arbitrary practices necessarily engender the idea that it is 'normal' when certain groups of people break the law: 'Both in the mental conceptions and practical relations of commodity owners of varying economic power, there develops a mixture of formal legal equality and juridical or practical inequality (status-bound privileges), that reveals the alterations undergone by classical bourgeois ideology to adapt it to the new epoch'.[137]

Mandel criticises political responses to the crisis symptoms of late capitalist society which seek to solve partial problems – for example, with advanced technology – without recognising the overall context from which these problems emerge. A real understanding of the way in which all these crisis symptoms are connected necessarily prompts, in his view, a critique of the capitalist mode of production as a whole – a mode of production ill-equipped to harness the potential for real social progress created by new technologies:

> The crisis of capitalist relations of production hence appears as the crisis of a system of relations between men, within and between units of production (enterprises), which corresponds less and less to the technical basis of labour in either present or potential form. We can define this crisis as a crisis not only of capitalist conditions of appropriation, valorization and accumulation, but also of commodity production, the capitalist division of labour, the capitalist structure of the enterprise, the bourgeois national state, and the subsumption of labour under capital as a whole. All these multiple crises are only different facets of a single reality, of one socio-economic totality: the capitalist mode of production.[138]

To repudiate and overcome this capitalist mode of production is all the more urgent for Mandel since its dangerous tendencies have greatly intensified: 'On the other hand, the objective opposition between partial rationality and overall irrationality, which is rooted in the contradiction between the growing social-

---

137 Mandel 1975d, p. 513.
138 Mandel 1975d, p. 571.

ization of labour and private appropriation and is a hallmark of the capitalist mode of production, acquires such explosive potential that the overall irrationality of late capitalism threatens in the medium term not only the existing form of society, but human civilization altogether'.[139]

For Mandel, the prime source of disintegration of bourgeois ideology in late capitalism is the contradiction between the abundance of articles of consumption and the underdevelopment of social consumption. All needs whose satisfaction has become part of the socially established standard of living of the average wage-earner, and which are satisfied with social services such as health, education, housing etc., can be barely or only insufficiently met by capitalist commodity production. Thus, in the bosom of this late capitalist society there arises the need for a form of distribution beyond the commodity and money economy, one that is irreconcilable with capitalism. More than three decades after the publication of Mandel's *Late Capitalism* it is almost impossible to read the following sentence without feeling nostalgic and, at the same time, bitter about the ideological triumphs of contemporary mainstream neoliberalism: 'The declarations of the British politician Powell that needs for medical care are "unlimited" and that therefore their price should be determined by a "free market economy", are already felt to be barbaric by a majority of the population of many, if not most of the industrialized countries'.[140] As a second factor, Mandel cites growing discontent with the fact that the bosses of large corporations make decisions of far-reaching consequences, despite the fact that these decisions are often in no way 'rational' from the standpoint of society's needs. The third factor that undermines bourgeois ideology is the contradiction between the large corporations' reliance on state support and the simultaneous safeguarding of their autonomy and business and banking secrecy. Fourthly, the advancing internationalisation of productive forces, the enormous problems posed by environmental destruction that are completely unmanageable in individual countries, the mass production of useless and straightforwardly harmful commodities (e.g. weapons of mass destruction) and the disuse of huge productive capacities due to mass unemployment and the inadequate utilisation of facilities. According to Mandel, these aspects all undermine the bourgeois nation state and the division of the world into nation states. However, this problem cannot be solved within the confines of the capitalist mode of production.[141]

---

139   Mandel 1975d, p. 575.
140   Mandel 1975d, p. 587.
141   Mandel 1975d, p. 588.

Mandel summarises the political conclusions from these 'contradictions' as follows:

> The appropriation of the means of production by the associated produ-
> cers, their planned application to priorities determined democratically by
> the mass of the workers, the radical reduction of working time as a pre-
> condition of active self-administration in economy and society, and the
> demise of commodity production and money relations are the indispens-
> able steps to their solution. The final abolition of capitalist relations of
> production will be the central objective of the mass revolutionary move-
> ment of the international working-class that is now approaching.[142]

4 Long Waves of Capitalist Development

Ernest Mandel's book on the *Long Waves of Capitalist Development*, originally
published in English in 1980, is based on a series of lectures given by the author
at the University of Cambridge in 1978.[143] According to his own account, he
gradually turned his attention to this topic from the mid-1960s onwards.[144]
Indeed, a Mandel essay discussing this concept appeared as early as 1964,
namely in the French journal *Les temps modernes* edited by Sartre and others,
under the title 'L'apogee du néo-capitalisme et ses lende-mains'. *Late Capitalism* contains a chapter dedicated to 'Long waves in the history of capitalism'.[145]
For Mandel, these 'long waves' are first and foremost an empirically established
fact; its Marxist explanation is essentially based on the long-term fluctuations
of the profit rate, which, in turn, ultimately determine the pace of capital accumulation (i.e. economic growth and expansion in the world market). With
regard to theoretical history, Mandel refers to the Marxist origins of the concept
in the works of Parvus, Kautsky, van Gelderen and Trotsky, as well as its adoption by 'bourgeois' economists such as Kondratieff, Schumpeter, Simiand and
Dupriez. He regrets that the concept is largely rejected by Marxists today.[146]
When speaking at a symposium devoted to Mandel's contribution to Marxism, Francisco Louçã traced the historical context of the idea.[147] Long waves of

---

142   Mandel 1975d, p. 589.
143   Mandel 1995c.
144   See Mandel 1995c.
145   See Mandel 1975d, p. 108.
146   See Mandel 1995c, p. 1.
147   See Achcar 1999a, p. 104 et seq.

the capitalist business cycle are upward or downward movements that occur independently of the 'normal' and regular capitalist business cycles whose laws Marx has demonstrated, and which within a few years (seven to ten) go through an upturn and a boom and culminate in an (overproduction) crisis. This economic crisis routinely carries within itself the conditions for a new upturn. Mandel cites two crucial indicators that empirically confirm the existence of 'long waves', namely industrial production and the growth of exports as a whole. The data indicates the following time periods with an ascending or a stagnating-depressive tendency: 1826–47 features a long wave with stagnating-depressive tendency; 1848–73 a long wave with expansive tendency; 1874–93 a long wave with stagnating-depressive tendency; 1894–1913 a long wave with expansive tendency; 1914–39 a long wave with stagnating-depressive tendency; from 1940 (for Europe only from 1948) to 1967 a long wave with expansive tendency; from 1968 on again a long wave with stagnating-depressive tendency. As to the upper and lower limits in relation to the above indicators, the differences between the two types of long waves are between 50 and 100 per cent. By way of exception, however, it is possible to achieve above-average growth rates even within the framework of a long wave of stagnation and depression if all efforts are concentrated on industrial production, as was the case in the USA after the Civil War or in Japan in the twentieth century.[148] Mandel remained convinced until his death that capitalism was globally going through a long wave with a stagnant-depressive undertone – and despite a number of findings to the contrary, the favoured position among his followers is that the long wave continues to this day.[149]

1826 saw the first modern capitalist overproduction crisis. Whether the period leading up to the crisis can be described as an expansive long wave is an

---

148   See Mandel 1995c, p. 2.

149   This debate was initiated in *Inprecor* (no. 447, May 2000) with contributions by Maxime Durand: 'Apropos d'un mini-krach', pp. 9–13, Marc Bonhomme: 'Crise mondiale ou nouvelle onde expansive?', pp. 13–15 and Francisco Louçã: 'Les flux du changenment: la culture dans une perspective historique', pp. 19–21, later systematised in *Inprecor* (no. 451, October 2000) by a summary of the questions posed by Jan Malewski: 'Une 5ème monde longue du capitalisme mondial?', p. 11 and contributions by Gianni Rigacci: 'Le systeme capitaliste n'a pas surmonte l'onde longue de stagnation', pp. 12–15 and by Henri Wilno: 'Un nouvel ordre productif?' In *Inprecor* (no. 463/464, October/November 2001), Michel Husson drew a balance of the economic boom that had recently ended and was, according to him, caused by a mainly 'speculative bubble': '2001 ou le grand retournement conjoncturel', pp. 29–34. The debate was provisionally concluded with a contribution by Claudio Katz, who processed a great deal of empirical material to show that no transition to a new expansive wave was in sight: 'Etappe, phase et crises, ou les singularites du capitalisme actuel' (in *Inprecor*, no. 478/479, pp. 51–65).

open question as far as Mandel is concerned – the reason being that this was a very early phase in the realisation of the capitalist mode of production.[150] The Marxist approach to the selection of indicators must be based on the primacy of material production. Under capitalist conditions, therefore, the decisive factor is the production of value and surplus-value, which has to be examined in the context of the world market. According to Mandel, it thus makes sense to take industrial production and global exports as criteria and measure them.[151]

Subsequently to the expansion of industrial production, which was closely linked to the implementation of the capitalist mode of production, there were three further technological revolutions. For Mandel, these were not decisive in triggering long waves with an expansive undertone, even if he is sometimes misunderstood in this way, and even though these revolutions were in some way linked to these waves.[152] The focus, however, is on the tendencies of capital accumulation and therefore the profit rate. From a Marxist point of view, long-term industrial growth (under capitalism) is unthinkable under conditions of a falling rate of profit. Insofar as, again from a Marxist perspective, the long-term tendency of the rate of profit to decline is claimed for the overall development of capitalism, there obviously arises the problem of explaining prolonged phases of growth.[153] From this emerges the need not only to examine the fluctuations of the rate of profit in the context of the business cycle and its secular tendency, but also to introduce a third time frame, namely 'long waves'. The sudden rise in the average rate of profit over a prolonged period could be explained with a number of factors. Mandel cites a sudden rise in the rate of surplus-value as the first. A sudden slowdown in the growth of the organic composition of capital, a sudden increase in the rate of capital turnover, or a combination of these factors is also possible. Mandel cites other potential causes, such as a sharp increase in the surplus-value mass and a strong flow of capital to countries with a significantly lower organic composition of capital than in metropolitan areas.[154] In general, expansive long waves occur when the factors that counteract the fall in the rate of profit have a strong and synchronous effect. However, we must also try to explain why the counteracting tendencies do not prevail within the individual long wave. According to Mandel, the fluctuations of the 'reserve army', i.e. the relative weight of unemployment, play an important role there.[155]

---

150   See Mandel 1995c, p. 5.
151   See Mandel 1995c, p. 6.
152   See Mandel 1995c, p. 7.
153   See Mandel 1995c, p. 8.
154   See Mandel 1995c, p. 11.
155   See Mandel 1995c, pp. 12–13.

One of Mandel's main theses is that in contrast to the normal capitalist busi-ness cycles, where transitions to depression and to recovery both correspond to internal laws of the capitalist economy, the transitions to a long wave with an expansive basic tendency must be explained by non-economic ('exogen-ous') factors. This is precisely why Mandel, unlike Kondratieff, does not speak of 'long cycles', but of 'long waves'. In his opinion, the 'long wave' with a depress-ive basic tendency does not contain in itself, in purely economic terms, the conditions for changing over to a 'long wave' with an expansive basic tend-ency, while conversely a 'long wave' with an expansive basic tendency contains in itself the conditions for turning over to a 'long wave' with a stagnating-depressive tendency. To explain the sudden and permanent increases in the average rate of profit after 1848, 1893 and 1940 (1948), Mandel identifies specific non-economic factors for each of these periods.[156] The year 1848 was char-acterised by revolutions, conquests and the discovery of the Californian gold fields. These three factors brought about a qualitative expansion of the capit-alist world market. Industrialisation and the technological revolution associ-ated with it were massively advanced. This process was marked above all by the transition from steam engine to steam motor, and by the transition from the artisanal to the industrial production of fixed capital.[157] This allowed for a spectacular increase in labour productivity and, due to the increase in relative surplus-value, also in the rate of surplus-value. In addition, the use of steam-ships, telegraphs and railways brought about a revolution in transport and tele-communications technology, accelerating the speed of capital turnover. This was augmented by the spread of joint-stock companies and the emergence of large department stores, which boosted the realisation of surplus-value. According to Mandel, all this combined led to a permanent growth in the rate of profit.

The analogous explanatory features for the onset of an expansive long wave after 1893 coincide with the main features of incipient 'imperialism' in Lenin's sense: the division of the world between the developed capitalist industrial countries, an increase in capital exports to the poor, backward and depend-ent countries, and a fall in relative commodity prices. The growth rate of the organic composition of capital declined, and the technological revolution

---

156   See Mandel 1995c, p. 16.
157   This process has not yet been completed and yet it already began in nineteenth-century capitalism: 'Large-scale industry therefore had to take over the machine itself, its own characteristic instrument of production, and to produce machines by means of machines', Marx wrote in *Capital* Volume I in Chapter 13 about the production of relative surplus-value – Marx 1990, p. 506.

brought about by general electrification in the rich industrialised countries in turn enabled increased production of relative surplus-value.[158]

For the expansive long wave since 1940 (in the US) and 1948 (in general), Mandel cites 'historical defeats of the international working class' as the main explanatory factor. Fascism and Nazism were responsible for the destruction of the labour movement in the affected countries. World War II, the subsequent 'cold war' and the McCarthy era in the US were further huge setbacks for the organised labour movement and its ability to effectively defend the interests of wage earners. All these factors together allowed for sensational increases in the surplus-value rate, in some cases up to 300 per cent. Once again, the growth of the organic composition of capital slowed down, this time due to cheaper access to Middle Eastern oil, a further drop in raw material prices, and a price drop for elements of fixed capital. A renewed revolution in telecommunications and lending, the emergence of a real international money market, and the proliferation of multinational corporations were all factors in the new situation. For Mandel, the expansion of arms production with state-guaranteed profits does not play the decisive role in this context, but nonetheless a very important one.

Mandel argues that, while 'exogenous factors' ought to be viewed as 'triggers' in the respective instances, they unleashed a dynamic process that was self-perpetuating for decades, which in turn can be explained with the aid of the traditional Marxist categories of the critique of capitalist economy.[159]

What role do the technological revolutions play in Mandel's explanatory model, then, if he does not believe that they can trigger periods with an expansive basic tendency? In the period of long waves with a stagnant, depressive basic tendency, a 'reserve' of technological innovations develops, but they are not introduced into the production process on a massive scale. The same is true for money reserves. Only a change in the economic climate and accordingly higher profit expectations prompt massive investment with the purpose of using these innovations in production. During an expansive wave, the average labour productivity in the technologically more advanced companies determines value. Companies that use more advanced technology for production realise extra-profits. This is where value is determined by the new industrial sectors that drive the technological revolution and have the highest production costs. Hence, they not only generate surplus-value at the expense of less productive companies, but also drive up the average rate of profit.

---

158   See Mandel 1995c, pp. 17–18.
159   See Mandel 1995c, pp. 18 and 23.

At the beginning of an expansive long wave, the working class still suffers from the consequences of the previous era and is therefore not in a position to stop the decline in wages relative to profits at once. Real wages begin to rise in the subsequent period, but only very gradually – notably more slowly than productivity is increasing in 'department II' (the production of articles of consumption). A greater rate of immigration also counteracts the increase in real wages. For this reason, the surplus-value rate may continue to grow for quite some time despite the rise in real wages. Expansive waves typically contain business cycles with longer and more pronounced phases of boom and shorter and less pronounced crises, milder forms of which are perceived as 'recessions'. During a stagnating depressive wave, the opposite is true, although even during such long waves there are, of course, periods of economic boom.[160] Further aspects that Mandel adds to his explanation are long-term trends in competition between the leading capitalist nation states and fluctuations in gold production. The first two expansive long waves coincide with British hegemony, the third with the hegemony of the US as the leading imperialist power. In Mandel's view, the significance of the hegemonic country's power to manage global crises is obvious – therefore, the relative decline of US dominance makes it more difficult to counter a generalised crisis-like development. In general, drastic changes in the political balance of power in the world arena are important (non-economic) factors that shape the general economic climate of the era.[161] Mandel mentions that many economic historians have been 'fascinated' by the thesis, based on the work of Gustav Cassel, that long waves are determined by the long-term fluctuations in gold production. However, he considers this thesis untenable from a Marxist point of view. Its flaw is that the average value of commodities, and therefore the general trend of prices, is not determined by the quantity of gold but by its value. In the nineteenth century, factors of 'chance', such as the discovery of rich new gold fields, played an important role since they radically pushed down the value of gold, thus helping to boost the rate of profit through general price rises. In the twentieth century, in contrast, gold mining itself became a capitalist industry and therefore subject to the logic of capitalist production since the discovery of South African gold mines.[162]

For Mandel there is an interplay between technological revolutions, advances in science, and the internal logic of capitalist development. He argues

---

160   See Mandel 1995c, pp. 24–6.
161   See Mandel 1995c, pp. 25–7.
162   See Mandel 1995c, pp. 25–7. Ernest Mandel does not agree with the thesis of 'demonetarisation'. In his opinion, gold retains an important function for the capitalist world economy and its currencies. See Mandel 1975d, pp. 408 et seq.

that it is a fundamental tendency of capitalism to transform scientific labour into a specific form of wage labour. This tendency has only been comprehensively realised in late capitalism.[163]

It was preceded by two phases. In the first, the experimentation of craftsmen was the direct basis for most advances in manufacturing. In the second, the observations of engineers made this process more systematic. In this way, a synthesis of 'abstract science' and 'concrete technological inventions' appeared: 'applied science'. According to Mandel, the tendency to subsume scientific labour into the production process stems from capital's 'unrelenting thirst for more surplus-value' (because it drives the production of relative surplus-value) and is interconnected with the rhythmic movement of capital accumulation.[164] Of course, there will be some investment in research in the course of a long wave with a stagnating and depressive undertone, but the main objective will be technological breakthroughs aimed at radical cost reductions; the typical investment will be rationalisation investment. Investment expenditure aimed at the massive introduction of new technologies into the production process generally begins about ten years after the beginning of an expansive long wave. While the basic correlation is clear, Mandel warns that we must not interpret it too mechanically. The same is true, according to him, for the correlation between a particular, fundamentally new technology and specific types of labour organisation. However, the following four machine systems all broadly correspond to four different types of labour organisation: craftworker-operated and craftworker-produced machines driven by the steam engine; machinist-operated and industrially produced machines driven by steam motors; assembly line combined machines tended by semiskilled machine operators and driven by electric motors; continuous-flow production machines integrated into semiautomatic systems controlled by electronics. The introduction of each of these successive radically different types of technology historically involved strong resistance from wage labourers. The reason for the introduction of new systems of labour organisation was in each case an attempt by capital to break down growing obstacles to further increases in the rate of surplus-value. The rhythmic long-term movement of capital accumulation is thus connected to capital's greater or lesser push toward radical changes in labour organisation. This interest is less urgent for most of the duration of a long wave with expansionary undertone, where the need to reduce social tensions and mitigate the causes of resistance and rebellion predomin-

---

163 See Mandel 1995c, pp. 28–9.
164 Mandel 1995c, pp. 29–30.

ates. Conversely, when an expansionist wave ends and a wave with stagnating-depressive undertone begins, capital's interest in radical changes in labour organisation will increase despite the risk of growing social tensions, which cannot be avoided anyway.[165]

As can be seen from the above, in *Long Waves of Capitalist Development*, Mandel tried to establish a correlation also with 'class-struggle cycles', i.e. with the ups and downs of working-class mobilisation in defence of class interests, or indeed with the surging and declining intensity of struggles between labour and capital:

> Conversely, toward the end of an expansionist long wave and during a large part of the subsequent depressive long wave, the decline in the rate of profit is pronounced, and that rate remains generally in a trough much lower than during the preceding expansionist long wave. There is then a growing and powerful incentive for capital to radically increase the rate of surplus-value, which cannot be achieved simply through increases in the work load, speedups, intensification of the existing labor process, etc., but demands a profound change in that process. Likewise, toward the end of the expansionist long wave, the class struggle generally intensifies for reasons linked to the very long term acceleration of capital accumulation itself (numerical strengthening of the working class, relative decline in unemployment, growing unionization, etc.). Precisely because intensification of the class struggle has already become an objective trend, the hesitation of the capitalist class to further increase social tensions by changing the labor organization will decrease (or, at least, the balance between the divisions inside the capitalist class related to those questions will tend to tilt in favor of those who want to go over to a stronger offensive against the working class).[166]

Taylorism (assembly line labour) and semi-automation (electronics) were each introduced for the first time or experimentally near the end of a long wave with expansionist undertone, but were not generally applied until the subsequent long wave with stagnant-depressive undertone. Thus, conveyor belt work was introduced in the years 1910–14, but only generalised after World War I. From 1940 (or 1948) to 1968, the organisation of continuous flow labour was limited to a few industries (nuclear power plants, oil refineries, petrochemical

---

165   Mandel 1995c, pp. 31–3.
166   Mandel 1995c, p. 34.

plants, canning factories, bottling and packaging plants) and was only generalised later with the emergence of microprocessors. According to Mandel, these findings confirm the following correlation to 'long waves': Initially, new technologies have an 'innovative character' and push up the average rate of profit. Then, in the long periods during which the take the form of generalisation, they push down and hold down the average rate of profit. Furthermore, any revolutionary innovation in labour organisation grows out of attempts to break down working class resistance to further increase the rate of surplus-value, i.e. the rate of exploitation. The first technological revolution was therefore also a response to the working-class struggle for a shorter workday. The second one was closely related to the resistance against stricter and more direct control by management over the work process (which boiled down to increased exploitation through intensified labour). Finally, the third technological revolution was a response to the growth of trade union organisation and the efforts of workers and their unions to weaken the power of control of management over conveyor-belt production.[167] The interplay of 'subjective factors' (the strength, confidence and class consciousness of the proletariat) is decisive for the capacity of reversing a long-term trend in the rate of surplus-value and therefore also in the rate of profit. Thus, the consequences of the class struggle of a whole historical period appear to Mandel as 'exogenous factors' determining the turning points. This is the dialectic between objective and subjective factors, in which the latter is characterised by 'relative autonomy'. Mandel assumes a cycle of class struggle that is interwoven with 'long waves', although it does not simply run parallel with them. He formulated and substantiated this concept once more in his essay 'Partially independent variables and internal logic in classical Marxist economic analysis'.[168]

According to Mandel, major historical events and the outcomes of major historical conflicts cannot simply be deduced from the laws of capitalist movement. That would be crude 'economism'. Nevertheless, major trends have objective economic roots. The profit expectations of entrepreneurs are always a considerably more important factor for strategic investment decisions.[169]

Mandel did not conceive of the periodisation of the history of capitalism by 'long waves' as a homogeneous progression. For him, World War I and the 1917 October Revolution marked an epochal break – a deep rupture. Prior to this historical turning point, the capitalist mode of production generally enjoyed its

---

167   See Mandel 1995c, pp. 34–6.
168   See Mandel 1985c and Mandel 1975d, p. 456.
169   Mandel 1995c, pp. 40–3.

historical peak, regardless of the way in which was accompanied by long waves and economic cycles. After this historical rupture (i.e. with the advent of the age of 'imperialism' in Lenin's sense or with the beginning of the 'era of socialist revolutions' since the October Revolution in Russia), capitalism entered its epoch of decline, also evident in its geographical pushback. For Mandel, World War I and the subsequent major political events were an expression of deepening contradictions and a structural crisis of the capitalist system.[170] Mandel asks whether a new upturn and renewed rapid growth in the productive forces are possible despite this structural crisis. He does not rule out the onset of a new expansionist long wave, but he stresses, if such an expansionist wave does come, that its nature will be significantly different from earlier expansionist waves. This is because capitalism is historically no longer in the ascendancy.[171]

The fiat currencies of leading capitalist nation states have always dominated the capitalist world (first the British pound sterling, then the US dollar). Despite the importance of this hegemony, Mandel does not see it as an 'exogenous factor' because in his view, governments cannot control the markets through their monetary policies. Behind the hegemony of a currency, he argues, is labour productivity, the quality of commodities produced, and the production capacity of the country in question. Mandel thinks that the hegemony of the US will be undermined by the fact that the US economy produces with lower labour productivity in key sectors than the economies of some countries competing with the US.

He argues that the United States would be unable to stop erosion of the US dollar hegemony could even by using its continued political and military supremacy. The crux of the matter is this: the hegemony of the British pound sterling expressed not only the superiority of British capitalism at the time; it also reflected the historical ascendancy and confidence of the capitalist system in general, despite economic downturns and even in the context of a long wave of stagnation and depression.[172] Mandel views the hegemony of the US, on the other hand, as signalling a general period of capitalist decline. Because it began after the October Revolution and because of the existence of the Soviet Union, it posed a much greater threat to this system than any previous crisis. When in 1975 the spectre of another generalised crisis appeared on the horizon once again, almost all capitalist governments therefore switched to 'Keynesianism', i.e. essentially crisis-suppressing measures by inflationary means. Without permanently growing debt, there could not have been an expansionist long wave

---

170　Mandel 1995c, pp. 49–50.
171　Mandel 1995c, p. 51.
172　Mandel 1995c, pp. 51–3.

after World War II. After World War II, capitalism was therefore dependent on using artificial incentives to work its way out of the stagnating and depressive tendency: namely by means of permanent inflation, state interventionism and permanent armament. Hence, the expansionist long wave after World War II had a different character than the previous expansive long waves. In this context, Mandel warns against analogies that are 'too elegant'.[173] In the long run, he argues, it is so difficult for capitalism to keep up a high rate of capital accumulation because – and this is an 'endogenous' point of view – the discrepancy between the development of productive capacity and the purchasing power of the 'final consumers' is built into the system and inevitably grows as a result of all the laws of capitalist movement. Each crisis of overproduction is simultaneously a crisis of the overproduction of commodities and of capital; the function of permanent inflation must be examined in this light. Credit inflation played a dual role in stimulating the post-World War II economic boom: firstly, it created a widely expanded market for cars and houses, and secondly, it allowed business firms to expand by getting deeper and deeper into debt. Despite a slight decline in this trend, in Mandel's view it is still true that expansion after World War II was only possible by the floating of a sea of debts (the only recourse for the capitalist system).[174] In this sense, Mandel thinks that the Keynesians were quite 'right', and the positive consequences of their remedies speak for themselves: less unemployment, a rise in the standard of living of broad sections of the wage-earning population, including in some countries of the so-called 'third world', and so on. Although linked to a general growth in debt, the third long wave of expansionary fundamentals was therefore a 'real wave', not a 'fictious' one. It was not 'artificially' induced by inflation – though inflation did help to bridge over the inner contradictions of the new long-term upward trend of capitalist expansion or mitigate its effects. The 'hour of reckoning' was delayed further and further. The remedies advocated by Friedman, Hayek and other neo-liberals, on the other hand, while indicating that Keynesianism had reached its limits, did not help in the least – and this is still the case today.[175]

Which contradictions, then, were key in ending the most recent long wave with expansionist undertone at the end of the 1960s?

The first of these contradictions results from the constant growth of the organic composition of capital, which corresponds to the tendency to displace

---

173   Mandel 1995c, pp. 59–60.
174   Mandel 1995c, pp. 59–61.
175   Mandel 1995c, p. 64.

living labour from the production process. Aware that this view is not undisputed and has led to controversy among economists, Mandel addresses all the relevant objections. Firstly, he concedes a difficulty in establishing the findings:

> We gladly concede that this rise in the organic composition of capital was less pronounced, especially during the first part of the expansionist long wave, than would follow from the very definition of the third technological revolution (i.e., semiautomation). One should not forget that within the framework of Marxist analytical concepts, the purely physical substitution of machines for manpower ... is not a correct indicator of the rising organic composition of capital. This concept concerns value relations (linked to technically predetermined relations), not physical quantities. Furthermore, it concerns not the value of equipment compared with the industrial wage bill (variable capital), but rather the price of equipment currently used, plus the costs of raw materials and energy, divided by wages. Another difficulty consists in the fact that from the point of view of Marxist economic theory, only the wages of productive labor must be taken into account, not the national wage bill. Statistical verification of the rise in the organic composition of capital is therefore impossible on an aggregate basis, starting from the GNP.[176]

Mandel argues that it is therefore necessary to examine certain key branches of the economy by way of example. He provides two examples to prove the asserted trend: The drastic reduction in the number of working hours required by the French telephone and telecommunications industry, which, with the introduction of fully electronic connections, was to fall to 80 per cent of what was previously required, and the transition from the production of chips, which were quite expensive at the time, in production plants worth $2 million in the late 1960s, to the production of much cheaper chips at a minimum level of profitability in production plants costing $50 million.[177]

Mandel sees the *second* contradiction in the fact that the possibilities of technological rents and extra profits are exhausted over time. Again, the example of chip production demonstrates the way in which this kind of process can take place. Another example is the chemical industry, where hopes for big profits from the discovery of new molecular combinations are dwindling, while new technologies – such as the production of chemicals from raw plant

---

176   Mandel 1995c, pp. 64–5.
177   Mandel 1995c, pp. 65–6. This trend is certainly continuing today in many areas.

materials and genetic engineering – nowhere nearly justify the kind of profit expectations that were normal in the pioneering days of synthetics production. Another barrier is posed by the need of big capital to recover as much as possible from huge past investments (such as in nuclear energy) before massively investing in new technologies and product lines again. *Third*, Mandel argues that further increases in the velocity of capital turnover became more difficult because the immense acceleration of money transfers do not correspond to the transportation of goods – not only for technical reasons, but also because the institutional boundaries inherent in capitalism (private property, nation states, unequal distribution standards) impose narrow limits.[178] *Fourth*, Mandel argues that it is especially in periods of accelerated growth that the disproportion between the rate of growth in productive capacity, on the one hand, and that in the raw materials sector, on the other hand, increases. The latter is more closely tied to natural conditions and is therefore less flexible. After a long period of declining commodity prices, the year 1972 was a turning point in this sector. *Fifth*, Mandel uses statistical data to demonstrate that a constant increase in (productively unused) overcapacity took place in the area of large-scale capitalist industry, and this despite an unchecked increase in consumer debt.[179] *Sixth*, a sustained and heavy increase in the rate of surplus-value really is the appropriate means of counteracting the fall in the rate of profit and reversing the trend – and indeed, this was achieved at the beginning of the expansionist long wave through a steep rise in labour productivity in department II (the sector where articles of consumption are produced) and thus through increased production of relative surplus-value. However, this process faced two obstacles: the end of the boom era of technological innovation and relative full employment, which pushed the profit rate down again.[180] *Seventh*, Mandel argues that the attenuation of crisis tendencies through debt also has its limits, since constant new inflationary surges ultimately only have the effect of postponing the 'hour of reckoning' again and again. Eventually, the effect inevitably turns into its opposite, and the dwindling credibility of the prospects of creditors being served becomes an obstacle to investment. *Eighth* and last, the growing importance of transnationally operating corporations reduces the scope for regulatory intervention by the governments of nation states.[181] For Mandel, the long waves of the business cycle are not only empirically ascertainable, but historical realities, 'segments' of the overall history of

---

178   Mandel 1995c, p. 69.
179   Mandel 1995c, pp. 69–71.
180   Mandel 1995c, pp. 72–3.
181   Mandel 1995c, pp. 72–4.

capitalism that have definitely distinguishable features, with each representing their own historical 'totality'.[182] This is evidenced by the ideological reflection of the 'up and down' of long waves. Thus, despite the untold catastrophes in the period leading up to it, the period from 1948–68 was a period of optimism, faith in science and progress, whereas the transition to a long wave with stagnant and depressive tendencies was the hour of pessimists and prophets of doom. According to Mandel, the rise of ideologies such as those of the French 'new philosophers' and the re-emergence of irrationalism, social Darwinism and sociobiology was characteristic for this.[183] The ideological turn away from Keynesianism to monetarism was an expression of a fundamental change in the capitalist class's priorities in the class struggle: the focus was no longer on integration, as had been the case in the ascending wave, but on increasing the rate of surplus-value. Similarly, the interwar period was marked by irrationality and mysticism, in sharp contrast to the rationalism and faith in science prevalent in the previous period.[184]

So far as contemporary ideological trends are concerned, Mandel distinguishes their irrational sides from their rational core. Critique of the prospects of 'unlimited growth' (with limited natural resources), the emphasis on responsibility for future generations, the rejection of the capitalist model of consumption – all of this is, in his view, justified and converges with the socialist view: from a certain stage of saturation with use-values within the framework of general emancipation, 'non-material' production will become predominant. Nevertheless, on the whole, the ideological change of direction is a threat, with anti-humanist, anti-egalitarian and anti-democratic tendencies prevailing.[185]

Concluding his presentation, Mandel discusses whether a new long wave with an expansionist undertone could occur and what the consequences would be. In his view, the prerequisites for this would be an increase in the rate of eco-

---

182   Mandel 1995c, p. 76. According to this, the first long wave corresponds roughly to the period of the industrial revolution and the emergence of a world market for manufactured goods from 1789 (French Revolution) to 1948, with the downward trend setting in from 1826. This was followed by the period of the capitalism of 'free competition', which passed its peak in 1873, although there still ensued a stagnant phase until 1893. 'Classical imperialism' came next, in turn entering its period of decline from 1914. In 1940 (or 1948 in the case of Western Europe and Japan), the golden age of the late capitalist phase of imperialism began, which in turn entered its stagnating-depressive period of decay towards the end of the 1960s (see the chronological scheme in Mandel 1995c, p. 82).

183   Mandel 1995c, p. 79.

184   Mandel 1995c, pp. 76–9.

185   Mandel 1995c, pp. 81–3.

nomic growth above the average of the 1970s and 1980s, a spectacular increase in the rate of accumulation, an equally strong expansion of the capitalist commodity market and a considerable increase in the rate of surplus-value. This would require a long period of high mass unemployment in order to significantly reduce real wages. To get there, in turn, the confidence and resilience of the working class would have to be decisively broken. A strong devaluation of capital would be another prerequisite. This would entail the bankruptcy of many small companies and a number of very large ones, as well as a new surge in international capital concentration. Moreover, the existing technological innovations would have to be introduced into the production process *en masse*, and the capital turnover rate would have to be drastically accelerated again.

Mandel believes that all of this is conceivable. Thanks to the development of microprocessors, the technical prerequisites are available too. In practice, this would mean a leap forward towards full automation and a massive application of genetic engineering methods, in particular in the production of drugs and in agriculture.[186] One consequence of this, however, would be the further displacement of living labour from the production process and consequently a reduction in the mass of surplus-value, which could not be offset by a simultaneous increase in the production of relative surplus-value. The potential increase in the rate of surplus-value would have to be considered marginal in relation to the immense costs associated with the generalisation of fully automated production. A significant rise in the profit rate is therefore not conceivable by this route. It would be impossible for the service sector to absorb 'laid-off' employees, since this sector would also be subject to strong rationalisation. Moreover, massive unemployment not only has unforeseeable social and political consequences, but also aggravates the problem of realisation since the declining mass purchasing power cannot be effectively offset by an increase in the consumption expenditure of the capitalists (through an increase in luxury consumption).[187] In Mandel's view, a further necessary prerequisite are either suitably large-scale industrialisation processes (and increases in welfare) in some of the poor countries – which seemed to him to be out of the question under the world conditions prevailing at the time – or a 'qualitative increase in the degree of integration of the USSR and China into the international capitalist market'.[188] In this context, Mandel does not consider whether

---

186 Mandel 1995c, pp. 84–5.
187 Mandel 1995c, pp. 84–6.
188 Mandel 1995c, p. 87.

the systems of post-capitalist countries might collapse and embark on capitalist restoration. However, he cites a huge credit expansion involving 'several hundreds of billions of dollars' as a prerequisite for a new expansionist wave, namely a credit expansion on a larger scale than that which flooded a number of countries in the so-called 'third world' in the second half of the 1970s – with well-known consequences and predictable serious shocks to those countries.[189]

Mandel does not offer an overall prognosis – only a conditional forecast. According to him, everything depends on the outcomes of social and political struggles internationally and on how the balance of power between classes develops. The offensive of capital and austerity policies, he argues, have indeed succeeded in increasing the rate of exploitation, even where real wages have not yet fallen. But these results have so far been far from sufficient for a 'reversal of the trend'. As yet, the bourgeoisie has not decisively broken the resistance of the working class in the rich industrialised countries. A 'victory' in this respect would also result in massive restrictions on democratic rights, up to and including the establishment of dictatorial regimes. But this would have to be preceded by a series of partial struggles, the outcomes of which would by no means be decided beforehand. The liberation movements in the countries of the so-called 'third world' would likewise have to suffer decisive defeats beforehand. Hitherto changes in the international division of labour and the relocation of production to low-wage countries should not be confused with an expansion of the world market – what is settled in one place will be lost in another. Ultimately, the transition to a new expansionist long wave of capitalism would depend on major confrontations between capital and labour, 'if not a series of international wars and civil wars'.[190] According to Mandel, capitalism's ability to adapt and respond should not be underestimated, but the high 'costs' of human suffering and the devastating consequences of a new upturn in this mode of production need to be highlighted. Ecological problems can only be solved if science is no longer stifled by the private profit motive, and the implementation of a socialist solution is preferable to paying the 'costs' of a successful capitalist 'crisis management'.[191]

---

189   Mandel 1995c, p. 91.
190   Mandel 1995c, p. 92.
191   Mandel 1995c, pp. 93–5. In the early 1990s, Mandel found the main conclusions of his Marxist interpretations of 'long waves' substantially confirmed by new empirical findings – see Mandel 1992c.

5   Worldwide Inequality

Mandel's point of departure for his critique of present-day capitalist class society is the observation of extreme social inequality, both in individual countries and worldwide. This reality is the starting point of his popular accounts of Marxism. In introductory seminars in his home country of Belgium and in the US, for example, he presented a number of global figures as evidence of the extreme inequality in contemporary capitalism:

> Four per cent of the citizens occupy the top of this pyramid, owning half the private wealth of the nation. Less than one per cent of Belgians own more than half the stocks and shares in the country. Among these, 200 families control the big holding societies which dominate the whole of the nation's economic life ... In the USA, a Senate Commission has estimated that less than one per cent of American families possess 80 per cent of all shares in companies, and that 0.2 per cent of families possess more than two-thirds of these shares.[192]

Mandel assumes that drastic inequality, as much as it is justified by the ideologues of the ruling classes and therefore accepted in the dominant consciousness, contradicts a desire for equality that is deeply embedded in human nature. It is therefore a source of latent dissatisfaction.[193] But he also underlines that inequality in the existing social order has a direct impact on the quality of life, to the point of different infant mortality rates in bourgeois and in working-class families.[194] The same applies to global inequality:

> Nowadays it is not enough just to take stock of the social inequalities which exist in each country. It is even more important to take into account the inequality between a small handful of advanced countries (from the point of view of industrialisation) and the majority of humanity, living in the so-called under-developed countries (colonial and semicolonial countries). The USA accounts for nearly half of the industrial production and consumes more than half of a great number of primary industrial materials in the capitalist world. Five hundred and fifty million Indians have less steel and electrical energy at their disposal than nine million Belgians. The real per capita income in the poorest countries of the world

---

192   Mandel 1979a, p. 11 et seq.; see also Mandel 1973b, pp. 29–30.
193   Mandel 1968b p. 30 et seq. and 655; Mandel 1973b, pp. 36–7.
194   See Mandel 1979a, pp. 11–12.

is only eight per cent of the per capita income in the richest countries. Sixty-seven per cent of the world's population receive only 15 per cent of the world revenue. In India in 1970, 20 times as many women per 100,000 births died in childbirth as in Britain. As a result an Indian's daily calorie intake is only half the daily intake in the West. Average life expectancy, which in the West is more than 65 years, and in some countries reaches 70 years, is barely 30 in India.[195]

When Mandel articulates his basic programmatic beliefs in order to prove that the capitalist mode of production is outdated, his starting point is always the interrelation between the two major, tendentially widening inequalities in the individual countries, on the one hand, and on a global level, on the other. In *The Reasons for Founding the Fourth International*, he cites this link as the first of the 'fundamental contradictions of our epoch':

> Since 1914, the capitalist mode of production has entered its period of historic decline. The huge productive forces built up by that system periodically enter into contradiction with the capitalist relations of production, the private mode of appropriation and the nation-state ... While capitalism in the 20th century undermines the fruits of past progress in parts of the world it blocks progress in other parts. The polarisation of haves and have-nots in each capitalist country, in spite of the resources available, is interconnected with a world-wide polarisation between relatively rich and relatively poor nations.[196]

Similarly, in his account of Trotsky's contribution to Marxism ('Trotsky's Place in the Twentieth Century'), Mandel cites as the first point the fixed nature of global inequality as a phenomenon linked to the ongoing imperialist era of capitalist mode of production: 'In the imperialist epoch, the Marxist evolutionary schema, according to which the advanced nations hold up to the more underdeveloped the image of their own future, is turned into its opposite. Imperialism blocks the radical modernization and industrialization of the underdeveloped countries'.[197]

In his economic writings, such as in *Marxist Economic Theory* and *Late Capitalism*, Mandel tried to determine the continuities and changes in the imperialist world system in the context of bourgeois class rule in the monopoly

---

195   Mandel 1979a, pp. 12–13.
196   Mandel 1988, chapter 2.
197   Mandel 1995a, p. 1.

capitalist age. We shall return to the political concepts he deduced from this for socialist programme and strategy in our subchapter on 'Permanent revolution and international dimension of socialist strategy'.[198] Here we will deal with some general conclusions that follow directly from Mandel's analysis of global realities.

In 1991, as part of his engagement to cancel the debts of the 'third world', Mandel gave an interview in which he succinctly outlined his views on global inequality.[199] His starting point was 'classical' imperialism causing dependency and blocking development for most of humanity located in the global 'south':

> The backwardness in development and prosperity of the countries of the so-called 'third world' against the imperialist metropolises has significantly deteriorated during the imperialist era. This period begins around the 1890s. It is characterised particularly by the fact that in the metropolitan areas, the export of capital becomes the pursuit of the large industrial and financial corporations instead of the export of commodities. These corporations thus gradually become monopolistic groups.
>
> For this reason, political control of the countries to which capital is exported becomes a necessity. If you export commodities, the problems are solved when the commodities are paid for, usually after three months. When you export capital, it remains put and is not fully amortised and utilised for years. Permanent political control aims to ensure the profitability and amortisation of capital in the long term.
>
> This is why the imperialist powers transform most underdeveloped countries into colonies. In Asia and Africa, only Ethiopia, Iran, Afghanistan and China evaded this fate (the Ottoman Empire was in a crisis of disintegration, but scarcely survived until World War I). However, despite retaining their formal political independence, they increasingly became semi-colonies, i.e. countries that are financially and economically controlled by the imperialist powers. This was also the fate of the Latin American and the Balkans (and, after World War I, the countries of eastern Europe). Under imperialist rule, the modernisation of the colonial and semi-colonial countries is blocked in two ways. On the one hand, the metropolises impose an economy on them that complements that of the imperialist countries. They confine them to the production and export of raw materials and agricultural products. These economies are also often

---

198   See Chapter 5, section 6.
199   See Mandel 2001.

characterised by monocultures or even the exclusive cultivation of one single product. The prices for these products are completely determined by the world market, which is controlled by the big corporations and big banks, and they are subject to strong fluctuations. This leads to the gradual ruin of small producers, to misery and chronic unemployment. For this reason, the internal market of these countries is very limited, which poses an additional obstacle to industrialisation.

On the other hand, the colonial powers have mostly helped the traditional propertied classes of these countries, who undertook a semi-feudal exploitation of the peasants, to remain in their old social position. Ground rents got very high. The peasants became increasingly indebted. They were subjected to the stranglehold of usurers. There is thus a combination of capitalist and pre-capitalist exploitation. The maintenance of barbaric oppression systems such as the caste system in India exacerbates this super-exploitation.

All this can be summarised as follows: modernisation is blocked. In countries like India or China, it was even the case that the beginnings of modernisation that had previously been underway were pushed back.[200]

After World War II, this system did not continue unabated – colonialism was replaced by neo-colonialism:

> It is true that the surge of liberation movements in the colonies since the formation of the Indian nation-state in 1942–43, powerfully boosted after the war by the revolutions in Indonesia and Vietnam, and then more than anything by the victory of the Chinese revolution, caused the colonial powers to gradually abandon the direct political rule of their colonies. The fact that the hegemonic imperialist power after World War II, US imperialism, only had a few colonies, contributed to this as well. The abandonment of colonial structures paved the way for US supremacy, which replaced that of the old colonial powers. Egypt, for example, was no longer ruled by Great Britain, but came under the patronage of the United States. The old colonies thus gained political independence, but aside from the exceptions of Indochina and North Korea, this did not mean that they won real independence from imperialism. Direct rule became indirect rule. Colonialism became neo-colonialism. Just as in the semi-colonies,

---

200   Mandel 2001, pp. 16–17, our translation; see also Mandel 1968b, p. 441 et seq.; Mandel 1979d, p. 67 et seq.

economic, financial and quite often military dependence still prevailed. In this way, the obstacles to economic development and to general social modernisation remained in place.[201]

On the other hand, significant industrialisation processes did indeed take place in the 'third world' – even in countries where capitalism was not overthrown. Mandel cites simplistic analyses that considered such developments impossible:

> In this respect, many ideologues – both Marxist and non-Marxist – have made major analytical and prognostic errors, especially in the 1960s. In fact, some 'third world' countries have seen the onset of industrialisation and modernisation, namely in two waves. The first one spanned from 1935 to 1955, especially in Latin America. The second came later, particularly from the '70s onward, in a number of Asian countries, Brazil, South Africa, Egypt, Iraq (while the same process began earlier in India and Egypt). Those who drive this incipient industrialisation process represent a coalition of forces in power that is quite different from the old ruling structures. The latter were based on an alliance between foreign imperialist capital, the domestic so-called *comprador* bourgeoisie (mainly trade and usurious capital), which was very closely linked to foreign capital, and the big landowners and other traditional ruling classes. The new coalition comprises a modernist wing from the military hierarchy, a nascent domestic monopoly bourgeoisie and some imperialist multinationals betting on the semi-industrialisation of the 'third world'.[202]

In *Marxist Economic Theory*, Mandel had already referred to these limited but significant industrialisation processes in countries of the 'third world'. He also pointed to various categories of causes for these processes, which provided the material basis for various (ultimately illusory or misleading) models of 'catch-up development' and for a modified relationship between the ruling classes of the metropolises and those of the periphery:

> The system of indirect domination – neo-colonialism or neo-imperialism – is not only an inevitable concession by the metropolitan bourgeoisie to the colonial bourgeoisie. It also corresponds to an economic

---

201   Mandel 2001, p. 17, our translation; see also Mandel 1979d, pp. 68–9.
202   Mandel 2001, p. 17, our translation.

change in the relations between the two classes. The industrialisation of the colonial and semi-colonial countries is an irreversible process. It undermines one of the pillars of the old colonial system – the role of outlets for goods of current consumption which is played by the backward countries ... It is exports of capital goods that more and more take the place of the old type of exports, in so far as the under-developed countries still have to furnish a safety-valve for the tendencies to periodical overproduction which are inherent in capitalist economy. These exports are compatible with a higher degree of political and social independence of the colonial bourgeoisie in relation to imperialism. They even necessitate, to some extent, increased intervention by the State, which alone is capable of setting up large heavy-industrial enterprises in the under-developed countries.[203]

Following on from this, Mandel refers to 'foreign aid' as a means to facilitate the 'redistribution of profits ... to the advantage of the monopoly sectors which export capital goods, at the expense of the "old" sectors (textiles, coal, etc.)'.[204] Despite 'foreign aid', the exploitation of the 'third-world' continues, primarily through 'deteriorating exchange relations', and the result is in fact even greater deterioration: 'Incidentally, the balance of "aid" shows a loss rather than an increase in the reserves of the "third world"'.[205]

The rise in exports of capital goods led to a new division of labour in the world economy, with parts of the 'third world' becoming suppliers of certain light industry products (textiles, leather goods, canned food, etc.) to the rich countries. However, according to Mandel, even 'moderate' partial industrialisation encountered 'insurmountable obstacles' because of the existing social structure in these countries.[206] In addition, however, there were also political motives for 'foreign aid' and the ideology in which it was cloaked that were linked to the east-west bloc confrontation (these have now therefore largely disappeared): 'It goes without saying that the "cold war" has stimulated the movement for aid to the under-developed countries, alliance with the colonial bourgeoisie being the only way in which imperialism can meet the con-

---

203   Mandel 1968b, p. 480.
204   Mandel 1968b, p. 481.
205   Ibid. Mandel proves this with a statistic of the official gold and foreign exchange reserves
       of industrialised countries, on the one hand, and of the non-industrialised countries, on
       the other, in their respective development from 1954 to 1960, with a clear increase for the
       rich countries and a decrease for the poor countries.
206   Ibid.

tinual strengthening of the anti-capitalist forces in the world. But the change in the structure of world trade to which neo-imperialism corresponds must be regarded as a factor working in that same direction in any case, even regardless of the conflict between West and East'.[207]

Mandel consistently stressed the limitations of these new developments. He did not see in them any possibility for countries of the 'third world' to catch up with the rich industrialised countries within the capitalist world system like Japan succeeded in doing:

> For one, the countries that have undergone semi-industrialisation rep-resent only a small minority of the countries of the 'third world'. The vast majority of these countries continue to struggle under severe underdevel-opment. Furthermore, it really is a semi-industrialisation rather than a progressive cumulative industrialisation. The modern capitalist sector usually remains combined with an archaic sector (Taiwan and South Korea being the two exceptions to this rule). This is transparently the case in India, Brazil, South Africa and Mexico. For this reason, a strong depend-ence on imperialism remains, especially in technological and financial terms, but also in the fields of trade and the military. Sudden turns of the international economic situation cause the standstill or even decline of development. This confirms the structural vulnerability of these coun-tries.[208]

In *Late Capitalism*, Mandel writes along similar lines: 'The decisive fact con-tinues to be the impossibility of any thorough industrialization of the under-developed countries within the framework of the world market, in the age of late capitalism and neocolonialism, just as much as in the age of "clas-sical" imperialism. Inter-zonal differences of development, industrialization and productivity are steadily increasing'.[209]

In Mandel's view, new problems arose in contemporary capitalism for poor and dependent countries, leading even deeper into the swamp of dependence, stunted and deformed development:

> Technological and financial dependence causes an outflow of resources to the imperialist metropolises, mediated by the unequal exchange that is

---

207   Ibid.
208   Mandel 2001, p. 17, our translation.
209   Mandel 1975d, pp. 375–6.

based on different levels in average labour productivity compared to the metropolises. This outflow of resources naturally slows down economic development in the long term. The new 'ruling bloc' attempts to counter this handicap by putting pressure on wages ('labour costs'). However, since industrialisation stimulates the development of the working class and therefore the emergence of a militant workers' movement, it often resorts to imposing dictatorial regimes or applying very harsh repression to stem the labour movement surge. This, in turn, limits the development of the internal market, renders the process of industrialisation dependent on the success of an unrestrained export policy, and thus increases dependence on the multinationals that dominate the world market.[210]

For the countries of the 'third world', a negative dynamic, a deterioration of the situation has ensued. This does not simply mean that they lag behind the developed capitalist countries, but rather that this dynamic affects the fate of many millions of people. In his speeches, Mandel did not hesitate to compare the millions of children who die of hunger and easily curable diseases with the victims of the world wars.[211] In a 1991 interview, he compared the living standards of the one billion worst-off people in the world with those of prisoners in Nazi concentration camps 'before 1941' (not to be confused with the Nazi extermination camps):

> It is true that the relatively most developed countries of the 'third world' have more resources and are therefore easier to plunder than the poorest countries from which little can be robbed. Therefore, the lion's share of the notorious 'third world debt' is concentrated in a relatively few underdeveloped countries: Mexico, Brazil, South Korea, Argentina, etc. Yet this is a general plundering phenomenon. The deterioration in the terms of trade alone (the ratio of the prices of poor countries' export products to the prices of their import products) has led to more losses for the 'third world' than has debt service within ten years. The combined effects ... [of] growing debt [and] the slowdown in growth due to the poor international economic situation meant a dreadful increase in misery in the 'third world' ... One billion people living in the poorest parts of the 'third world' have suffered a 30 to 40 % deterioration in their average standard of

---

210   Mandel 2001, p. 17, our translation.
211   The author remembers relevant statements made by Mandel at events in Brussels, Liège, Aachen and Cologne.

living. If you know how low that standard of living was previously, you can imagine how terrible this development is. Their nutrition is comparable to that of prisoners in Nazi concentration camps before 1941. 16 million children die every year in the 'third world' from starvation and easily curable diseases. There is an acute rise in epidemics typical of miserable conditions, such as cholera, which has been spreading from Peru to the rest of Latin America since 1991. So-called natural disasters that regularly affect Bangladesh are in reality caused by the fact that too little work is invested in infrastructure – in other words, by underdevelopment. Even from the point of view of the imperialist powers, this is a disastrous policy. The consequences of this increase in terrible misery in the 'third world' are spreading to the West and to Japan. The 'third world' is not an insignificant client of the imperialist powers. Its misery stifles the expansion of world trade.[212]

The so-called 'debt crisis', which had begun to escalate in the first half of the 1970s, marked a turning point and initiated a further change in relations between the ruling classes of the rich industrialised capitalist countries and those of the poor and dependent countries. It became another source of the drain of wealth from the poor to the rich world. There is a wealth of literature on this subject and on the disastrous consequences for large sections of the population in the countries concerned caused by 'adjustment plans' negotiated by the International Monetary Fund (IMF) and the World Bank (institutions acting in the interests of big capital and the banks of the rich developed countries) in the context of debt collection.[213] Mandel placed this 'third world' debt crisis in the context of his critique of contemporary capitalism as a whole and treated it as part of a more general phenomenon, as shown by an essay published in German in April 1986: 'The growing debt in no way stems from the failure of the underdeveloped countries, their ruling classes or their governments; it is only a particular expression of the key role that credit inflation – and thus inflation of all forms of debt – has played in promoting growth (or better still, in delaying the crisis) in all capitalist states and economic sectors after World War II'.[214] As Mandel points out here, according to figures from the mid-1980s, the public sector debt in the USA amounted to 2 trillion dollars, the debt of private companies in the USA to 2.8 trillion dollars, the debt

---

212   Mandel 2001, p. 17, our translation.
213   An example of this is Körner, Maaß, Siebold, Tetzlaff: *Im Teufelskreis der Verschuldung. Der Internationale Währungsfonds und die Dritte Welt*, Hamburg 1984.
214   Mandel 1987c, p. 75, our translation.

of private households in the USA to 1.9 trillion dollars – the total 'third world' debt had reached 950 billion dollars.[215] Mandel deduces from this the unreasonable nature of the complaints of bankers from the rich north about 'third world' debt: 'The complaints brought forward by banking circles only reflect a bourgeois wisdom: "You only lend to the rich", which, translated into a more frank language, means: "You should only have lent to the rich"'.[216]

The main cause of 'third world' debt is that capital was looking for investment opportunities, or more precisely for alternatives to investment in industrial production in the rich developed countries. For Mandel, this is in itself a symptom of the crisis of the capitalist system, namely a symptom of the tendency of the rate of profit to fall – or at least of the temporary exhaustion of possibilities to make extra profits through productive investments in the most developed industries. The issue was in particular the recycling of petrodollars, which had caused the assets of some US and British banks to expand after the oil shock of 1973. The banks therefore offered money to 'third world' countries, but also to a certain extent to non-capitalist states – at higher interest rates than was usual at the time for the rich developed countries, adjusted for inflation, but in the hope that the economies of the semi-industrialised countries would flourish and thus make them solvent. The redistribution of money was certainly in the interest of the capitalist system as a whole, given that the oil-importing 'third world' countries would no longer have been in a position to import goods on a significant scale because of the consequences of the 'oil crisis'.[217]

In a sophisticated analysis, Mandel cites different factors which by the mid-1980s jointly led to a six- or sevenfold increase in 'third world' debt from the initial 150 billion dollars. He also points out that even then, the debts already paid exceeded the sum of the credits, and that repayment was unthinkable. Thus a vicious circle of ever-increasing debt had been created. This was partially due to the increasing willingness of some executive staff of the major banks to take incalculable risks in order to maximise profits quickly, but also because it was fundamentally impossible to control the overall situation under the conditions of a market economy and the law of value. The increase in interest rates exacerbated the debt crisis, and the drop in oil prices – after a temporary surge – caused difficulties first for oil-exporting countries and then for a number of oil-importing 'third world' countries. Only some of the money

215   Mandel 1987c, p. 76.
216   Ibid.
217   See Mandel 1987c, pp. 78–80.

borrowed was invested productively. A larger share served to maintain production or infrastructure, and members of the propertied classes of the respective 'third world' countries invested a significant share directly in the metropolises. This increased the flow of capital flight. Finally, new loans were used to finance the payment of debt.[218] Mandel's diagnosis is that the whole international banking and credit system is threatened by the debt crisis. According to him, forcing poor countries to divert funds for debt service only exacerbates their lack of capital: 'Or in the words of Paul Prebic: "The therapy of the International Monetary Fund is bleeding an anaemic patient!"'[219] But the massive pressure on these countries to expand their exports in turn narrows the market for the exports of the rich countries (especially the US). Generally speaking, a section of imperialist capital is profiting from the 'debt crisis' (especially the creditor banks and the speculative capital organised through them), while other sections (capital invested in industry and in the export economy) tend to suffer from it. According to Mandel, this also explains the nuances in the policies of the various imperialist powers. While the US and Great Britain act as tough lobbyists for creditors, Germany and other EU countries are pushing for a 'softer' attitude, especially for Latin America, because this is more in line with their interests.[220] Mandel did not believe in the inevitability of a major crash ('This does not mean, however, that a real general banking crash is certain'). He stressed that the imperialist countries and their international institutions were likely to intervene with a vengeance if major banks or large corporations – i.e. the pillars of the capitalist system in all countries – were in danger of collapsing. For him, the official dispute is essentially about the distribution of sacrifices: for the ruling classes of the 'third world' countries, it is about deadlines and about the burdens that result from rescheduling and postponing debt. On the other hand, Mandel did not take it as a given that bailouts would always work. What he considered certain was who would pay for their costs: 'One part at the expense of the working masses of the imperialist states and the other part at the expense of the popular masses of the "third world" countries themselves'.[221] Worse exchange relations between typical 'third world' commodities and the typical commodities of developed capitalist countries contributed (and still contribute) to the deepening of the debt crisis. Fidel Castro gave a vivid example in his justification of the call for the cancellation of 'third world' country debt:

---

218 See Mandel 1987c, pp. 80–3.
219 See Mandel 1987c, p. 87.
220 Ibid.
221 See Mandel 1987c, p. 88.

24 years ago, you had to spend 200 tons of sugar to buy a bulldozer of 180 HP, today you need 800 tons of sugar for the same bulldozer at world market prices. And if you look at the coffee, cocoa, banana, ore exported by Latin America, the quantities produced to import a bulldozer or any other equipment for construction, transport, agriculture or industry from the developed countries are three or four times higher than what was needed at the time. If we compare with 1950, the deterioration in trade relations looks even worse.[222]

Mandel, who fiercely supported Castro's demand for debt cancellation, notes the same state of affairs, regarding its negative impact on the countries of the affected world regions as even more significant than debt itself:

Leaving aside the brief sensational speculative price rise from 1971–1973 and, in the case of oil, the two oil shocks of 1973–74 and 1979, the prices of raw materials and semi-finished products rose more slowly than the prices of finished goods – that is, assuming they did not fall. This negative development in the terms of exchange, which only some semi-industrialised countries such as South Korea have been able to evade (and even then, only temporarily), weighs down heavily on the poorest countries, whose debt, even if lower in absolute terms than that of semi-industrialised countries, is an intolerable burden. The average overall price of raw materials, if we consider 1979–81 to be 100, had fallen to 72 by September 1985. The losses in export revenue therefore still exceed the amount of debt.[223]

For Mandel, these exchange relations were only a part or an expression of a broader problem, namely of the unequal exchange between the economies of the developed capitalist countries (i.e. the imperialist countries) and those of poor and dependent countries. In his view, extra profits from unequal exchange played a lesser role in the phase of 'classical' imperialism than in what he called 'late capitalism', although this can only be demonstrated in an approximate fashion:

Although it is difficult to make statistical calculations, it is nonetheless clear that both before the First World War and in the interwar period

---

222   Mandel 1987c, p. 36, our translation.
223   Mandel 1987c, p. 85, our translation.

unequal exchange was quantitatively less important than the direct production and transfer of colonial surplus-profits. Colonial surplus-profits were hence the chief form of the metropolitan exploitation of the 'third world' at that time, unequal exchange being only a secondary form … The proportions changed in the late capitalist epoch. Unequal exchange henceforth becomes the main form of colonial exploitation, the direct production of colonial surplus-profits playing a secondary role.[224]

As mentioned earlier, for Mandel the development of exchange relations is connected to this. For him, the basis of unequal exchange on the world market is the difference in labour productivity. While for the exchange relations we consider the baskets of commodities typical of the respective world regions or countries that enter into world trade, for unequal exchange we imagine the same type of commodity (for example, a shirt or a tool) that requires a different number of working hours to produce in different regions of the world:

This unequal exchange meant that the colonies and semicolonies tended to exchange increasing quantities of indigenous labour (or products of labour) for a constant amount of metropolitan labour (or products of labour). The long-term development of the terms of trade was a gauge of this tendency, although other determinants also influenced them: among other things, monopoly control over markets for raw materials and colonial output of these materials by large imperialist companies from the metropolitan countries, and so on.[225]

For Mandel, the fact that this unequal exchange plays the main role in contemporary capitalism has a number of causes (including political causes linked to the transition from direct to indirect rule of most dependent countries) but is also an organic product of the development of capitalism globally. In late capitalism, the lion's share of capital export takes place in the metropolises. The structure of exports to 'third world' countries has changed, as has the structure of production in poor and dependent countries, where the production of articles of consumption plays an increasingly important role next the production of raw materials. In Latin America, for instance, the loss of export earnings from 1951 to 1966 far exceeded the loss due to capital drain caused by the profits of foreign corporations.[226]

---

224 Mandel 1975d, pp. 345–6.
225 Mandel 1975d, p. 345.
226 See Mandel 1975d, p. 350.

Where then does the loss or gain of value underlying unequal exchange come from? Marx gave a clear answer to this question, which represents an application of the general labour theory of value to international trade. In the epoch of capitalism, unequal exchange ultimately derives from the exchange of unequal quantities of labour. Within the framework of the capitalist world economy there are basically two sources of unequal exchange:

1.   The fact that the labour of the industrialized countries counts as more intensive (hence more productive of value) on the world market than that of the underdeveloped lands (or, what amounts to the same thing, by contrast to the situation within a national market, less intensive and productive labour receives normal remuneration, hence more intensive and productive labour receives a higher remuneration).

2.   The fact that no equalization of the rates of profit occurs on the world market, where different national prices of production (average rates of profit) exist side by side and are articulated with one another in a manner described in Chapter 2.[227]

It will suffice to briefly summarise the arguments concerning the 'structure of the capitalist world market' to which Mandel is referring here.[228] According to him, the fundamental differences in the social structure of the different world regions and countries of the south, which still retain their semi-capitalist and pre-capitalist conditions, are just as essential for this as the role of the nation states in the formation of markets to which no structure corresponds at the world level. The existing differences are in each case starting points from which specific roles of the economies of various countries emerge in the framework of the capitalist world market and consolidate into a global 'division of labour'. A general mobility of capital and labour as a prerequisite for a global levelling of profit rates is not achievable within this framework 'division of labour'. In this regard, the respective average wage level is not a cause but a consequence of the respective regime of capital accumulation as well as the particular structure of the industrial reserve army. The integration into this global system consistently prevents any attempts to catch up in terms of development.

Precisely because of these differences in the value of commodities and the productivity of labour between each country integrated into the cap-

---

227   Mandel 1975d, p. 351.
228   See Mandel 1975d, pp. 75 et seq.

italist world market, the law of value inexorably compels the backward countries with a low level of labour productivity to specialize on the world market in a manner disadvantageous to themselves. If they wish, despite this fact, to embark on the production of high-value industrial goods (in small series and with colossal costs) they are condemned to sell these at a loss on their internal market, because the difference in production costs compared with those of the industrialized nations is too large, and exceeds the normal margin of profit on the domestic market. Russia and China escaped this fate after their socialist revolutions only by a protective monopoly of foreign trade.[229]

Given Mandel's assessment of the global situation – and also in view of the eye-opening comparison of the available evidence with respect to the consumption of resources, the standard of living, etc. between the 'first' and the 'third' world – the question arises on what global solidarity, i.e. a community of interests of dependent workers, the exploited and oppressed, should be based. Evidently, reality has unfolded differently from Marx's expectations when he wrote that the developed capitalist countries were holding up the mirror of their own future to the underdeveloped countries, that the proletarian class is in the process of being homogenised across borders, and that their objectively unified interest is offering the opportunity to act subjectively to pursue this class interest. For Mandel, however, it was clear that ultimately the common class interest of waged workers would outweigh the diverging interests of the various strata among them. As one reason for this, he cited the fact that the role of colonial extra-profits had relatively declined (the main capital flows run within the imperialist 'triad' USA-Nafta/EU/Japan-Asean). Thus the exploitation of waged workers in the capitalist developed countries is decisive for the surplus value that big capital generates:

> There is no doubt that the over-exploitation of 'third world' producers is a source of extra profits for the monopolies and the big bourgeoisie of the metropolises in general. These extra profits help to facilitate material concessions to the waged workers of Western countries. But the share of these extra profits in the total profits of this bourgeoisie is quite limited. By far the greatest share of the surplus-value that the imperialist monopolies appropriate is produced by waged workers in the imperialist countries: we estimate 80% or more. When profits decline in the West, the main

---

229   Mandel 1975d, p. 74.

response of big capital is to take action against its own workers – i.e. austerity policies, attacks on the real wages and social property of its own wage earners. These attacks waged by capital lead to a more moderate reduction in the standard of living than is the case in the 'third world' countries. But in absolute terms, the mass of global resources that capital accrues in this way is much greater than those coming from the 'third world'.[230]

What is more, Mandel believes that there is no basis for a permanent division based on objective interests between the workers and general non-proprietors of capital in the 'rich north' and in the 'poor south'. Rather, he views the social reality of the world as much more complicated and intricate. Through his concept of a social 'pyramid', for instance, he points out that the 'poor and marginalized' of the rich countries are worse off than, say, industrial workers in the poor countries. The following picture painted by Mandel may be debatable in light of various indicators (how do we compare the standard of living of a Brazilian industrial worker with that of a German welfare recipient, for example?). However, it encourages us to turn away from a one-sided north/south dichotomy that ignores the respective specific interests involved and look for potential new approaches to cross-border solidarity:

> Generally speaking, global reality must be understood as being based on a pyramid of power, wealth, resources and misery. At the top of the pyramid are the great imperialist monopolies. Then there are the 'new' and 'old' super-rich of the 'third world', who have enriched and continue to enrich themselves in an exceptionally scandalous fashion. Then we have the middle classes of the so-called rich countries. Then come the middle classes of the so-called poor countries. Then the western proletariat. Then the proletariat and poor peasants of the poor countries. Then the poor and marginalised of the rich countries. And at the very bottom are the marginalised of the 'third world'. A realistic view of this hierarchy will refute those who claim that the prevailing struggle today is between nations or even races. More than ever, the fundamental antagonisms are class antagonisms and those between major class factions.[231]

In Mandel's view, it is precisely the pursuit of one's own interest, properly conceived, that can lead the workers of the rich countries to adopt an internation-

---

230   Mandel 2001, pp. 18–19, our translation.
231   Mandel 2001, pp. 18–19, our translation.

alist stance. The actions and the agitation by the capitalist side are ultimately based on playing off the interests of the workers and the dispossessed in the different countries and world regions against each other. Even a firm rejection of 'undercutting wages', i.e. of blackmail based on the existence of 'cheaper' labour elsewhere in the world, would amount to rejecting the logic of competition and create solidarity. However, Mandel does not confine himself to an argumentation based directly on interests – he adds that workers in the rich countries do need be aware of the misery of the poor countries. For him, class consciousness in a universal sense also implies a political and moral attitude. His concluding remarks in the aforementioned 1991 interview illustrate the tension between the two aspects:

> The multinationals, i.e. big monopolistic capital, increasingly pursue a global strategy. They move production facilities, workers, and harmful waste from one country to another, from one continent to another, from one ocean to another. They relocate production facilities to countries with lower wage levels (and incidentally, not only to 'third world' countries) as a permanent means of blackmail and pressure against the labour movement and the metropolitan working class: 'Accept wage cuts or we'll move production to a place where wages are lower'. But because the multinationals will always find countries where wages are even lower, to accept this blackmail would be to enter into a vicious circle of permanent decline in living standards in all countries.
>
> The only effective response to this global offensive by big capital is to counter it by the joint action of waged workers across the world. In other words: 'All together we reject wage cuts, wherever they occur in the world. We will fight against redundancies everywhere, especially by pressurising for shorter working hours.' We must help trade unions in the 'third world' to raise wages in their countries instead of lowering wages in the west towards 'third world' levels. This is not an obstacle to 'third world' development. It implies a different model of development, one which emphasises the expansion of articles of consumption, the domestic market and the gradual elimination of poverty.
>
> The initial impulse must come from the wage earners of the imperialist countries. This is a solidaric duty and in line with material interest. This solidaric duty involves a struggle to make the peoples of the west aware of the misery of the 'third world', it involves the fight for the total cancellation of 'third world' debt, and it also involves a ruthless struggle against all forms of racism and xenophobia.[232]

---

232 Mandel 2001, pp. 19, our translation.

CHAPTER 3

Socialism: The Utopian Dimension in Mandel's Work

1 The Free Association of Producers: A Stateless, Classless Society

The task of defining the socialist goal, i.e. the envisioned society that shall replace capitalist class society, plays an important role in Mandel's political thinking. It 'governs' his ideas of the way that should be taken towards this goal, about the transitional society between capitalism and socialism, and about mobilising the working class alongside all the exploited and oppressed towards a process of self-liberation and social revolution.

In his educational and propaganda activities, Mandel consistently placed special emphasis on the depiction of the socialist goal. He took great joy in talking about this specifically. At a weekend seminar of the Belgian section of the Fourth International in 1972, he said that it was much more pleasurable to discuss the future socialist society than, say the need to develop a programme of transitional demands. The enthusiasm with which he presented his visions of the future made him appear credible and inspired others – more than a few young listeners soon began to dream of this liberated society, see it as a tangible option, and committed themselves politically to making it a reality.[1]

The utopian dimension of Mandel's conception of socialism is also unmistakable in his writing, even if he usually used the term 'utopia' in a negative sense, i.e. in the sense of ideas that are insufficiently rooted in a critical conception of reality and therefore not realisable. 'Do these analyses contain any element of utopia, or of expecting a "paradise on earth"? We do not think so. If you follow these thoughts, it will become clear that they are not cranky products of the imagination, but extrapolations of tendencies that are already apparent under the most favourable conditions of capitalist development today'.[2] What is more, in interviews and debates, Mandel occasionally commented with a touch of irony that the socialist objective does not claim to solve all problems; rather, it is 'only' a matter of solving about half a dozen of the most

---

1   This author's recollections; see also the eyewitness testimony by Winfried Wolf and with Helene Jungclas, Hans Peiffer and Helmut Wendler.
2   Mandel 1981a, pp. 151–2.

pressing problems, i.e. to banish from the earth hunger, early death caused by scarcity, easily curable diseases, wars, epidemics and the destruction of natural resources.[3] This, he argued, was in essence the purpose of establishing a global socialist society.

His depictions of the new society, however, stood in sharp contrast to what was understood and referred to as 'socialism' by the 'official' Communist movement and by bourgeois ideologues. Mandel painted the picture of a universal process of liberation and of the realisation of lofty humanist ideals. At the end of the process, a new human being emerges who, free from material constraints and hardships, devotes himself to his own self-realisation in solidarity with other people. The utopian vigour of this notion becomes very clear, for instance, in the penultimate chapter of *Marxist Economic Theory*, 'Socialist Economy', especially in the last section titled 'Man's limitations'.[4] Mandel essentially denies that such limits exist, albeit again in the form of a question. The last passage of this section seems almost exuberant:

> Human freedom is not a 'freely accepted' constraint, nor is it a mass of indistinctive and disorderly activities such as would degrade the individual. It is a self-realisation of man which is an eternal becoming and an eternal surpassing, a continual enrichment of everything human, an all-round development of all facets of humanity. It is neither absolute rest nor 'perfect happiness', but, after thousands of years of conflicts unworthy of the man, the beginning of the real 'human drama'. It is a hymn sung to the glory of man by men aware of their limitations who draw from this awareness the courage to overcome them. To the man of today it seems impossible to be both doctor and architect, machine-builder and atomsmasher. But who can speak of limitations that man will *never* be able to break through, man who is stretching out his arms towards the stars, who is on the brink of producing life in test-tubes, and who tomorrow will embrace the entire family of mankind in a spirit of universal brotherhood?[5]

For Mandel, socialism is the social condition that will lead humanity to communism. But for him, socialism is by no means a society that can emerge immediately after the fall of capitalism. In his terminology, initially only transitional

---

3   See Mandel 1978c.
4   Mandel 1968b, p. 654.
5   Mandel 1968b, p. 686.

societies situated somewhere between capitalism and socialism can emerge after the working class of individual countries has conquered political power. The vital characteristics of full socialism are the ultimate disappearance of social classes, the withering away of money and commodity economy and simultaneous satisfaction of basic needs for free, and the dying away of the state. For Mandel, this stage can only be reached when the non-capitalist world dominates the globe.[6]

If this conceivable socialist society – which in Mandel's understanding cannot emerge overnight but can nevertheless become reality in a tangible future, (and which even at this early stage is so completely different to today's capitalist class society that it appears 'utopian' to most people today) – is itself only a transitional stage, what is the 'higher' communist goal? In a brief summary, Mandel defines it as follows:

> The stage of communism, characterised by the complete application of the principle 'from each according to their ability, to each according to their needs', by the disappearance of the social division of labour, by the disappearance of the separation of town and country. Humanity will reorganise itself into free communes of producer-consumers, capable of administering themselves without any separate organ for this purpose, at one with a restored natural habitat and protected from any threat of destruction of the ecological balance.[7]

To divide a future that one considers both desirable and possible into different time periods is certainly problematic. In Mandel's view, however, the distinction of transitional societies between capitalism and socialism, on the one hand, and socialism and communism, on the other, has important ideological and objective reasons.[8] However, in Mandel's conception the boundaries between these 'stages' are not rigid but fluid, while the conquest of political power by the working class to overthrow the rule of capital is the real, crucial rupture. The essential part is to set a dynamic in motion that leads in the direction of the communist goal:

> However, in a post-capitalist society where the workers and not a bureaucratic layer hold effective power, there will be no need of revolutions and

---

6 Mandel 1979a, p. 149.

7 Ibid.

8 The equation of societies in transition to socialism with socialism is a result of Stalin's thesis of 'building socialism in one country'. See Kellner 1989.

similar sudden shifts to move from one stage to the next. They will result from the progressive evolution of production and social relations. They will be the expression of the progressive withering away of commodity categories, of money, of social classes, of the state, of the social division of labour, and of the thought processes which resulted from the inequality and social struggles of the past. The main thing is immediately to begin these processes of withering away and not to leave them to future generations.[9]

With respect to his notion that even the socialist stage implies a classless and stateless society and an abolition of money and commodity economy, Mandel sees himself in the tradition of Marx, Engels, Lenin, Trotsky, and in the authentic tradition of the Marxist socialist and communist left in general. In this intellectual tradition, the socialist revolution, the overthrow of the rule of capital and the conquest of political power by the working class do not create socialism overnight: 'The abolition of private ownership of the means of production is a necessary, but not a sufficient condition for the existence of a socialist society.'[10]

In *Critique of the Gotha Programme*, Marx distinguished the 'lower stage of communism' (later commonly referred to as 'socialism') from the period of transition (the 'dictatorship of the proletariat').[11] In his pamphlet on *Marxism and the State*, Lenin interpreted the relevant sections in the same way.[12] In the Soviet Union, an acute awareness of the problems involved in using these terms arose in the dispute between the Stalin leadership and the Left Opposition around Trotsky (since 1923) over Stalin's truly 'innovative' assertion that 'socialism in one country' was feasible. Mandel's use of these terms corresponds to the original Leninist and Bolshevik tradition, at least to the extent that those were formulated in a conscious and theoretically correct fashion.[13] I myself have shown on occasion that Stalin, too, initially conceived socialism as a classless and stateless society and used the term socialism accordingly.[14] In any event, Mandel sees socialism as an already 'higher' mode of production in relation to capitalist class society. It is not confined to the socialisation of the major means of production, but also no longer relies on the 'private appropri-

---

9   Mandel 1979a, pp. 149–50.
10   Mandel 1981a.
11   See chapter IV in Marx 1970.
12   See Lenin 2006, p. 71.
13   See Simin 1985.
14   See Kellner 1989.

ation of the social surplus product'.[15] Since classes no longer exist, there is no working class and therefore no one who might be forced to sell their labour for wages. The liberation of the working class has been achieved – that is, its self-abolition as a class. The 'contradiction between a mode of production based on collective ownership of the major means of production and collective appropriation of the social surplus product, on the one hand, and on the other, the private interest which continues to operate as chief driving-force of individual economic activity', has therefore been abolished.[16] To the extent that the bulk of labour is no longer performed on the basis of material incentives, the concept of 'work' has acquired a completely new meaning: '"Labour", regarded as the full development of all the potentialities of each individual, and at the same time as conscious service by the individual to society, is a concept which in the long run is incompatible with the concept of "labour" as the way of "earning one's living", of ensuring one's means of subsistence, or appropriating, so far as possible, all the goods and services that enable an individual to satisfy his needs'.[17]

To create a 'new man', to overcome competitiveness and the struggle of 'everyone against everyone' is unthinkable for Mandel until people have had the practical experience that society can reliably satisfy their basic needs, i.e. that distribution is no longer rationed through the purse: 'This experience must have produced a conscious awareness of the new situation, and, more than that, new habits and customs, for the psychological revolution to occur and for the "old Adam" to die and give place to the socialist or communist man of the future'.[18]

Mandel consistently places particular emphasis on the material foundation of his emancipatory project: 'The new way of life cannot be born otherwise than from the *integration* of a new mode of production and a new mode of distribution. It is not a matter of preaching socialist morality, but of creating the material social and psychological conditions for this morality to be applied by the great majority as a matter of course'.[19]

Dissociating himself from the overall balance of post-capitalist systems so far, Mandel also tries to define socialism 'negatively', stating what most certainly cannot pass for socialism:

---

15   Mandel 1968b, p. 654.
16   Ibid.
17   Ibid.
18   Mandel 1968b, pp. 655–6.
19   Mandel 1968b, p. 656.

Socialism *cannot* be a society that maintains or even increases a great inequality in income, in the distribution of consumer goods, in education, in formation and the occupation of positions of political and social power. Socialism *cannot* be a society in which social priorities and the general direction of economic development are determined by a few individuals rather than by the mass of the working people after a public, democratic debate involving alternative proposals and other possible solutions. Socialism cannot be a society in which the production of commodities and money still crucially determine the behaviour of individuals and social groups – with all the consequences that entails. Socialism is not a society in which the scope for publishing literature, artistic creation, the free development of scientific research and the exercise of political liberties is more limited – instead of incomparably greater – than in bourgeois democracy. It is not a society in which repression of individual behaviour that deviates from the 'socialist norm' is more severe than in advanced capitalist countries.[20]

In such a negative demarcation the 'stages' of 'transitional societies' and 'socialism' again become blurred, because in Marx's terminology, which Mandel follows just as Lenin did in *The State and Revolution,* one can only strictly speak of 'democracy' as long as there is still 'domination' at all (even if it is the rule of the majority of wage-earners over the minority of formerly ruling exploiters). This is no longer true for socialist, i.e. classless and stateless society. This society may still have its conflicts of interest, disputes, votes and decisions, but people no longer rule over other people.

In *Marxist Economic Theory,* Mandel extensively discusses the characteristics of a socialist economy with respect to distribution.[21] His starting point is the distinction between individual wages and social wages. Mandel views this as an embryonic aspect in the reality of contemporary society and considers its expansion in a post-capitalist society as an essential feature of the construction of socialism. Individual wages mean the payment of a certain monetary price for a certain amount of labour or for the expenditure of an individual's labour capacity in a certain period of time. The wage-earner is compelled to do this work because it is the only way to gain access to the food on which he depends. Such dependency on wages exists in pre-capitalist, capitalist and initially also in post-capitalist societies. The nationalisation of the means of production, the

---

20   Mandel 1968b, pp. 144–5.
21   See Mandel 1968b, p. 656 et seq.

expropriation of the capitalists in favour of commonly owned socialised property does not change this at first:

> The argument according to which a wage-earning class no longer exists
> once there is collective ownership of the means of production, 'because
> a worker cannot sell his labour-power to himself', is a crude sophism.
> Collective ownership means ownership by the community, and not own-
> ership by each individual member of the community. A member of a co-
> operative may well sell a car, his individual property, to the co-operative
> he belongs to; in the same worker may sell, to the community he belongs
> to, his labour-power, which is his individual property. The *obligation* to
> carry out this sale in order to obtain the necessary means of subsistence
> proves the survival of the wage relationship both from the standpoint of
> the *form* of the act of exchange (sale for a definite price in money) and
> of its *content* (the workers surrenders the only commodity he possesses,
> and of which he cannot himself employ the use-value, so as to be able to
> acquire other commodities the use-values of which are essential for his
> continued existence and that of his family, and which he *cannot acquire
> without exchange*).[22]

In developed capitalism and with the emergence of the organised workers'
movement, a new situation results from a series of struggles: in addition to
the individual wage, a new form of remuneration appears, which Mandel calls
the 'social dividend' or 'social wage'. By this, he means the totality of commodities and services that society puts at the disposal of its members free of
charge (or for a very small, rather symbolic fee). Of course, the height of this
social wage varies according to the situation and social power relations. It may
include school education, school meals, health services, hospital stays, medical
supplies, use of public parks, museums, libraries, sports and recreational facilities, community-provided public lighting and space, and so on. For Mandel,
the scope of these benefits is an indicator of social progress. For the individual
they are 'free' (or extremely affordable and therefore almost 'free'), although of
course society has to invest a certain amount of labour to produce the necessary products or provide these services. The expansion of this 'social wage' in
a post-capitalist society is synonymous with the road to the dominance of a
socialist mode of distribution: 'This "social wage" foreshadows, at least potentially, the mode of distribution in the future, that is, of an economy directed

---

22   Mandel 1968b, pp. 656–7.

towards satisfying the needs of all individuals. An economy based on the satisfaction of needs differs from a commodity economy in so far as it satisfies these needs *a priori*, distributing goods and services *regardless of any exactly-measured counter-payment* (exchange) supplied by the individual'.[23]

Initially, though, this is just a nucleus. The money-form still predominates, and publicly distributed goods and public services bear the hallmarks of a society of relative need. They are therefore scarcely distributed in the sense that they are rationed, and often their quality leaves much to be desired. In a long process of further development of productive forces, by approaching a situation of relative abundance and increasing the volume and quality of goods and services provided free of charge to society, the system of distribution can acquire a socialist character. As long as this process is ongoing, society will remain dependent on precise accounting. It will initially distribute goods and services free of charge (and thus strip them from the commodity form) that are particularly suitable because of their physical characteristics, because of the particularly high elasticity of demand in view of increases in income or price reductions, because of their poor suitability as substitutes (and therefore as means of exchange) for other commodities and services, and because their free distribution ultimately costs society less than their distribution in exchange for money.[24]

Some everyday goods and services for which, according to Mandel, the conditions for a transition to free distribution already exist today include salt, bread and, in other regions of the world, rice, urban collective transport, education and health services. However, the extension of this method of distribution to other areas seems to depend on a substantial further increase in productive forces under the conditions of a planned economy in a post-capitalist society:

> The economic law which governs the withering away of commodity economy can be formulated like this: as society gets richer, and as planned economy ensures a mighty expansion of the productive forces, it acquires the resources needed to socialise the costs of satisfying an increasing number of needs for all citizens. And as the standard of living of the citizens rises, the elasticity of demand for more and more goods and services declines to zero, or even becomes negative, in relation to price reductions and increases in income. In other words, for these two reasons, the advances of planned economy make it possible to transfer more

---

23   Mandel 1968b, p. 657.
24   Mandel 1968b, pp. 658–9.

and more goods and services into the category of those which can be distributed in accordance with needs.[25]

Although tying the socialist vision to the material prerequisite of relative 'abundance', Mandel emphasises the limits of non-capitalist growth and resists the notion of an endlessly expanding production of goods on the grounds of the alleged limitlessness of human needs. Naturally, such a limitlessness would be irreconcilable with the transition to a distribution beyond rationing and the commodity and money form (although the latter is also a kind of rationing, albeit through the purse). Mandel counters the argument of the boundlessness of human needs with the thesis that historical experience in fact demonstrates that these needs have been 'amazingly stable': 'Any moderately serious study of anthropology and history will show ... how remarkably stable [our needs] are: food, clothing, shelter ... protection against wild animals and the inclemency of the seasons, the desire to decorate, the desire to exercise the body's muscles, the satisfaction of sexual needs, the maintenance of the species – there are half a dozen basic needs which do not seem to have changed since the beginnings of homo sapiens, and which still account for the bulk of consumer expenditure'.[26] Even if one added to this the expenditure on health and hygiene and leisure activities in the world's richest countries, practically all consumer spending is concentrated on a few basic needs. In Mandel's view, if we also consider the mature level of consciousness in a socialist society, the objection is 'disposed of'. Using the examples of nutrition, clothing, housing and furnishing, Mandel cites the evolving consumer behaviour of the ruling class, namely the rich capitalists themselves. In all these areas, excessive and ultimately unhealthy consumption, detrimental to well-being and comfort, has given way to a more rational way of eating, dressing, living and furnishing. In a socialist society, where domestic servants and even housewives have vanished due to the general living conditions and the disapproval by public opinion, this trend will increasingly come to dominate.[27]

For Mandel, to invoke the diversity and quality of products is likewise not a convincing argument against distribution beyond money and commodity economy. Much of this 'diversity' today is a sham, and the supposed autonomy of consumers in their choices does not really exist anyway. Only a few large fashion houses determine fashion, and for many items consumers have only a choice between a few mass-produced models. A socialist planned economy,

25   Mandel 1968b, p. 659.
26   Mandel 1968b, p. 660.
27   Mandel 1968b, p. 661.

on the other hand, would offer better possibilities to meet the rational and reasonable needs of the people. In a planned economy, there are no capitalists whose only concern is to make as much profit as possible. It can rely on opinion polls and democratic assemblies, and it can achieve an inelasticity of demand – a relative surplus – even with a very small margin of 'surplus' production, especially in the area of consumer durables. At the same time, it will not try to compel people to give up certain consumer goods – Mandel cites washing machines and dishwashers, for example, a need for which may continue to exist even if there is a sufficient network of laundries and restaurants, precisely because the need for regular seclusion is the 'dialectical counterpart' of the need for sociability. Likewise, a private car could still serve a purpose (for private leisure activities) even if a dense network of local and long-distance public transport is available.[28] What ultimately speaks against the unlimited expansion of needs is the limited nature of human life; according to Mandel, it is not an idealistic view of man, but a reasonable assumption that the 'lines of development of future consumption' will develop in analogy to the maturing process of the classes ruling today:

> Consumption on the basis of plenty and freedom, far from developing without any limit towards irrational caprice and waste, will increasingly assume the form of *rational consumption*. The requirements of *physical health and mental and nervous equilibrium* will more and more take precedence over the other motives of human behaviour. They will logically be the chief concerns of men whose basic needs have been met.[29]

In view of Ota Sik's distinction between 'economic' and 'non-economic' needs, Mandel points out that the intention here is not to conflate two different categories, namely goods and services that are still somewhat scarce today (e.g. elaborate musical instruments) and truly immaterial needs (e.g. the need to research, to be creative, to teach, etc.), since these are 'more elevated forms' of the need for activity, for 'human *praxis*'.[30]

For Mandel, the dynamics of development towards a socialist society cannot proceed in a linear fashion as far as the withering away of money and commodity economy. In the transitional society between capitalism to socialism, an increase in the standard of living will initially even serve to extend money and commodity economy, but in socialism it will serve to suppress it

---

28 Mandel 1968b, pp. 663–4.
29 Mandel 1968b, p. 664.
30 Ibid.

to the degree that the 'social wage' (the quantity of goods and services distributed outside of exchange) increases.[31] A declining number of commodities and services that can be acquired monetarily will run counter to increasing monetary incomes. Instead of skimming off this surplus money indirectly (via taxes etc.), it will then be more rational to take it out of the economic cycle step by step (increasingly pushing it to the periphery of economic life) and replace it with a new direct method of distribution. The choice of consumers will less and less consist in deciding what to spend their money budget on, and increasingly in deciding what kind of consumption they turn to and what they spend their time on. The sphere of production will become subject to the same logic of a withering away of money and commodity economy through automation and a gradual displacement of living labour from the production process, while wages will play an ever-smaller role in production expenditure. Money exchanges between socialised enterprises are more a matter of accounting in monetary units rather than transfers in real money. Much can be automated in the sphere of service too. For reasons of social priority, services where this is only possible to a limited degree should be the first to be made accessible to all irrespective of income – Mandel cites medicine and education in particular.

'In the end, automation will leave to money economy only the periphery of social life: domestic servants and valets, gambling, prostitution, etc. But in a socialist society which ensures a very high standard of living and security to all its citizens, and an all-round revaluation of "labour", which will increasingly become intellectual labour, who will want to undertake such forms of work?'[32]

The socialisation of the major means of production and social planning reduces real money (as opposed to mere accounting money) to two functions: the purchase of labour power and the purchase of raw materials produced outside the nationalised sector. But according to Mandel, socialisation will ultimately also prevail in agriculture:

> Successively, money thus retreats more and more from relations between enterprises, relations between enterprises and owners of labour-power, relations between enterprises and suppliers of raw materials. The withering away of money becomes general. Only 'units of account' survive, so that an economy based on accounting in terms of hours of labour may govern the management of enterprises and of the economy taken as a whole.[33]

---

31   Mandel 1968b, pp. 664–5.
32   Mandel 1968b, p. 667.
33   Mandel 1968b, pp. 667–8.

In Mandel's view, the gradual vanishing of existential worries and of the daily struggle for survival will spark a profound 'psychological revolution' and ultimately produce a new, free, cooperative, solidaric and socialist type of human who is far more in tune with his human nature than the stunted man under capitalism.[34]

The demise of classes and the state presupposes, in addition to the withering away of money and commodity economy, a radical reduction of working hours and a corresponding expansion of leisure time, which likewise relies on the progress of productivity. In its aims and implications, it far exceeds the extension of leisure time achieved so far. Far from guaranteeing real recreation for working people, free time as we know it today engenders alienated leisure which, in conjunction with alienated work and the commodity form of leisure activities, ensures that the producers remain subject to control and domination by others. According to Mandel, 'habitual' self-management (of companies and social institutions) will 'very likely' be achieved by halving the present working day (i.e. halving the 40-hour working week that was the standard at the time of writing). The extension of school education, the generalisation of higher education and the reduction of the retirement age may delay the reduction of working hours. Above a certain threshold, the way in which leisure time is used will change dramatically: away from the passive consumption of mass-produced entertainment, towards the creative production of culture (instead of films for an audience of millions, millions of amateurs making films). People will gradually evolve from being the passive objects of other people's products and calculations to become self-determined, productively active subjects.[35]

Responding to the objection that workers 'do not want to manage their enterprises', Mandel cites the limitations of existing experience. According to him, the willingness to participate in the management of an enterprise particularly depends on whether the important decisions are not, in fact, made by other people elsewhere. Automation strengthens the motivation for self-management in a socialist economy to the degree that it makes productive activity 'intellectual' and eliminates unskilled or 'manual' labour. The gradual abolition of the separation between manual and mental labour promotes both the capacity and the motivation for self-management.[36]

Mandel argues that the industrialisation of agriculture and the accompanying expansion of highly skilled labour for agricultural production will be the

---

34   Mandel 1968b, pp. 668–73.
35   Mandel 1968b, p. 675 et seq.
36   Mandel 1968b, pp. 676–7.

basis upon which the decisive dynamic towards the withering away of classes and the state will unfold. It will go hand in hand with the drive to overcome the divide between town and country and 'create integrated areas embracing greenery, cultivation, housing, recreation and social life, and zones of industrial production'.[37]

While official 'authority' will exist in the early stages as classes and the state are in the process of withering away, the steady reduction of such spheres will allow for self-managed producer and consumer communes. There, the rotation of individuals in administrative roles will replace special apparatuses, representatives and managers. The communist goal, according to Mandel, is a worldwide federation of such free communes, which appear 'utopian' today – wrongly so, considering that these possibilities are all contained in the advance of productive forces.[38]

In Mandel's view, there is no objective compulsion for economic growth in a socialist economy. The level of investment in relation to production for ongoing consumption is a matter of free choice for citizens. The abundance of goods and services in socialist society allows citizens a real choice between additional leisure time or additional material wealth. In such circumstances, it is only necessary to renew the machinery and, if required, allow the domestic product to expand in proportion with demographic growth, which is also something that society can plan consciously. According to Mandel, the objective is the rational and optimal satisfaction of human needs, which is materially attainable. The result are humans who are free from material worries as accounting and political economy become unnecessary.[39]

Using two quotations from *Grundrisse*, Mandel shows that his vision corresponds with Karl Marx's. Wealth, as conceived in socialist society, is measured by 'men's ... creative use of free time, directed towards their own development as complete and harmonious personalities'.[40]

Abolishing the division of society into classes is insufficient to attain this. Alienation from work derives not only from the lack of control over the products of labour, from working conditions, and from the compulsion to work for the benefit of others and under their command. It is also a consequence of the lifelong commitment to one specific type of work. According to the Marx-

---

37 Mandel 1968b, p. 677.
38 Ibid.
39 Mandel 1968b, p. 677 et seq. Mandel dedicated his final chapter in *Traité d'Economie Marxiste* (1964), which has not been translated into English, to the latter aspect: 'Origines, essort et dépérissement de l'economie politique'.
40 Mandel 1968b, p. 679.

ist tradition followed by Mandel, it is therefore necessary to abolish the social (societal) division of labour in order to really overcome alienation from work. For this, too, Mandel believes there are germs in existing society. In advanced capitalist society, the relative increase in leisure time has produced an explosion of creative activities that are pursued purely out of passion:

> In the nineteenth century – and, in wartime, even in the twentieth – the worker who busied himself with a vegetable garden had a 'material interest' in what he was doing. But the thousands of employees of Western Electric who grow flowers, make wooden furniture and toys, and devote themselves to every imaginable human activity, from ornithology to weight-lifting ... are living witnesses to the spontaneous desire to *offset* the uniformity of their jobs by differentiated, disinterested and free activities, proof that they instinctively strive to rediscover their own personalities, which economic life based on the division of labour must inevitably mutilate.[41]

Notably, people feel 'free' and 'at home' in these self-determined creative activities. Of course, the tyranny of the social division of labour has a more drastic effect the more mechanical, strenuous and boring a particular professional activity is. However, no one in present-day society is spared from its effects completely. Mandel objects to Galbraith, to whom he attests a mixture of clarity and apologetic limitation, as follows:

> True, the 'intellectual' of today is far from being a harmonious or happy person, even if he has been able to follow his vocation and is free of all material servitude such as would distort or coerce his spirit or his consciousness – conditions rarely fulfilled in capitalist society, any more than in a bureaucratic transitional society. He is still subject to the tyranny of an increasing degree of specialisation. As a rule he suffers from an unbalanced way of life, in which physical exercise and nervous equilibrium are not cultivated as conscious purposes, as they should be. Too often cut off from practical life, production or social activities, the present-day intellectual also suffers from another kind of alienation, alienation from praxis and from his social nature.[42]

---

41   Mandel 1968b, p. 681.
42   Mandel 1968b, p. 682.

Apart from allowing the pursuit of many different activities, the abolition of the social division of labour therefore by its very nature entails the elimination of the separation of mental and physical work, or in other words: the integration of mental and physical creative activity and self-development. Mandel's summary of his vision shows that he did not consider the abolition of alienated labour a more or less 'automatic' result of certain economic conditions. However, it is also true that certain expectations which he himself considered 'moderately optimistic' have not come to fruition:

> The generalisation of university education – which moderately optimistic observers foresee for the end of the twentieth century (Soule, Deutscher); the abolition of all routine work; the liberation of research and thought from all material slavery; the active participation of men in the management of the economy and of society; the abolition of the barrier between theory and practice; the socialist humanism which puts human solidarity and love of one's neighbour first among the motives of human action; all these elements of the withering away of the social division of labour are indispensable contributions to the birth of a new man, for which the economic conditions of plenty and socialism furnish only the general possibility, and for which conscious, pedagogical, therapeutic activity on the part of men, in the highest sense, will be the indispensable midwife.[43]

2 Socialist Council Democracy and Transition to Socialism

Closely following Marx's outlines, Mandel views the universal process of liberation after the defeat of capitalism as one involving the demise of classes and the state, the repression of the money and commodity economy, and the emancipation of labour. Work in class societies is usually exploitation because the ruling classes appropriate the surplus product. It is often 'alienated' because the producers have no control over the means of production – e.g. in slave-owning society or capitalism, but not e.g. in the case of tributary farmers. Where market mechanisms predominate, the products of labour are elusive to the producers and appear to them like an alien force. Furthermore, this labour is drudgery dictated by the social division of labour. It is one-sided and denies the human need for the comprehensive development of each individual's talents and abilities.

---

43   Mandel 1968b, p. 683.

Work in a modern factory is inhuman not only because the factory is a capitalist enterprise, but also because simply because it is a modern factory. It is indeed necessary to humanise labour, which involves the improvement of working conditions and reduction of working hours. Measured against the goal of emancipating labour, however – i.e. the elimination of work in the traditional sense – this is only a 'stopgap' for Mandel: 'The process of the humanisation of man will not be completed until labour has withered away and given place to creative *praxis* which is solely directed to the creation of human beings of all-round development'.[44]

The social surplus based on increased labour productivity has so far enabled the propertied classes to devote their time to activities that are more satisfying than the labour which is necessary to produce food. The aim of socialist emancipation is to allow all members of society to reap the benefits of increased labour productivity. It is only beyond necessary labour that the realm of freedom, of self-determined activity begins. This also puts an end to the one-sided nature of 'professions', of 'pure intellectual labour' or 'pure manual labour'. Mandel describes this ideal as a fusion of 'homo faber' and 'homo ludens':

> Free from the constraint of routine work, reintegrated in the collective community, socialist man will once again become both *faber* and *ludens*, increasingly *ludens* and at the same time *faber* ... The abolition of labour in the traditional sense of the word implies at the same time a new flowering of the chief productive force, the creative energy of man himself. Material disinterestedness is crowned by the creative spontaneity which brings together in the same eternal youth the playfulness of children, the enthusiasm of the artist, and the 'eureka' of the scientist.[45]

In contrast to 'positivist' interpretations of Marx and Engels's conception – which sometimes rely on Hegel's dictum of 'freedom as insight into necessity' – Mandel points to the conclusion of Friedrich Engels's popular text on the evolution of socialism from utopian to scientific, where the author describes freedom as freedom from authority and constraints. He also cites a well-known section from Marx's *Capital* Volume III:

> Just as the savage must wrestle with Nature to satisfy his wants, to maintain and reproduce life, so must civilised man, and he must do so in all

---

44   Mandel 1968b, p. 684.
45   Mandel 1968b, p. 685.

social formations and under all possible modes of production. With his development this realm of physical necessity expands as a result of his wants; but, at the same time, the forces of production which satisfy these wants also increase. Freedom in this field can only consist in socialised man, the associated producers, rationally regulating their interchange with Nature, bringing it under their common control, instead of being ruled by it as by the blind forces of Nature; and achieving this with the least expenditure of energy and under conditions most favourable to, and worthy of, their human nature. But it nonetheless still remains a realm of necessity. Beyond it begins that development of human energy which is an end in itself, the true realm of freedom, which, however, can blossom forth only with this realm of necessity as its basis. The shortening of the working-day is its basic prerequisite.[46]

Such visions, appearing as the vanishing point of a long-term development for which the massive growth of productive forces under capitalism has laid the foundations, have the disadvantage of being located in a fairly distant future. But what about the years immediately after the socialist rupture – i.e. when capitalism has been overthrown in a particular country or even several countries, but may still exist in others? The 'utopia', however 'concrete' it may be conceived, becomes unattractive if the transition to the realm of freedom promises to be another epoch of grey necessity, merely embellished with the promise of a bright future. For both Marx and Mandel, however, socialism is a process that commences from day one after the revolutionary rupture. It changes everyday reality in a radical and progressive fashion that has a strong impact on everyone's lives. The 'shortening of the working-day' cited by Marx is also central to Mandel's ideas. Not only is it an important demand in the class struggle inherent in the capitalist system, but also an important measure of the degree of emancipation achieved by a society in transition to socialism. The radical reduction of working-hours also constitutes an important material foundation for the political system of a socialist council [soviet] democracy. The basic principles of a council democracy as envisioned by Mandel are closely linked to Marx's account of the Paris Commune of 1871. The democracy of councils represents the 'dictatorship of the proletariat' that replaces the old bourgeois state

---

46   Marx 1991, p. 593. See also Engels: 'In proportion as anarchy in social production vanishes, the political authority of the State dies out. Man, at last the master of his own form of social organisation, becomes at the same time the lord over Nature, his own master – free' (Engels 1970, Part III).

machinery. It is a 'dictatorship' in the sense that it breaks the resistance of the old ruling classes, yet at the same time, it represents the self-government and thus political emancipation of the working class in power. This much is evident from the classical formulations in Marx's *The Civil War in France*, which in turn became the main source for Lenin's *The State and Revolution*:

> Paris could resist only because, in consequence of the siege, it had got rid of the army, and replaced it by a National Guard, the bulk of which consisted of working men. This fact was now to be transformed into an institution. The first decree of the Commune, therefore, was the suppression of the standing army, and the substitution for it of the armed people.
>
> The Commune was formed of the municipal councillors, chosen by universal suffrage in the various wards of the town, responsible and revocable at short terms. The majority of its members were naturally working men, or acknowledged representatives of the working class. The Commune was to be a working, not a parliamentary body, executive and legislative at the same time.
>
> Instead of continuing to be the agent of the Central Government, the police was at once stripped of its political attributes, and turned into the responsible, and at all times revocable, agent of the Commune. So were the officials of all other branches of the administration. From the members of the Commune downwards, the public service had to be done at *workman's wage* ... Not only municipal administration, but the whole initiative hitherto exercised by the state was laid into the hands of the Commune.
>
> Having once got rid of the standing army and the police – the physical force elements of the old government – the Commune was anxious to break the spiritual force of repression, the 'parson-power', by the disestablishment and disendowment of all churches as proprietary bodies. The priests were sent back to the recesses of private life, there to feed upon the alms of the faithful in imitation of their predecessors, the apostles.
>
> The whole of the educational institutions were opened to the people gratuitously, and at the same time cleared of all interference of church and state. Thus, not only was education made accessible to all, but science itself freed from the fetters which class prejudice and governmental force had imposed upon it.
>
> The judicial functionaries were to be divested of that sham independence which had but served to mask their abject subserviency to all succeeding governments to which, in turn, they had taken, and broken, the

oaths of allegiance. Like the rest of public servants, magistrates and judges were to be elective, responsible, and revocable.[47]

Incidentally, Marx himself pre-empts the misconception that this is just a new design for a city administration when adding:

> The Paris Commune was, of course, to serve as a model to all the great industrial centres of France. The communal regime once established in Paris and the secondary centres, the old centralized government would in the provinces, too, have to give way to the self-government of the producers. In a rough sketch of national organisation, which the Commune had no time to develop, it states clearly that the Commune was to be the political form of even the smallest country hamlet, and that in the rural districts the standing army was to be replaced by a national militia, with an extremely short term of service. The rural communities of every district were to administer their common affairs by an assembly of delegates in the central town, and these district assemblies were again to send deputies to the National Delegation in Paris, each delegate to be at any time revocable and bound by the *mandat imperatif* (formal instructions) of his constituents. The few but important functions which would still remain for a central government were not to be suppressed, as has been intentionally misstated, but were to be discharged by Communal and thereafter responsible agents. The unity of the nation was not to be broken, but, on the contrary, to be organized by Communal Constitution, and to become a reality by the destruction of the state power which claimed to be the embodiment of that unity independent of, and superior to, the nation itself, from which it was but a parasitic excrescence. While the merely repressive organs of the old governmental power were to be amputated, its legitimate functions were to be wrested from an authority usurping pre-eminence over society itself, and restored to the responsible agents of society. Instead of deciding once in three or six years which member of the ruling class was to misrepresent the people in Parliament, universal suffrage was to serve the people, constituted in Communes, as individual suffrage serves every other employer in the search for the workmen and managers in his business. And it is well-known that companies, like individuals, in matters of real business generally know how to put the right man in the right place, and, if they for once make a mistake, to

---

47   Marx 2010, p. 25.

redress it promptly. On the other hand, nothing could be more foreign to the spirit of the Commune than to supersede universal suffrage by hierarchical investiture.[48]

These detailed quotations show how much Mandel's ideas of socialist democracy stand in the tradition of Marx. By the same token, any authoritarian conceptions of the new society – or even of the steps to be taken on the way there – lay claim to Marx without justification. Despite the peculiarities of the commune, or perhaps even because of them, Marx left no doubt as to the general significance of this historical experience. Another quote from *The Civil War in France* may serve to illustrate this:

> The multiplicity of interpretations to which the Commune has been subjected, and the multiplicity of interests which construed it in their favor, show that it was a thoroughly expansive political form, while all the previous forms of government had been emphatically repressive. Its true secret was this: It was essentially a working class government, the product of the struggle of the producing against the appropriating class, the political form at last discovered under which to work out the economical emancipation of labor.[49]

Marx wrote this a long time before humanity gathered decades of experience with parliamentary democracies of the kind that became typical of the rich industrial capitalist countries especially after the war. In the nineteenth century, universal and equal suffrage was the exception (the default was a census voting right that only granted property-owning male citizens the vote). Even in the British bourgeois democracy of the time, the notion that workers' parties might one day send representatives to parliament was unthinkable. The French bourgeois revolution had brought the 'Third Estate' to power, but not the great mass of the plebeian 'Fourth Estate', whose outrageous disenfranchisement inspired all the early socialist aspirations.

Yet in the meantime, parties that emerged from the workers' movement (especially social-democratic and 'official' Communist parties) have boasted strong parliamentary factions. On many occasions, this allowed them not only to participate in the legislature, but also to participate in governments or even lead them. Never has this harmed the capitalist economic system in the slight-

---

48   Ibid.
49   Marx 2010, p. 26.

est. But even so, is not the fact that a political system permits such political representation evidence that it is sufficiently democratic – that it need not be replaced by a socialist council democracy?[50]

For Mandel, bourgeois parliamentary democracy in its modern form is merely another political system designed to maintain the rule of the bourgeois class. While he considers democratic liberties useful for the working class and argues that they must be defended, he fundamentally believes that even the most democratic bourgeois parliamentary republic is insufficiently democratic. This is because it is only an indirect democracy, based on formal equality but *de facto* perpetuating inequality, and because in the practice of everyday life, the economic and social power of the propertied translates to the subjugation of the propertyless:

> First of all, bourgeois parliamentary democracy is indirect democracy, within which some thousands or tens of thousands of mandated persons (deputies, senators, mayors, local councillors, etc.) participate in the administration of the state. The vast majority of citizens are excluded from such participation. Their only power is that of putting a ballot paper in the box every four or five years. Secondly, political equality in a bourgeois parliamentary democracy is a purely formal, and not a real equality. Formally, both rich and poor have the same 'right' to launch a newspaper – with running costs totalling hundreds of thousands of pounds. Formally, both rich and poor have the same 'right' to purchase air-time on the television, and thus the same 'possibility' of influencing the elector. But as the practical exercise of these rights presupposes access to powerful material resources, only the rich can fully enjoy them. The capitalists will succeed in influencing a large number of voters who are materially dependent on them, will buy newspapers, radio stations and time on television thanks to their money. The capitalists 'control' parliamentarians and governments through the weight of their capital. Finally, even if one ignores all these characteristic limits of bourgeois parliamentary democracy, and wrongly supposes that it is perfect, the fact remains that it is only political democracy. For what is the use of political equality between the rich and poor – which is far from the case! – if it goes hand in hand with permanent, enormous economic and social inequality, which is growing all the time? Even if the rich and poor did have exactly the same political rights, the former would still have enormous economic and social power

---

50   Mandel 1979a, pp. 91–2.

which the latter lack, and which inevitably subordinates the poor to the rich in everyday life, including the practical way in which political rights are applied.[51]

These fundamental limits of bourgeois democracy are not transcended by universal suffrage or by the opportunity to elect workers' representatives to parliament. Suffrage and parliaments are but one aspect of the bourgeois-democratic republic – to be precise, one whose importance is waning in the course of development:

> It is typical of the bourgeois state that, as the working masses gain universal suffrage and their representatives enter parliament in large numbers, the centre of gravity of the state based on parliamentary democracy inexorably moves from parliament towards the apparatus of the permanent bourgeois state: 'Ministers come and go, but the police remain.' This state apparatus is in perfect harmony with the middle and big bourgeoisie because of the way it is recruited, its selectivity and career structure, and its hierarchical method of organisation. Indissoluble ideological, social and economic links tie this apparatus to the bourgeois class. All its top officials earn salaries which allow accumulation of capital (sometimes modest, but real for all that), giving these people an interest even as individuals in the defence of private property and the smooth running of the capitalist economy.
>
> Moreover, the state founded on bourgeois parliamentarism is linked body and soul to capital by the golden chains of financial dependence and the National Debt. No bourgeois government can govern without constantly calling for credit – controlled by the banks, finance capital and the big bourgcoisie. Any anti-capitalist policies that are so much as sketched out by a reformist government come up immediately against financial and economic sabotage by the capitalists. The 'investment strike', the flight of capital, inflation, the black market, a decline in production, and unemployment quickly result from this counter-attack.[52]

From the point of view of the mass of wage-earners, the repressive functions of the bourgeois state can fade into the background in normal periods, when the

---

51 Mandel 1979a, p. 94.
52 Mandel 1979a, pp. 92–3. See also Mandel 1979a, pp. 78–9 for Mandel's appraisal of the Paris Commune.

regular functioning of the capitalist economy and society ensures the supremacy of bourgeois ideology and inviolability of class rule. But this is different in
times of crisis, when it turns out that even in a bourgeois democracy, the state –
as analysed by Marx and Engels – is ultimately just a body of armed men at the
service of the ruling class.[53]

Mandel greatly stresses that the political system inaugurated immediately
after the socialist revolution needs to be more democratic than even the most
democratic republic. The general formulations he makes on this topic show the
similarities between his and Marx's positions (or those of Lenin in *The State
and Revolution*, to which he repeatedly refers). Moreover, there are certain par-
allels to the anarchist notion of a society free from domination. However, in
the Marxist tradition we are still dealing with a 'state', albeit one that bears the
germ of its own demise:

> The workers state will be more democratic than the state founded on par-
> liamentary democracy in that it will extend direct democracy. It will be a
> state which will begin to wither away from its birth, leaving entire areas of
> social activity to the self-management and the self-administration of the
> citizens concerned (post, telecommunications, health, education, cul-
> ture, etc.). It will gather together the mass of working people in workers'
> councils which exercise power directly, abolishing the fictitious border-
> line between executive and legislative powers. It will eliminate careerism
> in public life by limiting the earnings of all officials, including the most
> highly placed, to the salary of the average skilled worker. It will cut across
> the formation of a new caste of administrators by introducing compulsory
> rotation as a principle in all delegation of powers. The workers state will
> be more democratic than the state based on parliamentary democracy
> inasmuch as it will create the material bases for the exercise of demo-
> cratic freedoms by all. The printing presses, radio and television stations,
> and assembly halls will all become collective property, and will be put at
> the disposal of any group of workers which wants to use them. The right to
> establish various political organisations and parties, including opposition
> ones; to create an opposition press, and the right of political minorities to
> express their views in the papers, on the radio and television – these rights
> will be jealously defended by the workers' councils. The general arming of
> the working masses, the suppression of the regular army and the repress-
> ive apparatus, the election of judges, the hearing of all cases in public;

---

53   Mandel 1979a, p. 96.

these will be the best guarantee that no minority can assume the right to exclude any group of working people from the exercise of democratic freedoms.[54]

The matters to be decided democratically in a council democracy are also more comprehensive than those that fall within the decision-making compet-ence of bourgeois parliaments. Apart from political decision-making, decisions concerning the overall direction of the economy are of primary importance. Because the major means of production have been nationalised with a view to genuine rather than just formal socialisation, they need to be managed by society. Problems that concern society as a whole and that cannot be left to self-management bodies in the individual enterprises are also addressed since they are important for the future of society. Whether or not to build a nuclear power plant cannot be decided by the staff of a single company or by a municipality alone. How to use the surplus product in general is also a question of general social importance. There are always different options: should advances in labour productivity be used to grant more holidays or to create more universities? Should working hours be reduced even further, or should more resources be invested in the optimisation of energy produc-tion? And if all of the above is desired: in what proportion should the vari-ous concerns be addressed? One very important question is the investment ratio – that is, the distribution of social expenditure between the growth of production (the future) and the expansion of consumption in the broad sense (the present). Mandel by no means excludes the possibility of error when such questions are decided democratically – but he believes that mistakes made through democratic channels have better chances of being corrected. For him, socialist democracy is not only a political and moral requirement on account of the emancipatory essence of the socialist goal, but also a means to ensure the economic efficiency of a planned economy in a society in trans-ition:

> The revolution effected by socialism in the economic and social struc-ture implies that decisions aiming at the devotion of part of the resources available for potential current consumption to the development of the productive forces must be taken by the mass of those concerned, in per-son. In contrast both to capitalism and to bureaucratic planning, these sacrifices thereby become *freely-agreed sacrifices*.

---

54   Mandel 1979a, pp. 97–8.

This may in some cases mean a growth rate lower than the optimum, though this is not at all certain. But even in such cases, the mistake made is most educative, and will not soon be repeated. Only in a system of bureaucratic planning, exempt from all public discussion and frank criticism, could such crying mistakes of economic policy ... be persisted ... without being corrected.[55]

Mandel's almost 60-page introduction to a 1971 anthology on workers' control, workers' councils and workers' self-management is a remarkably concise summary of his overall political conception, to which we will return in our chapter on strategy matters.[56] The text is also useful, though, for illustrating Mandel's position on socialist democracy, both with respect to the nature of its institutions and the relationship between the political rule of the working class, the self-management of companies and social institutions, and democratic planning of the economy as a whole. For Mandel, the connection between strategy and goal is always defined by the collective self-activity of producers, who are transformed from objects into subjects. This model can only succeed if a high degree of political, cultural and administrative activity of a large number of these producers is maintained. This alone shows why a radical reduction of working hours is so crucially important. In Mandel's view, advanced forms of workers' self-organisation in the class struggle produce elements of the future socialist republic in embryonic form. Grassroots democracy is a characteristic trait of these embryonic components:

> If you observe the development of a local general strike; if then democratically elected strike committees are formed not only in one factory, but in all factories in the city (rather still in the region, in the country), elected by the general assemblies of the strikers; if these committees merge, centralise and create a body that regularly meets its delegates, that is when territorial workers' councils emerge – basic cells of the future workers' state, emerge. The first 'soviet' in Petrograd was nothing more than this: a council of delegates from the strike committees of the most important factories in town.[57]

According to Mandel, the conduct of the struggle must be democratic in character in order to be successful, just as, by analogy, the state that emerges from

---

55   Mandel 1968b, pp. 631–2.
56   See Mandel 1971c.
57   Mandel 1971c, p. 14, our translation.

the working class conquest of political power must be democratic, both to run the economy efficiently and to meet the emancipatory objective: 'The socialist revolution, which aims to transform the overwhelming majority of the workers, exploited and oppressed from objects into subjects of history, from alienated individuals into people who determine their own destiny, cannot be made without the conscious participation of the masses. This revolution cannot be carried out behind the backs of the interested parties any more than an economic plan can be implemented "behind the backs" of those who administer the economy'.[58] Marx did not explain concretely in what ways the exercise of working-class political power should be linked to the conscious planning of the economy. For Mandel, hitherto experiences of non-capitalist economies have ranged from bureaucratic centralism (later called 'command economy') to the Yugoslavian model of workplace self-management. In his view, neither 'left communist' notions of managing the economy through 'industrial councils' nor the idea of entrusting the unions with factory management, which played a role in the early Soviet Union, provided satisfactory solutions.[59]

Mandel advocates the self-management of enterprises by the workforce, yet he opposes the kind of autonomy of individual enterprises that institutes competition and the market as decisive economic regulator ('This autonomy cannot but reproduce a series of evils inherent to the capitalist regime').[60] He highlights the contradiction between enterprise self-management and a perpetual, institutionally entrenched leadership that can neither be democratically controlled nor replaced. Central economic and political decisions need to be made, and there can be no talk of working-class rule or working-class management of the economy if these decisions are not majority decisions arrived at in democratic debate.

> Since the central economic decisions concern fundamental economic problems, real workers' self-management entails the right of the 'self-managing' staff, even at the company level, to actively engage in economic policy nationally – in other words, it demands the right to be involved in politics. It therefore involves the right of every workers' council to make counter-proposals to the government's economic policy plans, to seek allies for these alternative projects and plans nationally, to inform

---

58   Mandel 1971c, p. 15, our translation.
59   Mandel 1971c, p. 41.
60   Mandel 1963.

and influence the public on the alternative it is facing, etc. If this kind of socialist democracy does not exist, then self-management is essentially bureaucratised and deprived of its emancipatory substance.[61]

For Mandel, the pluralism of views and the right and the material means to express them, combined with the freedom of organisation and party plurality, are crucial features of a true socialist democracy. These features alone guarantee that democratic choices between coherent alternatives can be made. They also ensure that action can be taken against the consolidation of the self-interest of elites: as experience teaches us, historically or practically justified rights of elites soon turn into privileges, and their defence and expansion then become the essence of government policies – hence, no opposition is tolerated. Indeed, a plurality of political parties is considered incompatible with Marxism or Leninism according to both bourgeois ideology and Stalinist tradition. The Marxist school of thought to which Mandel feels committed is equated with the rule of a more or less monolithic party and state monopoly on ideas. Yet the bodies of the Paris commune comprised different political tendencies – and even Lenin did demonstrably not consider one-party rule the norm, as Mandel repeatedly points out.

> Neither Marx nor Lenin ever considered it a matter of principle that there could only be one party under the dictatorship of the proletariat, or even that the working class itself could only be represented by one party. On the contrary, the whole experience of the workers' movement proves that a diversity of tendencies and parties laying claim to the working class corresponds to both social differentiation and the inevitable ideological differences within the proletariat. This experience calls for factional freedom and for the freedom to form new parties within the context of the socialist constitution and socialist legality ... Many of the problems facing the worker's state will be new problems, and ultimately only practice (and long-term practice at that) can decide which solutions advocated by the various tendencies are correct. By suppressing the right to form new workers' parties, the party in power inevitably suffocates internal party democracy. This kind of democracy requires the right to form factions; and how could one fail to view a faction that is fighting over questions of principle as the potential seed of a new party? By obstructing internal party democracy, the party's capacity to avoid political errors

---

61   Mandel 1971c, p. 47, our translation.

is automatically diminished, and the time period during which an error remains unrectified is prolonged.[62]

For Peter von Oertzen, the radically democratic stance is Mandel's distinguishing feature, a pillar of the programmatic identity of the revolutionary Marxist tradition he represents, and an important reason why he regards Mandel's ideas as close to his own (another reason is his interpretation of transitional demands as structural reforms with an anti-capitalist thrust). This, despite the fact that Oertzen was a left-reformist social democrat in practice and a council socialist with sympathies for anarcho-syndicalism in theory.[63] When in 1972 the west German minister of the interior, Genscher, imposed an entry ban on Mandel, von Oertzen protested with explicit reference to Mandel's categorically democratic beliefs.[64] To a degree, Mandel's positions on socialist democracy, including party plurality, and on the democratic self-management of the economy simply channel the traditional political programme of the Fourth International. After all, the founding document of the Fourth International, the *Transitional Programme* of 1938, reads:

> Democratization of the soviets is impossible without legalization of soviet parties. The workers and peasants themselves by their own free vote will indicate what parties they recognize as soviet parties ... Factory committees should be returned the right to control production. A democratically organized consumers' cooperative should control the quality and price of products. Reorganisation of the collective farms in accordance with the will and in the interests of the workers there engaged![65]

This position was, in turn, the expression of a programmatic development. The Left Opposition from which the Fourth International had been formed initially fought for a change of course by the ruling (Stalinist) Communist Party and Comintern, also aiming for the restoration of a democratic regime in these organisations. Trotsky's own attitudes continued to bear the hallmarks of the bans on other Soviet parties and on factions within the Bolshevik Party, both of which he was partly responsible for, for years to come. In what Mandel referred to as Trotsky's 'dark years', he even theorised these decisions, which were taken

---

62   Mandel 1971c, p. 40, our translation.
63   See eyewitness testimony from Peter von Oertzen.
64   See GIM and RKJ 1972a.
65   Trotsky 2002, pp. 41–2.

by the entire Bolshevik leadership in a difficult situation.[66] From 1933, the Left Opposition no longer considered itself part of the official Communist movement, but set about building new communist parties and a new international instead. Moreover, it no longer advocated a perspective of reforming the Soviet system, but spoke of the need to overthrow the Stalinist bureaucracy – a 'political revolution'. In this context, it fleshed out its ideas of socialist democracy, including the demand for party pluralism. For Trotsky, this was in a sense a return to his earlier, radical democratic positions. Incidentally, these had been very close to those of Lenin and the early Bolshevik tradition – indeed, in the early days of the Soviet Russia they had merged with them. The dry words of the *Transitional Programme* quoted above contain an important nuance: the legalisation of parties is not linked to any *a priori* definition as to which parties can or cannot be considered legitimate countries of the soviet republic. Rather, the 'workers and peasants' are to decide this through their votes. It is clear that this implies complete political freedom. For Mandel, this side of the 'orthodoxy' of 'Trotskyism' was particularly important.[67]

It is impossible to understand the debates and disputes on the question of socialist democracy, including party pluralism, in the Marxist-inspired socialist movement in general and in the Fourth International in particular without taking into account what real difficulties these ideas were contending with. They are not, after all, abstract concepts that exist outside concrete circumstances. 'Dictatorship of the proletariat' and 'soviet (council) democracy' denote one and the same political system; in one instance the necessity to suppress the class enemy is emphasised, in the other the democratic organisation of the rule of the proletariat is foregrounded. In practice, the oppressive aspect will play a greater role in some situations than it will in others, and the distinction between oppressing the oppressors, on the one hand, and oppressing sections of the formerly oppressed – i.e. sections of the working population – on the other, is easier to make on paper than in practice. Mandel was certainly aware of this, but from the outset he highlighted the democratic aspect and the demise of the state, which he always considered an instrument of repression:

---

66   See Mandel 1995a, p. 81 et seq.; Mandel 1992a, p. 177 et seq. Mandel called Trotsky's polemic against Kautsky's criticism of the Bolshevik government, *Terrorism and Communism*, the 'worst of his books' because, like Lenin in the same period, Trotsky identified the dictatorship of the proletariat with the dictatorship of the party of the proletariat. See Mandel 1992a, pp. 119–20.

67   See Mandel 1995a, p. 89 et seq.

Suffice to say that a practical and faithful application of the principles of socialist democracy is a function of real class struggle and not a function of abstract pious wishes. Whenever bourgeois rule was under threat, even the most liberal bourgeoisie rescinded the democratic freedoms it had tight-fistedly granted to the people, erected dictatorships, and carried out bloody terror against the oppressed – countless times. Driven by the determination to defend their newly won freedom, the workers will fiercely defend themselves against any attempt by capital to restore its defeated power. The less severe this struggle, the more stable the workers' state. The more social relationships relax, the more the restrictions imposed on all opponents of the new regime in the exercise of democratic freedoms will be reduced and lifted. The workers' state, a state in the service of the great majority and aimed at repressing only a small group of exploiters, must in any case be a state of a special kind: a state which begins to wither away from the moment of its inception, so to speak.[68]

In my view, this tension between the necessity for radical democracy for the self-liberation of the working class with a view to the universal emancipation of human society, on the one hand, and the need to suppress the former ruling classes and counter-revolution, on the other is already present in Auguste Blanqui's thinking. Blanqui was convinced of the necessity of a revolutionary dictatorship. The problem strongly resembles that of petty-bourgeois revolutionary Jacobinism. The *terreur* likewise sought to suppress the oppressors in order to establish radically democratic conditions with true equality for all citizens. And yet, it carried 'the terror' into the ranks of the oppressed too. Blanqui, who championed the idea of revolution brought about by the determined action of a conspiratorial community of revolutionaries, envisioned a second stage during which democracy would be put on a clear class basis along the lines of the Paris Commune. Of course, this is based on the notion of an unproblematic transition from a very short-term minority dictatorship to the rule of the working class, which will probably grant the majority of seats in its governing bodies to the revolutionaries, or at least to various socialist and communist currents.

However, there is a 'pedagogical dictatorial' aspect to Blanqui's concept of the dictatorship of the proletariat that is peculiar to the whole French revolutionary tradition of the nineteenth century and which constitutes part of the

---

68   Mandel 1971c, pp. 40–1, our translation.

debate in the Marxist and Bolshevik traditions. In 1830, 1848 and 1871 in France as well as in Russia in 1917 (or in China or in other countries of the 'third world') we are dealing with societies with a predominant peasant majority. Peasants turned into small proprietors by bourgeois agrarian reforms; small producers on whom feudal and big bourgeois reaction was happy to rely, or tried to rely. After their liberation from feudal bonds, they had become powerful supporters of the bourgeois revolution – but later also of the Russian revolution. This rural milieu was under the influence of the clergy and backward in comparison with urban society in revolutionary times.

Whenever the quasi-plebeian, semi-proletarian revolution in France raised its head before 1871, it debated the question of general elections. In the revolutionary year 1848, for instance, there was a period of transition towards a social republic: upon Blanqui's advice, the urban revolution sent its commissars to the villages to break the influence of reaction and clergy among the peasants. Without such measures, the urban revolution would have risked losing any free elections. Of course, what the revolutionaries had in mind was a matter of months or at most a few years – not decades.[69]

This same concern can be found in Marx's work. We have quoted a passage from *The Civil War in France* to illustrate Marx's radically democratic conclusions. However, as is well-known, this text also contains sections that criticise the Paris Commune for its excessive leniency and attest to its almost suicidal high-mindedness. The problems arising from an overwhelmingly rural population, and the need to give it a certain amount of education to begin with, are also evident in this work. However, it strongly emphasises that the Commune, because it was fundamentally the rule of the working class (joined by the majority of the urban middle classes, whom the Commune had freed from their debts), had to bring about communal self-government 'down to the smallest village': 'The provincial French middle class saw in the Commune an attempt to restore the sway their order had held over the country under Louis Philippe, and which, under Louis Napoleon, was supplanted by the pretended rule of the country over the towns. In reality, the Communal Constitution brought the rural producers under the intellectual lead of the central towns of their districts, and there secured to them, in the working men, the natural trustees of their interests'.[70]

Marx talks about these peasant interests and of the ways in which the urban proletariat accommodated them by reducing the tax and mortgage burden, etc.

---

69   See Bergmann 1986, p. 120 et seq.; 263 et seq.
70   Marx 2010, p. 26.

Nonetheless, the mention of 'intellectual lead' in this quotation also suggests an early awareness of what would later become a central problem of the Russian Revolution.

The alliance (the *smychka*, the 'splicing') of workers and peasants under the 'leadership of the proletariat' (Lenin), the conquest of political power by the proletariat 'backed by the peasantry' (Trotsky), were not only strategic formulas for linking the interests of the urban working class, which was a minority in Russia at the time, with the mass of small peasant owners in struggle with the big landowners. They also had an institutional content represented by early Soviet Russia's system of councils (*aka* soviets). In the elections to the All-Russian Congress of Soviets, the working class was about five times stronger than the rural population. Moreover, a rapid transformation of the large majority of the population into wage labourers in early Soviet Russia, a country that was backward compared with western Europe and the US, would probably not have been conceivable without terrible distortions.[71]

Mandel, who abhorred the notion of the educational dictatorship, often stressed the difficulties of achieving a socialist democracy in 'backward' countries that only had a working-class minority, even if he supported its implementation to the greatest extent possible. Similarly, he often highlighted the growth of the proletariat as a worldwide class of propertyless people who have nothing to sell but their labour, and who depend on it for survival.[72] The 'normal' path originally envisioned by Marx was the conquest of political power by the working class in the developed industrial capitalist countries. Certainly, everything would be easier under such circumstances – i.e. on a far superior material basis, not to mention that today's working class can look back on decades of cultural and political traditions developed under bourgeois parliament-

---

71   The All-Russian Congress of Soviets consists of the representatives of the city soviets (one deputy for every 25,000 voters) and of the representatives of the governorate soviets (one deputy for every 125,000 inhabitants). (Constitution [Basic Law] of 10 July 1918 of the Russian Soviet Socialist Federal Republic). See *Die ersten Dekrete der Sowjetmacht*, Berlin 1987, p. 235. The Bolsheviks openly advocated the concept of the hegemony of the proletariat and its leading role in the revolution and in the soviet system before the vast peasant majority of the population of Russia. In the appendix to *Geschichte der KPDSU (B)*, *Schulungsmaterial von Grigori Sinowjew*, Erlangen 1972, there is an official appeal 'To the Labourers of the Union of Soviet Socialist Republics' on the occasion of the 25th anniversary of the Communist Party of Russia (Bolsheviks) (p. 202 et seq.) as well as a proclamation on 'The Bolsheviks and the Hegemony of the Proletariat' (p. 208 et seq.), in which Zinoviev proclaims that this position is 'the soul of revolutionary Marxism and thus also of Bolshevism'.

72   Mandel 1983, p. 14.

ary regimes. Until today, however, capitalism has only ever been overthrown in 'backward' countries. Although the horrors of the worst period of Stalin's terror were not repeated anywhere else, it is also true that no post-capitalist country ever lived up to the principles of socialist soviet democracy advocated by the Fourth International. The Fourth International did feel politically closer to the Castroist regime than, say to the Soviet or Chinese regimes, and it advocated a democratic reform of that system rather than a political revolution. But neither regime implemented democratic freedoms such as the right to public expression of dissenting views, the right to build independent trade unions, or the right to form alternative political parties that might contest elections and win majorities. The Fourth International therefore faced the task of having to demonstrate that its position was not idealist or normative, that it reflected the true Marxist position and, on the whole, did justice to the problems faced by relatively poor and backward post-capitalist transitional societies. That is why the FI wanted to clarify its position, present the result to the public and put it up for debate on the left.

These problems provided the basis for the discussion of 'Socialist Democracy and the Dictatorship of the Proletariat', which was launched with a draft resolution of the United Secretariat of the Fourth International in July 1977. The debate was only concluded at the twelfth world congress of the Fourth International in 1984, where the greatly revised resolution was finally adopted. In between those dates, only a preliminary consensus was reached at the eleventh world congress in 1979 after the Socialist Workers' Party (US) and its international affiliates withdrew their original support for the draft. At least one-third of delegates voted in favour of an alternative document, which was only narrowly rejected due to many abstentions and no-shows at the vote.[73]

Mandel took a very active part in this dispute. He was the author of the original draft and contributed the changes that were incorporated over the years, partly on his initiative. The first versions of the text contained hardly any references to Lenin and very little reflection on the repressive side of a revolutionary dictatorship, which Mandel himself was personally not very fond of.[74] A comparison between the finally adopted text and the draft submitted by the United Secretariat in 1977 reveals as much. Notably, the final version (see Fourth International 1985) is much more detailed and addresses a number of problems missing from the initial condensed versions.

73   See Fourth International 1985.
74   Message from Charles A. Udry – see Introduction.

In fact, a 'Bolshevik faction' had formed in the Fourth International, with Nahuel Moreno as its most prominent representative. The Argentinean PST was by far the strongest force in the FI, boasting substantial membership and supporter numbers compared to the other sections. Previously it had been part of the 'Leninist-Trotskyist Tendency' (LT'T), whose leading force was the Socialist Workers' Party (US). It broke this link in the course of debates concerning its position on revolutionary politics in Portugal and the conflict in Angola at the time, and in both cases different conceptions of 'socialist democracy' played a key role. At the end of the '70s, it left the Fourth International altogether. Moreno has extensively criticised the majority position of the Fourth International on 'socialist democracy'. In his opinion, Mandel and the majority of the Fourth International were committed to democratic standards that were neither supported by historical Bolshevism nor by the inevitable bitter necessities of a socialist revolution, especially one taking place in a poor and dependent country, surrounded by enemies. For its part, the 'Bolshevik faction' emphasised the tough necessity of repressive measures on the part of the proletarian dictatorship. It took the view that an extension of democratic freedoms to the point of permitting a multi-party system would inevitably be exploited by domestic and foreign counter-revolution – especially by imperialism with its immense resources – to annul all and any revolutionary gains.

Mandel saw these positions as an expression of the leadership's desire to justify a tight internal party regime and a manipulative relationship with the movements that it influenced – after all, the organisation was extremely marginalised in its country and could not be further from the real issues involved in exercising power.[75]

The questions involved in the factional dispute with the SWP-led LTT also influenced the debate. Mandel and the international majority tendency had made some efforts to defuse the dispute and come to a fruitful cooperation with the SWP leadership. The opportunity to develop a common position on the question of socialist democracy was perceived as very positive in this context. The SWP leadership combined a sometimes quite literal Trotskyist orthodoxy with a strong emphasis on exclusively peaceful mass actions and the democratic respectability of its position. Suffice to say, it tried to defend itself against state attempts at criminalisation and dispel the anti-communist pre-

---

75   These are this author's recollections. The discussion was also held in the German section of the Fourth International, the Group of International Marxists (GIM). In preparation for the World Congress, Mandel introduced the position of the international majority at the GIM conference.

judices so widespread among the American masses. For a certain period, the SWP leadership therefore had a basis for developing a common position with the international majority tendency on the question of socialist democracy. However, the SWP leadership at that time began to move very close to the Castroist leadership (in some statements the SWP appeared almost like a foreign section of the Cuban Communist Party). It counted on the opportunity to build a new, broader international also involving the Cuban leadership, the Sandinista leadership, and some similar tendencies. This was a very delicate issue with respect to the Fourth International's common position on socialist democracy. Clear criticism of the shortcomings of Cuban political institutions and of the undemocratic practices of the Castroist leadership would have greatly enhanced the consistency and credibility of the FI's official position on this issue. Probably for the sake of maintaining unity with the SWP (which was eventually lost anyway), the resolution only briefly touched on the subject of Cuba.[76]

These intersections between the debate on socialist democracy, the factional dispute and the miniature *realpolitik*, as it were, of a small, internationally organised movement show that Mandel and his close comrades' wording of the FI majority position was not just cheap propaganda. That is to say, it was not merely an exercise in promising a democratic pie in the sky all the while one was completely detached from the problems of exercising power – after all, the FI majority was in the same position as Moreno in this respect. But it all came at a price. The Fourth International lost its then strongest organisation in Latin America. By adopting the resolution with its categorical statements on the pluralism of opinions and indeed parties, and by clearly distancing itself even from the more laid-back, 'paternalistic' forms of undemocratic rule, it diminished its chances of being recognised as a small but serious partner by the Castroist leadership one day (Cuba solidarity had played an important role for the organisations and groups of the Fourth International since 1963). Ultimately, this clear position on socialist democracy also proved to be an obstacle to rapprochement with other groups from the 'Trotskyist' tradition that considered and

---

76   See Fourth International 1995. There, Tomás Borge is quoted in an interview with the Cuban newspaper *Granma* of 7 October 1984. He recommends open debate with critical and even reactionary positions as a necessary 'gymnastics' that 'prevents stiff joints and passivity'. Fidel Castro is also quoted as saying: 'The revolution must be a school of unfettered thought'. This is followed by the rather cautiously critical comment: 'Even if practice has not always lived up to these pronouncements, they are in line with the programmatic continuity of Marxism on the subject and must be defended tooth and nail against all who would deny them' (Fourth International 1985).

presented themselves as very 'orthodox'. Such groups often equated democracy more or less with bourgeois democracy – or else, they only thought that only a proletarian dictatorship fortunate enough to be led by the right leadership, ideally one's own sect, could be considered a socialist democracy. In the eyes of such 'orthodox Trotskyists', the members of the Fourth International had finally revealed themselves as pseudo-revolutionary, anti-Leninist, revisionist-reformist conformists by adopting the resolution on 'Socialist Democracy and Dictatorship of the Proletariat'.

This document, which clearly bears Mandel's handwriting while also being a product of the discussion of many, stresses the extension of democratic rights and liberties, of self-management at all levels of social life, and it emphasises the pluralism of views and parties. It describes general congresses of councils as advanced forms of representative democracy, supplemented by instruments of direct democracy such as referendums, but also by independent trade unions and a labour law that guarantees the right to strike.[77] Crucially and in stark contrast to bourgeois parliamentarism, decisions on economic policies are to be made democratically:

> Who will establish these priorities, which involve the well-being of tens and hundreds of millions of human beings and whose implications, consequences, and results in turn influence the behaviour of the mass of the producers and the toilers?
>
> Basically, there are only two mechanisms which can be substituted for the rule of the law of value: either bureaucratic choices imposed upon the mass of the producers/consumers from the top (whatever their origin and character may be, from benign technocratic paternalism to extreme arbitrary despotism of Stalin's type), or choices made by the mass of the producers themselves, through the mechanism of democratically centralised workers' power, i.e., through the mechanism of socialist democracy. This will be the main content of political debate and struggle, of socialist democracy under the dictatorship of the proletariat.[78]

Furthermore, the document envisions autonomous social movements instead of state-controlled 'mass movements', a dialectical process of democratic centralisation, and the decentralisation of decision-making. It firmly rejects workerist restrictions of democracy to productive workers. It calls for a strict separ-

---

77   See Fourth International 1985.
78   Ibid.

ation of parties and the state. And it calls for a strict limitation of the powers of other administrative apparatuses, which must be subject to elections and monitoring by the organs of council democracy.[79]

Parties and political organisations are to play an important role in socialist council democracy. This includes revolutionary vanguard parties. However, their leading role must not be institutionally enshrined. They can only acquire and maintain this role and win majorities in the institutions of council democracy by persuasion. Establishing firm roots in the working class and organising its vanguard are important safeguards, as is the elimination of all kinds of privileges. Finally, membership in an international revolutionary organisation can also function as a corrective for a ruling party.[80]

The resolution states that a 'clear stand on socialist democracy is necessary to win the proletariat for the socialist revolution and the dictatorship of the proletariat'.[81] The chapter thus titled warns that any ambiguity will help the enemies of the revolution: under the pretext of defending democratic rights, they can rally workers who live in bourgeois democracies in the developed countries to the defence of bourgeois democratic institutions.[82] Socialist democracy corresponds to the 'historical needs, and way of thinking ... of the working class itself' and is 'in no way a "luxury" reserved for the workers of the "richest countries", while its concrete application might suffer certain limitations because of the excessively reduced weight of the working class in some countries'.[83]

The latter touches on a delicate point that was part of the aforementioned original 'pedagogical-dictatorial' dilemma of the early socialist and communist movements. This is openly stated in the resolution just a few lines below, which to some degree betrays the desire to justify the Cuban system:

> When social conditions are such that a major part of the toiling population is illiterate, the bureaucratic degeneration of the forms of rule is made easier. This explains Lenin's insistence, in his last writings, on the need to raise the cultural level of the masses. The literacy campaigns conducted in Cuba and Nicaragua are models that should be followed.

---

79   Ibid.
80   Ibid.
81   Ibid.
82   Page 39 argues against the conflation of hard-won democratic rights with the functioning of parliamentary institutions in the rich capitalist countries on the grounds that these institutions are inseparable from the imperialist character of these states.
83   Ibid.

Moreover, in backward countries, during an initial phase, the dictator-ship of the proletariat may not follow proportional representation of the different segments of the population. It may openly choose to give added weight to the representation of the working class, particularly in relation to the peasants, as the Soviet Constitution of 1918 did.[84]

This statement is not found in the 1977 document, which is much closer to Man-del's original draft. Instead, it stresses that cases such as China and Vietnam are 'exceptions' that are unlikely to be repeated in other colonies or semi-colonies, and certainly cannot be transposed to advanced industrial countries. While favourable circumstances and the weakness of the bourgeoisie led to the over-throw of capitalism, these regimes were 'doomed' to bureaucratisation from the outset. This was due to the absence of democratically elected workers' and peasants' councils, even if the subsequent growth of the proletariat in these countries created the possibility of an authentic socialist democracy.[85]

The finally adopted 1985 resolution addresses the question why the over-throw of capitalism has hitherto only led to minority dictatorships. It names a complex interaction of several objective and subjective factors: for instance, the backwardness of the countries concerned, the role and consequences of protracted civil wars in the conquest of power, the political education of the leaderships concerned (instead of proclaiming these countries 'doomed' to bureaucratisation from the outset, the resolution now simply states that they had virtually no authentic proletarian council democracy until today), and finally, the decades of defeats and setbacks for the world socialist revolution. Nonetheless, the resolution states that the programme of socialist democracy is not an abstract standard, but the conceptual expression of a real historical tendency, of the increasingly evident 'instinctive' urge of the working class for democratic self-organisation wherever it acts independently. According to the resolution, the strength of this working class is now growing in a number of dependent countries as well, and the rejection of authoritarian political sys-tems is becoming more and more entrenched in its ranks, including in the bureaucratised workers' states. The program of socialist soviet democracy is therefore by its nature universal.[86]

The notion that self-assertion against imperialism inevitably results in un-democratic relations is rejected in a manner that clearly bears Mandel's

---

84   Ibid.
85   Ibid.
86   Ibid.

handwriting: 'We reject likewise any concept that the workers-council power would be in any way "impractical" as long as imperialism survives, i.e., as long as the problems of self-defence of the victorious proletarian revolution and of its international extension remain central under the dictatorship of the proletariat. On the contrary, we believe that workers-council democracy strengthens the capacity of self-defence of the workers state, and strengthens its power of attraction to the workers of the capitalist countries, i.e., favours the struggle against imperialism and for an international extension of the revolution'.[87]

Similarly, the greatly expanded section on the 'response to the dogmas of Stalinist origin' resembles just as clearly many of Mandel's statements and texts on this topic. In a nutshell, the resolution denies that the principle of infallibility underlying the Stalinist conception, whether openly or implicitly, is compatible with the fundamental Marxist socialist struggle for emancipation. How can a minority, a leadership or even an individual leader, like in the Middle Ages, claim to be more competent than everyone else and claim the sole prerogative not only of expression but also of decision-making? A rule 'on behalf' of the working class implies that the class itself is incapable of ruling. It engenders a monolithism that perceives any 'deviation' as a mortal threat and therefore tends to subject all of civil society to its control. The ability of a genuine revolutionary vanguard party to articulate the universal historical interests of the working class and link them to its immediate interests in a correct fashion can only be proved in practice. The text argues that even the most deeply socially rooted vanguard party can only reduce the probability of error, but never exclude its possibility. The principle of one party representing one class is wrong. Both the internal stratification of the working class and the constant emergence of new problems, for which even the best available theoretical texts do not provide any blueprints, require a multitude of factions and parties formed on different occasions (there may be several revolutionary parties in any given country, which have to strive for cooperation and unity). The working class can only learn and reach higher levels in a process of self-education that comprises the freedom to make mistakes. Finally, a regime that suffocates cultural diversity and the freedom of science in the name of an official state 'Marxism' is incompatible with Marxism:

---

87   Fourth International 1985. In the German-language version of the document available at the International Socialist Organisation (ISO) website, this section ends with an Engels quote: 'You – the party – need socialist science and this cannot exist without freedom to develop' – see 'Sozialistische Demokratie und Diktatur des Proleteriats' at Intersoz.org and Marx and Engels 2010, p. 181.

Any monopoly position accorded to Marxism (not to speak of a particular interpretation of Marxism) in the ideological-cultural field through administrative and repressive measures by the state can lead only to debasing Marxism itself from a critical and revolutionary science, as a weapon for the emancipation of the proletariat and the building of a classless society, into a sterile and repulsive state doctrine or state religion ... Marxism, which is critical thought par excellence, can flourish only in an atmosphere of full freedom of discussion and constant confrontation with other currents of thought, i.e. in an atmosphere of full ideological and cultural pluralism.[88]

This was, by way of example, precisely the content of Mandel's first intervention at the Bahro Congress, where 3,000 people gathered to demand the release of Rudolf Bahro. Bahro was arrested and later deported to the west because of his (socialist) critique of the GDR and, more generally, of the political system of the USSR and its allies. The congruence between the two texts goes as far as to cite the same Engels quote. At this congress, Mandel denounced the contradictory attitude of those who (whether as social democrats, Maoists or representatives of the 'official' Communist movement) condemned restrictions on freedom of expression in the power sphere of their adversaries, but justified them for their own power sphere.[89]

The FI resolution explicitly supports the right of worker's states to defend themselves against internal and external counter-revolution. To make socialist revolution means to break the power of capital. The private appropriation of the means of production and the private employment of workers, for instance, will be prohibited. The social foundations of council rule will be enshrined in the socialist constitution just as private property is enshrined in a bourgeois constitution. The resolution stresses the difference between opinions and actions. In the system of socialist council democracy, even bourgeois positions should be expressed freely, and they must be fought with ideological and political means rather than administrative or repressive ones. At the same time, the resolution pleads for an 'extension of the most progressive achievements of the bourgeois-democratic revolutions in the field of criminal law and justice' based on written legislation. This would involve the rejection of retroactive culpability; a burden of proof for prosecution; the presumption of innocence for the accused; the self-determination of the accused concerning their defence; the

---

88   Mandel 1985b, Chapter 9.
89   Mandel 1979c, p. 15 et seq.

immunity of lawyers for their defence; a rejection of all collective liability; the prohibition of torture and of any coercion to extort confessions; the abolition of the death penalty (except in times of war and civil war); the generalisation of public jury trials; the democratic election and recall of judges; and finally, the gradual involvement of the masses in the administration of justice, initially at local level and for 'minor offences', in order to initiate a process of dismantling the professional judiciary.[90]

'The fundamental guarantee against all abuses of state repression lies in the fullest participation in political activity of the toiling masses, the broadest possible socialist democracy, and the abolition of any monopoly of access to weapons for privileged minorities, i.e. the general arming of the proletariat.'[91] Under conditions of revolution and insurrection, but also under conditions of civil war or defence against counter-revolutionary intervention from the outside, repression is exercised and the democratic rights of the bourgeoisie and others involved in counter-revolutionary activity are restricted (Mandel repeatedly mocked the idea of a fundamental exclusion of the 'bourgeois' from socialist democracy, asking where to draw the line when left-wingers often characterise each other as 'ultimately or essentially bourgeois').[92] Historical experience has shown, the document continues, that in a time of inevitable restrictions on democratic rights, 'the more swiftly and more radically the armed resistance of the bourgeoisie is broken ... the lesser will be the costs in human life of the social transformation'.[93] However, no matter how difficult the situation, revolutionary measures must always be linked to the emancipatory goal in order to be effective: 'Only those measures of expediency against the class enemy are really efficient, even under conditions of civil war, which raise and do not lower the class consciousness and self-confidence of the working class, its faith in its capacity to build a workers state and a classless society, its active support of and participation in the administration of its own state, its capacity for mobilisation and self-organisation'.[94]

The military self-defence of workers states must be ensured as well. This involves the creation of special institutions for counter-espionage etc.[95] The draft resolution of 1977 contains a rather unclear statement on the question of secret services: 'Of course, any workers state must develop a modern mil-

---

90   Mandel 1985b, Chapter 9.
91   Ibid.
92   See Mandel 1979d, p. 44.
93   Mandel 1985b, Chapter 10.
94   Ibid.
95   Fourth International 1985.

itary and intelligence defence system against hostile capitalist states, but the support of the international working class is a thousand times more effective for self-defence than a powerful secret police continually in search of "foreign infiltrators" and "spies". In the long run, police methods generally weaken the capacity for self-defence of the victorious proletariat against foreign enemies'.[96]

From this, we can only conclude that it was a mistake to set up the Cheka in early Soviet Russia at all, or that it's a mistake to have any kind of police force in a newly formed socialist democracy; but on the other hand, it is deemed 'natural' to maintain a 'modern ... secret service defence system'. There can be no doubt about Mandel's own position on this issue, put on record without equivocation in one of his later works.[97] In a passionate defence of the October Revolution, slandered and dragged through the mud after the epochal break of 1989–90, Mandel emphasised that it was an authentic workers' revolution. He proved its popularity by providing testimony from some of its worst enemies, and he denounced the bestiality of the white terror while justifying the red terror, which had claimed far fewer victims and had a defensive, reactive character. At the same time, he analysed measures that contributed to the later bureaucratic degeneration of the revolution. We will return to this paper when discussing Mandel's critique of 'substitutionism' and in our last chapter. A subchapter of Mandel's paper deals with the Cheka. Mandel states at the outset:

> The question of the Cheka is very different from what we have just been talking about: temporary measures during a cruel civil war. The Cheka was the creation of an institution, an apparatus, with the inevitable tendency of any institution and any apparatus to become permanent, and to escape any control. A fascist torturer can be shot after a public trial, even a summary one. But a secret political police cannot be submitted to public control.[98]

Mandel shows that 'the worm was in the fruit from the very beginning, despite the personal honesty of Felix Dzerzhinsky, the first leader of the Cheka, who nobody suspects of improper intentions'.[99] He bases this assessment on facts and documents that had only come to light through Gorbachev's 'glasnost' policy. The members and informers of the Cheka gave themselves a bonus

---

96   Fourth International 1977.
97   He expressed it to this author in personal conversation as early as 1972.
98   Mandel 1992b, pp. 31–2.
99   Mandel 1992b, p. 32.

(a part of the 'spoils') for any goods seized from 'speculators' or from those who committed 'economic crimes': 'there is no doubt of the dynamic to corruption this represents'.[100] However, as a rule, the Cheka was only able to gain the upper hand against the People's Commissariat of Justice whenever the Soviet regime came under acute threat.[101] Mandel relates (albeit without proof) that Lenin obtained a passport for Martov (a former comrade from the days of *Iskra* and a left-wing Menshevik whom Lenin had fought politically but held in high esteem personally). He advised him to leave immediately, for the Cheka was after him and Lenin would not be able to prevent his arrest. (Peter von Oertzen vividly recalled this anecdote in an interview.)[102] Mandel goes on to describe Lenin's support for Kamenev's proposals to limit the powers of this secret service in the context of its transformation into the GPU, the State Political Administration with the People's Commissariat of Internal Affairs (NKVD). In his note to Kamenev on this issue, Lenin advised to 'limit the competence of the Cheka' and 'as regards arrests, limit its rights even further'.[103] The resolution adopted by the Fourth International in 1985 is less categorical on the issue of police intelligence services, but stresses that the activity of such services must not lead to the repression of politically undesirable individuals on the pretext of combating genuine hostile foreign activity (as was notoriously and excessively the case under Stalin):

> Military preparedness of the workers states against threats of imperialist aggression must include special measures against espionage, saboteurs sent in from abroad, and other forms of anti-working class military action that could persist for years if not decades. But special technical measures for self-defence by the workers' state should in no way restrict workers' democracy, by calling citizens who are exerting their right of criticism and opposition 'spies' or 'saboteurs'. In fact the higher the political activity, awareness, and social cohesion of the broad masses which can be realised only through a full flowering of socialist democracy – the more difficult does it become for real spies and saboteurs to operate in a resolutely hostile milieu and the stronger becomes the capacity of self-defence of the workers' state.[104]

---

100   Ibid.
101   Ibid.
102   See eyewitness testimony from Peter von Oertzen.
103   Mandel 1992b, p. 32.
104   Fourth International 1985.

As far as the army question is concerned, the 1977 draft contains only rather general statements, but this seems to be owed to the very concise character of the text. The resolution adopted in 1985 pleads in the spirit of Mandel for 'workers' and people's militias', while the maintenance of standing armies and their specialisation in complex technical weapons systems is considered a temporary evil. Nonetheless, a proletarian army must be organised differently from a bourgeois army, in particular by abolishing ranks and replacing them with functional command structures based on soldiers' councils and the election of officers.[105]

Mandel often stressed that he considered a number of developments in present-day society favourable with regard to chances of establishing an authentic socialist democracy with comprehensive self-government and a vastly reduced risk of deformation. In this context, he pointed to the growing numbers of wage earners, but also to the greater importance of highly skilled workers in enterprises, social struggles and strike movements.

> Workers, white collar workers, technicians increasingly self-managing their own struggles, their mass strikes, their general strike, will not be pushed away so easily from the management of the companies they have taken over ... The western working class – and also that of today's Soviet Union, not to say today's GDR and CSSR – is at an incomparably higher level of technical qualification and cultural development than that of Russia in 1917 or 1927, let alone China in 1945, 1949 or 1965. The practical possibility of self-management has therefore entered a qualitatively higher stage that even Marx of *Grundrisse* could hardly have imagined.[106]

Mandel consistently stressed two key prerequisites for a system of socialist democracy to function without new elites becoming permanent and a law unto themselves: the radical reduction of working hours, and the masses experiencing in practice that their decisions are actually implemented and lead to the expected results. In his view, these two factors combined can ensure that the masses do not sink into apathy, that they do not, after a short period of revolutionary upswing, succumb to passivity and consequently fail to resist

---

105   Ibid.
106   Mandel 1980a, p. 137, our translation. In the period of 'citizens' initiatives' and the formation of the German Green Party, the relevance of socialist perspectives on the basis of advanced mass struggles with a high degree of self-organisation, which Mandel energetically advocated in this conversation, appeared to many like a highly optimistic struggle against everything that was fashionable at the time.

gradual bureaucratisation. Whether or not Mandel's idea of a post-capitalist future is feasible therefore depends to a large degree on the actual possibility of implementing radically reduced working hours and on the practicability of the proposed mechanisms of socialist democracy. They are institutionalised forms of collective self-activity, but nevertheless dependent on whether they are really filled with the active life of a great numbers of people. In a conversation with Johannes Agnoli, he states categorically on the 'radical reduction of working hours':

> This not only corresponds to the deep desire of the majority of the working people, but is an absolute, material prerequisite of real rather than mystified self-management. Labourers who spend seven or eight hours a day with mechanical, uncreative work as producers or workers in the factory, who have to travel another two, three or four hours to work and back, and who need to eat, simply have no time for self-management. The slogan of reducing the working day by half has today replaced the peace, land and bread slogan of the Russian October Revolution. The first victorious proletarian revolution in an industrially advanced country will not only write it on its banner, but implement it immediately.[107]

According to Mandel, this will give workers the time to take care of administrative matters and receive further training. Computers facilitate the development of socialist democracy because they allow everyone to obtain socially relevant information. The reduction of working hours will 'create time to attain new skills. It forms, as it were, the infrastructure of the continuous process of self-education of the working people, which is the very basis of the construction of a classless society'.[108] Greater self-activity can be achieved to the degree that 'broader masses experience in practice that they can actually decide their own fate ...'.[109] Conversely, if people are only consulted, or only allowed to decide on trivialities while important decisions are made over their heads, then they rightly remain passive, disinterested and indifferent in production. They wonder: 'Why should we strain ourselves if the direction and distribution of the results of our efforts are decided by others on our behalf? And why should we run the risk of being caught in a dilemma of ever-increasing efforts with ever-decreasing marginal benefits for our own lifetime, for our own real purpose in life?'[110]

---

107   Mandel 1980a, p. 138, our translation.
108   Mandel 1980a, pp. 138–9, our translation.
109   Mandel 1980a, p. 139, our translation.
110   Ibid.

Mandel's appreciation of Marxist role models like Leon Trotsky and Rosa Luxemburg was strongly linked to their attitudes to council democracy and the self-organisation of the working class, i.e. socialist democracy. He acknowledged that Trotsky had brought the concept of 'self-organisation' into the debate. According to Mandel, he was the first – namely as early as 1905 – to grasp the essence of the council [soviet] movement. Trotsky considered it more or less the universal twentieth-century form of alternative state power from below. He recognised that it was very flexible, that it appeared in a variety of guises and embryonic forms, and that it was appropriate for the working class. As Trotsky later correctly understood, the revolutionary vanguard party must use political means to struggle for hegemony within the councils in order for the revolution to succeed and endure.[111] Although Mandel considered Luxemburg's harsh criticism of the early Soviet state a brilliant premonition of its later bureaucratic development, he did not concur with her and blamed it largely on her lack of access to information in prison. Nonetheless, he approvingly quoted her view of socialist democracy:

> It is the historical task of the proletariat, when it comes to power, to create in the place of bourgeois democracy, socialist democracy, not to do away with democracy itself. Socialist democracy begins, however, not in the promised land after the substructure of socialist economy has been formed, as a ready-made Christmas present for the good people who in the meanwhile have loyally supported the handful of socialist dictators. Socialist democracy begins simultaneously with the tearing down of class rule and the building up of socialism. It begins with the seizure of power; it is nothing else than the dictatorship of the proletariat.
>
> Yes, dictatorship! But this dictatorship consists in the manner in which democracy is employed, not in its abolition; in vigorous, decided intrusions into the well-established rights and economic relations of bourgeois society, without which the socialist overturn cannot be actualized. This dictatorship must be the work of the class, and not of a small minority in the name of the class; that is, it must proceed at each step with the active participation of the masses, be subject to their direct influence, stand under the control of unlimited public opinion, proceed from the growing political education of the masses.[112]

---

111   See Mandel 1979f pp. 60–1.

112   Luxemburg 1935, pp. 18–19. In 1972 Mandel jokingly described himself to this author as an 'orthodox Leninist with slight Luxemburgist deviations'.

Half a decade after the last experience with at least embryonic council-like structures in a capitalist country has passed – namely in Portugal in 1974–75 after the toppling of the dictatorship – Mandel wondered why the masses identified so strongly with bourgeois parliamentary democracy and what hope there was for socialist council democracy to gain greater legitimacy one day? Was the problem perhaps that there was no prolonged experience with authentic socialist council democracy to look back on? Mandel's initial answer was that such experiences had in fact been made, for instance in Spain:

> Between July 1936 and May 1937, the Spanish and especially Catalan committees developed the experience of direct democracy beyond the limits of the bourgeois regime in numerous fields – in particular, in local administration, industry, public supply and health – and were felt to be great achievements by the Spanish masses. It is not widely known that under the administration of the workers industrial production grew markedly and that the functioning of restaurants, theatres, education, health, and justice in Barcelona, stimulated by – among others – our ex-comrade Andres Nin, was a remarkable example of broad mass participation in the carrying out of appointed tasks. A considerable body of literature exists on this extremely advanced experience of proletarian democracy (and not just in the semi-mythological writings of anarchist authors).[113]

On the other hand, Mandel says that broad masses will be attracted to council democracy not primarily by studying previous historical experiences, but rather through their own practical experience of council democracy as a higher form of democracy. This will be based on 'experience of struggle ... before the outbreak of a revolutionary crisis – by the development of higher forms of self-organisation and of anti-capitalist demands, by strikes and factory occupations. The direct democracy of workers' councils will develop more out of that than out of historical comparisons of a theoretical nature'.[114]

Mandel concedes that even a council system is not simply 'direct democracy', but, like parliamentarism, contains a representative aspect. Moreover, he advocates a centralisation of the operational and local organs of council rule, because without this, an alternative to the bourgeois state cannot even arise. In contrast, he considers 'guarantees' against functionaries pursuing their own self-interest, proposed by Marx in his comments on the Paris Commune

---

113   Mandel 1979d, p. 21.
114   Ibid.

and by Lenin in *The State and Revolution* (or the remarks of Luxemburg and Trotsky on this subject), to be necessary factors in promoting the 'withering away' of the new state 'from the outset'. However, in his view they are not sufficient answers. The classical safeguards he cites are the eligibility of all offices, the recallability of office-holders, perhaps even the tying of mandates to the instructions of the electorate, and the limitation of the incomes of office-holders and elected officials to the average worker's wage.

Mandel adds three more features to this. The first is the greatest possible decentralisation of administration and therefore the real first step towards the 'dissolution' of the state. Only matters that need to be decided centrally by their very nature are to be decided centrally – in particular the distribution of any given country's resources:

> It should be the Congress of Workers' Councils that takes decisions concerning the allocation of national resources. For it is the working class that bears the sacrifice of not consuming a share of what it produces, so it is up to the working class to decide the extent of the sacrifice it is prepared to accept. But once it has been decided to devote 7, 10, or 12 per cent of national production to education of health, there is absolutely no need for state management of the education or health budgets. It is pointless for the Congress of Workers' Councils to take on this task of management, which can be much better assumed at the more democratic level of school or higher educational councils, and councils of medical staff and patients. The people who sit on these bodies will be different from those who are delegated to the Congress of Workers' Councils. This breaking up of the functions of the central state means that dozens of councils will be meeting at the same time and involving tens of thousands of people on a national and continental scale. And the same kind of process will be occurring at the regional and municipal level, this 'breaking up' will allow hundreds of thousands or even millions of people to participate in the direct exercise of power.[115]

The second aspect is the rotation of offices. No individual should be able to receive the same mandate twice. Under today's conditions, this would be much easier to implement than, say in the young Soviet state and allow an even greater number of men and women to be involved in self-management and political democracy. Mandel advocated this idea, which played an important

---

115   Mandel 1979d, p. 22.

role in the alternative movement and the early Green parties, from early on (incidentally with reference to Lenin), for example in his text on bureaucracy.[116] Thirdly, he argues that it is important to push from the very outset for the elimination of the social division of labour according to the social functions of producers, administrators and politicians. This should not be confused with the professional social division of labour, which can only be overcome in a very long process on the road towards communism. This is the purpose of genuine 'self-management'. Producers must be hugely involved in the production process, and to achieve this, working hours must be radically cut. Mandel does not consider it a given that the revolution will inevitably lead to a decline in production. He thinks it possible, at the current level of productive forces, to simultaneously reduce working hours, increase production, and satisfy the most important basic needs beyond the market and money.[117]

Mandel tries to show to social-democratic and liberal left audiences why only a socialist position, i.e. a commitment to socialist democracy, represents a consistent defence of universal human rights and liberties. Given the capitalist monopoly over the media, for instance, freedom of speech is largely a fiction. Mandel argues that in a socialist democracy, there will not only be greater freedom of expression, it will also be much better implemented. In answering how this would be achiever, Mandel shows his tendency to create 'concrete utopia':

> The vast majority of the population does not have the necessary material means to actually make use of press freedom. A radical commitment to human rights therefore requires, first of all, the creation of material conditions that make its implementation possible in the first place. In concrete terms, this might include the following: each group of citizens has free access to printing houses in accordance with its numerical size: for x subscribers or buyers, there is a daily newspaper; for x divided by 5: a weekly newspaper; for x divided by 19: a fortnightly newspaper; for x divided by 20: a monthly newspaper; for smaller groups: a page in a 'general gazette' (daily or weekly); for an individual, a column.[118]

According to Mandel, this general access to mass media should be created without any regard for economic profitability and without any authorisation

---

116   Mandel 1973c.
117   Mandel 1979d, p. 25.
118   Mandel 1989b, pp. 235–6, our translation.

from higher authorities. As in other matters, the central bodies of socialist democracy only determine the proportion of resources to be allocated. These should be majority decisions; but if strong minorities want a different allocation of resources, then compromises addressing their concerns ought to be possible.[119]

In the cited article, Mandel responds to an objection that might be summed up with Brecht's dictum, 'food first, morals later'. He concedes that starving people who lack the basics of life cannot organise socialist democracy. Therefore, it is all the more important to satisfy the basic needs of all first – and the capitalist system is not capable of doing this. He, moreover, denounces the objection as a sophism: according to him, it are precisely the neediest people who have no power or say in this system. This means that socialist democracy is not a 'luxury' for the rich countries, but a global necessity.[120]

Another problem that Mandel raises in this context is the question of expert knowledge. Many consider a socialist democracy to be unfeasible because 'ordinary people' do not have the competence of technicians or scientists to comprehend complex relations. They argue that a real mass democracy could therefore only become possible after a long process, when a level of education completely unlike today's standards has been reached. Mandel rejects this argument by narrowing down the significance of expert knowledge, on the one hand, and the scope of political decisions on the other. He uses a simple example:

> Certainly, the right to self-determination and self-management does not boil down to the power of ignorance. It is not possible to vote on how to build a bridge so that it does not collapse under maximum truck load. But one must conceptually distinguish the technical articulation of decision-making power from actual decision-making power. Whether we build a bridge, how many social resources we allocate for this purpose, and what other use of resources we are prepared to sacrifice – these are not technical, but socio-political decisions. You do not have to be a graduate engineer to make these decisions ... Experts, under the control of the public, must ensure that these decisions are based of the broadest, most appropriate information. But the right of decision lies with the masses.[121]

119   Mandel 1989b, p. 236.
120   Mandel 1989b, p. 237 et seq.
121   Mandel 1989b, p. 240, our translation.

Once again Mandel concludes his article with a plea for the radical reduction of working hours as a precondition for the leap into the 'realm of freedom'.[122] It is clear that experts of all kinds (including those of dubious competence) can have a manipulative influence on political decisions because of their advanced knowledge. Just consider debates about the introduction of any new technology from an ecological point of view – in this regard, the approach suggested by Mandel is not a miracle cure. However, socialist democracy is not designed as a system free from conflict, but as a system in which conflicts are dealt with in a particular way. The organs of bourgeois democracy, too, are accustomed to expert hearings where controversial expert opinions are considered. This does not exempt members of parliament, nor indeed the councils of socialist democracy that Mandel proposes, from taking decisions. In the bourgeois system, it is important to consider who is paying the experts in question. In Mandel's vision of a universal emancipatory process towards socialism and communism, the sources of conflict arising from educational differences and knowledge-based advantages will gradually disappear in a socialist democracy.

When a few years later, shortly after Germany's so-called *Wende* [turnaround] and 'reunification' of 1989–90, Mandel addressed an audience that had lived through the GDR and seen the fall of the SED regime, he presented Trotsky's intellectual legacy as an 'alternative' to both bourgeois parliamentarism and bureaucratic coercion from above.[123] Trotsky's position does not appear here as a ready-made answer, but as the product of a long-lasting clarification process during which setbacks also occurred (especially the 'Dark years 1920–21').[124] What played a major role in the final 'synthesis' of Trotsky's views was the recognition that it was a normal state of affairs to have a plurality of political parties and organisations, a plurality of tendencies within proletarian trade unions, and indeed a plurality of tendencies and views within a revolutionary proletarian vanguard party – and that any suppression of this plurality hindered the envisioned learning processes. For Mandel, what applies to the various components of the workers' movement and to the socialist movement struggling for the overthrow of capital should also apply to the post-capitalist 'workers' states' and to the organisation of political power within them ('with possible exceptions in the event of an imminent civil war'):

---

122   Mandel 1989b, p. 241, our translation.
123   See Mandel 1995a.
124   I will discuss these questions in detail in Chapter 4, section 4 on 'The temptation of substitutionism: roots of substitutionist politics'.

The leading role of the party is realized by a process of political persuasion and not by means of administrative measures, certainly not by means of repression directed against sections of the working class. It can only be realized, as used to be said in the GDR, by the application of the 'rentability principle' (*Leistungsprinzip*) to politics. This means: strict separation of state and party; direct exercise of power by the democratically elected organs of the working people and not by the vanguard party; a multi-party system – the workers and peasants must be free to elect whomsoever they wish.[125]

Mandel explicitly makes a connection between the efficient leadership of the workers' struggle and the efficient construction of a post-capitalist economic and social order:

Socialist democracy, internal trade union democracy and internal party democracy (the right to form tendencies and factions) have a mutual effect on each other. They are not abstract norms but practical preconditions for an effective workers' struggle and for an effective construction of socialism. Without proletarian democracy, the proletarian united front and therefore success in the workers' struggle is at best made difficult, at worst made impossible. Without socialist democracy, an efficient socialist planned economy is also impossible.[126]

Towards the end of his life, Mandel had the opportunity to once again voice his thoughts on the subject of socialist democracy in another anthology, published to honour Peter von Oertzen on his seventieth birthday. His contribution bore the title, 'All power to the councils. Confession of a notoriously unflinching leftist'.[127] The defiant subtitle implies that the developments that Mandel had hoped for had not occurred. The tone is different from earlier contributions: socialist council democracy is presented less as a tangible possibility arising from current mobilisations and more as an aspiration to be pursued.

Is council socialism a utopian project in the common sense of the word, i.e. unrealisable even in the long term? Certainly, there is no majority of citizens who are already convinced of this model or who could be con-

---

125   Mandel 1995a, p. 88.
126   Ibid.
127   Mandel 1994, p. 19.

vinced democratically. And by its very nature, council socialism requires
the active commitment of such a broad majority.

But this fact is by no means sufficient to declare council socialism to
be impossible to attain even in the long run. Such a conclusion would be
just as unscientific and dogmatic as the belief that its victory is inevitable.
Only history can decide on this question, and the decision is uncertain.
So far, no one has succeeded in scientifically substantiating the opposite
thesis.[128]

Mandel would certainly strongly dispute that this passage implies a change of
position. After all, he formulates in a way that retains continuity with what
he has always said: naturally, there is no such thing as a socialism that will
prevail 'either way', in a fatalistic historical sense. But Mandel had always perceived and portrayed every major movement of the exploited and oppressed
internationally, especially self-organised proletarian movements, as evidence
of the burning relevance of the overthrow of capitalism and its replacement
by a socialist council democracy. Often, Mandel depicted potential outcomes
as having almost been achieved. Now, however, he places the question in a
'broader historical context', compares it with the long road of the bourgeoisie to
power and its implementation of mere formal equality. Moreover, he points out
that the emancipation process is not straightforward, but has many setbacks,
some of them brutal.

> But it is precisely because these relapses of historical progress are undeni-
> able that council socialism has a historical chance to prevail in the long
> term. After all, a growing number of men and women are rebelling against
> the aforementioned ills. The scope of this rebellion is not diminishing
> but growing, although not in all countries and to varying degrees in
> each country. To be sure, this massive revolt is still mainly characterised
> by 'single issue' objectives. It therefore remains largely fragmented and
> inconsistent and does not quite lead to the pursuit of an alternative social
> order.[129]

'A historical chance to prevail'! Mandel's tone has certainly changed. On the
other hand, he contrasts this 'long-termism' with the danger of collapse if the
self-organisation of the working class, the exploited and the oppressed does not

---

128   Mandel 1994, p. 24, our translation.
129   Mandel 1994, p. 25, our translation.

develop sufficiently soon to enforce a socialist alternative. Thus he once again underlines the urgency of the socialist project.[130]

Apart from this, the article contains the same positions on socialist democracy as before, even if in some cases the examples that Mandel provides have slightly different accents. Mandel consistently distinguishes between what is desirable (e.g. car-free cities) and the right of producers to decide freely and within the framework of available resources what will be carried out and what not. He insists that individuals must have the greatest possible autonomy in deciding how to use their time.[131] Mandel's article also links 'council socialism' and the radical reduction of working hours with the interests of women: 'This alternative is more likely to promote the emancipation of women, in part because it guarantees a radical reduction in working hours (the 20-hour week) and a permanent, high-quality system of childcare for all women who want to make use of it. Women's material independence is guaranteed, as is free access to the material infrastructure of domestic labour for all women and men. The misery of double or even triple work days is thus eliminated for all women'.[132] What Mandel means by free access to the 'material infrastructure of domestic labour' is unclear. Traditionally, the Fourth International has advocated the 'socialisation of domestic work', although it did not regard the question of the equal distribution of domestic work between the sexes as a political issue (which began to change around the mid-1970s under the influence of the 'new women's movement').

Socialist council democracy is the very core of Ernest Mandel's political conception. It represents a state that immediately prepares the 'real beginning of human history' in Marx's sense. It results from the class struggle of a highly active, organised and politically conscious working class that strives for solidaric solutions to all urgent social problems. It is the axis that connects the desired future of universal emancipation with today's mobilisations, struggles and debates. It is the linchpin of 'orthodox Marxism' in Mandel's sense, which is inseparably linked with the workers' movement and the historical interests of the class of wage earners. It is inseparably linked in particular with the interest of this class in its self-abolition as a class, and therefore the abolition of all classes. According to a famous Marx dictum often cited by Mandel, Marxism wants to be nothing but the conscious expression of the class movement objectively taking place before everyone's eyes (or at least before the eyes of all intelligent observers).

---

130   Mandel 1994, pp. 25–6.
131   Mandel 1994, pp. 20–1.
132   Mandel 1994, p. 20.

3   The Material Prerequisites for Universal Emancipation

In the Marxist tradition, the notion of socialism – the society of associated producers and the process of universal emancipation it initiates – is based on the
productive forces that have developed under capitalism and on the potential
for a further growth of productive capacity through liberation from the fet-
ters of the capitalist mode of production. Real freedom is not conceivable in
a society of scarcity where people spend most of their time looking for the
necessities of survival. Mandel construes as well as substantiates Marx's project as the withering away of money and commodity economy based on a
relative abundance of consumer goods, a radical reduction of working hours,
and a massive release of self-management drive and self-determined creativity. This vision requires clear answers: is there really a sufficient material basis
for its realisation – or can a sufficient material basis be created? The question of material basis is of particular relevance for the initial steps after the
revolutionary rupture, i.e. for societies that have a socialist democracy operating in Mandel's sense, but have only just begun to build a classless socialist society. Regardless of the specific problems of the post-capitalist societies
that really existed after the October Revolution of 1917 (bureaucratisation, the
near absence of democratic rights, undemocratic planning, etc.), Mandel fundamentally assumes that a transition period is necessary.

By this, he does not mean the 'period of friction' after a socialist revolution that Bukharin addresses in *Economics of the Transformation Period*. Such
problems are essentially attributable to political factors, i.e. factors that are
'exogenous' from the economic point of view. Mandel is mainly interested in
the economic ('endogenous') problems that justify the necessity of a transition
period.[133] Now, it goes without saying that we will necessarily have to deal with
transitional societies in some countries as long as the capitalist system continues to exist in other parts of the world. This is because the socialist-communist
project is based on the seizure and transformation of the whole world economy, which was created under capitalist conditions. It is also clear that the
need for military defence not only devours resources, but is scarcely compatible with the withering away of the state – which is, after all, an apparatus of
force. Moreover, Mandel justifies the necessity of a transition period even on
the assumption that the world socialist revolution prevails. If capitalism were
abolished across the world, commodity production could also be abolished
and production adapted to the day-to-day needs of all people. But the result

---

133   Mandel 1968b, p. 608.

would be a rather ascetic world: 'The only condition for such a rapid and far-reaching transformation would be restriction of needs to the most elementary ones: men would have to be content with eating just enough to appease their hunger, dressing quietly, living in a rudimentary type of dwelling, sending their children to schools of a quite elementary kind, and enjoying only a restricted health service'.[134]

Of course, Mandel's statements quoted here and later in this chapter are based on empirical data and estimates that date back to the late 1950s, since Mandel's first major economic work appeared in 1962.[135] They are furthermore based on certain judgements that Mandel found unable to maintain later in life, mainly because of the increased awareness of ecological problems in society, in the labour movement and on the left (we shall return to these in due time). The debate on the material foundations of universal emancipation continues today (including in the Fourth International), and it has not necessarily become any less complex.[136]

According to Mandel's assessment at the time, the state of productive forces at the beginning of the 1960s would have allowed the basic needs of the whole world population to be met without additional industrial expansion. However, for this to happen, all forces would have to be concentrated on the construction of agricultural machinery, on food production, clothing, housing and health, and a considerable part of global production would need to be directed towards poor countries.[137]

In response to objections that even this is not possible, Mandel argues that the production of artificial fertiliser could easily be increased, citing statistics on the growth in agricultural productivity since 1947. It is interesting that this is exactly the same argument that Friedrich Engels used against Malthusianism.[138] However, the satisfaction of basic needs is not enough when people's needs and expectations in the wealthy industrialised countries have become much broader: '[The worldwide expansion of the production and circulation of goods] has brought about a universalising of needs which is merely a first awareness of the unlimited possibilities of free human development'.[139] This, Mandel argues, is even true if we leave aside the 'artificial or artificially

---

134   Ibid.
135   *Traité d'économie marxiste*, first published in English in 1968 as *Marxist Economic Theory*.
136   'Ecologie et socialisme', resolution of the 15th world congress of the Fourth International, February 2003 in *Supplément à Inprecor* no. 488, December 2003, pp. 39–40 plus relevant debate in *Supplément à Inprecor*, no. 457, April 2001 and no. 459/60, June/July 2001.
137   Mandel 1968b, p. 608.
138   Mandel 1968b, p. 609.
139   Mandel 1968b, p. 610.

inflated' needs generated by the commodity-producing industry. It is not possible, according to him, to abolish the industries that serve to satisfy these
greater needs without reducing the standard of living for a large part of the
population in the industrialised countries: 'It would mean a sort of "socialism of poverty" in which rationing by ration-card and the restricted variety
of products available would replace rationing by the purse. Instead of making possible a universal development of human potentialities, a "socialism"
like this would produce a man even more stunted and less satisfied than the
average inhabitant of the advanced capitalist countries of today.'[140] Moreover,
the inhabitants of the poor countries have also become aware of the possibilities of a higher standard of living and would not agree to strict rationing.[141] In
order to provide a standard of living for all that corresponds to today's needs
and expectations, the production of goods would have to be increased many
times over. Mandel argues that after the abolition of capitalism, the productive forces must therefore be developed further. This justifies the necessity of
a transition period, a period of 'socialist accumulation', especially since some
culturally advanced needs have so far only been very partially met even in the
industrialised countries, and since a 'tremendous productive effort' would also
be necessary in Europe to guarantee the 'optimum standard of life' that corresponds to the current state of science and technology.[142]

'During this period, on the basis of socialisation of the chief means of production and exchange, and of world-wide economic planning, a degree of
development of the productive forces (both mechanical and human, the latter
implying a gigantic educational drive) can be attained which will make possible an economy distributing its goods and services in such a way as to cover
all the needs of the people involved in it'.[143]

Consequently, there is a need to discuss the sources of this 'accumulation'.
Mandel examines them separately for the level of world economy and the level
of industrialised countries, on the one hand, and poor countries on the other.
We will now summarise the most important arguments at all three levels.

According to Mandel, world economy is the ideal framework for socialist accumulation. Within this framework, the international division of labour
could be used rationally and modified to make the best use of existing resources
and productive possibilities.[144] Furthermore, Mandel thinks that it is perfectly

---

140   Ibid.
141   Ibid.
142   Mandel 1968b, p. 612.
143   Mandel 1968b, p. 611.
144   Mandel 1968b, pp. 612–13.

possible to accelerate the rate of accumulation, including through the industrialisation of poor countries, and at the same time increase consumption levels worldwide through the rational use of all resources. After all, there is an 'immense fund of unproductive consumption', namely arms expenditure, which he estimates at 120 billion dollars per year worldwide (today, as is generally known, it is many times that amount). Based on official UN figures, Mandel calculates that for the 'third world', 'industrialisation without tears' would be possible within thirty or forty years. The industrialised countries would not have to sacrifice anything for this to succeed. They would simply have to switch arms production to civilian production and train teachers, engineers, doctors, nurses and psychologists instead of officers, fighter pilots and armaments technicians. In the poor countries, industrialisation would not have to replicate the history it had in today's industrialised countries, but could commence its development with the latest technological achievements. The gigantic costs imposed on humanity by the continued existence of nation states, not to mention military expenditure, are indeed good arguments for this programme.[145]

Mandel argues that in the industrialised countries, a new upturn in productive forces with a simultaneous increase in living standards can be achieved by eliminating the waste and destruction that is typical of capitalism. For these countries, Mandel names five 'sources of socialist accumulation': 1. making full use of the existing productive forces (tools and labour), which are periodically left idle under capitalism, with a large proportion of assets remaining unused even through the cycles; 2. eliminating expenditure on extravagant luxury and harmful or demoralising consumption (alcohol, gambling); 3. reducing distribution costs by eliminating trade profits, middlemen and the skyrocketing expenditure on advertising; 4. elimination of obstacles that are necessary for the capitalist system of competition but superfluous for an economy planned according to needs, e.g. patents, trade secrets, delay in the introduction of innovations due to the influence of monopolies, destruction of resources and values when companies and industries collapse – this source flows from replacing rationality limited to individual companies by its extension to the economy as a whole, 5. freeing of the creative powers, inventiveness and ingenuity of the workers, whose subordinate role in the capitalist enterprise largely prevents the development of this potential. Moreover, in a system of this kind, innovations are implemented if they save labour at the same cost, not just when

---

145   Mandel 1968b, p. 613 et seq. Later, Mandel maintained his view that it was materially possible to equalise the standard of living across the world while raising it for the workers of the industrialised countries, if only by eliminating the enormous waste of resources, especially arms expenditure (Mandel 1979d, p. 236).

they promise profit. Many more sources would gradually open up from all of the above. Once the basic needs are satisfied, all subsequent growth will produce more goods and services to satisfy greater needs, and then a time of plenty and the withering away of commodity economy will rapidly draw nearer.[146] Without the aid of the industrialised countries it will be far more difficult to make such calculations for underdeveloped countries, Mandel continues. In any case, the low level of development necessitates dramatic decisions when setting priorities. However, the thesis that the poverty of the poor countries is the cause of the vicious circle of underdevelopment (according to which low investment funds lead to low investment, thus perpetuating underdevelopment) is wrong. With reference to Paul A. Baran, Mandel lists four components of the social surplus product that are largely lost to the productive accumulation fund: 1. the social surplus product appropriated by the big landlords; 2. the social surplus product appropriated by traders and usurers; 3. the social surplus product exported from the country by foreign firms; 4. the part of the social surplus product appropriated by the 'lumpenbourgeoisie' and state bureaucracies.[147] In addition, there is a great potential of unused labour through mass underemployment. Access to farmable land combined with the provision of appropriate work equipment would help to achieve sufficient self-sufficiency in food without compulsion (a prerequisite for increasing the productivity of labour) and then an increase in the surplus product. For other meaningful work on the infrastructure of poor countries, it is advisable to take the needs of the respective communities as an immediate point of departure – this way, they soon feel their situation improving. The mobilisation of these resources of accumulation is obviously incompatible with the present ownership structure; it will only be achieved when large land ownership is abolished (i.e. a comprehensive agrarian reform will be necessary) or, as far as Equatorial Africa is concerned, when the exploiter alliance of capitalist firms with tribal chiefs is broken.[148] Mandel adds a few additional observations to this list of sources of accumulation in poor countries (assuming a non-capitalist path). The most important of these is the distinction between maximum and 'optimum' rates of accumulation, by which he primarily rejects the idea that maximum growth can be achieved by restricting consumption as much as possible. The latter notion, according to him, was one of the sources of error of the

---

146   Mandel 1968b, p. 618.
147   Mandel 1968b, p. 619. Mandel uses this term to denote capitalists who operate on the fringes of legality or illegally and in proximity to organised crime (see Mandel 1987a on the increasing convergence of crime and bourgeois society in late capitalism).
148   Mandel 1968b, p. 621.

Stalin-era Soviet model. From 1923, the Left Opposition suggested that industrial growth be accelerated and wages increased at the same time, and this
was not unrealistic. Unproductive expenditures (for example, for a bloated bureaucratic apparatus, far above-average remuneration of senior staff, army and
weaponry, etc.) would, however, have to be restricted as much as possible. Wage
expenditure – or the expenditure for the consumption fund of the working
people as a whole, which also comprises social benefits and social services –
cannot, however, be equated with unproductive expenditure. The lower the
general standard of living, the more an increase in this expenditure is likely to
result in an increase in labour productivity. Conversely, its stagnation or drop
below a certain level lowers labour productivity. There is certainly no mechanical relationship between the various key variables (renewal fund, productive consumption fund, unproductive consumption fund, necessary minimum
reserve fund, potential investment fund), and it is necessary to determine the
relationship between them in each specific social context in order to achieve an
optimum rate of accumulation.[149] In Mandel's view, this cannot be achieved on
a purely theoretical basis or by means of economic accounting through a planning apparatus. Rather, what is needed is a process in which 'trial and error' are
permitted to a degree, and where such experience becomes visible and can be
articulated. Subjective factors also play an important role.

> The optimum rate of accumulation, the one that makes possible the
> quickest growth ... can very probably not be determined except through
> a series of experiments, successive approximations and broadly demo-
> cratic discussions. Indeed, the workers' reactions to different variations
> in their standard of living are not given once for all time. On the con-
> trary, they are an extremely variable element, which depends on historical
> factors (the past and present standard of living), psychological factors
> (their relative confidence in the leadership of the country) and social
> factors (the extent to which they effectively participate in the manage-
> ment of the economy and of the separate enterprises). These reactions
> may even vary within a single country from period to period, according
> to circumstances.[150]

Accordingly, Mandel rejects the erstwhile Soviet dogma of the primacy of
developing the manufacturing sector. He refutes it using model calculations,
while conceding that this primacy can be necessary for a limited period of time

---

149   Mandel 1968b, p. 621 et seq.
150   Mandel 1968b, p. 626.

if the starting point of economic development is very low.[151] On the other hand, he justifies the importance of socialist democracy, without which the superior traits of planned economy over capitalist market economy cannot unfold, by arguing that only a voluntary renunciation of consumption (measured by the maximum possible) based on personal decision can maintain the identification of working people with the economy that they themselves manage. This, in turn, is an important factor for productivity (labour productivity in this context understood as the output of goods per hour worked).[152]

Potential socialist accumulation on a world scale, in the industrialised countries and in the so-called developing countries, is initially based on the existing productive forces that have developed under capitalism. According to Mandel's calculations, these forces would have been sufficient to provide at least elementary supplies for all of humanity as early as the beginning of the 1960s. His assessment of the productive forces at that time focuses on the 'third industrial revolution'. While the first technological revolution was characterised by the introduction of the steam engine and the second one by electric and internal combustion engines, the use of nuclear energy and the introduction of electronically controlled machines (as an important prerequisite for automated production processes) have been characteristic of this latest technological revolution. Mandel cites nuclear energy first.

> The productive deployment of atomic power is the first answer human ingenuity has discovered to the problem, which some regard as an agonising one, of the loss of world power resources. The second and doubtless final answer will be the employment of thermo-nuclear and solar energy. Already now, atomic power could cut the costs of industrialising certain under-developed areas (Latin America, large parts of India or China) where coal is scarce or hard to transport, and where hydro-electric power is more expensive than atomic power.[153]

However, humanity in the process of liberating itself would have to renounce nuclear energy (at least this is the position of the Fourth International today), not only because of the health risks involved, but also in view of the unsolved problem of nuclear waste disposal.[154] Today, more than 40 years after Man-

---

151   Mandel 1968b, p. 627 seq.
152   Mandel 1968b, p. 631 et seq.
153   Mandel 1968b, p. 605.
154   See *Ecologie et socialisme*. Since the 1970s, Mandel himself advocated the participation in the environmental movement with 'maximum loyalty' and considered the objective

del wrote the above statement, the use of nuclear energy is undoubtedly still an open question. Photovoltaics continues to play a growing but still marginal role today, and it remains a matter of dispute to what extent it will be able to replace fossil fuels. How much energy could be produced using which technologies in an ecologically responsible and economically viable manner remains a complicated discussion. In other words, on this important point Mandel's assessment of the world's productive forces was, in my opinion, based on a now obsolete premise. At the time of writing, the problem of nuclear waste disposal was virtually unheard of and remains unmentioned. Mandel was aware of some of the risks of nuclear energy even then, but he invoked them in support of the need for socialisation:

> The third industrial revolution is breaking through the framework of private property. In every country, it has been possible to develop atomic power only in public laboratories and enterprises. Its transfer pure-and-simple into the private sector would involve the risk that mankind might be at the mercy of a madman with the power to blow up entire countries. Nuclear technique is the first modern technique for which advanced forms of public control are indispensable, not only for the sake of profitability, health or injustice, but in order to safeguard the very survival of mankind. Even in the hands of capitalist states, this technique is a thread to the existence of mankind, in so far as it implies an arms race and the risk of atomic war.[155]

The second cornerstone on which Mandel's diagnosis is based is the transition from semi-automatic to automatic production processes through the introduction of electronically controlled measurement and control systems. This technology allows for a very far-reaching elimination of human labour from the immediate production process up to and including maintenance and control. Mandel goes very far with his conclusion: 'Present-day technique has thus found a "final" answer to the oldest of objections to a socialist economy: "Who, under socialism, will do the hard, unpleasant and unhealthy types of work?" Today the answer is clear: machines will perform all these tasks, by themselves'.[156]

---

of preventing the construction of a nuclear power plant to be 'correct', comparing it to equally correct demands 'for a 5 percent wage increase' or '3 hours less work' (Mandel, Bahro and Oertzen 1980, p. 225).

155   Mandel 1968b, pp. 606–7.
156   Mandel 1968b, p. 606.

However, apart from nuclear energy there are several other established or developing product lines that are hard to reconcile with today's ecological awareness. This even applies to the very foundations of computer technology and contemporary information technologies in general (disposal of electronic waste, radiation exposure, etc.). The vision of a world in which all humans are provided for at a high level, and where they are free to use their time as they wish because machines perform all the non-creative and unfulfilling labour, no longer seems credible in light of all this. In any case, anyone entertaining the concept must confront the question as to what production and what product lines are justifiable. This also applies to the world food problem. Mandel's solution of a multiple increase in the production of artificial fertiliser misses problems that have become highly visible in the meantime. Even today, the whole of humanity could be supplied with elementary nutrition practically overnight. But the extensive agriculture that makes this possible is destroying the arable land and the groundwater supply. We can safely assume that the ecologically responsible agricultural production of healthy and appealing food would be more costly and require more labour. It is claimed that genetic engineering can solve such problems. However, this seems to be an illusion, especially since this technology is associated with other incalculable risks. In this field, assessing the consequences of human intervention in nature amounts to little more than reading tea leaves.

Mandel concludes *Marxist Economic Theory* with a statement that identifies him as an optimist fascinated by the modern productive potential, including questionable contemporary innovations, and infected by the feasibility mania of the 1960s: 'But who can speak of limitations that man will *never* be able to break through, man who is strengthening out his arms towards the stars, who is on the brink of producing life in test-tubes, and who tomorrow will embrace the entire family of mankind in a spirit of universal brotherhood?'[157]

Space travel has lost much of its glamour, and no one really knows what missions to the moon and Mars can contribute to humanity. When it comes to biotechnology today, people tend to think of limits that humans should not cross. The implications are clear: given today's state of affairs and awareness of various problems, Mandel's vision of a global society in which everybody enjoys a high standard of living and works radically reduced working hours, where goods and services are increasingly distributed according to need – in other words, the classic Marxist vision – must either be discarded or founded anew. This involves a critical examination of the productions and product

---

157   Mandel 1968b, p. 686.

lines on which general prosperity is to be based, as well as exploring potential paths of development that are in many respects very different to what has been developed so far (quite apart from all the extensive ecological 'repair' work that has become necessary).

In *Late Capitalism*, which Mandel wrote ten years after *Marxist Economic Theory*, he approvingly cites Leo Kofler's work on this subject and criticises 'technical rationality' as the characteristic ideology of contemporary capitalism: 'Belief in the omnipotence of technology is the specific form of bourgeois ideology in late capitalism. This ideology proclaims the ability of the existing social order gradually to eliminate all chance of crises, to find a "technical" solution to all its contradictions, to integrate rebellious social classes and to avoid political explosions'.[158] Mandel regards this ideology as a mystification concealing the actual contradictions and problems of the capitalist social order at several levels.[159] Mandel, again in line with Leo Kofler, cites the objectification of human relationships as the first aspect of this mystification. Irrespective of human needs and objectives, irrespective of the class structure of society and the corresponding conflicting interests, this ideology presupposes an 'omnipotence of technology' from which no one can escape. In this context, Mandel quotes Jürgen Habermas's claim that: 'so long as the organisation of human nature does not change, and we have to sustain our existence by social labour and tools that are labour-substitutes, it is impossible to see how we can ever discard technology, indeed our technology, for a qualitatively different one'.[160] Mandel disagrees with this: 'It remains a mystery why men and women under different social conditions, increasingly liberated from mechanical labour and progressively unfolding their creative capacities, should be unable to develop a technology answering to the needs of a "rich individuality"'.[161] According to Mandel, Bukharin fell for the same kind of absolutisation of dominant technology, while Herbert Marcuse (who perceived modern technology as almost omnipotent) came very close in *One-Dimensional Man*.

This is also Mandel's answer to the environmental question. With reference to Barry Commoner's *The Closing Circle*,[162] he explains that the significant environmental problems that have accumulated, including air pollution, are not the result of any 'constraints' but of concrete technological mistakes made under the pressure of competition in the market. Mandel cites the monstrous

---

158   Mandel 1975d, p. 501.
159   Mandel 1975d, pp. 503–4.
160   Habermas 1969, pp. 56–7.
161   Mandel 1975d, p. 503.
162   Commoner 1971.

development of the big cities since the emergence of industrial capitalism as an example, describing it as an evil that has brought about inhuman conditions resulting from the interests of private companies. He argues that different (socialist) social relations would allow for decisions that meet human needs and do not harm the environment.

In Mandel's view, the belief in the omnipotence of technology, which furthermore entails a cult of 'experts', merges with other elements to form a late capitalist ideology that is in tendency inhuman, social-Darwinist, sceptical of education, and considers people to be incorrigible and fundamentally lazy. This ideology has replaced the early bourgeois belief in the ability of individuals to grow and evolve. Late capitalism produces university degrees for growing numbers of people, yet on the other hand it preserves the hierarchical structures of companies and bureaucracies. This, Mandel writes, is a source of new frustrations, which manifest themselves in irrationalism such as the proliferation of astrology, fortune-telling, commercialised eroticism and commercialised sadism.[163] Mandel denounces the peculiar kind of 'growth' and 'consumerism' that this entails: 'The massive psychological frustrations induced by late capitalism, among other things by the systematic inculcation of consumer dissatisfaction with consumption – without which a durable rise in consumption would be impossible – plays an important role here'.[164]

Mandel sees a further aspect of ideological mystification in the belief that late capitalism can overcome the contradictions and fundamental problems of the capitalist mode of production and ultimately integrate workers into the system. In reality, it can only offer alienated labour.

According to Mandel, theoreticians who proclaim the inability of the proletariat to challenge this system are parts of an ideological mechanism designed to persuade the proletariat of its own incapacity in the interest of the bourgeoisie.[165] He cites Adorno's appeal to technical military constraints on the rebels of the late 1960s: '"The pseudo-revolutionary gesture is the complement of the technical military impossibility of a spontaneous revolution ... Against those who control the bomb, barricades are ridiculous; one therefore plays at barricades, and the masters temporarily let the players have their way"'.[166] In contrast, Mandel argues that even Auschwitz and Hiroshima were not simply products of technology, but ultimately an expression of the unfavourable development of the social relations of power due to the historical defeats of the

---

163   Mandel 1975d, p. 505.
164   Ibid.
165   Mandel 1975d, p. 506.
166   Ibid.

working class. That is why there was no 'repetition' after World War II. On the contrary, the Vietnam War demonstrated that the resistance of the population in its own country can have more weight than military technology. Likewise, the students who were supposedly only 'playing' in May 1968 unleashed a general strike of 10 million workers. Mandel asserts that under certain social conditions, that is when large masses are on the move, even the most sophisticated technical means of repression can become less effective. Therefore, to promote a belief in the futility of revolt in the face of modern military technology is to aid the interests of the ruling class.[167]

Mandel accuses those who overestimate the capacity late capitalism to integrate rebellion of forgetting the contradiction between use value and exchange value. Much ado, he writes, is made about the fact that capitalism can turn 'everything into a commodity', even Marxist revolutionary literature. But even if it is possible to make a profit with the mass distribution of such literature, its use value is that of raising consciousness critical of capitalism. Consequently, it does not stabilise this system but contributes to undermining it.[168]

In the same context, Mandel also returns to the environmental issue. He views it as a problem from which further arguments against the capitalist mode of production can and must be drawn:

> A very recent example of the contradictory nature of the 'process of ideological integration' is furnished by the rapidly increasing awareness of industrial dangers to the environment in the imperialist countries. From the standpoint of the production of commodities and of value this development can undoubtedly open up new markets for the late capitalist economy: a whole 'ecology industry' is now in the process of emerging. But merely to perceive this immediate aspect of the problem, without also seeing that systematic explanation of the nature of the threat to the environment, as an effect of the capitalist mode of production itself which cannot be overcome within it, can be a powerful weapon against capitalism (not just in the sphere of 'abstract theory' but also as a 'stimulus to action' and mass mobilizations), is to be blind to the complexity of the social crisis of late capitalism.[169]

Ultimately, Mandel considers capitalist rationality to be a 'contradictory combination of partial rationality and total irrationality'. The pressure for exact

---

167   Mandel 1975d, pp. 506–7.
168   Mandel 1975d, p. 452.
169   Mandel 1975d, p. 508.

economic quantification that arises in the production of commodities 'comes up against the insuperable barrier of capitalist private ownership, competition and the resultant impossibility of exactly determining the socially necessary quantities of labour actually contained in the commodities produced'.[170] Every investment boom 'leads to overcapacity and overproduction, any acceleration in the accumulation of capital leads to the devalorisation of capital'.[171] The attempt to save the maximum human labour in the factory as much as possible leads to the increasing waste of labour in the overall social context.[172]

'The real idol of late capitalism is therefore the "specialist" who is blind to any overall context; the philosophical counterpart of such technical expertise is neo-positivism'.[173]

For Mandel, the productivity of labour is an important criterion for measuring human progress and comparing different social systems, insofar as it relates to the 'satisfaction of rational human needs and the optimal self-development of individuals'.[174] As elaborated by Marx in *Grundrisse*, the contradiction between the partial rationality and the overall irrationality of capitalism results in a contradiction between the maximum valorisation of capital and the optimum self-realisation of men and women.

> The reified autonomy of the means – of exchange values – is triumphant today. Partial rationality always consists of the best combination of paid-up economic resources for the profitability of the individual firm. Hence it excludes anything that has 'no (or only a very low) price'. Even in purely economic terms, of course, it is far inferior to a social 'globalization' of 'costs' and 'returns'.[175]

In a society with a global economy democratically planned according to needs, we would not be concerned with the 'price' of something, but with the consequences of certain types of production or particular product lines for humans. This would naturally include the issue of consequences for the natural foundations of life. This is Mandel's position, which he reiterates at the end of book on *Late Capitalism*:

---

170   Ibid.
171   Mandel 1975d, pp. 508–9.
172   Mandel 1975d, p. 509.
173   Ibid.
174   Ibid.
175   Mandel 1975d, p. 510.

The increasing internationalization of forces of production, the vast and unsatisfied needs of the semi-colonial masses, and the global spread of the threat to the environment render conscious planning of basic economic resources on a world-wide scale imperative ... All these searing problems will remain insoluble so long as control over the forces of production is not wrested from the hands of the capital. The appropriation of the means of production by the associated producers, their planned application to priorities determined democratically by the mass of the workers, the radical reduction of working time as a precondition of active self-administration in economy and society, and the demise of commodity production and money relations are the indispensable steps to their solution.[176]

However, *Late Capitalism* does not contain an updated detailed discussion of the material basis for this emancipatory social project, that is, the state of the productive forces and the sources of socialist accumulation. His later writings likewise fail to provide a detailed update of his discussion of these issues in *Marxist Economic Theory* in the light of new ecological insights. The year of the publication of *Late Capitalism* (1972) was also the year in which the Meadows report and the subsequent letter from Sicco Mansholt to the EEC Commission were published. It was the year of Dennis and Donella Meadows's *The Limits to Growth* and another upsurge in ecological awareness. This trend did not only provide new arguments for a socialist revolution. On the contrary: few people were under the impression that the countries of 'actually existing socialism' were better equipped to solve the 'problems of industrial societies', and the necessity to renounce further growth now proclaimed by many seemed to contradict both Marx's and Mandel's original socio-political objectives. Mandel responded to this challenge with an essay that appeared in the November/December 1972 issue of the magazine *Mai* in Brussels under the title 'La dialectique de la croissance. A propos du Rapport Mansholt'.[177] In this article, Mandel tries to refute the 'fairy tale' that 'Marx was first of all an admirer of technology', which had 'reared its head again following the publication of the Meadows Report and Sicco Mansholt's famous letter to the European Commission'.[178] He reconstructs Marx's position as one that was exclusively oriented towards human interest. According to Mandel, Marx did not indulge in growth fetishism, but wanted all humans to enjoy a decent life. His aim was the optimal

---

176   Mandel 1975d, p. 589.
177   See Mandel 2020a.
178   Mandel 2020a.

development of human beings – and after all, 'humanity's wealth consists of the wealth of human relations, in other words, social relations'.[179]

However, with respect to the possibilities of human development, Marx attached great importance to the development of the productive forces. He thought that the development of a rich social individuality would be impossible without a corresponding material basis.

'Marx firmly rejects a communism of poverty or asceticism, precisely because he is aware that such "communism" would disfigure human beings, make it impossible for them to develop their talents, imprison them in the environment in which they happen to be born, subject them to the tyranny of unrestrained natural forces, and, precisely because of this poverty, deprive them of the material means to fully develop their knowledge and needs'.[180]

One might argue that Marx praised Ricardo in *Theories of Surplus-Value* precisely because of Ricardo's productivism, i.e. because he elevated the growth of production into an end in itself. And indeed, Marx wrote about Ricardo:

> He wants *production for the sake of production* and this with *good reason*. To assert, as sentimental opponents of Ricardo's did, that production as such is not the object, is to forget that production for its own sake means nothing but the development of human productive forces, in other words the *development of the richness of human nature as an end in itself*. To oppose the welfare of the individual to this end, as Sismondi does, is to assert that the development of the species must be *arrested* in order to safeguard the welfare of the individual ... [Such reflections] reveal a failure to understand the fact that, although at first the development of the capacities of the *human* species takes place at the cost of the majority of human individuals and even classes, in the end it breaks through this contradiction and coincides with the development of the individual; the higher development of individuality is thus only achieved by a historical process during which individuals are sacrificed ....[181]

However, Marx distinguishes Ricardo from those who want not 'production for the sake of production', but production for the sake of profit. He criticises capitalism not least for developing production and the productive forces only insofar as this corresponds to profit interests and profit expectations. Indeed, production for the sake of capital does not aim to improve society or develop

179   Ibid.
180   Ibid.
181   Marx 1863, chapter 9.2.

and satisfy human needs. Rather, the two clash continually.[182] Marx appreciates in Ricardo that, although he was an ideologue of the bourgeoisie, this was 'only because, and *in so far as* their interests coincide with that of production or the productive development of human labour. Where the bourgeoisie comes into conflict with this, he is just as *ruthless* towards it as he is at other times towards the proletariat and the aristocracy'.[183]

Marx did not uncritically accept the suffering of the 'victims of progress', as one might conclude from the first quotation. Rather, his critique aimed at creating conditions in which the interests of the whole would coincide with the interest of the individual. He therefore refused to counterpose the welfare of the individual with the welfare of the whole in an abstract fashion.[184]

Mandel sees Marx as the 'brilliant forerunner' of the ecologists because he foresaw that the productive forces would threaten to turn into destructive forces if capitalist society persisted. After all, Marx wrote in *Capital* Volume I: 'Capitalist production, therefore, only develops the techniques, and the degree of combination of the social process of production by simultaneously undermining the original sources of all wealth – the soil and the worker'.[185] Of course, if this diagnosis is correct, it also entails the obligation to review the situation after a certain period of time and determine which possibilities for comprehensive emancipation are offered or have been lost by the present state of the productive or destructive forces!

Capitalism involves advanced commodity production and the fragmentation of production into private industries. Market competition prevails, and profit is the purpose of production. Anything that cannot be sold is disregarded. The point is not to meet needs, but to meet solvent demand. The time frame for investment decisions is limited by the amortisation of capital. All these aspects are immanent reasons for the ruthlessness of this method of production, even in relation to the natural resources of life. Even Marx and Engels wrote about some of the symptoms back in their day: e.g. the overexploitation of cultivable soil to the extent that it is cheaply available, air pollution, and the inhuman hypertrophy of cities. Mandel quotes Friedrich Engels, who denounced these

---

182   See Marx 1991, pp. 356–7.

183   Marx 1863, chapter 9.2.

184   Wolf 1983, p. 116 et seq. Illuminating the aforementioned relations in his remarkable study, Wolf approaches the relationship between Marxism and ecology quite in Mandel's sense, but he examines the subject more profoundly than Mandel ever did.

185   Marx 1990, p. 638. See also Mandel 2020a. In the latter text, Mandel invokes Marx's warning against the transformation of the productive forces into destructive forces under capitalism.

phenomena as early as 1845 in his work *The Condition of the Working Class in England*, and Marx, who wrote in *Capital* Volume I:

> Capitalist production collects the population together in great centres, and causes the urban population to achieve an ever-growing preponderance. This has two results. On the one hand it concentrates the historical motive power of society; on the other hand, it disturbs the metabolic interaction between man and the earth, i.e. it prevents the return to the soil of its constituent elements consumed by man in the form of food and clothing; hence it hinders the operation of the eternal natural condition for the lasting fertility of the soil. Thus it destroys at the same time the physical health of the urban worker, and the intellectual life of the rural worker.[186]

The Meadows report addresses the issues of pollution, the drain on natural resources and population growth. Mandel takes these issues seriously, but takes issue with the way in which the report deals with them. On pollution, he accuses the Meadows report of extrapolating current trends. Mandel's main argument against this method is that our present technology is not the only technology possible: industrial technology does not tend to undermine the ecological balance in and of itself. It was not until 1946 that environmental pollution increased massively. The real reason was the decision to opt for certain technologies (e.g. cars with internal combustion engines and high compression, petrol with a high octane rating, the introduction of chemical cleaning agents). What was advantageous for the large capitalist corporations turned out to be disadvantageous for the human species.[187]

In Mandel's view, the point is to develop other technologies using a combination of economic, social and natural 'costs' as the yardstick for investment decisions – something that will only become possible in the context of global socialist planning: 'The environmental debate ultimately leads to the conclusion that humanity can no longer afford the wealth of private profit – i.e. capitalism – being the engine of economic growth. The discussion leads to a rejection of a growth that is irresponsible from the point of view of humanity's long-term interests, and not to a rejection of "growth" as such'.[188]

However, this was not actually the conclusion of the Meadows report, nor was it the main thrust of the public debate. Instead of denouncing the profit

---

186   Marx 1990, p. 637.
187   Mandel 2020a.
188   Ibid.

motive in production, the ecology debate ended up providing justifications for attacks on the hard-won living standard of workers. The argument went that a price needed to be put on natural resources that had previously been free of charge – fines and taxes imposed on companies would stop pollution. As Mandel explains, this 'solution' would place a greater burden on ordinary consumers and the public than on the actual culprits – and if the costs became too high for the capitalists, they would simply stop making the necessary investments. Previously, the standard of living achieved in the rich industrialised countries of the west after World War II had been regarded as a major advantage by the proponents of the system. They thought of it as the price that had to be paid for the pacification of the working class and therefore as inviolable. But now, the Meadows report 'cheerfully' proposed that the living standard of the US population should be reduced by 50 per cent by 2000! There also emerged an environmental protection industry, which developed environmental repair and pollution prevention into a new source of profit.[189]

Mandel cites Harry Rothman's book *Murderous Providence: A Study of Pollution in Industrial Societies*, which in his view examined the ecological problem from a Marxist point of view for the first time. He appropriates Rothman's critique, according to which 'measuring' the 'cost of pollution' in monetary terms amounts to setting a price for human life, calculated on the basis of what returns a person might produce: 'We are here squarely in the realm of inhumanity'.[190]

Mandel notes that the ecology debate 'puts the prophets of doom, for long relegated to the background, back in the limelight'.[191] Instead of providing arguments for socialism, they argue that socialism is impossible – *any* kind of socialism, quite apart from 'actually existing socialism', which is indeed hardly an attractive example from an environmental point of view. (Mandel argues that the partial continuation of commodity production in the Soviet Union, the calculation of the profitability of individual enterprises introduced as a criterion by Stalin, and the bureaucratic administration of the economy resulted in ecologically disastrous decisions.)[192] They claim that socialism is unfeasible because of environmental problems and the depletion of natural resources: while socialism requires an abundance of consumer goods, the scarcity of resources makes shortages inevitable. In their view, the market economy has proved to be the best and most flexible mechanism for the distribution of

---

189   Ibid.
190   Ibid.
191   Ibid.
192   Ibid.

scarce resources.[193] Mandel, in contrast, cites the waste of resources under capitalism through armaments, the poor use of capacities, and the waste of raw materials for the production of unnecessary 'clutter'. He also shifts the burden of proof: according to him, no one is in a position to determine the actual reserves of natural resources and the untapped possibilities of new technologies. The adaptability of humankind to ecological challenges therefore remains unknown: 'But nowhere has it been demonstrated that the earth's present riches would not be sufficient to reasonably feed, clothe, house, educate and nurture every citizen of the world, and enable them to develop their human personality in the way that most suits them once primary needs have been met'.[194]

Mandel criticises the neo-Malthusianism responsible for the Meadows report on the possibility of feeding the world population adequately. According to the report, one acre (0.4ha) of arable land is needed to feed one human being, but there are only 7.5 billion acres of arable land on the entire globe, the most fertile and accessible parts of which are already being cultivated. It is too expensive to develop and irrigate most of the remaining arable land, and so on.[195]

Mandel points out that in the US the amount of cultivated land is constantly decreasing while agricultural production is increasing. He cites the possibilities of hydroculture and the large differences in agricultural productivity in different parts of the world. Most of all, he rejects the argument that the development of new arable land is 'too expensive': after all, 120 billion dollars a year are wasted on weapons production, and generally speaking, such profitability criteria are unacceptable when the survival of billions of people is at stake. Either way, in the Central Valley desert in the US, the watering of 1.5 million acres of land costs 1.5 billion dollars because the price has been driven artificially high by speculation. At that price, the irrigation of 2 billion acres of desert land would cost $2,000 billion (two trillion) dollars – a sum easily spent on pesticide production within three to four years.[196]

It is difficult to say whether the unavoidable ecological consequences of such gigantic projects can be justified. Mandel certainly believed that such problems could be solved, although it is questionable whether his belief was factually sound. Anyone calculating whether a high standard of living can be achieved for the whole world population (which is constantly growing) must consider

---

193   Ibid.
194   Ibid.
195   Ibid.
196   Ibid.

the existing and potential productive opportunities. As soon as certain conditions are identified as problematic, the argumentation must be modified. As we have seen earlier, in *Marxist Economic Theory* Mandel mentioned the possibility of multiplying the production of artificial fertiliser. At the same time, it is well-known that the present state of food production is characterised by large cereal monocultures. Mandel realised that this type of production would in the long run destroy the soil and the groundwater reserves, which is why in 1972 he argued differently than in 1961: 'The abnormal development of cities in our time is accompanied by an "industrialization" of agriculture, whose negative effects on the environment are particularly obvious; these negative effects are mainly due to the rapid transition to monoculture. An example: in the past, animal manure was used to restore soil fertility. Nowadays, artificial fertilizer threatens to poison the soil and its products, while natural manure is discharged into rivers and poisons the water'.[197]

But if it is necessary to reduce the use of artificial fertiliser and abandon industrial agriculture in favour of more environmentally friendly methods to produce varied, healthy and appealing food, then the global food supply base will have to be recalculated on the basis of different data and figures. Of course, there is also the possibility of offsetting: agriculture could become more productive, for example, if grassland used for burger, steak and methane gas production were converted to cultivate grain and vegetables. Let us note, in any case, that Mandel does not attempt any such new calculation.

As far as the 'population explosion' is concerned, Mandel cites the importance of supplying the population with contraceptives (while rejecting 'barbaric sterilisation practices'), but mainly points out that population growth is a function of social conditions. In the rich industrialised countries this growth has declined, and if the inhabitants of the 'Third World' achieve a similar standard of living, there will no longer be a 'population explosion' there. Incidentally, the recent experiences of the 'Green Revolution' and similar projects have made the dangers of any 'partial solution' very clear.[198] 'Zero growth' would mean condemning a large part of humanity to starvation. Mandel vehemently rejects this and instead pleads for 'controlled' and planned growth through democratic socialist planning. Such growth would need to (1) meet the primary needs of all people, (2) 'seek new and different forms of technology to replenish the reserves of scarce natural resources', and (3) develop the intellectual capacities of all through appropriate education and meaningful recreation.[199]

---

197   Ibid.
198   Ibid.
199   Ibid.

Assuming that all the means available to humanity today are applied rationally, free from the coercion of private profit, and assuming that the human potential comes to fruition when hundreds of millions of people, who now have to perform alienating and alienated labour, develop their creative gifts, there is no reason to suppose that the standard of living of the inhabitants of the northern hemisphere would fall at all. The standard of living in the southern hemisphere will by necessity rise by leaps and bounds.[200]

For this to succeed, the associated producers need to 'take control of production' instead of remaining slaves to 'blind economic laws' or 'technological compulsion'.[201]

In later statements on the subject, Mandel consistently tried to highlight Marx and Engels's early ecological awareness. In a 1980 book containing a conversation with Johannes Agnoli, he added a few Marx and Engels quotes in a footnote to underline this. They are largely the same passages he had already used in his 1972 essay (see above).[202] Mandel's attitude towards the ecology movement was both critical and solidaric. He identified reactionary tendencies within the environmental movement – for him, they were part of an ideological backlash associated with the beginning of a long wave with stagnant and depressive undertone. Irrational hostility to progress and technology had begun to resurface. After the 1950s and 1960s, which were characterised by a belief in science and technology not unlike the sentiments prevailing in the days of early capitalism, general pessimism began to proliferate again. An anti-scientific, social-Darwinist, socio-biological and inhuman climate began to take hold, and sections of the ecological movement also played a part in this. On the other hand, Mandel thought that the movement had objectively emerged from burning and pressing problems, and that it was drawing attention to very real dangers and shortcomings.[203]

By the time of his conversation with Agnoli, Mandel had become a supporter of the anti-nuclear movement. He expected that the opposition to nuclear energy would also prevail in the workers' movement and win out against the conservatism of the trade union bureaucracy – e.g. in the German IG Metall union – and the corporatist reflexes (rather than class reflexes) of workers

---

200   Ibid.
201   Ibid.
202   Ibid. See also Mandel and Agnoli 1980.
203   Mandel and Agnoli 1980.

employed in the energy sector.[204] He accused a part of the ecology movement of playing the game of capital when hedging its bets on small alternative farms and a parallel 'small economy', thus unwittingly helping capital to save on social expenditure. If generalised, this would also reduce labour productivity and bear disastrous consequences for humanity.[205]

In *Marxist Economic Theory*, Mandel still referred to nuclear energy as the first of two pillars of the 'third technological revolution' and – alongside nuclear fusion and solar technology – as an essential part of the solution to the energy problem. Suffice to say that on this point, too, a new assessment of the existing productive forces and potential sources for socialist accumulation from the point of view of sustainability would have been necessary. Mandel did not attempt this, and he does not seem to have explicitly self-criticised after his shift in attitude towards nuclear power.[206]

---

204   Ibid.
205   Ibid.
206   Having examined numerous of Mandel's contributions to the debate, this author has found no explicit self-criticism.

Critique of Bureaucracy

1   Mandel's Explanation and Critique of Bureaucracy in the Workers' Movement

Ernest Mandel regards the bureaucracy in the workers' movement as the most important 'secondary group' that needs to be analysed by contemporary Marxism (social classes being the primary groups). For him, the bureaucracy is not a class, but rather a distinct part of the working class that emerges under certain conditions and becomes an obstacle to the emancipation of the class to which it belongs, or from which it has risen. According to Mandel, the problem of bureaucracy in the workers' movement first appeared in the last years of the nineteenth century: 'Twentieth-century Marxism discovered the phenomenon of bureaucracy because this problem, born within the working-class movement in the last years of the nineteenth-century, had grown and acquired increasing importance in the life and practice of working-class organizations'.[1]

In his seminal essay on this question, Mandel views the origin of the problem of bureaucracy as being almost exclusively linked to the emergence of workers' mass organisations:

> The problem of bureaucracy within the working-class movement poses itself in its most immediate form as the problem of the apparatus of working-class organizations: the problem of full-timers and petty-bourgeois intellectuals who come to occupy the middle or top functions within the working-class organizations. As long as these organizations are limited to tiny groups, to political sects or self-defence groups of limited numerical strength, there is no apparatus, there are no full-timers and the problem does not arise. At the very most, there is the problem of the relationship with petty-bourgeois intellectuals who come to aid in the formation of this as yet embryonic working-class movement.[2]

In the context of a more comprehensive work on bureaucracy, namely *Power and Money: A Marxist Theory of Bureaucracy*, Mandel later devoted more atten-

---

1   Mandel 1973c, p. 1.
2   Mandel 1973c, p. 2.

tion to the seeds of bureaucratisation even in small organisations, in revolutionary movements, and in the 'heroic days' of workers' organisations.[3]

According to Mandel, the creation of 'apparatuses' of full-time functionaries is unavoidable for large trade union and political mass organisations, even if this brings with it the seeds of bureaucratisation, i.e. it bears the danger that these apparatuses assume a dynamic of their own and become unaccountable: 'Within capitalism [the social division of labour] assigns the labour of current production to the working class, while the production and assimilation of culture – as well as all the tasks of accumulation – are the near-monopoly of other social classes and layers. The nature of its labour – physically and emotionally exhausting and, above all, time-absorbing – does not allow the majority of the proletariat to acquire and assimilate scientific knowledge in its most advanced form, or even to engage in continuous political and social activity ...'.[4]

Abstaining completely from creating such apparatuses would condemn the workers' movement to 'primitivism' and ultimately even have an anti-emancipatory effect.[5] The contradiction between the need for professionalism and the problematic emergence of special layers with special interests compels Mandel to invoke the need to build revolutionary organisations before offering suggestions for how to tackle the problem of bureaucracy in mass organisations: 'A working-class organization whose members are only manual workers engaged fulltime in the productive process is far more easily conquered by bourgeois politics and ideology than an organization which makes a conscious effort to educate and select the most conscious workers and form them into professional revolutionists'.[6]

The problem of material privileges of paid full-timers, although important to Mandel, is not the focus of his criticism of bureaucracy:[7]

'As materialists we cannot, of course, separate the problem of the bureaucracy from that of its material interests: this bureaucracy enjoys material privileges and is determined to defend them. However, to reduce the problem of bureaucracy solely to this particular aspect would not help us to understand its origin and subsequent development'.[8] For example, the salaries received by full-timers of many Communist Parties in both rich and poor capitalist countries did not amount to material privileges that were worth defending – often,

---

3 We will return to these questions in Chapter 4, section 4 on 'Substitutionism'.
4 Mandel 1992a, p. 60.
5 Ibid.
6 Mandel 1973c, p. 9.
7 See also Mandel 1992a, p. 73 et seq.
8 Mandel 1973c, pp. 5–6.

they did not exceed the income levels of skilled workers. And yet, these parties were significantly bureaucratised.

A more general problem that Mandel regards as the underlying reason for the danger of bureaucratisation is what he calls the 'dialectic of partial conquests'.[9] By this, he means the contradictory interplay between positive and negative effects of workers' movement gains as long as bourgeois society and the hegemony of capitalism dominate globally. He designates as negative the 'identification of the aims with the means, of the bureaucrat with the organization. This identification, as we have said, gives rise to deep conservatism and this conservatism often comes into violent opposition with the interests of the working-class movement'.[10] Partial conquests of the class struggle and by the working-class organisation are reflected in wage levels that exceed the minimum subsistence level, in shorter working hours, in social protection and social security systems, and so on. In every country and globally, certain sections of the wage-dependent class enjoy more, sometimes considerably more of these gains than the relatively disadvantaged strata of this class. Mandel quotes a key sentence from the *Communist Manifesto*: 'The proletarians have nothing to lose but their chains'. However, as soon as this 'nothing' is superseded, a 'new frame of mind' emerges: 'The pros and cons of every new action now come to be weighed and balanced: might not the projected move forward, instead of achieving something new, result in the loss of what has already been gained? This is a fundamental root of bureaucratic conservatism, found already in the social-democratic movement before the First World War and in the bureaucracy of the Soviet Union even prior to the extreme peak of the Stalinist era'.[11]

For Mandel, this is a real contradiction, which cannot be resolved simply 'by a formula'. Defending past gains is indeed necessary, and to refrain from this would not help to win new victories. The conservatism of 'both the reformist and Stalinist bureaucracies' consists in making this task central and in fetishising the organisations and apparatuses built with consideration to the limits of the present system. Those who fear struggle and shy away from any 'revolutionary leap forward' because they believe that it jeopardises the past gains of the working class become fundamentally conservative. However, in Mandel's view there is no way of eliminating the cited contradiction (and thus the prob-

---

9   Mandel 1973c, p. 4. See also Mandel 2000, p. 66.
10   Mandel 1973c, p. 6.
11   Mandel 1973c, p. 5. [In the German version of Mandel's text, published in 1976, this passage begins with the sentence 'It is not true that the working class has nothing left to lose', which is omitted from the English version – Translator.]

lem of bureaucracy in the workers' movement) by virtue of pure insight and corresponding decisions:

> The dialectic of partial conquests, linked to the phenomenon of fetishization characteristic for a society of generalized commodity production organized around an extreme division of labour, expresses an important aspect of the process of bureaucratization. As such it is inherent in the development of the working-class movement in the historical stage of the decay of capitalism and transition towards a socialist society. The real solution to the problem of bureaucracy lies not in trying to abolish it through decrees or magical formulae, but in creating the best subjective and objective conditions for it to wither away.[12]

Apart from the bureaucracies that have emerged historically and are linked to the two major traditional tendencies of the labour movement (Social Democracy and Stalinism), Mandel thus regards the existing conditions as providing the basis for a trend towards the bureaucratisation of workers' organisations. Its deepest root is the social division of labour, in particular the separation of manual and mental labour.

Therefore, when new mass organisations of workers are created, a re-emergence of this phenomenon is to be expected. The struggle against it is certainly made easier by insight into its causes and possible consequences, but is not sufficient to solve the problem. The privileges of a bureaucracy are always a function of the relative passivity of the grassroots. Since the permanent and wide-ranging activity of these grassroots is not feasible under the prevalent conditions, an inclination towards bureaucratisation of workers' mass organisations always exists under capitalism. However, bureaucratisation involves various stages and can have very different consequences.

Material privileges can vary in scope. Their weight is relative to the normal working class living standards in the respective period, and 'these social privileges are also privileges of authority and power to which people attach great importance'.[13]

---

12   Mandel 1973c, p. 5. The 1978 German version of the text reads: '... The real solution to the problem of bureaucracy lies not in trying to abolish it through decrees or magical formulae, but in creating the best subjective and objective conditions for *the seeds of this bureaucracy, which at the present historical stage is present everywhere in society and in the workers' movement,* to wither away' [my translation and emphasis – Translator].

13   [Our translation. This sentence is missing from the English edition, but is contained in the German version of the text – Editor.]

In the trade unions and Social-Democratic parties before World War I, full-timers enjoyed rather modest material conditions. Given the long workdays and harsh workplace conditions at that time, though, leaving the place of production in favour of full-time work for the organisation represented 'an unquestionable social promotion, a certain degree of individual self-emancipation'.[14] But this did not yet create a 'privileged social layer': 'The early secretaries of working-class organizations spent a considerable part of their lives in prison and lived in more than modest material circumstances. All the same, from an economic and social point of view, they lived better than the rest of the workers at the time'.[15]

But Mandel also identifies a psychological side of the problem, which extends beyond relative material privileges:

> At the psychological level, it is obviously infinitely more satisfying for a socialist or communist militant to spend all his time fighting for his ideas than to spend his days performing mechanical work in some factory, knowing that the result of his labour will only serve to enrich the class enemy ... Those who occupy such positions quite simply want to carry on occupying them; they will defend their status against anybody who wants to establish instead a rota system, whereby each member of the organization would at some time fill these posts.[16]

It is noteworthy that Mandel invokes the rotation principle positively, as he indeed does elsewhere when invoking it, with reference to Lenin, as an anti-bureaucratic tool in a workers' state. The rotation of leadership posts, the exchange of managerial staff and the steady recruitment of new members to leading positions: these types of measures comprise a part of Mandel's proposals for reducing the risk of bureaucratisation or at least mitigating its effects.

Social privileges of a new quality emerge at a later stage, when the movement and its organisations are pushed to occupy positions within capitalist society: 'There is then the question of electing advisers, MPs and trade-union secretaries who are capable of negotiating directly with the bosses – and thus, to some extent, of co-existing with them. Similar considerations apply when appointing newspaper editors or representatives to take part in the additional activities through which the organization intervenes at all social levels'.[17]

---

14   Mandel 1973c, p. 6.
15   Ibid.
16   Ibid.
17   Mandel 1973c, p. 7.

Mandel does not believe that is a straightforward matter to prevent a layer that has its own autonomous interests from emerging among professional functionaries simply by following Marx's old rule. While in principle he subscribes to the notion that full-timers should not be paid more than the average skilled worker's wage, he recognises that this is usually only feasible for the most politically conscious elements. With all others, he sees a danger of 'negative selection': a strict application of the rule would result in the loss of many able journalists, doctors, engineers and architects in communities managed by the labour movement. They would get 're-absorbed into the bourgeois milieu' and thus be lost to the workers' movement.[18]

The construction of a kind of communist island within capitalist society is impossible, except perhaps 'for a nucleus of highly conscious revolutionaries, but a large workers' movement is much more firmly integrated into capitalist society and communist principles are thus much more difficult to put into practice within it. Consequently there is a tendency for the obstacles specifically erected against the danger of bureaucratization to be gradually abandoned'.[19]

According to Mandel, one can consciously create obstacles against bureaucratisation. However, in light of the relative integration of a workers' mass movement into capitalist society (especially under conditions of bourgeois-parliamentary democracy, which offers many opportunities to this end), these obstacles will become gradually less effective and eventually disappear.

The temporary culmination of such developments, its final consequence, so to speak, is a complete change of political orientation: 'conscious integration into bourgeois society' alongside 'class collaboration'. The latter means that the systematic confrontation between the working class and the capitalist class on the basis of antagonistic interests is abandoned and a commonality of interests posited (especially against competitors at home and abroad). In Germany, this ostensible commonality of interests between work and capital has traditionally been dubbed 'social partnership' (*Sozialpartnerschaft*). Social democracy has helped to achieve this final stage in a 'perfect' fashion:

> In this historic phase of capitalist decay, the dialectic of partial conquests assumes its fully developed form of conscious integration into bourgeois society together with the politics and logic of class collaboration. All obstacles to bureaucratization disappear, privileges multiply, the social-

---

18   Ibid. [The German version of the text speaks of re-absorption into the 'petty-bourgeois' rather than 'bourgeois' milieu – Translator.]

19   Ibid.

democratic leaders no longer give a part of their parliamentary salary to the organisation nor content themselves with the wages of a full-timer. Indeed, these functionaries come to represent an electoral client layer inside the working class. From this point on, bureaucratic deformation can only leap forward towards bureaucratic degeneration.[20]

Mandel explicitly rejects 'ultra-left' solutions, which deny the necessity of building any kind of apparatus and see a 'future Stalin' in every professional revolutionary.[21] In his estimation, they do not understand it is impossible to achieve any progress if you reject any organisation that contains germs of bureaucratisation. As individuals, the workers are exposed to the dominant bourgeois ideology. If they build organisational structures without employing full-timers and without any apparatus, they fall under the influence of bourgeois intellectuals. 'Workers' autonomy', i.e. the independent permanent organisation of waged workers in bourgeois society, is only possible if the potential danger of bureaucratisation is accepted.[22] If the working class comes to power, it cannot instantly abolish all wage and salary differentials without perpetuating substantial material and cultural deficits, thereby slowing down or even blocking the process of eliminating inequality in society. 'By maintaining some modest difference in wages, skills increase and so does the material basis favourable to the withering away of bureaucratization and privileges'.[23]

Mandel's 'revolutionary Marxist solutions' of the problem cover three main problem areas: the question of political organisation or party, the question of mass trade unions and similar organisations, and the question of 'workers' states', i.e. societies in which the power of capital has been broken and which are in a state of transition from capitalism to socialism. We will address the last issue more thoroughly in the next section.

On the question of political organisations and parties, Ernest Mandel explicitly argues for revolutionary vanguard organisations that remain in a minority until revolutionary situations arise. In a footnote he clearly states: 'The numerical size of social-democratic parties, far from being an obstacle to their bureaucratization, is in fact a major cause of it. It is far easier to prevent the bureaucratization of an organisation which only recruits members who already have

---

20   Mandel 1973c, p. 7.
21   Mandel 1973c, p. 9.
22   Ibid.
23   Mandel 1973c, p. 10.

a basic minimum of political consciousness, experience and activity since this makes it impossible for the phenomenon of "clientelism" to appear on any large scale'.[24]

Mandel refers here to the 'Leninist theory of the party'. He insists on considering not only Lenin's classic 1902 writing *What Is To Be Done?*, which is based on the creation of the core of a revolutionary party under conditions of illegality, but also Lenin's additions and corrections after the experiences of the mass strike movement and the Russian Revolution of 1905. According to Ernest Mandel, the revolutionary party must not 'substitute' the working class – in other words, it must not act in its place or on its behalf. This would be a violation of Marx's idea, according to which the 'emancipation of the proletariat can only be accomplished *by the proletariat itself*' (which Mandel quotes with this emphasis). In extraordinary revolutionary situations, the objectives formulated by the 'vanguard party' can and must be supported by the conscious decision and practical action of the working class if self-liberation is to be achieved. Prior to this, however, the growth of the party beyond a certain threshold would only promote the recruitment of due-paying but otherwise passive members, the bureaucratisation of the party and its integration into the system. For Mandel, the concept of the 'professional revolutionary' is, however, not inconsistent with the emancipatory role of the party, provided that there is a dynamic exchange between the organisation and politically active workers. This includes the recruitment of new full-timers from their ranks, who always retain the possibility of returning to work: 'The latter must never be separated permanently from the masses; he must always be ready to return to the factory floor and cede his place to another comrade, in order that he too can acquire the necessary experience. This is the theory of the rota system, which establishes a real "circulation of life-blood" between the proletariat and its vanguard'. Nevertheless, Ernest Mandel never made his argument for building small revolutionary vanguard organisations into an absolute. Rather, he enthusiastically welcomed the emergence of new independent parties of waged workers (such as the Brazilian Workers Party – PT in the late 1970s) and argued that revolutionaries should work inside such parties. At the same time, however, he thought that their continued existence within the capitalist system brought with it a dynamic of adaptation, the development of a work routine immanent to that system, and finally bureaucratisation and the gradual assumption of a fairly conservative role compared to the radical orientation of the early days. Revolutionaries involved in such parties should therefore, in his

---

24   Mandel 1973c, p. 37.

view, maintain their own structures and means of expression (especially publications) and become part of a clearly anti-capitalist left wing within these parties.[25]

His pamphlet *On Bureaucracy* contains important references to this subject in a chapter on historical experiences of bureaucracy in the workers' movement, especially in the subchapter on Rosa Luxemburg's contribution. He also dealt with this topic more succinctly in his talk at a conference on 'trade union theory today' held in March 1970 at the German Federation of Trade Unions school Bad Kreuznach. There, Ernest Mandel made the case for mass trade unions that would be 'critical of the system' and explicitly committed to the sociopolitical objective of overcoming capitalism, led by 'conscious socialists'.[26]

In Mandel's view, just as 'two souls, alas, are dwelling in Faust's breast', trade unions have a dual character. Originally, they were a product of the early period of capitalism in which workers were compelled to sell their labour power under value. One difference between labour power and other commodities is that you cannot simply take it off the market in order to push up its price. Wage labourers have to offer it at current market prices because they risk starvation otherwise – they are existentially dependent on regular income. The creation of trade unions is an attempt by wage labourers to improve this situation by selling their labour power collectively rather than individually.

> In and of themselves trade unions under capitalism are no threat to the system. They are not a means to abolish capitalist exploitation, but merely a means to make exploitation more tolerable for the masses of wage earners. They are intended to raise wages, not abolish wage labour as such. Yet at the same time, the trade unions are not compliant with the capitalist system in and of themselves. They contain the fall in real wages and can, at least periodically and under certain conditions, exploit favourable fluctuations in labour power demand and supply in order to raise the market price for this commodity. In this way, they enable the organised working class to exceed the bare minimum of consumption and needs. Only as a result of this, the class organisation, class-consciousness, and growing self-confidence of workers emerge on a broader scale and create the preconditions for a more comprehensive mass struggle against the system.[27]

---

25   See Mandel 1980b.
26   Mandel 1978a, p. 282.
27   Mandel 1978a, p. 266, our translation.

Mandel uses this ambiguity of the character of trade unions to explain why concepts that are perfectly compliant with the system exist and often even predominate in them. In order to fulfil their role as integral parts of the system – i.e. defend effectively the immediate material interests of wage labourers or at least significant sections of them – the trade unions depend on certain conditions that are not always in place. In particular, a certain economic situation is necessary, a situation in which more jobs are created than destroyed overall, and in which the capitalist class does not consider its fundamental interests undermined by the determination of wage levels through the fluctuations of the labour market. 'Historically, these conditions have only been realised in the west and only in the early imperialist phase of monopoly capitalism, roughly from 1890 to 1914'.[28]

Trade union organisations remain powerless in the event of long-term structural mass unemployment; and in times when the capitalist class sees its vital interests threatened by independent trade unions, it puts an end to their existence in one way or another.[29] Mandel certainly does not link the system-compliant orientation of trade unions with the problem of bureaucratisation in a mechanical fashion. This orientation is also the expression of a conception – illusory, in Ernest Mandel's view – that does not see the need for a revolutionary break with the capitalist system. Instead, it relies on the notion that the system can be gradually reformed. As was also the case with Bernstein's 'revisionism', this is linked to the prospect of a sustained, largely shock-free development of capitalism. It is also incompatible with the perspective of permanent mass unemployment, which is shifting the balance of power to the disadvantage of wage labourers. Mandel points to the world economic crisis of 1929–32 and the great catastrophes of the twentieth century, but also to the existence of post-capitalist societies spanning one third of the globe at the time of writing. The evolutionist belief in progress did not sit well with actual history. From this arose the need to adapt reality to one's own conception (originally envisaging a gradual, step-by-step abolition of the capitalist system). But the consequence was that the basic task of representing workers' interests often fell by the wayside:

> The trade union theories that were born out of hopes of gradual, uninterrupted progress proved incapable of solving the new historical tasks ... Holding on to pure trade union theory and practice inevitably led to the

---

28 Ibid, our translation.
29 Mandel 1978a, pp. 266–7.

conclusion that only a strong and healthy capitalism could grant wage increases. For this reason some were prepared to act as doctors at capitalism's sickbed ... The contradiction culminated when wage cuts were accepted in order to create a 'healthy' capitalism, i.e. to obtain wage increases later on. A trade union movement that could arrive at such absurd conclusions had obviously reached an impasse.[30]

It is only after this passage that Ernest Mandel invokes the material interests of the bureaucracy, which are tied to the continued existence of the trade unions themselves, but also to the institutions of class collaboration and therefore to bourgeois democracy. According to Mandel, late capitalism has pushed this situation in a new direction from the nineteen-forties onward, introducing a new quality of integration into the existing system. Yet, the same time, it has put the basis for the continued existence of the trade unions at risk, therefore jeopardising the status of the bureaucracy.

In late capitalism, due to the reduced turnaround time of fixed capital and the trend towards permanent technological innovation, there is a need for big business to budget its expenses – including wage expenditure – as precisely as possible. Wage costs and expenses for social benefits lend themselves to decision-making by way of politics and by involving the trade union leaders in relevant agreements. 'This automatically narrows the trade unions' traditional field of activity'.[31] The idea is to persuade them to refrain from fighting for substantial wage increases and social reforms even when the economic conditions are favourable.

At the same time, this fundamental trend of late capitalism in economic and social policy offers the trade union bureaucracy new prospects. Using the power of the organisation against the employers' representatives at the negotiating table is no longer the sole task. Now workers also have to be represented in the numerous state bodies of in the semi-state economic administration ... Ideologically, this deeper integration of the trade union bureaucracy into the late bourgeois state apparatus reflects the same desire for class collaboration and the same gradualist illusions as the previous wave of co-option did. Because 'social progress' is presumed to be determined by economic growth, it seems that the workers consequently have to take political responsibility for this growth ....[32]

---

30   Mandel 1978a, p. 268.
31   Mandel 1978a, p. 269, our translation.
32   Mandel 1978a, pp. 269–70, our translation.

But the integration of the trade union bureaucracy is, in turn, tied to certain conditions. First, the employers need the bureaucracy only for as long as they consider it capable of channelling workers' resistance from below. To succeed in this, the bureaucracy must to a certain extent retain the ability to act as a mobilising force. Moreover, the permanent debate about economic figures and their social implications brings the possibility of politicising broad sections of workers, thereby increasing their critical awareness and creating the 'danger' that they will experience and articulate dissatisfaction with their leadership's conformist policies.[33] Mandel invokes the great French mass strike movement in May 1968 (almost 10 million striking workers) and the one in Italy in 1969 (almost 15 million). According to him, the distinctive trait of these movements was that they went beyond plain demands for higher wages and shorter working hours. Instead, they posed questions about working conditions and the hierarchy in the enterprises, and ultimately even challenged the authority of the entrepreneurs and representatives of capital in the workplace.[34]

Naturally, Mandel continues, one should refrain from overly generalising the significance of these experiences. But at the very least, a trend towards new forms and objectives of struggle has emerged, which have a tendency to run free and evade the control of the bureaucracy. The ruling class tries to solve this problem by allowing 'co-management' – i.e. by involving workers in sharing responsibility for the success of capitalist enterprises. For Mandel, the hypothetical endpoint of such a development would be 'vertical unions' in which the bureaucrats become 'labour directors' representing the bosses, and where the union management agrees to wage cuts 'in the interest of the company'. Mandel writes: 'A "system-compliant" union integrated not only into the bourgeois state apparatus but also into the daily industrial management of capitalism would soon cease to be a real trade union at all'.[35] It would then turn from being a free trade union into a component of the administrative state apparatus, with the special task of administering a highly unpredictable commodity called labour power. Although this scenario has not fully materialised yet, the first steps in this direction of 'self-denial' have been taken in western Europe. Mandel's prognosis is optimistic, albeit subject to certain conditions: 'There is every reason to believe that the more class-conscious, radical and militant sections of the western European working class will reverse this process in due time. In the long run, however, this reversal will only be possible if the trade union movement thoroughly overhauls and reshapes its attitude to the problem of internal

---

33   See Mandel 1978a, p. 270.
34   See Mandel 1978a, p. 273.
35   See Mandel 1978a, p. 276, our translation.

trade union democracy, to the new tasks arising from the specific situation of late capitalism, and to the ultimate socialist goal of the labour movement'.[36]

According to Mandel, it is clear that the trade unions, unlike political organisations and parties, are not associations of like-minded people, but ideally comprise all workers regardless of their political beliefs. Programmatic trade union questions should therefore be treated differently from the programmatic questions of political parties. On the other hand, it takes a certain level of class consciousness to become a trade union member of your own free will. Normally only a minority of wage earners make this step, even if they number in the millions. For Mandel, the task of defending the elementary interests of workers cannot be logically separated from the struggle for an economic order that is subject to public economic imperatives rather than the private pursuit of profit.

In Mandel's view, the centralisation of trade unions is necessary in the face of the centralised power of big business, precisely in order to protect the interests of the weaker sections of wage earners. However, bureaucratic over-centralisation paralyses especially the most militant sections of the movement. Under pressure from the employers' side, the trade union bureaucracy assumes a disciplinary function against these sections. Bureaucratic 'deformation' corresponds to the growing 'passivity of trade union members'. This entails the danger that the unions can no longer rely on the enthusiasm and mobilisation of their members to defend themselves against anti-union campaigns launched by employers or political forces close to them. In response to these problems, Mandel calls for a democratisation of the trade unions: 'The only way to avoid the excesses of trade union centralisation is through the broadest internal trade union democracy. This means not only the duty to extensively inform, consult and involve the membership and activists prior to every important decision, but also the right of minorities to form associations in order to coordinate their actions at trade union meetings, at least partially, as efficiently as the apparatus can'.[37] Mandel does not accept the well-worn argument that the mass of members are themselves to blame for bureaucratisation because they are too passive and often 'more moderate than the apparatus'. He believes that people can only learn through practice, in this case through organising their own actions. Periodically it becomes apparent that significant numbers of workers take their actions further than their leaders would prefer them to. On the other hand, these leaders have the responsibility to systematically encourage and educate their members to act on their own initiative. If they failed to do this, the most

---

36   Mandel 1978a, p. 277, our translation.
37   Mandel 1978a, pp. 278–9, our translation.

likely result would be growing passivity within the 'legitimate' trade union framework, combined with a penchant for periodic radical action outside that framework.[38]

Mandel cites workers' control of production as a way to stimulate grass-roots activity. Unlike 'co-management', this concept does not involve sharing responsibility for the success of capitalist enterprises. At the height of the insurrectionary movement in Italy in 1920, which saw numerous factory occupations, 'workers' control' was a central demand. Moreover, this demand also ties in with the experience of strike movements in various western European countries from the early 1960s onward and with the mass strike movement of the late '6os. Free collective bargaining for trade unions and co-management for the maximisation of profits are incompatible, he argues, as is defending the interests of workers with subjugating them 'to the laws of movement of the capitalist mode of production'.[39] Workers' control of production involves the independent self-organisation of workers in the enterprise and the use of veto and monitoring rights, especially with respect to working conditions. This not only sows the seeds of 'dual rule' and of 'council rule', but also creates a powerful stimulus for trade union activity and internal union democracy, as long as the trade union 'is and remains an expression of the growing involvement of the mass of the wage-earning population in economic and social disputes'.[40]

Furthermore, Mandel proposes to strengthen international trade union action, which in his view lags far behind the objective requirements – this too, he argues, will counteract over-centralised bureaucratic tendencies.

> Another new task that the trade unions have to face with the development of late capitalism pushes in the same direction of more flexible forms of centralisation and internal trade union democracy: the objective of stronger international cooperation and integration. In the age of the multinational corporation, this is the only way to prevent, at least partially, the rapid shifting of contracts from one country to another, the rapid pitting of relatively low-waged workers against relatively high-waged workers by these international corporations. So far, the big trade union apparatuses have completely failed on the issue of international action. We are still waiting for the first European strike even though there are already so many European corporations. And when we see workers of such corpora-

---

38   See Mandel 1978a, p. 279.
39   Mandel 1978a, p. 280, our translation.
40   Mandel 1978a, p. 281, our translation.

tions going on strike in only one country, or when we witness how strikers in one industry are severely undermined by the rapid import of competing produce from a neighbouring country, it becomes clear that the multi-million strong 'official' trade union movement has accomplished less for international solidarity than have small, radical minority groups.[41]

For Mandel, grassroots and workplace level activity should be complemented by activity at corporation level – this combination should determine the form of international action. Technical centralisation may well be combined with the decentralisation of decision-making powers. Since Mandel believes that the democratic self-management of enterprises and of the economy is only possible when capital has been overthrown and capitalism abolished, these notions of democratisation primarily relate to decision-making processes that concern the actions, demands and organisations of the workers themselves.

In his pamphlet *On Bureaucracy*, Mandel distinguishes different stages of awareness of the problem of bureaucracy in the labour movement. Most of his examples concern the danger of bureaucratisation after the conquest of political power. However, the sections on Rosa Luxemburg and Lenin discuss their explanations of the phenomenon of bureaucratisation of mass workers' organisations under capitalism. We shall therefore address them in the present context.

Rosa Luxemburg critically examined the trade union bureaucracy and the transformation of the Social-Democratic Party of Germany (SPD) into a reformist party. She recognised earlier than others that these developments were engendering a new conservatism that could lead to counter-revolutionary politics in socially acute situations. The most important experience on which Rosa Luxemburg based her work was the Russian Revolution of 1905. Back then, it had become apparent, particularly in the historically relatively young industrial centres of the Tsarist Empire (to which Poland partly belonged), that millions of workers, most of whom had previously been active neither in trade union nor in political organisations, had created their own organs in struggle. In normal times, only a minority of the class is organised (Mandel does not consider this observation to apply universally, citing contemporary capitalist countries where more than half of all workers are unionised as counterexamples).[42]

---

41   Ibid.
42   Mandel 1976a, p. 27. [These remarks of Mandel's do not appear in the English-language version of the text (Mandel 1973f) – Translator.]

In times of revolutionary upsurge, in contrast, organs of self-activity arise from below. They capture the majority of the class; they are created to solve concrete problems and establish the unity of workers in action. These council organs cannot be created artificially or according to a predetermined model. The point is rather to find an organisational form that is '... best adapted to the aspirations of a given working class, in a given country, at a given time, to the possibilities of a decisive development of working class consciousness'.[43]

The left of the worker's movement at the time (we are talking about the period from 1907 to 1914 and the disputes within the Second International and its parties) had already developed a tradition of criticising political opportunism (the willingness to participate in bourgeois governments, then called 'Millerandism') and revisionism (Bernstein's theorisation of gradualist and reformist Social-Democratic practice). In Ernest Mandel's view, Rosa Luxemburg's merit in this debate is great, particularly because she saw through the fact that the bureaucracy of the labour movement was developing into a layer with its own special interests that had a tendency to integrate itself into bourgeois society and its state institutions.[44]

Nonetheless, Mandel believes that Rosa Luxemburg exaggerated with regard to this matter. He warns against 'ultra-left' conclusions and especially against drawing the equation, 'mass trade union movement = reactionary bureaucracy = betrayal'.[45] 'Those who argue this are forgetting that "the mass trade union movement is the objective expression of the collective force of the class during the period of social calm". When representatives of such 'ultra-left currents' say that in the advanced capitalist countries, the trade unions have become 'institutions of social welfare', or insurance associations dealing mainly with pensions and family allowances, they are to a degree objectively correct. However, Mandel warns, we must not forget that if these trade unions did not exist, the workers would have to solve all these problems on an individual basis. The relationship of forces would then be much more unfavourable, and they would not have any chance of winning anything at all'.[46]

A more nuanced view is needed, simply because the existence of trade unions represents progress when compared to a purely 'atomised' state of the working class. It is an expression of the development of an elementary stage of

---

43 Mandel 1973f, p. 17. In the German edition of Mandel's text, the sentence continues as follows: '... in accordance with the real historical objective: to mobilise the greatest possible number of workers for a clearly defined goal' (Mandel 1976a, p. 27, our translation).

44 See Mandel 1973f, p. 17.

45 Mandel 1973f, p. 18.

46 Ibid.

class consciousness.[47] According to Mandel, the dual nature of the trade unions corresponds to the dual character of the trade union bureaucracy: 'It is necessary to start from this dual nature of the trade-union bureaucracy in order to understand why, after fifty years of repeated betrayals by the bureaucracy, the workers remain strongly attached to these organizations. The workers know very well that trade unions are crucial to their day-to-day struggle against the capitalist bosses and that therefore it is not in their interest to abandon them'.[48]

Mandel's position on Lenin's theory of a 'working class aristocracy' is similarly nuanced. In principle he agrees with the notion, but he thinks that it must be used 'with great discretion'.[49] For Lenin, the conservative bureaucracy of the labour movement in the era of imperialism is based on a privileged stratum in the working class whose position is facilitated by colonial super-profits. Mandel argues that these colonial super-profits make up only a very small part of the profits of the bourgeoisie of the rich countries and therefore cannot explain the existence of the bureaucracies. Secondly, it would be objectively more accurate today to claim that the workers of the rich capitalist countries as a whole constitute a kind of 'aristocracy' when compared with the workers of the poor countries. After all, differences in wage levels within a given country are much smaller than those between different regions of the world.[50] What is more, the better-off strata of the working class have historically often played a leading role in the movement – this does not sit well with the theory of a 'working class aristocracy' at all:

> The German Communist Party became a mass party in the early twenties by winning over the metal-workers, who were the best-paid section of the German working-class at the time. The same is true in the case of France: the growth of the PCF after 1934 was based on its growth among workers of large enterprises, where wages were among the highest in the country. Thus it was the Renault workers rather than the textile workers of the North of France who Joined the Communist Party in large numbers; the latter have remained faithful to social democracy.[51]

Mandel's proposals on how to counter the problem of bureaucracy in the labour movement might be summed up thus:

---

47   Ibid.
48   Ibid.
49   Mandel 1973f, p. 19.
50   Ibid.
51   Mandel 1973f, pp. 19–20.

The problem of material privileges needs to be addressed without making it absolute. The implementation of the demand to pay no more than an average skilled worker's wage to full-timers is a function of consciousness. Strictly applied, it will therefore only be feasible among the most politically conscious strata. If the workers' movement applied this rule everywhere and under all circumstances, it would have to do without the participation of certain qualified individuals and ultimately weaken itself.

In Mandel's view, the erection of full-time apparatuses is necessary even if it creates the possibility of bureaucratisation. To dispense with workers' mass organisations, including full-time apparatuses, would be completely wrong under capitalism. It is nonetheless necessary to unite the most politically conscious elements in revolutionary organisations. During 'normal' periods under capitalism, these elements only ever constitute minorities in the class, and one must decide on a case-by-case basis whether they are to operate as independent organisations or as organised tendencies in larger parties. It is easier to prevent the bureaucratisation of such smaller political organisations, especially if they cultivate a lively dialogue with the most politically advanced sections of the working class. For the workers' mass organisations, especially the trade unions, Ernest Mandel recommends the formation of class-struggle tendencies, which also counteract the conservative inclinations of the bureaucracy. This requires the democratisation of the trade unions, i.e. the most extensive possible involvement of 'normal' members in the decision-making processes, and the freedom to form organised tendencies which offer alternatives to the existing leadership. Secondly, demands and strategies that promote the mobilisation of these members and of the working class as a whole must be developed – if necessary, through self-organised structures that are built up from below and include non-members. This is only possible by breaking with class collaboration ('social partnership') and confronting the bosses, their organisations and political representatives. Class autonomy, i.e. the organisational and political independence from the bourgeois forces, is an important prerequisite. Since the inclination of the bureaucracy to become a law unto itself is ultimately a function of the division of labour in class society, all of Mandel's proposed solutions stand and fall with the possibility of mobilising workers in great numbers. The monopoly on decision-making and administration is always a function of the relative passivity of the base. We will encounter this basic underlying idea again when dealing with the other aspects of the bureaucracy problem – for example, the problem of bureaucratisation of post-capitalist societies.

2   Critique of Stalinism

Mandel advocated a conception of 'Stalinism' that was quite different from
those that explained the Stalin era by pointing to the peculiarities, character
flaws, criminal tendencies etc. of Joseph Vissarionovich Jugashvili, commonly
known as Stalin. He also objected to the reduction of the problem with Stalinism to the 'cult of personality', which marked the beginning of the post-Stalin
era introduced by Khrushchev's assumption of office and the twentieth party
congress of the CPSU.

> Why mass terror? Why mass repression? Solzhenitsyn does not have an
> answer to this question. Because Stalin was an arch criminal and surroun-
> ded himself with mass murderers? To say so is merely to repeat the shal-
> low thesis of the 'cult of personality', which explains nothing. In contrast
> to every serious philosophy of history, and not just Marxist philosophy, it
> draws on the oldest and most unfounded of all historical myths: the myth
> of 'great men' (good and wicked) who 'make history', irrespective of social
> conditions and contradictions and irrespective of social forces.[52]

Following Trotsky's analysis (particularly his text 'What is the Soviet Union and
Where is it Going?', later published and known as *The Revolution Betrayed*),
Mandel regards Stalinism as the political expression of the emergence and
consolidation of the bureaucracy in the Soviet state.[53] By virtue of his personality traits, his biography, his actions, and his politics, Stalin as an individual
became the embodiment of the special interests of this bureaucracy. Mandel vehemently objects to the view held both by Stalinists and by bourgeois
ideologists that Stalinism is in continuity with the revolutionary Marxist and
communist traditions, with Lenin and Bolshevism. He stresses that a radical
rupture separates Stalinism from the latter tradition. Almost the entire stratum
of Bolsheviks left over from the revolutionary years had to be literally wiped
out so Stalinism could prevail.[54] In his article '30 Questions and Answers on
the History of the Communist Party of the Soviet Union', Mandel demonstrates
that post-Stalinist official historiography, while abandoning some gross distortions of party history, was still far from telling the truth.[55] He points out that
most of the leading Bolsheviks from Lenin's days were murdered. Trotsky's 1939

---

52   Mandel 1974d, our translation.
53   See Trotsky 1996.
54   See Mandel 1974a.
55   Mandel 2016, p. 233.

article 'A Graphic History of Bolshevism' showed that literally the whole generation of leading Bolsheviks from Lenin's day fell victim to Stalinist terror.[56] The
successors of those who were liquidated were also liquidated shortly after. Evidently, Stalin and his faction needed to draw a bloody line between themselves
and the living memory of the October Revolution and its early years.[57] Initially,
Mandel links the victory of Stalinism in the Soviet Union, in the Communist
Party of the Soviet Union and in the Communist world movement to objective
tendencies. However, he does not present this development as inevitable. A different policy, such as the one formulated by the Left Opposition in the Soviet
Communist Party from 1923, would not only have helped to prevent the worst
excesses, but – despite all the problems inherent in the historical situation –
it might have helped the emancipatory tendencies to unfold. This alternative
concerned party democracy and economic and international policy (especially
the policies of the Stalinist-led Communist Third International and later the
Cominform), and from 1933 culminated in calls to restore Soviet democracy,
including party pluralism, and build new Communist Parties and a Fourth
International. In *Introduction to Marxism*, Mandel summarises the alternative
advocated by the Left Opposition as follows:

> The programme of the Trotskyist Left Opposition was aimed entirely at
> creating the favourable conditions needed to put the situation to rights:
> (a) by accelerating the industrialisation of Russia, thus increasing the
> specific weight of the proletariat in society; (b) by increasing wages and
> fighting unemployment, with a view to increasing the confidence of the
> working masses in themselves; (c) by immediately increasing democracy
> in the soviets and in the party, with a view to raising the level of political
> activity and class consciousness of the proletariat; (d) by accentuating the
> class differences within the peasantry: providing credit and agricultural
> machinery to help the poor peasants, while burdening the rich peasants
> with increased taxes; (e) by continuing to look towards the world revolu-
> tion, and by rectifying the tactical and strategic errors of the Comintern.[58]

Mandel's point of departure for assessing the reasons for the rise of Stalinism
is the international situation at the time, which was characterised by a series of
working-class defeats in the global revolutionary process. In his view, the failure of the German Revolution in 1923 was a definite turning point: it marked

---

56   See Trotsky 1939.
57   Ibid.
58   Mandel 1979a, p. 111.

the end of all revolutionary prospects for Germany for the time being (even if there were still revolutionary possibilities in some countries after that date, Hitler's seizure of power and the defeat of the Spanish Revolution consolidated the domination of conservative elements in the Soviet Union as well). It was only then that Stalin began to advance the slogan of 'socialism in one country', whereas the Bolshevik tradition had always regarded the fate of the early Soviet republic as being closely linked to the world revolutionary process, especially to the prospects of socialist revolution in the developed industrial capitalist countries. According to Trotsky, for the Soviet bureaucracy the slogan of building 'socialism in one country' was an adequate expression of its need for 'peace and order', for the maintenance and consolidation of what had been achieved – as opposed to uncertain world-revolutionary daydreams that might even have challenged its own privileged position if put into practice. These are the same conservative instincts that prevail in the labour bureaucracies in general. The only difference is that in this case the bureaucracy is not only based on trade union and party organisations, but on power over a state apparatus that has been gradually merged with the apparatus of the party.[59]

The Russian revolution of 1917 did not take place in a colony or in a dependent country. By Lenin's definition, Tsarist Russia was an imperialist country too, albeit a very weak one. Russia was a backward country with a large peasant majority – the working class constituted but a small section of the population. The conditions for initiating a process toward the realisation of the Paris Commune programme as interpreted by Marx – i.e. the management of the economy and country by the popular masses and comprehensive political democracy from below – were therefore conceivably poor. For this reason, the October Revolution was only the first link in a chain of revolutions as far as the Bolsheviks were concerned. These revolutions would eventually allow for the construction of socialism, based on the appropriation of the productive potentials developed within the framework of globally dominant capitalism.[60] In addition to backwardness, the Bolsheviks had to grapple with the consequences of civil war, including the need to repel foreign counterrevolutionary intervention. This involved not only material setbacks, but also the loss of a great number of people. Countless enthusiastic, politically committed workers and staunch Bolsheviks lost their lives. Many of the politically conscious workers who survived were sucked into the early administrative apparatus. Those who had opposed the October Revolution tried to come to

---

59   Mandel 1979a, p. 108 et seq.
60   See Mandel 1970e.

terms with the new system and find some comfortable place in it. In Mandel's view, it was the decline in revolutionary enthusiasm and in the self-activity of the working class, both in Soviet Russia and internationally, that so greatly contributed to the rise of the bureaucracy.[61] In the Soviet Union, even high-ranking officials initially had no material privileges in the real sense. People's Commissars and members of the politburo received only the 'party maximum' (i.e. the highest permittable party salary), which was equivalent to the average wage of a skilled worker. They did not have to starve, but they were expected to show special commitment and an exceptional willingness to make sacrifices. The first groups to gain privileges were specially qualified technicians and other skilled workers. The early Soviet government 'bribed' them, so to speak, with an above-average standard of living as an incentive for their cooperation.

With the rise of Stalinism, the 'party maximum' was abolished. A hierarchically tiered system of functional privileges took shape. Through their monopoly of power, those at the top of the hierarchy granted themselves a standard of living many times higher than that of ordinary workers. This was the basis on which the party and state bureaucracies merged. The special interests of this stratum of administrators in offices, the army and factories (where factory directors ruled with almost unlimited authority) largely determined economic policy, but also international policy. The interests of this bureaucracy were enforced by the secret services and, at its peak in the second half of the 1930s, by a wave of repression that took on monstrous proportions. Thanks to *glasnost*, Mandel was later able to exemplify the explosive development of bureaucratisation under Stalin's rule with precise data. One important factor was the number of full-timers: 'Much has recently come to light about the growth of the bureaucratic apparatus, the extent of its privileges and its near-absolute power in Soviet Russia since the early twenties. The apparatus of full-time functionaries in the Communist Party soared from barely 700 in 1919 to 15,300 in 1922 and more than 100,000 some years later. Whereas the initial 700 were elected by the rank and file, the 15,300 were appointed by the centre and welded into a clientele structure owing allegiance, and their own job security, to the Party Secretariat and its general secretary, J.V. Stalin'.[62]

Mandel cites an article by the Soviet historian Alexandr Podchekoldin, who describes how in 1922 central authorities such as the central committee instructors and the central committee secretariat gained decisive influence on the party-internal regional election processes. They also began to exercise con-

---

61   Mandel 1979a, p. 110; Mandel 1976a, p. 37 et seq.
62   Mandel 1992a, pp. 72–3.

trol over the local party organisations. The creation of hierarchically graded material privileges was an important instrument to ensure subservience and obedience among functionaries.

'Illegally violating the principle of the "party maximum", Stalin began to distribute hierarchically differentiated monetary and non-monetary advantages to members of the apparatus, whose total remuneration had reached ten times the average worker's wage by 1923–24. From the thirties on, these material privileges grew and became institutionalized in a monstrous way – bloated incomes, special shops, weekend houses (dachas), private rooms in hospitals, special education camouflaged as "schools for the gifted", reserved access to foreign travel, and so on'.[63] This situation was already fully fledged under Stalin and even more blatant than under Khrushchev and in the later post-Stalin era.[64]

By and large, it remained characteristic of the bureaucratic ruling stratum of the Soviet Union even after Stalin's death, though of course the fact that the period of mass liquidations was over made a serious difference. How little such privileges have to do with 'socialism' should be obvious. Mandel quotes from the autobiography of Boris Yeltsin, who described this system of carefully graded privileges not least with reference to his own position. You had a lot to lose if you did not conform to the wishes of the leadership:

> Obsequiousness and obedience are rewarded in turn by privileges: special hospitals; special sanatoria; the excellent Central Committee canteen; the equally excellent service for home delivery of groceries and other goods; the Kremlin-line closed telephone system; the free transportation. The higher one climbs up the professional ladder, the more there are comforts that surround one, and the harder and more painful it is to lose them ... It has all been carefully devised: a section chief does not have a personal car, but he has the right to order one from the Central Committee car pool for himself and his immediate staff. The deputy head of a department already has his personal Volga car, while the head has another Volga, fitted with a car phone. But if you have climbed your way to the top of the establishment pyramid, then it's 'full communism' ... Even at my level as a candidate member of the Politburo, my domestic staff consisted of three cooks, three waitresses, a housemaid, and a gardener with his own team of under-gardeners ... The dacha had its own cinema, and every Friday, Sat-

---

63   Mandel 1992a, p. 73.
64   Mandel dismisses claims to the contrary as 'Maoist myths'.

urday and Sunday a projectionist would arrive, complete with a selection of films. As for medical treatment, the medicines and equipment are all imported, and all of them the last word in scientific research and technology. The wards of the 'Kremlin hospital care' are huge suites, again surrounded by luxury: porcelain, crystal, carpets and chandeliers ... The 'Kremlin ration', a special allocation of normally unobtainable products, is paid for by the uppermost echelon at half its cost price, and consists of the highest quality foods. In Moscow, a total of some 40,000 people enjoy the privilege of receiving these special rations.[65]

Mandel did not compile such examples in order to discredit the Soviet Union and similar societies vis-à-vis the capitalist west. It was the contrast between socialist ideals and the cultivated social inequality of 'actually existing socialism' that he found particularly reprehensible and demoralising:

> Of course, we should never forget that such privileges are really trifling in comparison with the wealth of top monopolists and top gangsters in capitalist countries. Here we have billionaires: there we have mere millionaires, or people owning even less than the equivalent of a million dollars. Nevertheless, from a psychological point of view, these differences in structure and power hardly modify the indignation and sense of betrayal felt by working people in the post-capitalist societies. As Angelica Babanova pointed out long ago, it is one thing when a capitalist who never claimed to defend social equality and justice cynically enjoys luxury amidst mass deprivation. It is quite another thing when people claiming to be socialists or communists no less cynically draw comforts, be they minor or major, amidst much greater penury.[66]

Apart from the relevant sections in Trotsky's *The Revolution Betrayed*, the classic contemporary account of the changing mentality of political functionaries in light of their monopoly on power and materially privileged situation is found in a much earlier text, namely Christian Rakovsky's letter to Nikolai Valentinov, 'The "Professional Dangers" of Power' (1928), which had certainly inspired Trotsky.[67] This was the tradition that Mandel adhered to, and he defended Trotsky's assessment of the Soviet bureaucracy and Stalinism his entire life. For him, it represented an important contribution to the theoretical arsenal of Marxism:

---

65   Mandel 1992a, p. 73.
66   Mandel 1992a, p. 74.
67   Rakovsky 1928.

'Trotsky's main contribution was to transform the theories of bureaucratiza-tion of workers' organizations into a coherent theory of the bureaucracy in a workers' state'.[68]

Consequently, Mandel attempted an independent examination of the eco-nomic development of the Soviet Union after World War II within the outlines of this basic position, analysing the contradictions of a system that he con-ceived of as a bureaucratised transitional society stuck between capitalism and socialism. Mandel opposed the notion of a 'socialist market economy'.[69] For him, the continued existence of commodities was inevitable in transitional societies. However, he was in favour of pushing back money and commodity economy as far as possible, yet without resorting to a policy of allocation in the consumption sector. Crucial to his understanding of transitional societies was that economic priorities are not determined by the law of value, despite the inevitable survival of money and commodities. He considered these societies contradictory, expressions of a 'necessity' that must not be made a 'virtue'. Fol-lowing Marx (who had implied as much in *Critique of the Gotha Programme*), Mandel viewed the contradiction between socialised means of production and the persistence of 'bourgeois norms of distribution' as central to transitional societies between capitalism and socialism.[70] In his view, the introduction of profitability as a criterion, individual farms, and the strong position of factory directors had already been mistakes in Lenin and Trotsky's days. Under Stalin, these mistakes were carried to extremes when all means of workers' protec-tion against the management – the involvement of party, union and workers' representatives, the independence of unions, etc – were removed. Although in Mandel's view, this did not constitute a return to the capitalist mode of produc-tion, it was still an expression of social regression that undermined solidarity among workers.[71] In his later writings, Mandel provides an answer to a question that was never conclusively or satisfactorily answered by Trotsky and his associ-ates. When did the 'Soviet Thermidor' begin? Mandel firmly rejected the thesis (put forward by anarchists and others) that the victory of the bureaucracy had already been achieved by the October Revolution, through the measures taken by the Bolshevik leadership in the civil war, or with the introduction of the New Economic Policy (even if he expressed criticism of such policies). In Mandel's view, a bloody 'civil war' had been necessary for the bureaucracy under Stalin to triumph. However, he dated the beginning of the Thermidor to 1923, the year

---

68   Mandel 1973c, p. 20. See also Mandel 1979e, p. 87 and Trotsky 1995, p. 32 et seq.
69   Mandel 1968b, p. 569 et seq.
70   See Mandel 1968b p. 654 et seq.
71   Mandel 1973c, p. 29.

when Stalin had gained central control of the party apparatus, while material privileges for top officials had already gone through the roof:

> If, as a Marxist, one looks at the conflicts between the oppositional groups, mainly the Left Opposition, on the one hand, and the 'hard core' of the Stalinist faction (the big majority of whom were also victims of the terror) on the other hand, and if we take into account the massive scale of the terror (we repeat: one million communists murdered), then there can be very little doubt about the civil war-like character of the terror. Supporters of the Marxist theory of historical materialism do not explain civil wars as inter-personal conflicts but as conflicts between social classes or major sections of social classes. In this sense, the bloody mass purges in the Soviet Union were the civil war-like endphase of the political counter-revolution in that country. Trotsky's struggle against the counter-revolution expressed historically the socio-political conflict between the Soviet proletariat and the Soviet bureaucracy. For Stalin to win this bloody civil war, it was essential for him to exercise political power. This assessment of the nature of the Yezhovshchina enables us also to come to a conclusion on the question of the beginning of the Soviet Thermidor, a question that occupied Trotsky for more than fifteen years and on which he changed his mind a number of times. When did the Soviet Thermidor begin? The answer is: in 1923. At the Trotsky Symposium held in Wuppertal, Germany, in 1990, Professor Pechekoldin, who had access to secret Soviet archives, stated that in 1923 the standard of life of a top functionary at the regional level was nine times higher, of a top functionary at Central Committee level thirty times higher than that of the average skilled worker.[72]

Mandel shared Trotsky's perspective of a 'political revolution' in the Soviet Union and similar countries in order to restore authentic council democracy and clear the path toward socialism. Despite all the ills of bureaucratic administration, he viewed the state-owned industry and state monopoly on foreign trade as historic gains of the October Revolution that had to be defended against all attempts, internal or external, at capitalist restoration. According to Mandel, a conquest of political power by the working class, coupled with the toppling of the bureaucracy, would leave the non-capitalist foundations untouched, but fundamentally change the political situation. To the extent that

---

72 Mandel 1995a, p. 52.

the bureaucracy is understood as an 'outgrowth', a privileged stratum or usurp-atory Thermidorian caste within the working class, revolution does not imply that the rule of one class is replaced by the rule of another. That is why Man-del, like Trotsky, described it as a 'political revolution' as opposed to a social revolution. Such a revolution would nevertheless fundamentally change the management of the economy, the administration of enterprises, and the form and content (prioritisation) of the planned economy.[73]

> In the bureaucratised workers states, the masses rise up to obtain demo-cratic freedoms against the bureaucracy's monopoly over the exercise of power, against the reappearance of national oppression, against cor-ruption, waste, and the material privileges which characterise the bur-eaucratic management of the economy. They demand the running of the workers' state by the workers themselves, organised in their coun-cils (soviets) with a plurality of parties and full democratic rights for all, the management of the planned economy by a system of democratically centralised workers' councils. This is the strategy of the political antibur-eaucratic revolution.[74]

This prospect has not materialised. It is therefore important for our investig-ation of Mandel's conception to identify the reasons for its failure. We can-not accept the official 'Marxist-Leninist' position as an alternative because the 'superiority' of the 'socialist camp' has proved to be a chimera. On the other hand, when the apologists of this 'camp' argued against attempts at demo-cratic socialist change, they denounced any challenge to the existing Soviet system as a gateway to capitalist restoration. In this negative and very limited sense, they might feel vindicated in retrospect. It is true that what had begun as mass protest against those who ruled the system and as an attempt to reform it democratically culminated in a return to the capitalist market economy – to be precise, a deformed, weak, dependent capitalist market economy inferior to the metropolises and for the most part subservient to them. We must therefore investigate why and to what extent Mandel had underestimated the danger of restoration (we will return to this in the subchapters on Gorbachev and Man-del's reaction to the epochal rupture of 1989/90).

One alternative assessment to Mandel's more or less orthodox Trotskyist analysis of the Soviet Union and similar countries was the notion that a 'state-

---

73   Mandel 1973c, pp. 31–2.
74   Mandel 1979a, p. 127.

capitalist' system had developed. Tony Cliff was a prominent exponent of this thesis.[75] Mandel's main objections to this theory were these: In the Soviet Union, neither the major means of production nor labour power could ever be freely bought and sold in the market. They therefore never became commodities – state ownership and the monopoly on foreign trade prevented any such development. Although the law of value retained influence in those countries, it did not substantially regulate production. In contrast to the capitalist system, the centrally drawn-up plan – albeit bureaucratic and problematic in many regards – always determined the course of the economy.[76]

The important characteristic of the market economy is that it can only determine after the accomplished fact whether certain investments or work done was 'socially necessary' or 'superfluous'. Mandel argues that this generally did not apply to the economies of the Soviet Union and similar countries. Moreover, the actual capitalists, the bosses of the big corporations, and the bourgeois politicians of the western imperialist countries have always been well aware of these differences and acted accordingly. The scope of trade between the western and the 'state-trading countries' was always much smaller than between capitalist nations. The ultimate objective of restoring capitalism in these countries was the decisive factor in the confrontation between the 'western' and 'eastern' blocs.[77]

Unlike a capitalist ruling class, the bureaucracy is not deeply rooted in the relations of production to which it owes its parasitic existence (for Mandel, that mode of production is ambivalent, i.e. neither capitalist nor socialist). Mandel reckons that as soon as broad movements which cannot be suppressed without outside intervention emerge from below – especially movements fighting for democratic rights – the bureaucratic system of rule is therefore bound to collapse rather unceremoniously. Moreover, the notion that one capitalism ('state capitalism') was simply replaced by another does not explain why the collapse of the post-Stalinist regimes and restoration of capitalism came as a bitter setback and defeat of historic proportions not only to the 'official' Communist movement, but to the entire socialist and communist left – including the class-struggle trade union left and the harshest critics of bureaucratic rule. When all is said and done, this can only be explained by the fact that these systems were linked to the gains of the October Revolution. In this sense, Mandel felt vindicated against the exponents of the 'state capitalism' thesis until the end.

---

75   See Cliff 2018.
76   See Mandel 1969a.
77   See Mandel 1986c.

Those who identified the USSR with state capitalism are thus left in a quandary: how can capitalism be restored if the state is already under capitalism? It is of no avail to argue that state capitalism is different from private capitalism. For if the difference is qualitative, what is the point of calling them both capitalism? And if the difference is only quantitative, it becomes impossible to explain how such minor changes could have produced a profound, systemic upheaval in several East European countries. It would hardly seem a minor difference whether or not an economy is ruled by the law of value, but in the cases of the former GDR, Poland or Hungary that is now precisely what is at issue in the transition from one system to another.[78]

Contending against other alternative viewpoints such as the notion of 'bureaucratic collectivism' or the interpretation of the ruling bureaucracy as a 'new (exploitative) class' proved more problematic for Mandel. The following line of argument appears somewhat scholastic, for instance: 'Then there are those who see in the bureaucracy of the workers' states a new social class historically progressive in relation to the bourgeoisie. This position would lead the proletariat to support another class, the bureaucracy, in its struggle against the bourgeoisie and imperialism, i.e. it denies the proletariat the leading role in the world revolution'.[79] The same problem is evident in the fact that Mandel always remained faithful to the traditional Trotskyist terminology when discussing this subject (even though Trotsky himself had expressed the hope that more adequate terms would eventually be found). In the Soviet Union and in similar countries, the working class remained disenfranchised for decades, and it goes without saying that did not exercise political rule. Even so, expressing his partisan defence of these countries against the bourgeois forces, the orthodox Trotskyist Mandel spoke of 'workers' states' until the end, despite all criticism and despite his call for a political revolution. We ought to add that he always specified that these workers' states were either 'bureaucratically degenerated' or 'bureaucratically deformed from the outset'.[80] Mandel argued that a political revolution would make the task of defending these states against world capitalism much easier. The erection of a socialist-democratic regime would make them far more attractive to the western working class and socialist intelligentsia.

---

78   Mandel 1992a, pp. 1–2.
79   Mandel 1973c, p. 34.
80   Mandel 1979d, pp. 153–4. Winfried Wolf criticises Mandel's clinging to these terms – see Wolf's eyewitness testimony.

Mandel did not define bureaucratic privileges as 'exploitation' in the scientific Marxist sense since they remained functionally tied and linked to the state ownership of the means of production. Once again, he felt his critical stance thoroughly vindicated by later developments: because bureaucratic rule did collapse relatively 'easily' (certainly a striking argument against the theorists of totalitarianism, according to whom these systems could not have been overthrown from the inside at all):

All those who characterized the bureaucracy as a new ruling class look even more misguided in the light of events in Eastern Europe. What kind of new ruling class is it which goes so far towards liquidating itself, which abdicates a large part of its power with lightning speed, in Poland and Hungary not even under the pressure of a revolutionary mass movement? A new ruling class which proves incapable of reproducing its rule after being in existence for three-quarters of a century? A new ruling class which rules through no distinctive form of appropriation of the social surplus product?[81]

The collapse of bureaucratic rule in favour of capitalist restoration (or enabling a process that would culminate in restoration) did not yield any progress in an emancipatory sense. The economic and social disaster in these countries and their relapse into direct dependence on the capital of the developed (imperialist) industrial capitalist countries was, in Mandel's eyes, proof that the defence of state-owned planned economies – however rudimentarily, potentially or incompletely socialised – was politically necessary.

In his later statements on this topic, Mandel self-criticises only his failure to recognise the erosion of the subjective conditions for a political revolution or a development towards socialist democracy. 'Revolutionary Marxists', he argues, underestimated the corrosive effect of decades of bureaucratic-authoritarian rule on class consciousness in these countries:

We have to admit that revolutionary Marxists seriously underestimated the disastrous long-term effects of Stalinism and bureaucratic dictatorship on the average level of consciousness. The balance-sheet which the great majority of toilers in these countries have drawn from their exper-

---

81   Mandel 1992a, p. 2. [In the German edition of Mandel's text, this section ends with the following additional sentence: 'It is difficult to refute what we predicted many years ago: if a new ruling class were to emerge in the USSR, it would not be "new" at all, but the good old capitalist ruling class', our translation – Translator.]

ience is that bureaucratic dictatorship totally failed to assure the level of consumption and freedom to which they aspire. As decades of Stalinist indoctrination – supported by the bourgeois ideological offensive – told them that these bureaucratic regimes were socialist, the bankruptcy of Stalinism appeared in their eyes as the bankruptcy of communism, Marxism and even socialism tout court. This created in their midst a tremendous ideological-moral vacuum. And since society, like nature, abhors a vacuum, ideological currents distinct from and opposed to socialism – from pro-capitalist social democracy and bourgeois liberalism to religious fundamentalism, racist chauvinism and outright fascism – have found it possible to penetrate these societies and make considerable headway.[82]

We shall return to the question to what extent Mandel underestimated or misjudged other factors and therefore remained too optimistic about chances for emancipatory movements in these countries or saw the existing developments in too rosy a light – at least in hindsight in light of the actual results. In the quoted text, which he wrote late (after 1990 in any event), he argued that in the Soviet Union, which has 'the strongest working class in the world, and one of the most skilled and most cultivated', capitalist restoration was 'not inevitable'.[83] Underlying this were certain analytical deficiencies, which were perhaps partly owned to a lack of information, but to some degree also linked to the analytical tools and theoretical and programmatic prior knowledge with which Mandel approached the information available to him. In any case, it will make more sense to discuss this question later, i.e. once we have evaluated Mandel's assessment of the 'crisis of Stalinism' and of 'glasnost and perestroika'.

Mandel's critique of the foreign policy of the Soviet Union and the international policy of the 'official' (Stalinist and post-Stalinist) Communist movement revolves around the argument that it was determined by the diplomatic interests of the Soviet Union and/or the Kremlin bureaucracy.[84] Even the Left Opposition had criticised the subordination to a Social-Democratic trade union bureaucracy in the case of the Anglo-Russian Committee, the subordination to the bourgeois Kuomintang in China, the failure in the struggle against Nazism, and subsequently the policy of the 'popular front'. It did not deny that the Soviet Union had a right to manoeuvre between the hostile imperialist powers and form different alliances depending on the situation. However, it

---

82   Mandel 1992a, p. 5.
83   Ibid.
84   See Mandel 1970e.

objected to the way in which the policies of the Communist Parties were subordinated to these manoeuvres: During the period of the Hitler-Stalin Pact, for instance, the Communist parties stopped agitating against Hitler and German imperialism, and they suspended agitation against bourgeois rule in the western parliamentary democracies when entering an alliance with the western imperialist powers. Even the Communist International was formally dissolved in 1943, and in conversation with an American journalist, Stalin referred to the idea that he and his comrades were pursuing a socialist world revolution as a 'tragi-comic misunderstanding'.[85]

Following on from Trotsky and the Left Opposition's criticism of this policy, Mandel regarded the policy of 'peaceful coexistence' as an expression of the interest of the Soviet bureaucracy in maintaining the status quo internationally. This line was wrongly attributed to Lenin, who only stated that periods of ceasefire between states were necessary, including normal diplomatic and trade relations – as opposed to a permanent state of war. According to Mandel, in the pre-Stalinist period the Bolsheviks saw the defence of the Soviet Union as an integral part of the overall goal of world socialist revolution. They would never have taken a diplomatic measure which entailed that the Communist Parties in the capitalist countries suspend revolutionary propaganda. Bureaucratic conservatism, however, led to a situation in which the Communist Parties, kept on a leash by the Kremlin, stifled revolutionary opportunities instead of promoting them. Thus, under Stalin, the pact with Hitler entailed the abandonment of the anti-fascist struggle, while the alliance with the western powers translated into the abandonment of any anti-capitalist activity by the western Communist parties. Such was the policy of the Stalinist-led Communist parties in western Europe after World War II: sticking to the diplomatically agreed outcomes of the war, they supported bourgeois governments and did much to ensure that countries such as Italy, Greece and France took a capitalist road again. Socialist revolutions driven by an upsurge in the self-activity of the working class in the developed capitalist countries would have been the death knell for the Kremlin bureaucracy and its allies.[86]

In principle, the Kremlin bureaucracy was quite willing to expand the borders of its sphere of influence, but only if it could maintain military, police and political control of such changes, and therefore not fundamentally challenge the rule of imperialism. More than anything, it was wary of triggering a wave of self-activity, i.e. an independent movement of the working class: 'When neces-

---

85   Ibid.
86   Ibid.

sary this bureaucracy does not hesitate to cross national boundaries and extend its power over other countries – provided this can be accomplished without the proletariat becoming re-politicized on a dangerous scale in the process'.[87]

Mandel does not promote an adventurous policy of permanent political-military confrontation with imperialism, as advocated, for example, by Posadas, who in the latter part of his life suffered from megalomania (he called for 'pre-emptive nuclear strikes' against the US, which proved a welcome occasion for the apologists of 'actually existing socialism' to reassert once more just how irresponsible 'the Trotskyists' were). However, he favours a policy which, within the existing balance of powers, is aimed entirely at expanding the non-capitalist part of the world through independent mass movements. For him, any theorising that could hinder the development of socialist class consciousness and sow confusion in the minds of advanced workers must be avoided in the context of such a policy. He therefore thinks it wrong to fraudulently appeal to Lenin and speak of 'peaceful coexistence' in the strategic sense, making a virtue of the reality of existing power relations. Ultimately, the imperialist bourgeoisie must be disarmed, and it is the duty of socialists and communists to encourage the workers and all strata of the exploited and oppressed to overthrow bourgeois rule. Mandel summarises his alternative to the policy of 'peaceful coexistence' as follows:

> The alternative to the illusions of 'socialism in one country' and 'peaceful coexistence' is not 'revolutionary war' launched by Moscow, 'preventive nuclear war', or 'simultaneous revolution' everywhere which is irresponsible adventurism. It is a comprehensive and coordinated strategy of world revolution, which is based upon support for revolutionary uprisings in a successive and growing number of countries, as a function of the maturing of favorable conditions for these uprisings inside the respective countries. It is, in a word, class struggle united in a dialectical way, on a world scale. And in the long run, the class struggle and the socialist revolution in the imperialist countries themselves will play the key role in the final test of strength globally.[88]

---

87   Mandel 1973c, p. 31. [In the German edition of Mandel's text, this section contains another sentence that is missing from the English version: 'This occurred in a number of countries after World War II, but only where the Red Army was strong enough to prevent a workers' uprising that might have unleashed a political revolution on an international scale', our translation – Translator.]

88   Mandel 1970e.

If we accept Mandel's view that the bureaucratisation of the Soviet system and the associated triumph of Stalinism was based on objective conditions, but not inevitable – at least in the extreme form in which it occurred – and if we further assume, following Mandel, that Trotsky and the Left Opposition proposed the right solutions at the time, then the question arises how the Stalin faction was able to prevail. Taking into account the conditions at the time, namely the ban on other Soviet parties and on factions within the only remaining legal party, we must ask why it was not possible to win majorities against Stalin and for a resolute fight against the bureaucratisation of the leadership of the ruling Bolshevik Party.[89] Mandel does not explain this simply by pointing to material corruption. Rather, he argues that Stalin succeeded in eliminating all potential contenders for an effective counter-position against his policies and his own growing power one by one: 'True, between 1923 and 1936 most of the old Bolshevik-leaders came to realize the monstrous nature of bureaucratic power; but this realization came too late. Their failure to perceive the real danger in time, coupled with their inability to see the historical significance of the factional struggles in which they took part, meant that the process of bureaucratic degeneration proceeded uninterrupted'.[90]

Mandel later confirmed this assessment and, based on newly available material, examined the fate of Nikolai Bukharin by way of example. Bukharin and other 'old Bolsheviks' made a big mistake in their support for Stalin and when polemicising against the Left Opposition regarding the pace of economic construction, international strategy, policies with respect to small peasant owners, and so on: they underestimated the question of bureaucratisation, and most of all, they underestimated the extent to which the leadership of the party apparatus was merging with the leadership of the state bureaucracy. Towards the end of his life, Bukharin himself expressed extremely astute insights into this. But by then, his fate had already been decided, and Bukharin's pleas to his former ally in factional struggle, Stalin, could not change this.[91] However, Mandel also mentions that many members of the Left Opposition – e.g. Preobrazhensky and Radek – who had previously analysed the problem with great foresight, later made the same mistake: they wrongly believed that Stalin had more or less begun to implement the economic policy originally proposed by the opposition, especially when he turned 'against the kulaks' or to 'forced collectivisation'. It is true that this abrupt and brutal bureaucratic

---

89　We will address Mandel's criticisms of the ban on other parties and on factions in the Bolshevik Party in our subchapter on 'Substitutionism'.

90　Mandel 1973c, p. 27.

91　See Mandel 1992a, p. 131 et seq.

U-turn indirectly confirmed the economic policy arguments of the Left Opposition (or the United Opposition, where Stalin's former main allies against Trotsky, Zinoviev and Kamenev, were active). But this did not change the main
issue, namely that the new policy served to consolidate the bureaucratic dictatorship rather than strengthen the working class economically or politically.[92]

New aspects of Mandel's critique of Stalinism, especially with respect to
labour organisation under conditions of a bureaucratised non-capitalist society, can be found in his relatively late text *Power and Money*. The continuing inner hierarchy in the enterprises means that the labour process is controlled from above, which results in deep frustration. Consumption offers an
escape and is encouraged by the bureaucracy as a lesser evil compared to self-
management aspirations. In this way, the workers' disinterest in 'their' workplaces (referred to as such by officialdom) increases even more. According to
Mandel, the fact that in transitional societies the 'professional' or 'technical'
division of labour is continued for prolonged periods should not tempt us into
arguing that the social division of labour must be perpetuated in production
itself. The emancipatory goal of self-determined development through socialised labour can only be effectively pursued through abolishing the social division of labour between planners and implementers, between administrators
and managers, between those who give instructions and oversee their implementation and the producers.[93]

3   Breaking Up Stalinist Monolithism and the 'Socialist Camp'

After the end of World War II, the few members of the Fourth International
were faced with many new problems. The new developments had not been
expected to happen in this way. Despite significant revolutionary surges, which
nonetheless remained rudimentary or isolated, capitalist society, especially in
western Europe, had not been upset in the same way as in the period after
World War I. For the members of the FI, the revolutionary experiences from
1917 and 1918 had been the blueprint for their designs for a new post-war period,
as anticipated in the *Transitional Programme*. Another unexpected important
outcome was that the ruling bureaucracy of the Soviet Union had consolidated its power and extended its sphere of influence. The third was the victory

---

92   Mandel 1992a, pp. 140–1.
93   Mandel 1992a, p. 78 et seq.

of revolutions in Yugoslavia and China that involved the elimination of bourgeois rule and the abolition of capitalism, but were led by parties that were at least formally part of 'official' Communism rather than 'Trotskyist' forces. All of this continued for decades – until the collapse of the Soviet Union and its allied regimes. The Kremlin bureaucracy remained in power. New revolutions occurred, like those in Vietnam and Cuba, and the same that applied to China and Yugoslavia was also true for them. For decades, those who adhered to Trotsky's analyses and the programmatic foundations of the Fourth International had to face the challenge of analysing the new situation and revaluating their theoretical and programmatic tradition against it. As is well known, different responses to this challenge have led to in divisions in the Trotskyist world movement.[94]

At a young age, just after World War II, Ernest Mandel was already a leading figure in the Fourth International alongside Pablo (Michel Raptis). He was regarded as a kind of prodigy, owing to his intellectual proficiency, his already vast knowledge, and his ability to think independently, offer captivating analyses of social processes, and articulate revolutionary-socialist perspectives in a compelling fashion.[95] From then on, he played an important role in the development of the Fourth International's positions on these issues. Because he always endeavoured to ensure continuity with Trotsky's most important positions and the programmatic legacy of the Fourth International, his own theoretical contribution in the stricter sense is not always easy to discern. For him, anything 'new' was best analysed with the Trotskyist 'grid'. Even so, Mandel made an independent contribution in this field, and the fact that the Soviet Union and the bulk of the 'official' Communist movement have disappeared calls for a retrospective appraisal of his various analyses, positions and concepts. Catherine Samary described Mandel's theoretical point of departure in her examination of his views on the question of 'transitional societies' in this way: 'Although [Trotsky] left open the hypothesis of the bureaucracy transforming itself into a class if it could destroy workers' capacities for resistance, Trotsky posed the fundamental alternatives as either a socialist, anti-bureaucratic revolution or a capitalist restoration: one or the other was supposed to occur rapidly'.[96] Samary was certainly able to present a number of Trotsky quotations to support her argument that Trotsky expected both a relatively short timescale and the 'either-or' scenario cited above. However, I have

---

94   Bensaïd 2002, p. 64 et seq.; Kellner 2004, p. 78 et seq.
95   See eyewitness testimony from Livio Maitan.
96   Achcar 1999a, p. 158.

a slightly different interpretation of the relevant section in his classic text on bureaucracy (written 1935/36), to which she is evidently referring. From today's point of view, one of the conditional prognoses that Trotsky makes there anticipates real developments in an almost astonishing fashion. There is no talk of timescales, and besides, the text speaks of three rather than two possible main paths of development. This is somewhat obscured by the fact that Trotsky indeed initially only discusses the two possibilities of a political conquest of power by the working class or, alternatively, bourgeois counter-revolution.

But then he presents a third possibility:

> Let us assume to take a third variant – that neither a revolutionary nor a counterrevolutionary party seizes power. The bureaucracy continues at the head of the state. Even under these conditions social relations will not jell. We cannot count upon the bureaucracy's peacefully and voluntarily renouncing itself in behalf of socialist equality. If at the present time, notwithstanding the too obvious inconveniences of such an operation, it has considered it possible to introduce ranks and decorations, it must inevitably in future stages seek supports for itself in property relations. One may argue that the big bureaucrat cares little what are the prevailing forms of property, provided only they guarantee him the necessary income. This argument ignores not only the instability of the bureaucrat's own rights, but also the question of his descendants. The new cult of the family has not fallen out of the clouds. Privileges have only half their worth, if they cannot be transmitted to one's children. But the right of testament is inseparable from the right of property. It is not enough to be the director of a trust; it is necessary to be a stockholder. The victory of the bureaucracy in this decisive sphere would mean its conversion into a new possessing class. On the other hand, the victory of the proletariat over the bureaucracy would insure a revival of the socialist revolution. The third variant consequently brings us back to the two first, with which, in the interests of clarity and simplicity, we set out.[97]

In Mandel's succinct popular account, the three hypotheses, which in the last analysis boil down to two opposite potential outcomes (counter-revolution resulting in the restoration of capitalism or political revolution resulting in the construction of a socialist council democracy), are essentially reduced to a single positive outcome. If mass movements against the post-Stalinist regimes

---

97   Trotsky 1996, chapter 9.

emerge, then, in his view, this can only lead to the desired political revolution. The following section from *Introduction to Marxism* is truly apodictic in this respect:

> Until now these mass movements have been suppressed by the military intervention of the Soviet bureaucracy. But as the same process ripens in the USSR, no exterior force will be able to halt the tide of political revolution in Eastern Europe and the USSR. Soviet democracy will be re-established. All danger of the restoration of capitalism will disappear forever. Political power will be exercised by the workers and poor peasants. The struggle for the socialist revolution in the rest of the world will be greatly advanced.[98]

To understand this perspective, we need to examine the meaning of the term 'crisis of Stalinism', as elaborated by the Fourth International in the decades following World War II. The victory and consolidation of Stalinism was ultimately ascribed to the terrible setbacks of the world socialist revolution, the catastrophic defeats of the working class and a dramatic decline in the independent class activity of the proletariat (and of the exploited masses more generally) both in the Soviet Union and internationally. Nonetheless, the first victories in this process of world socialist revolution, which was still deemed to be ongoing, i.e. the elimination of capitalism in a number of countries – partly thanks to the victories of the Red Army and partly due to independent revolutionary conquests of power – and the partial recovery of room for manoeuvre for the proletariat in several countries appeared as a trend likely to undermine bureaucratic rule in the Soviet Union and the Stalinist domination in the Communist movement. While the advances of the world revolution were once again confined to underdeveloped countries and their impact with regard to undermining Stalinism therefore remained limited, the process seemed to reach the rich capitalist countries, where the success or failure of the world revolution is ultimately decided, with the revolts of the late '60s. Thanks to the non-capitalist nature of its economic system and despite all the shortcomings of bureaucratic planning, the Soviet Union had itself become a developed industrial country with a potentially powerful proletariat, which could ultimately only aid this trend. Seen from this angle, the class struggle from below was a greater threat to the Kremlin bureaucracy and its junior partners in other countries (whether in power or not) than capitalism.

---

98   Mandel 1979a, p. 116.

The decline of the international revolution after 1923 and the backward state of the Soviet economy: those were the two main pillars of bureaucratic power in the USSR. But both have been gradually undermined since the end of the 1940s. Twenty years of defeats for the revolution have been followed by a new rise in the world revolution, at first confined to equally under-developed countries (Yugoslavia, China, Vietnam, Cuba), extending into the West since May 1968. After years of effort aimed at 'socialist accumulation', the USSR has ceased to be an under-developed country. Today it is the second industrial power in the world, with a technical and cultural level as high as that of many advanced capitalist countries. The Soviet proletariat, along with that of the USA, is numerically the strongest in the world. In these conditions, the basis for the passivity of the masses in countries dominated by the Soviet bureaucracy has begun to disappear. The beginnings of oppositional activities have been accompanied by splits within the bureaucracy itself, which has been undergoing a process of growing differentiation since the Stalin-Tito rupture in 1948. The interaction between these two factors favours a sudden eruption of political action by the masses, who have taken up the tasks of the political revolution, as in October–November 1956 in Hungary, or during the 'Prague spring' of 1968 in Czechoslovakia.[99]

What appears here like a simple and coherent summary of a decades-long historical process culminating in the final and global success of socialist democracy is, in fact, the culmination of a whole series of debates and analytical efforts. In these analyses, Mandel and his comrades in the leadership of the Fourth International tried to link the unforeseen developments after World War II to the traditional basic programmatic positions of their organisation. It was not their intention to close their minds to new developments. However, given the perspectives and hopes of most Fourth International members at the time of its formal establishment in 1938, now frustrated by the actual developments, they wanted to ascertain whether the small and marginalised Trotskyist movement was at least potentially viable.

The Trotskyists had entertained no doubt about the outbreak of World War II since Hitler's seizure of power and since the defeat of the Spanish Revolution against Franco at the latest. They expected that its outcome would largely follow a similar pattern to the developments at the end of World War I. The Fourth International, small though it was, was hoping to become the leadership of a

---

99   Mandel 1979a, p. 217.

socialist revolution, emerging from a wave of new mass movements, that would sweep away the old masters. They were hoping that this would also put the traditional leaderships of the working class, social democracy and Stalinism, in their place. Thus, the *Transitional Programme* of 1938 stated:

> At the beginning of the war the sections of the Fourth International will inevitably feel themselves isolated: every war takes the national masses unawares and impels them to the side of the government apparatus. The internationalists will have to swim against the stream. However, the devastation and misery brought about by the new war, which in the first months will far outstrip the bloody horrors of 1914–18 will quickly prove sobering. The discontents of the masses and their revolt will grow by leaps and bounds. The sections of the Fourth International will be found at the head of the revolutionary tide. The program of transitional demands will gain burning actuality. The problem of the conquest of power by the proletariat will loom in full stature.[100]

Along similar lines, according to the programme, the Fourth International could achieve a leading role through advances in colonial revolution – which had been misled into defeat by Stalinist leaders, e.g. in China in 1925–1927 – and through the forthcoming awakening of the proletariat of the USSR: 'Only the victorious revolutionary uprising of the oppressed masses can revive the Soviet regime and guarantee its further development toward socialism. There is but one party capable of leading the Soviet masses to insurrection – the party of the Fourth International.'[101]

Mandel was of course aware of the discrepancy between this perspective and the actual development. After all, almost everything had turned out differently than expected. Nonetheless, he broadly defended the perspectives of the *Transitional Programme*. Mandel tried to show that critics who dwelled on the disparity between expectations and reality were overstating the short-term economic aspects (in the sense of relatively short-term forecasts of revolutionary developments and the associated collapse of Stalinism) and therefore underestimating the long-term validity of the fundamental Trotskyist pronouncements. He also highlighted the difference between prognoses based on social science and history, on the one hand, and political-programmatic statements, which mainly serve as guide to political action and therefore can

---

100   Trotsky 2002.
101   Ibid.

hardly foreground worst-case scenarios. Mandel argued that the founding of the Fourth International was justified by the fundamental contradictions of the historical period, and the fact that the short-term perspectives of 'different groups of Trotskyist cadres in various countries ... in the late 1930s and early 1940s' were let down should not be confused with this broader context.[102] What Mandel calls the 'short-term perspectives' of various cadres, however, seems to be rather consistent with the sections of the *Transitional Programme* – the formal founding document of the *Fourth International*, after all – quoted above. Mandel describes these perspectives as follows:

> It has been alleged that the founding of the Fourth International had been determined by two predictions of Trotsky which turned out to be wrong. First, that the Second World War which was then imminent, would lead to a huge revolutionary upsurge by the international working class which would be greater than the one after the First World War and would largely bypass the traditional working class organisations and give a genuinely revolutionary current the historical opportunity for a decisive breakthrough. Second, that the Stalinist bureaucracy would come out of the war greatly weakened, if not overthrown, thereby losing its political stranglehold over the more militant sections of the international working class and anti-imperialist movement.[103]

Even if we accept Mandel's reasoning and interpret the early programmatic documents of the International Left Opposition (ILO) and the Fourth International (or Trotsky's relevant fundamental theoretical writings) not as 'short-term perspectives' but as political perspectives for the long term, it is not difficult to imagine the political morale of the few surviving members of the Fourth International in the years after World War II.

Why did the great revolutionary upsurge fail to materialise? Why could Stalinism successfully consolidate itself and gain new prestige through the victory of the Red Army over Nazi Germany – and why was the Kremlin bureaucracy able to extend its sphere of influence to the future Eastern Bloc states, whose ruling strata were, after all, organised in its image and more or less its vassals? Why were none of the subsequent victorious independent revolutions and mass movements led by Trotskyist parties or sections of the Fourth International, but rather by forces from the 'traditional' Communist movement more

---

102   Mandel 1988, chapter 1.
103   Ibid.

aptly described as 'Stalinist' (e.g. the Titoists and Maoists and later the Vietnamese leadership)? Why did the Fourth International remain a very small
organised with very little scope to influence reality? The need to find satisfactory answers to these questions was a crucial motivation behind Mandel's
analytical and journalistic activities and his involvement in the debates of the
Fourth International after World War II.

The first contradiction appears to be this: Stalin and the Kremlin bureaucracy had apparently emerged hugely strengthened from World War II, basking
in the glory of victory over Nazi Germany. Yet, in a sense, both despite and
because of this victory, they actually got caught up in the contradictions that
Mandel and his comrades in the FI leadership had theorised as the 'crisis of
Stalinism'. The height of the Stalinist terror and of Stalin's omnipotence as the
supreme arbiter of bureaucrats competing with each other for posts, material benefits, power and prestige had certainly been the period of the Moscow
show trials from 1936 to 1938. Virtually all serious historians today agree that
Nazi Germany's invasion of Russia, which Trotsky had predicted for some time,
came as a complete surprise to the dictator, who had executed most of the
best Soviet military leaders or had them deported to the camps of the Gulag
archipelago. The Soviet Union was poorly prepared and in the first months
of the war came close to a crushing defeat. To turn the tide, Stalin not only
had to bring back a number of Red Army military elite, survivors of the camps
and reinstate them in leading positions, he also had to severely limit his own
direct interference in military matters. Konstantin Simonov's trilogy of novels (*The Living and the Dead, Nobody is Born a Soldier*, and *The Last Summer*), published during the period of 'thaw' period in the Soviet Union, is not
least a literary reflection of this process. In his book on World War II, Mandel reveals that before the tide turned with the battle of Stalingrad, the Red
Army was on the verge of total defeat more than once. A dramatic reorientation and reorganisation of the command structures took place in the summer
of 1942:

> The threat of a total collapse and disintegration of the Red Army gal-
> vanized the Soviet command. 'Mass political work' in the army, whose
> morale had been badly shaken by defeat after defeat, was reorganized.
> Mass conscription of Communist Party members was greatly accelerated.
> An angry revolt of the younger officers resulted in the military command
> securing an all-important margin of autonomy from the political admin-
> istration (run by the NKVD). Zhukov, Vasilevsky, Rokossovsky and a score
> of other able commanders now rose to the top, with Zhukov obtaining
> the post of first deputy defence commissar. The high command rever-

ted to the dual command Supreme Commander-Front Command, with Zhukov and Vasilevsky bridging the gap between the two. At the front, the unitary command, which had been abandoned during the great crisis of the autumn of 1941, was reintroduced. A real and rapid modernization of the Red Army was now in the offing: tank-mechanised corps, air corps, air armies and a long-range bomber force emerged to provide the much needed strike power. Slowly and painfully, after defeats and despair, the Red Army was turning into a viable and modern fighting machine. Its decisive test would come at Stalingrad.[104]

After the victory, the extension of the Kremlin bureaucracy's sphere of influence to the later Eastern Bloc countries was quite double-edged from the point of view of stability. The social outcomes remained unclear at first: initially, bourgeois-capitalist conditions were envisaged for the 'people's democracies'. The Trotskyist tradition provided the theoretical tools for two possible scenarios. Because of its fundamental conservatism, the Stalinist bureaucracy tended to shy away from abolishing bourgeois-capitalist property relations outside the Soviet Union. On the other hand, as Trotsky had already noted, the occupation of territories by the Red Army brought with it a tendency to align ownership structures with those in the Soviet Union – even if the Stalinist bureaucracy feared the independent movement of the masses and tried to keep everything under military and police control. The second world congress of the Fourth International in the spring of 1946 found that the bourgeois ownership structures of the countries in the Soviet 'buffer zone' had not changed.[105] In the course of 1947, however, the logic of the 'cold war' changed all this: the economic organisation and property relations, but also the political structures, were assimilated to those of the Soviet Union. The Fourth International noted this and endorsed corresponding analyses by its governing bodies, in which Mandel had a major part, at the Third World Congress in 1951.[106]

> The first [resolution] dealt with the 'people's democracies'. Restating a document adopted by a session of the International Executive Committee held in April 1949, the resolution characterised the East European states as 'bureaucratically deformed workers states'. Unlike the Soviet Union, a workers' state born of a proletarian revolution but which had bureaucratically degenerated, these states were essentially a result of the Kremlin's

---

104   Mandel 2011, pp. 120–1.
105   See Frank 2001, p. 38.
106   See Frank 2001, p. 56; p. 39. See also eyewitness testimony from Livio Maitan.

military-bureaucratic intervention, supported at best by a limited and bureaucratic mobilisation of the masses. These 'people's democracies' had never experienced a true revolution and were born with bureaucratic deformations.[107]

We will see later in what ways Mandel revised this assessment. For the time being, the term 'crisis of Stalinism' does not seem justified, since the Kremlin bureaucracy was ultimately able to keep everything under control and create loyal vassal bureaucracies. It should be noted that a minority of the Trotskyist movement turns a blind eye to this reality to this day, believing that nowhere in the world has there ever been a non-capitalist regime except in the Soviet Union. The official statement on the nature of the people's democracies and a rigidly interpreted Trotskyist dictum on the counter-revolutionary character of the Stalinist bureaucracy has clouded their vision. We are talking here about the tendency from which the French Union Communiste (trotskyste), better known as Lutte Ouvrière, emerged.[108]

The concept of the 'crisis of Stalinism' emerged in the Fourth International in the wake of Yugoslavia's defection. Tito's break with Stalin marked the first clearly visible break with Stalinist monolithism. Pablo, Mandel and their associates developed a position of critical solidarity with the Communist Party of Yugoslavia, which had gained power thanks to an independently organised anti-fascist resistance movement and decided that it would no longer obey Stalin's dictates. For a short time, there seemed to be an opportunity to take advantage of the differences that had emerged in the Communist world movement as a result of the 'Titoist' break in order to build new unified non-Stalinist parties – indeed, one such attempt was made by the Independent Workers' Party of West Germany (UAPD). Then the right turn of the CPY leadership, especially its opportunistic adaptation to the western imperialist powers in the context of 'cold war', put an end to this. And yet, despite all reservations (stemming not least from the fact that the Communist Party of Yugoslavia guarded its monopoly on power with a jealousy thoroughly worthy of Stalinism) the 'Yugoslavian model' retained a special significance for the Fourth International for a long time to come – in particular because of its greater freedom of expression and its self-management of enterprises by workers. The Stalinist chain to which the Communist world movement was tied had suffered its first crack there. It was characteristic both of Pablo and of the young Mandel that they

---

107   Frank 2001, p. 46.
108   See Bensaïd 2002, p. 56 et seq.

were willing to assess such new developments without prejudice and with relative confidence in terms of their own theoretical and programmatic conceptions.[109]

This is also evident from Mandel's early contributions on the Chinese revolution and the role of the Maoist leadership, which had, after all, not formally
broken with the Kremlin leadership during Stalin's time. Mandel nevertheless
recognised that it was pursuing its own path and leading an authentic revolution, a real anti-imperialist war of liberation. He combined his critique of the
contradictions in the leadership's orientation of with an envy-free enthusiasm
for its successes and its inherent anti-capitalist potential.[110]

And indeed, Maoism eventually brought about the second major schism
in the Communist world movement, resulting in a break between the Maoist
leadership and the post-Stalin Soviet leadership. Although the Maoist leadership invoked the legacy of the late Stalin – or rather, an idealised myth of
Stalin – against Khrushchev, a break with the Stalinist orientation had in fact
been necessary to lead the Chinese revolution to victory and therefore onto a
non-capitalist path. This, along with an optimistic interpretation of Mao's cultural revolution as an anti-bureaucratic, anti-conservative, and anti-restorative
'revolution within the revolution' led mainly young people who had been politicised in the revolts of the late 1960s to embrace Maoism as the authentic
'Marxism-Leninism', on which they based their party projects. The Fourth International critically supported the Maoist leadership in the Sino-Soviet conflict
and initially praised its foreign policy – especially with regard to the poor and
dependent countries and anti-colonial struggles – as more in accord with internationalist standards than the foreign policy of the Kremlin. However, 'ping-
pong diplomacy' and the 'three worlds theory' brought the big setback, and
the Maoist leadership declared the Soviet Union to be the 'social-imperialist
main enemy'. In retrospect, Mandel summarised the differences and similarities between the two varieties of 'Marxism-Leninism' thus:

> While Stalinism is at the same time the product and expression of a polit-
> ical counter-revolution within a victorious proletarian revolution, Mao-
> ism is the expression both of the victory of a socialist revolution and of the
> bureaucratically deformed nature of this revolution from its very begin-
> ning. It therefore combines characteristics of a more flexible and eclectic
> approach to the relations between the apparatus and the masses with the

---

109   See eyewitness testimony from Livio Maitan.
110   See Mandel 1950.

characteristic trait of smothering any independent action or organisation on the part of the masses, especially on the part of the urban proletarian masses ... After declaring war on the power of the bureaucracy in the USSR, the Maoists end up defending a regime of bureaucratic command which is very similar to that existing in the USSR, even if it is topped off with a bit of fancy icing in the form of 'participation' of the masses in decision making. Maoism does not accept the Leninist theory of the dictatorship of the proletariat, based on the exercise of power by freely and democratically elected workers' and peasants' councils, any more than Stalin, Khrushchev or Brezhnev.[111]

The Twentieth Congress of the Soviet Union put an end to the 'personality cult' around Stalin. The year 1956 could thus be seen as confirmation that the assessment of the 'crisis of Stalinism' was justified. Mandel nonetheless recognised the narrow limits to this renewal of the 'official' Communist movement. Bureaucratic rule as such was not questioned, and the politically conservative character of Kremlin policy was rather accentuated. Even so, there was some relaxation in the wake of this turn of events, for example in cultural policy, and the time of bloody 'account settling' in leadership circles was over. You were no longer shot, but merely put on ice, often under quite comfortable conditions. Official historiography corrected some of the worst Stalinist falsifications, if only to maintain a 'softer' form of falsified historiography.[112]

For Mandel and the Fourth International, the Cuban Revolution was another milestone in the break-up of Stalinist monolithism. Although the revolutionaries of the '26th of July Movement' were initially only seeking democratic transformation, they arrived at socialist and communist positions through the logic of domestic and international conflicts with the ruling classes in Cuba and the US. Entirely in the spirit of Trotsky's strategy of 'permanent revolution', 'Che' Guevara proclaimed that there would be 'either a socialist revolution or a caricature of a revolution'. In contrast to the Stalinist 'stages theory' and 'peaceful coexistence', which preached the self-restraint of the revolution, the Guevarist-Castroist movement promoted the continuation and international expansion of the revolution, at least in Latin America and in the poor and dependent countries in general. While the Castro regime was paternalistic and authoritarian, the leadership had a very different relationship with the masses than the leaderships of the other Communist Parties in power.[113]

---

111 Mandel 1979a, pp. 120–1.
112 See Mandel 2016.
113 See Frank 2001, p. 90 et seq.

For Mandel, the constant attempts by the leaderships of the USSR and similar countries to carry out economic reforms testified to the contradictions of bureaucratic planning and, in this sense, to the crisis of Stalinism. Agricultural production had to be increased. But industrial production had to be upgraded too. And after the 'third technological revolution' in the capitalist west, there was a pressing need to improve quality. On the one hand, the idea was to increase efficiency and reduce waste by providing incentives for factory managers. On the other hand, such measures in turn created bureaucratic special interests. To the same degree that factory directors became more autonomous in their decision-making, unemployment and other ills resurfaced. Liberalisations took turns with reactive measures to restore a more narrowly conceived command economy. Mandel criticised both the neglect of the law of value, which continued to operate through the distribution of consumer goods for labour wages (money), and – in opposition to the notion of a 'socialist market economy' – the failure to recognise that the law of value was no longer the dominant regulator of the economy (since means of production and labour power were no longer commodities). In any case, since all economic reforms shared the common objective of side-stepping the only truly alternative way of regulating a non-capitalist economy, namely through democratic organs of the working people, Mandel thought that they could only lead into dead ends.[114]

Mandel and the Fourth International regarded the mass revolts repeatedly erupting in the Soviet sphere of power as particularly blatant testimony to the gradually worsening crisis of Stalinism. They interpreted them as signs of a 'political revolution' to restore or establish a socialist council democracy: Hungary and Poznan (Poland) in 1956, the Prague Spring in 1968, Poland in 1970. As a matter of fact, at that time the protesters were still waving red flags and speaking of a democratic renewal of socialism or a real dictatorship of the proletariat. Even at the beginning of the Solidarność era in 1980–81, when an independent trade union with millions of members adopted a programme that was not socialist, the official texts and speeches, at least, spoke of the 'self-management' of companies and society, not of capitalist restoration. Once again, Mandel viewed this revolt as the beginning of a 'political revolution'.[115] In our last chapter, we will discuss what severe complications Mandel's reading of the events had to contend with subsequently. It is, in any event, beyond dispute that these rebellions provided severe shocks to the post-Stalinist system of rule.

---

114   See Mandel 1979a, p. 116 et seq.
115   Mandel 1979a, pp. 115–16.

Changes in the Communist Parties of the west, especially in the western European capitalist countries, were another symptom of the crisis of Stalinism. Only national branches of the 'official' Communist movement that were small and without any influence served the diplomatic interests of the Kremlin bureaucracy for decades without being negatively affected by the constraints imposed by that bureaucracy. Wherever a Communist Party had a mass following in the working class and the general population, on the other hand, wherever it was rooted in important sections of the trade union movement and boasted numerous elected representatives in city councils, local and national parliaments, there tended to emerge a logic of conflict between its ties to the Kremlin bureaucracy and its social roots. Against this background, the 1970s saw the emergence of further distinct identities and new critiques of Stalinism – also in response to the deepening crisis of Stalinism, and the increasing implausibility of 'actually existing socialism' even to those generally sympathetic to communist or socialist ideas, especially, though not exclusively, in the rich capitalist countries. Moreover, the leaderships of mass communist parties not in power displayed a new boldness, expressing the will to determine their own policies independently of the Kremlin bureaucracy. This process culminated in the phenomenon of 'Eurocommunism', which Mandel analysed in detail. Naturally, the new critique of Stalinism articulated by leaders and intellectuals of the Italian and Spanish Communist Parties, among others, made it easier to bring Trotskyist positions into the debate. But Mandel did not fail to recognise that Eurocommunism involved a drift of the parties concerned to the right, towards greater integration into the system of the respective bourgeois nation state. For him, this development had already been implicit in the logic of Stalin's concept of 'building socialism in one country'. The disintegration of Stalinist monolithism unfolded as a break-up of the one, Russian-Soviet 'national messianism' (Trotsky's term) into many communist 'nationalisms': the 'Chilean Road to Socialism', 'Socialism in the Colours of France', etc. In his discussion of 'Eurocommunism', Mandel explained the early origins of this disintegration in detail:

> The adoption of the theory of 'socialism in one country' led to five transformations that were to convulse the theory, strategy and organization of the Communist parties and the Third International, radically modifying their objective function in the contemporary world:
> – It implied a revision of the very concept of world revolution and of its relevance … From this flowed a no less fundamental modification of the relationship between the defence of the isolated proletarian state in Russia (and of the *beginning* of socialist construction within this

state) and the international revolution. Defence of the 'bastion' was proclaimed the number one task of the communist movement and the world proletariat, which gradually dictated a subordination of the interests of the international revolution to the (supposed) interests of the defence of the 'bastion'.

– This subordination led to the transformation of the Communist parties from forces acting for the revolutionary overthrow of capitalism in their respective countries ... into instruments primarily for the defence of the Soviet fortress which increasingly entailed the automatic adaptation of the tactics of these parties and of the Communist International to the zigzags of Kremlin diplomacy.

– Such an adaptation inevitably led to Soviet 'national messianism' (in reality, the petty-bourgeois nationalist messianism of the Soviet bureaucracy), for this systematic subordination could be justified only on the basis of the decisive importance attributed to the USSR, the Soviet proletariat, and the Communist Party of the Soviet Union for humanity as a whole. The concepts of the guiding state and the guiding party, which played such a central role during the Stalin era and which Khrushchev and Brezhnev tried to salvage from the wreckage of Stalinism, originate in this petty-bourgeois messianism. Their inevitable organizational corollary was monolithism within the Communist International and the Communist parties, the suppression of any debate or critical reflection that threatened to upset the tranquillity and interests of the leaders of the 'guiding state', and the bureaucratization of the Communist International as a by-product of the bureaucratization of the CPSU and the Soviet state.

– Precisely because this theoretical, political and organizational degeneration undermined the bases upon which the programme and existence of the Comintern had been founded, it inevitably acted to decompose the Third International in the long run. The bureaucracies of the Communist parties submitted blindly to the orders of the Kremlin – which ever more obviously corresponded neither to the interests of the proletariats of their respective countries nor even to the interests of their own apparatuses – only to the extent that they saw no alternative, either because of their material dependence on Moscow or because of their view of medium-term national and international political perspectives.

Once this situation changed, it was only a matter of time before Stalin's 'iron monolithism' collapsed like a house of cards. The 'national messianism' of the CPSU was to produce as many 'messianisms' as there were powerful Communist parties materially independent of the Kremlin. The 'single centre' was to give way to polycentrism. 'Proletarian internationalism' identified with the 'defence of the Soviet bastion' was to lead to a proliferation of 'national communisms'. *In this sense, the threads of Eurocommunism were woven into the future of the world communist movement from the very moment the theory of 'socialism in one country' was adopted.*[116]

This long quotation illustrates very well the connection between Mandel's analysis of social reality in the (post-)Stalinist-dominated countries and his political conception, which, in line with Trotsky, ties in with the Communist 'orthodoxy' of the pre-Stalinist Communist International. With regards to the analysis itself, Mandel would address some of the problems underlying the concepts of the Trotskyist movement and his own in a long interview in the early 1980s. To what extent could the 'people's democracies' be called 'degenerated workers states' when they never encountered a proletarian revolution in the sense of the 1917 October Revolution? And how could one justify extending the concept of a 'deformed workers state' to these countries if Lenin had already defined the Soviet Union as a 'workers state with bureaucratic deformations' as early as 1921?[117] As regards the monopoly on power held by the merged party and state apparatus, the 'people's democracies' were generally not far behind the Soviet Union, at least not in the sense of a qualitative difference. Mandel's reply to these questions was this:

> I agree that it is semantically incorrect to call the East European countries degenerated workers' states. It would be more accurate to say bureaucratically deformed workers' states. But this formula creates another problem, namely how to distinguish them from, say, the Soviet Union in 1921, which was also bureaucratically deformed (as Lenin pointed out), but where the workers still exercised incomparably greater direct political and economic power than they do in Eastern Europe today. I would prefer to use a single formula to apply to all the states in which the bureaucracy holds a monopoly of power: bureaucratized workers' states, or bureaucratically-ruled workers' states. This formulation avoids that confusion.[118]

This might strike the reader as a relatively simple and convenient, even banal definition of terms. The definition is linked to the prospect of 'political revolu-

---

116   Mandel 1978b, pp. 15–16.
117   See Lenin 2002.
118   Mandel 1979d, pp. 153–4.

tion' in these countries. In this sense, Mandel predicts that it will probably break out in these countries before it reaches the Soviet Union, although he admits that he has too little information to say when the process will reach the Soviet Union itself. He believes it possible that the Kremlin bureaucracy will no longer be able to intervene militarily on a large scale if revolutionary movements break out in several eastern European countries. The demoralising effect of previous interventions by Red Army soldiers, who consequently had to be withdrawn, especially in the CSSR, testifies to this.[119] An entirely different question is why Mandel insists on talking about bureaucratised workers states at all. After all, according to his own assessment, the working class in these countries does not rule, but is ruled. It has been politically expropriated and lacks even the democratic freedom that it has won in the rich capitalist countries. Mandel admits that the use of this terminology may not be plausible to 'common sense' and points to the analytical framework of Trotskyist terminology.

> Trotsky spoke of a broken-down automobile that had crashed head-on into a wall. The difficulty here is the difference between science and pedagogy. The formula 'bureaucratized workers' state' refers to criteria of the Marxist theory of the state. For Marxism, there is no such thing as a state that stands above classes. The state is in the service of the historic interests of a given social class. If one drops the adjective 'workers', it can be replaced by one of two other terms. It can be called either a bourgeois state, or a state of a bureaucracy that has become a new ruling class.[120]

Mandel rejects both ideas. He explains that adopting either concept would make it extremely difficult to navigate the really occurring class struggles:

> ... when the fourth international – following Trotsky – asserts that there is still a bureaucratically degenerate workers' state in the Soviet Union, and that in this sense the Soviet Union still preserves a form of dictatorship of the proletariat, it does so in a quite precise way which implies no more than it says. Up to now this state has objectively continued to defend the structures, the hybrid relations of production, born of the October Revolution. Thus up to now this state has prevented the restoration of capitalism and the power of a new bourgeois class; it has prevented the re-emergence of capitalist property and capitalist relations of production.[121]

---

119   Mandel 1979d, pp. 154–5.
120   Mandel 1979d, p. 145.
121   Mandel 1979d, pp. 145–6.

Mandel uses the term 'workers' state' only in this sense, and not without an additional provision: he speaks of a 'bureaucratised workers state'. It is, at the same time, still a 'transitional society' between capitalism and socialism. He responds to the objection as to why there could be decades of such a transition by referring to historical analogies – the transition from slave-owning societies to feudalism also took a very long time, as did the transition from feudalism to bourgeois society. Moreover, the Stalinist simplifications have obscured the fact that there has been no predetermined, unambiguous sequence of modes of production (slave-owning society, feudalism, capitalism, socialism). After all, the age of absolutism might be described as an age of absolute monarchies serving the interests of the feudal landlords, even if these monarchies in reality prepared the ground for the rule of the bourgeoisie. In history, there have always been forms of bureaucratic rule by certain class factions that excluded the rest of the respective class from the immediate exercise of power.[122] According to Mandel, a period of 'transition' could well last a long time: the important point is that you are on a bridge; you have neither stayed on one river bank nor arrived on the other.[123]

Mandel explicitly states that in one respect he goes beyond the limits of Trotsky's analysis. The key to this is the distinction between the mode and the relations of production. According to Mandel, the fact that neither the capitalist nor the socialist mode of production have been established in the Soviet Union and similar countries in no way means that certain conditions of production do not prevail there. A typical feature of these relations is their hybrid character:

> But this hybrid combination gives rise to something specific – and it is perhaps from this standpoint that we have advanced somewhat over Trotsky's analysis ... I refer to the distinction between the notion of *specific relations of production*, which characterize any given social formation ... and the notion of *mode of production*. Although it is correct to say that there is no social formation without specific relations of production, it is false to say that any specific relation of production necessarily implies the existence of a specific or predominant mode of production. One of the essential distinctions between transitional periods and the great 'progressive stages' of history outlined by Marx in the preface to his *Contribution to the Critique of Political Economy* is precisely that the former do

---

122   Mandel 1979d, p. 146.
123   Mandel 1979d, p. 159 et seq.

not have a specific mode of production, whereas the latter are by definition characterized by such modes.[124]

According to Mandel, modes of production are heavily shaped by their inner
logic, while relations of production located between two 'progressive modes
of production' are subject to their respective contradictions. This, according to
Mandel, opens the possibility that they will disintegrate under their own contradictions. In any case, this argument puts the time frame for the Soviet Union
and similar countries into perspective: the dimensions are neither epochal, as
with the 'great progressive mode of production' that is capitalism (which, of
course, has had its day as far as Mandel was concerned), nor a short 'transition'
in the sense of an episode lasting a few years.[125]

Another problem highlights a further modification of Mandel's position in
relation to the Trotskyist tradition he defended. It takes us closer to the question of the basic political outlook. In relation to the perspective of political
revolution, Trotsky spoke of the necessity for workers to 'drive the bureaucracy
and the new aristocracy out of the new Soviets'.[126] Following his radically democratic conviction, Mandel – though advocating a broad understanding of bureaucracy and, notably, not restricting it to the circle of top officials – emphasises that a council democracy through which the working class exercises its rule
(a 'dictatorship of the proletariat' in Marx's sense) will not exclude anyone: 'The
term "expulsion of the bureaucracy from the soviets" is itself ambiguous, for its
meaning depends on how broadly the notion of bureaucracy is defined.[127] It
threatens once again to limit the freedom of choice, the political freedom, of
the workers. I believe that this freedom must not be subject to any limitation'.[128]

One last aspect which becomes apparent in the cited interview is Mandel's
certainty that the bureaucracy is neither able to introduce socialist democracy
on its own initiative nor initiate capitalist restoration. Mandel can certainly
see tendencies pointing in the latter direction, especially the inclinations of
factory directors to claim decisive powers for themselves and the desire of top
bureaucrats to transition from functional privilege to more secure, inheritable
ownership – but it is precisely the non-capitalist, bureaucratically run economy
that has remained the foundation for these privileges. Mandel stresses in any
case that restoration, like political revolution, could only come about with great
convulsions:

---

124   Mandel 1979d, pp. 120–1.
125   Mandel 1979d, p. 122.
126   Trotsky 1938.
127   Mandel 1979d, p. 152.
128   Ibid.

The gradual restoration of capitalism in the Soviet Union through a 'cold' process (or through the 'palace revolution' detected by the Maoists, Bettelheim, and some other theoreticians) is equally as impossible as the gradual overthrow of capitalism in Western Europe through a series of reforms. To believe otherwise is, to use an apt phrase of Trotsky's, 'to unwind the reformist film in reverse'. In sum, the restoration of capitalism could occur only through new and disastrous defeats for the Soviet and international proletariat, through violent social and political upheavals.[129]

This statement may give the reader a rough idea what problems Mandel would later face up to with the emergence of the Gorbachev phenomenon and especially with the world-historical watershed of 1989–90. It would then become evident just how limited the capacity of the Soviet bureaucracy for self-reform actually was. Its capacity and strength to resist capitalist restoration (*nota bene*: without direct capitalist-imperialist military intervention from the outside) was limited too – far more limited, indeed, than Mandel was inclined to believe.[130] To make matters worse, the actual course of events has revealed how the working class and the general population really acted politically once the ruling bureaucracy's monopoly of power had been broken by mass protest. Mandel believed the masses would push towards a socialist democracy. If such aspirations existed, then only for a very short time (for example, in the GDR in 1989). The desire to join the capitalist west turned out to be the main political aspiration after the collapse of bureaucratic rule in the name of communism. We will later return to the question of whether Mandel's convictions were vindicated or refuted in the face of real historical experience. For now, we can be certain that Stalinism has collapsed and that its remnants cannot expect a significant breakthrough in the future. It is also evident that for many people in the former Soviet Union and in eastern Europe, the capitalist path has turned from a dream into a nightmare.

4   The Temptation of Substitutionism: The Roots of Surrogate Politics

In Mandel's view, it is indispensable for the workers' movement and its parties and organisations to build apparatuses staffed with full-timers and run a press with paid editors. Without these things, we cannot move beyond a certain

---

129   Mandel 1979d, p. 150.
130   See Mandel 1991a, p. ix et seq. (preface); p. 182 et seq.

primitive level of resistance. To do without paid full-time staff also means to expose oneself to the prevailing influence of petty-bourgeois intellectuals who have the time and the ability to acquire a certain level of education. According to Mandel, it is not even all that easy to follow Marx's advice from his commentary on the Paris Commune and pay full-time officials no more than a workers' wage. One may be well advised, for instance, to break this rule to employ qualified editors whose skills could otherwise not be used – or used by the adversary.[131]

The 'dialectic of partial conquests' and the gradually evolving material privileges of paid functionaries are the foundations for the rise of bureaucracy in workers' organisations. Their conservative orientation becomes an obstacle to the realisation of the original emancipatory objectives.[132] 'Substitutionism', for Mandel, is a set of lines of reasoning used by the representatives and ideologists of these bureaucracies to justify their position and practices, whether in parties and trade unions under capitalism or in post-capitalist states. In their classical forms, Social Democracy and Stalinism embody different types of 'substitutionism' (the important difference is that social democracies tend to merge their leadership staff with the institutions of the bourgeois parliamentary republic, whereas Stalinist-type bureaucracies hold state power in post-capitalist countries). For Mandel, the none-too-common concept of 'substitutionism' stands for any ideology that justifies one type of surrogate politics or another. Marx's dictum that the liberation of the workers can only be achieved by the workers themselves is an unalterable principle for him. He therefore evaluates all actions and positions in the workers' movement and in the socialist and communist left by whether they promote or hinder this process of self-liberation. In Mandel's works, 'substitutionism' appears primarily as a phenomenon that has only emerged with the growth of the labour movement mass organisations and the bureaucracies that have developed within them:

> The problem of bureaucracy within the working-class movement poses itself in its most immediate form as the problem of the apparatus of working-class organizations: the problem of full-timers and petty-bourgeois intellectuals who come to occupy the middle or top functions within the working-class organizations. As long as these organizations are limited to tiny groups, to political sects or self-defence groups of limited numerical strength, there is no apparatus, there are no full-timers and

---

131   See Mandel 1973c, p. 7.
132   Ibid.

the problem does not arise. At the very most, there is the problem of the relationship with petty-bourgeois intellectuals who come to aid in the formation of this as yet embryonic working-class movement.[133]

The cited work on bureaucracy dates back to talks that Mandel gave at educational seminars in 1965 and 1967. It is therefore a relatively early text. But even there, it is already evident in some places that Mandel's notion of the problem of 'substitutionism' was not restricted to the emergence of more or less privileged bureaucracies in powerful mass organisations. He identifies early signs of relevant patterns of thinking in the beginnings of the labour movement, when its leaders enjoyed no material privileges and were exposed to considerable risks due to the nature of their involvement (of course, this situation can also occur today wherever a workers' movement and a socialist left are newly emerging or moving beyond the embryonic stages). It is possible to extend Mandel's notion of 'substitutionism' to relatively small organisation without too many reservations:

> Leaving the place of production, especially in the conditions prevailing at that time (twelve-hour working day, total absence of social security, etc.), in order to become a full-timer represented for a worker an unquestionable social promotion, a certain degree of individual self-emancipation. It would be wrong to equate this with 'bourgeoisification' or the creation of a privileged social layer. The early secretaries of working-class organizations spent a considerable part of their lives in prison and lived in more than modest material circumstances. All the same, from an economic and social point of view, they lived better than the rest of the workers at the time.[134]

The similarities with smaller left-wing organisations that have emerged more recently and only have a few, poorly paid full-timers, become even clearer when Mandel cites a partly psychological, partly social effect:

> At the psychological level, it is obviously infinitely more satisfying for a socialist or communist militant to spend all his time fighting for his ideas than to spend his days performing mechanical work in some factory, knowing that the result of his labour will only serve to enrich the class

---

133   Mandel 1973c, p. 10.
134   Mandel 1973c, p. 6.

enemy. The phenomenon of social and personal promotion unquestion-
ably contains the potential seeds of bureaucratization. Those who occupy
such positions quite simply want to carry on occupying them; they will
defend their status against anybody who wants to establish instead a rota
system, whereby each member of the organization would at Some time
fill these posts.[135]

To be sure, Mandel consistently stressed that one must not confuse the germs
of potential future bureaucratisation with the emergence of a real bureaucracy
that has clearly recognisable special interests, including interests of the material kind. All the same, he warns against the creeping displacement of an organisation's objectives by an interest in the self-preservation of these organisations
or their small apparatuses (however modest), and it is reasonable to conceive
this as a critical warning even with regards to organisations that are thoroughly
revolutionary-minded and also 'embryonic'. Precisely because of their margin-
alisation, these groups are always in danger of becoming a kind of cult.[136]

In addition to the privilege (cited by Mandel) of being able to devote much
of their time to their ideals, the poorly paid full-time staff of such organisations also enjoy, in my experience, another advantage: in the narrowly confined
space of their political movement, they have a considerable prestige and relish
in instructing, guiding, and directing others. Even without material privileges,
and even when they are badly underpaid, the loss of such a position can be tantamount to falling into an abyss. The general situation certainly also determines
to which extent this phenomenon takes hold: with relative full employment,
'rotation' becomes easier. Depending on age, the loss of a very poorly paid job in
times of steadily growing unemployment can mean a small biographical catastrophe, or at least be subjectively perceived as such, even for people with a
certain educational background.

Mandel exemplifies how the predominant motive of 'preserving the organisation' can turn self-destructive by invoking the behaviour of leaders of large
organisations such as the General German Trade Union Federation (ADGB) and
the Social-Democratic Party of Germany at the end of the Weimar Republic: the
ADGB leadership justified participation in the May Day celebrations organised
by the Nazis in 1933 on the grounds of that the organisation must be preserved –
on the following day, the trade union offices were stormed by the Brownshirts.
On a smaller scale, similar motivations can be found among the leaders of

---

135   Ibid.
136   See Kellner 2004, pp. 139–40.

minor organisations. Faced with the choice of whether to get involved in a larger political movement or shy away, the fear of losing one's own 'little troupe' can be the deciding factor. This, then, is a sectarian variant of 'substitution': the goal of creating a larger, more effective organisation of the left is abandoned in favour of preserving one's own small organisation.[137]

Following the development of Mandel's position on 'substitutionism', we can observe a shift of emphasis: later on, Mandel stresses that 'substitutionism' is a fairly universal temptation for the workers' movement and the political left. To establish as clear a distinction as possible to Stalinism and counter it with his own theoretical and programmatic orthodoxy based on Luxemburg, Lenin and especially Trotsky, Mandel often stressed that there is no justification in the foundational texts of Lenin and Trotsky for replacing the dictatorship of the proletariat with a dictatorship of the revolutionary proletarian party. He would argue that this was a subsequent falsification of the Bolshevik tradition by Stalinism.[138] There is certainly some evidence to support this view, but it seems somewhat overstated even in light of Mandel's own writings on the problems of the early Soviet Union. Even in relatively early texts, Mandel dissociated himself from the momentous 'substitutionist' actions and positions of Lenin and Trotsky in the pre-Stalinist Soviet Union, and this distinction became even clearer in later texts.

In his account of Trotsky's political ideas, originally published in English in 1979, the measures taken by the Bolshevik leadership in 1920–21 are initially presented as inevitable and born of necessity. Instead of passing a clear judgement, however, Mandel writes with a certain sense of doubt: 'Under the severe strain of mass famine and a dangerous decomposition of working-class strength – including in the physical, numerical sense of the word – the Bolshevik government was forced in the 1920–21 period to severely restrict soviet democracy by suppressing soviet opposition parties and formations, and eliminating the right to form factions in the Bolshevik Party itself. Trotsky wholeheartedly supported these measures. Whether they were unavoidable in order to save the dictatorship of the proletariat, only a detailed critical historical study could demonstrate'.[139]

However, Mandel outright rejects Trotsky's theorisation of these measures at the time: 'He tried to justify them theoretically, going so far as to state boldly that, under certain circumstances, the revolutionary party has to substitute for

---

137   Ibid.
138   See Mandel 1973c, p. 11.
139   Mandel 1979e, pp. 61–2.

the working class in the exercise of political power. He thus turned a theoretical somersault, denying everything he had espoused for nearly two decades with regard to self-organisation of the class, and expressing exactly that substitutionist deviation which he had (wrongly) attributed to Lenin in the 1902–4 debates'.[140]

In the same vein, Mandel refers to several passages in Trotsky's pamphlet *Terrorism and Communism* as 'not enriching' Marxism and as unacceptable apologia for the authoritarian measures of the Bolshevik leadership in this period. At the same time, he emphasises that Trotsky later changed his position and quotes the following passage from *The Revolution Betrayed* as evidence: 'The suppression of soviet parties led to the suppression of factions. The suppression of factions led to the consolidation of the bureaucracy'.[141] He also quotes a sentence from Trotsky's 1934 article 'If America Should Go Communist', which accentuates the same at least implicitly self-critical statement even more (compared with Trotsky's overall analysis of the bureaucratisation process in the Soviet Union, in which objective factors play an important role, it even does so one-sidedly): 'With us, the soviets have been bureaucratized as a result of the political monopoly of a single party, which has itself become a bureaucracy'.[142]

Subsequently, Mandel denied the possibility of a 'third road' between the rule of workers' councils based on a multi-party system and with institutional incentive for working class political activity, on the one hand, and administrative rule by a bureaucracy in place of the working class. In this respect, he agrees with Rosa Luxemburg's 1918 criticism of the Bolshevik leadership: 'And in our opinion, history has shown her to be right, at least on this point of her critique of the Bolsheviks (by no means on all other points). Trotsky's 1936 formula seems to indicate that he arrived at similar conclusions'.[143]

A comparison of this account with Mandel's statements on the same subject in the early 1990s shows that his appraisal of these Bolshevik measures and Lenin and Trotsky's justifications became more categorical. In *Trotsky as Alternative*, he stresses the inevitability of the cyclical ups and downs of the revolutionary enthusiasm and activity of the working class and the exceptionally difficult conditions in the Soviet Union: the backwardness of the country, the devastated industry, the physically decimated working class, the demoralising consequences of the civil war, the low living standards, the low levels

---

140   Mandel 1979e, p. 62.
141   Ibid.
142   Ibid.
143   Ibid.

of culture, the absence of revolutionary victories abroad. Because the working class had shrunk to 35 per cent of its 1917 numbers, the leader of the Workers' Opposition in the Bolshevik Party, Shlyapnikov, could taunt Lenin: 'I congratulate you, Comrade Lenin, that you exercise the dictatorship of the proletariat in the name of a non-existent proletariat'.[144]

However, Mandel then qualifies the medium-term scope of these extraordinarily unfavourable conditions by stating that under the influence of the NEP (the new more liberal economic policy that replaced 'war communism'), industry and the working class and their potential 'class power' began to grow again, and that there was therefore a basis for relying more on workers' democracy and the self-activity of this working class.[145] While in the late 1970s, he wrote that a thorough investigation would have to clarify whether the measures taken by the Bolshevik leadership out of necessity were inevitable, he now unambiguously rejects this:

> The key question, in view of the quantitative and qualitative growth of the Russian working class from 1922, is whether the concrete political measures of the Bolshevik leadership, its medium-term and long-term strategy on this question of the exercise of power, promoted or hindered the self-activity of the working class. Today, the answer to this question seems clear. From 1920–21 the strategy of the Bolshevik leadership hindered rather than promoted the self-activity of the Russian workers. What is more, the theoretical justification and the generalization of this 'substitution' made the situation even worse.[146]

Mandel denounces the ban on Soviet parties and the ban on factions in the Bolshevik Party even under the concrete circumstances of the time. He construes a passage from Trotsky's *The Revolution Betrayed* as explicit self-criticism: 'The prohibition of oppositional parties brought after it the prohibition of factions. The prohibition of factions ended in a prohibition to think otherwise than the infallible leaders. The police-manufactured monolithism of the party resulted in a bureaucratic impunity which has become the source of all kinds of wantonness and corruption'.[147]

Mandel dubs the theoretical justification of these measures by Lenin and Trotsky 'horrendous'. The title of the section clearly shows that he now dis-

---

144   Mandel 1995a, p. 82.
145   Ibid.
146   Ibid.
147   Ibid.

counts this period from the Marxist tradition to which he adheres: 'The "Dark Years" 1920–21: Trotsky's "Substitutionism"'. He quotes a section from a Trotsky speech at the second congress of the Communist (Third) International where this 'sliding towards substitutionism' becomes blatantly apparent:

> Today we have received a proposal from the Polish government to conclude peace. Who decides such questions? We have the Council of People's Commissars but it too must be subject to certain control. Whose control? The control of the working class as a formless, chaotic mass? No. The Central Committee of the party is convened in order to discuss the proposal and to decide whether it ought to be answered. And when we have to conduct war, organize new divisions and find the best elements for them – where do we turn? We turn to the party. To the Central Committee. And it issues directives to every local committee pertaining to the assignment of Communists to the front. The same thing applies to the agrarian question, the question of supplies and all other questions.[148]

It goes without saying that the political system that Trotsky is justifying in this speech has nothing to do with the 'self-government of producers' that Mandel has always passionately advocated. Although Mandel considers the proposals of the Workers' Opposition unrealistic, he nonetheless rejects Trotsky's reproach at the tenth party congress of the Bolshevik Party in 1921. There, Trotsky argued that the opposition had placed the workers' right to elect representatives above the party, 'as if the party were not entitled to assert its [sic] dictatorship even if that dictatorship temporarily clashed with the passing moods of the workers' democracy.'[149] The 'sic' in square brackets was inserted by Mandel, who thinks it significant that Trotsky speaks of the 'dictatorship of the party' as a matter of course, while 'workers' democracy' only appears as a supplement – after all, it is permitted to ignore its 'temporary moods'. Mandel also criticises Trotsky's promotion of coercion and forced labour during this period (though like in earlier contributions, he rejects the 'myth' that Trotsky's position in the 1920 trade union debate was primarily characterised by this aspect). Moreover, he describes Trotsky's *Terrorism and Communism* as his 'worst' book, which he used to 'justify and defend substitutionist practice without considering its political and social consequences'.[150] Mandel points out that it does not

---

148   Mandel 1995a, p. 83.
149   Ibid.
150   Ibid.

say a word about the independent role of the workers' councils or contain any commitment to the separation of party and state.[151]

He also objects to later such defences and justifications – not so much of the state terror and extreme repression under Stalin, but of milder forms of authoritarian 'substitutionist' dictatorship by the merged party and state apparatus. Such justifications, while inevitably invoking the low political consciousness of the masses, assert the need to govern with an iron fist: opening up to greater democratic freedoms and rights for the masses would leave the country at the mercy of the agents of capitalist restoration. Mandel rejects these ideas just as categorically as the justification tactics of the leading Bolsheviks during the 'dark years' of 1920–21. Indeed, he believes that the oppression of majority populations by governments calling themselves 'socialist' or 'communist' plays into the hands of bourgeois forces.

> What the events of 1989–90 in Eastern Europe and the severe crisis of the system in China have demonstrated is that it is impossible, in the long run, to realize the project of constructing socialism without the conscious support, co-operation and self-activity of the working class. The rebellion of a manipulated people is sooner or later unavoidable. To respond to this with repression is not only unsocialist but inhuman. It is also ineffective, as the examples of Albania and Romania have demonstrated. It simply pushes the masses into the arms of the bourgeois politicians. Stalinism and neo-Stalinism are no alternatives to restorationist tendencies. They can only lead to growing crises and explosions. They have no future.[152]

Mandel prefers to think of Trotsky as someone who underwent a learning process. In his mind, Trotsky became aware that bureaucratic degeneration was the main danger for the Soviet Union and the Communist world movement from 1923, which is why he took up the struggle against it. In the course of this struggle, he went beyond his original demand for the restoration of internal party democracy and began calling for the restoration of Soviet democracy with full democratic rights for the working masses and a plurality of political parties. Mandel draws a number of quotations to substantiate that Trotsky returned to the main tenets of his political life, so to speak: except in the 'dark years', he had always advocated the overthrow of capitalism and the exercise of political power by the working class with a view to building a classless society – but com-

---

151 Ibid.
152 Mandel 1995a, p. 84.

bined with broad, self-organised activity on the part of the workers and, more generally, the exploited and oppressed sections of the population.[153]

In his late work on the problem of bureaucracy, originally published in English the 1990s under the title *Power and Money* (a revised and expanded German version saw the light of day in September 2000), Mandel develops his critique of bureaucracy more systematically and in a broader context than was the case in his earlier works. Several aspects that did not appear in earlier writings, or at least were not developed in detail, are addressed there. The book contains, not least, an entire chapter in which Mandel examines the temptation of 'substitutionism'. He gives a number of examples, which we will discuss in detail below.[154]

In the first chapter of *Power and Money*, Mandel describes the bureaucracy that emerges in the labour movement, including when it exercises state power, as a product of the social division of labour, relative scarcity and continued commodity production. According to Mandel, a 'deformation' has arisen from a hybrid of 'market economy and bureaucratic despotism', and a specific 'state-commodity fetishism' is at the 'the heart of bureaucratic ideology'. When small, self-appointed elites make all the important decisions and market laws dictate developments, then we are dealing in both cases with processes that take place 'behind the backs' of those affected, the producers. All the undeniable advantages of a planned economy over the capitalist market economy (even in its bureaucratic variety) ultimately disintegrate, according to Mandel, to the extent that the authoritarian hierarchical organisation of business coincides with increased demands for critical technological expertise, on the one hand, and an expansion of the scope for macro-economically effective market mechanisms on the other.[155]

For the first time, this book of Mandel's also contains a detailed examination of the 'growth of bourgeois bureaucracies' both in the bourgeois state and in large capitalist corporations. Mandel objects to the notion that bourgeois state power is neutral or can be used by the socialist left for its own purposes (an idea especially characteristic of 'Austromarxism', but also, in a more general sense, a typical justification of workers' parties for their transition from a revolutionary socialist to a system-conformist practice).[156] There is also an examination of Max Weber's 'alternative theory of bureaucracy', which Mandel mainly reproaches for exaggerating the 'rational' character of bureau-

---

153   Mandel 1995a, p. 85.
154   Mandel 1992a, p. 103 et seq.
155   Mandel 1992a, p. 44 et seq.
156   Mandel 1992a, p. 163.

cratic administration and therefore in large measure apologising for state bureaucracy. Weber fails to grasp the irrational character of bureaucracy, which
becomes apparent when bureaucratic activity becomes an end in itself, a pre-
tence of competence and expertise, and an expression of the special interests of
professional administrators.[157] Similarly, Mandel criticises Joseph Schumpeter,
whom he describes as the 'real father' of the theory of 'convergence between
the two systems' in view of his late work on bureaucracy (*Capitalism, Socialism
and Democracy*). In the end, a bureaucratically planned economy seemed more
likely to Schumpeter than capitalism with large private sector monopolies and
mass unemployment, and he believed that majorities in the capitalist countries
could opt for this kind of 'socialist' path. For all his sympathy for Schumpeter's
turn towards a sceptical attitude to capitalism, Mandel criticises him, as he did
Weber, for overestimating the 'rational' character of bureaucratic administration.[158]

Mandel concludes the chapter with a comparison between the power of big
money wealth and the power that results from state apparatuses that have
become only relatively autonomous in relation to the capitalist ruling class
(including the combination of both):

> Power corrupts. A lot of power begets a lot of corruption. But in the
> epoch of capitalism, no power can be absolute, because in the last ana-
> lysis money and wealth rule. Big wealth corrupts as much as, if not more
> than, big power. Huge sums of money beget huge power and therefore
> corrupt absolutely. You can eliminate near-absolute power only if you do
> away both with the strong state and with huge money wealth.[159]

The fact that Mandel never relativised his opposition to the bourgeois apparatuses when fighting the conservative bureaucracies that emerged in the labour
movement is also evident from his peculiar pamphlet on the history of the
crime novel.[160] The booklet is a product of processing and reflecting on experiences while indulging in one of his favourite pastimes: reading crime novels.
In the final chapter he sarcastically notes an unstoppable fusion of 'state, business and crime' for contemporary capitalism.[161] There is a section in *Power and
Money* that harks back to Mandel's early writing on bureaucracy ('Organiza-

---

157   See Mandel 1992a, p. 180 et seq.
158   See Mandel 1992a, p. 185 et seq.
159   Mandel 1992a, p. 188.
160   See Mandel 1987a.
161   Mandel 1987a, p. 111 et seq.

tion and the Usurpation of Power'). Mandel first describes the positive effects of building workers' mass organisations on the self-confidence, class conscious-ness and cultural level of large numbers of workers.[162] Then he describes how the bureaucratic apparatuses have become self-perpetuating and what the neg-ative repercussions with respect to the goal of working class self-liberation are. In each case, he draws on the contemporary analyses of several workers' movement leaders, including Parvus-Helphand, Henriette Roland Holst, Lux-emburg, Bebel, Wilhelm Liebknecht, Marx, Antonio Labriola, Lenin, Trotsky and Gramsci. At the same time, he presents a history of ideas that relate to the development of awareness of both issues. New in this context are, for example, a detailed examination of 'bureaucratic enterprise organisation' and the eval-uation of materials and testimony on the problems of political and economic administration in the GDR (made accessible from 1989–90).[163]

An important aspect of the ideology of bureaucracies in power is, accord-ing to Mandel, that they tend to deny their own existence. Since they are not the ruling classes of a great 'progressive mode of production', they are structur-ally incapable of developing their own ideology (in the strict Marxist sense of the word). As a substitute, they use set pieces from Marx's capitalism critique and from the socialist and communist tradition in general. These are distorted to serve a state-sanctioned worldview and used pragmatically and arbitrarily. Their 'schizophrenic self-consciousness' ultimately generates a politically and morally deep identity crisis, especially among top bureaucrats who have not cut the umbilical cord to their proletarian origins.[164]

In his commentary on 'organisational fetishism', Mandel transcends the lim-itations of his earlier texts.[165] He now explicitly ascribes a less significant role to the deliberate betrayal and deception by social-democratic, Stalinist and other bureaucratic leaderships. The same is true for direct material corruption combined with the 'dialectic of partial conquests', the impact of the social divi-sion of labour on the workers' movement, and the growing tendency to run the organisation as an end in itself. Instead, he now emphasises a character-istic self-delusion on account of which many of these people were sincerely convinced that they were working for the interests of the working class, social-ism or socialist revolution. He identifies a presence of this feature especially in

---

162   Mandel 1992a, p. 59 et seq.

163   See Mandel 1992a, p. 40 et seq. [The evaluation of GDR materials referred to by the author is contained in the German edition of the book (see Mandel 2000, p. 85 et seq.), but not in the English edition (Mandel 1992) – Translator.]

164   Mandel 1992a, p. 87 et seq.

165   Mandel 1992a, p. 65 et seq.

the early period of bureaucratisation, but also in later periods: the leaders and paid officials of the major Communist Parties in western capitalist countries, for instance, were unlikely to enjoy material privileges even after World War II. Mandel criticises the justificatory patterns of 'substitutionism' less along the lines of the old 'theory of priest deception' formulated in the age of Enlightenment, and more in the manner of Marx's critique of ideology, i.e. as 'false (bourgeois) consciousness', which must be understood as 'real illusion', since it is rooted in a 'false' reality and in a 'false' daily practice of those involved.[166] At the same time, this false practice engenders great bitterness and resignation. Mandel advocates a policy that systematically promotes solidarity-based struggle for class interests, self-activity and self-organisation from below – but in the end, he returns to the need to build a political 'vanguard organisation' that in non-revolutionary times is necessarily a minority and systematically devoted to this purpose. He avails himself of the drastic accusation of 'crime', putting in a nutshell what he most resents about the bureaucratised leaderships:

> The role of the victim often engenders bitterness and scepticism. Only permanent activity in a political organisation that is dedicated to the general interests of the working people can offset these effects – and only a relatively small minority of the vanguard commits itself to such activity. Many thousands of fighters end up broken and give up their activism. Herein lies one of the worst crimes committed by bureaucrats as defenders of the steadily increasing limitations on class solidarity and of its denial: they are cadre killers in the literal sense of the word.[167]

The chapter on 'Substitutionism and realpolitik: the politics of the labour bureaucracies' nonetheless makes evident to what degree Mandel had become aware that even the purest, most emancipatory and mass-orientated revolutionary sentiments do not offer sufficient protection against the temptation

---

166   The 'theory of priest deception' divided the people into deceivers and the deceived: according to this theory, the enlightenment of the deceived about the real material desires and machinations of the deceivers would infallibly bring the liberation the deceived. The problem with this viewpoint is that both the deceiver and the deceived can to a certain extent be caught up in the same socially mediated false consciousness. (See Kurt Lenk's (ed.) introduction in *Ideologie, Ideologiekritik und Wissenssoziologie*, Darmstadt/Neuwied 1976, p. 3 et seq., and my master's thesis of 1980: 'Die Rolle der Projektion in Feuerbachs Religionskritik', published as *Feuerbach's Critique of Religion*, Frankfurt am Main 1988, p. 6.)

167   Mandel 2000, p. 76, our translation [the English edition of Mandel's text, *Power and Money* (Mandel 1992) does not contain this passage – Translator].

of 'substitutionism'.[168] Mandel discusses the typical substitutionist justificatory patterns of social-democratic, Stalinist and Maoist coinage, including
their inner affinity. He also explains how leading personalities of the historical socialist and Communist movements, whose revolutionary commitment
and exceptional awareness of this problem he views as beyond question, suc-
cumbed to more or less substitutionist positions and practices during certain
periods.

With respect to Lenin and Trotsky's 'dark years' of 1920–21, Mandel reiterates
the substance from his earlier writings that we have summarised earlier. Again,
he does not in the slightest justify measures such as the bans on Soviet parties
and on factions in the Bolshevik party. Now, however, he uses a series of quotations to show to what extent Lenin and Trotsky's justifications of surrogate
politics, which he considers a reflex to a spectacular decline in mass activity,
contradicted their own positions on council democracy as the incarnation of
the proletarian dictatorship, on the crucial role of the independent self-activity
of the proletarian masses, and on the internal regime of a revolutionary party.
With reference to *The State and Revolution*, but also drawing on statements
Lenin made in periods when building a party under conditions of illegality was
not the issue, Mandel describes Lenin's party conception as downright 'liber-
tarian' when compared to prevailing ideas (held by the Stalinist tradition and
mirrored by bourgeois prejudice, but also present among many other left trends
that lay a claim to Lenin's party conception).

According to Mandel, both Lenin – who recognised the problem of the bureaucratisation of party and state earlier than Trotsky, but had far less time to
address it systematically – and Trotsky returned to their former positions once
they realised the enormous danger posed by a party-cum-state-apparatus that
was becoming unaccountable and escaped any control.[169]

The Austromarxist Otto Bauer showed an acute insight into the dangers
of 'substitutionism', including in his critical writings on the situation in early
Soviet Russia. Significantly, though, in the period following the catastrophic
defeats of 1933 and 1934 in Germany and Austria, he himself arrived at distinctly
substitutionist positions. On the question of illegality – a situation comparable
to that in which Lenin had written *What Is To Be Done?* – he advocated and
theorised an organisational concept that lacked any autonomy for local organisations. Although he criticised the excessive power of factory managers in the
Soviet Union, he thought that the Soviet workers should at most be granted

---

168   Mandel 1992a, p. 103 et seq.
169   Mandel 1992a, p. 117 et seq.

a right to be heard. Much like the bourgeois apologists of the state bureaucracy, he justified the role of an elevated economic administration as mediator between conflicting interests, and he rejected the self-management of companies on the grounds that it would give rise to 'factory egoism' and 'corporatism'.[170]

Mandel cites as classic consequences of such substitutionist positions the willingness to justify coercive measures against strikes and ultimately even state terror against dissenters. In the name of 'efficiency' in production, Bauer turned from an admonisher against bureaucratic tendencies in the years 1918–20 to a partial defender of extreme repression under Stalin and of fairly unbridled authoritarianism. Mandel cites a particularly 'eloquent' quote by Bauer from 1935, in which Stalin, endowed with all kinds of martial secondary virtues, appears as a 'substitute' for class, party and even party leadership, and – in a sense – as the one on whom all good things depend:

> At a time when economic problems were piling up like mountains ... in a period like this, a party that permits free debate and free elections would find it impossible to deal with all the economic hardship suffered and all the resistance offered by a hundred million people – only a unified, tough and fearless resolve can triumph. During this period, the dictatorship had to select a leader from its ranks. Under such historical conditions, the man with the strongest nerves, the greatest tenacity, the greatest determination and ability to impose the most terrible sacrifices on the popular masses for victory's sake and for the sake of the future – in other words, the man with the strongest will, the toughest, the most ruthless – had to triumph over his rivals ... Selection is justified by performance. Stalin's achievement is the industrialisation and collectivisation of the economy of the Soviet Union, an achievement that has transformed not only the image of the Soviet Union but the image of the world.[171]

Of course, there have been many more shocking statements from politicians who submitted to the Stalinist apparatus or bended over politically and morally in the interests of 'discipline' and to meet the demands of a bureaucratic leadership. Mandel cites several examples of this as well. However, Bauer's evolution – not unlike that of various intellectuals who, as 'friends of the Soviet Union', defended Stalin in the struggle against any opposition – illustrates the deeper political motives behind the drift towards 'substitutionism'. It expresses

---

170   See Mandel 1992a, p. 126.
171   Mandel 2000, pp. 136–7, our translation [the English edition of Mandel's text *Power and Money* (Mandel 1992a) does not contain this quote – Translator].

a desire to find a substitute for the self-activity of the masses, which is no longer evident or can no longer be counted on (temporarily or permanently). In a sense, it is an illusory 'shortcut' on the road to the socialist goal of working-class self-liberation.[172] In the case of Antonio Gramsci, it is precisely because of his famous theoretical contributions on the need to achieve a broad political and cultural 'hegemony' of revolutionary communist ideas that few would suspect him of occasionally giving in to the temptation of 'substitutionism' too. However, Mandel shows that in a time of 'temporary retreat of the mass movement', Gramsci developed strategic concepts that were in blatant contradiction to the views he had previously held, as well as inconsistent with the notion of mass self-activity and self-organisation. Gramsci even granted 'the party' and, under certain circumstances, a 'small group of party leaders' the right to exercise a 'policing function' not only against the ruling classes, but also against 'backward part of the masses'. Mandel quotes the following section from Gramsci's prison notebooks: 'The war of position demands enormous sacrifices by infinite masses of people. So an unprecedented concentration of hegemony [of power] is necessary, and hence a more "interventionist" government, which will take the offensive more openly against the oppositionists and organize permanently the "impossibility" of internal disintegration – with controls of every kind, political, administrative, etc., reinforcement of the hegemonic "positions" of the dominant group, etc.'.[173]

Rosa Luxemburg was long thought by 'official' Communism to have excessive leanings in favour of the 'spontaneity of the masses'. Mandel held her writings in high esteem – particularly those on the importance of mass activity, the need for socialist democracy, the right to debate freely, the conservative character of the trade union bureaucracy, and the connection between the authoritarianism and the conservatism of the Social-Democratic leadership. Despite all this, it is well-established that even she led the illegal Social-Democratic Party of Poland with a fairly iron hand, relying not least on Leo Jogiches's organisational skills for this purpose. Mandel was familiar with Luxemburg's defence of the October Revolution, including of extreme measures taken during the civil war, and he approved of it. This was in stark contrast to today's widespread reduction of Luxemburg's positions to her warning to the Bolsheviks, written in prison, against pursuing surrogate politics and stifling the self-activity of the masses, and to the dictum 'freedom is always the freedom of those who think differently'. Mandel, too, invokes both statements as examples of proph-

---

172   Mandel 2000, p. 137.
173   Mandel 1992a, p. 126.

etic clear-sightedness, albeit with some reservations about their consistency with the actual situation in Soviet Russia in 1918. However, he adds in a footnote: 'Objectivity requires us to note that Rosa herself had her "dark years". In 1912–14, when faced with a dissident faction in the Warsaw party that included Hanecki and Radek, she did not hesitate to accuse them of being manipulated by the Tsarist secret police'.[174]

All this shows that for Mandel there is a correlation between a low level of working-class self-activity and the virulence of 'substitutionist temptation'. He does not deny the real problems that periods of receding or low-level mobilisation pose with regard to revolutionary socialist aspirations. However, he advocates a political method aimed at encouraging and promoting the activity of the working class, however difficult the situation. Without this, he argues, the project of self-liberation cannot be realised. Using Nikolai Bukharin's political biography as an example ('Substitutionism and policy choices: the tragedy of Bukharin and the old Bolsheviks'), Mandel tries to show how one can become an ally of the bureaucracy, embodied by Stalin, due to political errors of judgement – similar to Otto Bauer's, but with much more dramatic consequences. Mandel identifies the failure to recognise of the problem of bureaucracy as the problem number one. Bukharin, who in 1918–22 saw the danger that the working class might become oppressed by its own functionaries (in the 1920 'trade union debate', he promoted the slogan of a 'production democracy' alongside Trotsky and others; he rejected the notion that the trade unions were defensive organisations for the workers' immediate consumer interests, but he also opposed calls for the authoritarian administration of factories). Under the influence of internal struggles in the leadership of the CPSU, he largely ignored this aspect from 1923–28.[175] In this period, the debates and controversies in the field of economic policy had the greatest importance for him, which turned him into the fiercest opponent of Trotsky and the anti-bureaucratic Left Opposition. According to Mandel, he and many of the other 'old Bolsheviks' did not realise that for Stalin, factual disputes were at best secondary: 'For the General Secretary was essentially interested not in this or that political orientation but in the exercise of total power inside the Party, with the unity and integrity of its full-time apparatus as the number one priority'.[176]

The disputes within the leadership of the Bolshevik party over the direction of economic and international policy were important. These really were burning issues. Mandel, however, believes that the importance of these matters

---

174   Mandel 1992a, p. 147.
175   Mandel 1992a, p. 131 et seq.
176   Mandel 1992a, p. 132.

must still be put into perspective when measured against the immense danger posed by the special interests of the increasingly autonomous and powerful bureaucratic apparatus.

> Whatever the importance of the issues with which the Old Bolsheviks were obsessed – the tempo of industrialization, the growing weight of the kulaks, the 'price scissors', the relationship with the world market, the immediacy or otherwise of the war danger – it is hard to deny today, with hindsight, that they were all subordinate to the question of who, which group of people, actually exercised power in the USSR. The development of Soviet society and of the CPSU and its policies in the second half of the 1920s serves to confirm the accuracy of this analysis. For it was because the Stalin faction and the bureaucracy held the reins of state power that they were able to move overnight from the NEP to top-speed industrialization and forced collectivization, from growing integration in the world market to a large degree of autarky. And the vagaries of Stalinist and post-Stalinist economic policy, from 1924 to 1953 to 1990, only become comprehensible if we see that their principal motivation was the defence and expansion of bureaucratic privileges and of the power monopoly that sustained them.[177]

Bukharin became the intellectual leader of the so-called 'right' opposition, which advocated an expansion of the NEP, a slower pace of industrialisation, and a peaceful integration of the peasants (including rich peasants) into socialism. Only when he was stripped of power and finally became a victim of Stalin's repressive apparatus himself did he begin to speak of 'degenerate bureaucrats' and his 'helplessness before a hellish machine' – a machine that could accuse any party member of being a 'spy' and liquidate them.[178]

Mandel leaves the question open to what extent Bukharin's personality traits, or his need to justify his earlier political role, played a role in the fact that he never launched an open political struggle against Stalin – despite the fact that, according to various testimonies and sources, from 1929 he largely shared Trotsky's position on the Stalinist power apparatus. However, as with other 'old Bolsheviks', Mandel believes that an agreement with Stalin to keep controversies confined to the tiny inner leadership circle played an important role. This made it easier for Stalin to eliminate his real and potential adversaries within

---

177   Mandel 1992a, p. 141.
178   Mandel 1992a, p. 138.

the party one after the other.[179] Suffice to say, these attitudes were 'substitutionist' in the extreme: not only the working class, but also ordinary members of the ruling party were completely kept out of crucial disputes. This stance was complemented by a willingness to support 'political verdicts' passed by courts according to the criteria of political expediency. The horrible consequence of this is that the guilt or innocence of defendants loses all significance. Mandel quotes a section from a *Pravda* article of 3 October 1988, where the academician Smirnov testified that at a plenary session of the central committee, Bukharin's closest associate Rykov supported such a procedure with respect to the Shakhty trial.[180]

Mandel adds that many members of the Left Opposition – and Trotsky himself made too many concessions in the years 1929–30 – basically made the same mistake as Bukharin, albeit from an opposite position, in the disputes over economic policy. The fear of a possible restorative role on the part of the peasant upstarts ('kulaks'), which they overestimated, led them to misapprehend the danger of a 'thermidor', or in other words: a (bureaucratic) counter-revolution within the revolution.[181]

Mandel cites the political fates of Mao Zedong and Deng Xiaoping as consequences of wrong political choices in a revolutionary process. Unlike the Russian revolution of 1917, this process was bureaucratically deformed almost from the outset because it was based on the already established bureaucratic control of rural territories that had been liberated from imperialist troops and from the domestic state apparatus.

Even during the so-called 'cultural revolution' launched by Mao – which for Mandel, quite apart from revolving around inner-bureaucratic rivalries, at least had the potential for anti-bureaucratic correction in the CCP and the People's Republic of China – the 'great helmsman' finally chose the path of military and police suppression of the same 'red guards' and young people that he himself had mobilised. From then on, he could only survive politically as a figurehead, representative and guarantor of the overall interests of the party and state bureaucracy.[182]

Mandel's conclusion from the cited experiences does not provide a simple recipe against the dangers of bureaucratisation. He does, however, urge us to recognise and consciously combat tendencies towards substitutionism: 'A rejection of the substitutionist dogmas is an essential condition for consist-

---

179   Mandel 1992a, p. 139.
180   Mandel 1992a, p. 140.
181   Mandel 1992a, pp. 140–1.
182   Mandel 1992a, pp. 141–2.

ent struggle against the bureaucratic degeneration of workers' organizations and workers' states. It in no way entails any spontaneist illusion about the class struggle, and is fully compatible with the much needed efforts to build revolutionary vanguard parties. But it does require a correct view of the dialectical interrelation between the self-activity and self-organization of the class, on the one hand, and the vanguard party on the other'.[183]

In his chapter on substitutionism in *Power and Money*, Mandel also tries to summarise the 'substitutionist dogmas' of social-democratic and Stalinist coinage in the form of a whole series of erratic doctrines. The common denominator lies in an emphasis on, firstly, the existing leadership and organisational structures and, secondly, the kind of political activities in which the working class and ordinary members of parties and mass organisations only play a passive role.

The most common apologetics for substitutionist practices are references to the 'immaturity' of the masses, to their passivity (despite the fact that this is often a retroactive effect of the apparatus's substitutionist policies), and their reverse inclination to 'imprudent' and risky outbursts. In Mandel's view, a particularly dangerous culmination of substitutionism is reached by the apparatuses of large organisations when they are willing to use violence against the rebellious base 'if necessary', or take action against the base when it acts without the blessing or against the intentions of the leadership.[184]

---

183   Mandel 1992a, p. 144.
184   See Mandel 2000, pp. 109–10; 122 et seq. Mandel's comments on the 'psychological dimension of substitutionism' (Mandel 1992a, p. 129 et seq.) are also interesting: according to him, bureaucracies subject people to a 'process of negative selection' (p. 129) and 'institutionalise' the 'obsessive-compulsive neurosis', which is in fact an individual condition typical of bureaucrats.

Socialist Strategy

1   Prefigurative Forms of the New Society: Mass Strike and Self-Organisation from below

Marx took the view that the ideology of a given epoch is that of the ruling class, especially in capitalist society. This is not mainly so because of the possibilities for the rulers to manipulate the ideas of the ruled, but because the everyday social reality that surrounds the ruled produces and constantly reproduces that 'necessarily false consciousness'. On the other hand, Marx was committed to a socialist revolution consciously carried out by the working class. In his 'Theses on Feuerbach', he indicated in a very general fashion how the contradiction in society between the dominant bourgeois consciousness and the consciousness necessary for socialist revolution could be resolved: through 'revolutionary practice', i.e. the 'coincidence of the changing of circumstances and of human activity or self-changing', for it is essential to 'educate the educator himself'.[1]

Mandel's conception of socialist transformation in the developed capitalist countries and its preconditions can be read as an attempt to put this approach into concrete terms. First of all, he thought that the objective conditions for a socialist revolution on a worldwide scale were present (we have heard some critical commentary on this position in our subchapter on the 'Material preconditions for universal emancipation'; in the last chapter, we will address this issue from a number of different angles):

> Since the First World War, the necessary material conditions have existed for the building of a socialist society. Big factories have become the basis of production. The world division of labour has reached a high level. The interdependence of all people – the 'objective socialisation of production' – has been largely achieved. Hence it becomes objectively possible to replace the system of private property, of competition and market economy, by a system based on the association of all producers and the planning of production in order consciously to satisfy determined needs.[2]

---

1   Marx 2005.
2   Mandel 1979a, p. 122.

Moreover, Mandel argues that the objective weight of the working class, in his view the potentially revolutionary class (defined as those who own nothing but their labour power and sell it to live) is strong and that it continues to grow. What is more, at 'periodic intervals' situations arise in which the ability of the ruling bourgeois class to govern society is wavering and the working class rebels against bourgeois rule through independent action and mobilisation. Other questions to be taken into account are the subjective conditions, the politics of the present leaders of the working class, their political consciousness and maturity, and the influence of the revolutionary forces within their ranks.[3]

Mandel does not deny the aforementioned problem; he stresses that under 'normal' conditions of modern bourgeois society, the working class remains trapped in bourgeois ideology in its role as an object of exploitation, in its feeling of hopeless inferiority to the class enemy, and in its fragmentation into competing individuals. However, it sees a chance to change this during its periodic breaks from this everyday existence: 'One of the main aspects of the direct action of the masses, of their strikes or mass mobilisations, is the raising of their level of consciousness through the growth of their confidence in themselves'.[4] Thus arises the possibility of a 'psychological revolution', which is 'needed for the victory of the socialist revolution'.[5] The democratic 'self-organisation' of the working class in the solidaric struggle for its interests is the key concept in Mandel's political conception. For him, it is not only an opportunity for consciousness-raising, but also a bridge to the socialist democracy of councils that will replace the bourgeois state: 'Democratic assemblies of strikers electing strike committees, and every similar mechanism in other forms of mass action, play a vital role in developing the self-organisation of the masses. In these assemblies the masses learn about self-government. In learning to conduct their own struggles, they learn to run the state and economy of tomorrow. The forms of organisation to which they become accustomed are thus the embryonic forms of the future workers' councils, the future soviets, the basic forms of organisation of the workers state to be'.[6]

Although there are many different approaches and forms of self-organisation of the working class – providing a focal point for all of the exploited and oppressed 'popular masses' in general – Mandel focuses on only two of them. For him, the strike committee is the prototype of this kind of self-organisation, and workers' councils their highest form. They are also an expression of, and a

---

3 See Mandel 1979a, p. 122 et seq.
4 Mandel 1979a, p. 128.
5 Mandel 1979a, p. 129.
6 Ibid.

means for, the realisation of broad working-class unity. For Mandel, class unity and democracy are mutually dependent. One important criterion for these organs of self-organisation is that they do not exclude anyone, that they comprise those who are not organised in trade unions or political parties too, that all working-class political groups are represented and can articulate themselves in the councils. Minorities are most likely to respect majority decisions, Mandel argues, if they know that they will have the opportunity to put their position up for debate again when new experiences have been gained. This belief in the importance of democratic and pluralistic forms of organisation is deeply rooted in Mandel's thinking. It is closely linked to his concept of revolution and to his idea of a post-capitalist society: 'If this democracy is respected, the minorities in their turn will respect the majority decisions, because they will still have an opportunity to modify these in the light of experience. Through this affirmation of workers democracy, the democratic forms of organisation of workers' struggles also proclaim a characteristic of tomorrow's workers state: the extension and not the restriction of democratic freedoms'.[7]

In terms of intellectual history, Mandel situated his position on the democratic self-organisation of the working class and of the key role of the councils as its highest form in a process by which the workers' movement became conscious of relevant experiences and their significance. A whole range of Marxist, socialist and communist theorists were involved in this knowledge process. Mandel considers the works of Rosa Luxemburg and Leon Trotsky as milestones in the theoretical examination of this experience. In 1971, he published an anthology as testimony to this process of knowledge-gathering and prefaced it with an introduction dated 1 May 1970, which remains the most detailed systematic account of his positions on the subject.[8] The text does not directly mention revolutionary syndicalist or anarchist positions because Mandel thought they had been sufficiently dealt with in the works of the Dutch council communists.[9] An obvious decisive difference between Mandel and them is that he attaches great importance to political trends and parties, especially revolutionary ones, in council and self-organising bodies.

The anthology contains writings by Marx, Engels, Kautsky; Trotsky on the Petersburg Soviet of 1905; Lenin and Trotsky on the experiences during and after the October revolution of 1917; Anna Pankratova on factory committees, Comintern positions on councils and workers' control; Bolshevik theorists from 1918–21 (Valerian Osinsky, Nikolai Bukharin, Yevgeni Preobrazhensky,

---

7 Mandel 1979a, pp. 129–30.
8 See Mandel 1971c.
9 Mandel 1971c, p. 9.

Karl Radek, Alexander Shliapnikov); Rosa Luxemburg on the programme of the Spartacus League and early KPD and on the Russian revolution; Gabor on the 1919 councils in Hungary; O'Connor and Dowson on the committees of the general strike in Seattle and Winnipeg in the same year; Murphy et al. on the British shop steward movement of 1918–20; Oertzen and Levine on socialisation, workers' control of production and the German councils of 1918–20 (plus documents of the left-wing trade union opposition and a 1919 appeal by the workers' and soldiers' councils of the Ruhr region); Gramsci on the Italian works and factory councils of 1919–20 and the programme of *L'Ordine Nuovo*; Kautsky, Bauer, Marx and Adler on the dictatorship of the proletariat, the road to socialism, democracy and council rule; Lukács on Lenin's position; Korsch on socialisation and on labour law for works councils; Gorter and Pannekoek (of the Dutch 'council communists') on Lenin and on workers' councils; Trotsky on the programme of the Left Opposition, workers' control, socialist revolution and the transitional programme; Mao on the council movement in China (soviets in the Jinggang Mountains); Agnes Smedley on the Maoist 'long march'; Danos and Gibelin on the experiences in France in June 1936; Rama, Broué and Temime on Spain 1936–37 (collectivisation in Catalonia, role of workers' committees). This is all followed by accounts of experiences after World War II: Bilandžić and Marković on workers' self-management in Yugoslavia; Sarel on independent workers' initiatives in East Germany 1945–53; Colquiri on the position of the Bolivian mineworkers' trade unions (and records of experiences with workers' control in Bolivia in 1953–63); an eyewitness account of the Hungarian council movement of 1956 by Töke; Borowski et al. on the Polish workers' council movement of 1957; an appeal by Modzelewski and Kuron titled 'For workers' councils'; Raptis (real name of 'Pablo', who after World War II was an important leader of the Fourth International) on self-government in Algeria during the struggle for independence; Ananata on independent workers' initiatives in Indonesia until 1964; on the more recent debate in western Europe: Coates on whether workers can manage their own factories; Mandel on workers' control; Gorz on the strategy of the workers' movement under contemporary capitalism; Maitan on workers' control. There are also some documents concerning May '68 in France; on 'People's Power in Nantes' and the 'Central Strike Committee of Saclay'; and an extract from a 1969 speech by the editor-in-chief of a Czechoslovak trade union journal (at the Seventh British Conference on Workers' Control in Sheffield) dealing with the formation of workers' councils during the 'Prague Spring' of 1968.[10]

---

10   Mandel 1971c, p. 5 et seq.

By making these writings accessible, Mandel wanted to give an overview without any claim to completeness. He argues that there is a general tendency for workers to take over enterprises and the economy and reorganise them in accordance with their needs and in the spirit of self-management. Mandel believes that this is borne out by a whole century of experience on all five continents.[11] Every major, sustained workers' struggle raises the question of organisational forms that contain the seeds of challenging capitalist rule. This, according to Mandel, is precisely why the Prussian minister Puttkamer said: 'Every strike contains the hydra of Revolution'.[12]

Although struggles for immediate demands such as higher wages are intrinsic to the system, they can contain the seeds of challenges to the authority of the capitalists and even the bourgeois state – for example, when pickets begin to act as 'traffic police'. Experience in such cases shows that the state does not remain neutral. The struggle for control over the supply of labour by the whole working class conflicts with the supposed 'right to work' that translates as capital's right to buy labour power under favourable conditions. According to Mandel, the seeds of alternative rule from below evolve particularly with the regional, national or even international expansion of self-organisation, which initially emerges on a local or limited sectoral scale. The transition from purely passive strikes to factory, workshop and office occupations, combined with a high level of activity up to and including a resumption of labour by the workers under their own direction, ultimately raises the question: who is the master of the enterprise, of industry, of the economy, of the state – the working class or the bourgeoisie?

Mandel argues that in this kind of struggle, 'counter-power' is expressed in concrete terms in the workers' organisation – its driving force is the striving for leadership of the struggle. This requires, for example, committees and authorised groups that collect and distribute money, distribute food and clothing, block and control access to the premises, organise leisure, carry out public relations work, gather information about the intentions of the opponents, etc. All of this marks the beginnings of working-class rule, which increasingly gains power in areas such as finance, supplies, security (armed militias), information, leisure and intelligence. With territorial expansion, other problem areas such as industrial production, planning and foreign trade come into play as well. Even initial attempts in this direction showed a tendency to involve as many strikers as possible in the direct exercise of power, which amounted to

---

11   Mandel 1971c, pp. 9–10.
12   Mandel 1971c, p. 11.

a tendency against the social division of labour between administrators and managers. Even when 'moderate' reformist leaderships were at the head of such movements, the central strike committees of broad strike movements tended to take over functions of supply and public services. Mandel cites a relevant situation that he himself had experienced: in 1960–61 in Liège, Belgium, the strike management organised all car traffic in the city, and trucks were allowed into town only with its consent. The authority of the strike management was recognised even by the bourgeoisie during this period.[13]

In contrast to 'bureaucratic strike management', and even in contrast to an otherwise democratic strike management that is confined to those organised in trade unions, Mandel advocates a grassroots democratic management by all strikers, with elected strike committees and regular general assemblies. This, in his view, is not only effective as regards the immediate goals, but also the beginning of a process of emancipation and self-liberation: one turns from being an object of the bosses and of the market into a subject. A sensation of freedom and plain joy of life is therefore typical for this kind of mass action.[14]

The expansion and centralisation of such strike committees to territorial workers' councils creates, in Mandel's view, 'base cells of the future workers state'. After all, the first soviet in Petrograd was nothing more than a delegates' council of strike committees from the city's main factories.[15]

In his later defence of the October revolution, Mandel returned to the exemplary nature of the Bolshevik-led council [*soviet*] movement and its conquest of political power in October 1917 (according to the old calendar) in Russia. He tried to refute the widespread view that this was a 'coup' and, based on numerous quotes from non-Marxist historians and opponents of the Bolsheviks, underlined the mass character of self-organisation that made the conquest of political power possible. Indeed, at the time when the Bolsheviks finally gained the majority in the council movement in the large industrial cities, they were still the only party that stood for the seizure of power by the councils ('All power to the soviets' had been their slogan since April 1917). The Bolsheviks' substantial roots in the urban working class is precisely what made it possible for them to seize political power with a very small number of casualties (even compared to the February Revolution of the same year, 1917, when the Tsar was overthrown).[16]

---

13   See Mandel 1971d, pp. 11–12 and Mandel 1961.
14   See Mandel 1971d, p. 13.
15   Ibid.
16   Mandel 1992b, pp. 10–13.

Normally, the periodically emerging seeds of workers' power never grow beyond their initial nucleus forms. Apart from the insufficient scope of such movements, Mandel considers the lack of political maturity and a very unequally developed political consciousness to be the main reasons for this. In order for a strike committee to be transformed into a 'soviet', a number of conscious decisions have to be made. The basic feature of socialist revolution is that the working class can only take possession of the means of production and of the national assets if it seizes political power. It cannot rule the factories permanently without eliminating the power of the capitalist state and taking all major means of production into its own hands. This is precisely why conscious and centralised action is needed. Movements which contain the possibility of this type of revolution are initially more or less 'spontaneous'. But subsequently, a chain of 'conscious ruptures' is necessary, and no link in the chain should be left out (with the penalty of failure). The conscious participation of the masses is indispensable, precisely because the revolution is a matter of their self-transformation from objects into subjects of history.[17]

According to Mandel, pre-revolutionary situations are triggered by a combined crisis of the capitalist mode of production, state power and all spheres of the 'superstructure' (jurisdiction, representation, ideology, culture, etc.), and by disunity, fluctuation and uncertainty in the ranks of the ruling class. Other factors are growing discontent and frustrated expectations in the working class; the increasing confidence of the workers in their own strength and therefore a greater willingness to fight; a change in the balance of forces in their favour; minor preparational struggles in which the workers assert their strength or successfully defend themselves; and the consolidation of a vanguard (which is not necessarily a revolutionary party with mass influence).[18]

Mandel argues that under such circumstances, any incident can provoke an explosion. Strikes may go beyond the usual economic objectives and traditional forms of organisation. Whether the line of 'dual power' is crossed depends mainly on the consciousness of the workers' vanguard. The systematic political work of a revolutionary organisation among advanced workers in the years leading up to the strike is an important factor for this.[19] 'These conditions were present in Russia in 1905 and in Spain in 1936, but not in Italy in 1948 or in France in 1968'.[20]

---

17 See Mandel 1971c, pp. 14–15.
18 Mandel 1971c, pp. 15–16.
19 See Mandel 1971c, p. 16; Mandel 1971a.
20 Mandel 1971c, p. 16.

Mandel writes that the ruling ideology is usually the ideology of the ruling class not just because of manipulation by the bourgeois media, but especially because of the everyday effects of the market economy, the reification of social relations, and the enslavement through wage labour and resulting alienation. Fragmentation, isolation and competition between working people creates 'false consciousness', because these are not simply illusions, but – as Marx put it – 'real appearance' produced by capitalist conditions. Workers are usually compelled to behave according to the prevailing conditions of generalised money and commodity economy. However, when in certain situations dissatisfaction manifests itself on a massive scale, the awareness that the general conditions are unacceptable emerges: the command of the entrepreneurs, the treatment of labour as a commodity, the periodic losses of income and employment due to overproduction, and so on. For this reason, the workers always 'instinctively' try to revolutionise these conditions, or at least begin to do so.[21]

According to Mandel, they feel a sense of collective power, unity and strength when they alone are in charge of the factory and hold economic power in their hands. They then establish a counter-power; their councils assume authority and begin to intervene in all spheres of social and political life. Once such 'dual power' has come into existence, the struggle is over whether it will replace the old state or be crushed again. This is the question of the revolutionary break. It is where consciousness and the influence of an adequately prepared revolutionary leadership come in.[22]

After outlining the role of the revolutionary left and the strategy of transitional demands (especially the slogan of workers' control) for the development and success of more or less 'spontaneously' emerging council movements, Mandel turns to the conditions of contemporary capitalism, which he considers more favourable to a revolutionary process in the sense described. The third industrial revolution, the reduction of the turnover time of fixed capital, and the faster pace of technological innovation require that the amortisation of fixed capital and the accumulation of new fixed capital by large monopoly groups be planned in advance, including expenses, and especially wage expenditure. From this, he argues, there arises a tendency towards national and even international 'economic programming'. Late capitalism can no longer

---

21   Mandel 1971c, p. 17.
22   Mandel 1971c, p. 18. By 'organs of dual power' Mandel does not mean bodies that combine the rule of two classes. Rather, he means bodies that the working class creates from below. If the old 'bourgeois' state, which represents the rule of the capitalist class, continues to exist, 'dual power' emerges in this way.

afford the 'luxury' of catastrophic overproduction crises (as in 1929–32). It is therefore compelled to use anti-crisis measures, which are fundamentally based on bank loans and the inflation of paper money.[23] Mandel believes that in this situation, the monopolies must try to avert major strikes at almost any cost and involve the unions as much as possible (through negotiated pay policies, social plans, 'concerted action' by employers' associations, unions and governments, etc.). This involvement undermines the authority of the trade union apparatus vis-à-vis the trade union base in the long term, which is why the trade union leaderships are particularly tough on 'wildcat' strikes. The climate of general inflation and rapid technological change is also leading to a growing awareness among workers of issues such as work organisation, assembly line rates, job security and the general direction of investment. Moreover, near full employment does not 'automatically' secure wages without relevant action. On top of this, under late capitalism there is the tendency for the significance of unskilled labour to decrease. Higher education, on the other hand, leads to dissatisfaction with the extreme hierarchy of the enterprises.[24]

Thus the problems of the class struggle shift from questions of mere distribution to questions of work organisation and even production of national income. The work rhythm becomes important, as does the location where a new factory will be built. The same is true for the use-value of commodities, the need for elected delegates instead of master craftsmen or foremen; looming redundancies and job losses become a problem, as does, because of the permanent climate of inflation, the cost of living. For Mandel, all this boils down to a tendency to challenge the rule of capital in business and in the economy, to reject the logic of capitalism and the logic of profit – and this points to the latent need of wage-earners to restructure the economy according to their own interests and therefore along socialist lines.[25]

The opposing side tries to divert this revolt towards 'class collaboration', 'participation in decision-making' or 'co-management', assisted by the trade union apparatus. However, Mandel insists that any workers' co-responsibility for capitalist-run enterprises must be rejected. Any secrecy with respect to questions concerning workers must be rejected too: there needs to be full disclosure of all business transactions to all workers, not just to a small circle of experts and trade union leaders. This involves the verification of facts at the workplace by the workers themselves. In Mandel's view, this idea of 'workers' control' depends on resistance to the institutionalisation of relevant employee

---

23   Mandel 1971c, pp. 22–3.
24   Mandel 1971c, pp. 23–4.
25   Mandel 1971c, p. 24.

bodies and their interaction with the management as this could only result in class collaboration again if the ownership structure remained unchanged.[26]

Mandel takes the view that any participation in the management of capitalist enterprises, their profits, or their ownership through 'people's shares' encourages the identification with the interests of the enterprise against competing companies, and that it therefore intensifies competition among workers. Competition undermines class organisation and elementary class consciousness. It is necessary to counter this with voluntary association, cooperation and solidarity beyond 'one's own' company. Likewise, the individual profitability of individual enterprises must be countered with the notion of collective solidarity and the rights of all working people.

Lay-offs and unemployment must therefore be rejected, irrespective of the profitability of this or that enterprise. In any event, it is necessary to oppose the acceleration of the working pace and the further fragmentation of the workforce through certain remuneration systems. For Mandel, this 'spirit of rebellion' is also rationally justified: The profitability of a national economy is more than just the individual profitability of all companies combined, and only a democratically centralised, planned economy can reap its benefits. Even before a revolutionary situation arises and the question of constructing a council democracy becomes acute, sections of the working class must gather various advanced experiences of struggle for radical demands and assimilate them into their consciousness over substantial time periods.[27]

Mandel also emphasises that the abolition of general competition – i.e. of the capitalist struggle of 'everybody against everybody' – starts with cooperation and collegial solidarity in the workplaces, which have always been the basic cells of potential workers' power. Television, decentralised consumption, residential districts, and individualised leisure activities instead of leisure spent in public buildings and assembly halls weaken the cohesion of the class – and this increases the importance of the workplace.[28]

Greater travel distances to the workplace and representation by bigger and bigger, more complex and less transparent trade unions engender detachment and result in increasingly mediated proxy decisions that undermine the members' decision-making power. With the bureaucracy becoming increasingly unaccountable and following its own sectional interests, these decision-makers ultimately turn against the interests of those they represent. Nonetheless, Mandel believes that the anarcho-syndicalists are wrong when they

---

26   Mandel 1971c, pp. 25–6.
27   Mandel 1971c, pp. 26–7.
28   Mandel 1971c, p. 30 and footnote 20.

conclude that that workers' power can only be exercised at workplace level: those are ultimately petty-bourgeois, backward-looking ideals that lead to further fragmentation. The basic tendency in contemporary capitalism (despite counter-tendencies that constantly undermine it) is the centralisation and socialisation of labour. Mandel also argues that the overthrow of bourgeois state power can never be the 'automatic' result of a mass strike because the bourgeoisie will use its police and military apparatus as well as its means of communication. It is therefore necessary for the self-organising workers to build a centralised workers' power structure across enterprises that can coordinate conscious centralised action in order to replace the bourgeois state with a workers' state.[29]

The present stage of development of the productive forces requires the coordination of economic activities. This is only possible with conscious planning or through the market. According to Mandel, allowing any kind of market economy to operate because one is wary of authoritarian centralism will lead back to the dead end of alienation because the 'laws of the market' will assert themselves behind the backs of those involved.[30]

Mandel does not consider self-managed businesses within the framework of capitalism an alternative, nor a path to a universal alternative. Isolated cooperative enterprises under capitalism are doomed to rapid failure or, alternatively, to capitalist exploitative relations with the outside world and self-exploitation – after all, they compete with capitalist enterprises. In times of revolutionary crises, workers can play a positive role in driving the revolutionary crisis forward if they take production in individual companies into their own hands. As a general slogan, however, 'self-management' under capitalist conditions cannot serve to raise consciousness. This is only possible through mobilisation for practical action in which broad sections of the population gradually initiate the overthrow of the capitalist regime. Unlike the slogan of workers' control, self-management as a general slogan only serves to sow confusion. The aim is for to workers to conclude, based on their own experiences and daily hardships, that the capitalists must be driven out of the workplaces and removed from power as a class. A further drawback of calls for 'self-management' is that it diverts the energies of fighting workers to a terrain where they can only lose in the long run.[31]

Mandel views strike committees as natural organs of the proletarian exercise of power that have historically emerged again and again. The resultant coun-

29   Mandel 1971c, pp. 34–5.
30   Mandel 1971c, pp. 35–6.
31   Mandel 1971c, pp. 36–7.

cils have been highly adaptable and have taken a variety of forms, emerging not only at workplace level, but also in the form of functional and territorial councils (workers', soldiers', students', sailors' councils, etc.). For Mandel, these types of bodies are the best way to ensure that all participants in the struggle are involved in decision-making. They enable control by the masses through the transparency of the decision-making process, universal suffrage and universal recallability, therefore offering an ideal framework for proletarian and socialist democracy. They are forums for settling differences between all tendencies and parties of the workers' movement, but they also set rational limits on these disputes by imposing a necessary modicum of discipline that must be respected by everyone in the face of the enemy (participation in a strike committee implies participation in the strike). 'It is unlikely that completely new forms of organisation for workers' rule will emerge in forthcoming revolutions. But it is equally unlikely that these organisations will be plain imitations of the Russian soviets that emerged at various stages of the revolution in the Tsarist empire. We will see many variations of the type of organisation known as the workers' council, but the basic features outlined earlier will undoubtedly apply in the majority of cases'.[32]

In this sense, Mandel considers the council form a universal feature of proletarian emancipation before and after the abolition of capitalism: it is the connecting thread, a point of continuity between the time immediately before and after the revolutionary break. For him, its politically pluralistic character is justified by the fact that nobody can claim to have solved all problems of the class struggle, the conquest of power and socialist construction in advance. It is necessary to constantly absorb new experiences through democratic debate. For Mandel, the practical application of the principles of socialist democracy is a function of class struggle. The dynamic towards socialism, towards a society free from class and domination, involves a long-term process during which all oppressive functions are mitigated and their causes gradually eliminated.[33]

Mandel bases his strategic concept of working-class self-organisation in the struggle against capital on the idea that certain tendencies of contemporary capitalism favour this kind of working-class self-liberation. The role of the peasantry and the old middle classes has continually declined, while the importance of the liberal professions and the 'new middle classes' is no greater than it was before the economic crisis of 1929–32. In the industrialised countries, the number of dependent wage-earners (i.e. the working class according to the

---

32   Mandel 1971c, p. 38, our translation.
33   Mandel 1971c, pp. 39–40.

Marxist definition: those who are forced to sell their labour) has risen to 70–85%. The differences in wages and social status between blue collar workers, white collar workers, and lower and middle civil servants have become smaller when compared to the situation before the 1930s. On the whole, a homogenisation of the wage-earning class has become evident.[34]

France in May 1968 with 10 million strikers and the wave of 24-hour general strikes in Italy in 1969–70 with 15 million strikers and significant participation of white-collar workers, civil servants, educators, and even senior managers ('cadres' in French), are experiences that testify to the new possibilities of potentially anti-capitalist mass action. These mass strikes were partly pushing demands that were a direct challenge to capitalist relations: against the authoritarian structures in factories, offices and workshops, against the right of capital and its state to control workers and the means of production.[35]

Equally positively, Mandel cites student demands such as student control, student power, self-administration of schools and universities and demands concerning the 'margins' of economic life whose significance would, in his view, increase with the development of the productive forces: researchers, scholars, doctors, hospital staff, journalists, actors, theatre staff, and so on. The reason is the comprehensive reintegration of mental labour into the production process in the form of wage labour, which also forms the objective basis for an alliance of workers, students and intellectuals. Since labour remains more than ever a commodity, mental labour too is undergoing proletarianisation. This process involves aspects of alienation such as extreme specialisation and the subdivision of tasks, the subordination of all individual skills and interests to the profit interests of big capital, the emergence of a labour market for intellectual labour with corresponding pre-selection, and frequently de-skilling. This was the objective material basis for the revolt of students and sections of the intelligentsia. They are important allies for the workers' movement not only for the struggle against capitalism, but also for socialist construction later on. Mandel interprets this objective process taking place in late capitalism mainly as an opportunity for the working class as a whole to become better at facing complicated tasks, both before and after a socialist revolution.[36]

Mass spontaneity and vanguard organisation are not mutually contradictory. In Mandel's view, vanguard organisations lead the mass movement to success in times of revolutionary upsurge and provide support in times of political setbacks. A revolutionary vanguard party articulates itself within the self-

---

34   Mandel 1971c, pp. 48–9.
35   Mandel 1971c, p. 49.
36   Mandel 1971c, pp. 50–1.

organisational structures of the working class and oppressed masses, i.e. the councils. There, it tries to advance positions and demands aimed at the exercise of power by the proletariat. In Mandel's view, it is perfectly legitimate that an organisations' greater activity increases its influence in the movement, but this does not entail any special privileges. In any case, no organisation shall become a vanguard by self-appointment. It will only become a vanguard when significant sections of the exploited and oppressed put its proposals into practice. There is no contradiction between political persuasion and leadership, on the one hand, and the self-activity of the organised masses.[37]

Mandel concludes with a quote from the *Communist Manifesto*, according to which the communists have no interests separate from those of the proletariat as a whole. They 'only' highlight and advance the interests of the proletariat independently of nationality and always stand for the interests of the movement as a whole: 'The Communists, therefore, are on the one hand, practically, the most advanced and resolute section of the working-class parties of every country, that section which pushes forward all others; on the other hand, theoretically, they have over the great mass of the proletariat the advantage of clearly understanding the line of march, the conditions, and the ultimate general results of the proletarian movement'.[38] It should be critically noted, though, that this is no small claim made by Marx in the name of 'the Communists' and appropriated by Mandel. The claim that one is in a position to formulate the correct political line by virtue of superior insight, in contrast to all other parts of the proletariat, seems to me to contain the seeds of the arrogance and self-importance later used by self-proclaimed 'vanguards' to justify practices of authoritarian coercion and sterile sectarianism.

When asked in the late 1970s what historical situations can be described as 'revolutionary crises' or at least as 'pre-revolutionary crises' – e.g. the events of June 1936 in France, the liberation from German occupation in 1944, or the movement of May '68 – Mandel cautiously replied: 'There is a certain lack of precision in the relevant concepts used by the Marxist classics, and, despite the modest theoretical gains of recent years, the Fourth International has still not entirely eliminated this imprecision'.[39] In his view, they only become a revolutionary situation or a revolutionary crisis when an upsurge in the mass movement coincides with the growing inability of the bourgeoisie as the ruling class to continue to rule: 'In Lenin's brilliant formulation, a revolutionary crisis

---

37   Mandel 1971c, pp. 52–3. Mandel 1971a.
38   Marx 2004, chapter I.
39   Mandel 1979d, p. 6.

breaks out "when the lower classes" no longer want to be ruled in the old way, and when the "upper classes" cannot carry on ruling in the old way".[40]

Mandel argues that there was no genuine revolutionary situation in May '68 because de Gaulle's government had never lost its ability to govern or take political initiative. De Gaulle was clever enough not to attack the mass movement head-on; he manoeuvred and waited for the right moment to go on the counter-offensive. With the active help of the French Communist Party (which prevented the movement from breaking the limits of the existing system), he succeeded in bringing the situation back under control.[41]

Drawing on the experience of previous revolutionary crises in Europe (he cites Russia 1917, Germany 1918–19, Hungary, Spain 1936–37, Yugoslavia 1941–44 and 'perhaps even' Portugal 1975, adding that this list is 'not exhaustive'), Mandel highlights two complementary prerequisites: a fairly advanced stage of decomposition of the repressive state apparatus and the emergence of 'organs of workers' and popular power' which represent a potential alternative state power from below. If the staff of the banks refuse to obey the instructions of their superiors and instead accept the instructions of the workers' councils, and if this phenomenon extends, for instance, to the police, then the process is fairly advanced. What is additionally necessary is a 'crisis of legitimacy of the state institutions in the eyes of the great majority of the working class', and this majority has to regard the new structures that have emerged from self-organisation from below as far more legitimate than the old state institutions.[42] These are far more substantial shifts of popular sentiment than merely the feeling of no longer being represented by a particular government in parliamentary elections. Until majorities hold such views, it is necessary that they gain advanced experience in struggle, including sharp clashes between the council or council-like movements and the old state institutions.

Despite his statements, Mandel rejects a codification of abstract concepts and advocates a scientific approach to historical experience combined with a willingness to test and verify concepts in practice:

> Our concepts are still rather imprecise, even if we are approaching a greater rigour. Once again, all this must be studied in the light of the historical experiences in Western Europe since 1917 and a thorough balance-sheet drawn up, categorizing, classifying, and comparing the revolution-

---

40   Mandel 1979d, p. 7.
41   Ibid.
42   Mandel 1979d, pp. 8–9.

ary and pre-revolutionary situations. I think that it is by this historico-genetic method that we will succeed, rather than by an abstract attempt to work out concepts that may well be challenged by the next historical experiences. It is only the balance-sheet of history and revolutionary practice that will teach us to think more correctly.[43]

Mandel notes that there is a difference between cool-headed historical analysis and political statements aimed at influencing the open outcome of any given situation. In June 1936, for example, Trotsky said that the 'French revolution had begun' – only to correct himself in retrospect, characterising the situation merely as a 'caricature' of the February 1917 revolution in Russia. In Mandel's view, Trotsky's original statement should be understood as implying that everything must be done to bring about a truly revolutionary situation in the context of the emerging mass movement and the June 1936 general strike in France. Revolutionaries need to dispassionately analyse the events – and recognise, for example, that many who take part in the general strike merely want to give the Popular Front government a 'friendly push' to strengthen rather than transcend it. But on the other hand, they cannot be just passive spectators: 'Any self-respecting revolutionary organisation which is more than a mere sideline sect has to attempt to change the pre-revolutionary situation into a revolutionary one'.[44]

Whether in June 1936, during the period of liberation from the Nazi yoke immediately after World War II, or in May '68: in all these instances, the role of the existing traditional leaderships of the labour movement must not be underestimated. It was they who had the decisive influence in the working class and in the movements, and it was their stance that influenced the course of events. If a movement of this kind did not develop into a truly revolutionary situation, then this should not be blamed on too many 'objective factors'. On the other hand, Mandel is very aware of the limits of an assessment that is based on hypotheses of what would have happened if the existing leaders had acted differently: '... but of course with the aid of "ifs" one can rewrite the whole of world history!'[45]

Mandel's praise of Rosa Luxemburg's role in the struggle against the 'tried and tested tactic' of Social Democracy (which in his opinion had become obsolete at the turn of the century), namely to organise more and more workers to win more and more votes until, at some point, there are enough to vote

---

43   Mandel 1979d, p. 10.
44   Ibid.
45   Mandel 1979d, p. 12.

capitalism out is rooted in his idea of a self-education process by the proletarian masses through direct action and self-organisation. When Engels argued against the anarchists that the idea of a general strike was 'nonsensical', he misjudged the dynamics of such mass movements, according to Mandel. The reformist trade union leader Legien – although he himself would later call for a general strike that brought down the Kapp putsch – condensed this position into the formula 'general strike is general nonsense' and used it in the mass strike debate against Luxemburg and the party left. Engels's and later Legien's argument against the general strike was: if you already have a majority, you do not need it (you can then immediately seize political power), and if do not have a majority it will fail precisely because you do not have one. Luxemburg, in contrast, not only recognised that the age of imperialism had also put an end to the period of peaceful 'evolution', but also that proletarian mass movements become revolutionary by constantly drawing new strata into their activities and struggles, and that these masses gain and assimilate experiences very quickly when compared with 'normal' times when they are passive objects. In this way, their political consciousness can very quickly change in the direction of clearly revolutionary resolve.[46]

Mandel's concept is internally coherent and based on the analysis of several of experiences, although the focus seems to be on the first rather than the second half of the twentieth century (his relativisation of the significance of May '68, which can hardly be placed in the same category as Russia in 1905 or 1917 or Germany in 1918–19, would suggest so). However, it stands and falls with the question of whether contemporary capitalism really produces the social preconditions for periodic spectacular upsurges of the proletarian mass movement, and whether these upsurges result in council-like structures of self-organisation, or in council movements that contain at least the seeds of an alternative state power, harbouring within them the prospect of a socialist revolution in Mandel's sense. Some of the conditions that Mandel cites certainly have to be critically re-examined today – e.g. his thesis of a gradual 'homogenisation' of the working class.

At the same time, let us note that Mandel assumes fairly protracted pre-revolutionary or revolutionary situations in which the masses have the opportunity for collective learning and self-education. Revolutionary accomplishment in the sense of Mandel's ideas therefore also depends on a surge in mass activity from below that is neither broken nor reversed before an opportunity to seize political power rears its head.

---

46   See Mandel 1971d.

2   Strategy of Transitional Demands

Advocating a strategy of transitional demands, Ernest Mandel stood in the tradition of the *Transitional Programme*, the programmatic founding document
of the Fourth International of 1938. At the same time, he was seeking a way
out of a dilemma which he thought had long been a typical feature of socialist programmes. His central text explaining this strategic approach, written in
the spring of 1971, begins by stating: 'There is a red thread running through the
whole history of the modern workers' movement in western Europe: the practical division between day-to-day demands and struggles, on the one hand, and
the struggle for the ultimate goal on the other'.[47]

The *Transitional Programme* substantiates the need for transitional demands thus: 'Classical Social Democracy, functioning in an epoch of progressive capitalism, divided its program into two parts independent of each other:
the minimum program which limited itself to reforms within the framework
of bourgeois society, and the maximum program which promised substitution
of socialism for capitalism in the indefinite future. Between the minimum and
the maximum program no bridge existed. And indeed Social Democracy has no
need of such a bridge, since the word socialism is used only for holiday speech-
ifying'.[48]

Both for the founders of the Fourth International and for Mandel, the belief
that the objective conditions for socialist revolution exist on a global scale is a
central prerequisite. This is why they consider it important to work on the subjective conditions and fight for the creation of a new political leadership that
can equip the proletariat intellectually. The transitional programme makes this
very clear: 'All talk to the effect that historical conditions have not yet "ripened"
for socialism is the product of ignorance or conscious deception. The objective
prerequisites for the proletarian revolution have not only "ripened"; they have
begun to get somewhat rotten. Without a socialist revolution, in the next historical period at that, a catastrophe threatens the whole culture of mankind'.[49]

For Ernest Mandel, 'periodic outbreaks of huge mass struggles (mass strikes,
general strikes, general strikes with factory occupations, etc.) are inevitable in
the era of the general crisis of capitalism'.[50] We will later examine the similarities and differences between the *Transitional Programme* and Ernest Mandel's
work in their assessment of contemporary capitalism's propensity to crisis in

---

47   Mandel 1978d, p. 283, our translation.
48   Trotsky 2002, p. 5.
49   Trotsky 2002, pp. 1–2.
50   Mandel 1978d, p. 287, our translation.

more detail. In both cases, the view that capitalism in its imperialist stage is a doomed social system – i.e. since 1914 at the latest – underpins the notion that there is both a need and a possibility to build a bridge between day-to-day struggles/demands and the struggle for the conquest of political power by the working class. This is why the obstacles on the road to socialist revolution are not deemed 'objective' but 'subjective'. In the *Transitional Programme*, this is highlighted by the sentence: 'The historical crisis of mankind is reduced to the crisis of the revolutionary leadership'.[51]

This perspective entails the belief that Social Democracy and Stalinism have historically failed as mass tendencies of the workers' movement and that their practice has become an obstacle to the success of socialist revolution. If the problem lies in the immaturity of subjective conditions, then this means that the insufficient development of class consciousness is the reason for the absence of victorious socialist revolutions. A new leadership, a new organised political movement, a new party and a new international must replace the old leadership. However, they cannot be built simply through propaganda for the goal of socialist revolution and socialist society. It is necessary to develop the workers' consciousness through their struggles, to participate in these struggles, and to introduce transitional slogans that can lead to advanced struggle experiences and ultimately to a challenge to the system by the proletarian mass movement.

In *Introduction to Marxism*, Mandel succinctly summarises this approach thus:

> In our epoch, capitalist exploitation and imperialist oppression again and again arouse the masses to major struggles. But by themselves the masses generally do not go beyond the formulation of the most immediate aims of these struggles: the defence or increase of real wages; the defence or conquest of certain fundamental democratic freedoms; the fall of particularly oppressive governments, etc. The bourgeoisie can grant concessions to the masses in struggle to prevent these struggles from developing to the point where they threaten capitalist exploitation in its entirety. It is even more willing to do this because it possesses innumerable means of neutralising these concessions, of taking back with one hand what it has given with the other. If it accepts a rise in wages, an increase in prices can maintain profits. If working hours are reduced, the rhythm of work can be stepped up. If the workers win measures of social security, taxes can be

---

51   Trotsky 2002, p. 2.

increased so that they themselves end up paying for what the state seems to be handing out, etc. To break this vicious circle, the masses must be won to the adoption of transitional demands as the objectives of their present struggles – demands whose realisation becomes more and more incompatible with the normal functioning of the capitalist economy and the bourgeois state. These demands need to be formulated in such a way that they can be understood by the masses – otherwise they will just remain demands on paper. At the same time, their nature should provoke, by their very content and the depth of the struggles unleashed, a challenge to the entire capitalist system and the birth of organs of self-organisation of the masses, organs of dual power. Far from being valuable only in times of acute revolutionary crisis, transitional demands – such as the demand for workers' control – tend precisely to give birth to such a revolutionary crisis by encouraging the workers to challenge the capitalist system in action as well as in their consciousness.[52]

The history of political movements that lay a claim to socialism, especially the history of the Communist movement since its Stalinisation, has led to the strategy of transitional demands being regarded as a kind of whim or sect speciality of 'Trotskyism' to this day. However, a study of the debates and resolutions of the Third and Fourth Congresses of the Comintern reveals that the Fourth International took up a tradition originally developed by the Communist world movement and later buried in the course of its Stalinisation. Back in the early days, the defence of partial and transitional demands against 'leftist' critics was closely linked to the united front policy. Both were connected to the task of winning majorities for communist principles and socialist revolution among the working classes of the capitalist countries.

The theses on 'tactics' adopted by the third world congress of the Comintern and the commissioner on this question, Karl Radek, justified the struggle for partial and transitional demands in a similar way as the 'Trotskyist' tradition later would. Subsequently, the fourth congress of the Comintern discussed a general programme to substantiate the necessity of transitional demands. The debate was not concluded at this congress or during Lenin's lifetime (the plan was to continue it at the fifth world congress). However, since some aspects remained unclear at the fourth world congress, and since particularly Bukharin's contribution seemed to be a 'left-communist' objection to adding a validation of transitional demands in the Comintern programme,

---

52   Mandel 1979a, pp. 125–6.

Lenin pushed through a statement on behalf of the Russian delegation (which, remarkably, also bore Bukharin's signature and was presented by Bukharin) that is revealing enough:[53] 'The dispute over how the transitional demands should be formulated and in which section of the program they should be included has awakened a completely erroneous impression that there exists a principled difference. In light of this, the Russian delegation unanimously confirms that the drawing up of transitional slogans in the programs of the national sections and their general formulation and theoretical motivation in the general section of the program cannot be interpreted as opportunism'.[54]

Three out of five points in the motion adopted by congress to continue the programme debate address the issue of transitional demands:

3. The programmes of the national sections must clearly and decisively establish the necessity of the struggle for transitional demands, making the necessary reservations about the dependence of these demands on the concrete circumstances of time and place.

4. The theoretical basis for all transitional and partial demands must be clearly stated in the general programme, and the fourth congress likewise decisively condemns the attempt to depict the inclusion of transitional demands in the programme as opportunism, as well as all attempts to gloss over or replace the fundamental revolutionary tasks by partial demands.

5. The general programme must clearly explain the basic historical types of the transitional demands of the national section, in accordance with the basic differences in the economic and political structure of the different countries, for example England on the one hand, and India on the other.[55]

The wording reveals controversial debates and important nuances of opinion behind the largely unanimous nature of the declaration ultimately adopted. An analysis of the debates that took place at the congress would suggest so too, although this is not the place to elaborate on this any further. For our purposes, it is relevant to note that these formulations, as well as Ernest Mandel's in *Introduction to Marxism*, clearly show that it is not enough to set out a strategy of

53   See Communist International 1922.
54   Mandel 1971a, chapter 10.
55   Frank 1967.

transitional demands as a general idea. A blueprint 'beyond time and space' instructing revolutionaries how to work among the masses would be at odds with its strategic approach. They must instead try to understand the contradictions of the social situation in any given country, its effects on the situation of the exploited and oppressed classes and strata, and their mentality and level of consciousness. It is also necessary to determine what demands and calls for action that transcend the limits of the capitalist system can be linked to the workers' objective interests and perceived needs. Mandel, beyond arguing for this strategy in general, was himself involved in the drafting of action programmes in different periods and in different countries, and he tried to put them into practice.[56]

> What Marx said on this subject more than a century ago remains as true today as it was then. If the working class abandoned the struggle for these immediate demands, the sale of labour power as a commodity below its value would become the general rule, and as a result, the working class would become increasingly atomised and demoralised. The decisive point here is whether we restrict ourselves to this traditional routine or whether we know how to integrate objectives into the daily struggle that correspond to the qualitative needs of the working masses in this educational and emancipatory sense ... and that cannot be integrated into the capitalist system because they fundamentally exceed its boundaries [*systemsprengend*].[57]

Transitional solutions are linked to the prior knowledge that the capitalists have systemic ways and means at their disposal to undermine or reverse partial gains that have been won. Wage increases can be offset by price increases. Shorter working hours can be made up for by lay-offs and labour intensification. By proposing solutions that challenge the power of capital to impose its interests against workers' interests, and by applying standards of solidarity rather than profit, the consistent implementation of transitional demands effectively amounts to imposing another society – a society of associated producers – against the existing capitalist society. The aim is to overcome the political power of capital through the conquest of political power by the working class. An alternative logic to the capitalist logic of competition and profit will

---

56   See eyewitness testimony Livio Maitan, Helene Jungclas, Hans Peiffer and Helmut Wendler.

57   Mandel 1978d, p. 289, our translation.

not result from abstract deliberations, but from the consistent development of the struggle for proletarian interests that is linked to a maximum increase in proletarian self-organisation.[58]

The *Transitional Programme* uses the terms 'sliding scale of wages' and 'sliding scale of hours', which are difficult to understand today. Their example shall be used to show how, according to the concept, transitional solutions are supposed to work. 'Sliding scale of wages' means the automatic adjustment of wages to price developments. As mentioned earlier, this is based on the prior knowledge that wage increases previously won can be eroded by price rises. The consequence of this is that the trade unions' wage demands in collective bargaining talks follow the devaluation of money ('inflation adjustment') before real wages increase and a redistribution in favour of wage earners can even occur. The stronger an inflationary tendency, the more pressing such demands become. But the question immediately arises as to who determines how the price development for the average basket of goods of a wage-dependent household is to be determined. It is in the logic of transitional demands that this question is not left to the business side or to the authority of the bourgeois state, but that price control committees consisting of workers and consumers are set up, constantly examining this development and determining the results.

The ongoing broad discussion and the appropriation of authority and power to determine what basket of goods corresponds to the present real wage will encourage and enable proletarians in their roles as producers as well as consumers to develop alternative self-organised structures and an alternative decision-making logic to capitalism.

The 'sliding scale of hours' refers to the demand to reduce general working hours 'until everyone has work'. This is a simple and logical response to the capitalist contradiction by which mass unemployment coexists with increasing labour intensity and the massive use of overtime. One need not be a socialist to consider this a just and rational demand. However, its consistent implementation would challenge important features of the capitalist system. These include the freedom of capitalists and their management to hire and fire as they please, depending on the situation and interests of their businesses. Unemployment is always an important regulating factor in this system because it keeps real wages within certain limits or pushes them down. In general, the more unemployment there is, the more difficult it is to defend the workers' immediate interests. Reducing working hours until everyone has work will consequently eliminate

---

58   See Mandel 1978d, pp. 304–5.

the possibility of mass unemployment and substantially alter the balance of class power in favour of the wage earners.[59]

If such a demand were to be enforced through massive mobilisation and strikes, the inevitable question would be how to prevent the employers' side from offsetting a radical reduction in working time through other measures, such as intensifying work as well as enforcing greater 'flexibility' in the use of labour. This puts the question of workers' control over hiring and firing and over working conditions – essentially over the whole production process – on the agenda. To establish this kind of control, representative bodies are elected at the various levels of departments, enterprises and corporations, and it is part of the strategy of transitional demands to provide these bodies with all manner of important information about the enterprise and its situation. To facilitate the flow of such information, business books and business correspondence must be made public – and this uncompromising encroachment on 'business secrets' is fundamentally a challenge to the capitalists' status as masters of their enterprises, which is indispensable for capitalism. What is more, 'control' means the exercise of veto rights over all decisions that are in any way relevant to the interests of the workforce – and thus the 'master-in-my-own-house position' of the entrepreneur is called into question permanently.[60]

The strategy of transitional demands is not confined to problems that affect enterprises but, closely linked to the united front policy, aims at the overall social and political level. It seeks to establish the unity of wage labourers in the struggle against capital. Special attention is paid to the interests of the most disadvantaged layers to avoid creating a kind of illusory unity based on the neglect of their interests. This unity must not be based solely on the interests of the privileged 'labour aristocracy' layers of the class, which tend to come to an arrangement with capital once they have won more or less stable gains for themselves. For wages policy, this means, for instance, that attempts must be made to replace percentage demands with fixed-term deposit demands so that the gap between the highest and lowest wages does not widen further. This class unity is represented organisationally through bodies where organised and otherwise unorganised wage labourers work together regardless of their political views. The highest form of such class unity organs are councils (soviets). In political terms, however, unity can only be sustained if the fighting strength of the workers grows such a degree that political power is seized. But the strategy of transitional demands starts from the assumption that the majority of the

---

59   Alles 1989, pp. 66–7.
60   Alles 1989, pp. 70–1.

working class has not yet been won to the notion that capitalist private ownership of the means of production should be replaced by socialised ownership and the collective management by associated producers. The practice of workers' control and the resolute enforcement of workers' interests is expected to lead the majority of workers to this conclusion once they have processed their experiences and insights won in the class struggle.[61]

Under normal circumstances, the overwhelming majority of workers will not contemplate this objective. It can reach the opinion well in advance that it would be advantageous and necessary to have a government that represents the interests of the working class as consistently as the bourgeois parties represent the interests of the capitalist class. This is why action programmes inspired by the strategy of transitional demands usually culminate at government level, demanding that parties claiming to represent the interests of the working class form a government and purely bourgeois parties are excluded. We will discuss the related problems of 'workers' governments' in more detail in our subchapter on united front tactics. In the present context, the idea that the working class needs practical experience with such governments in order to gain awareness of the need for a completely different system rather than any form of bourgeois rule (including bourgeois parliamentary democracy) is of crucial importance: a system based on the self-organised structures that is has created in the struggle for its own interests, i.e. a socialist council democracy.[62]

Of course, debates on whether a particular demand is transitional are not the be all and end all of the strategy of transitional demands – such debates easily lead to scholasticism. The socialist or communist organisation in question has the task of working out an entire system of social, economic, democratic and political demands and corresponding proposals for action. These demands must be based on the objective concrete problems of the class struggle as they appear in a given historical situation and as they are felt by the majority of the working class. Moreover, they must direct the self-organisation of the working class on all levels towards the objective of breaking the power of capital and seizing political power (this is the beginning of the actual process of socialist transformation).[63]

A comparison between Mandel's essay 'A Socialist Strategy For Western Europe' (1964) and his treatise on the 'Strategy of Transitional Demands' (1971)

---

61   See Mandel 1969n.
62   See also Mandel 1970a, pp. 17–16.
63   See Alles 1989, p. 65.

reveals a number of different accents, despite the fact that the political method remains the same (as do its relatively new lines of argument when compared with the 1938 *Transitional Programme*, in that Mandel invokes certain tendencies of 'neo-capitalism' and 'late capitalism').[64] These accents indicate not so much a development on Mandel's part; rather, they imply that the milieu that he seeks to address has changed. Moreover, they imply a change in the political climate in which he is trying to communicate his views.

In *Socialist Strategy for Western Europe*, Mandel rejects the notion favoured by the long-lasting post-war boom, Keynesian state intervention and the continuous rise in living standards that a more or less crisis-free capitalism has been achieved, and that this rules out significant mass mobilisations that could challenge the system.[65] The fundamental contradictions of the capitalist mode of production and its vulnerability to crises have remained, Mandel writes, and the living standards by no means eliminate the possibility of significant mass struggles.[66] Taking this as a starting point, he argues for a 'Strategy of structural reforms' (the name of the relevant subchapter). His line of argumentation shows that there is no fundamental difference between this and the 'strategy of transitional demands'. It is rather the case that Mandel starts from a concept of reforms rooted in the left-social-democratic milieu in order to transition to an understanding of the transitional strategy:

> The main purpose of the strategy of structural reforms – invented by the left wing of the Belgian working class movement and now increasingly adopted by its counterparts throughout Europe is to effect an integration between the immediate aims of the masses and the objectives of the struggle which objectively challenge the very existence of the capitalist system itself. It does not mean in the slightest that the workers' movement abandons wage claims, demands for shorter hours, the insistence on a sliding scale to combat the rising cost of living, etc ... But it does mean that the movement does not limit itself to these immediate objectives or to a combination of struggle for these objectives together with vague propaganda for the 'socialist revolution', the 'socialization of the means of production' even 'the dictatorship of the proletariat', which, while they are not part and pared of the daily struggle, can exert no influence on the practical development of the class struggle. It means that the

---

64   See Mandel 1965 and 1978d, p. 283 et seq.
65   See Mandel 1965.
66   Ibid.

working-class movement, *in its day-by-day struggle*, combines the fight
for immediate objectives which, rooted in the immediate interests of the
masses, go on to challenge objectively the operation of the capitalist system.[67]

Mandel argues that such 'anti-capitalist structural reforms' should not be di-
luted for the sake of a reformist strategy. For him, the notion of depriving capital
of power 'step by step', beginning with the capture of 'outlying positions', is
the wrong path to take. Likewise, he warns against the 'institutionalisation'
of organisations and structures of 'workers' control'. In contrast to such left
social-democratic notions of a more or less 'harmonious' development towards
overcoming capitalism, he advocates a strategy of conflict that seeks, as far as
possible, to win the struggle for power at all levels – a strategy that aims from
the outset at the centres of capitalist control and the political power of the
bourgeoisie.[68] In the last two subsections of the essay – and this may well have
run counter to the intuition of most politically committed people, including
the left-wing social democrats of those years – he suggests that political activity be based on the anticipation of forthcoming mass struggles carrying within
them the potential of growing radicalisation and internationalisation.[69]

In 1971, Mandel speaks a different language to some degree. There is no
longer a need to defend the anticipation of new crisis-like developments and
broad mass struggles as realistic. May '68 in France, the Italian 'creeping May'
of 1969, a new cycle of broad class struggle mobilisations, the radicalisation of
young people in the late 1960s, and the emergence of a new political generation
open to revolutionary and socialist ideas have become a fact of modern history.
In western Europe, the Fourth International has abandoned its entrist tactics –
this, despite the fact that even young people organised in 'traditional parties'
of the labour movement became receptive to left wing socialist ideas after
1968 – and is trying to build organisationally independent open sections. It is
doing so in competition with other tendencies and organisations – not just the
social-democratic left and the more or less Moscow-oriented ('Stalinist' or post-
Stalinist) Communist Parties, but also Maoist, spontaneist, and other groups
and tendencies. In this new climate and situation, Mandel argues – while looking 'to the left' as well as 'to the right' – for the same strategic approach as in
1965:

---

67   Mandel 1965, pp. 7–8.
68   Mandel 1965, p. 9.
69   Mandel 1965, p. 13 et seq.

Therefore, a socialist strategy that starts from the inevitability of periodic outbreaks of great mass struggles – the theoretical justification and empirical confirmation of this thesis seems unquestionable to us – has to concentrate as far as possible on those forms of daily agitation that give the working masses the necessary struggle experience and insights that are necessary in order for revolutionary initiative and consciousness to develop at the 'breaking points' of objective development (the outbreak of mass strikes, the sudden outbreak of a great financial, monetary or military crisis; the beginning of a serious economic recession, etc.). This is the central function of the strategy of transitional demands, which has the struggle for workers' control as its axis.[70]

Instead of using the idea of 'structural reforms' as a starting point for communicating his own strategic approach, as in 1965, Mandel now rejects this notion and presents it as the flawed, inadequate alternative of left-wing social democrats and reform-oriented communists:

The main weakness of 'reforms to overcome the system' [systemüberwindend] consists in an insufficient understanding of the structural character of the capitalist mode of production, i.e. the immutability of the two central ... nerve centres of this form of society: relations of production and state power (state apparatus). Neither can be changed gradually. They can either continue to function or be paralysed in a severe social crisis. But if this crisis does not lead to their abolition, they will inevitably rise from this paralysis towards a new 'normalisation'.[71]

According to Mandel, reforms are either compatible with the functioning of the capitalist economy, in which case they cannot 'overcome the capitalist system' or they are not, in which case the struggle for them necessarily culminates in a decisive power struggle against the capitalist class and the replacement of the capitalist mode of production with another. A state of limbo between the two is inconceivable, since a modern industrial society would collapse rapidly if people stopped working. Investment by entrepreneurs would decline to the extent that one incentive after the other would be taken away from them. Without replacing profit with another incentive, production would come to a standstill, and the propertyless workers would be the first to be existentially

---

70   Mandel 1978d, p. 289, our translation.
71   Mandel 1978d, p. 290; p. 319 footnote 4, our translation.

affected in a most unpleasant way. Nor is it sufficient to obtain a majority of votes in elections or majorities in parliament, because this does not change the bourgeois nature of the state. According to him, a number of experiences proved that the willingness of 'left-wing' governments to carry out reforms was shattered by the balance of power in the economy and the state. Likewise, the idea of an immediate introduction of workers' self-management without the prior abolition of capitalism, which emerged in left-Catholic circles of the labour movement, does not add up: such self-managed companies are subject to competition with other capitalist enterprises and forced to take all kinds of measures against their own workforce.[72]

Mandel reproaches the Italian 'Manifesto' group, which demands 'communism now!' and wants the immediate abolition of all social division of labour, without considering that this would require a prolonged process of activating, educating and self-educating. As a propaganda slogan, i.e. a slogan that is not embedded in a system of transitional slogans, Mandel considers this idea to be unproductive: it does not contain any 'instructions for working class mass actions that might burst the limits of the system [systemsprengend]'.[73] Ernest Mandel nevertheless regarded the emergence of such slogans as characteristic of specific features of the renewed outbreak of the social structural crisis in late capitalism. The contradiction between the increasingly social character of production and the private form of appropriation appeared not so much as a conflict between an increasingly impoverished workforce and increasingly wealthy capitalists, but almost the other way round: as a kind of unredeemed promise contained in the level of productive forces achieved, but with the barriers inherent in the capitalist mode of production preventing real steps from being taken towards the realm of freedom. The mass movements and mass strikes since 1968 raised questions about a self-determined life, about eliminating the company hierarchy and authoritarian structures, indeed about a completely different life – as expressed, for example, by the slogan 'all power to the imagination' in May '68. Mandel did not argue against these emancipatory impulses, but against the idea that marginal groups in society – even if they were 'millions of hippies' – can bring about emancipation, bypassing the necessary process of self-liberation by the working class and all exploited and oppressed strata of society. Mandel, a proponent of overcoming economist self-restraint, opposed the various forms of 'voluntarism' represented by Maoist groups and stressed that sending intellectuals 'into production' for limited periods of time did not

---

72   Mandel 1978d, p. 290 et seq.; pp. 292–3.
73   Mandel 1978d, p. 294, our translation.

amount to abolishing the old division of labour.[74] Mandel tries to show that more recent workers' struggles had an objectively anti-capitalist and generally emancipatory character. However, revolutionary organisations must intervene to help them to develop this character and become fully aware of it. They have to develop appropriate forms of action and ultimately make it their conscious objective to overthrow the capitalist system and replace it with a one in which the organs of workers' power begin to establish socialist relations.

The central role of 'workers' control' in Mandel's theory throws up a complicated problem. While Mandel's general argumentation for 'transitional demands' seems quite plausible, there is no question that the slogan of 'workers' control' was popular in western European countries only in exceptional cases, and not at all in west Germany. Not even the most advanced sections of west German workers were familiar with the great historical experiences associated with this slogan. Historical experience had shown that, after the conquest of political power in a country with a predominantly peasant population like Russia, workers' control served a preliminary stage to the expropriation of the capitalists. The Bolsheviks, who did not have a predefined plan for the nationalisation of industry, found that the regime of workers' control in the factories could not be maintained for long. Entrepreneurs could not come to terms with it, and the workforce pushed for more radical solutions.[75] Other experiences had shown – as in Italy at in 1919–20 – that the transition from strikes for higher wages to the occupation of factories, combined with a generalisation of the slogan for workers' control, amounted to a decisive showdown with enterprises and bourgeois rule as a whole. The dilution of this demand ('trade union control') and disorientation of the mass movement that had been enthusiastic about it was the prelude to fascism's rise to power.[76]

But in West Germany, even in the early 1970s, not many people were able to make sense of this terminology. The logic of a strategy of transitional demands can only work if it takes existing consciousness as a starting point – this is precisely what is supposed to prevent it from becoming sterile propaganda. Here, however, Mandel finds himself confronted with a workers' vanguard (hegemonised by social democracy) that is indeed familiar with the slogan and to some extent also with the practice of 'co-determination', but for whom 'workers' control' is rather an alien concept or, at best, the exotic peculiarity of a very small political movement – Trotskyism.

---

74   Mandel 1978d, pp. 294–5.
75   See Mandel 1992b, p. 10.
76   See Scheuer 1996, pp. 70–1.

This is why Ernest Mandel discusses Fritz Vilmar's counter-proposal (in *Gewerkschaftliche Monatshefte* of March 1970, in *Frankfurter Rundschau* of 9 May 1970 and in *Konkret* of 22 November 1970) to replace 'workers' control' with 'co-determination at the workplace' (in contrast to co-determination in supervisory boards, which are detached from the workforce) without insisting on the literal use of the term 'workers' control'. Instead, he warns workers' representatives against any acceptance of 'co-responsibility' for 'their' capitalist enterprise. The more they allow themselves to be involved in such co-responsibility, the less, for example, works councils can consistently represent the interests of their staff. The obligation of industrial peace and confidentiality (i.e. the binding confidentiality of information in participatory bodies) have a demobilising effect on the workforce and weaken it in the long term. What is decisive is not what words one uses, but the observance of certain principles: no subordination to the logic of capitalist profitability or to the interests of one's 'own' company; the promotion of solidarity between workers as a decisive aspect of their actions; the exercise of veto rights against entrepreneurial decisions instead of co-responsibility; public negotiations with the bosses' side, complete transparency in front of the workers; systematic demands for the abolition of business and banking secrecy and the full disclosure of accounts and business correspondence; the introduction of a *de facto* veto right for the workforce in all matters concerning labour organisation.

'If someone insisted on describing these ... demands as "co-determination in the workplace", then it would of course be pointless to argue over words. But then we would still face the additional problem of infusing the official German Trade Union Confederation (DGB) proposals with this content instead of the content they have today. As long as this problem is not solved, it would only create additional confusion to use the same term for diametrically opposed projects'.[77] The crucial difference, Mandel argues, is whether one envisages a policy of class reconciliation, i.e. the promotion of class collaboration, or a policy of class confrontation, i.e. the independent class struggle of workers, which precisely translates into the concept of workers' control. Here one might also notice Mandel's interest in promoting the development of his own organisation in Germany, the German section of the Fourth International (Gruppe Internationale Marxisten or GIM, which was quite small and lacked influence), by giving priority to the defence of 'original' concepts over the pedagogical intention of meeting left-wing social-democratic thinkers where they were at

---

77   Mandel 1978d, p. 308, our translation.

the time. At any rate, Mandel was quite optimistic at this time about the growth potential of Fourth International organisations in the western European countries. He certainly contemplated the possibility that they might be in a position to lead sizable political forces to the left of the 'traditional' currents of the labour movement in the foreseeable future. An exaggeration of political pedagogy in relation to reformist circles may have been counterproductive for Mandel in view of such prospects (although, as the discussion with Vilmar shows, he did try to engage in dialogue with reformist trends in this phase). Mandel counters objections to the strategy of transitional demands 'from the left' – i.e. from left-wing student circles and successor organisations to the Socialist German Student League (SDS) – by pointing out the 'revisionist' and 'Kautskyan' roots of the 'clean' separation of day-to-day struggles from the ultimate goal. According to Mandel, the substance of these objections – i.e. that it is irresponsible or even deceptive to campaign for workers' control because this cannot be implemented without first overthrowing the capitalist regime – is based on an exaggerated schematic separation of non-revolutionary and pre-revolutionary situations. The point is precisely to encourage the transition from one to the other, from economic strikes to strikes with political objectives, from purely trade unionist to revolutionary consciousness: 'And in order to solve this problem, the scholastic fiddling about what is "unrealistic" and what is "semi-realistic" under these conditions does not help in the least'.[78]

In Mandel's view, an analysis of workers' struggles in late capitalism reveals trends that we should base our strategic orientation on. He believes that the German working class, too, will adapt to the working-class movements in other western European countries. Considering all specific circumstances when formulating specific demands is one thing, general direction another: 'whether class consciousness is 'purely trade unionist' or 'semi-socialist' depends, among other things, on whether important sections of the working class can be freed from the fallacious dilemma of 'either a hard-line entrepreneurial and authoritarian state or social-democratic class reconciliation and co-management'. And a gradually expanding and increasingly resonating campaign for workers' control (i.e. a campaign of propaganda, education and practical experience through struggle) [would] decisively help to overcome his dilemma, in which the vast majority of the west German workforce remains trapped today'.[79]

---

78   Mandel 1978d, p. 309, our translation.
79   Mandel 1978d, p. 310, our translation.

This conditional prognosis has obviously not materialised to this day. Whether in the future, under different conditions, substantial strata of the working class will adopt transitional slogans in general, and demands for workers' control in particular, is an open question. Negative experience, at least, certainly seems to support Mandel's proposals: the workers' movement, especially in Germany, has become more and more defenceless because of its preoccupation with social partnership, and no purely propagandistic anti-capitalism on the part of left-wing groups has helped the movement to change this course.

Late capitalism involves broader sections as potential allies of the proletariat in the struggle for demands that are at odds with the capitalist organisation of society (student youth, educational staff, progressive health professionals, etc.). This is why it offers more favourable conditions for a universal social mobilisation in which the working class becomes the centralising force of emancipatory sub-movements. The cross-fertilisation with other liberation movements, in turn, has a positive effect on the politics and on the consciousness of the working class.[80] Similarly, Mandel identified a trend towards the increasing internationalisation of class struggles. For him, the growing popularity of anti-imperialist solidarity campaigns in the course of the radicalisation of the youth was not mainly a 'distraction' from the necessity of fighting at home. Rather, he saw it as a prelude to the internationalist objective of building an international revolutionary organisation – one that would really begin to coordinate class struggles in the different countries and regions of the world. In Mandel's estimation, the two traditional wings of the labour movement had done much to stifle the internationalist aspect of socialist struggle through the routine of working 'in their own countries'. However, the transition to a socialist society entails overcoming the nation state, which is rooted in the old bourgeois class society. The logic of a strategy of transitional demands therefore necessarily entails the systematic promotion of international solidarity and of common working-class struggles across the borders of nation states. But it is precisely this aspect of the development of class consciousness that, in Mandel's view, can least be left to the 'spontaneity' of the masses or even that of their 'natural vanguard': '[These tasks] require an international revolutionary vanguard organisation, just as the effective development and application of a socialist strategy in a national context requires a national revolutionary vanguard organisation'.[81]

---

80   See Mandel 1971c.
81   Mandel 1978d, p. 318, our translation.

3   The Dual Character of the Trade Unions

The capitalist mode of production produces a highly unequal balance of power between the owners of the means of production and those who have nothing to sell but their labour, yet are forced to sell it in order to live. In the Marxist analysis of capitalism, the relationship between the individual capitalist and the individual proletarian is a relationship between commodity owners freely exchanging on the (labour) market what they (can) offer: labour power for wages. But because wage earners depend on wages for their daily survival, they cannot act like other commodity owners, who can push up the price of their commodities by withdrawing them from the market indefinitely. The capitalist is in control because he has greater endurance. As individuals, wage earners are in competition with one another. The capitalist can therefore play them off against each other by hiring whoever is willing to sell their labour at the lowest price.[82]

According to Mandel, this is the reason why there is a tendency for workers to organise themselves and take collective action in to assert their interests. They set up joint funds that enable them to stay out of work and survive for certain periods of time. Strikes are the means of enforcing higher wages, shorter hours without loss of pay, and better working conditions. Experience soon shows that it is more advantageous to create permanent trade unions than to restrict oneself to temporary coalitions. To some degree, the proletarians eliminate competition between themselves through joint action and organisation, and they create the conditions for acting in solidarity. Their freedom of organisation, the right to form trade unions and other mass organisations is a crucial matter because it determines whether they can establish a more favourable balance of power with the owners of capital and assert their interests much more effectively than as individual contractual 'parties'.[83] According to Mandel, trade union organising and collective action for one's own immediate interests testify to an elementary level of class consciousness. They reflect an understanding of the need to unite against the employers regardless of differences on other issues. This does not yet amount to political class consciousness, i.e. the insight that there is a need for political organisation independent of the bourgeoisie, and that one must conceive of one's interests as political and defend them politically. Historically, the labour movement entered the political stage as the radical left wing of the bourgeoisie or petty bourgeoisie. The British Chartist

---

82   See Mandel 1973b, p. 18 et seq.; Mandel 1968b, p. 143 et seq.
83   See Mandel 1979a, p. 73 et seq.

movement's struggle for universal suffrage is an early example of an independent organisation of workers fighting at the level of politics.[84]

In the absence of trade union organisation, workers systematically sell their labour below value especially in periods of high unemployment. Trade unions are a reaction to this. Rather than aiming to abolish competition and wage labour relations completely, they merely aim to ensure the sale of the commodity labour at its value in the context of capitalist relations of production. Nonetheless, Mandel advocated trade union organisation as one of the preconditions for advanced struggles and advanced stages of consciousness:

> Trade unions as such are therefore not potentially revolutionary [*systemsprengend*] under capitalism.[85] They are not a means to the end of abolishing capitalist exploitation, but only a means to make exploitation more bearable for the masses of wage earners. Their objective is to raise wages, not abolish wage labour altogether. But at the same time, trade unions as such are not unproblematically compliant with the capitalist system [*systemkonform*]. By halting the decline in real wages and by exploiting, at least periodically and under certain conditions, favourable fluctuations in the demand and supply of labour on the market in order to raise the price for this commodity, they make it possible for the organised working masses to exceed the minimum of consumption and needs that is usually granted to them. Only in this way can class organisation, class consciousness and confidence emerge on a wider scale and create the preconditions for a revolutionary struggle that involves broad masses.[86]

Mandel's attitude towards the unions is one of critical identification and support. In his view, trade unions have a dual character: they are products and instruments of resistance against capital, but they are also institutions within the capitalist system. The success of their campaigns depends on certain basic conditions that are not guaranteed in every phase of capitalist development or in every country with a capitalist mode of production. Industrial capitalism has to expand and create more jobs than it destroys so that improvements for the

---

84   See Mandel 1979a, p. 75.

85   [The German word *systemsprengend* (literally: system-bursting) refers to something that is exploding the limits of the present system; something that exceeds the capacity of the system and cannot be contained within it. We will translate it in different ways depending on context and add [*systemsprengend*] in square brackets in each instance – Translator.]

86   Mandel 1978a, p. 266, our translation. The quoted essay, 'Systemkonforme Gewerkschaften', first appeared in 1971 in *Gewerkschaftliche Monatshefte*.

benefit of workers can really be won. At the same time, the ruling class must be able to afford to let the price of the commodity labour power be determined by the 'free play of forces' on the labour market under the conditions of the existence of mass trade unions. When it sees its vital interests threatened in this scenario, the bourgeoisie shuts down the possibility of forming mass trade unions or smashes the existing ones in order to secure the conditions for the valorisation of capital. Functioning mass trade unions are historically an exception, and in poor capitalist countries it is often not possible to build such organisations.[87]

For all his criticism of the 'system-compliant' ways in which unions have usually been run, Mandel's identification with the trade union movement is based on his view that the level of real wages and the living and working conditions of wage labourers under capitalism are to a certain extent variable. He objected to interpretations of Marx that assume an 'absolute immiseration', expressed primarily in an inevitable epochal tendency for real wages to fall. The wage earners' collective advocacy of their own immediate material interests is therefore a factor of great importance, even if it does not (yet) have a potentially revolutionary [*systemsprengend*] character.

> Many authors have promoted the myth that Marx defended, in one way or another, the theory of an 'iron law of wages'; this theory originated with Malthus and Ricardo and was adopted in the socialist movement above all by Lassalle, whereas Marx always opposed it. Marx's theory of wages is a 'theory of capital accumulation' that examines the effects of lower or higher waves of accumulation on both supply and demand of the commodity labour power within the combined action of all other laws of movement of the capitalist mode of production. Moreover, Marx explicitly highlighted the partially autonomous character of wage movements, which are determined ... by the struggle (and balance of forces) between capital and labour as antagonistic social classes.[88]

According to Mandel, there is neither an epochal trend towards increasingly lower wages nor towards ever-higher wages (as suited the 'reformist' mentality of the post-war era). What we have instead is a 'cyclical fluctuation' of wages, although late capitalism, the 'long wave with a depressive undertone' since the mid-1970s, and long-lasting structural mass unemployment have put great pres-

---

87   See Mandel 1978a, pp. 265–6.
88   Mandel 1984a, p. 34, our translation.

sure on real wages. In addition, there is a 'relative impoverishment' of wage labourers because they receive a diminishing share of the value they create – due to the increase in labour productivity, this is even possible in periods when real wages rise. The increase in labour productivity, in turn, creates new needs through the greater strain on the labour force, through the creation of new lines of mass consumption, and through changes in the social infrastructure (e.g. longer journeys to work). These are not met even with modest increases in real wages, and certainly not with stagnating or falling real wages.[89]

This does not yet answer the question of the relationship between the two poles of Mandel's assessment, according to which wages are to be understood as a function of capital accumulation, on the one hand, and as the result of the 'system-immanent' class struggle between labour and capital on the other. Mandel addressed this question in a detailed introduction to an English edition of *Capital* Volume 1 by Karl Marx.[90] There, Mandel also asks why many authors have attributed a position of inevitable absolute impoverishment under capitalist conditions to Marx. The first answer is obvious: because 'Marx, in his youthful writings, did in fact hold such a theory – for example, in the *Communist Manifesto*'.[91] In the *Communist Manifesto* we can read for instance:

> Hence, the cost of production of a workman is restricted, almost entirely, to the means of subsistence that he requires for maintenance, and for the propagation of his race. But the price of a commodity, and therefore also of labour, is equal to its cost of production. In proportion, therefore, as the repulsiveness of the work increases, the wage decreases. Nay more, in proportion as the use of machinery and division of labour increases, in the same proportion the burden of toil also increases, whether by prolongation of the working hours, by the increase of the work exacted in a given time or by increased speed of machinery, etc.[92]

Mandel points out that Marx had not yet worked out his economic theory at that point. This is also easily seen from the fact that Marx speaks here of the 'price of labour', while in his mature economic writings he uses the categories of value and price of labour power – an innovation in relation to the bourgeois economists that he was particularly proud of.

---

89   Mandel 1984a, pp. 34–5.
90   See Mandel 1991c, p. 12.
91   Mandel 1990, p. 70.
92   Marx 2004, chapter 1.

Mandel cites two other factors that have led many authors astray. Firstly, many confused the category of the value of the commodity labour power with the category of real wages. According to him, the value of the commodity labour power depends on the value of the consumer goods that workers can buy with their wages, but real wages depend on their quantity. Both could well move in the opposite direction under capitalism, especially when labour productivity rises. In addition, sections of *Capital* that refer to 'increasing misery' and the 'accumulation of misery' have often been misinterpreted.[93] The context shows that these passages refer to those sections of society that have been thrown into unemployment and whose impoverishment can also be seen in contemporary capitalist welfare states.[94]

For Mandel, Marx's distinction between the physiological and 'moral' needs of wage labourers is crucial. The physical subsistence level is not equal to the social subsistence level, i.e. the range of needs whose satisfaction is considered 'normal' in a particular social context. This 'minimum' varies considerably from country to country and from period to period, and the more developed a capitalist industry, the higher should the working class standard of living normally be.[95] On the other hand, Mandel continues, Marx explained the fluctuations of the price of the commodity labour power within the economic cycles of capitalism as arising from the movements of the reserve army of labour: 'He indicated, however, that there was nothing automatic about this movement, and that the actual class struggle – including trade-union action, which he considered indispensable for this very reason – was the instrument through which workers could take advantage of more favourable conditions on the "labour market" somewhat to increase their wages, whereas the main effect of depression was that it would weaken the resistance of the working class to wage-cuts'.[96] On the other hand, according to Mandel, Marx consistently 'stuck to his theory of value with regard to wages'.[97] As prices for the commodity labour power they fluctuate around its value. Compared to the short-term fluctuations of prices within the cycles, the changes in the value of labour power predominate in the longer term. Marx's explanation of these changes is very different from all demographic schools of thought (à la Malthus). For Marx, the long-term development of the value of the commodity labour power is 'a function of the accumulation of capital in the five-fold sense':[98]

---

93   Marx 1990, p. 71.
94   Ibid.
95   See Marx 1990, p. 66.
96   See Marx 1990, p. 67.
97   Ibid.
98   Ibid.

a)   All other things being equal, the accumulation of capital implies a decline in the value of consumer goods included in the standard of living of employed workers. As a result, there is a tendency for the value of the commodity labour power to be depressed. This can also occur when real wages rise.

b)   Since capital accumulation not only lowers the value of consumer goods, but also entails an expansion of the mass production of consumer goods, workers can, if the conditions are favourable, force the inclusion of these new goods in the 'accepted minimum standard of living', which increases the value of the commodity labour power.

c)   Under conditions of near full employment (as, for instance, was the case in the US for a long time), the accumulation of capital will favour the increase in value of labour power through regular increases in real wages. In Europe, wages only started to rise when massive overseas emigration began to reduce the supply of labour.

d)   The accumulation of capital forms the upper barrier which no increase in the value or the price of labour-power can break; otherwise it will slow down due to a strong decline in surplus-value, which in turn leads to massive unemployment, an 'oversupply' of labour and a further drop in wages. It is quite possible under capitalism, however that wages drop to the bare physiological minimum.

e)   The accumulation of capital ultimately increases the value of labour power only at the cost of an intensification of the production process and therefore an increased attrition of labour power. The results are greater exhaustion and an increased need for consumption. Once wages decline below a certain level, (especially under the effects of wars or brutal dictatorships), the productive output of the workers also declines.[99]

Mandel's main focus is the relative impoverishment of workers through the effects of the accumulation of capital. However, following Marx, he also sees 'a trend towards periodic absolute impoverishment, essentially in function of the movement of unemployment'.[100] Support for trade union struggle is consistent with these assessments – if only to combat a decline in the price of labour power (i.e. wages) below its value. But this is also true of measures to combat mass unemployment (reduction of working hours without wage losses through proportional recruitment and the control of working conditions by workers), which have a special significance in Mandel's strategical conception. There is

---

99   See Marx 1990, pp. 68–9.
100   Marx 1990, p. 72.

no 'wall' that divides immediate demands from struggles aimed at pushing and bursting the limits of the existing system. Trade unions are not necessarily and terminally 'only' organs that represent workers' interests within the limits of the capitalist system – and if that is what they are, they arguably represent their interests in a far from satisfactory way.

Their dual character is reflected in the existence of different ideas in their ranks. As a rule, only left-wing minorities have tried to develop the anti-capitalist potential of trade unions as 'schools of class struggle'. Just as the English trade union confederations were 'neutral' on political issues (hence the negative connotation of the term 'trade unionism'), in the European trade unions originally founded by socialists or Social Democrats, forces prevailed that sought to limit trade union activity to opposing certain excesses of capitalism, fighting for small improvements, and safeguarding organising as such. This was consistent with Eduard Bernstein's 'revisionism', i.e. the idea of gradual progress within the framework of capitalist society, a gradual alleviation of class antagonisms, and a peaceful, almost imperceptible transition into a new social order [*hinüberwachsen* – to 'grow over' into something].

The trade union leaderships were well-disposed towards this approach (if not in theory, then in practice). It corresponded with the routine of organisational life and with the way in which the means (organising) were becoming end unto itself. In this sense, it also reflected the tendency of the unions towards bureaucratisation. Mandel argues that this tendency stood in contradiction to the real dynamics of social development, which in the twentieth century was crisis-ridden and explosive. In the long term, it also undermined the more modest role of trade unions as bodies designed to represent workers' interests:

> The adherence to pure trade union theory and practice was bound to lead to the conclusion that only a strong and healthy capitalism could provide wage increases. That is why they were prepared to act as doctors at the bedside of capitalism and, instead of putting an end to this sick man, they tried to cure capitalism of its illness by all means possible. The paradox culminated in accepting wage cuts in order to create a 'healthy' capitalism, i.e. to achieve subsequent wage increases. A trade union movement coming to such absurd conclusions had evidently reached a dead end.[101]

---

101   Mandel 1978a, p. 268, our translation.

Generally speaking, in a society based on generalised commodity production and social division of labour, there will always be a tendency for organisations originally conceived as vehicles for change to become ends in themselves. For Mandel, the integration of trade union leaderships and parties of
the labour movement into bourgeois society is not a *mechanical* consequence
of the material self-interest of a privileged layer of bureaucrats. It is indeed also
the result of the internal logic of a position which seeks to combine the representation of workers' interests with the practical, and ultimately ideological,
acceptance of the capitalist system and its persistence. But even so, the material interests that underlie such concepts cannot be ignored.[102]

According to Mandel, late capitalism is characterised by a tendency to permanent technological innovation and reduction in the turnover time of fixed
capital. Consequently, managers of large corporations are under growing pressure to plan long-term investment and expenditure. This expenditure naturally
includes wage costs. While even under monopoly capitalism only indicative
economic planning is possible – the profitability of any action taken or decision
made can only be established after the fact – wage cost planning (via collective agreements entered for the longest possible period, 'wage guidelines' and
involvement of the trade unions in 'concerted action' and other forms of the
social pact) tends to be imperative in nature. As a result, the traditional field of
trade union activity – the struggle for real wages – tends to get smaller in late
capitalism.[103]

This substitute for this loss is the increasing involvement of trade union leaders in the various bodies of joint 'administration', 'planning' and 'consultation'
in large corporations and at various levels of society. Some union leaders view
or sell this development as amounting to a transformation of society in the
workers' interest, or as a 'stage' on the road to a new society. The idea is not
entirely new and was originally articulated before the era of late capitalism:

> The archetype of this behaviour was provided by the old French trade
> union leader Jouhaux, who after World War I presented the decree that
> appointed him to the administrative council of the Banque de France to
> trade unionists, beaming with joy and exclaiming: 'The first nail in the
> coffin of capitalism!' French capitalism, however, seems to have survived
> these nails very well for fifty years. It is as alive today as it was in 1919 ....[104]

---

102   Ibid.
103   See Mandel 1978a, p. 269.
104   Mandel 1978a, p. 270.

According to Mandel, however, this behaviour is running into problems in late capitalism. Firstly, there is a risk that the rank and file is becoming increasingly alienated from the trade unions (the still ongoing debate on the crisis in the German Trade Union Confederation and the need for reorientation is a proof in point). On the other hand, the involvement of trade union representatives in bodies where economic developments and decisions at various levels of social policy are discussed also promotes the politicisation of workers. Following the traditional Marxist designation of trade unions as a 'school of class struggle', Mandel thinks it possible that in this way trade union activists go through a kind of 'higher school of class struggle'.[105]

This optimistic-sounding thesis is based on the mass struggles of the late 1960s, which had ended not long before Mandel wrote his key essay on trade union strategy. Mandel saw the rise of a 'spontaneous tendency' among employed workers to challenge the capitalist mode of production, starting from the 'right' of capitalists or of the management to determine autocratically the content of production the working and living conditions of workers. Beside wage levels, questions were raised about atomising forms of wages that promoted competition between employees, the division of labour, the hierarchy within the company, etc. Moreover, the revolts of the late 1960s brought new and better educated sections to the fore (both youth and white-collar workers), who were not inclined to be mere objects of the decisions of others.[106] If parts of the bourgeoisie issued slogans of 'participation' (De Gaulle) or 'co-management', this was an intelligent reaction aiming to integrate these new tendencies into the existing system. It is typical of the backwardness of the German bourgeoisie to fight a bitter struggle against 'participation' instead of welcoming it as a means of integration into the system. In any case, it is a fraudulent manoeuvre. The possibilities of influence through worker participation are limited within the context of the capitalist mode of production, and any hopes one attaches to it usually turn out to be a chimera. Without abolishing the capitalist market economy itself, Mandel argues, no authority will be able to freeze prices or profits in the long run, or prevent the increase in exploitation in the workplace in response to wage increases or shorter hours.[107]

In Mandel's view there are limits to the integration of trade unions into the system. If a certain line is crossed, they degenerate and cease to be independent trade unions. This ultimately also threatens the position and privileges of

---

105   Mandel 1978a, pp. 270–1.
106   Mandel 1978a, pp. 271–2.
107   Mandel 1978a, pp. 277–8.

the trade union bureaucracy because capital and the state can no longer trust it to control the workers and channel their activism. Under certain conditions, such processes can produce 'vertical' pseudo-unions, such as those that have evolved in the US, or those that have been characteristic of fascist and dictatorial regimes (e.g. the Franco regime in Spain, which was not overthrown until 1976). Voluntary trade union dues are then replaced by a compulsory levy, a kind of second income tax that workers have to pay. The managements of such pseudo-unions become part of the management and state administration, tasked with managing the 'commodity labour-power'.[108]

Despite trends in this direction, Mandel considered the degeneration process of the trade unions to be far from complete. Because of the growing concentration of capital, he thought the concentration of trade unions needed to keep pace too in order to counter capital's growing power. To resist this would be to act in the interests of capital. However, the process produced contradictory results. This was linked to the fact that the trade unions, even though in principle organisations for all waged workers, need to rely on a modicum of class consciousness in order to function as independent trade unions. The effects of the growing concentration of the trade union movement, in turn, can undermine this.

> Yet the same centralisation that allows poorer wage earners to negotiate more favourable wages and working conditions than they could achieve on their own threatens to turn against the militants and radicals once a trade union apparatus is bureaucratically deformed and self-perpetuating. It threatens to undermine the whole basis of trade unions if it degenerates into systematic passivity on the part of trade union members. An ever-smaller circle of functionaries takes the central decisions – including compromises in collective bargaining – without involving a broader layer of activists in the decision-making process.[109]

According to Mandel, capital is also putting pressure on union leaders to discipline activists and 'clear out' the 'unpredictable' militant elements from enterprises and union organisations. Mandel counters this with a demand for the 'broadest internal trade union democracy': 'This means not only the duty to inform, question and consult widely with the membership and activists before any important decision is taken, but also the right of minorities to associate

---

108   Mandel 1978a, p. 276.
109   Mandel 1978a, pp. 277–8, our translation.

in order to coordinate their efforts at trade union meetings, at least to some extent, just as effectively as the apparatus can'.[110]

Mandel considers it typical that, as soon as the right wing of the trade union becomes a minority, it always takes this right to organise as a minority for granted. The privileges of leaders and apparatuses are often defended with the argument that the grassroots are at fault because of their own passivity. Mandel concedes that this argument contains a 'grain of truth', but he points out that at the end of the 1960s, great numbers of trade union members were running ahead of the apparatuses rather than following them. Moreover, the question is precisely whether the actions of the leaderships encourage or discourage grass-roots activity in the long run. A strategy must be developed that systematically teaches people to take initiative, become active, have a say and participate in decision-making. Failing this, the unions will encourage a passive attitude, on the one hand, and produce a climate in which periodic activity from below will explode outside the framework provided by the trade unions.[111]

Mandel argues that especially in late capitalism, the struggle for 'workers' production control' should be placed at the centre of trade union strategy, in explicit demarcation from 'participation'. Any acceptance of co-responsibility for the maximisation of profits ultimately contradicts the struggle for maintaining the collective bargaining autonomy of the unions. Defending the interests of wage labourers is not compatible with subordination to the laws of movement of the capitalist mode of production. Instead of participation, it is therefore vital to fight for workers' veto rights and control rights at all levels. Mandel draws on André Renard, the syndicalist-oriented leader of the Walloon socialist trade union movement, with whom he had worked closely in the second half of the '50s. His slogan was: 'Workers' control under capitalism; participation in decision-making under socialism'.[112]

The struggle for workers' control, promotes the self-organisation of all workers in the enterprise and their independence from the institutions and bodies of capital. This ultimately points to dual power, i.e. the seed of socialist council rule. However, Mandel does not counterpose the emergence of such bodies to continued work in the trade unions. Rather, such a dynamic stimulates both the activity of the members in the unions and the development of internal union democracy in the context of 'increasing participation of wage earners in economic and social conflicts'.[113]

---

110   Mandel 1978a, pp. 278–9, our translation.
111   Mandel 1978a, p. 279.
112   Mandel 1978a, p. 280.
113   Ibid.

Another aspect of late capitalist reality is the progressive internationalisation of capital, which must be responded to with a progressive internationalisation of trade union action. For example, although the big corporations are increasingly operating Europe-wide, Mandel points out that we are still waiting for the first Europe-wide strike movement (*nota bene* that Mandel lamented this several decades ago, and there have still been virtually no steps in this direction). Small radical groups have hitherto achieved more in terms of international solidarity than trade union federations with millions of members, Mandel continues. It is the duty of union leaderships to demonstrate in practice that the increasing centralisation brought about by technological progress can be combined with growing self-activity and self-determination from below.[114]

Even according to the forecasts of bourgeois economists, technological development combined with the further concentration of capital threatens to create a monopoly on access to information and decision-making power for only about 200 large corporations worldwide. It is incomprehensible to Mandel that people still speak of 'free enterprise' in view of such prospects. For him, a promising trade union strategy can only be developed with the prospect of a fundamental system change, and only if trade unions are guided by this perspective in their day-to-day practice.[115]

Mandel favoured unified trade unions for all workers regardless of their political affiliation and opinion, as opposed to unions based on political orientation. Even so, he argued that these unified trade unions should orientate their activities towards the struggle for the 'final goal of socialism', i.e. a society based on common property managed by the producers themselves. Mandel saw no contradiction in these two aspects. And indeed, there is no such thing as a 'politically neutral' trade union leadership. Ultimately, class struggle tendencies are formed in trade unions – e.g. in unions led by social democrats – with a view to creating majorities to steer the unions in a socialist class struggle direction that poses an explicit challenge to the existing system [*systemkritisch*] – and, of course, produce a corresponding leadership. Consequently, Mandel concludes his central essay on this topic with the dictum: 'There can be no "system-compliant" [*systemkonform*] trade unions in late capitalism. "System-challenging" [*systemkritisch*] trade unions critical of the system, however, require a conscious socialist leadership'.[116]

For Mandel, trade unions not only play a strategic role in the workers' struggle under capitalism, but also in defending their interests in a transitional

---

114   Mandel 1978a, p. 281.
115   Mandel 1978a, pp. 281–2.
116   Mandel 1978a, p. 282, our translation.

society that is evolving towards socialism. He supports the continued existence of independent trade unions even after the overthrow of capitalism.[117]
Mandel always rejected the abstract idea that the interests of the working class
would not require any direct representation since they would be represented
by socialist democracy, council democracy, or the dictatorship of the proletariat (all of which are synonyms for Mandel). Nor did he defend Trotsky's position in the 'trade union debate' at the ninth congress of the Bolshevik party
(even if he pleaded for a more nuanced view of Trotsky and Bukharin's position). Instead, he attributed Trotsky's stance to the 'dark years' during which
he had a tendency towards 'substitutionism'.[118] Mandel's vision of the emergence of a socialist democracy, its 'withering away', and the emergence of a
society without classes or a state entailed an awareness of the perils found
on this path – in particular the risk of privileged strata becoming a law unto
themselves. For him, independent trade unions were an important aspect in a
multitude of preventive measures against such dangers.

4   Class Consciousness and Building Revolutionary Parties

At first glance, Mandel's stance on the construction of revolutionary parties
seems to contradict his views on the central strategic role of working-class initiative and self-organisation (as well as the self-organisation of all the exploited,
oppressed and propertyless). Of course, revolutionaries are not the only ones
who deliberately try to influence the working class, and this is the first justification for the notion of building 'revolutionary vanguard parties'.

In *Introduction to Marxism*, Mandel in fact deduces 'the need for a vanguard party' primarily from the historical development of the labour movement, specifically the existence and function of 'reformist opportunism'.[119] This
opportunism, according to him, became a political force that 'accentuated the
adaptation of the mass labor movement to the "prosperous" capitalism of the
imperialist countries'.[120] He considers all the defeats and missed opportunities far from inevitable: 'It would have been possible [in Germany – author]
to launch extra-parliamentary action and broader and broader mass strikes in
the years leading up to World War I. These actions would have prepared the
working masses for the tasks of revolutionary upsurge that coincided with the

---

117   Mandel 1995a, pp. 86–7.
118   Mandel 1995a, p. 133.
119   Mandel 1979a, p. 84 et seq.
120   Mandel 1979a, p. 84.

end of the war'.[121] What is needed, then, is a political force in opposition to the reformist opportunism that seeks to contain struggles and channel them into the framework of what already exists.

At the same time, Mandel clearly places himself in the tradition of 'Leninist party theory', which follows the ideas developed in early, Marxist-oriented Social Democracy by Karl Kautsky, among others. According to this theory, the most advanced socialist class consciousness must be brought into the working class 'from the outside', because this kind of consciousness presupposes that one has assimilated a critical science of society, i.e., scientific socialism. This assimilation cannot be accomplished spontaneously by the working class due of its conditions of existence under capitalism. How this position ties in with Mandel's emphasis on the self-liberation of the proletariat, and to what degree it is compatible with his rejection of 'surrogate politics', has to be examined primarily with reference to his essential treatise on this subject, 'The Leninist Theory of Organisation'.[122] In any case, in the course of our discussion it will become clear that Mandel took roughly the same position in later writings, although in a less doctrinal and absolute manner. After the 1905 revolution with its powerful upsurge of proletarian self-activity and the emergence of the council movement, even Lenin's writings begin to contain certain relativisations of his earlier notions that socialist consciousness must be brought into the class 'from the outside', or that on its own devices, the working class can only obtain trade union consciousness. In his foreword to a new edition his seminal 1902 text *What Is To Be Done?*, published with the experience of the 1905 revolution in mind, Lenin wrote that there are certainly situations in which the mass of workers can become 'spontaneously Social-Democratic' (this meant 'socialist' in the terminology of the time).[123] But even so, he thought that the problems that make the construction of vanguard organisations necessary continued to exist.

Mandel's opening points indicate that his understanding of Lenin's party theory runs contrary to any pragmatic-organisational interpretation. He argues that Lenin's theory is not a supra-historical 'recipe' for tackling organisational issues. Any serious discussion of Lenin's contribution to party theory must begin with determining its place in the historical evolution of Marxism:

> Approached in this way, the Leninist theory of organisation appears as
> a dialectical unity of three elements: a theory of the present relevance

---

121   Mandel 1979a, pp. 84–5.
122   See Mandel 1970b.
123   Lenin 2004.

of revolution for the underdeveloped countries in the imperialist epoch (which was later expanded to apply to the entire world in the epoch of the general crisis of capitalism); a theory of the discontinuous and contradictory development of proletarian class consciousness and of its most important stages, which should be differentiated from one another; and a theory, of the essence of Marxist theory and its specific relationship to science on the one hand and to proletarian class struggle on the other.[124]

The 'actuality of the revolution' does not imply that the revolutionary conquest of power by the proletariat is always on the agenda everywhere. The deep contradictions of the capitalist system inevitably produce periodic social upheavals, the most important aspect of which is the massive upsurge in the mobilisation and self-activity of workers. This leads to pre-revolutionary and revolutionary situations whose outcome depends not least on the ability of a revolutionary party to lead the mass movement to victory. This role of the party arises from the specific features of the socialist revolution when compared to all previous revolutions, e.g. the bourgeois revolutions (see below). Lenin's concept of the 'actuality of the revolution' was first taken up by György Lukács in *History and Class Consciousness*. The second aspect Lenin addresses concerns the conditions for the formation of proletarian class consciousness. Mandel stresses that Lenin was not the first to formulate the idea that socialist class consciousness must be brought into the working class 'from the outside'. He cites not only Friedrich Engels and Karl Kautsky, but also the 1889 Hainfeld Programme of the Austrian Social Democrats as earlier examples: 'Socialist consciousness is something that is brought into the proletarian class struggle from outside, not something that organically develops out of the class struggle'.[125] The third element is the relative autonomy of Marxist theory, which is conditioned by the proletarian class struggle, but not its 'mechanically inevitable product'. Rather, it follows its own logic and only gradually merges with the class struggle through a long and complex process.[126] Even though Lenin's conception is rooted in the classical Marxist tradition, Mandel views it as a further development and expansion of its subjects, and in this context he also points to certain limitations in the reception of Marx before the early twentieth century, when *The German Ideology* in particular, and therefore also the category of 'revolutionary practice', was unknown.[127] Mandel names four spe-

---

124   Mandel 1970b.
125   Mandel 1970b, footnote 1.
126   Mandel 1970b.
127   Mandel 1970b, footnote 2.

cial features in which the proletarian socialist revolution differs to all previous revolutions in history.[128] The bourgeois revolutions, which are historically the best studied and have traditionally been the paradigm of Marxist
political theory formation, are used for comparison. All these special features
amount to a focus on the 'subjective factor', i.e. the factor of consciousness-
raising.

Firstly, he argues, the proletarian revolution is the first to be carried out by
a social class that previously had no economic wealth whatsoever (as distinct
from access to consumer goods). By contrast, the bourgeois class was already
rich and powerful within the feudal social order before it set about the conquest of political power. *Secondly*, the proletarian revolution is the first aimed
at a consciously planned overthrow of existing society and does not seek, to
restore a previous state of affair. This goal therefore initially only exists at the
level of thought – it is anticipated only as 'theory' or a 'programme'. *Thirdly*,
proletarian self-liberation can only be accomplished through a long-term transformation of all social relations. The conquest of political power is therefore
not the end but the starting point of the process of social change. *Fourthly*,
this proletarian revolution is international and universal in character: it is a
world-revolutionary process that is not straightforward and uniform but contradictory, with many advances and setbacks.

All these special features come down to the fact that an 'automatic' or purely
'spontaneous' success of socialist revolution is unthinkable. Mandel argues that
Lenin's theory of organisation provides the key to solving this problem. Success
depends not only on 'objective conditions' (the fact that the capitalist mode of
production has outlived its historical purpose), but also on 'subjective conditions'. 'Subjective conditions' consist in the level of activity and consciousness
in the proletariat and in the maturity of its political leadership. Mandel sees in
the special concern with this subjective factor, conceived in this way, a distinct
tendency and tradition within Marxism compared to the 'objectivist' variant.
He views Lenin as not the sole representative of this trend, and in fact he himself identifies with it: 'The Leninist theory of organisation represents, then,
broadly speaking, the deepening of Marxism, applied to the basic problems of
the social superstructure (the state, class consciousness, ideology, the party).
Together with the parallel contributions of Rosa Luxemburg and Trotsky (and,
in a more limited sense of Lukacs and Gramsci), it constitutes the *Marxist science of the subjective factor*'.[129]

---

128   Mandel 1970b.
129   Ibid.

The political dilemma to which Mandel seeks an answer is this: on the one hand, he wants to place the activity and self-organisation of the proletariat at the centre of a strategy of proletarian self-liberation (and therefore the liberation of human society as a whole). On the other hand, he considers the construction of political vanguard organisations as indispensable for this self-liberation. Mandel's point of departure is Marx's famous dictum, 'The ideas of the ruling class are in every epoch the ruling ideas'. If therefore bourgeois ideology is the dominant ideology in capitalist society, then the proletariat necessarily remains trapped in this ideology, and there is no telling how this social class might be able to assert its self-liberation against the bourgeois class. Mandel argues that a number of theorists, including Marcuse, have remained trapped in this dilemma, but: 'The problem can be solved by replacing the formalistic and static point of view with a dialectical one'.[130]

The ruling bourgeois class controls the means of ideological production. However, its control over the members of bourgeois society (including the workers) by bourgeois ideology is not exerted purely through ideological manipulation, but 'above all through the actual day-to-day workings of the existing economy and society and their effect on the consciousness of the oppressed'.[131] Under conditions of generalised commodity production, competition, a working day determined by others, fatigue, lack of opportunities for development due to lack of free time etc, even the workers cannot free themselves from the influence of bourgeois ideology. This is only possible through 'revolutionary practice': 'Only when the workings of this imprisonment are blown apart by a revolution, i.e., by a sudden, intense increase, in *mass activity outside of the confines of alienated labour* – only then can the mystifying influence of this very imprisonment upon mass consciousness rapidly recede'.[132] 'The majority' of the working class can only liberate itself from bourgeois ideology in the revolution itself.[133] However, even before the conditions that harbour this possibility arise (i.e. pre-revolutionary and revolutionary situations) there are already struggles and political conflicts. The outcomes and lessons drawn from these struggles are decisive for whether later opportunities will be seized upon or not – i.e. whether the proletariat will actually conquer political power.

In Mandel's view, bourgeois ideology only dominated absolutely during early, ascending and prosperous capitalism. Even then, significant sections of

---

130   Ibid.
131   Ibid.
132   Ibid.
133   Ibid.

the working class were already fighting for their own interests, even if using the 'formulas, ideals and ideologies of the exploiters'.[134] The more unstable bourgeois class domination becomes, the more the rule of bourgeois ideology is upset. At the same time, there develops a critical engagement with bourgeois ideology – an ideological struggle for the 'new ideals of the revolutionary class'. Mandel refers to Gramsci's concept of 'political and ethical hegemony', which needs to be conquered before political power can be captured, as a culmination of this idea.[135] The necessity for a conscious intellectual confrontation with the ruling ideas indicates one of the reasons for the need to build revolutionary organisations: their members must set themselves the task of accomplishing essential preparatory work for the victory of the socialist revolution long before revolutionary situations arise.

Despite his emphasis on the 'subjective factor' and the paramount role of consciousness formation, Mandel's view stands in distinct contrast to subjectivist schools such as Italian *operaismo* (workerism). According to *operaismo*, the working class only constitutes itself in the struggle against capital and in the context of the corresponding formation of consciousness in general.[136] To support his position, Mandel refers to Marx's and Engels' views after 1852, which – in contrast to the formulations found in the *Communist Manifesto*, for instance – were based on an objective class concept: the proletariat exists because of its place in the production process, irrespectively of its awareness of this situation at different times. This objective concept of class is fundamental to the classical Marxist tradition represented by German Social Democracy and by Lenin. According to a formulation by Bukharin modelled on Hegel, this tradition is faced with the problem of how to transform the proletariat from an (objectively defined) 'class in itself' into a 'class for itself' (conscious of its situation and its corresponding historical tasks).[137] Divorced from the objective existence of the working class as a potential revolutionary subject, the concept of the vanguard party is a detached and hopeless elitism:

> It is only because there exists an objectively revolutionary class that can, and is periodically obliged to, conduct an actual revolutionary class struggle, and it is only in relation to such an actual class struggle, that the

---

134 Ibid.
135 Mandel 1970b, footnote 8.
136 See for instance Tronti 1971, pp. 32–3.
137 Ibid.

concept of a revolutionary vanguard party (including that of professional revolutionaries) has any scientific meaning at all, as Lenin himself explicitly observed. All revolutionary activity not related to this class struggle leads at best to a party nucleus, but not to a party. This runs the risk of degenerating into sectarian, subjective dilettantism. According to Lenin's concept of organisation, there is no self-proclaimed vanguard. Rather, the vanguard must win recognition as a vanguard (i.e., the historical right to act as a vanguard) through its attempts to establish revolutionary ties with the advanced part of the class and its actual struggle.[138]

As regards consciousness, Mandel continues, there are many differences and layers in the working class, which in turn are the result of the complex process of objective class formation. This is because the working class is composed of layers that have been proletarianised at different times and under different conditions – therefore, they have acquired very different degrees of experience in the class conflict against capital. Consequently, there are different 'levels' of class consciousness. The category 'advanced workers' refers to the section of the working class that has reached a much more mature class consciousness than the 'mass' of workers. Socialism as a science, which presupposes comprehensive knowledge and engagement with philosophy, history, economics etc., can ultimately only be acquired individually. For the same reason, socialist consciousness can be acquired by members of other classes and social strata.[139] The prerequisite for the revolutionary party is a selection process according to the criterion of socialist consciousness, which cannot spontaneously flow from 'working at a lathe or a calculating machine': 'Any other approach can lead only to an idealisation of the working class – and ultimately of capitalism itself'.[140]

For Mandel, not 'work on the lathe' is at the root of all experience from which 'elementary class consciousness' flows, but the mass actions (especially strikes) for higher wages, shorter working hours and better working conditions from which the elementary class organisations have emerged. Mandel generalises this statement: 'It is a general law of history that only through action are *broad masses* able to elevate their consciousness'.[141] Elementary class struggle

---

138 Ibid. Mandel cites Lenin, who described the organisation of the professional revolutionaries without the precondition of the ability of the working class to organise as a mere 'plaything' – see Lenin 1907.

139 Ibid.

140 Ibid.

141 Ibid.

and the experience derived form a 'residue' whose main characteristic is continuous organisation. The majority of those taking part in a mass action return to their everyday lives – which are characterised by competition and heteronomy – as soon as it is over. Some, however, try to continue the struggle by other means. This section of the working class is its 'natural vanguard'. Their activity continues in a different way the process initiated by mass action through the transition to permanent trade unions, workers' newspapers, workers' educational circles, etc.: 'It thus helps give form to a factor of continuity, as opposed to the necessarily discontinuous action of the mass'.[142] The consciousness of the 'broad vanguard' that carries this activity is essentially determined by practical experience of struggle and is therefore essentially 'empirical and pragmatic'. A revolutionary vanguard organisation that starts from a political and scientific viewpoint rather than practical experience in the class struggle must, in turn, get involved in the class struggle and try to forge ties with this broad vanguard. Mandel argues that the perspective of a process of fusion is characteristic for Lenin's theory of organisation, according to which individuals proceed from very different starting points to bring about the 'unity of theory and practice'.[143]

To illustrate the dynamics of this desired process of fusion, Mandel draws up a diagram that starts from the three categories 'masses', 'advanced workers' and 'revolutionary nuclei' and their distinguishing features: the 'masses' take action, gain experience through action, and reach consciousness through experience; the 'advanced workers' reach consciousness from experience and therefore take action; whereas the 'revolutionary nuclei' become active because of their consciousness and gain experience through action.[144]

While Mandel regards the fusion of the consciousness of revolutionary nuclei and the broad vanguard as the first important goal when building revolutionary parties, he also emphasises mass action, on the one hand, and the action of the revolutionary nuclei on the other. It is precisely the great weight of practical experience gained by the broad vanguard of advanced workers that makes it so difficult for them to take collective action: they are neither driven by the 'spontaneous explosivity' of revolting masses nor by the 'pure conviction' of the revolutionaries. These vanguard workers are cautious precisely because of their experience and are often reluctant to launch mass action because they know the risks and difficulties involved. Although these advanced workers are

---

142 Ibid.
143 Ibid.
144 Ibid.

key to the prospect of mass class activity, they are often imbued with a sense of conservatism: 'The greatest "temptation" of economism can be traced to this very point'.[145]

However, if broad mass action increasingly coincides with the activity of the broad vanguard, a pre-revolutionary situation matures. If additionally, the consciousness of the broad vanguard and revolutionary consciousness merge, a revolutionary situation erupts.

In this kind of situation, the masses establish 'organs of dual power' – i.e. potential organs of potential for the exercise of alternative power – and take up the fight for demands that can no longer be fulfilled by the capitalist system.[146] Before such situations emerge, the inherent conflicts of interest in capitalist society lead to mass struggles with immediate concrete objectives. For Mandel, the transition from this kind of system-inherent class struggle to a revolutionary class struggle especially depends on whether a sufficiently large section of advanced workers has already gained experience in promoting transitional demands; and secondly, whether there is a revolutionary organisation that has sufficient social weight and is capable of working out a comprehensive programme of transitional demands. This programme must not only meet the 'objective', scientifically verifiable demands, but also the subjectively perceived needs of the masses.[147]

Referring to Rosa Luxemburg's relevant critique of 1903–04, Mandel defends Lenin against the accusation of having an 'ultra-centralist' conception. It is a misunderstanding to believe that the emphasis of Lenin's argumentation is on organisational centralist streamlining, Mandel argues. Rather, the key issue is the need for political centralisation and a 'central strategic plan'.[148] The central point of *What Is To Be Done?* is the argument for party education and action that is not only 'economic' but comprehensive and political and has its eyes on developing general political class consciousness. The point of Lenin's emphatic dissociation from the 'economist' positions aimed at 'increasing the activity of the working masses' (as he calls it in *What Is To Be Done?*) is that he wants the political party to learn and teach to record and react to all classes of society and their interrelationships, and all political and social phenomena in their context. 'Those who concentrate the attention, observation, and consciousness of the working class exclusively, or even mainly, upon itself alone are not Social Democrats; for the *self*-knowledge of the working class is indissolubly bound

---

145   Ibid.
146   Mandel 1970b, footnote 20.
147   Mandel 1970b and Mandel 1979a, pp. 125–6.
148   Mandel 1970b.

up, not solely with a fully clear theoretical understanding – it would be even truer to say, not so much with the theoretical, as with the practical, understanding – of the relationships between *all* the various classes of modern society, acquired through the experiences of political life'.[149] Only in this way, argues Mandel, is it possible to join up the various local and sectoral struggles that are developing in the different sectors of society politically.

Objecting to Lenin, Luxemburg stated that 'the proletarian army is recruited and becomes aware of its objectives in the course of the struggle itself'. Mandel quotes this passage from Luxemburg's *Organisational Questions of Social Democracy*, only to claim that it has been 'refuted by history'.[150] It is remarkable that the idea expressed by Luxemburg is still very close to Mandel's own approach (Mandel emphasises the similarities between Lenin and Luxemburg more than the differences, especially with regard to the period between the outbreak of the German revolution and Rosa Luxemburg's assassination). For Mandel too, 'the proletarian army' is essentially 'recruited in the struggle itself'. In his view, the activity of revolutionary organisations is largely aimed at the emergence of such situations: the workers start moving *en masse*, gain completely new experiences on account of their own activity and, on this basis, form their consciousness anew. However, his assessment of all the great movements, uprisings, and revolutionary situations in modern capitalist history that did not lead to the working class conquest of political power is negative. From his point of view, what was missing was a political party acting in the Leninist sense and demonstrating its worth as a vanguard:

> Experience in struggle is by no means sufficient for clarity on the tasks of a broad pre-revolutionary, or even a revolutionary, mass struggle to be attained. Not only, of course, are these tasks connected to the immediate motives that set off the struggle, but they can be grasped only by means of a comprehensive analysis of the overall social development, of the historical position achieved by the capitalist mode of production and its internal contradictions, and of the national and international relationship of forces between classes. Without protracted and consistent preparation, without the education of hundreds and thousands of advanced workers in the spirit of a revolutionary program, and without the practical experience accumulated over the years by these advanced workers through attempting to bring this program to the broad masses, it would

---

149 Ibid. Mandel approvingly quotes a passage from Lenin's *What Is To Be Done?* in which the author argues for 'comprehensive political exposure'.

150 Ibid.

be absolutely illusory to assume that suddenly, overnight so to speak, with
the mere aid of mass *actions*, a consciousness equal to the demands of the
historical situation could be created among these broad masses.[151]

This requires the formation of a 'trained vanguard', and the Bolshevik Party
around 1905 and after 1912 (when mass movements re-emerged after the years
of reaction) was an organisation of this type: it facilitated a fusion between
socialist consciousness and the workers' vanguard.[152]

Beyond the problem of comprehensive political consciousness-raising,
Mandel identifies the revolutionary perspective itself, which entails a confrontation with the existing state and aims at the conquest of political power, as
another factor in political centralisation and – to a certain extent – an aspect
of 'Jacobinism' in revolutionary organisation (in Lenin's sense). He does not
mean this in the sense of forming a 'Blanquist squad of conspirators'. Rather, he
considers it necessary to complement the ebb and flow of the mass movement
with the permanent organisation of convinced revolutionaries who never stop
working for the revolution (similarly to the 'advanced workers' who maintain
elementary class organisation even in the quiet periods between strikes and
mass movements).

When assessing the Russian October revolution of 1917, Mandel stresses
the class and mass character of the council (soviet) movement that seized
power, but equally highlights the need for a consciously organised insurrection (which, as is well-known, Lenin passionately advocated in his *Letters from
Afar*). Without such organisation, it is easy to miss the relatively short moment
during which the representatives of the old order can only muster feeble resistance.[153]

Like Rosa Luxemburg, Mandel has a very high regard for spontaneous mass
action. Incidentally, he sees a convergence rather than an irreconcilable opposition between Luxemburg and Lenin, both in this question and with respect to
the role of the party. All the same, he considers it important to recognise the
limits of spontaneous mass action. The entire programme of socialist revolution cannot evolve from mass action, nor can the forces involved in mass action
be centralised at crucial moments to guarantee its success – such a thing cannot
simply be 'improvised'. What is more, if you scratch the surface, the theory of
pure spontaneity turns out to be a 'fairytale': behind every meaningful action

---

151   Ibid.
152   Ibid.
153   See Mandel 1979a, p. 104 et seq.; Mandel 1992b, p. 11.

there are ultimately conscious forces, left-wing trade union activists, revolutionary groups and other such elements driving it forward. The role of the revolutionary party is to coordinate the action of these vanguard elements. This is ultimately the meaning of Lenin's 'centralism'.[154]

Mandel considers this approach to constitute the counter-position to the 'mechanical fatalism' espoused by theorists like Otto Bauer ('Austromarxism', left Social Democracy) and Karl Kautsky (the 'centre' of German Social Democracy). Because of the contradictions imminent in capitalism, he argues, periodically reoccurring mass action is inevitable – however, it is impossible to predict the time, duration, the concrete occasion or the concrete forms that mass action will take. The revolutionary vanguard party has the task of aiming all forces at the current 'weakest link' of the old order. May 1968 in France and the autumn of 1969 in Italy saw 10 and 15 million workers, respectively, moving into action and striking for objectives beyond immediate, purely economic demands. Especially in Italy, the election of *delegati di reparto* showed that there was a dynamic heading towards the overthrow of the system. Using a metaphor borrowed from Trotsky, Mandel says that the 'steam' (the mass movement with revolutionary potential) was there, but the 'piston' (the revolutionary party) was missing, with the result that the steam evaporated.[155]

In building the revolutionary party, a unity of separation and integration must be sought in relation to the working class: separation between those who support the revolutionary programme and those who do not support it (yet), constant communication and exchange with the working class, especially with its most advanced sections. However, capitalist society is characterised by commodity production and the division of labour, and there is a tendency within this society to reify all relations. In the final analysis, this is also the root cause for self-perpetrating party apparatuses acting in their own interests and for the bureaucratisation of workers' organisations. In Mandel's view, Luxemburg and Trotsky were more clear-sighted in recognising this danger than Lenin, who regarded the influence of petty-bourgeois intellectuals as the main danger for revolutionary working-class organisation. In reality, Mandel continues, the main danger comes from the party bureaucracy itself, i.e. from its legalistic daily practice. Rosa Luxemburg warned against this as early as 1904 and Leon Trotsky wrote in 1906 that it could become an 'obstacle' to the revolution, whereas Lenin did not fully recognise the problem until 1914.[156]

---

154 Mandel 1970b.
155 Ibid.
156 Ibid.

From that point on, Lenin stressed that political class consciousness is not enough. What is also necessary is the formation of revolutionary class consciousness in the vanguard: the fusion between the revolutionary programme and the vanguard is the task of party building; it creates the conditions for winning the majority of the working class for socialist revolution.[157]

Because the project of building revolutionary vanguard organisations must be tied to the idea of the actuality of revolution in the historical sense, so as not to be arbitrary, the revolutionary organisation must focus its activity on future active participation in a revolutionary mass movement. This requires a 'pedagogical mediation' of its programme beyond pure propaganda even in non-revolutionary times. Mandel can certainly see the danger of integration into the system, but he does not consider it inevitable because there are counter-tendencies that can be reinforced: for instance, the integration into an international political organisation, participation in class struggles and mass movements, a 'selection of cadres in practice' (i.e. in revolutionary struggles), constant exchange with the social vanguard, the rotation of functions and institutional 'guarantees' such as limiting the pay of full-time workers to the average wage level of a skilled worker. Ultimately, the question of preserving revolutionary identity or, alternatively, slipping into bureaucratic-opportunistic degeneration is a struggle between two tendencies that objectively work against each other: it is the struggle between the degree of political self-activity of the workers' vanguard and the degree of special interests followed by full-time functionaries.[158]

If a workers' party is set up as an electoral association, it is much more at risk of bureaucratisation than a revolutionary fighting party. In the 'electoral club' type of party, the mass of passive members constitutes a kind of plebiscitary mass at the disposal of its leaders. In the revolutionary combat organisation, on the other hand, the activity of all members extends as much to the implementation as to the formulation of policies. In 1917, according to Mandel, Lenin won through with his *April Theses* and steered the course towards socialist revolution because his position was consistent with the aspirations of the advanced sections of the workers' vanguard already organised in the Bolshevik party. The sentiments prevalent among that vanguard, in turn, corresponded to the dominant trend of political mass radicalisation. Conversely, Stalin could later assert himself with his position of 'building socialism in one country' because this vanguard of workers had disintegrated (or indeed had been

---

157   Ibid.
158   Ibid.

physically destroyed by the civil war) and because it corresponded to a wide-spread passivity of the working masses.[159]

In Mandel's view, the need to build revolutionary parties in no way contradicts council democracy. On the contrary, he sees councils as a kind of 'unity in diversity', a united front of different political organisations acting together within the framework of the councils. If counter-revolutionary tendencies prevail within the councils (as in Germany in 1918–19), the revolution fails. Councils do not make parties superfluous because they do not emerge from a homogeneous political consciousness in the working class. Councils without parties would not result in a more democratic system – rather, they would ensure that the important questions of revolution are not debated in front of the masses. It is important for revolutionary parties to do everything in their power to encourage the activity of the working class – their activity is ultimately the strongest guarantee for their emancipation. The council system offers exceptionally favourable conditions for this.[160] Mandel does not believe that the desired high level of self-activity of the masses is in contradiction to Lenin's concept of organisation: 'The Leninist concept of organisation, built upon a correct revolutionary strategy (i.e., on a correct assessment of the objective historical process), is simply the collective co-ordinator of the activity of the masses, the collective memory and digested experience of the masses ...'.[161]

If a party, instead of promoting the self-activity of the masses, turns against it or even suppresses it by force, this reveals its non-revolutionary character, its commitment to interests that are alien to the class (bureaucratic or bourgeois). The argument that one should not build revolutionary parties because there is a potential for degeneration, however, is akin to the desire to return to quackery just because scientifically based medicine sometimes fails.[162]

In Mandel's view, the working class as a potentially revolutionary subject is not only non-homogeneous in its consciousness, but also quite 'contradictory' in itself. The development of class consciousness is therefore a contradictory process that does not occur in a linear fashion but in wave movements. The opportunist tendency in the labour movement tends to 'worship the worker of bourgeois everyday life' (or even 'worship his buttocks' – a formulation of Plekhanov's), whereas the sectarian only 'approves' of the worker who is willing to sign up to the whole sectarian programme here and now. The Maoist

159   Ibid.
160   Ibid.
161   Ibid.
162   Ibid.

movement in particular stands out for this kind of subjectivism. In extreme cases, the working class is simply proclaimed part of the bourgeoisie.[163]

'Extreme objectivism on the one hand ("everything the workers do is revolutionary"), and extreme subjectivity on the other hand ("only those who accept our doctrine are revolutionary or proletarian"), join hands in the final analysis when they deny the objectively revolutionary character of huge struggles led by masses with a contradictory consciousness'.[164]

This statement of Mandel's is meant to draw lines of demarcation, yet at the same time it indicates certain problems in his own approach to mass movements with 'contradictory consciousness'. After all, his claim implies that revolutionaries should judge the behaviour of mass movements primarily in terms of their imminent emancipatory and revolutionary potential, and only secondarily assess their shortcomings. This of course brings with it the danger of seeing movements through rose-tinted glasses and with too much 'revolutionary optimism'. Whether this danger takes its toll always depends on whether one's assessment is sober enough to consider the limits or even reactionary pitfalls contained in the 'contradictory' consciousness of existing mass movements.

Mandel discusses in the context of organisational theory which sections of the intelligentsia tend to have a negative influence and which do not. He distinguishes six different categories:

1) Foremen and other cadre personnel, who however only play a very minor role as agents of the interests of the employers in the labour movement.

2) The intermediaries between science, technology and production: laboratory assistants, scientific researchers, technologists, draftsmen etc., who take part in the production process in their own way (they are not exploiters because they do not live off surplus-value).

3) Those involved in the realisation of surplus-value: advertising experts, market researchers, etc.

4) Paid officials of the labour movement who act as intermediaries between the buyers and sellers of the commodity labour power.

5) The 'intermediaries between capital and labour in the sphere of superstructure' – i.e. the producers of ideology, bourgeois politicians, professors, journalists and artists.

6) The 'mediators between science and the working class', i.e. the 'theoretical producers, who have not been professionally incorporated into the

---

163   Ibid.
164   Ibid.

ideological production of the ruling class and are relatively able, being free from material dependency on this production, to engage in criticism of bourgeois relations'.[165] This also includes critical artists.

For Mandel, the social strata corresponding to categories 2) and 6) have a positive influence on the formation and development of class consciousness, whereas the others (especially 4 and 5) have a negative influence. The positive influence of the technical and critical intelligentsia mainly stems from its ability to equip the working class with knowledge, which enables the class to criticise bourgeois society and tackle the problems of production under its own direction and in free association. Those who promote anti-intellectualism against these layers of the intelligentsia objectively aid the other layers of the intelligentsia, thus increasing their harmful influence on the development of class consciousness. Ultimately, such anti-intellectualism serves to perpetuate the social division of labour, that is the separation of manual and mental labour. Revolutionary organisations, on the other hand, at least create starting points for breaking this division within the workers' movement.

Mandel believes that 'distrust towards intellectuals' is particularly entrenched in those sections of workers who work in small and medium-sized enterprises, who have worked their way up as autodidacts and through their own effort, and who have risen to the top of bureaucratised organisations.

The German-language version of Mandel's text *The Leninist Theory of Organisation* contains the observation: 'In other words, the social basis of economism, spontaneism, bureaucratism and hostility toward science within the working class is the craft layer, not the working class of the large factories and cities or of the expansive industries. These strata were also the main supporters of Majority Social Democracy in the decisive years of the German Revolution of 1919–1923'.[166]

Mandel argues that this was historically also the basis of the anarcho-syndicalist tendency. Any attempt to revive this approach under the pretext of 'workers' autonomy' today, in the era of the third industrial revolution, can only dissipate the forces of the vanguard and give a boost to the backward sections of the working class.[167]

This brings us to a point that should be discussed critically in light of recent social developments. According to the Marxist criteria applied by Mandel – but also, for example, by Heinz Stehr, chairman of the German Communist Party (DKP) from 1990–2000 (in an interview with *Sozialistische Zeitung* 8/2000) –

---

165   Ibid.
166   Mandel 1970f, p. 193, our translation.
167   Mandel 1970b.

the working class and therefore the potentially revolutionary subject is growing internationally. However, Mandel's organisational concept does not depend only on this. His emphasis on big corporations and 'expansive' sectors with advanced technology raises the question how his concept fits into a pattern of development that has seen not only the disintegration of traditional working environments, but also a decline in the importance of big enterprises and their core workforce – namely through mass redundancies, 'streamlining' of production, 'outsourcing', precarisation and pseudo self-employment. As a result, the 'handicraftsman's approach' is coming back in certain respects, the growing working class is increasingly fragmented, and the objective aggregation of the core strata of the working class in the large firms is countered by powerful tendencies. The question is what changes this necessitates for the conception of revolutionary organisation, or whether such a conception is still realistic in view of these development trends.

Mandel's reflections on the intelligentsia, on the other hand, have apparently remained relevant. His starting point is a quote from a draft chapter entitled 'Results of the Direct Production Process', which did not make it into the final version of the first chapter of Marx's *Capital* Volume I.[168] The quote is now well known, but it was not part of the debate until Hans-Jürgen Krahl cited it in his last work, 'On the general relationship between scientific intelligence and proletarian class consciousness' in December 1969:

> Since with the development of the *real subsumption of labour under capital* or the *specifically capitalist mode of production* it is not the individual worker but rather a *socially combined labour capacity* that is more and more the *real executor* of the labour process as a whole, and since the different labour capacities which cooperate together to form the productive machine as a whole contribute in very different ways to the direct process by which the commodity, or, more appropriate here, the product, is formed, one working more with his hands, another more with his brain, one as a manager, engineer, or technician, etc., another as an overlooker, the third directly as a manual worker, or even a mere assistant, more and more of the *functions of labour capacity* are included under the direct concept of *productive labour*, and their repositories under the concept of *productive workers*, workers directly exploited by capital and altogether *subordinated* to its valorisation and production process.[169]

---

168   See Marx 1864.
169   Marx 1864.

Mandel sees this as Marx's premonition of a process that would only unfold with the third technological revolution and bring a change in the role of the intelligentsia in the class struggle through the partial 'proletarianisation' of the intelligentsia – i.e. because of new, existentially insecure conditions that it will find itself in. This, according to Mandel, was the material basis for the student revolt of the late 1960s. He elaborates further on these ideas in his writing on the role of the intelligentsia in class struggle.[170]

In earlier times, student revolts sometimes emerged as harbingers of revolutionary mass movements, but the involvement of intellectuals in the workers' movement declined to the extent that the movement assumed a mass character. The student intelligentsia even became especially susceptible to extremely reactionary ideas. Modern late capitalist development, however, has produced an intellectual class that can no longer consider itself an immediate appendage or agent of the ruling class. Mandel sees this, above all, as an opportunity: since ignorance in the working class of the industrialised countries is no longer mainly the result of blatant misery, but of the concealing mechanisms of bourgeois everyday life and the manipulative techniques of bourgeois mass communication, the role of a broad stratum of intellectuals with a critical attitude towards society could be very beneficial to the development of class consciousness.[171]

The contemporary perspective from which Mandel wrote this becomes clear in a passage where he attributes the increase in mass consumption as well as the production of an entire class of social critics to contemporary capitalism.:

> As the contradiction between the objective socialisation of production and labour on the one hand, and private appropriation on the other, intensifies (i.e., as the crisis of the capitalist relations of production sharpens) ... and as neo-capitalism seeks to win a new lease on life by raising the working class's level of consumption, science will increasingly become for the masses a revolutionary, productive force in two regards: With automation and the growing mountain of commodities, it produces not only a growing crisis in the production and distribution process of capital, which is based upon generalised commodity production; it also produces revolutionary consciousness in growing masses of people by allowing the myths and masks of the capitalist routine to be torn away ....[172]

---

170   Mandel 1975b.
171   Ibid.
172   Ibid.

The learning processes that Mandel describes schematically in order to distil a concept for building revolutionary organisations correspond to real experiences. The question that nevertheless remains unanswered is whether these processes will in future assume such a scale that majorities for socialist revolution emerge in the rich industrialised countries and worldwide. This, however, determines the realism of the concept. For Mandel, there are 'three kinds of historical pedagogy' in the formation of class consciousness; revolutionary parties have the function of relating all three levels effectively with each other.[173] The masses learn through action – but action does not automatically produce revolutionary class consciousness. Still, the struggle for immediate goals and partial demands is very important because it produces confidence and self-assurance. Any revolutionary organisation must connect to these struggles and advance them by focusing them on transitional demands. Advanced experience in the struggle for transitional demands – i.e. demands that cannot be met by the capitalist system or co-opted – aids the formation of revolutionary class consciousness.

The 'natural vanguard' of the class, on the other hand, which comprises the crucial 'multipliers' in relation to the working class as a whole, learns from its daily experiences. It recognises the need for collective action, the need to co-ordinate and organise as a class independently of the class enemy, both in trade unions and, where appropriate, politically. The revolutionary vanguard organisation tries to influence this 'natural vanguard' into taking action that pushes through the limits of the capitalist system. A revolutionary organisation will be successful to the extent that it succeeds in developing this revolutionary attitude out of the actual needs of the natural vanguard. The prerequisite for this, however, according to Mandel, is precisely that the objective situation contains tendencies that make such consciousness formation possible.[174] No matter how 'correct' a political tactic or line may be in the abstract, there is no chance of a breakthrough in periods of declining class struggle – the illusion that this is somehow possible has caused many revolutionary groups to split. That being said, the tenacious and patient preparatory work of revolutionary forces is important even when the class struggle is on the decline. It will bear fruit later, when the natural vanguard of the class suddenly becomes ready to fight for demands that can shatter the capitalist system [systemsprengend]. To win the vanguard politically, of course, it is not enough to know the general concept and use it as a blueprint

---

173   Ibid.
174   Ibid.

because you have read about it in books. One needs to analyse concretely the present social reality and the present consciousness of the class and of the vanguard, and one needs to apply historical experience ('the lessons of history') in a concrete fashion.[175] Revolutionary theory in the full sense of the word can only evolve in this way. Differences of principle can arise from the real problems of practice and from the activity of revolutionary organisations, and there is no point in avoiding them. They must be fought out, because the consequences of taking one position or the other does lead to different actions.[176]

Ernest Mandel stresses he does not envision the revolutionary learning process as a one-way street. Rather, it is an interaction of teaching and learning that involves everyone, including the revolutionary cadres, who therefore have no reason to be arrogant on the pretext of their special knowledge. Theory only proves its right to exist if it succeeds in connecting with the real class struggle and transforming potential class consciousness into real revolutionary class consciousness (which also means 'saturating' and developing one's own theoretical consciousness with experience). The mediation of the three different ways of learning forms the 'unity' of the process of building the revolutionary party.

> The famous observation by Marx that the educators must themselves be educated means exactly what it says. It does not mean that a consciously revolutionary transformation of society is possible without a revolutionary pedagogy. And it is given a more complete expression in the Marxist proposition that 'In revolutionary activity the changing of oneself coincides with the changing of circumstances'.[177]

With this quotation, Mandel concludes his key text on the construction and role of revolutionary parties. For him, political and organisational theory is embedded in the ethical stance articulated by Marx that constitutes the foundation of revolutionary activity – even before the analysis of existing conditions proves its realism.

---

175 Ibid.
176 Ibid.
177 Ibid.

5   Critique of Reformism and United Front Policy

Those not familiar with the historical debates on the major disputes in the workers' movement usually think that revolutionary socialists reject the struggle for reforms precisely because they are for revolution. They often believe that critiques of reformism amount to a rejection of reforms aimed at improving the living conditions of workers in the context of capitalist society. Mandel does not reject the struggle for reforms, though – he criticises reformism for other reasons: 'For revolutionary Marxists, reformism is in no way identified with the struggle for reforms. Reformism is the belief that capitalism can be abolished gradually through the accumulation of reforms. But it is perfectly possible to combine participation in struggles for immediate reforms with the preparation of the workers vanguard for anti-capitalist struggles of such an intensity and size that they bring about a revolutionary crisis in society'.[178]

When Mandel criticises the reformist strategy, he does not suggest that struggles to defend the basic interests of workers under capitalism should be renounced. In his view, these struggles are valid – but they must be fought from a revolutionary perspective which aims at the abolition of capitalism and the conquest of political power by the working class.[179] This places him in the tradition of a critique of reformism famously formulated by Rosa Luxemburg, who dealt with Eduard Bernstein's 'revisionism' at the turn of the twentieth century ('revisionism' was the openly articulated revision of certain traditional Marxist positions in order to pursue a reformist rather than revolutionary strategy):

> Can the social democracy be against reforms? Can we counterpose the social revolution, the transformation of the existing order, our final goal, to social reforms? Certainly not. The daily struggle for reforms, for the amelioration of the condition of the workers within the framework of the existing social order, and for democratic institutions, offers to the social democracy the only means of engaging in the proletarian class war and working in the direction of the final goal-the conquest of political power and the suppression of wage labor. Between social reforms and revolution there exists for the social democracy an indissoluble tie. The struggle for reforms is its means; the social revolution, its aim.[180]

---

178   Mandel 1979a, p. 86.
179   See Mandel 1988d.
180   Luxemburg 2008.

In the quoted text, Luxemburg accuses Bernstein of introducing a distinction between the struggle for reform and the struggle for revolution in the first place, namely by coining the phrase, 'The final goal, no matter what it is, is nothing; the movement is everything'. For her, there is an 'inseparable' connection between the two. If the 'opportunist' orientation were to prevail, she argues, this would put the specifically socialist character of Social Democracy at stake – it would fall victim to the petty-bourgeois elements penetrating the workers' movement.[181] The idea that capitalism can be gradually overcome through more and more reforms, that the everyday class struggle as a means of self-education, of raising the political consciousness of the class can be neglected, inevitably leads one to abandon the standpoint of the working class. But it also implies that a consistent struggle for reforms is abandoned: in Luxemburg's view, capitalist reality does not permit a sustained improvement in the condition of the working class on account of its internal contradictions, which have a tendency to intensify. Luxemburg consequently rejected Bernstein's then-new idea that a prolonged peaceful development with steadily withering contradictions would be possible by virtue of the partial abolition of capitalist anarchy by cartels and trusts and the increasing importance of the credit system, which in his view counteracted economic crises.[182]

Mandel is just as vehemently opposed to 'ultra-leftist' sloganeering against struggles for reform, which are based on the pretext that a real and lasting solution can only be obtained through socialist revolution:

> The radical rejection of any struggle for reforms implies the passive acceptance of a deterioration in the situation of the working class until a moment when it would suddenly become capable of overthrowing the capitalist regime with one concerted attack. Such an attitude is both utopian and reactionary. It is utopian because it forgets that the workers, increasingly divided and demoralised by their inability to defend their standard of living, employment and elementary rights, are hardly likely to be able to overcome a social class invested with the wealth and political experience of the modern bourgeoisie. It is reactionary because objectively it serves the cause of the capitalists – who have everything to gain by lowering wages, maintaining massive unemployment, suppressing the unions and the right to strike – if the workers passively allow themselves to be reduced to the state of defenceless slaves.[183]

---

181   Luxemburg 2008, p. 100 et seq.
182   Luxemburg 2008, pp. 46–7.
183   Mandel 1979a, pp. 86–7.

According to Mandel, the self-liberation of the working class must be preceded by a period in which the strength, unity and confidence of the proletariat
is growing as a series of successful struggles take place – often, these will be
struggles for reform. Reformism can be defeated if the revolutionaries succeed
in organising extra-parliamentary struggles beyond the – necessary but not sufficient – propaganda for the socialist revolution, and if these struggles assume
an anti-capitalist thrust rather than merely aim at improvements within the
capitalist system. By the same token, revolutionaries need to participate in the
workers' mass trade unions to strengthen them where possible and to turn the
unions, as far as possible, into instruments of a real struggle against employers.[184]

In contrast, the reformist strategy usually relies on winning majorities in
bourgeois parliaments in elections. It wants to overcome capitalism on this
basis, i.e. through gradual changes by participation in government or by assuming governmental responsibility (this necessarily entails that the workers are
not the crucial actors in this process). It may seem exaggerated, but the Marxist
critique of reformism (and the 'electoralist' approach generally associated with
it, which is based on election victories in a bourgeois parliamentary republic)
in the tradition of Luxemburg and Mandel boils down to a paradoxical charge:
in the long run, it is reformism that undermines the struggle for reform and
renders the working class defenceless even with respect to its elementary day-
to-day interests rather than just its historical ones. Today this is blatantly obvious, with German social democracy not only having long since abandoned its
reformist policy of gradually overcoming capitalism when it formally adopted
the Godesberg Programme (logically so, as Luxemburg predicted over a hundred years ago), but also because it has turned the meaning of the word 'reform'
into its opposite when adapting it to the prevailing neo-liberal ideology of the
bourgeoisie. 'Reform' is now used as a term for measures that deteriorate rather
than improve the living conditions of the working class and the dispossessed
in general (or at least of substantial sections). The interests of capital are pursued for the sake of competition in the 'globalised' international marketplace
and to increase profits – on this basis, improvements for the workers can supposedly be won at some point in the future (not much needs to be said about
the credibility of this empty promise). During periods of prolonged economic
prosperity without major crises – for instance, at the time when Bernstein
developed his 'revisionism' or in the 1950s and '60s – this can be temporarily
concealed. In prosperous times, material concessions can be made – the bour-

---

184   Mandel 1979a, p. 86.

geoisie prefers this over risking a potential radicalisation of working people. But by the second half of the 1960s, the basic tendency of the protracted post-war boom had already begun to falter. Mandel began to criticise reformism, its electoralist strategy, and governments led by social democrats as early as 1968, denouncing this strategy as one that fails to achieve reforms and instead sets back the working class both materially and morally:

> The alternatives to socialist revolution continue to periodically go bankrupt. The experience of the Wilson administration in Britain is the latest striking example of this. Here we have the Labour Party in power on its own for the third time, with a substantial absolute parliamentary majority for the second time, and with the clear support of the majority of the people. But faced with the economic difficulties caused by the decline of British capitalism, this party does not show the slightest degree of socialist initiative, it shies away from confronting the rich and powerful, it does not challenge the wealth and scandalous luxury of a parasitic, decadent and impotent ruling class. Subject to the dictates of international finance capital, the party prefers to launch attacks on state subsidies for milk for children and medicines for the sick. In the course of a few days, it has pushed back the socialist institutions [i.e. the social institutions previously introduced by Labourism – author] by almost 20 years, which is something that no Conservative government would have dared to try. It has announced a wage freeze while at the same time providing enormous subsidies to private entrepreneurs. After shouting the need for technological modernisation from the rooftops, it ended up not approving the extension of compulsory schooling until the age of 16! It has showed no imagination, not a trace of boldness, not the slightest degree of independence from the propertied classes – nothing, in fact, but abject subservience. All this under conditions of a relatively prosperous capitalist world economy without war, without an immediate threat of civil war, and without any reason to fear sabotage by the bureaucracy of the bourgeois state.[185]

The more the stagnant, depressive, crisis-ridden tendency of capitalism reasserted itself, the less the government parties that had emerged from the workers' movement were willing to implement any reforms to improve the situation of workers, the dispossessed and the poor. And they enforced worse condi-

---

185   Mandel 1978a, pp. 32–3, our translation.

tions, arguing that otherwise 'the economy' could not be improved in any other way. Mandel reproaches social-democratic reformist 'opportunism', its 'system-compliant' strategy, and its revision of Marxism: all of this left the masses completely unprepared for any drastic changes or social upheavals.[186] Apart from its willingness to participate in bourgeois governments and refusal to combat one's 'own' colonialism and imperialism, the opportunist character of this tendency (and equally that of the social-democratic 'centre' around Kautsky, which made more and more concessions to this trend and dressed up opportunist day-to-day practice in 'Marxist' arguments) showed most clearly when refusing to accept Rosa Luxemburg's suggestion, based on the experiences of the Russian revolution of 1905, that mass strikes should also be launched for political ends.[187]

Mandel took a differentiated view on the causes of reformism and its overwhelming influence in the workers' movement over extended periods, considering a number of objective and subjective factors. We have already discussed all the essential relevant points in our subchapter on bureaucracy.[188] Mandel's nuanced analysis did not stop him from speaking of 'betrayal' when characterising the policies of social-democratic and other reformist leaderships in certain historical situations.

While such leaders like to refer to the 'backwardness' of the base in times of widespread passivity, they determinedly fight against revolutionary sentiments if and when they do arise. According to Mandel, the German experience shows that such leaderships consciously stifle revolutionary advances.[189] Moreover, he even refers to the Social-Democratic support for the imperialist war of 1914–18, which was initially opposed by only a small internationalist minority, as 'treason':

> But soon the predominant feelings within the masses turned into dissatisfaction, opposition to the war, and revolt. This time, however, the German social-patriot leaders Scheidemann and Noske and the French social-patriot leaders Renaudel and Jules Guesde did nothing 'to adapt to the predominant feelings within the working class'. On the contrary, they manoeuvred in every way to avoid the outbreak of strikes and mass demonstrations, entering into coalition governments with the bourgeoisie, helping it to suppress anti-militarist, strike and revolutionary

---

186   Mandel 1979a, pp. 84–5.
187   Mandel 1979a, p. 84.
188   See Chapter 4, section 1.
189   Mandel 1979a, pp. 84–5.

propaganda, and sabotaging the development of the workers' struggles. When revolutions finally broke out, the social democratic leaders, who had given their approval to the massacre of millions of soldiers for the cause of capitalist profit, quickly rediscovered their pacifism and begged workers not to have recourse to violence, not to provoke the spilling of blood. At the beginning of the war, while the masses were disoriented by bourgeois propaganda and the betrayals of their own leaders, only a handful of revolutionary socialists remained faithful to proletarian internationalism, refusing to take up a common cause with their own bourgeoisie: Karl Liebknecht and Rosa Luxemburg in Germany; Monatte and Rosmer in France; Lenin, a section of the Bolsheviks, Trotsky, Martov in Russia; the SDP in the Netherlands; John MacLean in Great Britain; Eugene Debs in the USA; while in Italy, Serbia, and Bulgaria, a majority inside the social democratic parties held internationalist positions.[190]

As regards the German Revolution of 1918–19, Mandel rejects the 'economic determinist' and 'fatalist' arguments employed by Otto Bauer and Karl Kautsky: according to them, the situation was objectively not ripe for a socialist revolution, the balance of power between the proletariat and the bourgeoisie was far too unfavourable for the proletariat, and the level of consciousness far too low. In contrast, Mandel emphasises the level of working-class organisation during this period and the evolving consciousness of a steadily growing section of the class until 1923. This was reflected in the formation of the Independent Social-Democratic Party of Germany (USPD), the majority of which joined the Communist International in 1920, and in the fact that the majority of the German working class ultimately leaned towards communism in 1923 – for which, he argues, there is quite convincing evidence.[191]

Nor is it true that the bourgeoisie and its state apparatus were too strong in 1918–19 to be overcome by a well-organized working class. As a matter of fact, their weakness was so pronounced that they remained almost completely inactive during the first weeks of the revolution, putting all their hopes in the SPD leadership of Ebert, Scheidemann and Noske. It was these right-wing social democrats who, the bourgeoisie hoped, would trick the workers into rebuilding a bourgeois republic instead of seizing

---

190   Mandel 1979a, pp. 99–100.
191   Mandel 1981a, pp. 48–9.

power, and who would be willing to build a new repressive army out of the disintegrating Imperial forces. This calculation proved to be correct.[192]

Despite the weight of the 'objective' factors, which from a Marxist point of view are ultimately the basis of 'subjective' factors, Mandel explains the defeats of the German working class up to the crushing defeat of 1933 essentially as a result of the interaction between the experience of struggle, the formation of consciousness and the balance of power between the various tendencies in the workers' movement: 'The secret of these defeats does not lie in the deep bedrock of the productive forces, nor in the immediate substratum of the class structure and the class relationship of forces in German society. Rather it is located at the quite different level of the relationship between the working class and its leadership; the balance of forces between different currents inside the organized labour movement; and the correlation of, on the one hand, certain levels of class consciousness and the conscious role of revolutionary leadership, and on the other, the accumulation of certain types of struggle experience'.[193]

Mandel's critique of the reformist strategy does not entail a voluntarist demand to make revolution always and everywhere. In his view, the essential task is to prepare for the revolution by organising certain experiences of struggle on a mass level – these have an impact on the development on political consciousness. For him, extra-parliamentary mobilisation and self-organisation up to the construction of council-like bodies of alternative state power takes precedence over working in the institutions of bourgeois parliamentary democracy to which traditional reformist work is ultimately confined. The difference between the two concepts cannot be reduced to divergent expectations as to the outbreak of revolutionary crises – it is essentially based on everyday practice, even in periods located outside revolutionary cycles.

> For revolutionaries, on the other hand, however important electoral-parliamentary activity maybe, it remains subordinated to the masses' self-activity and self-organisation, which is the real practice preparing the emancipation of working people. The emancipation of the workers can only be the work of the workers themselves and not that of parties or trade unions, whatever their indispensable role in this – not to mention that of parliaments or local councils. That is what Marxism is all about.

---

192   Mandel 1979e, p. 44.
193   Mandel 1979e, pp. 45–6.

Reformist strategy and revolutionary strategy are not only opposed to each other because the first writes off the inevitability, indeed even the possibility of revolutionary crises. They are in opposite corners when it comes to day-to-day activity in the class struggle even in a non-revolutionary conjuncture. Reformists more and more subordinate the defence of workers' interests to 'safeguarding the institutions' and 'social equilibrium', in other words, to class collaboration. Revolutionaries defend at all times and against all forces the interests of working people and the political independence of the proletariat, not only from bourgeois parties but also with respect to the institutions of the bourgeois state.[194]

Linking revolutionary positions to the unyielding defence of the interests and independence of the working class is very characteristic of Mandel's politics. Indeed, he repeatedly stressed that capitalism had been in decline since 1914 and, in the 'historical sense', the world socialist revolution had been on the agenda since then.[195] On the other hand, his statements also reveal how little a refutation of this diagnosis could have dissuaded him from his basic position that from a socialist point of view, the defence of the fundamental working class interests should not be subordinated to any other consideration, be it strategic or pragmatic. Beyond the purely subjective aspects, Mandel attributes the rise of reformism in the workers' movement and Luxemburg's prominent role in the struggle against it to an objective development that had led to the 'crisis' of the 'tried and tested tactics' of Social Democracy.[196] This 'tried and tested tactic' was not the invention of reformists trying to revise Marx's intellectual legacy, but rather matched the attitude that Friedrich Engels took in the last years of his life. In way of evidence, Mandel cites a section from Engels's 1895 introduction to Marx's *Class Struggles in France* that the proponents of reformist policies had repeatedly appealed to:

Everywhere, the German example of the utilization of the franchise and of the conquest of all possible positions has been imitated ... The 2,000,000 voters whom it sends to the hustings, plus the young men and women non-voters standing behind them, these form the most numerous, the most compact 'shock troops' of the international proletarian army. This mass already furnishes more than 25 per cent of the total vote cast ... Its growth is so spontaneous, so steady, so irresistible and yet at the

---

194   Mandel 1988d, chapter 5.
195   Ibid.
196   Mandel 1971d.

same time as quiet as that of a natural process. All governmental interference with it has proved futile. Today, we may figure with 2,225,000 voters. If this goes on, we shall at the close of the century win over the greater part of the middle social layers, petty bourgeoisie as well as small peasants, and we shall come to be the decisive power in the land, before which all other powers must bow whether they like it or not. To keep going this growth without interruption until it swamps the ruling governmental system, that is our main task.[197]

It is true, Mandel writes, that Engels's text was mutilated and falsified by the German Social Democrats, who omitted any trace of Engels's intact revolutionary spirit. However, the paragraphs quoted are still authentic. Even more convincing than appeals to the authority of the old mentor, however, was the experience that appeared to prove pragmatists like Bebel, Vandervelde and Victor Adler right for many years. Despite a number of setbacks, the electoral and organisational successes of the Social-Democratic workers' movement seemed unstoppable until the objective factors on which they were based were exhausted (as always, consciousness lagged behind the real development). A secular reduction of the 'reserve army of labour' through emigration and over-exploitation in the colonies and semi-colonies mitigated the contradictions in the capitalist core countries somewhat. But at the turn of the twentieth century, these contradictions began to intensify again and undermined the material basis for a more or less peaceful, uninterrupted boom of the Social-Democratic workers' movement.

'Rosa's merit was that she was the first to grasp clearly and systematically the necessity for a fundamental change in the strategy and tactics of the workers movement in the west, confronted by a changed objective situation: the dawning of the imperialist epoch'.[198] Mandel attributed Rosa Luxemburg's outstanding contribution in this debate to her personal skills and qualities, but especially to her position as a leading member of two Social-Democratic parties, namely the German and the Polish one. Poland was then part of the Tsarist Empire. Luxemburg had special insight into the new forms of struggle in Russia, but had also encountered the increasingly conservative tendencies in the German party and trade union leaderships and apparatuses.[199] In short, Luxemburg's position in the subsequent 'mass strike debate' – fuelled by analysis of the Russian revolution of 1905, which had been the first outbreak of mass

---

197   Engels 1895.
198   Mandel 1971d.
199   Ibid.

struggles with a revolutionary tendency since the Paris Commune of 1871 – had the distinction that she conceived of the mass strike as a means to overcome routine and kickstart a process of mass self-education. This could then rapidly lead to the formation of political consciousness and a tangible opportunity for socialist revolution. Until then, the Social Democrats, appealing to Marx, had always argued against the anarchists and their 'general strike panacea' that the organisational level of the masses had to be patiently raised and majorities won for socialist revolution. A general strike, according to them, was either a risky minority action or pointless because there is no need for a general strike when one already has the majority. This was also Engels's position: 'Paul spoke very well – a slight indication of the universal strike dream in it, which nonsense Guesde has retained from his anarchist days – (whenever we are in a position to try the universal strike, we shall be able to get what we want for the mere asking for it, without the roundabout way of the universal strike)'.[200]

When invoking Luxemburg, Mandel stresses that the 1905 revolution had weakened syndicalism in a way that seemed paradoxical, not least because the Russian Social-Democratic Party supported the mass strike movement. Experience had shown that in the context of every mass strike movement, new layers are drawn into action. The mechanical concept of mass action at the push of a button by board members – and equally, the abortion of mass actions at the push of a button – did not fit that bill. In other words, what Mandel particularly appreciated about Luxemburg's contribution was her insight into the infectious and self-educational dynamics of a mass move-ment revolving around the proletariat (and spreading beyond the proletariat to all exploited and oppressed strata). For him, the fact that the vast major-ity of Social-Democratic leaders did not understand this was one of the major ingredients that led to the 1914 disaster.[201]

Mandel believed that Rosa Luxemburg's work constitutes a 'unity', defined by her desire to assert a revolutionary conception of the tasks at hand against the 'tried and tested tactics'. He counted her analysis of imperialism and her anti-militarist and anti-monarchist agitation as part of this. In his view, all ele-ments of her political interventions were aimed at preparing the working-class vanguard for decisive confrontations with the bourgeois class and its repressive state apparatus in the context of an increasing internationalisation of the class struggle. Mandel regarded even positions of hers that he believed to be wrong as part of this 'unity' – e.g. her criticism of Lenin's 'ultra-centralism', when she

---

200 Ibid.
201 Ibid.

herself approved of the extremely centralist regime that Leo Jogiches had set up under very similar conditions in the illegal Polish party; or her misappreciation of the need to develop revolutionary cadres and build an organised left-wing tendency in the Social-Democratic Party as early as 1906 because she relied too much on the socialist education of the working class vanguard. The latter blunder took its toll when the Spartacus League and the newly founded KPD had to get down to this task in the fire of the revolutionary crisis.[202] In his view, these errors were closely linked to her deep-rooted distrust of officials and professional politicians too. Mandel conceded that Luxemburg had recognised the immense danger inherent in the conservatism of the bureaucratised trade union and workers' party leaderships far earlier than others, including Lenin, who, as is well known, had been so surprised by the German Social-Democratic Party's vote for war loans that he initially believed the report was a forgery. It was only after 1918, however, that she adopted Lenin's belief in the necessity of building revolutionary vanguard organisations. She abandoned the notion that it was enough to trust the verve or spontaneity of the masses to overcome the obstructive role of conservative functionaries (however, Mandel calls the cliche about Luxemburg's supposed spontaneism 'slander').[203]

What is certain is that Luxemburg was virtually the only one among the prominent socialist leaders of her time to be clearly aware of the obstructive role of this stratum before the 'mass strike debate' erupted in the SPD. In the course of this debate, the 'Marxist centre' around Kautsky and Bebel ultimately came to an agreement with the leaders of the trade union leadership, which had become openly 'revisionist'. She said the following to her confidants:

> Since my return from Russia, I feel rather isolated .... I feel the irresolution and the pettiness of our whole party more glaringly and more painfully than ever before. However, I can't get so excited about the situation as you do, because I see with depressing clarity that neither things nor people can be changed – until the whole situation has changed, and even then we shall just have to reckon with inevitable resistance if we want to lead the masses on. I have come to that conclusion after mature reflection. The plain truth is that August [Bebel], and still more so the others, have completely pledged themselves to parliament and parliamentarism, and whenever anything happens which transcends the limits of parliamentary action they are hopeless – no, worse than hopeless, because they then

---

202   Ibid.
203   Ibid.

do their utmost to force the movement back into parliamentary channels, and they will furiously defame as 'an enemy of the people' anyone who dares to venture beyond their own limits. I feel that those of the masses who are organized in the party are tired of parliamentarism, and would welcome a new line in party tactics, but the party leaders and still more the upper stratum of opportunist editors, deputies, and trade-union leaders are like an incubus. We must protest vigorously against this general stagnation, but it is quite clear that in doing so we shall find ourselves against the opportunists as well as the party leaders and August. As long as it was a question of defending themselves against Bernstein and his friends, August & Co. were glad of our assistance, because they were shaking in their shoes. But when it is a question of launching an offensive against opportunism then August and the rest are with Ede [Bernstein], Vollmar, and David against us.[204]

In his examination of 'Eurocommunism', Mandel harked back to all the arguments originally articulated in the course of the adaptation of Social Democracy to bourgeois society. Similar causes produced similar results. In some capitalist industrial countries of western Europe, 'official' Communist mass parties gradually built up a layer of professional politicians who held numerous offices and parliamentary mandates linked to the institutions of bourgeois democracy. This material base began to compete with, and overtake, the dependence on 'Moscow'.

In Mandel's assessment, 'official' Communism had long before adopted a reformist stance on account of the conservative character of the Soviet bureaucracy and imposed it in the parties of the former Comintern. However, Eurocommunist positioning went beyond this and drew directly on Kautsky's theorising after he had bowed to the needs of the Social Democratic bureaucracy – 'attrition strategy' instead of 'strategy of assault', conquest of the majority within the framework of bourgeois-democratic institutions instead of broad mass action, etc.[205] Following the same logic as the Social-Democratic leaderships, Mandel said that the 'Eurocommunists' inevitably became apologists for 'austerity policies', i.e. for the deterioration rather than improvement of the situation of workers and the poor. At the time, leading Eurocommunist figures maintained a convoluted and sometimes confusing discourse, combining, again analogously to the early Social-Democratic reformists (who believed

---

204   Luxemburg 2004, pp. 30–1.
205   Mandel 1978b, p. 160 et seq.

they had to play the role of the 'doctor at the sickbed of capitalism'), concessions to the spokesmen of the bourgeoisie (e.g. that it is initially necessary to fight inflation through wage sacrifices, etc.) with more or less radical visions of a mobilisation of the masses in order to safeguard their basic interests (e.g. strengthen their purchasing power). Aside from all the 'militant' rhetoric, however, in practice the Eurocommunists bowed to the alleged need for tough 'austerity policies' in the interests of capital, according to Mandel. For instance, he wrote about the Berlinguer leadership of the Italian Communist Party (CPI): 'When all the verbiage is eliminated and all the smokescreens are dissipated, one essential and immediate point remains: the leaders of the PCI have surreptitiously drifted toward a thesis that tallies with that of the employers, namely that wage increases are one of the essential causes of inflation, that the struggle against inflation is the top priority, and that this struggle demands an incomes policy that drives down real wages by no longer adapting them to the dizzying increase in the cost of living. Such is the unabashed content of the austerity policy'.[206]

In fact, the majority of the CPI subsequently proved to be allies of capital in abolishing the 'scala mobile', the automatic adjustment of wages to price developments. In line with Mandel's diagnosis of the 'social democratisation' of the Eurocommunist parties, the majority of the Italian CP actually ended up in the second social-democratic International, while a minority (which later formed Rifondazione Comunista) combined the critical reappraisal of the (post-)Stalinist past with a fundamental rejection of the capitalist social order and an openness to new social movements and non-Stalinist (even 'Trotskyist') revolutionary tendencies.[207]

While the opportunist leaders of the workers' movement, who are more or less bourgeoisified and whose argumentation appears 'reformist', have to rely on the social differentiation and division of the working class in the interest of cooperation with capital and its state institutions, seeking support in the relatively privileged strata, revolutionary Marxist tendencies strive to promote the unity of the working class against the bourgeoisie, its parties and its state.

Even before the crystallisation of politically diametrically opposed tendencies in the workers' movement raised the need for a special united front policy or united front tactics, the question of achieving the unity of the proletarian class already existed as a fundamental strategic task. For Mandel, the pursuit

---

206   Mandel 1978b, pp. 121–2.
207   In the meantime, however, Rifondazione Comunista has moved to the right and has begun to decline again.

of this goal remains the foundation for all 'tactical' steps aiming to achieve the united action of the various parties and tendencies of the workers' movement for concrete objectives of struggle. Under capitalist conditions, the working class is exposed to the influence of competition and is therefore fragmented. It is also sociologically heterogeneous. The proletarianisation of urban and especially rural small proprietors and their offspring is taking place in stages and is resulting in a working class composed of, on the one hand, people who have long been shaped by their position as wage earners in the industry and, on the other, those whose mentality is still influenced by the village, by their immediate past. Irrespective of this, capitalism draws on traditional social distinctions (between men and women, old and new, young and old, etc.) and adapts them to its needs. Past social struggles by sections of the working class that were able to organise themselves with greater ease and therefore establish a favourable balance of power relative to 'their' bosses can also produce a relatively privileged position relative to other sections of the proletariat. Since the ruling classes use and deepen such differentiations in their own interest according to the simple principle of 'divide and rule', the assertion of the interests of the working class as a whole is closely linked to the attainment of unity in the struggle for demands that all layers can support.[208]

For Mandel, the highest form of class unity is reached with the organisational form of councils, in which all parts of the class, whether unionised or not, can articulate their concerns. In this sense, the defensive aspect of class unity (joining together to defend oneself against capital) is always closely tied to the possibility of an offensive against the class rule of capital (the working class, self-organised in councils, feels that it can manage its own affairs, and therefore the affairs of society, by itself and sets out to challenge the rule of the bourgeoisie). Even if the forms that class unity takes are initially rudimentary (e.g. based on agreements between the leaders of different parties and tendencies), the confrontation of 'class against class' gives them an inherent emancipatory, consciousness-raising dynamic aiming at comprehensive solidarity and therefore socialist revolution.[209]

The deep divide between Social Democracy and Communism, which resulted from the majority of Social-Democratic leaders' support for 'their' nation state and turn away from the original revolutionary aims, raised the question of class unity in a more acute form. Reading the debates and resolutions of the first four congresses of the Communist Third International reveals how

---

208   Mandel 1987d, p. 151 et seq.
209   Mandel 1987d, p. 151.

the fledgling Communist movement struggled with this problem.[210] When it became clear in the first few years after World War I that no socialist revolution outside Russia would be prevail in the short term, and that in most cases Social Democracy would retain hegemony in the workers' movement, the attainment of workers' unity against the class enemy could no longer be confined to propagandistic attempts to wrest the majority of the class and its 'natural vanguard' from the Social-Democratic leaders. In addition to the strategy of partial and transitional demands, a united front policy was worked out at the third and fourth Comintern congresses. It was based on the assumption that the majority of Social Democracy's proletarian base would only break with its leadership as a result of advanced experience in the class struggle. In order to promote this, the Communist Parties were to systematically approach the Social-Democratic parties with proposals for joint action, up to the slogan of forming 'workers' governments'. These would carry out measures in the interests of the working class and against capital, thus achieving a broad class mobilisation to break the political power of capital. In the context of this tactic, it was seen as essential to appeal to certain positions that these more or less bourgeoisified leaderships articulated out of consideration for their proletarian base and its demands. The refusal of these leaders to accept offers of a united front were expected to trigger a learning process among their base, and even more so their acceptance of such offers, which would inspire a dramatic increase in mass activity and corresponding advances in consciousness.[211]

Following on from Trotsky's positions and programmatically in keeping with the Fourth International, Mandel made this tradition his own and argued for the application of the 'united-front tactic' according to the concrete circumstances in different countries. In his view, the Stalinisation of the Comintern had buried this tradition first in favour of the ultra-left politics of the 'third period' and then 'popular front' policies.[212]

For Mandel, defending the independence of the working class both politically and organisationally is fundamental. He categorically rejected cooperation with bourgeois political parties, especially at government level (i.e. 'popular front' policy). Nonetheless, he stressed the need for alliances with pettybourgeois forces of working small proprietors, especially in the context of national liberation struggles against colonial and imperialist oppression. In

---

210   See Communist International 1923.
211   Frank 1981, pp. 203–4.
212   Mandel 1979a, pp. 137–40.

response to the frequent accusation of 'dogmatism' directed at the Trotskyist critique of 'popular fronts', he stressed the point that alliances must be based on common interests if the interests of the lower classes and strata are not to be sacrificed to the 'common cause' or fall by the wayside, as had occurred so often in history.

> What we dispute is that an alliance between working class parties and bourgeois parties is necessary in order to reach a similar alliance among the labouring classes. On the contrary, the liberation of the peasantry and the urban petty bourgeoisie from the hold of the bourgeoisie also presupposes their emancipation from the support they tend to give to bourgeois political parties. The alliance can and ought to be based on common interests. The proletariat and its parties should offer these classes the social, economic, cultural and political objectives which concern them, and which the bourgeoisie is incapable of achieving. If experience confirms the will of the proletariat to seize power and implement its programme, it can obtain the support of a large part of the petty bourgeoisie who wish to achieve these objectives.[213]

In contrast, 'popular front policy', like any policy of cooperation with the bourgeoisie, could only lead to further catastrophes (considering that the refusal of the Stalinist-led Communist Party of Germany to seek a united front with Social Democracy had led to the catastrophe of the Nazi rise to power). For Mandel, the turn of the 'official' Communist movement to the popular front policy therefore marks the historical moment when it essentially (despite rhetoric to the contrary) became 'reformist' and was lost for the cause of revolution.

> From 1935, the Communist International under Stalin's leadership had taken up the old Menshevik and Social-Democratic strategy of the lesser evil, the policy of blocs with the 'liberal' against the 'reactionary' bourgeoisie. This so-called popular front policy, which was accompanied by a deep structural crisis of the capitalist economy and of bourgeois democracy as a whole – a crisis which could not be alleviated by any reforms – not only resulted in the squandering of another historic opportunity for the workers to seize power. This time it was the Stalinists who were to blame, as the Social Democrats had been in 1918–1923 (the same exper-

---

213   Mandel 1979a, p. 142.

ience was repeated for a third time in 1944–1948 in France, Italy and Greece, and the Communist parties are preparing for another repeat in south-west Europe).[214]

The debates in the early Communist International had already shown that the practical implementation of the united front policy in relation to the parties of Social Democracy was not easy. The principles laid down in resolutions on this subject provided no blueprint for steps or policy initiatives to be taken in each specific situation. In contrast to the later Stalin era, the united front policy was not designed to gloss over fundamental political differences with Social Democracy. For Trotsky and Mandel, who both stood in this tradition, an agreement with the Social Democrats involving even temporary moderation or suppression of public polemics and radical criticism would have been unacceptable, as would have been the case for the early Comintern.[215]

The Social-Democratic leaders, on the other hand, naturally saw through the 'game' and tried to undermine joint action in so far as this was compatible with the moods and attitudes of their own base. The leaderships of the Communist Parties, for their part, tended to turn the united front policy into a mere rhetorical and propagandistic 'unmasking tactic', especially when they were in a position to lead a substantial part of the working class into action on their own accord. But they could also be tempted, as the example of Paul Levi demonstrates, to absolutise the policy of a united front with Social Democracy to the point of branding even significant minority actions as 'putschist' deviations.[216] The critical debate surrounding the German Communist Party's 'March Action', which led both to Paul Levi's departure and to a political rejection of the tactics pursued during the 'March Action', contributed considerably to the intellectual 'armament' of the KPD leadership. In 1921 and 1922 it applied the united front tactic vis-à-vis Social Democracy very successfully. To this end, it had to take difficult political decisions on a monthly and sometimes weekly basis. In his impressive book, Arnold Reisberg has described this in great detail using original sources.[217] The complexity of the concept of the united front policy was particularly evident in debates over the slogan of 'workers' governments'. The distinction between 'real' and 'ostensible' workers' governments, for example, is almost reminiscent of medieval scholasticism. The real problem behind such complex distinctions was once again the difference between two

---

214   Mandel 1982a, p. 178, our translation.
215   See Mandel 1979e, p. 68 et seq.
216   See Frank 1981, p. 157 et seq.
217   See Reisberg 1971.

divergent approaches. The first was a purely propagandistic one, as adopted by some – including Zinoviev in particular – at the third congress of the Comintern, according to which the slogan of workers' governments could only be a popularised paraphrase for 'dictatorship of the proletariat'. There could only be a 'real' workers' government if it was run by Communists and immediately toppled the rule of capital. However, a different alternative view prevailed: even a government formed by Social-Democratic and Communist parties within the framework of a bourgeois democratic state could, under certain conditions, trigger a dynamic which, after a long process, might result in majority support for the Communists and the working class conquest of political power. Of course, at that time nobody thought of long-term cooperation with Social Democracy or with purely bourgeois parties in order to manage the capitalist system.[218]

Although the problems were already quite complex at that time, a sensible and practical application of the united front tactic later became even more difficult for small Trotskyist groups (who also lacked the moral prestige of representing a part of the world where the rule of capital had already been broken). Of course, it should be easy to reach agreements for joint action with other groups or tendencies – and even this can be a problem when sectarian rivalries are involved. But how can a marginal group develop a policy that at least increases the chances that the vanguard of the working class, and with it significant sections of the class itself, gets moving? Trotsky himself distinguished in his critical examination of the Socialist Workers' Party of Germany (SAPD), which had turned the argument for a united front of Social Democrats and Communists into a kind of fetish, between (meaningful) united front politics and (meaningless) united front propaganda. At that time, however, the 'Trotskyist' Left Opposition still identified, despite all Stalinist excommunication and persecution, as a part of the Communist International and the Communist Party of Germany, whose policies it wanted to correct. It refused to place itself 'between' the Social-Democratic and Communist camps. During the 'popular front' period in France, on the other hand, it had already broken with this self-image (namely in 1933) and set out to build independent parties and a new international to the left of Social Democracy and 'official' Communism. But even with respect to the situation in France at the time, when the united front that the Trotskyists had been demanding for so long had suddenly materialised before the eyes of the masses – albeit in the form of the 'popular front', that is, incorporating purely bourgeois forces too – Trotsky stressed that a small

---

218   See Frank 1981, pp. 206–7.

group could not claim 'an independent place in the united front'. This was one of the reasons that led to 'entrism', which in this instance meant the entry of the 'Trotskyist' group as a faction into the French Social-Democratic Party. In the politics of the various Trotskyist groups after World War II, one finds all kinds of application of traditional 'orthodoxy' – from purely propagandistic rhetoric to far-reaching political adaptation to the 'reformist' leadership of mass parties.[219]

In Mandel's case, too, it is evident how difficult it is for small organisations to find a practicable application of the traditional tactical arsenal of the united front policy. The Belgian section of the Fourth International elaborated, with Mandel's participation, the following response to the split in the Belgian workers' movement: There is a Christian trade union movement alongside the social-democratic one, and there can only be a chance of real class action if the two join forces. To raise this to the level of politics, the Belgian social democrats would have to form a coalition government with a Christian workers' party that has yet to be created and implement measures in the interests of the working class. This line of reasoning reflected the mood of a section of left-leaning social-democratic trade unionists and ongoing debates among certain circles of Christian trade unionists, who were not without influence. And yet – what a convoluted construct, especially since the (highly unlikely) realisation of such a coalition government would certainly produce anything but the government policy desired by Mandel and his friends![220]

A similar problem is evident in the policy of the French section, supported by Mandel, towards a 'Union de la Gauche' of social democrats and Communists, which actually took government office under Mitterrand in May 1981 – many people were dancing and celebrating in the streets of Paris in the hope of real *changement*! For years, Mandel and his friends had championed not only the joint action and preferably merger of the respective French trade unions with distinct political orientations, but also the joint action of the social-democratic (PS) and Communist (PCF) parties, right up to taking government office – but they had intended the policy of such a government to go beyond the programme of the Union de la Gauche. The idea was to implement measures in the interests of the working class in such a consistent manner that they would effectively challenge the rule of capital. In their view, failure to do so would inevitably lead to an accommodation to bourgeois politics – which is,

219   See also Daniel Bensaïd's commentary on the debates on the tactics of entryism at the International Institute for Research and Education website: https://www.iire.org/node/550.

220   See also Mandel (and Bahro, Oertzen) 1980d, pp. 286–7.

of course, what happened very quickly. In such cases, Mandel and his comrades were always hoping that the working masses, encouraged by the election victory and transfer of governmental responsibilities to 'their' parties, would become tremendously active to put their expectations, hopes and dreams into practice. The balance of forces and the consciousness of the masses would change rapidly, and the masses would become open to the ideas and positions of revolutionary tendencies. In France, however, the experience of the Mitterrand government led to long years of shattered hopes, resignation and the distinct weakening of left-wing tendencies.[221]

In France, with its two-round electoral system (the parties that come out strongest from the first round compete against each other in the second round), and in other countries where Fourth International groups were too weak to launch a candidacy of revolutionary forces themselves or in conjunction with others, attempts to apply the united front policy were often accompanied by appeals to vote for the big traditional parties of the labour movement. For Germany, Mandel argued into the 1980s that it made sense for left-wing socialist and revolutionary Marxist forces to call for a Social-Democratic Party of Germany (SPD) vote, even though the party was, by his own admission, pursuing bourgeois policies. According to him, it was important not to cut oneself off from social-democratic workers, and not to be blamed by them for a possible election victory of the purely bourgeois parties (especially with someone like Franz-Josef Strauss as candidate for chancellor, which was a distinct possibility in 1980). Mandel considered it vital that everything be done to enter into political dialogue with these workers.[222] One of the difficulties of this type of policy is that it can be perceived as incomprehensible, opportunistic and overly tactical by the left, let alone by politically interested workers who may be in the process of turning more critical and breaking with social-democratic influence. Ironically, such attempts to enter into political dialogue with greater numbers of social-democratic workers and trade union activists can easily have the effect of getting cut off even from people who are relatively close to you. Personally, I feel that the German section of the Fourth International, the Group of International Marxists (GIM), spoiled a number of opportunities up until the mid-1980s, not least under Mandel's influence. This was especially the case because the internal debates on electoral appeals and generally on the 'united front tactic' vis-à-vis social democracy were exceptionally factional and toxic.[223]

---

221   See *Inprecor*, 141, February 1982, pp. 23–4.
222   See Mandel, Bahro and Oertzen 1980, p. 290 et seq.
223   See Mandel 1974b.

6   Permanent Revolution and the International Dimension of
       Socialist Strategy

The concept of 'permanent revolution' may seem strange: 'revolution without
end' – it sounds like an esoteric, sectarian idea. It goes back to Trotsky's conception of the Russian revolution as formulated from 1905: although the Russian revolution had to fulfil the tasks of the bourgeois revolution (democracy,
agrarian reform, independent economic development, etc.), it could only
achieve this through the conquest of political power by the working class.
The working class would have to carry out 'socialist measures' also in its own
interest and inspire socialist revolution in other countries, especially in the
developed industrial capitalist countries. By the late 1920s, Trotsky generalised this concept to all countries that were more or less lagging behind the
developed capitalist ('imperialist') industrialised countries, including the
colonies and semi-colonies in particular.[224] Mandel always defended Trotsky's
concept of 'permanent revolution' as an essential component of revolutionary
strategy. This is how he summarised it in *Introduction to Marxism*:

> *In the colonial and semi-colonial countries*, the workers and poor peasants
> cannot wait until the workers of the industrialised countries come to their
> aid. Given the enormous burden of oppression and misery that imperial-
> ism has imposed on the masses in those countries, the eruption of vast
> mass struggles and vast revolutionary movements there is inevitable. The
> workers must support every anti-imperialist mass movement, whether it
> is directed against foreign political domination or against exploitation
> by foreign trusts; whether it is for the peasant revolution or the elimin-
> ation of bloody native dictatorships. Having won the political leadership
> of these mass movements through its resolve and energy in making the
> progressive demands of all the exploited classes and layers of the nation
> its own, the proletariat fights for the conquest of power, and at the same
> time overthrows the property and power of the native bourgeoisie. This
> is the strategy of permanent revolution.[225]

The first serious objection may be that Mandel is adopting a concept of Trotsky's in order to perform his role as an 'orthodox' exponent of Trotskyist ideas.
This, in turn, makes him the protagonist of a largely marginal dissident 'sub-

---

224   See Trotsky 1931a, chapter 10.
225   Mandel 1979a, pp. 126–7.

current' of Marxism and of the communist movement. To be able to pass judgement, we need to familiarise ourselves with the history of ideas surrounding the concept of permanent revolution at least in its basic outlines. The fundamental idea of a 'revolution in permanence' can be found in the works of Marx. In his 'Address of the Central Committee to the Communist League' of March 1850, Marx sought to learn the lessons of the failed German Revolution of 1848–49. As had been the case in the French Revolution of 1789, the political formations of the bourgeoisie and petty bourgeoisie were no longer prepared to consistently implement the democratic and national aims of the bourgeois revolution. While in France at that time the plebeian masses had represented the lowest strata of the people, in the meantime the modern proletariat had emerged, striving for its own liberation in the revolution. For fear of the workers' demands, the bourgeoisie preferred to make pacts with feudal monarchist reaction rather than assume political power in the form of a democratic republic. The radical petty bourgeoisie in town and country strove to relieve itself of the pressure of big capital, but wanted to end the revolution soon and keep it within a bourgeois framework.

> While the democratic petty bourgeois want to bring the revolution to an end as quickly as possible, achieving at most the aims already mentioned, it is our interest and our task to make the revolution permanent until all the more or less propertied classes have been driven from their ruling positions, until the proletariat has conquered state power and until the association of the proletarians has progressed sufficiently far – not only in one country but in all the leading countries of the world – that competition between the proletarians of these countries ceases and at least the decisive forces of production are concentrated in the hands of the workers.[226]

Marx argues for the independent political organisation of the working class, which must free itself from its role as the left wing of the bourgeois and petty-bourgeois democrats. While it should fight alongside these democrats for common objectives, its own class interests compel it to move beyond this as soon as it becomes necessary to overcome the conservative self-limitation of the revolution: 'But they themselves must contribute most to their final victory, by informing themselves of their own class interests, by taking up their independent political position as soon as possible, by not allowing themselves to

---

226 Marx and Engels 2006.

be misled by the hypocritical phrases of the democratic petty bourgeoisie into doubting for one minute the necessity of an independently organized party of the proletariat. Their battle-cry must be: *The Permanent Revolution*.[227]

A closer look at the debate on the concept of revolution in the Russian social-ist movement (initially 'Social-Democratic', from 1917 'Communist') reveals that Trotsky's notion of 'permanent revolution' was largely consistent with the real events of the October revolution. Tsarist Russia was a backward country with a vast majority of peasants. There was a small industrial proletariat of about three million people. Four fifths of the population lived as farmers in the coun-tryside. Industry was heavily dependent on foreign capital from the developed industrial capitalist countries of Europe. Early Russian Social Democracy had emerged as a result of a dispute with the Narodniks, who believed that a liber-ated, socialist or communist society could be achieved directly through revolu-tionary mobilisation of the peasants. The theorists of Russian Social Demo-cracy countered that a bourgeois revolution would be the first step to clear the way for the development of modern capitalism. Within this process, the prolet-ariat and its organisations would gain strength and eventually be able to take up the struggle for power.[228]

However, after the experience of the 1905 Russian revolution, in which the workers of industrial plants played an important role and for the first time formed council organisations, three different concepts of the forthcoming revolution emerged within Russian Social Democracy.[229]

The 'moderate' Social Democrats of the Menshevik faction held fast to the traditional idea of clearly distinct 'stages' of the revolution. According to them, Tsarism had to be overthrown first, and only the bourgeoisie could lead such a revolution and subsequently exercise power. The workers' party would remain in the opposition until its time came.

The Bolsheviks, a radical faction of the Russian Social-Democratic Party, agreed that the Russian revolution had to pave the way for modern capitalist development, and that the time had not yet come for a socialist revolution in such a backward country. But they did not trust the bourgeoisie to complete this revolution in a truly consistent manner. On the contrary, they expected that the bourgeoisie would make pacts with reaction for fear of the rising proletariat. The perspective was therefore a joint 'democratic dictatorship of the prolet-

---

227   Ibid.
228   See also Helmut Dahmer's introduction to Trotsky's *Results and Perspectives* and *The Per-manent Revolution* in the 1969 German-language edition of *The Permanent Revolution*, p. iv et seq. [the pages of the introduction are numbered with Roman numerals].
229   See Trotsky 2016.

ariat and the peasantry', linked to the expectation that the peasantry would produce its own political party with which the workers' could form a coalition government after the fall of Tsarism. The liberation of the peasantry from the feudal yoke of the big landowners would be – this was undisputed – the decisive content of this revolution.[230]

Trotsky, along with very few other Social Democrats, took a different stance that went beyond the Bolshevik position, drawing on Marx's ideas quoted above. In his paper *Results and Prospects*, Trotsky concluded as early as 1906 that only the conquest of political power by the workers and poor peasants, supported by the masses of the oppressed rural population, would provide a complete and lasting solution to the tasks of the bourgeois revolution (democracy, agrarian reform, economic development, liberation of the oppressed nations and nationalities).

Mandel bases his view that Trotsky was right on this issue on the actual course of the Russian revolution:

> In the years prior to the October revolution, the expression 'permanent revolution', associated almost exclusively with the name of Trotsky, meant simply that the coming revolution in Russia would place the working class in power and that once in power, the workers would be compelled to take radical measures against bourgeois property relations if they were to resolve the problems posed by Russia's lack of a bourgeois revolution. During those years, permanent revolution was counterposed on the one hand to the position of the Mensheviks, who held that the coming revolution would inevitably be bourgeois and that the leadership of it would therefore logically devolve to the liberals, and on the other hand to the position of the Bolsheviks, a more nuanced one which maintained that although the tasks of the revolution were bourgeois, they would be accomplished by an alliance of the proletariat and peasantry. Once that alliance had seized power, according to this view, it would inaugurate a 'democratic dictatorship of the workers and peasants'. Trotsky characterised this formular as 'algebraic' in the sense that the relative weight of the two classes in the alliance was left unspecified, as was the class character of the state dominated by that alliance.
>
> Now, in practice the Bolsheviks, under the impetus of Lenin, came to adopt the strategy of permanent revolution in the course of the upheavals of 1917 itself. I know of no evidence, however, to indicate that Lenin ever

---

230   See Trotsky 1906, chapter 5.

reconsidered permanent revolution from the theoretical standpoint. In effect, during the spring of 1917 he came to assign the peasant component of his algebraic formula the value of zero. This is what the April Theses represented, and they were so interpreted by the Bolshevik Old Guard, which initially received them as a 'Trotskyist' deviation. If the peasant component of the 'algebraic' formula of the 'democratic dictatorship of the workers' and peasants' were assigned the value zero, then the formula would simply equal 'dictatorship of the proletariat'.[231]

This is not to say that the peasants did not play a decisive role in the revolution – in both Mandel's and Trotsky's views, agrarian reform was a central task of the revolution – but that their most important demands could only be met by the working class in power. Both Trotsky and Lenin, the Bolshevik, saw the Russian revolution in an international context. Its lasting success would depend on whether it would inspire a series of revolutions in the developed capitalist countries. The perspective was that of world socialist revolution, without which the completion of the construction of a classless socialist society would be unthinkable.[232]

In the months between the February and October revolutions of 1917, Lenin indeed moved very close to Trotsky's position, which also made it possible for Trotsky and his followers to join the party created by the Bolshevik faction of the Russian Social-Democratic Labour Party in 1912 (equally important was Trotsky's realisation that Lenin had been right against Trotsky's 'conciliationism' on the important question of the dispute – namely in his appraisal of the Mensheviks and on the development of the Bolshevik faction into an independent party).[233] Lenin succeeded in 're-arming' the Bolsheviks when he published his *April Theses*. With the slogan 'All power to the soviets', they now focused their efforts on the conquest of political power and on socialist revolution. Thus Lenin broke with the old formula of the 'democratic dictatorship of the proletariat and the peasantry'.[234] It was not until the Stalinist era that the old 'stages' theory was revived and the strategy of 'permanent revolution' denounced as an ultra-leftist and disorienting fantasy. Trotsky had initially confined the idea of 'permanent revolution' to Russia. In the struggle against Stalin's faction, he tried to avoid polemics about the 'old issues' where he had previously crossed swords with Lenin and the Bolsheviks (as Pierre Broué noted

---

231   Mandel 1979d, pp. 85–6.
232   See Trotsky 1931a, chapter 9.
233   See Trotsky 1930, chapter 28.
234   See Lenin 1964.

in his French-language biography, *Trotsky*). Later, under the impression of the disaster of Stalinist policy in the Chinese Revolution of 1925–27, he generalised his conclusions and formulated them as a strategy for all countries that lagged behind the advanced capitalist countries, including colonies and semi-colonies.

> With regard to the countries with a belated bourgeois development, especially the colonial and semi-colonial countries, the theory of the permanent revolution signifies that the complete and genuine solution of their tasks, democratic and national emancipation is conceivable only through the dictatorship of the proletariat as the leader of the subjugated nation, above all of its peasant masses ... The dictatorship of the proletariat ... is inevitably and very quickly placed before tasks that are bound up with deep inroads into the rights of bourgeois property. The democratic revolution grows over immediately into the socialist, and thereby becomes a permanent revolution.[235]

In a sense, the 'naive' understanding of 'permanent revolution' as a revolutionary process in society that continues until the complete liberation from all exploitation and oppression has been achieved corresponds to this position. Trotsky emphasises that the conquest of political power by the proletariat 'only opens' the revolution. If the socialist goal is to be realised, the revolution must continue on a national and, above all, international scale. Even the conquest of political power in any one country or in a few countries is, from this point of view, only a partial achievement.[236]

Very little 'socialism' and emancipation can be accomplished with the limited material resources of poor countries. Every conceivable government in such countries will repeatedly find itself compelled to make very difficult decisions about the priorities of economic development and with regard to relations both with foreign corporations and the international institutions of the rich industrialised countries. This is why it is impossible to accomplish the goals of the revolution in an isolated country, especially a poor one. According to Trotsky's position, which remained valid for Mandel, the 'permanent revolution' is a link to a worldwide process of emancipation; they both conceived of it as a process of world socialist revolution. 'The socialist revolution begins on the national arena, it unfolds on the international arena, and is completed on the

235   Trotsky 1931a, chapter 10.
236   Ibid.

world arena. Thus, the socialist revolution becomes a permanent revolution in a newer and broader sense of the word; it attains completion, only in the final victory of the new society on our entire planet'.[237]

For Mandel, the view that the objective conditions for socialist revolution on a world scale are present, as reaffirmed in the 1938 *Transitional Programme* of the Fourth International, remains valid too. For him – as for Trotsky – the world-revolutionary perspective is inseparably linked to the organisational need to build not only revolutionary organisations in the individual countries, but also an international revolutionary organisation:

> The need for a revolutionary International which is more than the sum total of national revolutionary parties is based on solid material founda-tions. The imperialist epoch is the epoch of world economy, world polit-ics, and world wars. Imperialism is a cohesive international system. The productive forces have already been internationalised for a long time. Capital is increasingly organised internationally in multinational corpor-ations. The nation state has long been a hindrance to the furtherance of production and civilisation. The great problems of humanity (the preven-tion of nuclear world war; the elimination of hunger; the planning of eco-nomic growth; the equitable division of resources and income amongst all peoples; the protection of the environment; the utilisation of science for the people) can only be resolved on a world scale.[238]

Mandel also assumes that mass struggles in today's world have an inherent spontaneous tendency to spread internationally and spawn international movements. He warns revolutionaries not to fall behind this spontaneous tend-ency in their own practice.[239]

As regards 'permanent revolution' as a revolutionary concept for the poor and dependent countries, the question is why none of the revolutions in these countries have so far been led by forces that have laid claim to 'permanent revolution' or to the Trotskyist tradition in general. Moreover, there have been a number of radical changes without socialist revolutions, beginning with the political independence of most former colonies and ending with the partial industrialisation of a number of countries in the so-called 'third world'. Man-del therefore had to contemplate what balance to take decades after the theory of 'permanent revolution' was formulated.

---

237 Trotsky 1931a, chapter 10.
238 Mandel 1979a, p. 125.
239 Ibid.

He confronted this problem in a detailed interview on this subject, the book version of which he edited for the last time in early 1979.[240] The first question he faced was that of successes (especially the achievement of political independence) of revolutions in poor and dependent countries with bourgeois leaderships. Didn't these experiences mean that the adherents of the theory of 'permanent revolution' had underestimated the potential of bourgeois forces in these countries? After all, isn't the basic premise of this theory precisely the inability of the bourgeoisie in these countries to fulfil the tasks of bourgeois-democratic revolution?[241]

Mandel's initial response to this is to emphasise a 'correct' and not 'too narrow' interpretation of the concept of 'permanent revolution'. According to him, there had never been any question that some of the tasks of the bourgeois revolution in the backward, poor and dependent countries could not be solved under bourgeois leadership. Rather, the core statement was that they could not be solved completely, not really, not sustainably under bourgeois leadership.[242]

According to Mandel, these countries are entangled in the totality of the global capitalist economy as well as in a combination of archaic and modern structures, which makes it impossible for them to carry out a radical agrarian reform, develop a single market to which the mass of their population has access, and catch up with the developed industrialised countries 'because the law of uneven and combined development obviously continues to operate in the epoch of imperialism – more than ever, in fact'.[243]

Mandel emphasises the persistent barriers to development, the continued dependence (even if the rulers in these countries are no longer the recipients of orders, but nevertheless junior partners subordinate to the rulers of the metropolises), and the impossibility of establishing US-American – i.e. purely capitalist – conditions in agriculture in these countries.

> Now, what is the consequence of this? It is formidable: the failure of any of these countries to bring about this form of agricultural development has prevented the genuine modernization of these countries. What I mean

---

240 See Mandel 1979d.

241 Mandel 1979d p. 67 et seq.

242 Mandel 1979d pp. 70–1. Trotsky himself formulated the question not in terms of a partial but a complete solution of the democratic tasks: 'A backward colonial or semi-colonial country, the proletariat of which is insufficiently prepared to unite the peasantry and take power, is thereby incapable of bringing the democratic revolution to its conclusion' (Trotzki 1931b, chapter 10).

243 Mandel 1979d, p. 73.

by modernization is very simply this: the opportunity for more than one thousand million people – because that is the scope of the problem on a world scale – to escape from extreme forms of degradation, misery, semi-famine, obscurantism, and complete lack of possibility of development, capitalist or otherwise.[244]

Only 20 per cent of the population of countries such as Brazil and India are integrated into the market in the sense that they can buy a range of consumer goods.

'But this statistic can be expressed in an opposite form: 400 million people in India and 80 million in Brazil have been totally excluded from this process. Hence the formula: genuine and complete resolution of the democratic tasks of the bourgeois revolution is impossible under a bourgeois state. The process can only be begun, and there are sharp objective limits to its development'.[245]

According to Mandel, significant steps towards independent economic development have only been possible in poor countries where capitalism has been overthrown – especially in China and Cuba. He argues that the victory of the Chinese Red Army under Maoist leadership was possible – despite the 'stageist' official rhetoric about 'new democracy' – only because the Maoist leadership disregarded the instructions of the Kremlin and broke the power of capital. The Cuban revolution also pushed beyond the bourgeois framework, although the Cuban leadership had not originally planned it. Mandel saw in this the most important statements of the 'permanent revolution' confirmed. With his exclamation 'Socialist revolution or caricature of a revolution', which referred to Cuba and other poor and dependent countries of Latin America, Africa and Asia, Ernesto 'Che' Guevara certainly came closest to this concept among all known revolutionary leaders in both theory and practice.[246]

Only a planned economy in which the state has a monopoly on foreign trade – from a Trotskyist point of view a major achievement of the October revolution of 1917 in Russia – can break the vicious circle of dependency. It is not possible to achieve this without breaking with the capitalist system.

Michael Löwy, expert on Latin America and leading member of the Fourth International, drew the following conclusions a few years later, in 1987:

---

244   Mandel 1979d, p. 75.
245   Ibid.
246   See Mandel 1989f, p. 26 et seq.

Some countries – Mexico, Bolivia, Algeria, Peru, etc. – have undertaken relatively radical agricultural reforms, while others – Mexico, India, Venezuela, etc. – have established more or less stable parliamentary democratic states. Finally, some countries have achieved a high degree of political and economic independence from imperialism. Algeria, Burma, Egypt (at least in Nasser's time), Mozambique, etc. But these results must be qualified in two respects: firstly – each of these achievements has been incomplete, limited and often short-lived; secondly – no country has yet succeeded in successfully combining all three revolutionary-democratic transformations, and as a result explosive and unresolved contradictions remain at the very core of their social institutions.[247]

But Löwy also wonders whether Mandel's formulation of the problem – his emphasis on the completeness and sustainability of the solution of the tasks of the bourgeois-democratic revolution – might not also obscure the vision for concrete political tasks in any given country. Mandel's defence of the permanent revolution is linked to the importance of the self-organisation of the working class in his general theory. A truly 'revolutionary' development without or against this working class was not conceivable for him anywhere in the world. And yet, there have been drastic upheavals, such as the overthrow of the South African Apartheid regime, where capitalism was preserved and the working class heavily suppressed.

More recent developments in the course of so-called 'neoliberal globalisation', however, underline the limits of change under bourgeois conditions, which is something that both Mandel and Löwy emphasised. However important the conquest of at least formal political independence by the majority of former colonies, beyond the capitalist metropolises there is an escalating vicious circle of dependency, underdevelopment and maldevelopment. The International Monetary Fund and the World Bank increasingly wield direct power in the poor countries by way of 'adaptation plans' and such, pushing through the further dismantling even of meagre social gains, the privatisation of public enterprises and services, and a focus on exports for debt service financing. The dismantling of 'investment barriers' and free trade are forced upon weaker nations, whereas the rich industrialised countries practise shameless protectionism against products from the 'third world'. It is always the poor people from poor and dependent countries, the small proprietors and workers in both rural and urban areas, who pay the bill.[248]

---

247   Löwy 1987, pp. 161–2, our translation.
248   See Mandel 1987c, p. 55 et seq.

The situation in Africa, Latin America and large parts of Asia is still characterised by 'unequal and combined development'. Modern industries and exploitative conditions go hand in hand with outdated pre-capitalist structures, and new forms of slavery are emerging in slums, 'free trade zones', and through the excessive private debt of the poorest of the poor. Not only with the Argentinazo has the promise implied by concepts such as 'emerging economies' and 'Tiger states' has not vanished into thin air.[249]

Mandel did not confine himself to citing evidence for the validity of the concept of 'permanent revolution'. He also analysed changes in contemporary capitalism that are relevant to the assessment of revolutionary perspectives in poor countries. In the aforementioned extensive interview, for example, he points out that the Fourth International spoke at an early stage – as early as 1947 – of a general transition from the direct domination of colonies to indirect domination. It argued that the rulers of the poor countries were becoming something like 'junior partners' to the rulers of the metropolises in the course of this process, securing a higher (though still very limited) degree of 'autonomy'. This, it was argued, was a result of the shift in the balance of power. The boom of the colonial revolution made the rulers of the imperialist metropolises wary that capitalism might be overthrown in other countries, such as India, with potentially fatal consequences for the capitalist system as a whole. In light of this, granting political independence was seen as the lesser of two evils.[250] There is no contradiction between this development and the premises of 'permanent revolution', because this conception has never denied that some tasks of the bourgeois revolution can be carried out within a bourgeois framework.[251]

Mandel also refers to his analysis of contemporary capitalism, first developed in chapter 14 of *Marxist Economic Theory* and more extensively in *Late Capitalism*.[252] As soon as the sector of capital that produces and exports capital goods becomes predominant in the developed industrialised countries, there is also a massive interest in finding buyers in the 'third world'. This, however, leads to partial industrialisation of parts of the 'third world'.[253]

> This leads to a change in the ruling bloc in some of the key countries of the underdeveloped world. The classical ruling bloc was that of the big

---

249   See *Inprekorr* no. 366, April 2002, p. 3 et seq.
250   Mandel 1979d, pp. 85–6.
251   Mandel 1979d, p.
252   See Mandel 1968b, p. 485 et seq. and Mandel 1975d, p. 343 et seq.
253   Mandel 1979d, pp. 73–4.

landowners, 'comprador' bourgeoisie, and imperialist capital dominating the production of raw materials and primary products. That dominant blog had no interest in large-scale or rapid industrialization – quite the opposite.

Now there is a new dominant blog in some of these countries: a bloc of native capitalist monopolies, technocrats of the state and military apparatus, and multinationals interested especially in the export of industrial equipment. This bloc, unlike the previous one, has an interest in industrializing these intermediary economies up to a point. This shift in the composition of the ruling bloc in some countries is therefore linked both to structural changes in the metropolis of the imperialist bourgeoisie itself and to important changes in the social composition of the intermediary countries, for there have been major upheavals there.[254]

Mandel criticised the term 'emerging economies' because it suggests that some of the poor and dependent countries can catch up fully with the developed industrialised countries. At the same time, he recognised the emergence of new, more or less autonomous financial capital in some of these countries. This was linked to the emergence of a 'semi-industrialised' economy in countries like Brazil, Mexico, Argentina, South Korea or Iran and to the attainment of a greater degree of autonomy from metropolitan capital. In view of this, it no longer made sense to speak of 'semi-colonies'. Mandel nevertheless stressed the limits of these developments: for example, because this new financial capital has to operate in certain niches, and because the economies of these countries remain extremely sensitive to changes and crises in the world economy as a whole. These countries, even though they are no longer semi-colonies and are undergoing significant industrialisation processes, remain poor and dependent. The effect of 'unequal and combined development' is that in these societies, too, deeply archaic structures coexist alongside the most modern methods of production and exploitation, and the decisive breakthrough to a single market with massive absorption of mass consumer goods cannot succeed.[255]

As far as Mandel is concerned, these changes also have no bearing on the theory or strategy of 'permanent revolution' either (Mandel preferred the term 'strategy'), but he stressed that this strategy is based on an examination of social conditions, i.e. a 'theory'. On the contrary, in his view, these are processes that increase the weight of the working class, wage earners, and the

---

254 Ibid.
255 Mandel 1979d, p. 76 et seq.; also Mandel 1975c.

urban population over peasants and the rural population. They do not make the pursuit of 'permanent revolution' more difficult, but easier, because the proletariat should find it less difficult to lead revolutions when it constitutes a much greater proportion of the total population than, say in Russia in 1917 or in China in 1949. Mandel considers another criticism more valid, namely that '… Trotsky made a mistake in generalising the theory to countries that were so backward that the weight of the working class was negligible'.[256]

Another new development in contemporary capitalism has been the increased weight of oil-exporting countries and OPEC. Mandel points out that the level of their currency reserves has been propagandistically exaggerated by the custodians of the interests of imperialist capital so that scapegoats could be blamed for crisis symptoms in the capitalist world economy ('the oil sheikhs'). In reality, these funds are not sufficient to finance the independent industrialisation of these countries, with the result that many of them have actually run up balance of payments deficits. This is a reflection of their structural backwardness, their lack of adequate infrastructure, etc.[257]

More generally, the position of all countries of the so-called 'third world' on the world market, including the 'emerging economies', has always remained marginal. There is therefore no question of 'pure' socialist revolutions being on the agenda there; rather, the problem of 'permanent revolution' remains acute.[258]

At the beginning of a revolutionary process in a poor and dependent country, or in a country that is 'backward' in relation to the metropolises, demands for agrarian reform, democracy or independence may be central, depending on the situation. For Mandel, the political problem was that revolutionary processes cannot succeed on a purely spontaneous basis. Therefore he was particularly wary of the schematic fixation on certain limited 'bourgeois-democratic' goals in a given 'stage' of the revolution. Political leaderships that programmatically advocate such limitations often tend to defend them against the revolting masses in practice. They then keep the revolution confined to a bourgeois agenda and in this way prevent the complete and sustained accomplishment even of its bourgeois-democratic tasks. When organs of an alternative, proletarian state power begin to develop, such leaderships do not urge or encourage them to seize and exercise political power themselves – they are far more likely to repress them.

---

256 Mandel 1979d, p. 80.
257 Mandel 1979d, pp. 80–1.
258 Mandel 1979d, p. 83.

As we saw in Russia and in many other countries as well, such forms of proletarian self-organization tend to arise spontaneously out of revolutionary struggles. The problem is that although they arise spontaneously, they do not spontaneously strive to replace the existing state apparatus; they do not automatically challenge the legitimacy of the bourgeois state directly. This requires revolutionary leadership. And any political current that is blinded by the schema that a 'phase' therefore necessitates bourgeois-democratic state institutions will logically attempt to repress these embryos of self-organisation as premature, as not in conformity with the character of the stage – or phase, or whatever term is used – of democracy. A party with this line will play an objectively counter-revolutionary role – regardless of the intentions of its membership or even leadership. That is the trap that must be avoided.[259]

The internationalist dimension of 'permanent revolution' and of socialist strategy in general played a key role for Mandel. He tied it to the organisational conclusion that it was necessary to build revolutionary parties and a revolutionary international. The Fourth International (FI) was founded in 1938 in response to the 'crisis of leadership of the proletariat', which its founders considered a key problem. In the opinion of the FI founders, the objective conditions for world socialist revolution existed, but the 'traditional leaders' of the workers' movement, Social Democracy and 'official' communism ('Stalinism') were lost for the revolutionary goal. The FI would become the new revolutionary leadership the course of a resurgence of the proletarian mass movement.[260]

In 1988, on the occasion of the fiftieth anniversary of the founding of the FI, Mandel presented the reasons why, in his view, the general perspectives which had inspired the founding were still valid. In the process, he also had to confront the question why – contrary to initial expectations – the FI had remained a rather small organisation without much influence.

Mandel begins by rejecting critics' claims that the founding of the FI was based on two false predictions by Trotsky: first, that a great revolutionary upsurge after World War I would push back the traditional leaders of the workers' movement in favour of an authentically revolutionary current, and second, that the Stalinist bureaucracy would emerge from these events weakened at the very least.

---

259   Mandel 1979d, p. 92.
260   See Alles 1989f, p. 61 et seq.

'Undoubtedly these perspectives kept different groups of Trotskyist cadres in various countries motivated in the late 1930s and early 1940s. When they turned out to be wrong it had important consequences. Many of them broke with the Fourth International and often even with the workers' movement'.[261] However, Mandel continues, the FI was not founded on short-term prognoses, but on more fundamental considerations. Organisations built on cyclical conditions are 'built on quicksand'. The FI, on the other hand, corresponds to 'historical reality on an international scale'.[262]

Mandel's notion that the cited expectations were held only by 'various cadres' of the Trotskyist movement seems a bit of a stretch. In the FI's founding document, the *Transitional Programme* ('The Death Agony of Capitalism and the Tasks of the Fourth International'), arguments of principle do predominate, and the weakness of the forces of the FI itself is highlighted rather than glossed over. But the document contains the following prognosis with regard to the coming world war:

> At the beginning of the war the sections of the Fourth International will inevitably feel themselves isolated: every war takes the national masses unaware and impels them to the side of the government apparatus. The internationalists will have to swim against the stream. However, the devastation and misery brought about by the new war, which in the first months will far outstrip the bloody horrors of 1914–18 will quickly prove sobering. The discontents of the masses and their revolt will grow by leaps and bounds. The sections of the Fourth International will be found at the head of the revolutionary tide. The program of transitional demands will gain burning actuality.[263]

Elsewhere in the *Transition Programme*, the FI founders say of their own organisation: 'It has shown that it could swim against the stream. The approaching historical wave will raise it on its crest'.[264]

It is impossible not to notice the analogies to the outcome of World War I in the deliberations of the authors. It is also indisputable that these expectations, which were indeed officially formulated in the founding programme, did not come to fruition.

---

261   Mandel 1988, chapter 1.
262   Ibid.
263   Trotsky 2002, p. 26.
264   Trotsky 2002, p. 44.

However, Mandel quotes from the *Manifesto of the Fourth International on Imperialist War and the Proletarian World Revolution* of May 1940 (which he calls Trotsky's 'real political testament') to prove that the occurrence of certain events at certain times was less important to the FI founders than their analysis of the fundamental contradictions of the period:

> The capitalist world has no way out, unless a prolonged death agony is so considered. It is necessary to prepare for long years, if not decades, of war, uprisings, brief interludes of truce, new wars, and new uprisings. A young revolutionary party must base itself on this perspective ... The question of tempos and time intervals is of enormous importance; but it alters neither the general historical perspective nor the direction of our policy.[265]

Moreover, the fundamental decision in favour of founding the FI had already been taken in 1933, when the defeat of the working class was sealed in Germany, but not by a long way in France, Spain and a number of other countries. At that time, World War II was by no means imminent, and victorious revolutions could have prevented it.[266]

In 1988, Mandel named five 'fundamental contradictions' of contemporary capitalism that justify the necessity of building a revolutionary International. He articulated the positions set out below just before the historical rupture of 1989–91, the collapse of the Soviet Union and the Warsaw Pact:

1. The capitalist mode of production has been in decline since 1914. Although 'the productive forces' are not 'stagnating', as the *Transitional Programme* suggests, they are increasingly turning into forces of destruction. The continued existence of capitalism entails widening inequality worldwide and in the individual regions and countries of the world, a growing threat to every achievement of civilisation and even to the physical survival of humanity.

2. The rebellion of productive forces against the capitalist relations of production – against private appropriation, against the continued existence of nation states, etc. – is periodically manifested in great mass struggles of wage-earners and other oppressed sections of the population, who objectively and 'instinctively' put the replacement of capitalism by a socialist social order, based on solidarity, on the agenda. But socialist revolution can only be carried out consciously, and therefore the level of

265 Trotsky 1940.
266 Ibid.

proletarian class consciousness is important, as is the revolutionary quality of the leadership.

3. Because of the difficult objective conditions that a transitional society
    found itself in after a terrible civil war in a relatively backward coun-
    try, the October revolution of 1917, the first victorious socialist revolution
    of the twentieth century, ultimately gave rise to a bureaucracy that has
    assumed a monopoly on power. It has led to increasing social inequal-
    ity and stalled any progress towards socialism. This will generate anti-
    bureaucratic rebellions, which culminate in political revolutions against
    the bureaucracy. These are to be regarded as an integral part of the world
    socialist revolution.

4. Social democracy, Stalinism and reformist trade union leaderships are
    responsible for the fact that previous mass movements have not led to
    socialist revolution. The way in which the bureaucracies of the labour
    movement defend 'strongholds' and 'gains' not only prevents new victor-
    ies, but ultimately leads to the loss of these achievements too.

5. That is why there is a need for a new leadership and new workers' parties.
    This corresponds to a real process of political differentiation in the work-
    ing class, which constantly produces new layers of leadership. Their
    fusion with revolutionary Marxism – that is, their assimilation of the most
    important past experiences of class struggle – will produce new and up-
    to-date revolutionary leadership.

6. The productive forces, capital, and the working class itself have never
    been so internationalised as in the era of imperialism, which persists to
    this day, and this internationalisation is increasing in contemporary late
    capitalism. It is not possible to realise an advanced, socialist social order
    in just one part of the world. The only solution is a worldwide federation
    of socialist council republics. Conscious preparation for this perspective
    is only possible through international organisation. Without it, neither
    an adequate grasp of international processes, nor a successful struggle
    against nationalist influences, nor an effective coordination of struggles
    are possible.[267]

Mandel's verdict that capitalism offers 'no solution', and that it is a doomed
social order, is not based on a denial that contemporary capitalism has brought
any progress.

'Presenting the considerable increase in the production and mass consumption of foodstuffs, textile products, consumer durables, medical services, edu-

---

267   See Mandel 1988d, chapter 2.

cation, etc., as "a development of the destructive forces" is obviously to invite justifiable ridicule'.[268]

For sections of the population, contemporary capitalism has brought greater prosperity, and it has further developed the productive forces. Did the revolutionaries not underestimate the 'adaptability' of the capitalist mode of production? Mandel's first objection is that capitalism's progressive achievements were only possible at the price of enormous catastrophes and unspeakable suffering.

> How can one draw the balance sheet of the last fifty years without including the 100 million dead of the Second World War, without bringing in Auschwitz, Hiroshima, the millions killed in the colonial war since 1945, the holocaust of children dying of hunger and curable diseases in the Third world since 1945 .... Is it a secondary problem, this enormous mass of human suffering; is the concept of 'agony' so misplaced when we survey this overall reality?[269]

According to Mandel – who underlines this point with reference to Lenin – there will be no automatic collapse of capitalism. In the future, it will still be possible to reap the benefits of technical and economic progress, just as life expectancy has risen worldwide and infant mortality has fallen over the last 50 years. But such progress is paid for not just with the suffering of the past: the underlying driving forces are increasingly exhausted as we enter a long wave with stagnant and depressive undertone. There is a general trend towards the erosion of social and civilisational achievements. Mandel recalls that earlier visions of a more or less crisis-free capitalism in which more and more people would be doing better have proved illusory.

> What remains today of the dreams of 'guaranteed economic growth, full employment, and social progress'! Where are the real utopians if not in the camp of those who assumed that capitalism (sorry, the 'mixed economy') was capable of ensuring all that? They have egg on their faces now with 40 million people unemployed in the imperialist countries, hundreds of millions underemployed in the Third world, a fall in the real income of at least 10 % of the Western proletariat (the emergence of the 'new poor' is part and parcel of this) and a fall ranging from 30 % to 50 %

---

268 Mandel 1988d, chapter 3.
269 Ibid.

in real wages in most dependent semi-colonial and semi-industrialised countries.[270]

As Mandel points out, capitalism's 'adaptability' clearly has its limits. Increasingly irresponsible technologies, harsher and harsher super-exploitation of poor countries, the increasing destruction of remaining democratic freedoms, including the systematic state use of torture in more than 50 countries, and the fact that another world war would amount to self-destruction – in his view, all of these phenomena bear witness to this.

> Formerly, the alternative was presented as 'socialism or barbarism'. Today it has taken the form 'socialism or death'. For it is impossible in the long term to avoid these disasters without ending the egotistical and competitive behaviour that flows from the regime of private property and competition, which inspires double moral standards and the incapacity of extending real solidarity to the whole of the human race.[271]

Many admit that there are dangerous developments but accuse the revolutionaries of 'catastrophism'. They point out, for example, that although there are a great many unemployed, these unemployed – at least in the rich industrialised countries – are no longer starving. They see an increase in 'localised' wars, but argue that a new world war has become very unlikely. Mandel concedes that today's society is not permanently on the brink of total disaster. And yet, he believes that coming catastrophes might yet eclipse those of the past (if only because the destructive power of weapons is much greater than in the past, because the destruction of the natural foundations of life has a more global impact than it did in the past, etc.).

'As long as capitalism survives the threat of exterminating the human race will remain, whatever the level of consciousness world-wide, even among the bourgeoisie, of this threat'.[272]

But what about the working class, regarded in the Marxist tradition as the revolutionary subject capable of eliminating capitalism and initiating the construction of a new socialist society? Contrary to all notions of the 'integration' of the working class into capitalist society and its erosion and increasing heterogeneity and segmentation under the influence of modern economic trends,

---

270   Ibid.
271   Ibid.
272   Mandel 1988d, chapter 9.

Mandel apodictically adheres to the basic Marxist position: 'Only the working class is capable of overthrowing capitalism'.[273]

Mandel draws on the first programme of Russian Social Democracy drafted by Lenin and Plekhanov to define the term 'working class'. According to that definition, the term encompasses all those who lack access to capital and to the means of production and can therefore only sell their labour power to gain access to the means of consumption. Mandel argues that the working class thus defined is, in fact, numerically stronger and less heterogeneous today than ever before.[274]

> It is true that the billion-strong army of wage-earners throughout the world is not growing at the same rate in every country at all times, nor are their living standards and working conditions bringing them closer together than they were at all times in the past. The development of the working class does not progress in a linear way. It declines (and becomes de-skilled) in certain sectors, regions, or even countries while progressing and becoming more skilled in others. But there are no data that prove that the long-term, world-wide tendency is one of decline, far from it.[275]

In the capitalist countries, Mandel continues, the absolute number of wage earners has increased, as has their share in the total population. It remains an important task for this proletariat, especially in the poorer countries, to find allies especially among the urban and rural poor. But its weight is much greater than at the time of the October revolution, when peasants still made up 75 per cent of the active (producing) population globally. Moreover, the social situation of the proletariat enables it to carry out the kind of solidaric action that will produce the new society. The greater role of the 'new social movements' does not contradict the role of wage earners as the potentially revolutionary subject. The base of these movements is generally also 'proletarian' according to the aforementioned definition. Not its alleged petty-bourgeois composition, but a process of alienation from a largely conservative official labour movement, which is unattractive on many issues linked to emancipation, has led it to constitute itself 'outside'.[276]

---

273   Mandel 1988d, chapter 4.
274   Ibid.
275   Ibid.
276   Ibid.

This 'proletariat' has obviously not carried out a socialist revolution in any developed industrial country. However, Mandel highlights the periodic occurrence of broad mobilisations of wage earners. He argues that it becomes evident that they tend to challenge bourgeois society if one analyses their respective dynamics. In the long run, their objective ability to paralyse the power of the bourgeoisie (or even bureaucracy) and implement a rule of councils has only grown.

> We just have to compare the 10 million strikers of May 1968 with the 3 million of June 1936 in France, the 10 million Polish workers in Solidarnosc in 1979–80 with the ½ million who were involved in the general strikes of 1905–06 or the 1918–20 revolutionary movements in Poland, and those involved in the 1973–74 Portuguese revolution with the numbers participating in previous struggles there. We can see that at least in a number of countries (we do not say all countries) there is a clear tendency for the numbers involved to increase significantly.[277]

Of course, Mandel does not think that the 'spontaneous tendency' is enough. This is precisely what he sees as the decisive argument for 'conscious anti-capitalist theory and practice', i.e. for building organisations that assimilate the experiences of the past and carry the theoretical results into the working class. They have to mobilise as large a section of the class as possible, employing a strategy of transitional demands and running a smooth united-front policy. This must occur well before the decisive struggles take place. If such organisations are sufficiently active and self-organised, they have a chance of winning majorities for their programme and proposals in times of intensified class conflict.[278]

According to Mandel, the experiences in the Soviet Union and in countries with a similar social structure have shown that there is no way around a revolutionary transformation from below in those countries – that is, a political revolution: 'The bureaucracy cannot introduce an institutionalised socialist democracy'. The masses have risen up again and again. Attempts by sections of the bureaucracy to reform the system have met the limits of their self-interest as a privileged layer time and time again.

> In no way does this mean the bureaucracy is incapable of carrying out any reforms, sometimes even very bold ones, when this is the price it will

---

277   Ibid.
278   Ibid.

pay for its survival. The imperialist bourgeoisie and even the bourgeoisie of several semi-colonial or dependent semi-industrialised countries have incidentally shown a similar capability. Just think a moment of the workers' self-management set up by the Yugoslav CP in 1950, the concessions the Nagy faction made to the masses in Hungary in 1956, the reforms implemented by the Dubcek leadership in Summer 1968 in Czechoslovakia. Today's *glasnost* policy being implemented in the USSR is along the same lines. But these reforms come up against an insurmountable barrier of social interests when they endanger the material privileges of the bureaucracy.[279]

According to Mandel, the threat to the bureaucracy's monopoly on political power makes even its most reform-inclined parts shy away from a consistent reform policy. Sovereign workers' councils would certainly not be compatible with this monopoly of power. However, Mandel could imagine an interplay between the bureaucracy's attempts at self-reform and mass mobilisation, which could eventually trigger a revolution of the system:

> The interaction between divisions within the bureaucracy, triggered by internal contradictions of the system as well as by the first signs of popular opposition, *and* the subsequent development of an autonomous mass movement is part of the real process towards the anti-bureaucratic political revolution since 1948. The role played in this by de-Stalinisation (de-Maoisation) initiatives, such as the spectacular one of Khrushchev from 1955–56, comprising not only the famous 'secret report' to the CPSU's twentieth Congress but also the release of millions of prisoners, must also be understood.[280]

Since the mass movements against bureaucratic rule in these countries are an integral part of the world socialist revolution, Mandel argues it is a natural duty of revolutionaries and the workers' movement in other parts of the world to practice solidarity with them. This is particularly important because the way in which the socialist idea has been discredited by the bureaucratic systems of 'really existing socialism' is a major obstacle to the formation of socialist class consciousness worldwide. Mandel refers to the main statement of a FI resolution from 1963 (which he played a major role in drafting), the thesis of the

---

279   Mandel 1988d, p. 6.
280   Ibid.

'dialectic of the three sectors of world revolution', and applies it to the two sectors of 'bureaucratised workers' states' and 'developed industrialised capitalist countries':[281]

> Consequently there is an objective dialectic between progress towards the anti-bureaucratic political revolution on the one hand and progress to the proletarian socialist revolution in the imperialist countries on the other. The dialectic operates in both directions. In today's world no decisive progress of the world revolution is even thinkable without the unfolding of this dual dialectic. Without this victorious political revolution there will be no solution to the crisis in the USSR, eastern Europe, or China.[282]

For the members of the FI, one of the unexpected developments in the years after World War II was that even according to their own analysis, 'socialist revolutions' that had not been led by 'Trotskyist' organisations had taken place in a number of countries.[283] This was true of Yugoslavia and China, but also of Cuba and Vietnam and later Nicaragua and Grenada. At the time of its founding, the FI had declared that 'official' Communism ('Stalinism') had lost the capacity to lead socialist revolutions because it had been transformed into an agency for the defence of bureaucratic special interests. The FI regarded its members as the only remaining real Marxist revolutionaries. In the *Transitional Programme*, the FI founders say of their own 'cadres': 'Outside these cadres there does not exist a single revolutionary current on this planet really meriting the name'.[284]

And yet, the revolutions in the aforementioned six countries (Mandel reserves judgement on Albania and North Korea because he is not sure whether 'authentic popular revolutions' occurred there) did take place on planet Earth.[285]

First of all, Mandel makes clear that the drastic change in property and production relations in countries like Yugoslavia, China and Vietnam, i.e. the break with capitalism, is undeniable. He considers the attempts of certain 'Trotskyist' currents to deny this ridiculous. Obviously, neither a 'bourgeoisie' nor a 'petty bourgeoisie' is in power in these countries.[286]

---

281   Mandel 1988d, chapter 6.
282   Ibid.
283   See Frank 1974, p. 66 et seq.; Bensaïd 2002, p. 65 et seq.; Kellner 2004, p. 83 et seq.
284   Trotsky 2002, p. 49.
285   See Mandel 1988d, chapter 7, footnote 18.
286   See Mandel 1988d, chapter 7.

In Mandel's view, in order to lead successful socialist revolutions, the Communist Parties of Yugoslavia, China and Vietnam had to put the interests of the proletariat and the oppressed masses of their countries above the interests of the Soviet bureaucracy. That is why they also had to break with the Kremlin in practice, or at least with its political instructions, in order to be able to carry out these revolutions successfully. This resulted in the well-known 'schisms' in the Communist world movement, i.e. the cracks in Stalinist 'monolithism'. According to Mandel, it is wrong to invoke the 'pressure of the masses' in order to downplay the revolutionary role of these leaders (who in that case would have been revolutionary leaders against their will, so to speak, which does not seem very plausible). Such assertions imply that one underestimates the role of organisations and the subjective factor in general and, conversely, it vaguely implies that 'the masses' are to blame for defeats.[287] In Greece after World War II, in Indonesia in the early 1960s and in Chile in the early '70s, there was just as much 'pressure from the masses'. But the Communist Parties there acted very differently, and that is why counter-revolution prevailed.[288]

'The fact that the Yugoslav, Chinese, and Vietnamese CPs broke with Stalinism to lead the revolution in their countries *without having revolutionary Marxist parties* must not be blotted out of the analysis on the pretext that the only thing that counts is the seizure of power'.[289]

According to Mandel, the break of these leaderships with Stalinism was not complete, which is why they did not promote the establishment of authentic socialist council rule. The internal regimes of their parties and the state organs of power that had emerged from these revolutions were bureaucratised from the outset. Party and state apparatuses had been merged, the masses were restrained to various degrees and prevented from organising independently. According to Mandel, these shortcomings had grave consequences for the domestic and international policies of these leaderships. Thus, the victory of the Chinese revolution initially changed the balance of power considerably in favour of colonial revolution, but the bureaucratic form of the system that emerged from this revolution, combined with the ideological confusions of Maoism, considerably diminished the prospects of revolution, especially in Indonesia and India. Maoism also led to the disorientation of a large number of newly politicised young people in the late '60s, making it much more difficult to build new revolutionary parties in the west.[290]

---

287 Ibid.
288 Ibid.
289 Ibid.
290 Ibid.

As regards Cuba, Grenada and Nicaragua, Mandel points out that these leaderships and parties were not 'Stalinist' in origin. They were products of the differentiation and maturation of the revolutionary and socialist movements in the respective countries. This, for him, is a big difference with important implications. It is why in these countries, after the victory of the revolution, milder forms of bureaucratisation prevailed and quite significant steps towards building real popular power from below were made (albeit at a local rather than national level). Consequently, these revolutions – especially the one in Cuban – also gave significant impulses to the colonial revolution in the other poor countries.

> But here again the non-assimilation of the essential tenets of revolutionary Marxism has had serious political consequences. The absence of authentic socialist democracy in Cuba becomes increasingly a brake on further economic progress. The paternalist conception of the party involves serious risks of political and social conflicts. The subsequent identification of the party with the state limits greatly the internal influence of the Cuban leadership for promoting the revolution in Latin America. Inevitable diplomatic manoeuvres of the Cuban state tend to influence if not dictate the tactical, even strategic, advice given to revolutionary forces in the rest of the continent. The lack of revolutionary victories up to now in Latin America weakens in turn the position of the Cuban state against imperialism, increases its material dependence on the Soviet bureaucracy and deepens the dynamic of crises in Cuba itself. The question of supporting the revolutionary Marxist programme as a whole is not therefore an insignificant or secondary detail even in the case of Cuba and Nicaragua.[291]

Mandel does not rule out that there might be other cases of non-revolutionary Marxist forces leading victorious revolutions in the future: 'But we are convinced we are talking here of only a few exceptions'.[292]

In the past, at any rate, a constellation of very special circumstances had made such cases possible: the emergence of a leadership that had politically matured over years of struggle and was independent of the bourgeoisie as well as the Kremlin bureaucracy; a severely weakened or decomposing ruling class in the country in question; the relative paralysis of imperialism, which was

---

291   Mandel 1988d, chapter 7.
292   Ibid.

unable to intervene forcefully enough on account of certain global political circumstances; and a weak tradition of self-organisation of the proletariat.[293]

This latter characterisation of 'exceptional situations' shows that in Mandel's theory, the 'normal' path of socialist revolution begins from advanced forms of self-organisation of the proletariat unfolding in the industrialised countries. A shift of the process of world socialist revolution towards this main stream would also spectacularly strengthen the influence and role of 'revolutionary Marxism', the Fourth International, or at least politically very similarly oriented forces.

In 1988, Mandel identified a very uneven but genuine global regroupment process of the workers' movement that had historically begun with the Cuban Revolution and had continued to evolve through setbacks and advances ever since. The most spectacular case, according to him, was the emergence of the Brazilian Workers' Party (PT) as a socialist class party with a programmatic orientation towards socialist revolution. He also considered the independent mass trade unions in South Africa (COSATU) and Poland (Solidarność) to be part of this process. Mandel argued that in all these cases, organisations that influenced millions of workers had emerged, producing much more democratic internal structures in comparison to the traditional (social-democratic and Communist) parties of the workers' movement. In other countries, he identified similar processes at a lower level, including regroupment processes and mergers in the ranks of the revolutionary left, although these were of relatively modest weight.[294]

Mandel argued further that the grip of the reformist apparatuses on the working class remained largely unbroken and continued to present the most significant obstacle to revolutionary developments. However, he saw this influence prevailing mainly at the electoral level (although in some cases, as in Denmark, electorally significant forces were emerging to the left of social demo cracy), whereas it had declined spectacularly on the shopfloors and, in some cases, among trade union activists. Denouncement of the capitulations of the reformist leaderships, he argued, has to be combined with a smart united front policy.[295]

Overall, Mandel saw a 'transitional situation' in which a 'semi-political class consciousness' dominated among the broad vanguard. In his eyes, this situation certainly offered new opportunities for the construction of revolutionary

---

293   Ibid.
294   Mandel 1988d, chapter 9.
295   Ibid.

parties. The most important obstacle, however, was the burden of a whole range
of negative experiences.

> The great disillusionment caused by the classic Stalinist (post-Stalinist)
> and social-democratic political projects which for decades have failed and
> led to repugnant compromises; the lamentable situation in the USSR and
> China which is by and large accepted as such by these vanguards; the
> disastrous military interventions in Czechoslovakia, Poland, and Afgh-
> anistan as well as the horrific Pol Pot experience: All this burden of neg-
> ative experiences is not yet compensated by pilot experiences compar-
> able to the October revolution or even the 1936 Spanish revolution, which
> could really sustain hope on a historic scale for the world proletariat.[296]

For Mandel, the Brazilian PT is the closest thing to an authentic revolutionary
mass party preparing for socialist revolution, 'but even here the decisive test
is still to come'.[297] More serious for Mandel than the negative experiences of
the past, however, is the hitherto absence of a sufficiently big movement of the
class itself, especially in key countries such as the US and the USSR, but also in
states like Germany and Japan. If independent class movements and political
organisation of the working class emerged in the aforementioned countries,
Mandel thinks that they could scarcely be tamed by bureaucratic apparatuses.
Mandel advises revolutionaries to cooperate loyally in any concrete attempt to
reconstitute the revolutionary forces before such spectacular new movements
occur – without, of course, throwing their own insights and programmatic convictions overboard or sacrificing the integrity and operational capacity of their
own 'cadre'.

> Paradoxically, it is during non-revolutionary situations and phases that
> the essential contribution to building revolutionary leaderships and
> parties must be made. When the revolution starts there is too little time
> to go through certain stages of party-building. These tasks have to be well
> on the way to completion in the previous period.[298]

For Mandel, the global situation implies that neither a socialist orientation
in a single country nor a reinforcement of the 'socialist camp' are sufficient

---

296   Mandel 1988d, chapter 8.
297   Ibid.
298   Ibid.

to solve serious problems and avert the worst dangers for humanity. His fundamental disagreement with radical pacifists and ecologists does not lie in a different assessment of the level of threat, but in his belief in the inseparable link between the threat of global suicide by weapons of mass destruction and the erosion of the natural foundations of life, on the one hand, and the continued existence of the capitalist world system and its nation states. For him, the only solution is a world socialist federation arising from successive victories of socialist revolutions in the capitalist industrialised countries, political revolutions in the bureaucratised non-capitalist countries, and permanent revolution in the poor and dependent countries. Therefore, a real socialist strategy can only be an international strategy oriented towards global relations.[299]

Mandel now raises the question why the idea of building an international revolutionary organisation within what he calls the 'broad vanguard' has so far found so little resonance at the world level. In his opinion, the negative experiences of the past also play a decisive role here. The Second (Social-Democratic) International failed in the face of the decisive challenge of World War I, despite all the internationalist resolutions and promises. The Third International developed into an authoritarian, manipulative administrative centre already under Zinoviev's presidency, and later became an instrument of the power interests of the Kremlin bureaucracy. There were also recurrent negative experiences on a smaller scale, such as when Maoist groups allowed themselves to be tied to the diplomatic vacillations and manoeuvres of the Chinese leadership. In general, according to Mandel, there has been great scepticism as to whether it is at all possible to efficiently combine sufficient international commitment and a capacity to act internationally with the necessary autonomy for revolutionary organisations in their respective countries. After all, there are always special conditions that can only be assessed with sufficient precision in the country itself.[300]

On the other hand, he argues that the largely separate experience of the movements and left political forces in the 'three sectors of world revolution' has been a key impediment for the full development of revolutionary consciousness:

> Another objective reality weighs down over parties and currents emerging from the process of recomposition of the workers' movement (elsewhere than in Cuba and Nicaragua) and this is that the identity of interest

299 See Mandel 1988d, chapter 9.
300 Ibid.

between the three sectors of the world revolution, which is an historic reality, is not yet part of the day-to-day experience of significant sectors of the vanguard, not to speak of the broad masses. The desynchronisation and largely autonomous development of mass struggles in these three sectors is an important obstacle.[301]

According to Mandel, the possible positive combined effect of the Tet Offensive in Vietnam, the Paris May and the Prague Spring was largely nullified by the invasion of Soviet tanks. The experiences of the revolutionaries of Central America, the Polish workers of Solidarność, the British miners, the Fiat workers, the French workers, and the German metalworkers ran largely isolated from each other, and it was only very partially possible to break through this isolation with education and solidarity campaigns. As a result, both the mass struggles themselves and the assimilation of their experiences remained very fragmentary. Moreover, the most important battalions of the world proletariat have not yet entered the struggle. This too, Mandel argues, makes the project of building a new revolutionary mass international appear less credible.[302]

'In these conditions, only the Fourth International and a few small groups of equivalent size to its strongest sections, are fully behind a really universal class solidarity. Only the Fourth International has drawn the corresponding organisational conclusion – to simultaneously build national revolutionary parties and a world revolutionary party'.[303]

Because such a mass international cannot come into being spontaneously, Mandel argues that the building of this existing Fourth International should not be abandoned. The new mass international, which the FI will help to create, will probably be the result of a broader regroupment.[304]

Mandel considers the emergence of a socialist world federation to be impossible without prior mass experience of an international revolutionary organisation practising global solidarity. International cooperation requires at least a partial surrender of sectional sovereignties – and to commit to this is a far from obvious matter for many.

But you would have to believe in Father Christmas to think that after thousands of years of exploitation, oppression and violence by the strongest states against other ethnic groups, peoples, states, or weaker classes; after

---

301   Mandel 1988d, chapter 10.
302   Ibid.
303   Ibid.
304   Ibid.

a century of imperialist super-exploitation and oppression against colonial and semi-colonial peoples; after centuries of racial discrimination, violence and even extermination; after a half-century of oppression and discrimination by the Soviet bureaucracy against various foreign nations and nationalities inside the USSR ... that all peoples, oppressed minority groups, working classes and revolutionary parties will automatically and freely accept without any afterthoughts such a limitation of sovereignty as something quite logical. It seems indispensable that they first have to go through an experience teaching them that world-wide collaboration is possible on a strict basis of equality, where the 'small' forces will not have less rights and powers than the 'big' ones, where limits on sovereignty are applied first of all on the 'powerful' before being placed on the 'weaker', where all discrimination on the grounds of gender, race, nationality, ethnic group is strictly forbidden.[305]

For Mandel, this experience is most likely to occur first in a revolutionary international organisation, in which the constituent national organisations make policy autonomously in their country, and majority decisions in the international determine international policy. It is necessary to avoid both the hyper-centralism of the Third International, which amounted to bureaucratic centralism, and the extreme federalism of the Second International, which, according to a dictum of Rosa Luxemburg, led to a terrible perversion of the motto of the *Communist Manifesto*: '... the proud old cry, "Proletarians of all countries, unite!" has been transformed on the battlefields into the command, "Proletarians of all countries, cut each other's throats!"'[306]

Mandel cites two conditions for the success of his strategic approach. As far as he is concerned, the fate of humanity is sealed if these are not met. First, working class action must occur especially in the major countries, build on the most advanced struggles of the past, and overcome the fragmentation of the class movement into individual countries and regions of the world.

On condition that a sufficient number of cadres, solidly rooted in the working class, equipped with a correct programme and strategic vision, able to take appropriate political actions and initiatives, are grouped together in those situations, then the political, organisational, and geographical limits of the ongoing process of recomposition of the workers'

305   Ibid.
306   Luxemburg 1916.

movement will be progressively overcome. The building of new national revolutionary leaderships and a new mass revolutionary International will become possible.[307]

Mandel adds that he has no doubts about the realisation of this perspective and therefore continues to have faith of the future of humanity, the construction of a new mass international, and the ultimate victory of the FI.

He maintained this perspective with relatively minor modifications until his death six years later, notwithstanding the drastic changes in the world situation since 1989–91.[308]

---

307   Mandel 1988d, chapter 10.
308   See Mandel 1995b.

CHAPTER 6

Emancipation and Social Catastrophe

1   Mandel on Trotsky's Theory of Fascism

Fascism and National Socialism were historical catastrophes for the organised workers' movement, and they were international political catastrophes for humanity. Their respective 'seizures of power' were important prerequisites for World War II, which led to immeasurable suffering and destruction and resulted in 80 million dead. The Nazi dictatorship organised the systematic murder of six million who were killed simply because they were Jews or because their murderers classified them as Jews.[1] Since the collapse of the Italian Fascist dictatorship and of the German 'Third Reich', there has been no end to the debate about the nature of these movements and the reasons why they rose to power. Youth radicalisation and the new political-cultural climate of the late 1960s led to an upsurge in the study of the various attempts of the left to grasp the fascist and National Socialist phenomenon and work out ways to prevent a repeat. Mandel addressed this topic in an essay on Trotsky's theory of fascism in 1969. The text became the introduction to an anthology of Trotsky's writings on Germany that was first published in 1971.[2]

At the outset, Mandel emphasises that the various theoretical attempts at explaining the phenomenon are determined by political needs. For the German bourgeoisie, for instance, the Nazi era remains an 'unresolved past' because the (capitalist) social relations that provided the breeding ground for fascism and Nazism still exist. This creates a bias that makes it impossible for bourgeois ideologues to reveal the real picture.

> It is impossible to get at the roots of the fascist barbarism without laying bare this causal connection. Insofar as the restored rule of West German capital constitutes class rule, one can scarcely expect the exposure of these roots to shape university and secondary-school education. Since the past cannot (or will not) be exhaustively explained, it cannot be 'mastered'.[3]

---

1   Usually a figure of 50 million dead is cited. But Mandel speaks of a larger number: 'Eighty million people were killed, if one includes those who died of starvation and illness as a direct result of the war – eight times as many as during World War I' (Mandel 1986d, p. 168).

2   Mandel 1971b and Trotsky 1971.

3   Mandel 1971b, pp. 39–40.

With reference to the essay 'Ideological Components in the Theories of Fascism' by Wolfgang Fritz Haug et al., Mandel underlines that any attempts to paint the aspirations and mentalities of broad majorities of the population as the essential causes for the rise of fascism and Nazism have an exonerating function for the ruling class. They give the oppressed and the weak the blame for their own oppression.[4]

In Mandel's view, the rise of fascism was accompanied by the inadequacy of the predominant theories of fascism at the time – not only the bourgeois ones, but also those produced by the prevalent trends in the workers' movement. However, those were not the only existing theories of fascism:

> On the periphery of the organized political mass forces and their ideologists, there was an analytical intelligentsia working with an acuteness that today can only inspire astonishment and admiration. These theorists understood the new phenomenon. They early recognized the great danger it represented. They warned their contemporaries and showed how the threatening monster could be vanquished. They did everything that could be done in the theoretical sphere.[5]

Mandel is referring to Trotsky's contribution in particular. The bureaucratic apparatuses that dominated the mass organisations of the working class were, in his view, responsible for the fact that the correct theoretical understanding of fascism and the appropriate means to combat the peril were not adopted by the masses, and the catastrophe was therefore not averted. Even so, he considers it important that the theoretical gains of the past are used for the present and future anti-fascist struggle. The high esteem in which Mandel holds Trotsky's contribution to the theory of fascism and to the struggle against the growing Nazi movement is evident in all of his texts on this topic.[6]

For Mandel, the superiority of Trotsky's theory of fascism lies in the fact that it captures the totality of social and political relations that underlie the rise of fascist mass movements and the operation of fascist dictatorships. Most bourgeois approaches, in contrast, are characterised by a pitiful juxtaposition of economic and political factors and a debate as to which is predominant: 'With laborious pedantry, they try to interpret this or that action of the Hitler

---

4 The reference to Haug's essay is contained in the first footnote of the German version of Mandel's introduction – see Mandel 1993.

5 Mandel 1971b, p. 11.

6 See Mandel 1979a, p. 134 et seq.; Mandel 1979e, pp. 88–98; Mandel 1986d, p. 22; Mandel 1995a, p. 106 et seq.

regime, asking such questions as, "Was it to the advantage of big capital? Was it contrary to the expressed wishes of the capitalists?" They do not ask the more fundamental question – whether the immanent laws of development of the capitalist mode of production were realized or negated by that regime'.[7]

Mandel points out that many US bourgeois were bitter opponents of Roosevelt's 'New Deal', and yet there is no denying that in the long run this policy served to stabilise the capitalist mode of production, the profits of big corporations, and the expansion of the power of US capital. By the same token, he considers it irrelevant with what degree of enthusiasm and inner conviction, and when exactly, representatives of big business like Thyssen or Krupp began to support Hitler. The historical balance of the actions of the Nazi regime in relation to the objective interests of the German bourgeoisie as a class presents a much more decisive factor.[8]

Moreover, the inner logic of the war economy cannot be separated from the economically determined expansionary interests of the ruling classes of the imperialist countries, which ultimately had to be pursued by military means. The irrationalities of this war economy were ultimately the sharp expression of a distinct combination of operational partial rationality (in the enterprises, in the organisation of production, in the advancement of appropriate techniques, etc.) and irrationality in relation to the overall social outcome of all activities. This combination, Mandel argues, is inherent in the capitalist mode of production and its market economy in general.[9]

Mandel rebukes Ernst Nolte's attempt to appropriate Ernst Bloch's concept of the 'unsimultaneity' [Ungleichzeitigkeit] of history, although he considers it quite correct to cite the persistence of archaic forms of existence in contemporary societies as one of the factors explaining the emergence of fascist mass movements. Even Trotsky himself highlighted this aspect, especially in 'Portrait of National Socialism', which he authored in June 1933:

> Fascism has opened up the depths of society for politics. Today, not only in peasant homes but also in city skyscrapers, there lives alongside of the twentieth century the tenth or the thirteenth. A hundred million people use electricity and still believe in the magic power of signs and exorcisms. The Pope of Rome broadcasts over the radio about the miraculous transformation of water into wine. Movie stars go to mediums. Aviators who pilot miraculous mechanisms created by man's genius wear amulets

---

7 Mandel 1971b, p. 12.
8 Mandel 1971b, p. 13.
9 See Mandel 1971b, pp. 13–14.

on their sweaters. What inexhaustible reserves they possess of darkness, ignorance, and savagery! Despair has raised them to their feet, fascism has given them a banner. Everything that should have been eliminated from the national organism in the form of cultural excrement in the course of the normal development of society has now come gushing out from the throat; capitalist society is puking up the undigested barbarism. Such is the physiology of National Socialism.[10]

But Nolte goes so far as to say that if fascism is rooted in the archaic, then it is ultimately based in human nature and not in the capitalist mode of production. Mandel declares this conclusion trivial and compares it to Molière's remark that opium puts you to sleep because it has sleep-inducing properties. While psychological factors such as a latent readiness for aggression have always existed in humans, this does not provide any explanation for modern outbreaks of massive violence, the specific features of which are linked to modern society, its structures and technical means.[11]

According to Mandel, all attempts to explain fascism in terms of specific national mentalities suffer from a similar flaw. After all, fascism took hold between in many imperialist countries from 1920 to 1945, all of which had their own particularities. Blaming the rise of the Nazis on typically German discipline and subservience resulting from the belated abolition of serfdom in Prussia does not sit well with the example of Italy, which is regarded as an 'undisciplined' nation. What is more, Germany was the most advanced industrialised country on the European mainland, while Italy was relatively backward. Although such factors do play a role, explanations that foreground national peculiarities are evidently inadequate.[12]

As for a series of detailed studies on the attitudes and interests of certain factions of German capital before and during the Nazi period, Mandel considers them relatively trivial, particularly because most of their findings correspond to simple intuition. For example, it goes without saying that the interests of heavy industry and armaments corporations were more closely aligned to those of the Nazis than the interests of the light and consumer goods industries; IG Farben exerted a particularly strong influence on important decisions of the Nazi regime; the 'Aryanisations' did not play a significant role for the German economy; and so on. Once again, Mandel disagrees with Nolte, who considers

---

10   Trotsky 1971, p. 405.
11   Mandel 1971b, pp. 14–15.
12   Mandel 1971b, p. 15.

such findings proof that there was no particular connection between Nazism and capital as a whole.[13]

What is essential for capital, according to Mandel, is private ownership of the means of production and the possibility to accumulate. With respect to this, the figures speak a very clear language. According to Mandel, they provide striking evidence of just how closely the Nazi regime aligned with the interests of big capital, especially certain sections of big business:

> Profits from all industrial and commercial enterprises rose from 6.6 billion (thousand million) marks in 1933 to 15 billion marks in 1938. But while sales of the Bremen Woolen Mills stagnated and sales of AEG (Allgemeine Elektrizitat Gesellschaft – General Electric Company) increased only 55 percent, those of Siemens were doubled, those of Krupp and Mannesmann Tube Works were tripled, those of Philipp Holzmann, Inc., increased six times, and those of the German Weapons and Munitions Works rose tenfold. From these figures, there clearly emerges a collective economic interest of the capitalist class – one which is far from being merely a conceptual construction – while at the same time, within the framework of this collective interest, special interests arise and assert themselves repeatedly.[14]

For Mandel, the superiority of Marxism consists in its ability to integrate contradictory aspects, and Trotsky succeeded brilliantly in doing that: 'Trotsky's theory of fascism is a unity of six elements. Each element within this unity possesses a certain autonomy, and each passes through a certain development by virtue of its internal contradictions. But the unity can only be understood as a closed and dynamic totality in which these elements, not in isolation but in their intrinsic connection with one another, can explain the rise, victory, and fall of fascist dictatorship'.[15]

Mandel considers it particularly important to grasp the interplay of objective and subjective factors to explain the emergence and function of fascist mass movements. He cites the following six elements:

1. Fascism is the expression of a severe structural crisis of the capitalist mode of production. Its function is to bring about a sudden drastic improvement in the conditions of the realisation of capital.

---

13   Mandel 1971b, pp. 15–16.
14   Mandel 1971b, pp. 16–17.
15   Mandel 1971b, p. 17.

2. Fascism fulfils and simultaneously negates the tendency peculiar to imperialist monopoly capital, if the equilibrium within the 'normal' bourgeois-parliamentary form of capitalist rule is seriously upset, to move to authoritarian and even totalitarian forms of rule with increased executive power and direct access by the leaders of the monopolies to important political decisions. Fascism realises this tendency at the same time as it accomplishes the political expropriation of the bourgeoisie, which is much more directly and diversely involved in the immediate exercise of political power under the bourgeois-parliamentary form of rule.

3. Fascism can only smash the workers' movement and build an effective firewall of block wardens and informers against constant flare-up of class struggle from below if it is based on a big mass movement. This is the essential difference to military dictatorships and similar forms of authoritarian rule.

4. The mass base of fascism is the declassed petty bourgeoisie and the petty bourgeoisie threatened with social degradation, whose radicalisation (Trotsky spoke of 'counter-revolutionary despair') is stoked by nationalist and superficially anti-capitalist demagogy and aimed against the workers' movement. Once this violent mass base is in place, the fascist seizure of power requires the financial and political support of important sections of monopoly capital.

5. In order to triumph, a fascist mass movement must, over a certain period of time, manage to shift the balance of power in its favour and against the workers' movement. Its rise is tantamount to a permanent state of civil war, although it is not decided from the outset who will win the struggle. Successful working-class resistance against the fascist mass movement simultaneously creates a revolutionary situation in which the working class has a chance to come to power. Because of this risk, the bourgeoisie only pulls the 'fascist card' in extreme emergencies. Initially, there is only a section of the petty bourgeoisie 'gone mad' and prepared to do whatever it takes physically attacking the institutions and activists of the workers' movement. If it succeeds in intimidating and demoralising the workers' movement, the mass of the petty bourgeoisie and declassed will be pulled towards fascism. The more the working class defends itself resolutely and in a united fashion, the more the petty bourgeoisie will be inclined to join it.

6. After the fascist seizure of power, fascism is 'bureaucratised'. It merges with the highest levels of the state apparatus and suppresses the mass movement. Any aspects of 'anti-capitalist' demagogy end up in the dustbin. Fascism's adventurism shifts to foreign policy. Growing national debt

and devaluation of money eventually only leave wars of conquest as a way out.[16]

The writings by Trotsky that Mandel introduces were largely aimed at convincing members of the Communist Party of Germany (KPD) of the need for a united front with the Social Democrats (SPD) in order to counter Nazism and the physical threat it posed to the entire workers' movement. Moreover, Trotsky tried to convince Communists of the need to combine the defensive task of joint self-protection against the Nazi stormtroopers with a revolutionary perspective for the overthrow of capitalism and seizure of political power by the working class. Mandel highlights aspects of Trotsky's analysis of the fascist mass movement that played an important role towards these ends. In Mandel's text, these aspects add up to a comprehensive and coherent 'theory of fascism' coined by Trotsky.

The fourth congress of the Communist International in 1922 saw the first comprehensive discussion of the Italian Fascist movement. Reports from Radek and Bordiga and various other contributions to the debate show that the analysis of fascism had already established its key characteristics by that point: the mass character of the fascist movement; the fact that it is based on the counter-revolutionary despair of the impoverished petty bourgeoisie, disillusioned with its role and prospects and under threat of social dislocation; fascism's role as a battering ram aimed against the organised workers' movement and its threat to the physical existence of that movement; the difference between the petty-bourgeois character of the movement and its class-political function of defending the power and interests of capital and the monopolies; and so on.[17] Instead of speaking of a self-contained theory coined by Trotsky, it therefore seems more appropriate to stress that Trotsky continued a tradition of fascism analysis that had begun in the early Comintern and was buried in the course of its Stalinisation.[18] This was also evident in an impoverishment of the theoretical examination of fascism: fascism in power was described as the 'open terrorist dictatorship of the most reactionary, most chauvinistic and most imperialist elements of finance capital'.[19]

Mandel compares Trotsky's position with the fascism analyses by representatives of other tendencies of the left and the workers' movement. He concludes that it is clearly superior to these other assessments.

---

16 Mandel 1971b, pp. 368–9.
17 See Frank 1981, p. 208 et seq.
18 See Kellner 2000.
19 Dimitrov 1935.

Social-Democratic authors cite left radicalism as the most important cause for the defeat of the workers' movement – specifically the radical stance of the KPD when it comes to Germany. According to them, the Communist Party terrified the petty bourgeoisie and drove it into the arms of the Nazis. Mandel's main objection here is that the credibility of 'moderate' politics in line with the institutions of the bourgeois-democratic state had been steadily declining in the years before the Nazis seized power. In terms of electoral politics, too, Social Democracy was increasingly caught between the two 'extremes', the Nazi Party and the Communist Party. For fear of 'Bolshevism', the SPD became an unwitting helper for the Nazis. In the same vein, Mandel criticises the 'legalism' of the Social Democrats, who helped to strengthen the same repressive institutions they would later fall victim to when right-wing extremist personnel took over the top echelons of the state apparatus. Because it is an unconscious protest against existing conditions that has turned destructive, fascism cannot be defeated without winning broad masses to a radical anti-capitalist perspective.[20]

Another object of Mandel's criticism of Social-Democratic ideas of fighting fascism is their economism, which lies in an absolutisation of the economic crisis and unemployment as essential causes for the rise of fascist movements. Mandel cites the example of the leading Belgian Social Democrats Spaak and De Man, who, when in government, did everything possible within the limits of the system to stimulate the economy and curb unemployment, yet were unable to prevent the rise of the far-right movement in their country. Overcoming the economic crisis is not enough, he argues, since this does not resolve the deeper structural crisis of the system or redress the loss of credibility suffered by the institutions of bourgeois democracy. The economic and social situation as such does not determine the direction in which radicalisation will evolve, nor which direction will prevail. Economic and social factors can only have an impact in combination with factors like mobilisation, workers' self-organisation, and the level of initiative of the political forces of the workers' movement compared with those of the far right.[21]

As for the position of the 'official' Communist movement, Mandel concedes with reference to Clara Zetkin and Karl Radek, among others, that there were initially 'elements' of a 'Marxist theory of fascism' but these were soon crushed by the factional struggles within the Soviet Communist Party. The analysis of the anti-fascist struggle was sacrificed to the victory of Stalin's faction.[22]

---

20   See Mandel 1971b, p. 22.
21   Mandel 1971b, pp. 22–3.
22   Mandel 1971b, p. 24.

The theory that fascism was simply the expression of the most aggressive sections of monopoly capital and that Social Democracy was the 'twin' of fascism (i.e. the 'social fascism' theory) corresponded to the thesis of a gradual 'fascisation' of the Weimar Republic.[23] According to Mandel, the real danger was glossed over by the notion that socialist and Communist perspectives would prevail once Hitler had seized power and then quickly 'ruined himself'. This stance culminated in the KPD leadership's slogan 'After Hitler, it will be our turn'.[24]

The refusal of the KPD to adopt a united front policy vis-à-vis the SPD was a serious mistake. There are few in the 'official' Communist movement today who deny this. For all the differences concerning the respective roles of the Social Democrats and the Communist Party, the combined policies of the mass organisations of the workers' movement (SPD, KPD, the General German Trade Union Federation, and the federations they influenced) ultimately resulted in capitulation to the Nazis' assumption of power without a fight. Mandel's essay on 'Trotzkis Faschismustheorie' (Trotsky's theory of fascism) was republished in a pamphlet alongside a text from 1935 in the latter half of the 1970s [in West Germany – Translator].[25] The latter text, authored by a German supporter of the Trotskyist Left Opposition, is mainly documentary in character. It synoptically contrasts official pronouncements from the KPD and Comintern from early 1931 onward with those from Trotsky and the Left Opposition. Although the positions of the latter were held only by a vanishing (and marginalised) minority of the Communist movement, it is undeniable in retrospect that they treated the struggle against the Nazi threat much more realistically than the official leadership did.[26]

In fact, the very few instances in which the Left Opposition was stronger than official Communism and able to achieve joint action by all organisations of the workers' movement (especially in Bruchsal and Oranienburg) demonstrated that such a policy could change the balance of power and spectacularly push back the influence of the Nazis. Alas, the Left Opposition was too weak to generalise such a policy on a nationwide scale.[27]

---

23   Ibid.

24   Ibid.

25   'Trotzkis Faschismustheorie' is the German original of Mandel's introduction to Trotsky's
      The Struggle Against Fascism in Germany – see 1971k.

26   See Mandel and Fischer 1977. Oskar Fischer's text, printed in the pamphlet along with
      Mandel's essay, was originally published in 1935. It contrasts the positions of the leadership
      of the KPD and the Comintern with those of Trotsky and the Left Opposition in synoptic
      form.

27   See Mandel 1992a.

The turn to Popular Front politics at the seventh congress of the Comintern in 1935 is still regarded today, even by Communists who sharply criticise the Stalinisation of the Comintern, essentially as a correction of the 'ultra-left' line up to 1933.[28] Mandel follows the assessment of the Trotskyist Left Opposition on this question as well. He points out that the theoretical revision of the 'ultra-left' policy only took place 25 years after its practical revision, because an openly self-critical assessment of the Comintern and KPD line had previously been out of the question due to the cult of infallibility around Stalin. For Mandel, however, the opening up of the united front to bourgeois forces equally disoriented the anti-fascist struggle, since an effective defence against the fascist threat would imply a mobilisation that objectively challenged bourgeois class rule. To the extent that the Communist leadership did not want to allow any challenge to bourgeois property relations and to the legitimacy of bourgeois republics out of consideration for its bourgeois allies, it also had to put the brakes on anti-fascist mass mobilisation at decisive moments.[29]

In the early 1990s, Mandel augmented his account of Trotsky's critique of the Popular Front with a warning against positions that he describes as sectarian. He argues against a formalist interpretation of the rejection of 'popular front politics' and rejects dogmatism in applying Trotsky's positions to concrete present-day situations:

> Some sectarians have attempted to reduce the difference between the popular front and the workers' united front to the question of participation of bourgeois or petty-bourgeois politicians or parties in coalitions. This abstract, schematic approach is actually quite similar to that of popular front supporters. The latter see the alliance with liberal-bourgeois parties as a necessary precondition for the alliance with the middle classes. The sectarians see the participation of bourgeois politicians in the alliance as the inevitable prelude to class betrayal. What both overlook is the really decisive issue, namely, the free development of anti-capitalist mass action. If the participation of bourgeois politicians or parties results in – or is used as an excuse for – this mass action being reduced or prevented, then what we have is a popular front, that is, the surrender of the class political independence of the proletariat. The workers' parties then become the prisoner of the bourgeoisie. But if the participation of bourgeois politicians or groups in the alliance does not put a brake on

---

28   See also Günter Judick's insightful essay 'Der VII. Weltkongress und die Volksfront in Frankreich und Spanien', *Marxistische Blätter*, 3/2004, p. 31 et seq.

29   Mandel 1971b, p. 25.

the developing offensive against the bourgeois state, then these bourgeois politicians are objectively the prisoners of the working class.[30]

In other words, for Mandel, a rejection of 'popular front politics' does not mean rejecting in every instance the participation of bourgeois forces in any government led by working-class political groups or parties. What matters is who has hegemony in such a government alliance, and whether the bourgeois allies are able to protect bourgeois property and bourgeois state power. As an example, Mandel cites the Kuomintang politicians and generals who were part of the Maoist government from 1948/49 onwards. Although the Maoist leadership did stifle the self-organisation of the working class, it did not let the bourgeois allies and its 'stages theory' rhetoric prevent it from smashing the old state apparatus and disempowering the bourgeoisie. In all likelihood, Mandel also had the example of the Sandinista National Liberation Front of Nicaragua in mind when he wrote the relevant lines. Some tendencies that lay claim to Trotsky's legacy accused the Sandinista leadership of class collaboration, popular front politics, and dragging the revolution back into the bourgeois realm after the fall of Somoza, on the grounds that it co-opted bourgeois politicians into its government. By contrast, Mandel and the FI majority analysed this as analogous to the Chinese example and assumed that the Sandinistas had carried out a successful 'permanent revolution' and erected a 'workers' state' – even if they did not use these terms.[31]

For all his criticism of the Stalinist 'social fascism' thesis, Mandel emphasises that it was the policies of the Social-Democratic Party that paved the way for Nazism. The united front policy addresses the certainty that a victory for fascism will entail the destruction of the whole workers' movement, including its politically bourgeoisified Social-Democratic component. According to Mandel, the united front policy must be based on the recognition (and applied accordingly) that the defeat of the fascist mass movement through a broad working-class mobilisation will pave the way for the demise of capitalism and bourgeois parliamentary democracy, and therefore also for the demise of Social Democracy as the hegemonic political tendency in the working class.

---

30 Mandel 1995a, p. 124.
31 See also Livio Maitan, 'Encore sur gouvernement ouvrier et paysan: en guise d'autocritique', in *Quatrieme Internationale*, 16, March 1985. In this text, Maitan critically assesses the Fourth International position on the Sandinista revolution. For years, the FI characterised the FSLN conquest of power as 'dual rule of a special kind', then – in retrospect – as a socialist revolution that had led to a workers' state which persisted even after Violeta Chamorro's election victory (Maitan was himself still convinced of this in 1995).

Social Democracy did in fact prepare fascism's seizure of power by under-mining the workers' class struggle with its policy of class collaboration and by identifying itself with bankrupt parliamentary democracy. But the fascist seizure of power nevertheless means also the downfall of Social Democracy. The masses of Social Democrats, and not a few of their lead-ers, become increasingly aware of this as the moment of the catastrophe comes closer and casts its shadow beforehand in numerous bloody incid-ents. And this consciousness, which expresses all the contradictions of Social Democratic politics, can, if a correct united-front policy is pursued, be the starting point of a real unity in action and a real, sudden shift in the social and political relationship in Germany forces that can lead not only to victory over fascism but also to victory over capitalism and, in addition, to victory over the Social Democratic policies of class collaboration and class conciliation.[32]

Mandel reproaches the theorists who, following Rudolf Hilferding, analysed fascism and Nazism as expressions of the convergence of the monopolistic con-centration of capital and the utmost centralisation of political power (along similar lines as Paul Sering alias Richard Löwenthal with his thesis of National Socialism as 'planned imperialism'). He argues that this supreme centralisation must be combined with a political disempowerment of the bourgeoisie, which is why it is less an expression of the tendencies of monopoly capitalism or late capitalism than it is an expression of its deep crisis.[33]

August Thalheimer's analysis of fascism was fairly close to Trotsky's. However, in Mandel's view, Thalheimer exaggerated both his analogy with Marx's analysis of Bonapartism and the aspect of creeping 'fascisation'. The dis-tinctive feature of fascism – i.e. the complete destruction of the workers' move-ment instead of 'normal' repression by an authoritarian state apparatus – faded into the background. Moreover, Thalheimer's analysis of the balance of forces between the working class and the bourgeoisie did not take the structural crisis of late capitalist society into account. Thalheimer therefore failed to see that a way out of this crisis was objectively possible through a victory of the work-ing class. Mandel accuses Otto Bauer of a similar approach, even if he clearly regards his analysis of fascism as superior to the usual Social-Democratic and 'official' Communist explanations (and also as having much in common with Trotsky's assessment). In practice, Bauer's mechanical separation between the

---

32   Mandel 1971b, pp. 25–6.
33   Mandel 1971b, p. 26.

'defensive' and the 'offensive' merely left the Austrian anti-fascist forces to wait 'at the ready' and in the end lose a purely defensive struggle (the 'heroic battle of the *Schutzbund* in February 1934'). The fascist mass movement, itself an expression of the deep crisis of the capitalist system, can only be defeated if the conquest of political power by the working class is identified as the immediate goal.[34]

Mandel cites the historian Arthur Rosenberg's judgement that the bourgeois republic in Germany perished in 1930 because its fate was entrusted to the bourgeoisie while the working class was already too weak to defend it. For Mandel, this is objectivist reasoning – a different policy might have prevented Hitler's rise to power. Moreover, Rosenberg represents the goal of the anti-fascist struggle inaccurately: 'It escapes Rosenberg's fatalistic historiography that almost three years remained in which the working class, if its leadership had not failed, might have saved not bourgeois democracy certainly, but all the democratic elements worth preserving, by rescuing them from bourgeois democracy for socialism'.[35] According to Mandel, results of more recent research, of which Trotsky and other Marxist authors could not have been aware, confirm especially the thesis that the Nazi dictatorship acted in the interests of big capital. Quoting Jürgen Kuczynski's *Geschichte der Lage der Arbeiter in Deutschland, Volume 2: 1933 to 1946*, Mandel cites figures showing that average workers' wages in the Third Reich had remained far below the level of the period of sharp crisis in the late 1920s, despite full employment. The distribution of income also changed drastically in favour of capital between 1932 and 1938. The share of income from capital, industrial and commercial profits rose from 17.4% of national income in 1932 to 26.6% in 1938. Mandel cites measures that restricted the free movement of labour and established a wage maximum under pressure from monopoly capital, despite some initial hesitation (because this did not fit the image of a 'national community'). In his view, such policies give lie to the thesis of a 'primacy of politics over economics' espoused by a number of bourgeois commentators with respect to the history of the Nazi regime.[36]

The accumulation and concentration of capital also made significant advances under Nazi rule. To prove this, Mandel draws on research by Franz Neumann and Charles Bettelheim. It reveals a spectacular increase in the share capital of all German joint-stock companies, whose number at the same time

---

34   Mandel 1971b, pp. 28–9.
35   Mandel 1971b, p. 29.
36   Mandel 1971b, p. 44, footnote 51.

declined significantly. 'The share in this total capital of the largest companies – those with a capital of more than 20 million RM – rose from 52.4 per cent in 1933 to 53. 6 per cent in 1939 and 63.9 per cent in 1942'.[37]

Under the Nazis, the management of compulsory cartels and economic mergers was largely placed in the hands of big capitalists or their direct representatives. According to Mandel, this simple fact alone contradicts theses such as Tim Mason's, who believes that any collective representation of big business interests had disintegrated under Nazi rule. On the contrary, the representatives of big business defended their interests very efficiently – and these interests did not only run counter to those of wage-earners, but also to the interests of weaker competitors and the majority of the petty bourgeoisie. The Nazis' 'anti-capitalist' demagogy had very little in common with their practical policies.[38]

According to Mandel, this is reinforced by the price and profit margins in the arms industry and by the relationship between the private and the state sector. The general trend under Nazi rule was not towards more nationalisation, but rather towards the reprivatisation of industries. Mandel gives two examples that show how little the Hitler-led state and party bureaucracy was able to assert its ideas 'dictatorially' against the interests of big capitalists. In the middle of the war, in May 1940, the Flick Group was to receive 24 RM [*Reichsmark*] per grenade it would supply to the Reich, taking into account a 'fair' profit. The corporation demanded 39.25 RM and was granted 37 RM after negotiations. The second example refers to Wehrmacht factories built with public money and leased to corporations in return for a state share in the profits. In 1942, the Flick Group took over Donauwörth-GmbH at a book value of only 3.6 million RM – its market value was 9.8 million![39]

> If the Nazi state had systematically nationalized all armaments plants, if it had ruthlessly reduced profit margins to 5 or 6 percent, if it had insisted, for example, that at least half the directors of companies producing for the war effort be direct representatives of the state and the armed forces – certainly these demands derive from the needs of a more effective conduct of the war – then some question about the class character of this state would at least be partly justified. But the data unambiguously present just the opposite picture: brutal subordination of all interests to those of the big companies. And the ruthless subordination

---

37   Mandel 1971b, p. 30.
38   Mandel 1971b, pp. 30–1.
39   Mandel 1971b, pp. 31–2.

of all sectional claims to a 'total' conduct of the war that was waged in the interests of these companies ended the moment it touched on the alpha and omega: capital accumulation of the big corporations.[40]

Mandel's thesis of the 'political expropriation of the bourgeoisie' by the fascist regime goes hand in hand with his assessment of the clear class character of this type of rule. The bourgeoisie does not command the political decision-making bodies, which are delegated to the Fascist or National Socialist party and state apparatus. But big business can assert its immediate economic interests extremely efficiently when dealing with this political apparatus. The abolition of the freedom of association and the dismantling of independent trade unions further ensures an exceptionally favourable balance of power in favour of employers.

Drawing on post-war accounts, Mandel also sees Trotsky's essential statements on the Nazis' road to power confirmed. In the course of the Nazis' electoral upsurge, many big capitalists initially hesitated and shied away from the risk of financing the Nazi movement. But the agenda of the big industrialists (an authoritarian state, massive wage cuts, a revision of 'Versailles', etc.) dovetailed with Hitler's march towards his 'seizure of power' to the extent that he pushed back the left-demagogic wing of his own movement and – as in his speech at the Industrial Club on 27 January 1932 – allayed the concerns of big capitalists by guaranteeing private ownership of the means of production and promising to apply the 'Führer principle' in the factories. Had it not been for a change of heart among influential circles of big capitalists, the Nazi Party would not have been able to overcome its crisis and financial difficulties after the electoral setback of November 1932.[41]

According to Mandel, the notion that the Nazis could have been stopped by a broad united action front is confirmed by a wealth of memoirs, even if the authors did not necessarily set out to substantiate this thesis. Clearly, many trade unionists, members of the Social-Democratic Party and its paramilitary organisation, the Reichsbanner, and most Communist Party members were ready to fight and waiting for a signal from their respective leadership. But that signal never came, even if local examples of united action by Social Democrats and Communists increased shortly before Hitler's ascension to power.[42]

For Mandel, the practical benefit of understanding the past theoretically is that we are better equipped to tackle similar developments in the future. He

---

40 Mandel 1971b, p. 32.
41 Mandel 1971b, p. 33.
42 Mandel 1971b, pp. 33–4.

warns against extending the concept of fascism to phenomena to which only some of the six key characteristics cited by him apply.[43] Repressive governments like Brüning's or Schleicher's, 'normal' repression by an authoritarian state, the use of police and military in a bourgeois democracy, or even the policies of Social-Democratic parties that use the state apparatus as a means to repress workers are not the same as fascism or Nazism. An excessive use of the term blinds us to the real danger, leaving us unable to put up an effective resistance if and when it really arises. The trend towards a 'strong state', the growing power of the executive, the restriction of democratic rights, and the expansion of the arsenal of repression should not be equated with 'fascisation'.

Moreover, Mandel does not consider authoritarian regimes in the 'third world' fascist, even when they rely on reactionary petty-bourgeois mass mobilisation and brutally crack down on the working class and political opponents. In his view, the merging of the interests of the state and monopoly capital, an aspect that distinguishes true fascism, does not apply to them. The Peronist regime in Argentina, for instance, was an expression of the interests of a national bourgeoisie that stood between the working class of its country and the imperialist bourgeoisie of the metropolises. As the terrible Indonesian experience has shown, such dictatorships, when they side with imperialism and turn against the exploited and oppressed, can have hundreds of thousands murdered. However, the Argentinean example indicates that under such regimes the workers' movement can, under certain circumstances, rebuild itself and achieve an upsurge in its self-organisation and fighting strength.[44]

For Mandel, there was no acute fascist danger in the late 1960s, especially not in Europe. During this period, extreme right-wing groups were rather weak and not very well prepared for action in most countries. Mandel could most readily imagine a rapid development towards a fascist-type mass movement in the United States – for example, if racism, xenophobia, indifference to political murder and the various resentments that feed into right-wing extremism were to increase spectacularly.[45]

For Mandel, the political leanings of students were like a seismograph indicating broader socio-political tendencies. In earlier times, universities had been breeding grounds for the offspring of far-right movements. But in the second half of the 1960s, they produced a generation among which left-wing,

---

43   Mandel 1971b, pp. 34–5.
44   Mandel 1971b, p. 35.
45   Mandel 1971b, p. 37.

liberation-oriented politicisation prevailed. This militated against the notion that there would soon be an upsurge of far-right mass sentiment.[46]

Mandel further assumed that large sections of the petty bourgeoisie were rather comfortable and satisfied on account of the prosperity they were enjoying during the long wave with expansive undertone in the '50s and '60s. This, he argued, was reflected in their propensity to call for state repression against 'left-wing extremists', but not take to the streets and subject themselves to physical confrontations with protesters or strikers. Nonetheless, Mandel points out that the turn of the economic climate into stagnation and depression, along with the associated rise in unemployment and declassing of large sections of the population, may very well lead to an upsurge of fascist mass movements in the future.[47]

Mandel concludes his introduction to Trotsky's writings on Germany with an optimistic keynote, especially with regard to Germany:

> We said at the beginning that the reader of this book will be transfixed by Trotsky's analytical achievements. But the study of these writings calls forth anger and scorn even more than admiration. How easy it would have been to have heeded Trotsky's admonition and avoided disaster. This should be the great moral for us: to recognize the evil in order to fight it in time, and with success. The German catastrophe does not have to be repeated. And it will not be repeated.[48]

Later, conversely, Mandel would emphasise that even worse catastrophes were possible if a force similar to the fascist and Nazi movements were to take hold.

2   Mandel and the Holocaust

Trotsky predicted the extermination of the Jewish population of Europe by Nazi Germany in December 1938: 'It is possible to imagine without difficulty what awaits the Jews at the mere outbreak of the future world war. But even without war the next development of world reaction signifies with certainty the *physical extermination of the Jews*'.[49] The small Fourth International group in Belgium warned the Jewish population that the Nazis would make their threats

---

46   Mandel 1971b, p. 38.
47   Ibid.
48   Mandel 1971b, p. 39.
49   Trotsky 1945.

come true, which many did not want to believe at the time.[50] But for decades, little on this subject could be found in Ernest Mandel's writings.

His first known publication dealing with this question was a newspaper article from 1946, 'La question juive au lendemain de la deuxieme guerre mondiale'.[51] Mandel was 22 or 23 at the time of writing. As with Isaac Deutscher and many others, his starting point is the incomprehensibility of the scale of the catastrophe, the strain on the human imagination that it poses: 'Human reason refuses to admit that material interests pursued with cold calculation caused the extermination of these countless defenceless human beings'.[52]

Even so, Mandel places the fate of the European Jews in the general context of the crisis of capitalism and compares it to other horrors of the war and of the immediate post-war period – for example, the dropping of the nuclear bombs on Hiroshima and Nagasaki by the United States, British brutality against the masses of India, and the expulsion of the German population from east European countries. He holds 'all governments of the world' partly responsible for the Shoah because they failed to help the Jewish people. In addition to the millions of murdered Jews, there were '60 million victims of the imperialist war'.

Mandel argues that responsibility in a higher sense lies with capitalism in its epoch of decline: 'The barbaric treatment of the Jews by Hitler's imperialism only carried the usual barbaric methods of the imperialism of our epoch to extremes ... Far from being a solitary example or antithetical to the destiny of humanity, the tragedy of the Jews shows other peoples their future destiny in the event that capitalism continues its decline at the present rate. Capitalism is responsible for the tragic fate of the Jews'.[53]

Thanks to good luck and energy, the young Mandel had escaped the Nazi henchmen several times. For him, the Nazi crimes, including the murder of millions of innocent and defenceless Jewish people, were primarily an expression of the death agony of a doomed social order, i.e. imperialist capitalism. He regarded them as comparable to a series of other contemporary symptoms of barbarism. The young internationalist revolutionary from a Jewish background focuses his argumentation almost exclusively on denouncing the capitalist system. In the light of much later debates in Germany on the 'contextualisation' and 'relativisation' of Nazi crimes for the purpose of exonerating the German national conscience, the deficits of Mandel's position are striking. A prognosis

---

50   See subchapter 1.2.
51   See Mandel 1946.
52   Mandel 1946, p. 1.
53   Mandel 1946, pp. 2–3.

near the end of the aforementioned article that in retrospect seems utterly misguided underlines this impression: 'it is not only possible but even probable that a US-American fascist movement would surpass the brutality of Nazi antisemitism in its technical 'perfection'. If the next decade does not see a proletarian revolution in the United States, it will have hecatombs in store for US Jewry that will dwarf the horrors of Auschwitz and Maidanek'.[54]

Mandel's essay on Trotsky's theory of fascism, written much later in 1969 and discussed in the previous subchapter, examined the social causes and class character of fascism and National Socialism. It also addressed the failure of the main tendencies of the workers' movement (Social Democrats and Communists) to stop the Nazi Party's ascension to power. The function of fascism, according to Mandel, is the destruction of the organised workers' movement – by accomplishing this, it eliminates all obstacles from its path to another murderous world war and monstrous crimes. The extermination of the European Jews is not explicitly mentioned anywhere in this text of Mandel's. The introductory words only contain a general allusion to the magnitude of Nazi crimes and the historical turning point they marked:

> A new phenomenon suddenly appeared that seemed sharply to reverse a long-term historical trend of 'progress'. The shock experienced by attentive observers was all the greater because this historical reversal was accompanied by the even more direct brutality of physical violence against individuals. Historical and individual fate suddenly became identical for thousands of human beings, and later, for millions. Not only were social classes defeated and not only did political parties succumb, but the existence, the physical survival, of broad human groups suddenly became problematical.[55]

Ten years later, Mandel wrote a chapter entitled 'Fascism' in *Trotsky. A Study in the Dynamic of His Thought*. The 14 pages in question speak of the 'barbarism' of fascism and of the deadly threat it poses to large groups of people and to 'human civilisation' as a whole. The 'final solution of the Jewish question', however, is not mentioned.[56]

Mandel explains 'fascism' as a phenomenon to which all capitalist-imperialist countries are predisposed and that can re-emerge under certain sociopolitical conditions. He rejects any emphasis on this or that national specificity

---

54   Mandel 1946, p. 11.
55   Mandel 1971b, p. 9.
56   Mandel 1979e, p. 88 et seq.

as 'inappropriate' in this context. Norman Geras commented on the irritating impression this attitude can make even on people who largely share the viewpoints of 'Trotsky's theory of fascism': 'While I have, on one level, no quarrel with this, it is nevertheless an optic likely to discourage attention towards a certain specificity of German National Socialism and one of its policies'.[57]

Norman Geras's contribution, which I discuss in more detail below, is a useful starting point for a critical reflection on Ernest Mandel's political legacy, especially in relation to Germany's historical experiences and the ways in which these are addressed. The influence that Mandel and his writings exerted on the political orientation of Fourth International members in Germany, who until 1986 were organised in the Gruppe Internationale Marxisten – GIM, was significant. GIM's political education on this topic focused largely on the failure of the traditional mass organisations and parties of the workers' movement, the ADGB, SPD and KPD (especially their leaderships) in the face of the growing Nazi movement and Hitler's ascension to power, and on the need for a united front, on the one hand, and the link between anti-fascist struggle and a revolutionary socialist perspective on the other. In the socio-political analysis of 'fascism', the grave differences between the Italian original and German Nazism played virtually no role. Specifically dealing with the crimes of the Nazis was seen as a task that had been sufficiently dealt with by other political currents (especially left-liberal ones and those linked to 'official' Communism), who in turn refused to draw the right conclusions from the failures of the official workers' movement.

Later writings by Ernest Mandel demonstrate a greater awareness of the uniqueness ('singularity') of Nazi crimes and an increasing effort to differentiate without abandoning the original line of reasoning: Mandel's charges are still aimed against the capitalist system, the defence of working-class interests and the socialist perspective. The relevant statements in his book on the *Meaning of the Second World War* (1986) testify both to the evolution and to the continuity of his position.[58]

The characteristic feature of Mandel's attempt to explain World War II – which, significantly, begins with the terse statement: 'Capitalism implies competition' – is that he views it as a combination of different wars: an inter-imperialist world war for global hegemony and zones of influence in the image of World War I; a just war of self-defence by the Soviets against Nazi aggression and against the Nazis' attempt to turn their country into a colony and

---

57   Geras 2017, p. 143.
58   See Mandel 1986d.

destroy the remaining gains of the October Revolution (state ownership of the means of production, planned economy and foreign trade monopoly); a just anti-imperialist liberation war by the Chinese masses, which also led to a break with capitalism; the equally just anti-colonial liberation wars of various Asian peoples for national self-determination, some of which spilled over into a break with the capitalist world system (e.g. Indochina); and a just war of national liberation in the countries occupied by Nazi Germany, which in Yugoslavia and Albania also led to a break with capitalism, while civil wars pointing in a similar direction broke out in Greece and northern Italy.[59]

This perspective involves a clear dissociation from the kind of 'anti-fascism' that conceals the class interests of an imperialist bourgeoisie (or reactionary bureaucracy) which aims to limit the scope for working class action and political confidence and use it for its own special interests. Mandel provides quotations to prove that leading US politicians, for instance, were conscious of their imperialist motives and, contrary to the official anti-fascist proclamations, acknowledged them. Secretary of State Cordell Hull, for example, said in 1942: 'Leadership towards a new system of international relationships in trade and other economic affairs will devolve largely upon the United States because of our great economic strength. We should assume this leadership, and the responsibility that goes with it, primarily for reasons of pure national self-interest'.[60]

An obvious problem is the prioritisation of the various issues. Ernest Mandel's multifaceted and stimulating economic, social, political and military-strategic analysis of the Second World War, based on a wealth of material, contains only six and a half pages on the Holocaust in the German edition of 172 pages, excluding notes and references [five pages in the English-language edition of 164 pages sans notes and references – Translator]. Compared to his earlier writings, one notices a more multifaceted explanatory approach incorporating various social, ideological and psychological factors against the backdrop of the death throes of the capitalist system. In Mandel's view, racism, including the exterminatory pseudo-biological racism of the Nazis, ultimately stems from the guilty conscience and attempted self-justification of colonialists, exploiters and looters. Ernest Mandel also speaks here of the mass murder of six million European Jews as a 'unique' crime, yet without justifying why he

---

59 See Mandel 1986d, p. 45.
60 Mandel 1986d, p. 16. Mandel also cites the following statement by Robert E. Sherwood, who wrote about Roosevelt in 1950: 'The decision he [Roosevelt] made in 1940, on his own authority and without clarion calls, involved the commitment of the United States to the assumption of responsibility for nothing less than the leadership of the world'.

has adopted this term. In the same section, he once again focuses on situating the Jewish genocide within the history and perspective of heinous crimes committed in pursuit of capitalist and imperialist interests.[61] From the point of view of later debates on the German left, the notion that Mandel is 'contextualising' or even 'relativising' Nazi crimes might seem like an obvious reproach.

In 1990, an essay by Ernest Mandel, based on a 1988 lecture, was published in French: 'Prémisses matérielles, sociales et idéologiques du génocide nazi'.[62] In the text, Mandel refers to the Jewish genocide as the 'ultimate expression so far of the destructive tendencies existing in bourgeois society'.[63] Mandel rejects the alleged 'incomprehensibility' of the Holocaust, which he discards as a mystification that can only harm the anti-fascist struggle. Although in his view the biological racism of the Nazis does underlie the Holocaust, he considers this racism to be a product of the ideological dehumanisation of oppressed peoples by their oppressors and typical of imperialism. And in general, he regards the combination of extreme technical rationality and perfection in detail with complete irrationality of a whole as typical of capitalism. Overall, the essay shows a further refinement of Mandel's position: for example, he addresses the role of mentality when linking Germany's conformist and conservative tendencies to the belated abolition of serfdom and other particularities of German history.[64]

The German version of Mandel's book on the *Meaning of the Second World War*, published in 1991, contained the text 'Zum Historikerstreit' as an appendix. There, Mandel addressed the 'historical revisionism' of Ernst Nolte and his co-thinkers: 'On the historians' dispute. Origin, essence, uniqueness and repeatability of the Third Reich'.[65] In terms of theory, it is Mandel's 'last word' on the topic – we will therefore assess it below. Essentially, the position he espouses there is the same as in the essay published slightly earlier on the 'Material, social and ideological preconditions of the Nazi genocide'.

Norman Geras notes the 'formal resemblance' of Mandel's 'contextual relativisation' of the Holocaust with the apologetic relativisation by conservative German historical revisionists.[66] This formal resemblance indeed exists –

---

61   Mandel 1986d, pp. 92–3.
62   [See Mandel 2020b for the English translation – Translator.]
63   Ibid.
64   Ibid. Mandel does mention that the Nazis had 'several million accomplices', but stresses in the same sentence that 'the Germans strictly speaking doubtless [made up] no more than 50 to 60 per cent of the total'.
65   [An English translation has now been made available by the International Institute for Research and Education: see Mandel 2020c – Translator.]
66   See Geras 2017, pp. 155–6.

and this despite the fact that Mandel polemicises against the German apologists, denounces the conformism of the collaborators and confidants, and attempts to clarify his own position by emphasising the total and modern industrial character of the mass murder of the European Jewish population. However, a more accurate judgement of Mandel's position is only possible by relating his motives to his line of argument.

Nolte's and Mandel's motives are of course diametrically opposed. Like Rosa Luxemburg, who felt 'at home wherever in the world there are clouds, birds and human tears' and who wanted to reserve 'no special corner' in her heart for the suffering of the Jewish people (letter from prison to Mathilde Wurm), Ernest Mandel, the Belgian national who described himself as a 'Flemish internationalist of Jewish origin', was concerned with universality and general emancipation.[67] Perhaps in part because he felt a special affinity with the German workers' movement and its extreme left wing, his complete works leave us with the impression of an irritating under-examination of the mass murder of European Jews and Roma and Sinti committed by Hitler's 'Third Reich' – i.e. by the German state machinery with the complicity and passive acquiescence of a large part of the German population. What also appears underexamined are the specific causes of antisemitism and the necessity for all German social emancipation to ruthlessly account for the historical role of one's own nation. Mandel largely places the burden of this responsibility on the German ruling class and its political administrators.

It seems to me, however, that the liberation-oriented universalism of Rosa Luxemburg and Ernest Mandel paradoxically also draws attention to the fact that, for example, Polish Jews and potential or actual victims of imperialist or specifically German oppression cannot be held to the same standards as members of 'oppressor nations' (in Lenin's sense, who insisted that the nationalism of members of imperialist nations and that of oppressed nations be judged differently – a position shared by Mandel), especially members of the German nation.[68] Nevertheless, this distinction contains an element of invalidity precisely because of the claim to universality made by the likes of Rosa Luxemburg and Ernest Mandel. The claim implies, after all, the need to formulate positions that are correct and apply to all leftists equally, i.e. also to German leftists.

Mandel opens his examination of Nolte and other German 'historical revisionists' by denouncing their attempts to deny the uniqueness ('singularity') of

---

67   See Luxemburg 1978, p. 180. As for Mandel, the blurb on the inside cover of the German version of his book *Trotsky as Alternative* (Berlin: Dietz, 1992) states that he 'describes himself as a Flemish internationalist of Jewish origin'.

68   See Lenin 1914, chapter 4 and Mandel 1995a, p. 137.

Nazi crimes: 'The unsuccessful attempt by Professor Ernst Nolte ... to relativize this uniqueness has nothing to do with science. It cannot stand up to a minimum of critical research and evaluation of sources. It is an ideological-political project to at least partially absolve the German power structures before and during the Third Reich from these terrible crimes, or when their complicity cannot be completely denied, to plead mitigating circumstances'.[69] Mandel condemns Nolte's attempts to portray the Jews, the Communists and the workers' movement as being the cause, or at least partly responsible, for Nazi crimes. Even if Nazi Germany had not exterminated the Jews but treated them like prisoners of war or 'civilian internees' (Nolte's term) because, after all, Jewish civilian organisations had 'declared war' on Germany, only absurd constructions could provide a 'semblance of justification' (again, Nolte's term). According to Mandel, Ernst Nolte and Joachim Fest (the latter with his talk of the Gulag archipelago as the 'logical and factual precursor' to Auschwitz) are guilty of obvious anachronisms, for example when they omit that Hitler's racist biologism, antisemitism and insane determination to annihilate entire sections of the population had emerged long before the crimes committed under Stalin, and that there is no allusion whatsoever to any 'fear of Bolshevism' in Hitler's *Mein Kampf*. In reality, precisely because of his racist antisemitism, Hitler thought that the Jews possessed little ability to defend themselves, and he considered the Bolshevik-led Soviet Russia to be a 'colossus on feet of clay' that posed no threat to Germany whatsoever. In Mandel's view, Hitler instrumentalised bourgeois and petty-bourgeois fear of Bolsheviks and socialists for propaganda purposes, but was not driven by it himself. He also considers the German historical revisionists' contention that Marxists strive for the 'annihilation of entire social classes' absurd – as if one could compare the struggle for a society without classes to the crimes of the Nazis and their goal of physically annihilating entire sections of the population. Mandel reminds us of ruling class extermination campaigns against revolting slaves, peasants, and proletarians – for instance, the murder of 20,000 unarmed prisoners after the defeat of the Paris Commune. For him, the assertion of a 'disproportionate' participation of Jews in revolutionary movements is pure sophism (and a veiled equivalent of the delusion of a 'Jewish world conspiracy'), thus offering a certain degree of understanding for the antisemitic desire for extermination.[70]

Against Nolte and his ilk, Mandel defends the difference between revolutionary violence, which is motivated by liberation from exploitation and

---

69   Mandel 2020c.
70   Ibid.

oppression, and counter-revolutionary violence, which is aimed at averting the 'danger' that the oppressing and exploiting classes are disempowered and is based on the fear of losing privileges. This is precisely the context in which Mandel places fascism and Nazism: 'It was not "fear of Bolshevism" and "Bolshevik hatred" that stood at the cradle of Nazi ideology and practice, but hatred and fear of socialism, fear and hatred of progress, if not a fear of reason and hateful rejection of reason all together. In this context, fascism and National Socialism appear as the terminus of a long extremely conservative, counter-revolutionary tradition, development and practice'.[71]

By classifying fascism and National Socialism in this way, Mandel also rejects the idea that he is trying to divert attention from the Holocaust. Rather, he argues, it is impossible to fully grasp the causes of the Nazi crimes without linking them to the interests of the bourgeois ruling class in an analysis that takes many factors into account:

> These considerations are not marginal to the 'historians' dispute' controversy, nor are they distractions from the real issue of the causes of Nazi tyranny that culminated in the genocide of the European Jews. An investigation into the causes of this violence cannot in any way ignore the ideological, mass and individual psychological factors among the chain of causes. It misses its goal if it excludes, or relegates to a general background, the defence of material interests and social power by the ruling classes and its most important factions.[72]

This time, Mandel certainly addresses the complicity of a large number of Germans (he speaks of about one million) in the mass murder of European Jews. He warns that the importance of material resources should not be underestimated – in his view, earlier and later examples of mass extermination only lacked these industrial means to match the scale of the Nazi crimes. Mandel's argument considers the mentalities that made the execution of Nazi crimes possible, distinguishing between the motives of fanatical Nazis and those of fellow travellers. He mainly criticises the latter for their conservatism and conformism, which, according to him, are also driving the modern German historical revisionists. It is precisely the intensification of their values – fatherland, fulfilment of duty, and so on – that contains the potential for the emergence of a regime such as the Nazi dictatorship. The historical responsibility for the

---

71   Ibid.
72   Ibid.

Nazi crimes, whose real prelude was the German nationalism and imperialism of World War I, lies with state-loyalist and nationalist attitudes – not with their antithesis, i.e. revolutionary and internationalist sentiments and the inclination to dissent, revolt and rebel against exploitation and oppression. If the latter attitude prevails, crimes like those of the Nazis are made impossible.

Appeals to the 'rule of law' or claiming that political radicalism of every kind should be blamed obscures examples of brutal violence against rebellious colonial populations committed by states organised under the 'rule of law' (e.g. the French Fourth Republic in Algeria, the US in Vietnam, etc.).[73]

Aware what accusations his line of argument could attract, Mandel therefore poses the question himself: 'Does any attempt to historically and sociologically explain fascism in general and the Nazi dictatorship particular necessarily have an apologetic aspect, tending to relativise the responsibility of Hitler, of the Nazis, the Third Reich in general and its rulers for all the crimes committed?'[74]

His answer is: 'This depends on what the content of this "historicization" is'. As regards the possible content of historicisation, Mandel first of all distances himself from historical fatalism, including of 'vulgar Marxist' provenance. Social classes, political leaderships, organisations or individuals who act under absolute coercion and therefore have no other choice can of course not be held responsible for anything. However, in certain decisive years and periods (e.g. 1914, 1918–23, 1930–33), there were demonstrably always different options and different possible courses of action. Therefore, according to Mandel, the question of culpability does arise. He argues that an investigation of historical causes benefits the struggle against similar phenomena, while the thesis of inexplicability makes it more difficult: 'it is precisely the thesis that the Hitler regime was characterized by total irrationality, that the human mind is incapable of grasping and explaining the causes and extent of the Nazi crimes, that leads to conclusions which make the fight against fascism more difficult'.[75]

In view of the enormity of Nazi crimes, Mandel considers hatred understandable – however, hatred makes blind and makes it difficult to produce a maximum of intellectual weaponry in the struggle against fascism. Social scientific knowledge is part of this intellectual armoury, and scientific research is useful for the social struggle when it obeys exclusively scientific rules and is not guided by 'partisan' rules. The 'womb that gave birth to this beast' is indeed still

---

73   Ibid.
74   Ibid.
75   Ibid.

fertile.[76] Mandel illustrates this with the brutal practices of military dictatorships in Argentina and Brazil at the time and the absurd antisemitic conspiracy theories of Argentine generals, according to which the Montonero guerrillas were part of an international conspiracy to establish a 'second Jewish state' in Patagonia.[77]

It is in this section that Mandel substantiates the thesis of the 'singularity' of Nazi crimes. Of particular interest is the way in which he associates them – in the same breath, as it were – with other terrible extermination campaigns, situating them in the historical context of colonialism and capitalist imperialism:

> Here again we come up against the problem of the so-called singularity of National Socialist violence, of a more precise definition of this concept and its limitations. As we said, the systematic murder of six million European Jews simply because of their descent is without doubt unique in history. But it cannot be detached from the nature of the Third Reich. In its essence and in its self-conception, this was a fundamentally authoritarian, terrorist, imperialist state which, using ideological justifications, institutionalized and elevated to state doctrine the systematic use of violence against its enemies – real, supposed or alleged – at home and abroad.[78]

In a footnote, he adds:

> In purely numerical terms, the murder of the indigenous peoples of Central American exceeds the murder of the European Jews. Between the landing of Cortez and 1564, the population of Mexico and the Central American areas fell by 8.5 million. Only 1.5 million Indigenous people remained alive. The ratio is worse than for European Jews. However, there was no formal decision by the Spanish gentlemen to exterminate all indigenous men, women and children. But for the eight million innocent victims this was neither consolation nor a lesser evil.[79]

---

76   [A reference to a Bertolt Brecht's 1941 play *The Resistible Rise of Arturo Ui*, which its author intended as a satirical allegory to Hitler's ascension to power. The final monologue contains the sentence 'The belly is still fertile from which the foul beast sprang' – Translator.]
77   Ibid.
78   Ibid.
79   Ibid.

That is undeniable. Nevertheless, it is hard not to feel that one might find this quotation in the kind of literature that seeks to heap up historical examples of terrible crimes in order to relativise those of Nazi Germany. Such examples belong to the arsenal of talking points that serve to exonerate the German national conscience: The Young Turks' mass murder of Armenians; the British colonialists' concentration camps and their brutality against the Boer civilian population in South Africa; the exterminatory brutality of the Conquistadores and Spanish grandees against the Indians, etc. Certainly, Mandel is not trying to get at this. For him, the 'uniqueness' of Nazi crimes 'cannot be detached from the nature of the Third Reich. In its essence and in its self-conception, this was a fundamentally authoritarian, terrorist, imperialist state which, using ideological justifications, institutionalized and elevated to state doctrine the systematic use of violence against its enemies – real, supposed or alleged – at home and abroad'.[80]

Drawing on Trotsky and Nicos Poulantzas, Mandel characterises this type of regime as one of institutionalised permanent civil war in which one side is deprived, at least legally, of the possibility to defend itself, and where the victims of violence are bound hand and foot.

According to Mandel, the development that led to the mass murder of European Jews was not unique at least in its nuclear form. Since the end of the nineteenth century, it had appeared in many imperialist states, and the extermination of indigenous populations in the course of pre-capitalist colonialism had already given rise to the ideological dehumanisation of the victims.[81] But why did the Nazi empire come into being in Germany? why was the crime of the Holocaust, 'unique' despite all the comparisons one might make, committed there?

> The specificity of modern German history lies in the combination between the failure of a radical bourgeois (national-democratic) revolution as a result of the defeats of the German Peasants' War and of the Revolution of 1848 as well as the above-average growth of German big industry and big banks after German unification in 1871. This combination led on the one hand to a belated but extremely dynamic penetration of German capital into the world market. German imperialism was pressing from the outset for a new division of the existing spheres of influence. On the other hand, it resulted in a specific structure of the bourgeois state,

---

80   Ibid.
81   Ibid.

in which, compared to Great Britain, France and Italy, not to mention the USA, the specific weight of pre-capitalist strata and mentalities, specifically the East Elbian Junkers and the Prussian military caste (which played a decisive role in the foundation of the Reich) was disproportionate.[82]

While imperialist militarism is a product of modern capitalism rather than of pre-capitalist semi-feudal phenomena, Mandel argues that particular forms of imperialism and militarism are linked to their concrete history and prehistory. With reference to Fritz Fischer's *Griff nach der Weltmacht* (1964), Mandel argues that the particularly aggressive tendency of German imperialism had already become apparent during World War I. There is, according to him, a continuity from Wilhelmine Germany's aspirations for global domination to that of Nazi Germany.[83]

Mandel reminds us that Eastern Europe, especially Russia, had been the most important object of external aggression from the outset, which alone renders the thesis of the 'preventive' character of Nazi aggression against the Soviet Union untenable. This is further supported by the fact that neither the Wehrmacht, in the course of its advance on Soviet territory, nor anyone else ever found a single document remotely hinting at Soviet plans to attack Germany. Moreover, as is well known, the Soviet leadership did not expect a German attack and was extremely ill-prepared.

However, the quest for world domination was not limited to Germany but a general phenomenon of imperialism and late capitalism that demonstrably applied to Britain, Japan and the US as well. According to Mandel, distinct power relations between classes and the special features of the respective ruling classes gave this aspiration its specific national character. However, the general tendency of the imperialist age, including in its contemporary imperialist phase, is the creation of the possibility of a massive military build-up in a short period of time, and the latent readiness for military expansion as a means of economic expansion (with state arms orders at the same time counteracting the long-term stagnant and depressive tendency). Once again, Mandel dissociates himself from the 'relativisers' who, invoking such general tendencies, deny the uniqueness of Nazi crimes. In his view, their theses are scientifically untenable and have been conclusively refuted.[84]

The needs and apparatuses of the ruling classes are crucial for the formation of particular mentalities that predominate in certain historical periods:

---

82   Ibid.
83   Ibid.
84   Ibid.

There is no doubt that belief in authority, meekness, blind obedience, nationalist myopia and lack of moral courage prevailed among the German ruling classes, and among the middle classes they ideologically dominated. This, in turn, reflected the entire historical misery of the German bourgeoisie since the 16th century, even though an opposite, minority tendency also existed among German liberals and to some extent among Catholics. In Italy, where the popular attitude towards 'state order' was rather negative (after centuries of foreign rule) and where people were used to disobedience and scepticism towards the law, 85 per cent of the Jews survived.[85]

In the anglophone countries and especially in France, mentalities have been shaped by successful bourgeois revolutions and are therefore imbued with suspicion towards rulers and state apparatuses. However, an authoritarian current that is loyal to the state and glorifies war has been gaining ground: 'Since the Watergate affair and Thatcher's rise to power, at the latest, there has been a marked increase in a belief in authority, blind obedience, disdain, if not contempt, for democratic freedoms, and a growing willingness to sacrifice those on the altar of "state security" and "necessity".[86]

It appears that for Mandel, the crucial motivation for wanting to apply certain limits to the notion of the 'uniqueness' of the Nazi crimes and the Holocaust is the possibility that similar events might occur again – precisely because of the crisis-prone tendencies of contemporary capitalism. He wants us to be prepared so we can prevent it from happening. However, he formulates the pertinent conditional prognosis much more cautiously than he did in the 1946 text quoted at the beginning of this article:

> It can by no means be completely excluded that over the course of deepening structural crises of the late capitalist mode of production and increasing deterioration of the 'normal' accumulation of capital, there will be a qualitative change of the relationship of forces, to the disadvantage of the wage dependent class. Severe defeats of the labour movement and of the 'new social movements' could enable irrational, fanatical political adventurers to again seize power in major imperialist states.[87]

Mandel concludes:

---

85   Ibid.
86   Ibid.
87   Ibid.

Our thesis of the repeatability of extremely violent dictatorships in late capitalism, though possibly not in forms identical to those of fascism and National Socialism, is to be understood as a call to vigilance and resistance when there is still time and opportunity to do so. In this sense, it is a weapon for an effective struggle for democracy and human rights. An unhistorical approach to the appearance of the Third Reich, which makes its singularity absolute, makes it difficult to fight against renewed danger and against the continuing trend towards a relapse into barbarism.[88]

The Holocaust is thus a 'singularity', but its 'singularity' must not be 'absolutised'! It is difficult to say whether Mandel ever really adopted the concept of the 'singularity' of Nazi crimes with inner conviction.

As part of his conclusion, Mandel refers to his own study of the history of the crime novel. In that text, he highlighted the increasing criminalisation of late bourgeois society and the growing entanglement of the legal and illegal sectors of capital, as well as that of the legal state apparatuses (especially the military, police and secret services) with the illegal activities of right-wing extremists.[89] This interesting study (motivated primarily by Mandel's avowed passion for crime novels), which relates the different levels of development of bourgeois society to the plot patterns of popular crime novels in the respective periods, concludes with a general indictment of the capitalist social order. It underlines how important it was for Mandel to propose the rejection of capitalist class society as a political conclusion in all topics he dealt with:

> The history of the crime story is a social history, for it appears intertwined with the history of bourgeois society itself. If the question is asked why it should be reflected in the history of a specific literary genre, the answer is: because the history of bourgeois society is also that of property and of the negation of property, in other words, crime; because the history of bourgeois society is also the growing, explosive contradiction between individual needs or passions and mechanically imposed patterns of social conformism; because bourgeois society in and of itself breeds crime, originates in crime, and leads to crime; perhaps because bourgeois society is, when all is said and done, a criminal society?[90]

---

88 Ibid.

89 See Mandel 1987a, p. 105 et seq.

90 [Mandel 1987a, p. 135. The German version of Mandel's text, quoted in the original German-language edition of this book, contains the additional words: 'Bourgeois society was

If bourgeois society 'leads to crime on an ever-larger industrial scale', then this is reminiscent of the two essential arguments Mandel uses to substantiate the 'singularity' of Nazi crimes: that the murder of European Jews was perpetrated on an industrial scale and by industrial means, and that it sprang from an irrational desire to exterminate an entire people (a desire to exterminate that eventually turned into a desire to self-destruct). For Mandel, the combination of rationality in detail, on the one hand, and irrationality in relation to the whole is, in any case, characteristic of the capitalist mode of production in general. The conclusion he dispassionately draws from his preoccupation with the social history of the crime novel indicates how difficult it must have been for him to formulate a convincing justification for the 'singularity' of Nazi crimes, which he felt compelled to do in the context of the 'historian's dispute' and the 'revisionism debate' in Germany.

Norman Geras criticises Mandel's position, even if he broadly agrees with it. He considers Mandel's later expositions on Nazi crimes and the Holocaust a 'more qualified and enriched' view than offered in the first 1946 article on the subject, but the 'same weaknesses in one way or another were to remain'.[91] As noted earlier, Mandel himself wrote in 1946 on the mass murder of European Jews that the human mind 'refuses to admit that material interests pursued with cold calculation caused the extermination of these countless defenceless human beings'. His reflections, however, are aimed at dispelling the impression that this horrific reality is inaccessible to the critical mind. In his opinion, the tragedy can be explained with the tools of Marxist analysis. He views the horrifying crimes as an expression of capitalist imperialism and of the intensification of this system's crisis. To prevent a repeat or worse, the system must be overthrown. These are Mandel's essential lessons from the Holocaust. They remain unchanged in his later contributions, even when embedded in a more differentiated analysis, and even when enriched by the adoption of the element of 'singularity' and a stronger emphasis on the irrational – for instance, in *The Meaning of the Second World War*, where the 'uniqueness' of Nazi crimes is alluded to for the first time, albeit without further explanation, and most clearly in his 'last word' on the subject written on the occasion of the German historians' dispute.

Geras cites three opposite pairs of statements to clarify what he disagrees with. The 'destruction of the Jews of Europe is alternatively "singular" or

---

born out of violence, it constantly reproduces violence and appears to be permeated by violence. It originates in crime and leads – on an ever-larger industrial scale – to crime', our translation – Translator.]

91   Geras 2017, p. 143.

"unique"'; 'rationally explicable' or 'beyond comprehension'; it is 'the product of capitalism and imperialism' or 'due to some other combination of factors'.[92]

In his 1946 contribution, Mandel clearly chooses the first option in all three cases (later he takes a kind of 'intermediate position' at least for the first pair of opposites). Geras believes that this is wrong, that one must take a position somewhere between these poles.[93] Many people, including Marxists, have commented on the uniqueness of the catastrophe, the rupture in the history of civilisation, and the incomprehensibility of the Holocaust. Geras quotes Isaac Deutscher, the best-known Trotsky biographer:

> The fury of Nazism, which was bent on the unconditional extermination of every Jewish man, woman and child within its reach, passes the comprehension of a historian, who tries to uncover the motives of human behaviour and to discern the interests behind the motives. Who can analyse the motives and the interests behind the enormities of Auschwitz? ... [W]e are confronted here by a huge and ominous mystery of the degeneration of the human character that will forever baffle and terrify mankind.[94]

In Geras's opinion – and a wealth of contemporary literature contains similar reflections – the Holocaust cannot be explained completely. The decision to exterminate the Jews and the genocidal implementation of this decision cannot be totally elucidated and reappraised by social-scientific analysis (even if one takes into account 'mentalities') and political critique. There remains a residue that is not accessible to critical mind. Geras approvingly quotes Primo Levi, who also commented in this sense on the deficits of the common explanatory models: 'They are reductive; not commensurate with, nor proportionate to, the facts that need explaining ... I cannot avoid the impression of a general atmosphere of uncontrolled madness that seems to me to be unique in society'.[95] Levi preferred historians who 'confessed to *not understanding*' such a 'furious hatred'.[96]

The point Geras is aiming at by invoking the 'incomprehensible residue' is a far cry from Hannah Arendt's 'banality' of evil. He is talking about the frenzy of

---

92   Geras 2017, p. 142.
93   Ibid.
94   Geras 2017, p. 140. Geras takes this quotation from Isaac Deutscher's essay 'The Jewish Tragedy and the Historian' (in *The Non-Jewish Jew*).
95   Geras 2017, p. 150.
96   Ibid.

the mob, where individuals can commit the most horrible acts of violence with impunity. He means the Nazi hordes unrestrainedly brutalising the defenceless and becoming intoxicated from doing so. He means the soldiers and visitors who do not want to miss the cruel execution of prisoners. By elaborating what he means, Geras broadens the field of comprehension. His scepticism about the possibility of explaining everything completely thus proves to be a productive scepticism. It is not certain whether Mandel would have rejected his argument – more likely, he would have tried to incorporate it into his own explanatory paradigm. Nonetheless, as we shall see, there remains a methodological problem that points beyond what has been discussed here and concerns 'Mandel's Marxism' as a whole.

Early in his contribution, Geras quotes Trotsky's prophecy of December 1938 that we mentioned at the beginning of this article: 'It is possible to imagine without difficulty what awaits the Jews at the mere outbreak of the future world war. But even without war the next development of world reaction signifies with certainty the *physical extermination of the Jews*'.[97]

With certainty the physical extermination of the Jews! Geras highlights the astonishing aspect about this prophecy. Few contemporaries foresaw the mass murder of the European Jews. Many Jews did not believe that such a thing could happen and thought of relevant Nazi propaganda as a series of exaggerations, typical of the demagogy of extremist political tendencies. What is it that gave Trotsky such clear-sightedness? Geras turns against the unconditional rationalism with which Mandel, after enumerating a whole series of backgrounds and causes for the Nazis' rise to power and their barbaric policies, claims in *The Meaning of the Second World War*: 'The Holocaust only comes at the end of this long causal chain. But it can and must be explained through it. Indeed, those who understood the chain were able to foresee it'.[98]

This comment boasts the pride of the Marxist intellectual who regards himself as standing on Trotsky's shoulders – one who leads a political tendency whose theory and programme interprets reality correctly and can therefore foresee events of great consequence. Although this tendency is very far from having achieved any of its goals, its potential effectiveness is proven by its ability to grasp social reality in its entirety. Geras calls this the 'totalizing ambition' of Mandel's approach, which at that point turns into absurdity:

> Attempting to 'recover' the heterogeneity in the explanation by treating everything it as part of one unified chain, and then imagining that Trot-

---

97   Ibid.
98   Mandel 1986d, p. 92.

sky's 1938 prediction might really have been based on being able to foresee all the individual links in it *and* their connection. I cannot take the suggestion seriously. Especially not, remembering the context of general unpreparedness and incredulity vis-à-vis the Jewish calamity as it first loomed and then became a reality. Trotsky would have needed to be superhuman to have had this much understanding in advance.[99]

Of course, Geras does not believe that Trotsky only made his prediction out of some 'dark foreboding'. Naturally, his forecast was informed by all the elements of Marxist analysis and political insight known from his writings. However, according to Geras, an additional element of intuition was necessary that was based on Trotsky's personal experience. Geras quotes from the passage about the Jewish pogroms in Trotsky's 1905 book about the Russian revolution:

> [T]he gang rushes through the town, drunk on vodka and the smell of blood ... Everything is allowed to him [the member of the gang], he is capable of anything, he is the master of property and honor, of life and death. If he wants to, he can throw an old woman out of a third-floor window together with a grand piano, he can smash a chair against a baby's head, rape a little girl while the entire crowd looks on, hammer a nail into a living human body ... He exterminates whole families, he pours petrol over a house, transforms it into a mass of flames, and if anyone attempts to escape, he finishes him off with a cudgel ... There exist no tortures, figments of a feverish brain maddened by alcohol and fury, at which he need ever stop. He is capable of anything, he dares everything ... The victims, bloodstained, charred, driven frantic, still search for salvation within the nightmare. Some put on the bloodstained clothes of people already dead, lie down in a pile of corpses and stay there for a whole day, for two or three days ... Others fall on their knees before the officers, the policemen, the raider, they stretch out their arms, crawl in the dust, kiss the soldiers' boots, beg for mercy. In reply they hear only drunken laughter. 'You wanted freedom? Here, look, this is it'.[100]

'"In these last mocking words", Trotsky says, "is contained the whole infernal morality of the pogrom policy"; and he repeats once again, "capable of anything"'.[101]

---

99   Geras 2017, p. 146.
100   Trotsky 2006, chapter 12.
101   Geras 2017, p. 151.

Geras cites examples from the Nazis' murderous practice that are equally horrific. The Holocaust – or rather, an important aspect of the Holocaust – was already 'inherent' in the Jewish pogroms that Trotsky describes. In Geras's opinion, this experience had to complement Trotsky's cool-headed Marxist analysis in order to induce him to formulate his prophecy.[102]

Mandel was familiar with Trotsky's writings, and he was very familiar with Trotsky's 'What Is National Socialism?', from which Geras quotes some passages. They allude to the symbiosis of the archaic and the modern that is so characteristic of the social, intellectual and psychological background of reactionary mass movements, especially the Fascist and National Socialist movements (an example of the concept of 'unequal and combined development'): 'Everything that should have been eliminated from the national organism in the form of cultural excrement in the course of the normal development of society has now come gushing out from the throat; capitalist society is puking up the undigested barbarism'.[103]

Of course, Mandel would agree with this assessment, and in this general form he has always subscribed to it. However, in 'Material, social and ideological preconditions for the Nazi genocide', as in his other contributions on the subject, Mandel either bypasses the problem of sadistic outbursts of violence or only names fanaticism and the resulting willingness to use violence. He puts the emphasis on conformism and faith in the state:

> One of the factors that allowed the Holocaust to happen was of an ethical order, or if you like has to do with the motivation of behaviour. It took a particular turn of mind: The Holocaust was also the result, not just of the inclination to accept, celebrate, or even worship massive violence, but of the acceptance of the doctrine that the state has the right to require individuals to do things from which they should recoil, and in their hearts do recoil, from the point of view of the fundamental rules of ethics.[104]

I think it very likely that Mandel would have been able to integrate the aspect cited by Geras into his analysis without changing much about it. Psychological and mass psychological aspects were not alien to him as part of analysis, even if he usually contented himself with referencing them and pointing to relevant specialist publications (e.g. in *Marxist Economic Theory*). As regards method,

---

102   Geras 2017, pp. 151–2.
103   Trotsky 1933.
104   Mandel 2020b.

however, Mandel would certainly have strongly disagreed with Geras. A 'total-ising' approach was just as deeply ingrained in his beliefs as was an abhorrence of accepting that certain aspects of reality are fundamentally inexplicable. His confidence depended on his sense of being part of, and embodying, a tradition of thought that is capable of grasping the whole of social reality and its changes – in a reasonable approximation – and of providing a coherent, comprehensive explanatory model, thereby making an indispensable contribution to transforming reality in an emancipatory sense. For Mandel, this motivation was only outweighed by the basic conviction that it was justified to revolt against exploitation, oppression and inhumane conditions. The problems of this approach and the significance of Mandel's pre-scientific basic principles, as it were, are therefore the subject of our following, concluding chapter.

CHAPTER 7

Evaluation and Prospects

1 **Openness and Coherence: A Field of Tension**

In 1980, a conversation between Johannes Agnoli and Ernest Mandel on 'dogma, orthodoxy and the heresy of reality' was published in German language in book form under the emblematic title *Offener Marxismus* (Open Marxism). It is Agnoli who, in this conversation, introduces the concept of 'open Marxism' in distinction to a 'dogmatic' or 'orthodox' Marxism.[1] Mandel, meanwhile, lays claim to being an 'orthodox Marxist' and precisely for that reason not a dogmatist. However, he distances himself from 'official' orthodoxy – which, in his view, has deformed Marxism for apologetic purposes – as well as 'Talmudist' versions of Marxism, which are based only on quotations and textual interpretation. For Mandel, however, Marxism is not just a 'method', but consists essentially of coherent, mutually linked and verifiable substantive statements.

> When I say I am an orthodox Marxist, I mean the following: Marx's theory, which is not a purely economic theory but represents a general theory of the development of human society, which contains in particular a fully elaborated theory of the development of bourgeois society, and which has incorporated significant elements of all social sciences, has an incredibly strong and explosive internal coherence. You cannot randomly remove two or three pillars of this attempt at scientifically explaining the entire history of human societies and believe that the rest still remains intact.[2]

Mandel speaks of the 'openness' of Marxism primarily in terms of the need to absorb and process new experiences, empirical findings and insights. In his view, this enables the further development of Marxist theory. However, if any new findings or insights contradicted the fundamental statements of Marxism, then Marxism as such would have to be abandoned.

> It is necessary to recognise changes in reality, recognise changes in scientific knowledge – including knowledge of the past – and examine in an

---

1 See Mandel 1980a, p. 7.
2 Mandel 1980a, p. 13.

honest and reflective way in each case whether there is an explanation of these changes that is consistent with the basic statements of Marxism or whether there is no such explanation. If there is, then we have 'creatively enriched' open Marxism, as we used to say twenty years ago. If it turns out that this is not possible, then one is free speak of a crisis of Marxism or of abandoning Marxism.[3]

In general, Mandel's work is characterised by a tension between 'openness' and the insistence on 'coherence'.

He was 'open' in dialogue with dissenters and exponents of other tendencies, and he was prepared to assimilate their contributions into his version of Marxist theory. At the same time, their 'coherence' was very important to him. Thus, despite all his agreement with Popper's demand for 'falsifiability' as a criterion for the scientificity of all theory, he also embodied the type of 'system thinker' and 'workers' movement Marxist' that was much more widespread until the nineteen-twenties than it is today. His 'system' is complex and flexible and, precisely for this reason, more or less hermetically sealed off from the influences of other schools of thought. Mandel's extensive knowledge always allowed him to use many concrete examples to substantiate his arguments and, when necessary, relate them to accurately remembered quotations from the 'classics' of Marxism. His lectures were therefore lively, captivating and convincing. Conversely, in controversial discussion, his propensity for piling up heaps of examples could have an 'overwhelming' effect. You might feel that Mandel's generalising conclusions did not exactly fit the examples he offered, or that his interpretation of the examples he provided was somewhat forcibly made to fit his conclusions – and yet you were unable to refute his argument![4]

When submitting written polemics in the context of controversies within his own organisation, the Fourth International, Mandel was prone to using the 'coherence' of the revolutionary Marxist position, as embodied by him, as an argument against those who avowedly – or without admitting it – questioned certain parts of the traditional 'canon' of 'orthodoxy'. Here is an example.

In 1979, a long article by Mandel appeared with the telling title 'The 21 theoretical errors of comrades Clark, Feldman, Horowitz, and Waters'. It ends with a piece of 'good advice' to these leading US opponents in the inner-organisational factional dispute:

---

3 Ibid.
4 Personal memories of the author. See also eyewitness testimony from Helene Jungclas, Hans Peiffer and Helmut Wendler.

We advise them to stop and think, before they continue playing with theory, revising key elements of the Marxist theory of the state and of social classes. Marxist theory is characterized by an extreme degree of inner coherence, which they do not seem to be fully aware of. You loosen a few bricks in the foundations, you take out another couple of bricks in the walls, and before you have time to turn around, the whole house will come crashing down upon your heads.[5]

The international minority tendency led by the majority of the US-SWP (which called itself 'Leninist-Trotskyist') had long attacked Mandel and his close co-thinkers as 'diluters' of Trotskyist orthodoxy. Now the SWP leadership began to question 'pillars' of formerly shared positions, in particular the theory of permanent revolution, but also the concept of political revolution and the notion that there could be no third entity between a 'workers' state' (however bureaucratised) and a 'bourgeois state'. The background to this was a desire to adapt to the Castroist leadership and similar currents, in the hope that a more substantial attempt at international revolutionary organisation could emerge from this. Given this background, it is not surprising that Mandel takes pleasure in reproaching his opponents for deviating from orthodoxy. The emphasis on the coherence of his own edifice of ideas nevertheless springs from deep-seated needs. The cohesion of an organisation that is only imparted to an extremely modest degree by successes in practical action depends not least on the idea that the doctrine that the organisation stands for is in line with social reality and its tendencies of development. On what else can it base its hope of becoming a relevant political factor someday?

Mandel's fight for the integrity and confidence of his small international organisation occasionally led to a shift in the function of certain theoretical perspectives. In theoretical or educational contributions, for example, 'permanent revolution' and 'political revolution' appear as categories that articulate a correct analysis of the relevant social situation. They are therefore indispensable for formulating the right perspectives and orienting revolutionary action. Mandel called these concepts both 'theories' and 'strategies'.[6] However, in the context of factional disputes in the FI or polemics against other, more or less closely related political currents, such categories almost unnoticeably assume a different function. The issue then is to examine processes in which the organisation has little or no direct involvement and in which, in any event,

---

5 See Mandel 1981a, pp. 471–2.
6 See Mandel 1979a, cf. Mandel 1979d, p. 84 et seq.

other political forces play the leading role. If categories from the programmatic 'canon' (such as 'permanent revolution') prove to be inadequate for interpreting such processes, the cohesion of one's own organisation appears to be at stake. In such cases, however, theory serves less as a guide to action than as a means of reassuring oneself about the validity of one's own basic positions. Thus there is a certain 'apologetic' aspect to Mandel's Marxism too.

What is more, this aspect sometimes bore curious fruits. Apparently motivated by the idea that science proves its worth in borderline cases, Mandel vehemently advocated that a state today could only be either a bourgeois state or a 'workers' state', however hideously deformed. In the factional dispute in the FI, Mandel argued that the state that had emerged from the 1979 Sandinista revolution in Nicaragua was a 'workers' state'. However, he also took the view that Cambodia under Pol Pot had been a workers' state 'because' it had not been a bourgeois state. Mandel was also adamant that only a genuine revolutionary or counter-revolutionary rupture could turn a bourgeois state into a workers' state, or a workers' state into a bourgeois state – in his view, an inconspicuous creeping process was not enough to achieve such a feat.[7] On this basis, I find it difficult to argue that the Sandinista electoral defeat against Chamorro was a counter-revolutionary rupture that turned a 'workers' state' into a 'bourgeois state'. On the other hand, Mandel no longer claimed (and no member of the Fourth International claims today) that Nicaragua is still a workers' state.

2   The Revolutionary Potential of Western Europe

Mandel must have developed his considerable 'prognostic confidence' after he had correctly predicted at the beginning of the 1960s, on the basis of his analysis of contemporary capitalism as well as some major tendencies with respect to social forces and struggles, not only the turn to a 'long wave' with a stagnant and depressive tendency, but also a new upsurge of anti-imperialist struggles, anti-bureaucratic struggles, and class struggles in the developed industrial capitalist countries. In all of this, his predictions were vindicated by the actual development. In this way, he gave the members of the Fourth International and a number of activists in the left and workers' movements new hope: the perspective he offered them was that real tendencies in society would soon converge with their ideas of a process of universal emancipation. In particular, the 'dialectic of the three sectors of the world revolution', which may have

---

7   See Mandel 1979d, p. 112.

seemed speculative and over-optimistic to observers in 1963, seemed to begin to materialise in the late '60s. The left in general, and the FI in particular, emerged stronger from this process of radical change.[8]

Reading Mandel's essay 'A Socialist Strategy for Western Europe' from May 1965, one gets the impression, in retrospect, of a thoroughly realistic anticipation of events that were to unfold, and of a well-founded, moderate 'optimism of the deed'.[9]

At that time, Mandel did not rule out a nuclear war, which would amount to the suicide of the ruling classes, any more than he ruled out a catastrophic economic crisis like the one in 1929. However, he considered both scenarios improbable and, in any case, inadequate starting points to base a revolutionary strategy on.[10] On the other hand, the analysis of 'neo-capitalism' (a term Mandel still used at the time), the dynamics of expected class struggles, and the political conditions made it seem likely to him that, if anti-capitalist positions were sufficiently embedded in the vanguard layers of the working class, mass action with an anti-capitalist tendency could be organised. These would show a strong tendency towards self-organisation, up to and including the formation of organs of alternative state power. If pre-revolutionary or revolutionary situations were to develop in this way, then the 'subjective factor' would be decisive – i.e. the degree to which revolutionary socialist ideas were entrenched and influential in the movement.[11] As is well known, the expected surge of movements indeed came 'from below' in the years after he formulated this perspective. In retrospect, Mandel's essay 'On the Current Stage of World Revolution' from May 1976 leaves a completely different impression.[12] By this, I do not mean his general elucidations concerning the course of world history since '1914, if not since 1905', i.e. since 'the objective conditions for world socialism' had been present.[13] Nor am I referring to his account of the different stages of upsurge and downturn in the process of world revolution, his dissociation from the (post-)Stalinist 'two camps theory', and from certain theorisations of colonial revolution. What I mean are Mandel's extrapolations from more recent experiences in western Europe: he starts from the belief that the general direction of the upsurge of class struggles triggered by May '68 and its aftermath will continue. The fall of the western European dictatorships of Greece, Por-

---

8   See Bensaïd 2002, p. 96 et seq.
9   See Mandel 1974c.
10   See Mandel 1974c, p. 1.
11   See Mandel 1974c, p. 11.
12   See Mandel 1976b.
13   Ibid.

tugal and Spain, and especially the experience of the Portuguese revolution of 1974–75, reinforced his conviction. In other countries such as Italy and France ever broader circles of the population still seemed to be longing for a fundamental transformation of social conditions too (in France, it was precisely for this reason that the joint programme of the PS and the PCE, the programme of the 'Union de la Gauche', became so popular in the following years).[14]

In 'On the Current Stage of World Revolution', Mandel argues that the outcome of the global class struggle will ultimately be decided in the US. It will depend on whether the working class of the United States prevents US imperialism from using its weapons of mass destruction against revolutionary advances in other parts of the world. This analysis, Mandel continues, does 'not imply any tendency toward "capitulation to nuclear blackmail" by US imperialism'; rather, it implies that struggles in other parts of the world have an effect on the thoughts and psychology of the masses in the US – as the Vietnam war has shown.

'Only developments that aid the U.S. proletariat in finding the road to mass political action and socialist class consciousness will lead toward a disarmament of U.S. imperialism, through its overthrow. But socialist revolution in the United States is neither assured nor automatic. "Socialism or fascism in the United States" will be tomorrow's concrete expression of the alternative "socialism or barbarism" on a world scale'.[15]

Mandel then speaks of the upsurge of the European proletariat since 1968, whose present full 'unfolding on the Iberian peninsula' (i.e. in 1976) he attributes essentially to the growth of the productive forces, on the one hand, and the growing contradictions of capitalism on the other.[16] Increasingly large sections of the working class vanguard realise that social democracy and Stalinism are bankrupt. The working class has the instinctive desire to run a self-managed, democratically centrally planned economy, and it is capable of doing that. Mandel argues that the forthcoming wave of socialist revolution will take place at a higher level of consciousness than any previous attempts from 1917–23 or after World War II.

> The historic function of the European revolution – and the historic breakthrough of the Fourth International alongside the unfolding of that revolution – will be to decisively modify the *subjective* situation of the two

---

14 Ibid.
15 Ibid.
16 Ibid.

largest sectors of the world proletariat, the working classes of the United States and the Soviet Union, and, subsequently, of the entire world proletariat.[17]

Of course, in Mandel's mind, these western European revolutions would create model council republics with an irresistible appeal to the masses all over the world. The outline is clear. Socialist revolution in western Europe will kiss the two 'sleeping giants' awake: the proletariat of the US and the USSR. Fourth International members who adhered to this perspective certainly felt that they were fighting for a worthwhile goal. But in the historical moment in which Mandel issues this proclamation – while careful enough to speak of all kinds of obstacles and difficulties, above all the 'reformist and semi-reformist' illusions so deeply rooted in mass consciousness – the élan left over from the late 1960s was already exhausted.[18] The year 1977 marked the turning point, and the orientation towards short-term 'breakthroughs' now proved to be a boomerang. Mandel was good at inspiring people into action, but there was one thing than a whole generation of 'post-68ers' – or at least those who listened to him – could not learn from him, even if he himself certainly possessed the necessary stamina: to prepare for prolonged periods of setbacks.

Even in later years, Mandel never failed to draw attention to new positive developments in the revolt of the oppressed and, above all, in the self-organisation of the working class around the world. He would search for them, and when he found them, he would share his pleasure with others: the erosion of the South African apartheid regime; the emergence of mass trade unions in South Africa, South Korea and Brazil; the overthrow of the Shah regime by a broad mass movement; the Sandinista revolution and its unprecedented affinity with the values and democratic ideas of the Fourth International; the emergence of the Brazilian Workers' Party under the banner of an emancipatory development of socialist ideas (when compared to the traditional social-democratic and [post-]Stalinist currents of the workers' movement); and time and time again, mass revolts, strikes, and signs of a revival of the latent working class urge for self-determined action ...[19]

At a 1997 conference on Mandel's intellectual legacy, Francois Vercammen – after outlining the development of Mandel's prognoses and strategic positions from the beginning of the 1960s onward – put forward the hypothesis that

---

17   Ibid.
18   See Kellner 2004, p. 103 et seq.
19   See eyewitness testimony from Winfried Wolf.

Mandel's conception of the party had a distinctive weakness. This concerned less the positions that Mandel advanced theoretically, but rather ideas that appeared to be linked to the way he formed his positions.[20]

Vercammen pointed out that Mandel almost always started from predicting an ascending line of class struggle and mobilisation 'from below'. The focus of his expectations was a broad development of working-class self-organisation. To the extent that this working class detached itself from heteronomy and organised in its own autonomous structures, Mandel's confidence in its creativity and ability to learn was almost unlimited.

While it is true that Mandel also warned against the reformist inclinations that are deeply embedded in working-class consciousness, Vercammen believed this to be more of a complementary, less crucial 'add-on'. In Mandel's vision, a small revolutionary Marxist group would have a chance to grow stronger if it was 'carried' by such a movement (Vercammen spoke of 'surfing' on the wave of a rising movement), precisely because it correctly anticipated its revolutionary potentiality. Vercammen countered this with a different idea that he considered more 'Leninist': the notion of a revolutionary party that swims against the tide in the movement. This is precisely how it consolidates itself and prepares the desired victorious outcome in the future: the overthrow of the rule of capital.[21]

3   Reaction to Gorbachev

Mandel's conception of the non-capitalist countries as 'bureaucratised workers' states' and the associated perspective of social change towards socialist democracy were put to the test by dramatic events in the last ten years of his life. Mandel's reaction to the 'Gorbachev experiment' after four years of 'glasnost' and 'perestroika' shows both the strengths and weaknesses of the analytical and programmatic tools by which he approached the Soviet Union and similar countries. His discussion of the issue does not start with the ideas held by Gorbachev, his adversaries, or the intellectuals of various tendencies who, in the course of *glasnost*, were exploring their new possibilities of articulation – some of which he finds very encouraging, others worrying – but with an assessment of the social situation and the crisis-like developments in the

---

20   See François Vercammen, 'Ernest Mandel et la Capacité Révolutionnaire de la Classe Ouvrière' at Ernestmandel.org.

21   See Vercammen, 'Lenin und die Parteifrage', *Inprekorr*, 315, January 1998, p. 21 et seq.

Soviet economy. He conceives of Gorbachev's attempts at reform neither as an 'ideological deviation' that serves as a gateway for 'the west' and capitalism, nor as a coherent plan to solve the existing problems from the outset. In Mandel's view, they are tentative attempts from within the leading stratum to find ways out of a genuinely pressing situation.[22]

Mandel's point of departure is the contradiction between the dynamic growth of the Soviet economy up to the 1970s and the moment of stagnation that occurred on account of the power of the bureaucracy. Its obstructive influence became conspicuous under the new conditions of the Brezhnev era and the transition from extensive growth to the challenges posed by growth conditioned by new technologies. In the first half of the 1980s, the growth rates of the Soviet economy dropped spectacularly to the point of complete stagnation (zero growth), as diagnosed by some Soviet commentators in contrast to the official growth rate of 3.5%. The dramatic nature of the situation was further illustrated by more tangible aspects such as declining production in many sectors, a stagnation in government revenue for twenty years (with the exception of revenue from oil sales and alcohol taxes), a decline of consumer spending growth rates, etc. At the same time, long-standing problems remained unsolved, for example in housing: 10.2 square metres were available per person in Soviet cities in 1960 and 13.9 square metres in 1984. Mandel highlights the stagnation of grain production and the Soviet Union's need to import grain from western countries. In addition, it had become increasingly difficult to improve labour productivity.[23]

The persistent and growing discontent over stagnation in the standard of living and the apparent inability of the system to improve the quality of products and survive the race for technological innovation formed the background for the need for a long-term overhaul. It would have to go beyond previous cultural 'thaws' or economic 'liberalisations' in sub-sectors.[24]

Mandel highlights the contradiction between the high number of doctors and alarming figures such as increases in infant mortality. Devastating hygienic conditions in hospitals, the proliferation of time lost to filling out forms, and the emergence of an informal 'shadow economy' in the cracks of the official provision of goods and services were some of the symptoms to which Gorbachev and his co-thinkers reacted.[25]

---

22   See Mandel 1991b, p. 1 et seq.
23   Mandel 1991b, pp. 1–9.
24   Mandel 1991b, pp. 5–10.
25   Mandel 1991b, pp. 14–15.

Mandel did not paint a euphoric picture of the bureaucracy. In his view, the special interests of the bureaucracy rendered it incapable of a self-reform that might bring about a genuinely socialist council democracy. This was reflected in the limits of the certainly quite inspiring rehabilitation campaigns for the victims of Stalinist repression (according to Mandel, the Gorbachevists had the greatest difficulties with Trotsky because his positions were particularly diffi- cult for the liberal wing of the bureaucracy to co-opt) and especially in the con- tradiction between *glasnost* and *perestroika*.[26] Reforms in the political sphere pointing towards democratisation were essential to overcome *stagnation*, but also to address the discontent of the masses. Gorbachev and his co-thinkers had to rely on this all the more because they could not offer the workers any sub- stantial material improvements in the foreseeable future. But if *glasnost* were taken to its logical conclusion, then it would be all the more necessary to grant the workers complete freedom to organise themselves, choose their own rep- resentatives, and choose between different political options. And that would be incompatible with the one-party system and the political rule of the bureau- cracy. On the other hand, according to Mandel's assessment, *perestroika* was primarily an attempt to grant more autonomy to the management of individual enterprises and make steps towards a market economy – up to and including the 'right' to lay off workers. The objectives of *perestroika* therefore demanded that democratic rights be restricted anew, starting with the rights granted to workers. Otherwise, the workers would make massive use of their new rights, brought about by *perestroika*, to rebel against the deterioration in their living standards and security.[27]

As might be expected, Mandel's suggested alternative was a democratically planned economy beyond capitalism or bureaucratic administration. In hind- sight, the picture he painted of the controversies and prospects in Gorbachev's Soviet Union seems strangely at odds with the outcome of the events that led to the dissolution of the Soviet Union. The attempted coup by 'conservative' sections of the post-Stalinist bureaucracy corresponded to the most negative scenario envisaged by Mandel. Yeltsin's counter-coup and the restoration of capitalism it inaugurated, on the other hand, did not correspond to any pos- sibilities he foresaw. Looking at Mandel's reaction to these later developments, it becomes clear that there was a deeper reason for this. Mandel did not think it possible, or at least very unlikely, that the Soviet bureaucracy would push the aspect of the 'reforms' that might lead to capitalist restoration to its ultimately

---

26   See Mandel 1991b, pp. 92 and 164–5.
27   See Mandel 1991b, p. 56 et seq.

conclusion. Nor did he think it likely that the Soviet working class, equipped with new room for manoeuvre, would permit such a development more or less without resistance. These two aspects therefore indicate 'blind spots' in Mandel's analytical arsenal.

4   World Historical Rupture 1989–1991

Mandel had a propensity to overestimate the emancipatory potential of the anti-bureaucratic movements in the Soviet Union and similar countries, as well as underestimate the danger of restoration. The discussion in the Fourth International about the 1989–90 'turn' in Germany and the positions taken by Mandel in this debate show these weaknesses of his approach as if through a magnifying glass.[28]

Mandel interpreted the events in East Germany in the autumn of 1989 as the 'beginning of a political revolution'.[29] He supported this judgment by pointing out that a massive movement had emerged 'from below'. Although the large demonstrations were not complemented by a strike wave like in May 1968 or during the Italian 'creeping May' of 1969, he thought daily assemblies of workers in the large factories were sufficient evidence of considerable self-activity on the part of the working class. Mandel noted the good spirits, the humour, the creativity of these masses that had begun to move. He found that the demand for German reunification was not central, and that the prevailing sentiment seemed to point in the direction of a democratically reformed GDR rather than a copy of the 'western' system.[30]

As always, Mandel sought proximity to the events and to the people who were on the move – including in the GDR. He gave talks to many and had conversations with many. For the successor party to the SED, he was now no longer an 'unperson' but a recognised interlocutor. He defended his democratic and socialist views very convincingly, and it may well be that some of the agreement he gained in personal conversation was based more on his powers of persuasion than on real, deeper agreement.[31] The retroactive effect of such experiences on his own judgement certainly contributed to the fact that Mandel, in his own organisation, hindered rather than promoted a realistic grasp

---

28   See also Touissant 1987.
29   See Mandel, 'La révolution politique et les dangers qui la menacent', *Inprecor*, 297, 13 November 1989.
30   See Mandel, 'Ceux d'en bas se sont mis en marche', *La Gauche*, 21 November 1989.
31   Toussaint 1997, p. 2 et seq.

of what was going on until the German Democratic Republic was annexed by West Germany.

In March 1990, a resolution passed by the United Secretariat of the Fourth International, largely written by Mandel, stated that although the GDR had seen the beginnings of a political revolution, the most likely outcome was now capitalist restoration through the incorporation of East Germany into the Federal Republic of Germany. Between the original optimistic assessment and this statement lay the drastic shift in mass sentiment – from 'We are the people' to 'We are one people'. The resolution describes the impending 'annexation' of East Germany as a 'social counter-revolution' and predicts negative consequences both for the German masses and for Germany's international role as an imperialist power. On the other hand, the resolution is aimed at 'buying time' so that the masses have the opportunity to make their own initial experiences with such negative consequences and draw their conclusions. To this end, Mandel believed he could rely on two factors: on the one hand, the costs of 'reunification', on top the costs of introducing an EU currency, would be too high for the West German bourgeoisie; on the other hand, the Kremlin would neither tolerate NATO membership for a united Germany nor the stationing of Bundeswehr soldiers or soldiers from other western states on the territory of the GDR.[32] Mandel had realised by this time that the bureaucracy of the GDR would no longer offer any resistance to restoration and annexation. But this seemed to him to be owed to the special conditions in Germany. He could not yet imagine a comparable self-sacrifice for the ruling bureaucracies of the other east European countries and for the Kremlin bureaucracy.

The resolution was opposed by two other documents. A minority in the Fourth International (supported mainly by a minority in the French section) argued quite unrealistically for a 'socialist' reunification of Germany, despite the fact that the bourgeoisie was obviously holding the best cards at the moment.[33] A document of the United Socialist Party (VSP), the organisation of FI members in West Germany at the time, stated realistically that a political revolution in the sense of a seizure of political power by the working class was not on the agenda in the short or medium term. Moreover, there was no longer any prospect of a prolonged period of confederation on an equal footing with an independent GDR. The VSP argued in favour of defending the autonomy of the GDR as the only way to defend the gains of East German workers and

---

32   See 'La situation en RDA et noch tâches', *Inprecor* 305, 23 March 1990.

33   Toussaint 1997, p. 7.

women.[34] The majority position formulated by Mandel oscillated somewhere between these two 'extremes'.

From autumn 1989 until November 1990, when a resolution also drafted mainly by Mandel found the support of the majority of the FI leadership, the German members gradually influenced Mandel's positioning in the sense of a more realistic (and thus more pessimistic) assessment of the situation. Events confirmed their assessment. Consequently, the new resolution contained implicit and explicit self-criticism of the March 1989 resolution:

According to the new document, the most negative of the predicted potential scenarios had come to pass on 3 October 1990. Not only had there been no political revolution towards socialist democracy, there had also been no cautious process of rapprochement between the two German states. Such a process, unfolding in several stages, would have granted the masses time for a learning process. This might have resulted in a rejection not only of bureaucratic rule, but also of the rule of capital. The outcome of the 18 March 1990 elections in the GDR and the triumph of the twin organisations of the West German bourgeois parties, the document continued, had destroyed the democratic achievements of the movement of autumn 1989. The time of 'round tables' had come to an end, and the constitution of a reunified Germany was taking place without any democratic participation of the population. Germany would now become a global gendarme alongside other imperialist powers, dominate the single European market planned for 1992, and intensify all reactionary tendencies against refugees, immigrants, and the countries of the 'third world', exacerbate social inequalities on its own soil and further restrict democratic rights. Moreover, Germany would be in an ideal position to play a dominant role in the capitalist conquest of the east European countries.[35]

As we can see, not 'political revolution' but capitalist restoration under western domination was now suggested as the likely scenario for the east European countries as well. However, no comprehensive explanation of the reasons for this shift in analysis is provided.

However, the resolution contains explicit self-criticism when it states that unfavourable subjective conditions had previously been 'underestimated'. The working class of the GDR had not gained enough confidence in its own strength or political consciousness to be able to make a claim to political power. More-

---

34   This text was published as 'Position du VSP' in *Inprecor* 305 on 23 March 1990. The author of the present work already argued along these lines in *Inprecor* 302 on 9 February 1990: 'Unification au pas de course'.

35   Resolution of the United Secretariat of the Fourth International of November 1990. Published in *Inprecor*, 322, 18 January 1991.

over, the 'frustrated national sentiment' of the Germans had been underestimated. The latter statement stands in marked contrast to Mandel's almost hymnal touches of November 1989, when he wrote: 'Rosa Luxemburg's descendants have proven themselves worthy of her. Today, history says that she did not fight in vain and did not die in vain'.[36] As much as Mandel was aware of the extent to which socialist consciousness had been buried over many decades, he believed in the possibility of reviving the revolutionary legacy of the left wing of the German workers' movement. The outcome of the events in Germany and the Soviet Union was a bitter disappointment for him.

In the introduction to his work on the Marxist theory of bureaucracy, published posthumously in German, Mandel defends his assessment of the Soviet Union and similar countries, which he had based on Trotsky. There is an explicit correction only with regard to his assessment of the subjective factor, i.e. the level of working class consciousness: 'We have to admit that revolutionary Marxists seriously underestimated the disastrous long-term effects of Stalinism and bureaucratic dictatorship on the average level of consciousness'.[37]

But prior to this section – the text was written after the dissolution of the Soviet Union – Mandel describes the absorption of the GDR by capitalist West Germany as an exception and stresses that in order to fully restore capitalism in the eastern European countries and in the former USSR, the resistance of a working class that has much to lose would first have to be broken:

> Restoration of capitalism is possible only if that resistance is defeated, or at least so fragmented as to become practically inoperative. Such an outcome, however, is by no means certain. It is not inevitable in the former USSR, which has the strongest working class in the world, and one of the most skilled and most cultivated. The awakening of that mighty social force, with its first moves of independent intervention, is one of the most positive aspects of world developments in the last five years which could largely neutralize and even reverse the negative trends in Eastern Europe. But all this being said, it remains a fact that the low level of class consciousness of the East European and Soviet working class has created a situation which restorationists can exploit.[38]

---

36 Mandel, 'Ceux d'en bas se sont mis en marche', *La Gauche* of 21 November 1989; see also Mandel 1990a.
37 Mandel 1992a, p. 5.
38 Ibid.

5   Weaknesses of the Concept of 'Bureaucratised Workers' States'

Mandel defended his conception of 'bureaucratised workers' states' with convincing arguments against competing theories. He countered 'official Communism' with everything that the 'classical Marxists', beginning with Marx, had written on socialism, pointing to the obvious contradictions between this objective and the reality of the 'socialist countries'.[39] He showed the proponents of the theory of 'state capitalism' that the law of value, even if it continues to operate in non-capitalist economic systems, does not dominate there: neither the major means of production nor labour power are commodities in these systems.[40] To those who considered the bureaucracy a (new ruling) 'class', he cited the differences between typical ruling classes and ruling bureaucracies, whose members possess only functional privileges.[41] The collapse of these systems also seemed to confirm important aspects of his concept: If these had been 'socialist societies', or at least societies in transition to socialism in which the working class was in power, then this would render the more or less 'voluntary' transition to capitalism incomprehensible. If it was 'state capitalism' (i.e. only a 'variety' of capitalism), then it remains inexplicable why its collapse was a defeat and bitter setback for the working class, the workers' movement, and the left across the world. If, however, the bureaucracy was a 'ruling class' as defined by Marxist terminology, representing an independent mode of production that was tied to its rule, then it is not understandable why it did not produce its own self-conscious ideology (but rather drew ideologically from 'borrowed' Marxist revolutionary ideas, which were distorted according to need) nor why its leading representatives ultimately abdicated in the hope of gaining more for themselves under capitalist conditions by transforming themselves from privileged officials into genuine owners of means of production.[42]

But being more correct than others in certain aspects does not mean that one's concept is adequate to reality. This non-sequitur seems to me to be particularly important in view of Mandel's characteristic coupling of scientific efforts to arrive at an adequate approach to understanding social reality with his desire to promote emancipatory change – and put his own ideas and organisation in the best possible light. Even Trotsky did not find the term 'bureaucratically degenerated workers' state', which he himself had coined, particularly fortu-

---

39   See Mandel 1985a.
40   See Mandel 1969a.
41   See Mandel 1979b.
42   See Mandel 1979d, p. 148 et seq.

nate. He hoped that a better term would be found.[43] After all, by 'workers' state' he meant the Soviet Union under Stalin, a state in which the working class not only did not rule, but did not even have elementary democratic rights, let alone the freedom of trade union or political organisation. The term 'workers' state' was intended to express continuity with the fledgling Soviet Republic, where the working class had come to power through an authentic socialist revolution and genuinely exercised it through the councils. This continuity was embodied in the 'gains of October': the nationalised industry, the planned economy, the state monopoly on foreign trade. The bureaucracy was not construed by Trotsky as a new ruling class, but as a parasitic outgrowth of the working class, to which the working class had politically subjugated itself. By analogy, France under Napoleon was certainly a 'capitalist state', but one in which the bourgeoisie was not directly involved in the exercise of political power as would be the case in a 'normal' bourgeois-democratic republic.[44]

The problem, however, is not so much what terms are used or if the analogies are appropriate. A fundamental weakness of the concept seems to be that its starting point is a norm (or a good beginning), from which bad reality has deviated.

A similar weakness underlies Mandel's notion that there are 'historic detours': the socialist revolution should 'actually' have been initiated by the working classes of the developed industrialised capitalist countries; yet 'for certain reasons', it took a diversion through less developed and poor countries, with serious consequences; it is 'to be expected' that future events will rejoin the 'intended' course of history, by which the working classes of the most developed industrialised countries become the vanguard of the world socialist revolution. Similarly, the 'bureaucratised workers' states' are a (tragic) 'detour' of history, and 'normalisation' consists in a 'return' to authentic Soviet democracy.[45] This description may be somewhat exaggerated in the interest of clarity – granted, Mandel was trying to analyse social formations and systems starting from the contradictions that characterised their social reality rather than from abstract 'norms' – but it seems to me that it indicates a real problem.

At a seminar in Germany in 1987, German members of the FI expressed concern about the agreements between the International Monetary Fund and the Yugoslav government. They were wary this would trigger a dynamic that would culminate in a restorative process and make Yugoslavia dependent on the imperialist powers. Mandel did not share this concern at all. He argued that

---

43   See Trotzki 1942 p. 121; Mandel 1987b: pp. 159–60.
44   See Trotsky 1935.
45   See Mandel 1979d, p. 114 et seq.

the ruling class of a capitalist semi-colony stood in relation to the imperialist bourgeoisie like a servant to his master. The Titoist bureaucracy, he said, could not be compared to this – according to him, it was far more autonomous. It could, if it deemed it appropriate, decide from one day to the next to refuse paying debts and refrain from further borrowing. This was the first time I felt that Mandel was inclined to overestimate the (anti-capitalist) resilience of the bureaucracies of these countries, while of course being familiar with Trotsky's opinion that they would 'ultimately' prove to be the agents of restoration if not overthrown 'from below'. However, he had often opposed 'Trotskyist' groups who interpreted this position in such a narrow manner that they construed every step of the Kremlin leadership, even under Brezhnev, as 'ultimately' pro-capitalist, which inevitably led them to draw absurd conclusions.[46]

In the years leading up to the break-up of the Soviet Union and, under Yeltsin, to an open turn towards restoration, Mandel often expressed his high regard for the potential especially of the Soviet working class. At a conference in the early '90s, he emphasised to German FI members its willingness to strike, the emergence of miners' strike committees and strike committees of other sections of the working class in the Soviet Union, their justified (often very elementary) demands, and their demands to be involved in political decision-making. He did not share the scepticism of other contributors to this debate, for example, when they wondered whether workers demanding the right to freely trade the coal they produce on the world market was not too far a cry from even potentially socialist consciousness. He considered such misgivings to be rather small-minded and as betraying an uncritical acceptance of official opinion published in the bourgeois mass media.

In such discussions, Mandel frequently ridiculed the idea that workers who had 'just chased away their bureaucratic masters' might hand over 'their' factories to new masters, but this time capitalist ones.[47] However, if we substantially simplified matters, we could say that the real course of events did roughly proceed like this.

---

46 Author's recollections of events and discussions with Ernest Mandel.
47 Author's recollections. However, Mandel's attitude is also evident in his book on Gorbachev, for example, where in a chapter on the 'Future of the Gorbachev Experiment', he does not utter a single word of concern that this future might go in a capitalist direction – see Mandel 1991b, p. 182 et seq. He always sees the activity of the working-class masses as the decisive factor: 'Under those circumstances, any action against the interests of the workers would make it more difficult to mobilize their support for Gorbachev. Some sections of the workers would become passive, while other sections would give their support to the conservatives' (Mandel 1991b, p. 186).

The degree of alienation of Soviet workers from their 'workers' state' and its origins could not have been greater. Perhaps for Mandel this was obscured by the genuine mass discussion about the rehabilitation of the old Bolsheviks who were defamed and liquidated under Stalin. But only a short time after this political-moral victory, it became obvious that only a tiny, indeed vanishing minority in Soviet or ex-Soviet society gave a damn about the theoretical heritage of Bukharin, Zinoviev, Trotsky or even Lenin. Any notion of who had been a Soviet icon and who had been demonised largely disappeared in the mire of the general denigration of Marxist traditions.

Even if this were to change for the better in the future – any connection to the revolutionary period of 1917 and the subsequent few years would essentially be based on a resurgence and further development of similar ideas, not on a historical or structural continuity with the October revolution and the early Soviet republic. But this also means that the idea of the Fourth International as a tendency that would eventually assert itself against 'official' Communism as an 'authentic' embodiment of its origins, which was still very much alive in Mandel's time – and was nourished again by the rehabilitation debate under Gorbachev – has proven to be unrealistic and obsolete, to say the least.

In retrospect, the dispute with the political representatives of the (post-)Stalinist bureaucracy appears in part in a peculiar light. Certainly, 'Stalinism' is dead and 'generally', Mandel was right when he highlighted its crisis and analysed its causes. On the other hand, despite all their transformations and differences, the successor organisations of the (post-)Stalinist parties of the former Soviet Union and its former allied countries are still much stronger than the groups of the Fourth International or even tendencies vaguely related to the FI. In a hypothetical debate with the Fourth International, 'official' Communism might, in hindsight, be able to justify its suppression of democratic freedoms and oppositional views to an extent. Indeed, while Mandel believed that broad pro-democracy movements in these countries would advance the establishment of real workers' power, especially when large numbers of workers were involved, they actually proved to be gateways for capitalist restoration. Trotsky, in contrast, was aware that in the absence of a truly 'revolutionary leadership', or in the case of a very weak leadership, there was a possibility of capitalist restoration. Mandel himself often wrote how much depended on the 'subjective factors', on organising by conscious revolutionaries. Yet evidently, he often saw the dynamics of mass movements in too rosy a light.

However, the suppression of 'deviations' and of the freedom of the masses to organise had – and in this respect, I think that Mandel is right – a highly counterproductive effect on the development of mass socialist consciousness. Thus, one might say that repression 'in the name of socialism' has in fact produced anti-socialist consciousness.[48]

6   Historical Determinism

Mandel advocated a coherent theoretical concept that he repeatedly reformulated in various forms. Judging by the short educational chapters on 'materialist dialectics' and 'historical materialism' in *Introduction to Marxism*, for instance, the general philosophical foundations of his thought were not particularly inspiring.[49] He defended epistemological realism and the idea of an objective dialectic underlying the subject-object dialectic between human society and nature.[50] He saw the material production of food and the cognitive processes associated with it as the fundamentally decisive basis for all specifically human activities and ideas. He presented the relevant classical Marxist concepts in a way that would hardly have withstood a qualified philosophical debate. Examples he cites from certain scholarly fields are highly contestable.[51] Mandel's writing tends to be far much more sophisticated and engaging when he focuses on the development of class society and capitalism. His first relevant text, *From Class Society to Communism. An Introduction to Marxism*, sets out the characteristics of his conception of history.[52] *Marxist Economic Theory* reads like an (economic) history book partly because Mandel emphasises that capitalist society is embedded in the history of class society and in the history of commodity production.[53] A paper from 1968 on the emergence and development of Karl Marx's economic doctrine demonstrates that his conception of history is strongly informed by an interpretation of Marx that borrows heavily from the work of Roman Rozdolsky.[54] In his 1986 essay *The place of Marxism in history*, he presents this understanding in a more developed and mature manner.[55]

---

48   See Mandel 1974a and Mandel 1992a, p. 88.
49   Mandel 1979a, p. 151 et seq.
50   See Mandel 1979a, pp. 152–3.
51   For example, Mandel spoke of evolutionary transitions from plants to animals, from birds to mammals, from apes to humans – See Mandel 1979a, p. 161. This does not correspond to the real process of the history of nature.
52   See Mandel 1979a.
53   See Mandel 1968b.
54   See Mandel 1968a.
55   See Mandel 1979a, p. 161; 1986c.

In Mandel's work, Marxism appears as a conceptual expression of social relations that only fully matured with industrial capitalism and could therefore only be adequately understood and scientifically grasped in its time. Marxism is simultaneously the theoretical expression of a liberation movement that rebels against class society in general and against capitalist class society in particular. This revolt is not only a revolt against exploitation in its capitalist form, but against all exploitation and oppression and against aspects of alienation that are inherent in every class society, which are already present in commodity production even where it has not become generalised as capitalism.[56]

Mandel conceives of Marxism as a critical science of society that tends, as far as possible, to absorb and assimilate all the achievements of the human sciences and all valid theoretical approaches. In this way, he argues, it becomes possible to analyse an ever-changing reality. The path along which Marx and Engels developed their views serves as the model: their critical turn against conservative forms of Hegelianism and embrace of its emancipatory potential, their advocacy of the socialist aspirations of their time, and their critical analysis of the political economy to ensure there is real basis for revolutionary action.[57]

In Mandel's writings, however, Marx and Engels's ability to productively absorb all the emancipatory impulses and scientific findings of their time appears more unproblematic and unquestionable than it undoubtedly was. Thus it is not enough to point out, as Mandel does, that Marx and Engels defended Flora Tristan's 'feminism' and that Engels, following Morgan, turned his attention to the patriarchal nuclear family.[58] With a modicum of critical awareness, one should at least recognise that Marx considered the 'solution of the women's question' to be more or less imminent, because the bourgeois nuclear family no longer existed 'in the proletariat' of early capitalism, and that women's liberation would be a more or less 'automatic' by-product of the social-

---

56   See Mandel 1986b, chapter 1.

57   Ibid.

58   Ibid; Mandel 1984a, p. 105; see also the expanded edition of Mandel's *From Class Society to Communism – An Introduction to Marxism*, which contains a sub-chapter on the liberation movements of women and oppressed nationalities: Mandel 1982b, p. 146 et seq. However, Mandel qualifies his positive judgement of Marx and Engels in this field: 'Similarly, while they developed an acute awareness of the dual oppression of women in class society, and extended the analysis of the origins of that oppression to the very beginning of that society, Marx and Engels were not able to encompass all the necessary aspects of women's emancipation that progressively emerged in the 20th century'. Mandel 1986b, p. 33.

ist revolution.[59] In my opinion, a theoretically productive relationship between Marxism and radical feminism remains a task for the future rather than an achievement of the past even today.

For Mandel, there are three – extensively evidenced – basic statements at the centre of 'historical materialism'. Historical materialism stands and falls with these three statements: the determination of the various societies by their respective relations of production; the determination (in the final analysis) of the 'superstructure' by these relations of production; the role of the state as a means of class domination. Thereby, Mandel rejects the notion of necessarily successive modes of production. He refers to the long transitional periods when a new mode of production came into force (especially capitalism, which was preceded by an epoch of 'small commodity production', 'semi-feudal' absolutism and the more or less violent separation of a large mass of small producers from their means of production), and he also refers to the 'tributary' ('Asiatic') relations of production, which stand outside such an assumed sequence. He stresses that modern capitalism developed under very specific circumstances in western Europe, not somewhere else. He explains the fact that 'progressive' new modes of production prevail by their ability to significantly increase the productivity of labour. This creates more leisure time for self-development and creative productivity, although in class societies this is only true for a minority. The goal of the socialist workers' movement and, in fact, of all emancipative movements, is to make the fruits of this kind of progress equally accessible to all human beings.[60]

Mandel rejects a deterministic historical fatalism and, following Marx, emphasises that 'men and women make their own history'. But they do so under pre-existing conditions that they cannot circumvent. These conditions limit their possibilities of knowledge as well as change.

> This 'over-determination', however, is never so strict as to leave open only one path of historical development. Marx and Engels stressed that, out of the periods of acute social revolution – the epochs of decline of a mode of production –, there could arise either a superior mode of production, a superior organisation of society from the standpoint of the life and survival of humankind, thanks to the victory of the revolutionary class, or the mutual decomposition of the contending social classes, and a general decadence of society. This is what happened, for instance, with the

---

59   Marx 1990, pp. 620–1.
60   Mandel 1986b, p. 33.

decline of the slave mode of production in Ancient Rome. It is also the historical basis of the dilemma that we face today: 'Socialism or Barbarism'.[61]

The juxtaposition of these two opposing possibilities naturally justifies for Mandel the urgency of commitment, of revolutionary action. In the last years of his life, which offered fewer occasions for him to point to promising big movements, he stressed the alternative 'socialism or barbarism', 'socialism or death' with particular emphasis.[62] An obvious objection suggests itself, namely that there can be more than just two possible ways out of a complex situation. Mandel himself tried to develop a multifactorial determinism that encompassed a range of developmental possibilities and gave much space to the potentially drastic consequences of the conscious actions of individuals and groups.[63]

With the development of the capitalist mode of production, new determinant factors emerged, and thus the determinism based on 'historical materialism' gained its decisive evidence. Mandel tried to develop a general theory of the relationship between economic factors and the ebb and flow of the proletarian class struggle, based on his analysis of 'late capitalism' and his adoption of the theory of 'long waves of capitalist development'.[64] However, he did not conclude this investigation to a point at which it was ready for publication. In this context, he developed the category of 'partially independent variables', whose respective development plays an important role in the overall development of the capitalist mode of production, in addition to its fundamental contradictions.[65] Apart from aspects of this work that are of interest for a specialised economic discussion, it is worth highlighting the significance of this approach for the understanding of history and political strategy. Determinism becomes less dualistic and mechanical in this way as it draws on new insights that have found their way into social science debates since the late 1970s through the theories of chaos and self-organisation. Part of this is the recognition that even a process starting from a very limited number of determinants (initial conditions) can lead to unpredictable outcomes.[66]

Taking up such insights *expressis verbis* did not exactly come naturally to Mandel. He defended the independence of science, especially socialist science,

---

61   Mandel 1986b, p. 13.
62   Mandel 1985d.
63   Mandel 1991d, pp. 100–1.
64   Mandel 1979e, p. 66.
65   Mandel 1975d, p. 41.
66   See Bensaïd 1995.

from any political influence and political wishful thinking (in this context, he liked to quote Engels's words against the German Social-Democratic Party's executive committee when the latter hesitated, motivated by party interest, to reprint Marx's *Critique of the Gotha Programme*).[67] At the same time, the ability to predict certain developments (the recurrence of crises, for example) was virtually a benchmark of scientificity for him.[68] In his contribution to a lecture series in honour of Leo Kofler, he generalised the category of partially independent variables derived from economic analysis and speaks of a multifactorial 'parametric determinism'.[69] At the same time, he foregrounded the category of 'latency', which he had not used before.[70] Thus a picture of social conflicts and their development emerges in which the class struggle is an objective reality ('a datum', says Mandel) irrespective of the consciousness of those involved, yet its outcome is uncertain. Those who want to help a general emancipation movement to succeed rely neither on the certainty that they are acting in accordance with the laws of development of society, nor is there any certainty that a new mass movement will ensure their victory. They rely on the 'latency', i.e. on the likelihood inherent in the contradictions of existing society that such movements will always 'periodically' occur. The key 'latency' for Mandel in this context is that the working class 'latently' aspires to manage the economy and society itself.[71] Just as any given level of the productive forces can, according to Mandel, give rise to different relations of production – there is no rigid determinism here – relatively small shifts in the 'subjective factor' (including the correct actions of a relatively small group of people taken in the respective situation) can also play a crucial role: social development can suddenly take an unforeseen direction that most people would not have thought possible.[72]

On the whole, Mandel stands for a conception of history and a critical social science that encourages continued research in a variety of fields while also posing a challenge to all those who believe they can simply erase the fundamental Marxist positions at the stroke of a pen – especially their grounding in the critique of existing capitalist class society and its trajectories from its origins to its looming consequences should it continue to exist for much longer.

---

67   See Mandel 1984a, pp. 90 and 81.
68   See Mandel 1991c, pp. 23–4.
69   See Mandel 1991d, p. 100.
70   See Mandel 1991c, p. 103 et seq.
71   See Mandel 1991c, p. 108 et seq.
72   See Mandel 1991c, pp. 111–12.

Mandel's 'genetic' interpretation of Marx's categories of the critique of political economy and the way in which he is continuing the work of *Capital* cannot be separated from his desire to highlight real people's suffering and for liberation. In the same way, Marx's *Capital* is by no means exhausted in 'logical extrapolations', but depicts in vivid colours both the brutal violence at the cradle of capitalism and the everyday life of downtrodden workers in the capitalist factories.[73]

7   Karl Marx's 'Categorical Imperative'

For Mandel, the struggle for universal emancipation is by no means simply the result of 'scientific insight'. He repeatedly quoted – as in the aforementioned talk at the lecture series in honour of Leo Kofler – Marx's version of the 'categorical imperative' from the introduction to the Critique of Hegel's *Philosophy of Right*, namely '... *to overthrow all relations* in which man is a debased, enslaved, abandoned, despicable essence ...'.[74] Mandel makes the point that taking sides with the exploited and oppressed is a moral duty, even if all hopes of achieving the desired social liberation are shattered: 'Today, in bourgeois society, this implies siding with the working class and other oppressed strata of the population, poor peasants in the third world, oppressed women, oppressed youth, etc. This is a moral duty, a matter of conscience that does not stem from any certainty that socialism will prevail. Even if one is convinced that barbarism will triumph, one must not for a second abandon this moral, categorical imperative'.[75] In the same spirit, Mandel strongly agreed with a late statement by Trotsky: If the working class, contrary to the hopes and expectations of the Fourth International, should prove incapable of overthrowing world capitalism and ridding itself of bureaucratic rule, then the *Transitional Programme* will have to be abandoned; instead, a new minimum programme will be required to defend the interests of the slaves under new barbaric conditions.[76]

In addition to analysing the underlying conflicts and interests behind them, Mandel also applied Marx's 'categorical imperative' to crimes committed in the name of socialism, especially the terrible 'purges' under Stalin in the nineteen-thirties. He said that it is possible to be 'scientifically' convinced of socialism and morally behave 'like swine' for reasons of 'realpolitik'. But in the end, this

---

73   Mandel 1979a, p. 151 et seq.; Marx 1990, p. 871 et seq.
74   Marx 1843, introduction, original emphasis; see also Mandel 1991d, pp. 101–2.
75   Mandel 1991c, p. 102, our translation.
76   See Trotsky 1942, p. 9. Mandel 1979d, pp. 160–1.

leads to catastrophes even in 'realpolitik' terms. From the point of view of the 'working class and the real movement for emancipation', such behaviour is not beneficial (in the long run).[77] This is how Mandel linked an emotionally and morally based attitude with his conception of a new society, the transition to this society, and the methods he considered acceptable and useful to achieve the desired change.

Mandel's ethically based stance – the view that it's permissible to be wrong on many things, but not on this morally based commitment – was credible and convincing, and it united him with a number of devoted socialists of various tendencies who shared it, regardless of how unrealistic or excessively optimistic Mandel's outlook seemed to them otherwise.

In Marx's work, the aforementioned 'categorical imperative' follows on from the realisation (contained in Feuerbach's critique of religion) that 'man is the highest essence for man'.[78] A common objection to socialism is that it contradicts human nature. Mandel, of course, disagreed with this assessment. His understanding of human nature is characterised by the idea of a very far-reaching 'plasticity' of human behaviour and human potential for development.[79] The possibilities range from the most horrible and ruthless fighting of everybody against everybody to cooperative, considerate and loving behaviour. What is decisive are the circumstances. Under certain social conditions, it is possible to initiate a process of self-education and maturing that produces selfless people who seek happiness in creative self-development and loving relationships. The deep-rooted 'latency' that Mandel takes as his starting point, and which in his view is evident in all class societies from the outset, is our predisposition to dissatisfaction with unjust conditions, inequality, discrimination, exploitation and oppression. In Mandel's view, this reflects that such conditions do not correspond to the 'essence' of human beings, i.e. to their real, deep-seated needs. The desire for a return of a 'golden age' without inequality, without classes, without exploitation and oppression, which has always been the ideological expression of an incipient revolt, is in Mandel's view not pure fantasy, but rather a fantastically exaggerated longing for that classless state of affairs that the human species was acquainted with for the longest time of its existence (even if that condition was one of poverty and ruled by natural necessity). After all, class societies did not emerge until 10,000 years ago at the earliest, and even then, they by no means encompassed all human beings.[80]

---

77   See Mandel 1991d, pp. 102–3.
78   Marx 1843, introduction.
79   Mandel 1968b, p. 669.
80   Mandel 1968b, p. 670.

Michael Löwy believes that Mandel's characteristic 'revolutionary human-ism' is ultimately based on an optimistic view of humanity. Expressed in a simple formula, man is capable of anything (good or bad), but 'the good' in him is the germ waiting for the opportunity to flourish, so to speak. This is why human beings only really come into their own through emancipation from class society (similarly, Marx wrote that the 'real' history of humanity begins with communism, while the history of class societies is only 'prehistory').[81] Löwy aptly summarises Mandel's view thus:

> At the heart of Mandel's revolutionary faith lies a sort of *anthropological optimism*, i.e. an optimism based on the belief that 'in the last instance, the striving for emancipation (*Emanzipationsstreben*) has an anthropo-logical foundation.' Rebellion is inherently human: as long as human-kind continues to exist, the oppressed and enslaved will rise against their chains and the revolutionary species will never disappear.
>
> This does not mean that Marxists hold a naive and one-sided view of the intrinsic 'goodness' of human nature: they agree with modern psy-chology (Freud) that humans are contradictory and ambivalent beings. Their character combines individualism and socialization, selfishness and solidarity, destructiveness and creativity, Thanatos and Eros, irration-ality and rationality. However, as contemporary anthropology has shown, humans are social beings; this means that there exists the possibility of a society organized in such a way as to favour the human potential for creativity and solidarity.
>
> There are also historical reasons for optimism: the study of primitive societies shows that greed is not a component of 'human nature' but a product of social circumstances. Far from being an 'innate part' of the human character, the tendency towards private accumulation of wealth did not exist for thousands of years: cooperation and solidarity held sway in primitive, tribal or village communities. There is no a priori reason for them not to become universal human qualities once more, in a future, socialist world community. It is not accident that for many centuries, socialism was a dream of return to the lost 'golden age'.[82]

Focusing on Mandel's 'revolutionary humanism' and the reasons for the revolu-tionary optimism underpinning his conception of man might, of course, dis-

---

81   Achcar 1999a, p. 27.
82   Achcar 1999a, p. 33.

tract you from recognising the weaknesses in his argumentation and examining why his idea of what was really happening, especially at the end of World War II and in the 1980s and 1990s, proved so inadequate. Löwy manages not to fall into this trap – he calls the problem by its name. While acknowledging Mandel's 'anthropological optimism' as a productive factor for revolutionary commitment, he does not gloss over the fact that an unfounded optimism is likely to conceal shortcomings of analysis or method:

> But, when it ceased to be 'optimism of the will' in the Gramscian meaning (i.e. coupled with 'pessimism of the intellect') to become a sort of ungrounded 'optimism of the intellect', or rather just plain and simple over-optimism, it was a source of great weakness. It inspired some of his notoriously optimistic oracular predictions, so often repeated and so often falsified, about the 'impetuous rise of the masses', and the imminent revolutionary upsurge, in the USSR, in Spain, in Germany, in France, in Europe and in the whole world. This pattern that frequently reproduced itself, started very early as shown by the following example: in an article from 1946 'E. Germain' (Mandel) insisted that the uprisings of the years 1944–45 were only 'the first stage of the European revolution', soon to be followed by a second. There will be no 'relative stabilization', he said: the present situation is only 'the calm before the storm', a 'transition towards a general revolutionary upsurge'. Cutting short any counter-argument, 'Germain' concluded: 'this is not optimism, it is revolutionary realism' ... Mandel's over-optimistic predictions were short-lived. But his humanist/revolutionary message is as relevant as ever ...[83]

In his lecture on 'Mandel's revolutionary humanism', Löwy does not examine the reasons for the 'weakness' that was Mandel's 'ungrounded optimism of the intellect'. The best starting point in the quest for answers might be an examination of the tension between Mandel's focus on the broadest possible class movement in the struggle against exploitation and oppression, on the one hand, and his preoccupation with building a small international organisation on the other.

---

83   Achcar 1999a, p. 34.

8   Aporias of Marginality: Mandel's 'Last Word' on Sectarianism

Mandel's political-strategic thinking is permeated by a tension between his orientation towards the class movement of wage labourers and the entire range of emancipatory social movements, on the one hand, and his strong identification with his own, largely marginal organisation. On 11 November 1994, Mandel attended a meeting in New York at the invitation of what was then called the Spartacist Tendency (now the International Communist League). This organisation had the habit of publicly attacking the Fourth International and Mandel personally for alleged violations of Trotskyist tradition and a policy of 'liquidationism' (which, according to the Spartacist Tendency, had ruined the Fourth International, which therefore had to be 'rebuilt'). Mandel himself had challenged the Spartacist Tendency to debate him publicly, and the organisation had accepted the challenge. After some negotiations about the general conditions and speaking time, the event finally materialised. Close political friends had strongly advised Mandel not to risk his health, which was precarious after his second heart attack, for an event whose political value was difficult to discern.[84] Truth be told, the Spartacist Tendency is a true sect – and I am consciously using this term to distinguish it from small revolutionary organisations with sectarian traits that cannot, however, be reduced to these traits.[85]

Mandel then produced a substantially expanded written version of his talk under the title 'Sectarianism vs. Revolutionary Marxism. World Socialist Revolution Today'.[86] This is Mandel's last extensive piece of writing – in a sense, it can be regarded as his 'political testament'. It shows how strongly the aforementioned tension affected Mandel to the end, for this polemical treatise is sharply aimed against 'sectarianism' and at the same time irritatingly 'identitarian' in relation to Mandel's own organisation, the Fourth International.

Mandel explains why he is getting involved in a debate with 'sectarians' to begin with. By criticising the Spartacist movement, he says, he wants to confront all the sects that lay a claim to Trotskyism. After all, these sects comprise several thousand organised activists. Their dogmatism and their way of intervening in mass movements, which fluctuates between eruptive intervention and passivity, both engenders and reinforces anti-Trotskyist prejudices. They are 'cadre killers' because many of their former members are lost to revolutionary involvement as a result of their bad experience.

---

84   See eyewitness testimony from Livio Maitan.
85   See Kellner 2004 p. 143.
86   See Mandel 1995b.

In addition, in Russia they create the myth about allegedly existing 'different Fourth Internationals', obscuring the fact that there is only one FI which really exists and functions as such on a worldwide scale. The confusion which results from that myth makes it more difficult for Russian supporters of Trotsky to rebuild a Russian FI organization, which would certainly have been Trotsky's main purpose in his country.[87]

Why does Mandel confine himself to the example of Russia? The argument that there are many 'Fourth Internationals' is far more widespread. In fact, this remark couldn't be further from Mandel's usual argumentation, which tends to be based on global historical processes.

Mandel's starting point in his talk is the resolve, embodied by Marx since 'Theses on Feuerbach', to change the world in practice – and the notion that this possibility is grounded in reality, mediated through the self-liberation of the working class under capitalism. The unexpected fact that capitalist class rule was first overthrown in backward countries led to a 'desynchronisation' of the process of world revolution, but this uncomfortable state of affairs can be overcome. Great numbers of people, including in the developed industrial capitalist countries, have been continuously worse off since contemporary capitalism entered a prolonged stagnant-depressive period. Although capital is still on the offensive, there is an increasing tendency towards resistance and the emergence of movements from below, although the offensive of capital is far from over. In the Soviet Union, the old revolutionaries who were ostracised and murdered under Stalin have been rehabilitated – most recently even Trotsky, who, more than anyone, was not really in need of being rehabilitated by the representatives of 'official' Communism and the CPSU. However, Mandel argues that the practical result is hugely important: his writings are republished, and his ideas are taken up again by new generations.[88]

And yet, the 'sects' obstruct the construction of the Fourth International in Russia! One must bear in mind that there is not even a handful of FI members in the entire territory of the former Soviet Union today. It was not much different the time when Mandel gave his.[89]

Mandel does not completely discount the merits of the 'sects'. He mentions, for example, that the Lutte Ouvrière (LO) candidate received over 5% of the vote in the April 1995 presidential elections – and that the Militant Tendency

---

87   Mandel 1995b, p. 29.
88   Mandel 1995b, pp. 18–19.
89   Mandel 1995b, pp. 28–9.

played a key role in mobilising against the 'poll tax' in the UK. When Mandel wrote this, the French section of the Fourth International could only dream of such electoral success. It was only with the 4.25% success of the Ligue Communiste Révolutionaire presidential candidate Olivier Besancenot in 2002 (while Lutte Ouvrière candidate Arlette Laguiller got 6.1%) that this was put into perspective.[90] And compared with the Militant Tendency in the UK (now the Socialist Party of England and Wales, the British section of the Committee for a Workers International), the British section of the FI has long been vastly smaller and weaker – and it remains so today. The largest of British organisations broadly in the Trotskyist tradition, the British SWP (which regarded the Soviet Union as 'state capitalist' and is the leading section of the International Socialist Organisation), is also considered one of the 'sects' by Mandel.[91]

If you lump together genuine sects and other organised tendencies that have certain sectarian features, but are programmatically quite close to the FI – and in reality, no marginal organisation can easily withstand the pressure to sow sectarian illusions or adapt to much more popular tendencies or leaderships – then the FI, which likewise comprises but a few thousand members, can indeed appear like the 'real deal'. Mandel, for all his openness to participation in broader political formation processes, thus arrives in a convoluted way at a kind of 'exclusive authority claim', asserting a kind of 'birthright' because of the continuity of the existing FI with the organisation founded by Trotsky and his comrades in 1938. And that is a very questionable thing to do.

Mandel does admit self-critically to weaknesses of the FI at all kinds of levels (organisational weakness, occasional momentous misjudgements, etc). But he also repeatedly flatters his own organisation, even to the point of praising the many clever books written by FI members (and Mandel does not fail to mention his own books 'in all modesty'). Incidentally, one cannot fail but notice from the long list of authors that a number of them had left the FI in the meantime – which Mandel also notes without comment.[92]

Under the sub-heading 'An international to be proud of', we again find Mandel's extreme identification with his own organisation, albeit combined with Mandel's unconditional determination to build an international organisation not with the kind of illuminated types that sects are made of, but with completely 'normal' people:

---

90 In the meantime, the importance of LO has dwindled, while the LCR has launched a much stronger 'New Anticapitalist Party' comprising over 10,000 members at the time of writing – MK, 2009.

91 Mandel 1995b, p. 36.

92 Mandel 1995b, pp. 34–5.

I have never felt as proud and confident in the Fourth International,
that great movement of ours which we are collectively building through
the combined efforts of thousands of comrades. Fanatics attract fanatics.
Screwballs attract screwballs. But the overwhelming majority of humankind is composed neither of fanatics nor of screwballs. It consists of normal human beings, inasmuch as people can be normal in the inhuman
society we are living in. A revolutionary organization composed of normal people, that is what we strive to become.[93]

The truth is that the members of the FI are, as a rule, relatively 'normal'. The FI is
neither organised around a cult of personality, nor is it dominated by a 'mother
section', as is the case with most of the other groupings. Even during Mandel's
lifetime, however, the FI no longer upheld the claim found in the 1938 *Transitional Programme* of being 'the world party of socialist revolution'. At the world
congress held in the year of Ernest Mandel's death, it rather more modestly
declared that it is one of several international organised tendencies wishing to
make a contribution to the renewal of the workers' movement, the reformation
of an anti-capitalist left, and the formation of revolutionary parties and a mass
revolutionary international.[94] Mandel likewise said that the FI was prepared
to operate as an organised minority within a mass international supported by
much larger movements. However, one has to grasp the reservations implicit
in this declaration: for Mandel, the FI, the organisation that *authentically* preserved and developed the revolutionary Marxist tradition, was *the* nucleus of
the future great force and not merely one nucleus of many. Therein lies the
strongly 'identitarian' trait in Mandel's thinking.[95]

   The central feature of Mandel's distinction from sectarianism is the reference to the practical movement and the 'openness' of Marxism to new insights,
both in relation to the past and the present. What he considers characteristic
of sectarianism is the exaggeration of canonised texts and the preservation of
group identity by proving faulty positions or even just formulations among rival
groups:

> Sectarians are fanatical addicts of the Gospel according to St. John: 'In
> the beginning was the Word.' Everything depends on the right word being
> spoken or written everywhere. The belief in the power of the word be-

---

93   Mandel 1995b, p. 37.
94   'Building the International today' in Fourteenth World Congress – 1995, available at https://
      fourth.international/en/world-congresses/14th-world-congress-1995.
95   Mandel 1979a, p. 124 et seq.

comes like a belief in magic. Any consideration of actual time and place disappears. Terrible consequences are supposed to flow from a wrong formula here, a wrong headline there.[96]

The Spartacist League (not unlike other groups that had split from the Fourth International over time) accused the Fourth International of having 'capitulated to Stalinism' since the late nineteen-forties. Paradoxically, things were turned into their opposite over the decades, and the accusation against the FI is now that it opened the door to bourgeois forces through its opposition to the post-Stalinist bureaucracies, for example with its solidarity with Solidarność. Mandel therefore takes the opportunity to stress once again the rooting of Marxist politics in the project of working-class self-liberation, which implies a rejection of any kind of paternalism by 'higher authorities' and a commitment to self-management and socialist democracy. Marxist socialism or communism aspires to the real 'freedom' of individuals, and the path to such a state cannot completely run counter to the goal, because then the goal cannot be achieved.[97]

Although Mandel's attitude to the 'sectarians' he is debating is difficult to compare with theirs, he does give the impression – driven by rivalry between competing groups – of occasionally stooping to their level. For example, he accuses them of entangling themselves in 14 (!) contradictions, which he 'proves' to them in great detail. The 'final and supreme' contradiction reads as follows: 'All the sects supposedly intent upon "Leninist party building" haven't built anything resembling any really existing international organization; some have even abandoned all pretense of doing so. We and our cothinkers on the other hand, accused of "liquidationism" and other deadly sins, have built the Fourth International and assured its constant – though, to be sure, modest – growth for over thirty years'.

However, even if others have not achieved anything of significance, it is still a very shaky argument to highlight the organisational successes of the FI and attest to three decades of continuous growth. When I joined the FI in 1972, it stated much higher membership figures than even the staunchest member would be able to give with a modicum of honesty today.

Since groups that lay claim to Trotskyism, such as the Spartacists, frequently strike martial tones in order to appear particularly radical, they tend to dismiss any defence of freedom, human rights and self-organisation as bourgeois humanitarianism. Mandel, by contrast – and this is something he stresses

---

96   Mandel 1995b, p. 20.
97   Mandel 1995b, pp. 21 and 31.

in debate with the Spartacist Tendency – stood for the unconditional support for any movement of liberation and rejected the idea that the interests of the exploited and oppressed should be subordinated to any 'higher' (e.g. world-strategic or organisationally egoistic) motives. Mandel cites the defence of Sacco and Vanzetti by the young Communist Party USA and the Communist world movement, despite the fact that these two victims of bourgeois class justice were not Communists but anarchists, as an example worth emulating: 'This lesson from history should be generalized. We should resolutely stand in favor of fighting for basic human rights in all countries of the world, without exception'.[98]

By insisting that this should apply to all countries in the world, Mandel distances himself from the idea that the defence of human rights is 'Eurocentrist', i.e. that it imposes 'European' values on other cultures. Mandel does not accept torture, flogging or stoning under the pretext that such 'customs' correspond to certain cultural or religious practices. Naturally, Mandel did not support Jaruzelski's coup against Solidarność either, and even the fact that the restorative forces ultimately won out in Poland did not change his mind in retrospect.

Against those who believe in the magic powers of (correct revolutionary) words, Mandel cites the necessity of a certain organisational strength in order to make a difference. 'In order to successfully overthrow capitalism, it is not enough to have a correct program. While this is a key clement for success, you need in addition sufficient organizational strength and a sufficient implantation in the working class and the progressive mass movements, be it in large enough minorities of them'.[99]

Now, the organisations of the FI and the revolutionary movements in general are clearly far from having achieved such organisational strength and entrenchment among the masses. Mandel explains this with the deeply rooted hesitation of broad masses to break with their traditional leaderships, at least as long as they do not see an alternative force that looks like it could become a sufficiently strong and effective organisation in the foreseeable future. Because too many in its ranks underestimated the potential of new processes of radicalisation, the FI was also unable to take advantage of the late 1960s upsurge – except to some extent in France – to create parties capable of action, be it small parties. The successes of Maoism at the time, resulting from the appeal of a far too rosy interpretation of the Maoist 'cultural revolution', did not make things any easier. Above all, the credibility crisis of the socialist idea had continued to

---

98   Mandel 1995b, p. 21.
99   Mandel 1995b, p. 22.

intensify, not only because of the terrible Pol Pot regime, but also because of the increasingly tangible inability of the bureaucratically administered USSR and its allies to keep up with (let alone 'overtake') the developed capitalist countries in the third technological revolution.[100]

Mandel sees the possibility of achieving the necessary rootedness and strength to play a decisive role in new mass movements as well as during the outbreak of pre-revolutionary and revolutionary situations. Against the Sparta-cists, who regard such matters as bourgeois catastrophism, Mandel underlines the catastrophic developments that threaten humanity if the forces of socialist revolution do not prevail: the danger of a nuclear annihilation, the danger of ecological collapse, the danger of drowning in squalor, despair and barbarism. At the end of his opening, he calls out to his auditorium:

> Forward to a more human society. Given the threats weighting upon the future of our species, never in history was there a cause more worthy of defending than this collective endeavour of ours, more worthy of devot-ing one's whole life to it. So, comrades, to the World Socialist Federation that will safeguard the survival of the human race and usher in the higher and more human civilization of socialism, of emancipated labour. For-ward! Vperyod! Adelante![101]

One hopes that many more people will be inspired by Mandel's verve and let themselves be motivated to live his kind of life, yet without succumbing to ungrounded political confidence or to some of his more questionable ideas. Ultimately, any other than critical approval would not be in Mandel's spirit.

9   The Self-Organisation of the Working Class

Mandel's work is an important starting point for the revitalisation of the dis-cussion on socialist strategy. Since his death, we have seen a resurgence of struggles against wage and social cuts, the privatisation of public services and social insurance, as well as international protests and mobilisations against neoliberal globalisation. Mandel lived long enough to see the very early signs of the latter development, which would only enter public consciousness with the outcry in Seattle in 1999: 'The world is not a commodity! Another world is pos-

---

100   Mandel 1995b, pp. 22–3.
101   Mandel 1995b, p. 37.

sible!'[102] In the international movement, especially in the spaces for exchange and reflection that the social forum movement has created, people increasingly debate what kind of world, what kind of economic and social order can and should replace the existing one. Mandel's ideas of socialist democracy, i.e. of combining self-management in the enterprises and in all social institutions and sectors with democratic decision-making processes on all major political and investment choices, are an important contribution to this debate. Today, a revival of the ideals of the international that Mandel stood for – international solidarity and common international action, international articulation of positions and a sense of common destiny in this one world – is on the agenda more than at the time of his death.

The thread that runs through the whole of Mandel's work and through all of his political and strategic thinking is the idea of self-determined working class activity and organisation as the lynchpin of the desired universal process of emancipation.[103] Since the emergence of a social surplus product, the transition from absolute to relative scarcity, and the emergence of the social division of labour and class society, human society has been characterised by class division and class domination, by exploitation and oppression. Since then, freedom for self-development has always been reserved for a minority of society at the expense of the working majority. The domination of the majority by ruling minorities in class societies is based on direct subordination on the one hand. On the other, since the emergence of commodity production and money, it has also been determined by the anonymous forces of the market, whose laws are enforced behind the backs of participants as expressions of an illusory nature that they themselves have created, but which they do not consciously control.

In capitalist class society, which represents developed commodity production, these aspects of heteronomy and alienation are taken to extremes. They are threatening to turn into the annihilation of all human civilisation. On the other hand, a class of wage-earners has emerged that Marx called the working class or the proletariat, which according to Mandel today comprises one billion people, or even two billion if the poor rural semi-proletariat is included. Because of its size, position and role in the production process, Mandel still sees this class as the potentially revolutionary subject, whose self-liberation can trigger a comprehensive process of liberation from all exploitation, oppression and alienation. In Mandel's understanding, political organisation and the construc-

---

See Aguiton 2002.
103   See Mandel 1979a, p. 128 et seq.

tion of revolutionary organisations and 'vanguard parties' only make sense if they promote the self-activity of workers and the exploited and oppressed in general.[104]

In Mandel's view, socialist revolution is possible particularly in the advanced capitalist countries, which offer the best material basis for the construction of socialism, for the reduction of working hours and the pushing back commodities, the money economy and authoritarian hierarchies. In part, this notion is tied to the idea of the traditional large enterprise. If the workforce of such enterprises starts to act for its own interests, then its collective self-organisation to control its own working conditions and ultimately take over the enterprise in self-management comes more naturally than it does to a large number of producers scattered across small enterprises (or even producing or providing services on their own account on a pseudo-self-employed basis). For some years now, however, the large-scale industrial enterprise has been considered a phased-out model. It therefore seems to me a task for the near future to work out to what extent this trend undermines Mandel's classical notion of self-organisation at the workplace as the essence of socialist working-class self-liberation.

Mandel himself noted such trends. In his analysis of contemporary capitalism (especially in *Late Capitalism*), he argues that the concentration and centralisation of capital, the constant increase in labour productivity and the displacement of living labour from the production process as a predominant tendency is mediated by constant revivals of dispersion, new creation of smaller units and therefore also of producing with lower labour productivity in sub-sectors.[105] From Mandel's point of view, it is not just that the absolute number of wage-earners is growing worldwide; the potential fighting capacity of this class also appears greater to him than ever before in history. He views the proletarianisation of more highly educated classes as adding to the emancipatory potential. A strike of all bank employees or broad layers of highly qualified technicians lasting several weeks, for example, could economically undermine the ruling class faster and easier today than a miner or steelworker strike lasting several months could in the past. Moreover, Mandel's idea of a revolutionary process is by no means limited to the model of a large-scale workforce. This is because only an all-encompassing class movement spanning enterprises and industries, comprising the mass of the population down to the residential quarters and neighbourhoods, and extending to an entire country, can challenge

104   Mandel 1995b, p. 40.
105   See Mandel 1975d, p. 527 et seq.

bourgeois class rule. The precondition is the democratic centralisation of structures of self-organisation built from below. In this way, a new, democratically legitimised structure can emerge, while at the same time the great diversity of interests and opinions within the majority of the population is protected. This structure can replace the old bourgeois state apparatus.

Of all the things that have occurred since the World War II, the Portuguese revolution of 1974–75 came closest to Mandel's conception of revolution. As mentioned earlier, Vercammen hypothesised that Mandel's error lay, in a sense, in the belief that a revolutionary tendency could gain strength by 'surfing' on such a broad wave of independent mass activity and self-organisation.[106] Certainly, Mandel had a propensity to celebrate the creative potential of masses in motion very enthusiastically. His political proposals at the time were nonetheless at odds with the politics of forces far more influential than was the small FI group emerging in the wake of the 'Carnation Revolution'. In spite of giving the very strong impression of developing perspectives in line with the prevailing feelings and moods of the Portuguese workers, soldiers, small peasants and poor, Mandel was in a sense 'swimming against the tide'. What won out in the end – capitalist normalisation and a 'normal' bourgeois parliamentary democracy – was certainly not what he had hoped for.[107]

In opposition to the big traditional tendencies of the workers' movement, especially the social-democratic Socialist Party (PS), which had hegemony among the masses, Mandel advocated the need to continue to develop and expand the germs of self-organisation from below that had emerged, as well as centralise them regionally and nationally. This was meant to herald the beginnings of a new, socialist republic. Unlike the overwhelming majority of the radical left, i.e. the subjectively revolutionary elements to the left of the CP, Mandel advocated the necessity of a united front with the traditional parties of the workers' movement. This included the social democrats, even though – or perhaps for the very reason that – they were the most important force of the 'democratic counter-revolution', i.e. the force that channelled the upsurge of the mass movement and kept it within the framework of existing capitalist relations. However, the majority of the anti-capitalist left made this business easier for social democracy by limiting itself to denunciation.[108]

Mandel's understanding of revolution is strongly influenced by his reception of the 1917 Russian experience. The revolutionary mass movement wins demo-

---

106   See Vercammen 1997, 'Ernest Mandel et la Capacité Révolutionnaire de la Classe Ouvrière'
        at http://www.ernestmandel.org.
107   See Mandel 1975e, p. 18 et seq.
108   See Mandel 1979d, p. 47 et seq.

cratic freedoms and creates structures of self-organisation all the way to councils. These are initially dominated by 'moderate' forces that do not want to viol-
ate the bourgeois framework. But masses acting in a self-determined fashion
learn quickly, especially when there is a politically astute revolutionary party
that organises the bulk of the workers' vanguard and gradually advances the
learning process of the masses through its participation. In the end, the 'mod-
erates' lose their credibility, the revolutionaries win the majority in the councils, and the insurrection, the moment of taking power, becomes the logical
conclusion of this entire process (rather than a coup by a determined small
minority).[109]

Since Mandel has always presented his strategic thinking and his conception of revolutionary processes as an adaptation of Trotsky's ideas, and since
the views of the two indeed have much in common, it is not easy to distinguish Mandel's original contribution from the 'tradition' to which he appeals.
The same applies to Mandel's manner in which he appropriates Lenin's 'theory
of organisation'.

If one examines how Trotsky and Mandel uses the term 'dual power' respectively, one is struck by a not entirely insignificant difference. Like Lenin, Trotsky describes the 'regime' of dual power that emerged in Russia in February
1917 as a blatantly contradictory, ambiguous and untenable situation in every
respect. The government is bourgeois and relies on the 'conciliatory' majority in the workers' and soldiers' councils, which are the only real power in the
country, yet do not exercise power.[110] Mandel, likewise, believes that there are
ultimately only two possibilities when councils or council-like structures of
mass self-organisation emerge: either they prevail, and their authority replaces
of the authority of the old state apparatus; or the movement is defeated, the
structures of self-organisation are largely destroyed, and the bourgeois state
reclaims all power for itself. Nonetheless, unlike Trotsky, Mandel uses the term
'dual power' in a consistently positive sense.[111] For him, 'dual power' is a stage
through which the masses must pass if they are to attain socialist consciousness
and understand the necessity of socialist revolution. For revolutionary organisations, which must first obtain a modicum of strength and rootedness, this is
the only opportunity to win majorities for their ideas.[112] Mandel finds it difficult to imagine a revolutionary mass party emerging in a 'cold climate', i.e. at
low levels of mass movement and self-organisation from below. Such a party

---

109   See Mandel 1992b, p. 8.
110   See Trotsky 1932, chapter 11.
111   See Mandel 1979d, p. 32 et seq.
112   See Mandel 1970c.

would succumb to the pull of what exists rather than be able to uphold its revolutionary identity. A serious revolutionary organisation (to be sure, more than just a small propaganda group) that might stand a chance in a revolutionary situation, on the other hand, can and will usually only organise or critically influence a small minority of the participants at the beginning of a revolutionary process.[113]

The logical corollary of this concept is the desire for the stage of 'dual power' to last not just a few weeks, but for a relatively long time – many months, perhaps even one, two, three years. In this kind of scenario, the main social classes would keep each other in check, so to speak. With the repressive apparatus largely dismantled, the bourgeoisie would no longer be able to crush the mass movement and its organisations. The movement, on the other hand, in which the conscious revolutionaries are still a minority, albeit a growing one, would not yet be ready to articulate the conquest of political power as a desirable practical goal.

Once the socialist objectives and practical proposals of the revolutionaries have gained majorities and are accepted in the movement, the question of ending dual power in favour of the full exercise of power by the councils arises. If we try to imagine such a process as vividly and concretely as possible, it goes without saying that a whole series of uncertainties and unforeseeable factors might emerge. Above all, individual factors such as the degree of inability of the bourgeois state to act, on the one hand, and the degree of the political maturity of the mass movement, on the other, would have to be timed rather well and interlock smoothly in order for the matter to 'end well' in the sense of Mandel's idea of revolution.

On the whole, Mandel has made a very inspiring contribution to the idea of a plausible revolutionary process in industrialised countries as we know them today, reflecting the inspiring, positive sides of real contemporary experiences. It is up to us to critically examine this contribution by working through the negative possibilities that favour a 'bad' outcome, based on new experiences, reflections and debates. This is a broad subject and should not simply translate into 'developing Mandel's approach further', although this approach cannot be ignored if we are to the evolution of socialist revolutionary theory seriously. In the 'political testament' dealt with in the previous section, Mandel admits to 'gaps' in 'revolutionary Marxism', of which he was one of the leading exponents. The questions of ecology, women's oppression and women's liberation in particular have so far been inadequately integrated, both theoretically and

---

113   Mandel and Agnoli 1980, p. 130 et seq.

programmatically.[114] These are, of course, not minor issues. A real theoretical confrontation between the most advanced ecological analyses, scientifically founded forms of radical feminist thought, and Mandel's 'revolutionary Marxism' would certainly be a challenge, the outcome of which is neither certain nor can be predicted by anyone.

Mandel's attempt to critically revive the Marxist tradition as a whole, based on extensive empirical findings, can only be continued through collective work: that is, through collaboration between representatives of different interpretive traditions in Marxism and related branches of critical, emancipation-oriented social science. It is likely that the results of intensive interdisciplinary research in the future will not simply augment Mandel's legacy, but result in a less homogeneously conceived revolutionary theory, emerging from a variety of theoretical perspectives and with less concern for a coherence that covers all conceivable social theory.

---

114   See Mandel 1995b, p. 31.

Eyewitness Testimony (Tape Recordings from the Author's Own Archive)

Helmut Dahmer, Frankfurt (Main), 23 October 2000
Jakob Moneta, Frankfurt (Main), 23 October 2000
Rudolf Segall, Frankfurt (Main), 23 October 2000
Helene Jungclas, Thalhausen, 25 November 2000
Hans Peiffer, Cologne, 26 March 2001
Helmut Wendler, Cologne, 26 March 2001
Winfried Wolf, Berlin, 28 March 2001
François Vercammen, Brussels, 22 April 2001
Peter von Oertzen, Hanover, 7 June 2001
Livio Maitan, Paris, 18 June 2001

Bibliography

1 Literature by Ernest Mandel

Mandel, Ernest [alias E. Germain] 1946, 'Postface: La question juive au lendemain de la deuxième guerre mondiale' in Abraham Léon: *La Conception matérialiste de la question juive*, Paris: Paris Pionniers.

Mandel, Ernest 1950, *The Third Chinese Revolution*, available at https://www.marxists.org/archive/mandel/1950/05/china1.htm.

Mandel, Ernest 1961, 'Les greves belges: essai d'explication socio-économique', *Les Temps Modernes*, 180, April 1961: 1291–1310, available at http://www.ernestmandel.org.

Mandel, Ernest 1963, 'The Law of Value in Relation to Self-Management and Investment in the Economy of the Workers' States. Some Remarks on the Discussion in Cuba', *World Outlook = Perspective mondiale*, 1, 1963, available at the Ernest Mandel Internet Archive at http://www.lcr-sap.be/mandel/en.

Mandel, Ernest 1965, 'A Socialist Strategy for Western Europe', Nottingham: Institute for Workers' Control.

Mandel, Ernest 1967a, *An Introduction to Marxist Economic Theory*, available at https://www.marxists.org/archive/mandel/1967/intromet/index.htm

Mandel, Ernest 1967b, 'El debato economico en Cuba durante el periodo 1963–1964', *Cuadernos de Marcha*, 3, July 1967: 87–92.

Mandel, Ernest [alias Ernest Germain] 1967c, 'Marxism vs. Ultraleftism. Key Issues in Healy's Challenge', in *The Fourth International*, Paris.

Mandel, Ernest 1968a, *Entstehung und Entwicklung der ökonomischen Lehre von Karl Marx: 1843–1863*, Frankfurt am Main: Europäische Verlagsanstalt.

Mandel, Ernest 1968b, *Marxist Economic Theory*, London: Merlin Press.

Mandel, Ernest 1969a, *The Inconsistencies of State Capitalism*, London: International Marxist Group Education Commission.

Mandel, Ernest 1969b, 'The Debate on Workers' Control', available at http://www.marxists.org.

Mandel, Ernest 1970a, *Contrôle ouvrier, conseils ouvriers, autogestion*, Paris: Anthologie.

Mandel, Ernest 1970b, 'The Leninist Theory of Organization', available at http://www.ernestmandel.org.

Mandel, Ernest 1970c, 'The Laws of Uneven Development', *New Left Review*, 59, Jan/Feb: 19–38.

Mandel, Ernest 1970d, *Die Radikalisierung der Jugend*, Mannheim: ISP-Verlag.

Mandel, Ernest 1970e, *Peaceful Coexistence and World Revolution*, available at http://www.marxists.org.

Mandel, Ernest 1970f, 'Lenin und das Problem des proletarischen Klassenbewusstseins', in *Lenin. Revolution und Politik*, Frankfurt: Suhrkamp.

Mandel, Ernest 1971a, *The Leninist Theory of Organisation*, available at http://www .marxists.org.

Mandel, Ernest 1971b, 'Introduction by Ernest Mandel' in Leon Trotsky, *The Struggle Against Fascism in Germany*, New York: Pathfinder.

Mandel, Ernest 1971c, *Arbeiterkontrolle, Arbeiterräte, Arbeiterselbstverwaltung*, Frankfurt: Europäische Verlagsanstalt.

Mandel, Ernest 1971d, 'Rosa Luxemburg and German Social Democracy', available at http://www.marxists.org.

Mandel, Ernest 1972a, *Der Spätkapitalismus*. Frankfurt: Suhrkamp.

Mandel, Ernest 1972b, 'Besetzung der Fabriken – na klar' (interview), *Der Spiegel*, 11, 26 (6 March): 41–6.

Mandel, Ernest 1972c, 'Die Arbeiten des 20. Plenum des Internationalen Exekutivkommittees. Am Beginn einer neuen Etappe der entristischen Arbeit', in *Die Taktik des Entrismus: Dokumentation*, edited by Gruppe Internationale Marxisten, Cologne.

Mandel, Ernest 1972d, 'Wettkampf der Systeme', in *Probleme der internationalen Beziehungen*, edited by Ekkehart Krippendorff, Frankfurt: Suhrkamp.

Mandel, Ernest 1972e, *Der Spätkapitalismus*, Frankfurt: Suhrkamp. See also Mandel 1975d. [The German text contains some passages that are not in the English translation. Where such passages are cited in the present work, we reference the German edition of Mandel's text.]

Mandel, Ernest [alias E. Germain] 1973a, 'Zur Kritik der „Kompass"-Tendenz am Europäischen Dokument', *Internationaler Rundbrief*, 14: 1–14.

Mandel, Ernest 1973b [1969], *An Introduction to Marxist Economic Theory*, New York: Pathfinder.

Mandel, Ernest 1973c, *On Bureaucracy: A Marxist Analysis*, London: IMG Publications.

Mandel, Ernest 1974a, 'Solzhenitsyn's Assault on Stalinism and the October Revolution', available at http://www.marxists.org.

Mandel, Ernest [alias E. Germain] 1974b, 'On the Compass Tendency's Critique of the European Perspectives Document. A Reply and a Request for Clarification of Differences', *Internal Information Bulletin*/Socialist Workers' Party, 3: 13–20.

Mandel, Ernest 1974c, *A Socialist Strategy for Western Europe*, Nottingham: Institute for Workers' Control.

Mandel, Ernest 1974d, 'Solschenizyn oder Der unbewältigte Stalinismus', *Frankfurter Rundschau*, 30 (23 March), 3.

Mandel, Ernest 1975a, *Von der sozialen Ungleichheit zur klassenlosen Gesellschaft*, Zürich: Veritas-Verlag.

Mandel, Ernest 1975b, *Die Rolle der Intelligenz im Klassenkampf*, Frankfurt: Internationale Sozialistische Publikationen.

Mandel, Ernest 1975c, 'Les notres: Georg Jungclas', *Quartieme Internationale*, 22, Autumn: 5–6.

Mandel, Ernest 1975d, *Late Capitalism*, London: NLB.

Mandel, Ernest 1975e, 'Revolutionärer Aufschwung und wirtschaftlicher Niedergang', in *Wohin treibt Portugal?*, Frankfurt: ISP-Verlag.

Mandel, Ernest 1976a, *Die Bürokratie*, Frankfurt: Internationale Sozialistische Publikationen.

Mandel, Ernest 1976b, 'On the Current Stage of World Revolution', available at http://www.marxists.org.

Mandel, Ernest 1978a, *Revolutionäre Strategien im 20. Jahrhundert. Politische Essays*, Vienna: Europa-Verlag.

Mandel, Ernest 1978b, *From Stalinism to Eurocommunism*, London: NLB and Verso.

Mandel, Ernest 1978c, 'Der Mensch ist das höchste Wesen für den Menschen', in Fritz J. Raddatz, *Warum ich Marxist bin*, Munich: Fischer Taschenbuch.

Mandel, Ernest 1978d [1971], 'Die Strategie der Übergangsforderungen' in *Revolutionäre Strategien im 20. Jahrhundert*, Vienna: Europa-Verlag.

Mandel, Ernest 1979a, *From Class Society to Communism: An Introduction to Marxism*, London: Ink Links Ltd.

Mandel, Ernest 1979b, 'Why the Soviet Bureaucracy is Not a New Ruling Class', *Monthly Review*, 31, 3, July/August: 63–76, available at http://www.marxists.org.

Mandel, Ernest 1979c, 'Redebeiträge (1978)', in *Der Bahro-Kongress: Aufzeichnungen, Berichte und Referate*, Berlin: Olle und Wolter.

Mandel, Ernest 1979d, *Revolutionary Marxism Today*, edited by Jon Rothschild, London: NLB.

Mandel, Ernest 1979e, *Trotsky: A Study in the Dynamic of His Thought*, London: NLB.

Mandel, Ernest 1979f, *Trotzki. Eine Einführung in sein Denken*, Berlin (West): Olle und Wolter.

Mandel, Ernest 1980a, *Offener Marxismus*, Frankfurt: Campus-Verlag.

Mandel, Ernest 1980b, 'Report on the World Political Situation', in *1979 World Congress of the Fourth International. Major Resolutions and Reports*, New York: Intercontinental Pr.

Mandel, Ernest 1981a, 'The 21 Theoretical Errors of Comrades Clark, Feldman, Horowitz and Waters', *Intercontinental Press*, 16, May: 456–72.

Mandel, Ernest 1981b, 'Die Planungsdebatte auf Kuba', in *20 [Zwanzig] Jahre kubanische Revolution in der Analyse der IV. Internationale*, edited by the Political Bureau of the International Marxist Group (Germany), Frankfurt: GIM.

Mandel, Ernest 1982a, 'Der Klassencharakter der Sowjetunion', *The Review of Radical Political Economics*, 14, 1, Spring: 55–67.

Mandel, Ernest 1982b, *An Introduction to Marxism*, London: Pluto Press.

Mandel, Ernest 1983, 'Emanzipation, Wissenschaft und Politik bei Karl Marx', in *Marx heute. Pro und Contra*, Hamburg: Hoffmann und Campe.

Mandel, Ernest 1984a, *Karl Marx – Die Aktualität seines Werkes*, Frankfurt: ISP-Verlag.

Mandel, Ernest 1984b, *Delightful Murder: A Social History of the Crime Story*, London: Pluto Press.

Mandel, Ernest 1985a, 'Kein Sozialismus ohne Selbstverwaltung', in *Der Sozialismus an der Schwelle zum 21. Jahrhundert*, Volume 1, edited by Milo Nikolic, Berlin: Argument-Verlag.

Mandel, Ernest 1985b, *Dictatorship of the Proletariat and Socialist Democracy*, available at http://www.marxists.org.

Mandel, Ernest 1985c, 'Partially Independent Variables and Internal Logic in Classical Marxist Economic Analysis', *Social Science Information*, 24, 3: 485–505.

Mandel, Ernest 1985d, 'Ernest Mandel on the Necessity and Possibility of Socialism', available at http://www.IIRE.org.

Mandel, Ernest 1986a, 'Anatomy of a Split. Why the Australian SWP Left the Fourth International', *International Viewpoint*, 93, 24, available at http://www.marxists.org.

Mandel, Ernest 1986b, *The Place of Marxism in History*, Amsterdam: International Institute for Research and Education.

Mandel, Ernest 1986c, *In Defence of Socialist Planning*, available at http://www.marxists .org.

Mandel, Ernest 1986d, *The Meaning of the Second World War*, London/New York: Verso.

Mandel, Ernest 1987a, 'Les catégories marchandes dans la période de transition', in Ernesto 'Che' Guevara, *Ecrits d'un révolutionnaire*, edited by Michael Löwy, Montreuil: La Brèche-PEC.

Mandel, Ernest 1987b, *Die Krise. Weltwitschaft 1974–1986*, Hamburg: Konkret Literatur-Verlag.

Mandel, Ernest 1987c, 'Verschuldungskrise: Eine tickende Zeitbombe', in Jeffrey Bortz, Fidel Castro, Ernest Mandel and Winfried Wolf, *Schuldenkrise. In der Dritten Welt tickt eine Zeitbombe*, Frankfurt: ISP Verlag.

Mandel, Ernest 1987d, 'Marx, Karl Heinrich', in *Marxian Economics: The New Palgrave*, London: Macmillan.

Mandel, Ernest 1988, *The Reasons for Founding the Fourth International – And Why They Remain Valid Today*, available at http://www.marxists.org.

Mandel, Ernest 1989a, 'Einleitung', in *Die kommunistische Alternative: Texte der Linken Opposition und IV. Internationale 1932–1985*, edited by Wolfgang Alles, Frankfurt: ISP-Verlag.

Mandel, Ernest 1989b, 'Freiheitsrechte und Sozialismus', in *Soziale oder sozialistische Demokratie? Beiträge zur Geschichte der Linken in der Bundesrepublik*, Marburg: SP-Verlag.

Mandel, Ernest 1990a, 'Unter welchen Bedingungen die DDR tatsächlich zu einer neuen Hoffnung werden kann', in *Nichts wird mehr so sein, wie es war. Zur Zukunft der beiden deutschen Republiken*, edited by Frank Blohm and Wolfgang Herzeberg, Frankfurt: Luchterhand Literaturverlag.

Mandel, Ernest 1990b, 'Introduction by Ernest Mandel', in Karl Marx, *Capital*, Volume I, London and New York: Penguin.

Mandel, Ernest 1991a, *Kontroversen um 'Das Kapital'*, Berlin: Dietz.

Mandel, Ernest 1991b, *Beyond Perestroika: The Future of Gorbachev's USSR*, London: Verso.

Mandel, Ernest 1991c, 'Introduction by Ernest Mandel', in Karl Marx, *Capital*, Volume III, New York and London: Penguin.

Mandel, Ernest 1991d, 'Die Dialektik von Produktivkräften, Produktionsverhältnissen und Klassenkampf neben Kategorien der Latenz und des parametrischen Determinismus in der materialistischen Geschichtsauffassung', in *Die versteinerten Verhältnisse zum Tanzen bringen. Beiträge zur marxistischen Theorie heute*, edited by Thomas Brüsemeister et al., Berlin: Dietz.

Mandel, Ernest 1992a, *Power and Money: A Marxist Theory of Bureaucracy*, London: Verso.

Mandel, Ernest 1992b, *1917: Coup d'etat or Social Revolution? The Legitimacy of the Russian Revolution*, Amsterdam: International Institute for Research and Education. PDF available at http://www.IIRE.org.

Mandel, Ernest 1992c, 'The International Debate on Long Waves of Capitalist Development: An Intermediary Balance Sheet', in *New Findings in Long-Wave Research*, edited by Alfred Kleinknecht, Ernest Mandel and Immanuel Wallerstein, London: Palgrave Macmillan.

Mandel, Ernest 1992d, 'Introduction by Ernest Mandel' in Karl Marx, *Capital*, Volume II, New York: Penguin.

Mandel, Ernest 1993 [1969], 'Theorien über den Faschismus', in *Theorien über den Faschismus*, edited by Hans-Jürgen Schulz et al., Berlin: Gruppe Avanti, available at http://www.ernestmandel.org.

Mandel, Ernest 1994, 'Alle Macht den Räten: Bekenntnisse eines notorisch-unbeirrbaren Linken', in *Zwischen Rätesozialismus und Reformprojekt: Lesebuch zum 70. Geburtstag von Peter von Oertzen*, Cologne: SPW-Verlag.

Mandel, Ernest 1995a, *Trotsky as Alternative*, London: Verso.

Mandel, Ernest 1995b, 'World Socialist Revolution Today. Sectarianism vs. Revolutionary Marxism', *In Defense of Marxism*, 125, May/June: 18–41.

Mandel, Ernest 1995c, *Long Waves of Capitalist Development: A Marxist Interpretation*, London and New York: Verso.

Mandel, Ernest 1997, *Le troisieme âge du capitalisme*, second French edition, Paris: Edition de la Passion.

Mandel, Ernest 2000, *Macht und Geld*, Köln: Neuer ISP-Verlag.

Mandel, Ernest 2001, 'Das Verhältnis von Nord und Süd. Argumente für Weltbürgerschaft und Solidarität', *Inprekorr*, 352, February: 16–19.

Mandel, Ernest 2011, *The Meaning of the Second World War*, London and New York: Verso.

Mandel, Ernest 2016 [1962] [as Ernest Germain], '30 Questions and Answers on the History of the Communist Party of the Soviet Union', available at http://www.marxists .org.

Mandel, Ernest 2020a [1973], 'Ernest Mandel on Marxism and Ecology. The Dialectic of Growth', available at http://www.iire.org/node/924.

Mandel, Ernest 2020b [1990], 'The Material, Social and Ideological Preconditions for the Nazi Genocide', available at https://www.iire.org/node/902.

Mandel, Ernest 2020c [1991], 'The Origins of National Socialism. Singularity and Repeatability of the Nazi Crimes', available at https://www.iire.org/node/949.

Mandel, Ernest and Johannes Agnoli 1980, *Offener Marxismus. Ein Gespräch über Dogmen, Orthodoxie und die Häresien der Realität*, Frankfurt: Campus-Verlag.

Mandel, Ernest and Oskar Fischer 1977, *Trotzkis Faschismustheorie/Leninismus gegen Stalinismus. Die Lehren der deutschen Katastrophe*, Frankfurt: Internationale Sozialistische Publikationen.

Mandel, Ernest, Rudolf Bahro, and Peter Oertzen 1980, *Was da alles auf uns zukommt ... Perspektiven der 8oer Jahre*, Berlin: Olle & Wolter.

Mandel, Ernest and Winfried Wolf 1988, *Cash, Crash & Crisis: Profitboom, Börsenkrach und Wirtschaftskrise*, Hamburg: Rasch und Röhring.

2   Literature about Ernest Mandel

Achcar, Gilbert 1999a, *The Legacy of Ernest Mandel*, edited by Gilbert Achcar, London and New York: Verso.

Achcar, Gilbert 1999b, *Le Marxisme d'Ernest Mandel*, Paris: PUF.

Ali, Tariq 1995, 'Tariq Ali Interviews Ernest Mandel. The Luck of a Crazy Youth' (1989), *New Left Review*, 213, September/October: 101–6.

Alonso, Aurelio and Sergio de Santis 1973, 'Bewußtsein und Produktion. Eine Kontroverse zwischen Ernesto Che Guevera, Charles Bettelheim und Ernest Mandel über die sozialistische Organisation in der Ökonomie', in *Sozialökonomische Studientexte*, Volume 11, Giessen: Rotdruck.

Artous, Antoine 1996, 'Une réponse à Jean-Marie Vincent', *Critique communiste*, 144: 13–17.

Bendien, Juriaan 1987, *Ernest Mandel: An Attempt at a Bibliography of His Writings*, Christchurch: University of Canterbury.

Bendien, Juriaan 2000, 'Additions/corrections to the 1987 bibliography of Ernest Mandel's writings by Jurriaan Bendien, updated June 2000, chronologically ordered by year only (S.l.)', unpublished manuscript.

Berlin-West Senator für Wissenschaft und Kunst 1972, *Rätesystem, Revolution und Grundgesetz. Warum Ernest Mandel nicht berufen werden konnte*, West Berlin: Berlin Notgemeinschaft für eine Freie Universität.

Freitag, Peter 1992, *Eine unwissenschaftliche Arbeit. Eine unbewusst wissenschaftliche Arbeit als Versuch einer Dialektik des Lebendigen mit dem Mechanistischen über eine Kritik der 'Langen Wellen' des Ernest Mandel*, Frankfurt: R.G. Fischer.

GIM and RKJ (eds) 1972a, *Der Fall Mandel. Dokumentation und Analyse*, Hamburg.

GIM et al. (eds) 1972b, *Dokumentation zum Fall Ernest Mandel*, place of publication unknown.

Häckel, Erwin and Wolfram Elsner 1974, *Kritik der Jungen Linken an Europa*, Bonn: Europa-Union-Verlag.

Hilferding, Rudolf 1981 [1910], *Finance Capital: A Study of the Latest Phase of Capitalist Development*, edited by Tom Bottomore, London: Routledge & Kegan Paul.

Kellner, Manuel 1981, 'Der „wahre" Marxismus des Ernest Mandel – oder die Vorteile der Polemik mit einem Unbekannten', *Die Internationale*, 16: 100–5.

Krause, Günter 1977, *Das Elend der 'Linken'. Zur Kritik der politischen Ökonomie des Linksrevisionismus*, Berlin: Verlag für Theorie und Praxis der Wirtschaft.

Krause, Günter and Klaus Müller 1980, *Der 'wahre' Marxismus des Ernest Mandel. Zur Kritik der politischen Ökonomie des Linksradikalismus*, Berlin: Verlag für Theorie und Praxis der Wirtschaft.

Latteur, Nicolas 2000, *La gauche en mal de gauche*, Paris and Brussels: De Boeck Université.

Lubitz, Wolfgang and Petra 1996a, 'Ernest Mandel (1923–1995). A Bibliographical Tribute', *Journal of Trotsky Studies*, 4: 67–124.

Lubitz, Wolfgang and Petra (eds) 1999, *Trotsky. An International Classified List of Publications About Leon Trotsky and Trotskyism: 1905–1998*, Munich: Saur.

Lubitz, Wolfgang and Petra (eds) 2004, 'Ernest Mandel Biography', available at https://www.trotskyana.net/Trotskyists/Ernest_Mandel/Ernest_Mandel_Biography.html.

Mattick, Paul 1974, 'Ernest Mandels „Spätkapitalismus"', in *Kritik der Neomarxisten und andere Aufsätze*, Frankfurt: S. Fischer Verlag. English version available at https://www.marxists.org/archive/mattick-paul/1974/crisis/ch05.htm

Müller, Wolfgang (ed.) 1969a, *Wertgesetz, Planung und Bewußtsein. Die Planungsdebatte in Cuba*, Frankfurt: Verlag Neue Kritik.

Müller, Wolfgang 1969b, 'Marxistische Wirtschaftstheorie und Fetischcharakter der Ware', *Neue Kritik. Zeitschrift für sozialistische Theorie und Praxis*, 52/52, February: 69–86.

North, David 1997, *Ernest Mandel, 1923–1995. A Critical Assessment of His Role in the History of the Fourth International*, Bankstown: Labour Press Books.

Notgemeinschaft für eine freie Universität (eds) 1973, *Rätesystem, Revolution und Grundgesetz. Warum Ernest Mandel nicht berufen werden konnte*, Berlin.

Oertzen, Peter von 1972, 'Freiheitliche demokratische Grundordnung und Rätesystem', in *Zur Frage der Berufung marxistischer Wissenschaftler. Dokumentation zum Fall Ernest Mandel*, Berlin: Presse- und Informationsamt der Freien Universität Berlin.

Roth, Karl-Heinz 1971, 'Ernest Mandel, ein Vertreter der zeitgenössischen Kritik der politischen Ökonomie', *Proletarische Front*, 2/3: 58–74.

Senftleben, Günter 1985, *Die Theorie der langen Wellen*, Wuppertal: Fachbereich Wirtschaftswiss. d. Berg. Univ. Gesamthochsch.

Silberman, Bertram 1971, *Man and Socialism in Cuba: The Great Debate*, New York: Atheneum.

Sozialistisches Büro (eds) 1972, *Dokumentation zur neuen Sozialistenverfolgung, dargestellt am Beispiel Ernest Mandel*, Offenbach: Offenbach Verlag 2000.

Stutje, Jan Willem 2003, 'Ernest Mandels kleine oorlog. Revolutionaire socialisten in bezettingstijd, 1940–1945', *Bijdragen tot de Eigentijdse Geschiedenis/Cahiers d'histoire du temps présent*, 12, November: 275–6.

Stutje, Jan Willem 2009, *Ernest Mandel: A Rebel's Dream Deferred*, London: Verso.

Toussaint, Eric 1997, 'Notes a propos de l'approche d'Ernest Mandel par rapport a la crise en Allemagne de l'Est en 1989–90', *Cahiers Ernest Mandel. Bulletin de la Foundation Ernest Mandel*, Bruxelles, 1: 21–33.

Vercammen, François 1997, 'Ernest Mandel et la Capacité Révolutionnaire de la Classe Ouvrière', available at https://www.ernestmandel.org.

Vincent, Jean-Marie 1995, 'Ernest Mandel et le marxisme révolutionaire', *Critique communiste*, 144: 53–8.

3 Other Literature

Aguiton, Christophe 2002, *Was bewegt die Kritiker der Globalisierung? Von Attac zu Via Campensine*, Cologne: ISP.

Alexander, Robert 1991, *International Trotskyism 1929–1985. A Documented Analysis of the Movement*, Durham, NC: Duke University Press.

Alles, Wolfgang (ed.) 1989, *Die kommunistische Alternative. Texte der Linken Opposition und der IV. Internationale 1932–1985*, Frankfurt: ISP-Verlag.

Bensaïd, Daniel 1995, *La discordance des temps: essais sur les crises, les classes, l'histoire*, Paris: Passion.

Bensaïd, Daniel 2002, *Les trotskysmes*, Paris: PUF.

Bergmann, Karl Hans 1986, *Blanqui. Ein Rebell im 19. Jahrhundert*. Frankfurt and New York: Campus-Verlag.

Cliff, Tony 2018 [1974], *State Capitalism in Russia*, Chicago: Haymarket Books.

Commoner, Barry 1971, *The Closing Circle*, London: Cape.

Communist International 1922, 'Fourth Congress', *Resolution on the Program of the Communist International*.

Dimitrov, Georgi 1935, 'The Fascist Offensive and the Tasks of the Communist International in the Struggle of the Working Class against Fascism', available at http://www .marxists.org.

Engels, Frederick 1890, 'Marx-Engels Correspondence 1890: Engels to Laura Lafargue', available at http://www.marxists.org.

Engels, Frederick 1895, *Introduction to Marx's Class Struggle in France*, available at http://www.marxists.org.

Engels, Frederick 1970 [1880], *Socialism: Utopian and Scientific*, Moscow: Progress Publishers, available at http://www.marxists.org.

Fourth International 1963, 'The Dynamics of World Revolution Today', *Fourth International*, 16, October–December: 3–28.

Fourth International 1977, 'On Socialist Democracy (July 1977)', available at http://www .IIRE.org.

Fourth International 1985, 'The Dictatorship of the Proletariat and Socialist Democracy', available at http://www.internationalviewpoint.org.

Fourth International 1995, 'Building the International Today', available at http://www .internationalviewpoint.org.

Frank, Pierre 1967, *The Transitional Program*, available at http://www.marxists.org.

Frank, Pierre 1974, *Geschichte der Vierten Internationale*, Hamburg: ISP-Verlag.

Frank, Pierre 1981, *Geschichte der Kommunistischen Internationale*, Frankfurt: ISP-Verlag.

Frank, Pierre 2001 [1974], *The Fourth International: The Long March of the Trotskyists*, PDF available at http://www.revolutionary-socialism.com.

Geras, Norman 2017, 'The Longest Hatred: Antisemitism', in *The Norman Geras Reader*, edited by Ben Cohen and Eve Garrard, Manchester: Manchester University Press.

Habermas, Jürgen 1969, *Technik und Wissenschaft als 'Ideologie'*, Frankfurt: Suhrkamp.

Hilferding, Rudolf 1910, *Finance Capital*, available at http://www.marxists.org.

Hirsch, Joachim 1971, *Wissenschaftlich-technischer Fortschritt und politisches System*, Frankfurt: Suhrkamp.

Kellner, Manuel 1989, 'Der Name der Nelke. Begriffliche Voraussetzungen zur Diskussion der Kontroverse um den „Sozialismus in einem Land"', *SoZ-Magazin*, 4, 8/9, April: 24–9.

Kellner, Manuel 2000, 'Den Faschismus besser verstehen, um ihn besser zu bekämpfen', *Inprekorr*, 348/349, October/November: 44–54.

Kellner, Manuel 2004, *Trotzkismus. Einführung in seine Grundlagen – Fragen nach seiner Zukunft*, Stuttgart: Schmetterling-Verlag.

Lenin, V.I. 1907, 'Preface to the Collection of *Twelve Years*', available at http://www .marxists.org.

Lenin, V.I. 1964 [1917], 'The Tasks of the Proletariat in the Present Revolution' [aka 'The April Theses'], available at http://www.marxists.org.

Lenin, V.I. 1999 [1905], 'Two Tactics of Social Democracy in the Democratic Revolution', available at http://www.marxists.org.

Lenin, V.I. 2002 [1921], 'Once Again on the Trade Unions', available at http://www.marxists.org.

Lenin, V.I. 2004 [1905], 'The Reorganization of the Party', available at http://www.marxists.org.

Lenin, V.I. 2006 [1917], *The State and Revolution*, New York: International Publishers.

Lenin, V.I. 2008 [1916], *Imperialism. The Highest Stage of Capitalism*, New York: International Publishers.

Leon, Abram 1914, *The Right of Nations to Self-Determination*, available at http://www.marxists.org.

Leon, Abram [Abraham Leon] 2017 [1950], *The Jewish Question*, New York: Pathfinder.

Löwy, Michael 1987, *Revolution ohne Grenzen. Die Theorie der permanenten Revolution*, Frankfurt: ISP-Verlag.

Luxemburg, Rosa 1913, *The Accumulation of Capital*, available at http://www.marxists.org.

Luxemburg, Rosa 1916, 'Either Or', available at http://www.marxists.org.

Luxemburg, Rosa 1935, 'Leninism or Marxism?', *Council Correspondence*, 5, February, Chicago: United Workers' Party.

Luxemburg, Rosa 1978 [1917], 'To Emanuel and Mathilde Wurm', in *The Letters of Rosa Luxemburg*, edited by Stephen Eric Bronner, London: Routledge.

Luxemburg, Rosa 2004, *The Rosa Luxemburg Reader*, New York: Monthly Review Press.

Luxemburg, Rosa 2008 [1900], 'Reform or Revolution', in *The Essential Rosa Luxemburg*, Chicago: Haymarket.

Marx, Karl 1843, *Critique of Hegel's Philosophy of Right*, available at http://www.marxists.org.

Marx, Karl 1863, *Theories of Surplus-Value*, available at http://www.marxists.org.

Marx, Karl 1864, 'Results of the Direct Production Process', available at http://www.marxists.org.

Marx, Karl 1970 [1975], *Critique of the Gotha Programme*, available at https://www.marxists.org/archive/marx/works/1875/gotha/.

Marx, Karl 1990 [1887], *Capital*, Volume I, London and New York: Penguin.

Marx, Karl 1991 [1894], *Capital*, Volume III, New York and London: Penguin.

Marx, Karl 1992 [1885], *Capital*, Volume II, New York and London: Penguin.

Marx, Karl 2004 [1848], *Manifesto of the Communist Party*, available at http://www.marxists.org.

Marx, Karl 2005 [1888], 'Theses on Feuerbach', available at http://www.marxists.org.

Marx, Karl 2006 [1850], 'Address of the Central Committee to the Communist League', available at http://www.marxists.org.

Marx, Karl 2010 [1871], *The Civil War in France*, PDF available at http://www.marxists.org.

Marx, Karl and Frederick Engels 2010, *Marx & Engels Collected Works*, Volume 49, London: Lawrence &Wishart.

Rakovsky, Christian 1928, 'The "Professional Dangers" of Power', available at http://www.marxists.org.

Reisberg, Arnold 1971, *An den Quellen der Einheitsfrontpolitik. Der Kampf der KPD um die Aktionseinheit in Deutschland 1921–1922. Ein Beitrag zur Erforschung der Hilfe W.I. Lenins und der Komintern für die KPD*, Berlin: Verl. Das Europäische Buch.

Scheuer, Georg 1996, *Mussolinis langer Schatten. Marsch auf Rom im Nadelstreif*, Colonge: Neuer ISP-Verlag.

Simin, Alexander 1985, *Sozialismus und Neostalinismus. Eine Stimme aus dem sowjetischen Untergrund*, Frankfurt: ISP-Verlag.

Tronti, Mario 1971, *Extremismus und Reformismus*, Berlin: Merve-Verlag.

Trotsky, Leon 1906, *Results and Prospects*, available at http://www.marxists.org.

Trotsky, Leon 1930, *My Life*, available at http://www.marxists.org.

Trotsky, Leon 1931a, *The Permanent Revolution*, available at http://www.marxists.org.

Trotsky, Leon 1931b, *The Revolution Betrayed*, available at http://www.marxists.org.

Trotsky, Leon 1932, *History of the Russian Revolution*, available at http://www.marxists.org.

Trotsky, Leon 1933, *What Is National Socialism?*, available at http://www.marxists.org.

Trotsky, Leon 1935, 'The Workers' State, Thermidor and Bonapartism', available at http://www.marxists.org.

Trotsky, Leon 1938, 'It Is Necessary to Drive the Bureaucracy and the New Aristocracy Out of the Soviets', available at http://www.marxists.org.

Trotsky, Leon 1939, 'A Graphic History of Bolshevism', available at http://www.marxists.org.

Trotsky, Leon 1940, *Manifesto of the Fourth International on Imperialist War and the Proletarian World Revolution*, available at http://www.marxists.org.

Trotsky, Leon 1942 [1939–40], *In Defence of Marxism*, New York: Pioneer Publishers, available at http://www.marxists.org.

Trotsky, Leon 1945 [1937–40], 'On the Jewish Problem', available at http://www.marxists.org.

Trotsky, Leon 1971, *The Struggle Against Fascism in Germany*, New York: Pathfinder.

Trotsky, Leon 1996 [1936], *The Revolution Betrayed*, available at http://www.marxists.org.

Trotsky, Leon 2002 [1938], *The Death Agony of Capitalism and the Tasks of the Fourth International: The Mobilization of the Masses around Transitional Demands to Prepare the Conquest of Power: The Transitional Program*, PDF available at http://www.marxists.org.

Trotsky, Leon 2006 [1909], *1905*, available at http://www.marxists.org.

Trotsky, Leon 2016 [1939], 'The Three Conceptions of the Russian Revolution', available at http://www.marxists.org.

Vercammen, François 1998, 'Lenin und die Parteifrage', *Inprekorr*, 315, January: 21–28.

Wohlforth, Tim 1994, *The Prophet's Children: Travels on the American Left*, New Jersey: Humanities Press.

Wohlforth, Tim and Dennis Tourish 2016, 'Gerry Healy: Guru to a Star', in *On the Edge: Political Cults Right and Left*, edited by Tim Wohlforth and Dennis Tourish, New York/London: Routledge.

Wolf, Harald 1983, 'Marxismus, Produktivkraftentwicklung und Befreiung der Arbeit. Zur ökologischen Marxismuskritik', *Die Internationale*, 19: 116–58.

Wolf, Winfried 2000, *Fusionsfieber. Oder: Das große Fressen. Globalisierungsmythos – Nationalstaat – Wirtschaftsblöcke*, Cologne: PapyRossa-Verlag.

Index